W9-BZO-166

MANSTEIN

Erich von
MANSTEIN
Hitler's Master Strategist

Benoît Lemay

Translated by Pierce Heyward

CASEMATE
Philadelphia & Newbury

Published in the United States of America in 2010 by
CASEMATE
908 Darby Road, Havertown, PA 19083

and in the United Kingdom by
CASEMATE
17 Cheap Street, Newbury, Berkshire, RG14 5DD

© 2010 by Benoît Lemay
English translation © 2010 by Casemate Publishers

ISBN 978-1-935149-26-2

Cataloging-in-publication data is available from the Library of Congress
and from the British Library.

Printed and bound in the United States of America.

10 9 8 7 6 5 4 3 2 1

For a complete list of Casemate titles, please contact:

United States of America
Casemate Publishers
Telephone (610) 853-9131, Fax (610) 853-9146
E-mail casemate@casematepublishing.com
Website www.casematepublishing.com

United Kingdom
Casemate-UK
Telephone (01635) 231091, Fax (01635) 41619
E-mail casemate-uk@casematepublishing.co.uk
Website www.casematepublishing.co.uk

Mixed Sources
Product group from well-managed
forests and other controlled sources
www.fsc.org Cert no. SW-COC-002283
© 1996 Forest Stewardship Council

FSC

CONTENTS

Erich von Manstein in 1938.
Bundesarchiv, Bild 183-H01758/photo: o.Ang.

INTRODUCTION

Could one consider the German field marshal Erich von Manstein the greatest operational genius, if not the best strategist, of World War II? Although this may be the opinion of numerous specialists in the field, an understanding of his role in German military history remains to this day rather limited in the West. One could explain this by a certain centro-Americanist perspective, which has primarily focused on the West European and North African theaters of operations. Since the majority of Manstein's military achievements occurred on the battlefields of Bolshevik Russia, Anglo-Saxon and French historians have accorded him only the smallest amount of interest, in comparison, for example, to Field Marshal Erwin Rommel, whose principal military exploits took place in France and North Africa. However, relatively speaking, the latter had military responsibilities much less important than those of Manstein, given that the outcome of the war was decided on the Eastern Front, where the German Army had concentrated the largest proportion of its effort and suffered 85 percent of its losses, thus making Russia the "tomb of the German Army."[1]

Even if the majority of Western specialists recognize the primacy of the Eastern Front, it has not necessarily inspired the analysis of their works, which explains to a certain extent why Manstein's military role, for example, during the Battle of Stalingrad in the winter of 1942–43, remains to be fully defined. One could make a similar remark regarding his role on the Western Front, for a debate exists as to whether or not he was truly the author of the Sickle Cut Plan (*Sichelschnitt*), the basis of the Wehrmacht's lightning victory over the French and British armies in May and June 1940.

Be that as it may, leading military historians almost unanimously consider Manstein the greatest strategic talent and the cleverest practitioner of mobile warfare among the German generals of the Second World War. His understanding of the operational dimension of modern warfare, which in particular involved the dualistic relationship between armor and combat aircraft, and his capacity for improvisation and flexibility during unforeseen events, made him the most talented of the Wehrmacht's senior officers and the most feared by the Red Army's high command. A master in the art of commanding audacious offensives, and surprise and violent counterattacks, he was also able when necessary to orchestrate vast, methodical, and well-ordered withdrawals.

In his work *The Other Side of the Hill*, drawing from conversations and correspondences with German generals who were prisoners of war after 1945, the eminent military historian Basil Henry Liddell Hart writes: "The ablest of all the German generals was probably Field Marshal Erich von Manstein. That was the verdict of most of those with whom I discussed the war, from [Field Marshal Gerd von] Rundstedt downwards. He had a superb strategic sense, combined with a greater understanding of mechanized weapons than any of the generals who did not belong to the tank school itself. Yet in contrast to some of the single-track enthusiasts he did not lose sight of the importance of improving alternative weapons and defense. He was responsible, shortly before the war, for developing the armoured assault gun, which proved invaluable later." Liddell Hart confirmed this perspective several years later in his monumental *History of the Second World War*, underscoring there that Manstein "was considered by his friends to be the best strategist among the young generals."[2]

Another military historian of great standing, John Keegan, estimates that Field Marshal Manstein "possessed one of the best military minds in the Wehrmacht." In Christian Schneider's view, Manstein "was so brilliant that he was unanimously recognized—as much by his comrades-in-arms as by the military experts of Germany, as well as by both the victorious and neutral countries—as the most competent German general of the Second World War." Hitler himself considered Manstein "the best brain that the staff has produced." David Irving goes so far to declare that "Hitler's respect for General von Manstein's ability bordered on fear." Such a fear is without a doubt explained by Manstein's personal ambitions and the authority which he enjoyed within the officers' corps. "Von Manstein," asserts Albert Seaton, "was indeed very ambitious, a man of operational genius whose great abilities were clouded by a pose of arrogance and conceit; he wanted the powers of a von Hindenburg and the fame of the elder von Moltke, with a unified *Oberkommando* with himself at its head."[3]

In the preface to the 1958 English edition of Manstein's *Memoirs*, volume one, Liddell Hart writes: "The general verdict among the German generals I interrogated in 1945 was that Field Marshal von Manstein had proved the ablest commander in their army, and the man they had most desired to become its commander in chief." Richard Brett-Smith agrees wholeheartedly when he states that Manstein would have been accepted by all of the generals on the Eastern Front to fill the post of commander in chief with full operational authority. "Von Manstein," he adds, "was the greatest German general of the war, and probably the greatest of any participating nation."[4]

Many generals of the Wehrmacht shared this opinion, beginning with von Rundstedt, the eldest of the German field marshals. Colonel General Heinz Guderian, patriarch of the panzer divisions (*Panzer-divisionen*), stated that Manstein was "our most brilliant operational brain." Generals Walter Warlimont and Günther Blumentritt both asserted that he was "the most brilliant strategist of all our generals," while General Siegfried Westphal declared that: "[...] of all the general staff officers, von Manstein possessed the greatest strategic and military talents overall. With an eye on all of the possibilities of the future, always full of new ideas that were good and often brilliant, he was an organizational genius and a difficult subordinate, but a generous superior. He was also always among the first when the interests of the army were at stake."

Field Marshal Wilhelm Keitel, who was profoundly jealous of Manstein, corroborated this perspective, writing in his *Memoirs* while awaiting his Nuremberg trial these highly revealing words: "I myself advised Hitler three times to replace me [as the army's chief of staff] with von Manstein [...]. But despite his frequently expressed admiration for Manstein's outstanding talents, Hitler obviously feared to take such a step and each time he turned it down; was it sheer indolence on his part or some other unvoiced objection he had to him? I have no idea."[5]

"If anyone could have led a successful military revolt, it was Manstein," asserts Samuel W. Mitcham, referring to the immense respect that the field marshal earned in the Wehrmacht, and implying by that very fact why Hitler so feared him. Was Manstein not "undoubtedly Germany's most significant personality in the Second World War," as Andreas Hillgrüber, one of the most distinguished military historians, suggests?[6]

By virtue of his numerous military feats, Manstein equally merited the respect of his adversaries, such as the Soviet marshals Rodion Malinowski and Kyrill Kalinov. After the war, Malinowski spoke of Manstein in a most laudatory fashion: "We considered the hated Erich von Manstein as our most dangerous enemy. His technical mastery of everything, of every situation, was unparalleled. The situation would have perhaps become nasty for us if all the generals of the German Army had been of his caliber." For his part, Kalinov held very similar views of Manstein: "In the club, we often discussed the merit of the highest ranking German commanders. For many among us, the bastard Erich Lewinski, a.k.a. von Manstein, was the most dreaded. His army group appeared unbeatable to us, his technical qualities incomparable, and his understanding of our country exceptional. If all the German generals had been comparable to him [...]."[7]

His great strategic talent nonetheless provoked animosity and jealousy on the part of several colleagues both in the OKH, such as its commander in chief, Field Marshal Walther von Brauchitsch, and its chief of general staff, Colonel General Franz Halder, as well as in the OKW, such as Field Marshal Wilhelm Keitel, chief of staff, and Colonel General Alfred Jodl, chief of the operations bureau, which undoubtedly prevented him from attaining more important decision-making posts throughout the course of his career. He was equally under-appreciated by various members of the Nazi Party hierarchy, whether it was by Reichsmarshal Hermann Göring, who was Hitler's *prince* and commander in chief of the Luftwaffe, Propaganda Minister Joseph Goebbels, or the Reichsführer-SS Heinrich Himmler, chief of the SS and the Gestapo.

Despite his great admiration for the field marshal's military competence, the Führer feared his independent spirit and his strong character, which explains why he refused to entrust to him Brauchitsch's position, after he had dismissed the German Army commander from his duties in mid-December 1941 due to his failure in Operation Barbarossa. Moreover, it is for this reason that the Führer relieved Manstein on

March 30, 1944, after one of his most beautiful military operations, from the command of Army Group South.

Beyond Manstein's personal feats, a look at his career provides a new perspective on the nature of the war, particularly the war on the Eastern Front against the Soviet Union, which is the primary focus of this study on the field marshal. The dominant historiography on the Second World War has recognized for half a century that Germany's objective in launching the war was the conquest of *Lebensraum*, living space in the East at the expense of the U.S.S.R., and the destruction of part of its population, in particular the Jews and those representing the Bolshevik regime. However, it has only been in approximately the past ten years that these histories have taken into account studies claiming that the Wehrmacht participated, as a fully-committed member of Hitler's state, in the preparations for the wars of aggression, through the army's own actions and the criminal operations of the National Socialist regime. The army was thus not an entity separate from the Nazi apparatus, but rather an instrument that had voluntarily placed itself as an ally in service to the party.

There existed, therefore, a completely natural sense of community between the majority of the senior leaders of the army and those of the Nazi regime. Like members of the National Socialist Party, the military was against liberalism, democracy, Socialists, Communists, pacifists, and Jews. On the one hand, they favored the return of a strong authoritarian regime to Germany, permitting Hitler to rise to power and to overturn the republican system, and on the other hand, the restoration of a powerful army endowed with offensive capacities. Their common objectives included the destruction of any constraints upon German sovereignty imposed by the Treaty of Versailles, the formation of a unified Reich created by the annexation of Austria (*Anschluß*), the disappearance of Czechoslovakia and Poland, and above all by the conquest of living space in the Soviet Union, necessary to make of the German Reich a great continental and autarchic power. They were, indeed, allies sharing common preoccupations and perfectly compatible worldviews, particularly regarding the political-strategic objectives in Eastern Europe. In short, the Nazis and the army formed a mutual alliance and became veritable accomplices.

However, the political and ethical responsibility of the Wehrmacht during the Nazi period has most often been eclipsed thanks to the Cold

War and the demands of German rearmament, under the framework of the North Atlantic Treaty Organization (NATO), which necessitated the re-enlistment of former soldiers having served in Hitler's army. It should be stated that the support of qualified persons in the institutions of the Federal Republic of Germany, as in the bureaucracy, the justice department, the universities and, beginning in 1956, the Bundeswehr, necessitated a rather obvious discretion from the moment it became a issue of determining political and penal responsibility for the actors of the National Socialist era. This of course gave license to the senior officers of the Wehrmacht, in particular those who participated in the conscription of the Bundeswehr troops, to cast an unapologetic image of their own history.[8]

More than any of his peers, Manstein influenced, through his testimony and postwar *Memoirs*, historians who, drawing on theories of totalitarianism, had a tendency to render Hitler alone responsible for the war and the crimes committed during its course. In his *Memoirs*, there is absolutely no mention of the war of extermination against the Jews, officers of the Red Army, or Soviet prisoners of war, despite Manstein's active involvement, particularly in the Crimea. He chose instead to emphasize the actions and sacrifices of his soldiers during the war.[9] During the trial of the major war criminals before the Nuremburg International Military Tribunal, Manstein, as a witness, presented himself as guarantor of the Wehrmacht, attempting more than anyone else to exonerate the general staff and the high command of accusations of having formed a criminal organization.

It is thus hardly surprising that he became, after 1945, one of the principal moral pillars of Wehrmacht integrity. Nevertheless, he was condemned at Hamburg on December 19, 1949 by a British military tribunal to 18 years in prison for his role as commander in chief of a region of the U.S.S.R. where grave acts of brutality had been committed, particularly against prisoners of war. He was then released on May 7, 1953, one year after having received leave for medical reasons. Some in West Germany thus thought that he had been no more than a victim of "victors' justice," included in a collective punishment, and not a war criminal as such. This thus explains why he participated, at the request of the West German government, in the supervision of the reconstruction of the German Army in 1956.

Consequently, the predominant tendency of the historiography on

Manstein is to this day an assemblage of works in his defense, dealing with his various military accomplishments and his glorious feats of arms. This trend neglects the political and ideological aspects of the conflict, which are essential for an understanding of his true nature. And when these two aspects are examined, it is generally to assert that the field marshal should not be associated with the criminal dimension of the war, for the facts would demonstrate that he is beyond any suspicion. Furthermore, did Manstein not include among his critics Himmler and Goebbels, who reproached him for his disinterest in the Nazi cause, as well as for his origins, partly Slavic, if not Jewish, like 150,000 other Wehrmacht soldiers? But is the pertinent question not to know whether his military exploits are separate and distinct from the known issues of the war on the Eastern Front?

Manstein always insisted that the German Army had no share in the Nazi crimes, since they had been committed by units of the SS and SD. He claimed that the army was unaware in general of what was happening behind the front, i.e. the nature and scale of these crimes, but expressed its disappointment when it had knowledge of certain offenses. However, there is no longer any doubt today that the majority of the high-ranking officers who served on the Eastern Front collaborated closely with the police units of the Nazi regime who were in charge of the elimination or deportation of Soviet prisoners of war, political commissars of the Red Army, partisans, and Jews. The senior officers of the Wehrmacht, including Field Marshal Manstein, could not have remained ignorant of what was truly occurring. And since he was a key commander on the Eastern Front, a reappraisal of the postwar perceptions of his role is required.

In spite of the fact that he seems not to have been a true Nazi, Manstein nonetheless gave certain orders that encouraged his troops to commit criminal actions at the expense of the political commissars of the Red Army, partisans, and Jews. For example, it was under the title of commander in chief of the Eleventh Army in the Crimea that he ordered his soldiers on November 20, 1941, to vigorously support the policy of extermination of the Jews, demanding their understanding for the severe punishment to be inflicted, since the Jews were considered the spiritual representatives of Bolshevik terror. Since such a directive resulted in only further bolstering his troops' morale and their desire to fight, the field marshal appeared all the more guilty of the war crimes committed under his command in the Soviet territories.

Manstein knew full well that it was impossible to make a career for himself in a totalitarian regime without a degree of compromise, even more so in a regime which he and his German Army colleagues had decided to support as allies, even if they did not approve of all its policies. Consequently, Manstein intended to respect the oath of allegiance that he had declared to Hitler in the summer of 1934, a form of submission deliberately chosen and suggested by leaders of the Wehrmacht, future field marshals Werner von Blomberg and Walter von Reichenau. All throughout the war, Manstein remained faithful to the spirit of alliance which bound the army to the regime; he remained consistent with the choice that had made, i.e. to serve his country and his Führer to the very end. For him, the soldier was in service to the politics of the state, and it was his duty to restrict himself to military matters. One can thus better understand his refusal, in the winter of 1943, to follow Major Claus Graf Schenk von Stauffenberg and Colonel Henning von Tresckow, leaders of the military conspiracy against Hitler, and then to consider, in the summer of 1943, an invitation from Field Marshals Günther von Kluge and Erwin Rommel, as well as from Lieutenant Colonel Rudolf-Christoph Freiherr von Gersdorff, to take leadership of the Wehrmacht following a coup d'état that would have rid Germany of Hitler and his Nazi regime.

Manstein was affiliated with a group of talented senior officers who were greatly encouraged by the arrival of the Hitler regime. The massive rearmament and the expansion of military contingents had accelerated his promotions. Moreover, he was well integrated into the officers' corps which was preparing the war, and clearly part of the dominant mindset of the state. As such, the letter that he wrote on July 21, 1938, during the Sudetenland Crisis, to Colonel General Ludwig Beck, chief of the OKH general staff, in which he stated his insistence upon the necessity of eliminating Czechoslovakia, is both significant and loaded with meaning.

A great military figure, but a man who lacked a razor-sharp political sense, Manstein was very much representative of the Germano-Prussian military caste of his time. It is thus through him that the destiny of other high-ranking officers who fought during the Second World War, particularly on the Eastern Front, stands out. From here we may understand the importance of a biography on this figure who served his

Führer until the very end. Indeed, a study of Manstein's indulgent behavior with regards to Nazi abuses of power, during and after the war, further permits us to understand why the German Army voluntarily allowed itself to become the instrument of Hitler's expansionist policy. Such a biography is not only important for the history of the war and for the operational knowledge of an exceptionally talented strategist; it also permits us to penetrate into the world of thoughts, conceptions, and psychology of a high-ranking officer who played a key role in the preparation and supervision of the wars of aggression, in addition to the war crimes committed by the Wehrmacht on behalf of the National Socialist regime.

I

FROM THE IMPERIAL ARMY TO THE REICHSWEHR

Until the final collapse of the Third Reich, Field Marshal Erich von Manstein remained loyal to Adolf Hitler, his Führer, to whom he had pledged his oath of allegiance. He thus refused to join the ranks of the military opposition who wanted to assassinate Hitler and overturn the National Socialist regime so as to spare Germany the worst that was yet to come. While he admittedly distanced himself from his Führer after the war, he nonetheless continued to present himself as an advocate of the Wehrmacht and its actions. Manstein's family origins, education, and professional development permit us to understand the behavior and attitude of this figure who was very much representative of the Germano-Prussian military caste of his time, of which he was its most accomplished product. Equally so, they allow us to bring to light his indulgence for the abuses of the Nazi regime and his acceptance of Hitler's expansionistic policy.

Family environment and education

From a very early age, Erich von Manstein had been destined to lead a soldier's life, if only because of his family origins and his education. Born in Berlin, on November 24, 1887, he was the tenth child of General Eduard von Lewinski and the fifth child of the latter's second wife, Helene von Sperling. Her younger sister, Hedwig von Sperling, was married to Lieutenant General Georg von Manstein, with whom she had no children. In accordance with common practice at the time, the Lewinski couple had decided to entrust their next child to the Manstein couple. Thus even before his birth, it was agreed upon between the two families that Erich would be adopted at the moment of

11

his baptism. And so, on the day of this religious ceremony, Fritz Erich Georg von Lewinski took the family name von Manstein.

Both his birth and adoptive parents were born into aristocratic Prussian families who had military traditions dating back several centuries. The two families included among their forebears officers who had served Prussian kings for several generations. In fact, to be more precise, the military traditions of the Lewinskis and the Mansteins dated back to the Teutonic knights. And so it was that certain ancestors of Erich thus guarded the European borders in the thirteenth century. On the Lewinski side, as on the Manstein side, sixteen of his ancestors were officers who had served in the military, whether it was for the kaiser or the czar. The Lewinski family alone had provided the German Army with no less than seven generals throughout the course of the twentieth century. General Eduard von Lewinski, Erich's natural father, was an artillery officer who would climb the military echelons up to the rank of army corps commander. His adoptive father, Lieutenant General Georg von Manstein, was, in turn, an infantry officer who would become a division commander. The Sperlings also came from a distinguished military family of the Prussian nobility. Erich's maternal grandfather, Oskar von Sperling, was a general, as was the brother of his natural and adoptive mothers. Furthermore, the youngest sister of his birth and adoptive mothers was the wife of the future field marshal and president of the Reich, Paul von Hindenburg. Although the adoptive father of Erich von Manstein belonged to the Prussian nobility, he was not a landowner. Nevertheless, Georg von Manstein lived in comfort ever since his family and that of his wife's received an endowment for services rendered at the time of the Franco-Prussian War of 1870–1871, during which time his father had commanded an army corps, and his father-in-law had held the office of army chief of staff. Granted by the Reichstag, the endowment had guaranteed the Mansteins and the Sperlings financial independence by supplementing their salaries paid by the army.

The family environment of young Manstein thus destined him to a military career, all the more so since his father would provide him with an education straight from the tradition of the Prussian officers' corps. "The environment in which I grew up," he remarked after the war, "was the world of the Prussian soldier. [...] One can thus suppose that a certain military inheritance had been bestowed upon me." He then added: "It is not surprising that, from my most tender childhood, I wanted to become a soldier."[10] He would thus be raised, at both home and at cadet school, in accordance with the traditions and general moral code of the old Prussian military caste, to which it would be necessary to add a strong Lutheran puritanism.

From cadet school to the Imperial Army

Erich von Manstein was a child of delicate constitution. Yet, after having studied for five years at a Strasbourg high school, where his father had been posted, in 1900 he entered, at the age of thirteen, the Royal Prussian Cadets' Corps, first in Plon, then in Berlin. He remained there six years, a time during which his constitution strengthened to the point that when he entered the army in 1906, he was provisionally declared suitable for active service. During his time in Berlin, which lasted four years, he was appointed, as a member of the nobility, to the pages' corps in the court of Kaiser William II.

Exerting a substantial influence over the old German Army, the Royal Prussian Cadets' Corps was founded in 1717 by King of Prussia Frederick William I, who had decided to combine Berlin's various military academies into a single cadets' corps for boys between the ages of eleven and eighteen, and to place it under the nominal command of his son, the future Frederick the Great. Originally, admission was reserved only for the nobility. But this had hardly changed by the beginning of the 20th century, for the majority of cadets were still born into the families of Prussian officers and civil servants, as well as the *Junkers*, those local squires of the East. The primary mission of the cadet institution was to provide the necessary education to the young members of the nobility who aspired to become officers. Within the established curriculum, military training was only one facet among others, such as the instruction of academic subjects or the meaning of honor and duty. Indeed, emphasis was placed upon the development of character in order to create a harmonious combination which would include the best aspects of physical, academic, and religious education. Training quite obviously insisted upon loyalty towards the person of the emperor. Young Manstein and his classmates were thus educated in an environment where unconditional and chivalrous loyalty towards Germany prevailed, where the motherland was personified by the monarch, the supreme warlord. In the second volume of his *Memoirs*, Manstein recounts his years spent in the Royal Prussian Cadets' Corps with a certain amount of nostalgia. A sense of honor and duty, uncompromising obedience, and camaraderie were the principal values instilled in him and which, in his mind, molded his character in a highly positive way.[11]

Manstein was intelligent and capable of quickly mastering a subject. Furthermore, his report cards indicated that he could attain higher results if he were to apply himself more and take better advantage of his talents. In 1906, after having passed the exams required to enter into the cadets' academy at Lichterfelde, he was appointed as ensign to the prestigious Third Prussian Foot Guards Regiment. Stationed in Berlin and reserved almost exclusively for members of the nobility, the regiment included among its ranks officers who would play a key role in the history of their country, such as the future field marshal Paul von Hindenburg, commander in chief of the Imperial Army from 1916 to 1918 and president of the Reich from 1925 to 1934; the future lieutenant general Kurt Freiherr von Hammerstein-Equord, commander in chief of the army from 1930 to 1934; the future lieutenant general Kurt von Schleicher, chancellor and minister of the Reichswehr during the last year of the Weimar Republic; and the future field marshal Walther von Brauchitsch, commander in chief of the army from 1938 to 1941. And so at the age of nineteen, Manstein began his military career in earnest. For him, however, being a soldier was much more than a job. In fact, for him it was nothing less than a *raison d'être* intimately linked to his world vision.

The following year he was promoted to the rank of second lieutenant and became, by default, an officer of the German Army. In 1913, he entered the *Kriegsakademie* (War Academy) in Berlin where he underwent officers' general staff training, which he was unable to complete due to the outbreak of the First World War. "The best mind that the general staff has produced," as Hitler would one day declare apropos of Manstein, would thus never have at his disposal, during the course of his military career, a general staff officer's training in due form.

At the beginning of the war, Manstein was promoted to lieutenant and served as adjutant in the 2nd Guard Reserve Regiment, first in Belgium, then in East Prussia, and finally in Poland. It was with this unit that he served on the Western Front, in the Battle of the Marne and in the capture of Namur, and in the East, in the battle of the Mazury Lakes which, along with the Battle of Tannenberg, definitively halted the Russian advance into East Prussia and brought fame to his uncle, Field Marshal Hindenburg, commander in chief of the Eighth Army. In November 1914, Manstein was seriously wounded in a hand-to-hand battle in Poland by two bullets: one lodged in his shoulder, the other in his sciatic nerve. Despite the injury, he returned to service at the end of spring 1915. Attached to General Max von Gallwitz's army group, under the title of staff officer, he participated in the German offensives in northern Poland and Serbia. Promoted to the rank of captain in the summer of 1915, he served as adjutant at the headquarters of the Twelfth Army. In 1916, he served as staff officer, first in the Eleventh Army during the Battle of Verdun, then in the First Army under General Fritz von Below, the commander in chief, and Major General Fritz von Loßberg, chief of staff during the Battle of the Somme. The following year, he became a staff officer in charge of operations for the 4th Cavalry Division in Estonia and in Courland, which at this particular moment was fighting against the Bolsheviks. Beginning in the spring of 1918, he took on the same duties for the 213th Infantry Division deployed on the Western Front. He was thus able to take part in the massive German offensives of May and July, as well as in the decisive battles of Reims and Sedan. He served in this theater of operations until Germany signed the Armistice on November 11, 1918.

During the course the war, Captain Manstein was awarded two great military distinctions: the Iron Cross (First Class) and the House Order of Hohenzollern. Although he had not commanded any troops during the war, he nevertheless had the opportunity to demonstrate, within the scope of his various duties as a staff officer, an exceptional tactical talent and a remarkable understanding of the needs and demands of the high command at the time of an offensive. Even though he was only an adjutant of a rifle battalion, he had already proven the vast potential of his military talent. "He was the best adjutant I ever had," his commander later declared.[12]

The Reichswehr during the Weimar Republic: A state-within-a-state

Because of their social class and the education they had received in the cadets' academy—and also in the *Kriegsakademie* for certain ones among them—Prussian officers like Manstein were not in a position to understand the true causes of the events that took place in Germany in November 1918. Whether in the cadets' academy or in the *Kriegsakademie*, their education was essentially based upon an apprenticeship of military tactics, military history, armaments, fortifications, railroads, mathematics, physics, geography, and finally, military discipline. Little importance was granted to other disciplines, such as language, economics, or political and social science. German military education clearly demonstrated its insufficiency with regards to officers in the age of industrialization and, in particular, of mass armies and industrial wars. In a rather paradoxical way, the industrial revolution, socialism, and parliamentarism were concepts poorly understood by the officers, even as economic, social, and political factors had enormous impact on the role of the armed forces within the state and society. They were thus incapable of understanding the actual causes of the events of November 1918, believing rather that the war had been lost because of influential factors they hardly understood and which they had learned in the army to hold in contempt: socialism, liberalism, democracy, parliamentarism, and behind all of this, the Jews. Refuting modernism, confining itself to a reactionary traditionalism, the officers' corps had remained a state-within-a-state, which is to say an institution at the service of the king and his kingdom, not belonging to any political parties or society.[13]

Like his army colleagues, Manstein was thus profoundly and deeply distressed by the collapse of the Hohenzollern monarchy. For the officers, he recounted after the war, such a loss not only constituted a simple change of regime, it caused their very understanding of the world to dissolve. And just like his ancestors, Manstein had taken an oath of allegiance to the King of Prussia. It was precisely this oath of loyalty to the king that in Manstein's opinion was the foundation of a soldier's sense of duty, not the abstract idea of "state" or "people." Bound unconditionally to the person of the king by an oath of allegiance, the army, up to that point, seemed no longer conceivable without a monarchy. With the revolution and the Armistice, wrote Manstein, his military youth came to an end. Rather than to the Kaiser, he added, the soldiers were henceforth obliged to take an oath of allegiance to the Reich, a concept which he described as abstract, indeed mythical.[14]

As was the case for the majority of the officers, the Weimar Republic would remain foreign to Manstein. The German nationalist right considered this political regime a product of defeat and a foreign body imposed upon the German nation by the victorious powers. This same conservative right reinforced the discredit of the Republic by insisting that Germany had not been militarily conquered, instead crediting the idea that the army had been "stabbed in the back" by the socialist democrats, the Communists, and the Jews. Like his colleagues who had served the Kaiser, at least those who came from the nobility, Manstein would remain nostalgic for the Prussian monarchy and the central position formerly held by the army within the imperial regime.[15]

Regarding parliamentary democracy, Manstein's opinion was hardly positive. In volume two of his autobiography, he provides his perspective of the German state during the period of the Weimar regime: "It proved to be, neither more nor less, than the puppet of political parties and interest groups. It represented less a genuine authority than an apparatus used to implement all the upheavals. Moreover, its form unquestionably did not find its authority in the will of the majority of the people, but from the consequence of defeat, and the resultant wishes of the conquering enemies." In his view, parliamentary democracy was thus synonymous with political instability and a regime that could not win the acceptance of the general populace and which, in addition, attempted to rule without true authority. After attending a meeting of the Reichstag under special invitation, he would even reveal having been "disgusted by the indignant squabbles of the parties."[16]

Despite his profound aversion to the Weimar Republic, Manstein would remain loyal, particularly during its first tumultuous years. Following the example of the large majority of his colleagues in the officers' corps, he remained faithful to the oath of allegiance that he declared not to the president of the Republic, but to the Constitution. Accordingly, he approved his superiors' decision not to offer their support to Wolfgang Kapp. The latter, in March 1920, had attempted a coup in Berlin to overthrow the Weimar regime, with the assistance of the commander in chief of the northern armies, General Walther von Lüttwitz, and Captain Ludwig Erhard, chief of a Freikorps of 6,000 men that had just returned from the Baltic. The attempt had been made with the agreement of General Erich Ludendorff, formerly the assistant to Field Marshal Hindenburg when he was at the head of the German high command from 1916 to 1918. Concerning this event, Manstein wrote after the war that to support the Kapp Putsch would have not only been "totally contrary to the tradition of the German soldier, but would have seriously compromised the army's position vis-à-vis the people," because for them, "the soldier's role was not only to defend the homeland, but also to preserve order and authority within the state." He also explained that the decision of the Reichswehr—the name of the small German army born out of the Treaty of Versailles—not to intervene on the part of the putschists was out of a fear of provoking, on the one hand, division within the troops, or perhaps even the disintegration of the army, and on the other, a civil war that could have led to chaos and a rise in Bolshevik sentiment within Germany.[17] This rationale, which had motivated him to oppose the Kapp Putsch, would essentially be the same that caused him to refuse to take part in the conspiracy against Hitler during the Second World War.

It is obvious that, like the majority of his officer colleagues, Manstein had been profoundly marked by the troubles at the end of the war, for example the November 1918 revolution that provoked the collapse of the Hohenzollern monarchy, or the Communist revolutions of the Spartacist uprising at Berlin in January 1919 and at Munich the following spring. He came out of this traumatizing experience filled with a powerful anti-Communist sentiment which, throughout the Second World War, would not only lead him to support, but also to actively participate in the war of annihilation and extermination undertaken by National Socialist Germany in Bolshevik Russia. Nevertheless, the Freikorps or the army had interceded, at the demand of the provisional government, in each of the revolutions of 1918–1919 to crush the Communist revolutionary uprisings. From that moment on, it was clear that the existence of the young Weimar Republic depended more than ever on the Reichswehr. Not only did the latter appear as the ultimate recourse in case of internal crisis, but also as the guarantor of state and national unity.

Colonel General Hans von Seeckt, to whom was entrusted command of the army, had been opposed to any putsch, insofar as the Reichswehr's autonomy was safeguarded within the new regime, the Weimar Republic, which he considered as an anomaly, since it was born out of military defeat and political collapse, and was moreover the symbol of the Treaty of Versailles. He thus endeavored to maintain the spirit of the old imperial army, in other words, creating out of this organization a state-within-a-state, independent of political power. He therefore considered it necessary for the new army to retain the monarchic spirit of the old officers' corps.

In this respect, the young officer Manstein thought, just like Seeckt, that the fiasco of the Kapp Putsch, which had been defended by Generals Lüttwitz and Ludendorff, demonstrated that the officers' corps should steer clear of the politics and instead prepare itself for the day where outside security would be entrusted to the new army. Like Seeckt—and the same would apply for the majority of his peers—Manstein believed that the primary role of the officers' corps consisted in preserving the army as a safeguard for the protection of the nation itself and for the eventual resurrection of Germany as a great power. During the Second World War, when the conspirators approached him to gain assurance of his support for the attempt to rid Germany of Hitler and the Nazi regime, Manstein offered them nothing more than a straightforward refusal, not only stating the reasons that had motivated his behavior with regards to the Kapp putsch, but also presenting the argument that the soldier was in service to state politics, and that it was his obligation to restrict himself to military issues.

Obedience, loyalty, and a sense of duty, Manstein's three principal virtues, would remain with him during his entire military career. He thus described his profession through the traditional ideas of simplicity and chivalry, as well as through his personal concept of military honor. To a certain degree, he saw himself as a descendant of the monastic military order of the Teutonic knights, proud of his motto "knight without fear and without reproach." Whether it was for his extreme precision or for his discipline and strict character, he was a typical product of his environment. In fact, he was arrogant, intolerant at times, and even occasionally uncompromising with regards to discipline. However, he was very intelligent and possessed an exceptionally acute, clear, and sharp mind which relied upon, for the most part, his intuition. Authoritarian, distant, cold, and reserved, he was nevertheless an emotional man who had learned how to master his feelings. Above all, he had a great strength of character, refusing to bow before his superiors when he thought he was right and they were wrong. Thus, in the eyes of his colleagues whose rank was higher than his, he appeared as impertinent, insolent, disrespectful and immeasurably ambitious. Yet, at the same time, such traits helped him to distinguish and bring attention to himself within the officers' corps. Gifted with an unwavering self-confidence and a sense of superiority over others, as much with regards to his talent as his competence, he felt predestined from the very beginning of his career to hold the highest posts of the army, for reasons of prestige, no doubt, but also due to a motivation related to a profound desire to assume responsibilities of paramount importance.

The year of the Kapp Putsch also saw the marriage of officer Manstein to Jutta Sibylle von Loesch. On January 10, 1920, Manstein asked for her hand, only three days after having met her for the first time, during a hunting trip at Deichslau, in Silesia. The wedding took place five months later on June 10, at Lorzendorf, in the Namslau region of Silesia. They were a happy couple throughout their marriage, until the death of *Frau* Manstein in 1966. They had three children, Gisela, Gero, and Rüdiger, born respectively in 1921, 1922, and 1929. A lieutenant in the Wehrmacht, Gero lost his life on the battlefield in Russia, on the banks of Lake Ilmen on October 29, 1942.

Manstein's father-in-law, Arthur von Loesch, was an aristocrat and landowner in the Namslau region, where he owned three estates: Lorzendorf, Hennersdorf, and Butschkau. The latter was located in a district named "*Reichtaler Ländchen*," which the Allies had granted to Poland under the terms of the Versailles Treaty. In the second volume of his *Memoirs*, Manstein expresses his rancor against the expropriation of the Butschkau estate and the amputation of part of Silesia to Poland's advantage, a region which, in his opinion, never belonged to it and over which that country had no rights, from neither an historic nor ethnographic perspective. Concerning the people's right to self-determination, he stresses, this region was purely German. "Even within our own family, we too suffered the consequences of the Versailles diktat," he writes bitterly.[18] Furthermore, such resentment would explain, in part, his belligerent attitude during the preparations for the Poland campaign in the spring and summer of 1939.

The secret rearmament of the Reichswehr and preparations for the next war

In accordance with the Treaty of Versailles from June 28, 1919, Germany's military power was severely diminished, its army having been reduced to 100,000 men, of whom 4,000 were officers. Composed of seven infantry and three cavalry divisions, and distributed among seven military districts (*Wehrkreise*), the army was henceforth conceived of as a small force of border guards or police in charge of maintaining order, all the while being forbidden to possess heavy artillery, assault tanks, or combat aircraft. Additionally, it was banned from an entire section of the national territory, i.e. the demilitarized zone that included the left bank of the Rhine, to be occupied until 1935, along with 50 kilometers of the right bank. One must thus recognize that the disarmament was never accepted by the majority of the German population and its political leaders, and even less so by the officers' corps of the Reichswehr. As a result of the Treaty of Versailles, the disarmament appeared as an insult, as if the great nation's sovereignty had been confiscated. Consequently, it could be nothing more than provisional.

Because of his exceptional military aptitude, Manstein was among the 4,000 officers retained to protect the traditions of the old imperial army. Major General Fritz von Loßberg, president of the commission in charge of designing an army that had been reduced to 100,000 men, called upon Manstein to assist him in this undertaking in Berlin. Former chief of staff to the First Army, Loßberg had a great deal of esteem for Manstein's natural talents from the very moment he had worked under his direction during the Battle of the Somme. The officers working in the commission fulfilled their duties with the idea of rectifying and reconstituting a national army freed from any obstacle. For them, the new army had foremost to be composed of an elite group, an army of officers. Among the 40,000 officers of the interim Reichswehr of 400,000 men, which had emerged out of the defeat on the ruins of the imperial army, they had no difficulty in designating 4,000 officers to the new army of 100,000 men. These new appointed officers were chosen particularly for their honesty, authority, and above all, their competence. In fact, several of the selected candidates were staff officers.

Colonel General Seeckt, as commander in chief of the army, endeavored to offset, organizationally speaking, certain constraints imposed by the victors. The creation of the *Truppenamt* (Troop Office) had the objective of replacing, clandestinely, the general staff which the Treaty of Versailles had dissolved. Manstein had not been able to complete his staff officer training at the *Kriegsakademie* of Berlin, and his only true qualification for the general staff was the experience he had acquired within various staffs during the war. But above all, it was essential for him to gain command-level experience. On October 1, 1921, he thus received command of the 6th Company of the 5th Prussian Infantry Regiment at Angermünde, in Pomerania. He held this command for the customary period of two years. On October 1, 1923, he was transferred to the staff of *Wehrkreiskommando II* in Stettin (Szczecin), then, on October 1, 1924, to that of *Wehrkreiskommando IV* in Dresden, where he taught military tactics and history for three years to the young officers selected to serve on the staffs. During this period, the course was no more than a pretext for the training formerly provided at the *Kriegsakademie*, the activities of which the Treaty of Versailles had prohibited. After having been appointed to major on February 1, 1927, he was selected to serve, beginning on October 1, on the staff of the *Infanterieführer IV* in Magdeburg.

On September 1, 1929, he was posted to the Reichswehr Ministry at Berlin. There he oversaw Group One of the T1 department, which corresponded to the operations department of the *Truppenamt*, i.e. the general staff. Under Manstein's direction, Group One supervised the operations of the staff to the army's commander in chief and distributed work to all of the troops. It also organized the *Kriegsspiele* (war games which consisted of performing maneuvers on maps) and educational lectures, which were part of the operational training for high-ranking commanders and staff officers.

Within the Reichswehr's general staff, Manstein demonstrated a level of intelligence and competency clearly superior to that of his colleagues. His proposals often garnered the praise of his chiefs, thus leaving in the shade those put forth by his higher ranking colleagues, like Lieutenant Colonel Wilhelm Keitel, who would become the Wehrmacht's chief of staff of the supreme command from 1938 to 1945. From this moment on, Keitel suffered a profound jealousy for the ambitious and talented Manstein, and their relationship amounted to nothing more than a reciprocal hatred until the end of the Second World War.

The high command of the Reichswehr recognized Manstein's talent to such an extent that it relied more and more on his opinion concerning decisive military issues. In volume two of his *Memoirs*, Manstein expressed the great satisfaction that he felt for having his talent recognized for its true worth: "For me, this success had the consequence of giving henceforth a certain weight to my opinion as a member of the operations department."[19]

In his role as chief of Group One, Manstein developed the first mobilization plans for a Reichswehr of 100,000 men, at a time when the French Army was able to mobilize, with only a short delay, approximately thirty divisions, the Polish Army approximately twenty, and the Czech Army approximately fifteen. In order to confront the superiority of such enemies, he proposed to triple the number of infantry divisions from seven to twenty-one. For this he recommended, in accordance with accelerated training, that all enlisted men, officers or not, be able to assume in times of crisis the duties of two ranks superior to their own. However, the principal problem of expanding the number of infantry divisions did not stem from the training of enlisted men, but rather from the insufficiency of equipment and modern materials, despite a secret, limited rearmament initiated at the beginning of the 1920s.

Contrary to what has often been asserted, German rearmament was a reality long before Hitler's arrival in power. From the very first years of the Weimar Republic, the Reichswehr, under Seeckt's command, had proceeded with a discreet rearmament which benefited from the collaboration between German politicians and industrialists. The Reichswehr was developing prototypes of weapons prohibited by the Treaty of Versailles (tanks, combat aircraft, heavy artillery, etc.), which depended on German industry equipping itself for mass production in order to furnish, at the appropriate moment, the necessary armaments. Moreover, prototype fabrication on behalf of the Reichswehr expanded to other countries, not only in the U.S.S.R., but in Sweden, Switzerland, Spain, and the Netherlands. However, the Rapallo Treaty of 1922 had finalized the details of the secret military agreement that the leaders of the Reichswehr had signed the previous year with their Red Army counterparts, without the German political authorities' knowledge. The restoration of German military power, as a means to facilitate the revision of the Treaty of Versailles and the recovery of the Reich's pre-war position was, since the beginning of the 1920s, the primary object of the military and many German politicians. One even envisioned the war as an instrument of foreign policy, once the Reichswehr regained its ability to launch offensives and circumstances were favorable.

The senior officers of the Reichswehr believed that war was a legitimate prerogative of the state's sovereignty. They rejected, because of this, the Kellogg-Briand Pact of 1928, which condemned any recourse to war as an instrument of national policy. All things considered, the mentality of the generals had hardly changed since the time of Field Marshal Helmuth Graf von Moltke, chief of general staff of the Prussian Army from 1858 to 1888. In 1888, he described his world vision in the following terms: "Peace is a dream [...] and war is one element in God's world order. In war, one finds the greatest of man's virtues: courage, self-abnegation, sense of loyalty, and spirit of sacrifice. Without war, the world would succumb to materialism." At the beginning of the 1920s, Colonel General Seeckt, commander in chief of the army, abandoned pacifism, the League of Nations, and the principle of collective security based on a general disarmament to guarantee peace. "My personal training prohibits me from seeing in the idea of eternal peace anything other than a dream [...]." Lieutenant General Ludwig Beck, who would become chief of the army general staff after Hitler's rise to power, attempted to justify the war when he wrote at the end of the 1930s: "The last resort of the states in their mutual relations will remain in the future military power." He concluded logically: "We are not able to eliminate war."[20] In short, for the German officers, war was an historic fact of nature and, if it had not existed, it would have been quite simply necessary to invent it, for it was essential to any policy claiming to represent the interets of state.

Not only did the senior officers of the Reichswehr consider that another European war was inevitable, they deemed it necessary so that Germany could tear the Treaty of Versailles to shreds and find once again its genuine place in Europe. "The army can have only one thing in sight, war, and not eternal peace," declared, as early as 1920, Colonel General Seeckt. In a secret document from the minister of the Reichswehr, dating from April 1923, it was indicated that the Reich could only recover its liberty and national independence, as well its economic and political power, through war. In December 1923, Lieutenant Colonel Schleicher, chief of the Office of Ministerial Affairs within the *Truppenamt*, defined the objectives of the military leadership: "1. Strengthen state authority; 2. rehabilitate the economy; 3. rebuild a military capability; all are prerequisites for a foreign policy that has the goal of creating a Greater Germany." In May 1925, another secret document from the Reichswehr Ministry bluntly stipulated: "That Germany will in the future have to fight a war for its continued existence as a people and a state is certain." In a memorandum from March 6, 1926, Colonel Joachim von Stülpnagel, chief of the operations section of the *Truppenamt*, emphasized the importance of reinforcing the army, the instrument of expansionism responsible for recuperating territories that the Reich had lost through the Treaty of Versailles, of reestablishing German supremacy in Europe, particularly at the expense of France, and of preparing the ultimate battle for world domination against the Anglo-Saxon powers.[21]

Recent research has demonstrated that the German generals had planned and prepared a new war well before Hitler's accession to the leadership of the German state. In fact, the march to war began ten years prior to the National Socialists' rise to power. The occupation of the Ruhr by Franco-Belgian troops in 1923, because of Germany's non-payment of reparations due in accordance with the Treaty of Versailles, left its mark on the spirit of the Reichswehr leaders to such an extent that they decided from that moment to devise an ambitious plan aimed at establishing a great army, even larger than the one that had served the Kaiser in 1914. It was Seeckt who conceived of the secret plan to increase the army's offensive capacity to 2.8 million men, distributed among 102 divisions, under the command of 252 generals. Thus, on September 1, 1939, at the unleashing of the Second World War, the German Army indeed had at its disposal 2.8 million men, divided among 102 divisions, and at least 252 generals. It is interesting to note that it included among its ranks approximately 600,000 more men than the Kaiser's army in 1914.

One should also recall that, at the time Seeckt drafted this secret plan, Hitler was serving his prison sentence at the Bavarian prison of Landsberg and was contemplating *Mein Kampf*. He never thought, when he came to power ten years later, that the high command of the Reichswehr would have already laid the foundations for the creation of a powerful greater Germany. Moreover, without the military's preparation of a secret rearmament plan, it would be difficult to conceive that the Third Reich could have managed, in a period of only six years, to endow itself with a powerful instrument of war that would permit it to dominate the entire continent within the very first years of the war. One month prior to the launching of the Russian campaign, on May 26, 1941, an officer of the Wehrmacht accurately made the following remarks: "When Hitler rose to power, he realized that the Reichswehr had already laid the technical foundations necessary to carry out a large-scale rearmament." It would thus be false to claim that the

German generals would have wanted to develop nothing more than military force with only a defensive role, and that Hitler, once in power, would have compelled them to create a war machine endowed with offensive capacities.[22]

At the time, Manstein was aware that the Reichswehr, despite the quality of training and the motivation of the troops, was not only incapable of supporting a conflict against France, but also of waging war against Poland or Czechoslovakia. An insufficiency of weapons and modern equipment limited their professional standards. Because of the restricted number of forces and the inadequacy of its equipment, the German Army was able to do nothing more at this time than conduct diversionary battles, with the results being inevitably disastrous. In order to overcome these shortcomings, Manstein reinforced the border defenses with coils of barbed wire, anti-tank ditches, and thick-walled concrete pillboxes.

Already able to speak French well, and having learned Spanish in the meantime, Manstein took advantage of the credits granted to the army meant to encourage officers to travel abroad. In 1931 and 1932, he traveled to the Soviet Union. In the fall of 1931, he accompanied the head of the *Truppenamt*, General Wilhelm Adam, to the U.S.S.R., where they visited the principal Soviet military installations. He also met commanders of the Red Army in Moscow and Leningrad, in particular the people's commissar and defense deputy, General Mikhaïl Tukhatchevsky. In the summer of 1932, he returned to the U.S.S.R., this time as General Adam's official representative, and participated in military maneuvers in the Ukraine and the Caucasus.

These two trips to the U.S.S.R. intensified the flames of Manstein's anti-Bolshevism. After the war, he recounted that returning to Germany brought about an even greater sense of relief knowing that Bolshevik Russia was not part of Europe. With regards to this, he wrote in volume two of his *Memoirs*: "Even though the Soviet regime liked to refer to the Western ideas of Marxism and to eagerly acquire the latest technologies of the Western world, the Soviet Union was no longer part of Europe! The shadow of Asian despotism hung over the country, its people, and its events."[23] But even more importantly, his visits into Soviet territory confirmed for him the image that the German officers' corps had of the alleged "despotic Asian tyranny," embodied particularly by the political commissars of the Red Army. In other words, his visits reinforced his prejudices in which the cadres of the Red Army and the Communist Party were for the most part Jewish, and which led him, during the Second World War, to support Nazi Germany's war of extermination in the U.S.S.R. against the Jewish Bolshevik enemy.

II

THE WEHRMACHT: ARMY OF THE THIRD REICH

Like the majority of his colleagues in the officers' corps, Manstein enthusiastically welcomed Hitler's rise to power, the establishment of the National Socialist Party dictatorship, and the end of the Weimar Republic. If, for the aristocratic officers like Manstein, Hitler and the Nazis were no more than upstarts, they nonetheless shared a similar worldview, which would explain their willingness to collaborate in order to accomplish their common intentions: the creation of a powerful army endowed with strong offensive capabilities allowing Germany to assert its dominance in Europe.

The officers' corps and Hitler: A common worldview?

Just prior to his last trip to the U.S.S.R., Manstein was promoted to the rank of lieutenant colonel. At the time of Hitler's appointment to the Reich Chancellery on January 30, 1933, he had been in charge of the chasseurs battalion of the 4th Infantry Regiment at Kolberg (Kolobrzeg), in Pomerania, since October 1, 1932. For the conservative Prussian aristocrat, Hitler's rise to power incited more hopes than worries, for Manstein saw in him the ideal man for restoring Germany to the ranks of a great power, a position that would obviously be based on a powerful army. After all, was Hitler not the one who promised to break once and for all the chains of the Treaty of Versailles, which unjustly held the Reich in a weakened state vis-à-vis other European powers? Furthermore, did Manstein not have to draft, several years earlier and with the greatest of worries, mobilization plans for an army almost without defense against eventual attacks from neighboring enemies? The collapse of the Weimar Republic was thus for him a source of satisfaction, as his assessment of the regime's fourteen years indicates: "Divided on the inside, powerless on the outside."[24]

The abolition of democracy and its fundamental liberties, and the installation of a totalitarian regime governed by the National Socialist Party, were not only welcomed by Manstein, but also by a large majority of the officers' corps. One must admit that between Hitler and the officers of the Reichswehr, who were opposed to parliamentary democracy and to Communism, eager to accelerate Germany's rearmament, and concerned with preparing for the next war once any reservations contrary to the "Bohemian corporal" were overcome, there was a striking similarity of viewpoints and objectives. Moreover, the new German leader offered the officers a political perspective that was in line with their personal and professional ambitions.[25]

The German Army was often presented as an organization that would remain, due to a supposed apolitical stance, foreign to the National Socialist ideology. In fact, the anti-liberal and anti-democratic position of the army had never been as pronounced as it had been during the Third Reich. Already, prior to 1933, the officers' corps of the Reichswehr considered the Weimar Republic, with its liberal and democratic political system, an organization foreign to German political culture, a regime imposed on them by the victors of the First World War and, moreover, marked by the "infamous" Treaty of Versailles. Due to this, the Reichswehr rejected liberalism, democracy, and pluralism, the foundational political values of the Weimar Republic, a political regime that it judged not only as weak and decadent, but also as the source of national division. For him, the republican regime should only be temporary, providing enough time for Germany to recover its military power and to free itself from the constraints imposed upon its sovereignty by the peace treaty of 1919.

Considered a bastion of "traditional Germany" well in advance of the 1848 revolutions, the officers' corps advocated a return to an authoritarian political system in Germany—not necessarily monarchist, even though that was the wish of the majority among them—in which the army would find again the privileged position that it occupied within the Reich prior to 1918, as a pillar of the regime in power. Fundamentally reactionary, the majority of the officers were against the democrats, socialists, communists, pacifists, the Jews, Poland, and

Czechoslovakia. Concerning foreign policy, their objective was not limited to the simple revision of the Treaty of Versailles in terms of restoring the German borders of 1914, particularly those in the East, but also to create a powerful armament. Certain generals were already aspiring to expand the territories into Eastern Europe all the way to the Narva-Rostov line which the Brest-Litovsk Treaty of March 1918 had allowed Hindenburg and Ludendorff's high command to occupy, and which would make of the German Reich a true continental autarchic power.

This worldview on the level of domestic and foreign policy was common to both Hitler and his acolytes in the National Socialist Party. It is thus hardly surprising that the vast majority of the Reichswehr officers rejoiced at Hitler's rise to power, at the creation of a dictatorship by the National Socialist Party on the ashes of the liberal pluralist democracy, and at the replacement of the Weimar Republic with the Third Reich. Contrary to defensive opinions often put forth, the army was not part of the Third Reich as a simple apparatus to execute Hitler's policies. It knowingly participated in the Reich's mission.[26] And as someone who was well integrated into the officers' corps, Manstein was fully involved in the dominant ethos.

The latter, who at the time had approved of his superiors' decision to let Hitler's putsch attempt in Munich fail on November 9, 1923 (though it was assisted by General Ludendorff), and for the same motives as during the Kapp Putsch, now accepted, without any reservations, to serve the new legally constituted government. Hitler's program, which was a source of great pride, consisted in eliminating the system of parliamentary democracy, eradicating Marxism, restoring national unity by rallying the worker and peasant masses under the concept of national community (*Volksgemeinschaft*), extolling nationalism, giving absolute priority to the army, particularly by returning to it the rank and power which it had traditionally enjoyed within the state prior to 1918, and breaking the chains of the Treaty of Versailles, so that the Reich might recover its status as a great power.

Moreover, after the war, Manstein explained the principal reasons as to why the officers' corps had welcomed the National Socialist Party's rise to power: "By emphasizing the idea of nationalism and rising up against the Versailles diktat, the [National Socialist] Party made a great impression on the soldiers. It would be the same for its relentless battle against the Communists [...], as well as for its determination to surmount the division between the bourgeoisie and the workers in Germany. Indeed, one could consider such problems not only as the underlying reasons for the 1918 collapse, and for all the following upheavals in the Reich, but also as a serious danger for the future. How could Germany once again recover its standing as a great power and defend itself against foreign attacks as long as it had not put an end to these domestic rifts? One must recognize that the other parties would not have been able to repair these fractures. The Communists' objective was to establish a dictatorship following the Soviet model. The socialists always remained deeply loyal to the idea of class struggle. The bourgeois parties fought to maintain their ideological and economic positions or dreamed of returning to a time in the past."[27]

Lieutenant General Ludwig Beck, commander in chief of the 1st Cavalry Division and future chief of the army general staff, wrote shortly after Hitler's rise to power that the nature of the political regime change that occurred on January 30, 1933 was what he had desired for many years, and that, for this reason, was extremely happy that his hopes had not been deceived. "This is the first true glimpse of light since 1918," he added. During the same period, Lieutenant General Werner Freiherr von Fritsch, commander in chief of *Wehrkreiskommando III* in Berlin and future commander in chief of the army, declared that "'Nationalist Socialist thought'" was already "the sole vehicle of German intellectual life" and that the Wehrmacht had to become "one of the chief exponents and promoters of the National Socialist movement."[28] Such remarks can be considered as particularly representative of the position of the German military caste and without a doubt of Manstein himself, who would have considered Beck and Fritsch as his two mentors during the years when he would have worked with them at the army's high command.

In short, there was a completely natural community spirit between the senior officers of the Reichswehr and the leaders of the Hitler regime, which was built upon a hatred of Jews, democracy, liberalism, Marxism, socialism, and Bolshevism. Equally so, it relied upon the necessity of a militarization of German society and an excessive rearmament of the armed forces, both crucial for setting into motion a policy of power destined to destroy the Treaty of Versailles and to undertake in the East the conquest of a vital living space which would establish henceforth the German hegemony and domination of the entire

European continent. And so, on January 30, 1934, within the context of a speech marking the anniversary of his rise to power, Hitler emphasized the relationship between the armed forces and the National Socialist regime, declaring that the state was supported by two pillars: one political, represented by the national community (*Volksgemeinschaft*), brought forth from the National Socialist movement; the other military, embodied by the Wehrmacht. The theory that the armed forces constituted one of the two pillars which supported the state coincided perfectly with the aspirations of the military leaders and the officers' corps in general.[29]

On April 4, 1934, the minister of the Reichswehr and commander in chief of the armed forces, Colonel General Werner von Blomberg, could not have expressed any more clearly this shared sense of community, when he spoke of the German Army as "the protector and guardian of National Socialist Germany and its living-space." In December 1938, Colonel General Walther Brauchitsch, commander in chief of the army, delivered his day's orders to the officers' corps in which he underscored a worldview common to the Wehrmacht, Hitler, and National Socialism: "The Wehrmacht and National Socialism are from the same intellectual roots. They will accomplish great things for the nation if they follow the example and the teachings of the Führer, who embodies in his person the genuine soldier and National Socialist." In March 1939, Grand Admiral Erich Raeder, commander in chief of the Kriegsmarine, declared that "the Wehrmacht and the Party have become an indivisible whole in attitude and spirit." In short, the conviction formerly expressed by Colonel General Fritsch, commander in chief of the army from 1934 to 1938, in which the "'foundation of the modern army must be Nationalist Socialist," was widely shared among the ranks of the army.[30]

As his behavior and attitude would demonstrate during the war, Manstein clearly participated in this mindset, at least for the most part. His remarks after the war, asserting that the army had been impervious to Nazi ideology by remaining attached to its "traditional ideas of simplicity, honesty, and military honor," are, to say the least, fallacious. Such is the case in the passage from his *Memoirs* where he writes with regards to the Wehrmacht: "If Hitler was unable to accuse the army of lacking loyalty towards the state, he understood perfectly that it was unwilling to throw its ideas overboard in order to adopt the National

Socialist ideology, and that this attitude would make the army even more popular within such an expansive people's party."[31]

The introduction of racial legislation into the army and Manstein's protest

The principal military leaders, Colonel General Blomberg and his assistant Major General Walter von Reichenau, each recognized for their profound National Socialist convictions, did not hesitate to brush under the carpet Seeckt's axiom in which the army had to steer clear of political life, remain above political parties, and thus form a state-within-a-state. They were thus largely responsible for the army's integration into the Hitler regime and for its indoctrination into National Socialist ideology during the years following Hitler's rise to power. In their minds, the relationship between the army and the state had to be based on the absence of compromise between the two powers. Such a distinction was considered beneficial for each other, as soon as the state committed itself to satisfying the needs of the army and recognizing its primacy within the nation. Thus, not only did Blomberg and Reichenau celebrate the "bringing into line" (*Gleichschaltung*) of the whole of society according to National Socialist principles, but they promoted the "Aryan clauses" and the teaching of Nazi doctrine within the army.

On April 7, 1933, scarcely two months after Hitler's arrival in power, the National Socialist regime drafted the "Law of Restoration of the Civil Service" which, on the basis of the "Aryan paragraph" (*Arierparagraph*), removed Jews from the administration by forbidding them from practicing in civil service professions. One single exception, granted by intervention of the Reich president, old Field Marshal Hindenburg, concerned Jews who had served on the front or those whose fathers or sons died in combat. Four days later, a supplementary decree to the law defined as non-Aryan anyone who had three or four Jewish grandparents (*Volljude*), two Jewish grandparents (*Halbjude*), or even one single Jewish grandparent (*Vierteljude*). For the last two categories, the person in question was described as *Mischling* (mixed).

On February 28, 1934, Blomberg accepted, on his own initiative and without any insistence from Nazi leaders, the "Aryan paragraph" for the officers' corps. Although he did not question the exemption of non-Aryans who had fought during the Great War, his decision never-

theless led to the immediate dismissal of seventy officers. By crossing
this threshold, he was clearly indicating that Nazi ideology would func-
tion as a guiding principal, as much in theory as in the elaboration of
military policy. He therefore relinquished the traditional autonomy of
the Reichswehr in relation to political affairs.[32]

The racial legislation put into operation within the ranks of the
Reichswehr by its leaders met practically no opposition in the officers'
corps, which had been infused with a deep anti-Semitism ever since the
imperial era, an anti-Semitism which became even more radical with the
troubles at the end of the Great War and the advent of the Weimar
Republic. In the minds of many officers, there was no doubt that behind
the pacifists, the social democrats, and the Communists, whom they
held responsible for the 1918 military defeat and the collapse of the
imperial regime, hid the Jews.

In fact, of all the Reichswehr officers, only one protested against the
inclusion of the "Aryan paragraph" within the armed forces. His name:
Erich von Manstein. Promoted to the rank of colonel on December 1,
1933, then appointed general staff chief of *Wehrkreiskommando III* in
Berlin on February 1, 1934, Manstein had attempted, though in vain, to
come to the assistance of Klaus von Schmeling-Diringshofen, who was
dismissed from the army because he had a Jewish grandparent, which
made him a *Mischling* with regards to the racial legislation. For an officer like Schmeling-Diringshofen, to be discharged from the army was
the worst dishonor that he could have faced, as much from a professional perspective as from a social one. Like his fellow officers who had
suffered the same lot, it was difficult for him to understand why he
could no longer take part in the profession that he had chosen and
through which he had become so well known. He had thus written to
Manstein, his former commander at Kolberg, to inform him that
Germany would perhaps need him and his brother later, and that if such
a possibility should arise, they would be there to serve their country
once again.[33]

Colonel Manstein took the matter into his own hands and, on April
21, 1934, sent a memorandum to his superior, Lieutenant General Beck,
who had been head of the *Truppenamt*, i.e. of the general staff, since
October 1, 1933, to explain to him that the Schmeling-Diringshofen
case had led him to look into the establishment of the racial legislation
within the Reichswehr: "A few days ago, I learned the news of the

impending departure of a chasseurs battalion officer at Kolberg, due to the 'Aryan paragraph.' It concerns a young lieutenant for whom I have much esteem, particularly because of his character, his opinions, and his productivity. [...] I know that you are in a position to understand, *Herr* General, that as the former commander of this exceptional young officer who has faced such a tragic fate, I feel compelled and obliged to assist him in any what that I can. The case has led me to reflect deeply on the matter of any subsequent enforcement of the Aryan paragraph in the army [...]."

After having assured his superior that it was not his intention to blame the military leadership or to even criticize them, he informed him of his thoughts regarding the implementation of the "Aryan paragraph" in the army: "If the Reich is prepared to demand of a soldier the sacrifice of his life at all hours and for years, then legally it cannot now say to him: 'You are no longer a true German.' A man who has willingly become a soldier, who is thus ready to sacrifice his life at any moment for the German people, has rightly become, through his goodwill, a German. He has proven himself to be an Aryan, regardless if his grandmother was Aryan or not." Thereupon, the author of the letter stressed that "the honor of these young post-war soldiers is a matter of honor for all of us."

Colonel Manstein nevertheless reassured Lieutenant General Beck, particularly concerning his devotion to National Socialism and to racial ideology: "That we all approved of National Socialism and racial ideology, there is no doubt. But, in my opinion, we must not forget a soldier's honor who, until now, has inevitably united us all together." He also admitted that "Germans no longer wanted to serve under non-Aryans," even if this never before had any real importance. Although the leadership of the National Socialist Party could not appreciate what he was suggesting, Manstein declared that no officer would demand to see his lieutenant's family tree so long as he earned respect for his qualities as a good soldier. Clearly, he wanted the army to retain the right to judge its own members rather than abdicating such a prerogative to the civilians of the National Socialist Party. To this effect, he even considered the "Aryan paragraph" as the fruit of a campaign led by certain elements intending to destroy the officers' corps and to replace it, doubtlessly alluding to the Ernst Röhm's ambitions to swap the Reichswehr for the SA.[34]

In his move against the introduction of the "Aryan paragraph," Manstein was supported by his immediate commander, Lieutenant General Erwin von Witzleben. After having read it, Beck sent Manstein's letter to the Defense Ministry. Indignant about its contents, Major General Reichenau, whose nickname in the army was "General Nazi," then forwarded it to his superior, Colonel General Blomberg. He became so enraged by Manstein's written protest, which moreover appeared as meddling on the part of a subordinate officer in the area of expertise of a commander in chief of the armed forces, that he ordered General Fritsch, as army commander in chief, to take disciplinary measures straightaway against the officer in question. Fortunately for the latter, Fritsch took no action, thus avoiding for Manstein any consequences that could have been detrimental to his future career advancement. Despite his virulent anti-Semitism, Fritsch seems to have agreed with Manstein's position relative to the necessity of preserving the army's autonomy vis-à-vis the National Socialist Party. Manstein's written objection was thus not completely rejected. One does not know, however, the reverberation that it had within the officers' corps, nor if Blomberg even presented it to Hitler.[35]

Though recalcitrant towards the use of racial legislation in the army, Manstein nevertheless conceded that Jewish influence should be eradicated from society. However, with regards to his letter of protest, one must wonder if, for him, "Jewry" did not mean anything other than what Nazi ideology claimed it to be. Indeed, he appears to have broached the Jewish question according to a cultural perspective rather than through that of racial identity. In his eyes, a non-Aryan who had taken part in German culture through serving in the army became a German. Manstein was therefore most likely compelled to write such a letter to Beck not only because he wanted to be of assistance to his subordinate officer, Schmeling-Diringshofen, but also for his two grand-nephews, who were both solders in the Reichswehr and both *Mischlinge*. The two were children of his niece, *Frau* von Preuschen, née von Lewinski.

Furthermore, one must ask at what point his family, and therefore, his possible Jewish ancestry, motivated him to take the position against the introduction of the "Aryan paragraph" into the army. Much conjecture has circulated with regards to Manstein's potential Jewish ancestry. The fact that he was born under the Lewinski family name, and then adopted by the Manstein family has led several authors to presume that he was of Jewish lineage. They have suggested that Lewinski could be a variation of Levy, with the addition of the Polish patronymic suffix. Without ever being completely certain, Manstein himself worried that his great-great-grandfather Lewi could have been a rabbinical leader in Warsaw. At the very least, this is what Lieutenant Alexander Stahlberg, his adjutant during the Second World War on the Soviet front, and who also had Jewish ancestors, reported in his *Memoirs*. For his part, Manstein's son Rüdiger asserted that his family was perhaps of Jewish descent, but that there was no proof to confirm the supposition. The SS led an investigation into the ancestral origins of Manstein—whom it continued to call Lewinski—in April 1944, after his dismissal. However, the dossier was not completed, and whatever the SS could find with regards to the matter remains unknown.[36]

Though he raised objections against the "Aryan paragraph" and its use in the army, Manstein nevertheless remained highly ambiguous in his memorandum, particularly when he expressed his leanings toward National Socialism and racial ideology. For this reason one cannot truly talk about an act of resistance on his part against the Nazi regime and its fundamental principles. In fact, he only protested against a retroactive application of the dismissal of *Mischlinge* who were already members of the Reichswehr, and not against the future prohibition of admitting non-Aryans into the ranks of the army. In other words, he did not want the "Aryan paragraph" to have any retroactive effects for the *Mischlinge* who were serving in the army before its introduction, his clear intention being that Schmeling-Diringshofen, a subordinate officer for whom he had much respect, and his two grand-nephews could all remain in the Reichswehr. The introduction of racial legislation in the army forbidding future admission of all new *Mischling* into its ranks did not present a single problem for him. Evidently, neither political nor humane considerations had motivated his intervention. If he had opposed Blomberg's decree, it was simply because the latter was going against the principle of camaraderie in the army. Whatever the case may be, we must recognize that he demonstrated exceptional courage by daring, with regards to this issue, to place his career in jeopardy. This was nevertheless the last time he would dare to protest against a policy initiated by the regime.[37]

During the Second World War, he would implicate himself in war crimes against the Jewish populations of Poland and the U.S.S.R. Not only did he back the war of annihilation and extermination driven by the Wehrmacht in Eastern Europe, but he himself gave the orders authorizing and inciting the troops to act mercilessly towards the Jews in the occupied territories. Contrary to his attitude with regards to the *Mischlinge* of the German Army, whom he considered his comrades-in-arms, he behaved in a completely opposite manner towards the Jews of Eastern Europe, in particular those who were Communists, Slavs, or Asians. Personal ambitions in relation to his career advancement in the army, along with the prejudices prevalent in the officers' corps concerning the supposed menace of Jewish Bolshevism against the survival of the Reich, would explain such criminal anti-Semitism carried out in Eastern Europe.

The establishment of the "Aryan paragraph" in the army represented an important stage in the close integration of the organization within the Hitler regime. It marked the end of an era, that of the army's traditional autonomy in relation to political affairs. Henceforth, it was unmistakably no longer a question of a state-within-a-state, as was the case during the Weimar Republic. With the acceptance of National Socialism's racial principles in the army, one finds the seeds of future complicity on the part of the officers' corps in the racial and ideological war of extermination and annihilation in Bolshevik Russia, beginning in the summer of 1941.[38]

The "Night of the Long Knives" and the Führer's oath of allegiance

After the introduction of racial legislation into the ranks of the Reichswehr, the alignment of the armed forces to National Socialist ideology continued even more thoroughly, to Hitler's satisfaction as well has to the higher ranks of the army. When the leader of the National Socialist Party polled the leadership of the Reichswehr on April 11, 1934 to know if they would accept him as successor to the elderly Field Marshal Hindenburg, who was dying, and thus take on the two roles of president and chancellor of the Reich, they responded affirmatively. But the military leadership accepted him under one condition: he had to guarantee for them that the regime would safeguard the Reichswehr's monopoly over the military, in particular by carrying out a drastic reduction in the units of the SA, which would thus curtail any claims put forth by its leader Röhm. The latter saw in this paramilitary group of the Nazi movement, more than three million men strong, the seeds of the future German Army, which presupposed the suppression of traditional Reichswehr structures. He also envisioned his militia as the standard-bearer of a "second revolution," which he placed under the sign of socialism. The officers' corps, to which Manstein belonged, was evidently worried about such ambitions and did not cease, through the intervention of its leaders, to pressure Hitler into stifling the menace.

Hitler, who took into account that he would not have been able to come to power without the support of the Reichswehr generals, could do nothing other than comply with their conditions. Not only would he personally need the loyalty of his military leaders at the crucial moment when Hindenburg, the president of the Reich and commander in chief of the armed forces, would pass on, but also of the officers' corps, with all of its soldierly traditions and military talents, to achieve his dream of quickly building a powerful army, both well organized and disciplined, which would be destined to establish German hegemony in Europe through the conquest of vital *Lebensraum* in the East.

Already, at a meeting held on February 28 at the Defense Ministry, in which the senior officers of the Reichswehr participated, among whom in attendance was Colonel Manstein and the leaders of the SA and SS, Hitler rejected Röhm's ambitions with regard to the SA, preferring rather to entrust the latter with border protection and pre-military training. If Röhm came out of this meeting disappointed, it was not so for the Reichswehr leaders. Hitler's promise to grant the Reichswehr a monopoly over the military, to create a powerfully armed Wehrmacht, and to conquer living space in the East, was pleasing to the ears of the senior officers. Through such discourse, Hitler made a good impression on Manstein, all the more so since he was the embodiment, in his eyes, of legitimacy, like the Kaiser once was. He later recognized that: "This was the first time that I saw Hitler. [...] and I could not do anything but recognize that he had made a strong impression on me."[39]

Yet, rumors of an imminent putsch by the SA, fueled by Röhm's enemies, beginning with Blomberg, Reichenau, Hermann Göring, and Heinrich Himmler, the chief of the SS, provoked Hitler, to whom many of the SA leaders remained faithful, particularly Viktor Lutze, to strike to eliminate Röhm and reduce the SA's influence. The Reichswehr, which viewed the SA chief's ambitions more and more suspiciously, placed weapons, ammunition, and transportation at the disposal of the SS, which, through its modest numbers and its restriction to police work, did not yet present a threat to it. All the leaders of the Reichswehr, Blomberg and Reichenau initially, but also Fritsch and Beck, stood ready for imminent action against Röhm. Manstein's postwar assertion that the coup prompted by Hitler against the SA leadership on June 30, 1934, had taken the German Army "completely by surprise," is thus false.[40]

During the purge of June 30, 1934, the notorious "Night of the Long Knives," approximately one hundred victims were assassinated, including not only Röhm and the principal leaders of the SA, along with the supporters of the "second revolution," but also all those who, in Hitler's view, were liable to lead the slightest opposition. The chancellor took the opportunity to settle old debts by executing all those whose actions he could not forgive, first of all Lieutenant General Schleicher, former chancellor and minister of the Reichswehr during the final moments of the Weimar Republic, and Major General Ferdinand von Bredow, Schleicher's right arm.

At the end of the "Night of the Long Knives," the SA was placed under the command of Lutze, who endeavored to purge the organization's ranks. In the shadow of the army, its mission was to do nothing more than provide the reservists with political education and physical training, in addition to recruiting volunteers. Moreover, the carrying of weapons was strictly forbidden. The Reichswehr could thus consider itself satisfied.

Like his peers, Manstein welcomed Hitler's resolve which allowed him to crush the SA and to eliminate, as a result, the organization which not only seriously destabilized the regime, but also threatened the exclusive rights of the army in relation to the carrying of weapons. For having saved the German people from civil war, Hitler commanded nothing but respect from him. Admittedly, Manstein was incensed by the assassination of the two generals, which had led him, with the company of a handful of colleagues, to support Fritsch in his attempt to open an investigation on the fate of Schleicher and Bredow. But Blomberg, who was still celebrating the elimination of the SA and the support given by Hitler to the army's authority within the state, refused to pursue it.[41] Instead of returning to the attack, Manstein joined the large majority of the officers' corps who were completely occupied with cracking open the champagne to celebrate the destruction of the SA. The fact that his protest against the "Aryan paragraph" almost brought disciplinary action against him, which would have jeopardized his career, explains without a doubt his lack of motivation in this matter.

For a large number of army officers, Nazism, however flawed it may have been, was preferable to the Bolshevism that Hitler had succeeded in presenting as the only other alternative. The Hitler regime appeared to them as the best solution for Germany. The army's complicity in the events of June 30, 1934, had only served to unite it all the more closely with Hitler and his regime. But in doing so, it opened wide the gates for a crucial extension of Hitler's power when Hindenburg died on August 2, 1934. On the eve of the field marshal's death, the ministerial cabinet had decided that the functions of the president and the chancellor of the Reich would henceforth be fused together in Hitler's hands. The title of president was thus abolished; Hitler would be referred to as Führer and Chancellor of the Reich. In his role as minister of the Reichswehr, Blomberg was included among the signatories of this constitutional amendment. Following this, Hitler would automatically become the supreme commander of the armed forces at the time of Hindenburg's death. And so disappeared for the Reichswehr any possibility of appealing to the president of the Reich and supreme commander at the head of the government. But the Reichswehr leaders were not excessively concerned about it. To the contrary, they were pleased with the results of the referendum held on August 19, 1934, in which 89.9 percent of the population approved the powers, henceforth without limits, bestowed upon Hitler. At the end of the referendum, Blomberg gave orders to the army demanding that his officers and soldiers address Hitler as "*Mein Führer.*"

Additionally, Blomberg and Reichenau were resolved to forge ahead. They wanted to take advantage of the situation by linking Hitler even more closely to the armed forces. It was on their own initiative that they drafted the oath of unconditional allegiance to the person of the Führer, which each officer and soldier of the armed forces was obliged to take on August 2, during ceremonies organized throughout the country. In the eyes of Colonel Manstein and his fellow officers, the oath only helped to restore the type of relationship that had formerly existed with the Kaiser. From the moment they took the oath of allegiance, they felt united to the person of the Führer, similar to the past when they had been united to the German emperor and the King of Prussia.[42] Through such a personalized demonstration of loyalty, Blomberg and Reichenau were hoping to cement with Hitler a privileged bond that would strengthen the role of the army as the second pillar of the state, by the side of the party. Obviously, Hitler was quite overjoyed by this demonstration of loyalty towards him from the Reichswehr.

The oath erased any distinction between loyalty to the state and loyalty to Hitler. Because of this, opposition became even more difficult. This must have been a good pretext for those who, like Manstein, later hesitated to join in a conspiracy against Hitler. And yet, they had hardly hesitated when it came time to break their oath of allegiance to the Weimar Republic and immediately offer their loyalty to the person of the Führer. In fact, it was an oath that must have later presented a moral dilemma to a certain number of senior officers, when their leader set off in a direction that they knew could lead to nothing less than the destruction of their nation. The oath would also permit an even larger number of officers to exonerate themselves of all personal responsibility for the unspeakable crimes that they had perpetrated under the orders of the supreme commander, whose true nature had appeared to them during the "Night of the Long Knives."[43]

III

MANSTEIN AND THE
MARCH TO WAR

The acceleration in rearmament, expansion of the officers' corps, advancement in military careers, the empowerment of the army as the second pillar of the state alongside the National Socialist Party, and Hitler's first diplomatic successes all strengthened the armed forces' bonds to the regime. As part of a group of talented senior officers, Manstein was thus greatly favored by the arrival of Hitler in power. Massive investment and a rapid expansion of units accelerated his promotions, allowing him to quickly climb the echelons of the military hierarchy, from the rank of lieutenant colonel when Hitler took power, to lieutenant general on the eve of the war. Despite the fact that he had no formal staff officer training per se, he nevertheless held positions of primary importance within the army's general staff. The swiftness of his ascension was thus in many respects quite remarkable, and was a testament to the exceptional talents of an officer who, on September 1, 1939, did not even figure in the list of the fifty highest ranking members of the German Army.[44]

The Wehrmacht and the acceleration of rearmament

On July 1, 1935, Manstein was appointed chief of the operations branch of the army general staff, a particularly prestigious position because of its responsibilities. On October 1, 1936, he was promoted to the rank of major general and, five days later, to the position of first quartermaster, or chief of the logistics section, which made him the deputy chief of the army general staff. In his new role, he was selected to succeed General Beck who, as chief of general staff, was only subor-

43

dinate to Colonel General Fritsch, commander in chief of the army. As deputy chief of general staff, Manstein supervised, in addition to the operations department of the general staff, the departments of organization, fortresses, cartography, and engineering. From time to time, the chief of general staff's representative would organize *Kriegsspiele* with various army groups. Major General Manstein retained this key position until February 4, 1938, a crucial period during which the Third Reich tore apart the Treaty of Versailles by proceeding with an accelerated rearmament, reintroducing obligatory military service, and remilitarizing the Rhineland, thus achieving the restoration of national sovereignty.

Contrary to what Manstein and other German generals claimed after the war, it is not true that the military elite of the Reich sought to develop an army that was only defensive in nature.[45] We have seen how they proceeded with a secret rearmament from the beginning of the 1920s with the intention of developing the army's potential, permitting it to become once again the old imperial army, and how they created a plan for raising an army that would be even larger than the one that had served under the Kaiser before the Great War, and this, at the time of the Ruhr occupation by the Franco-Belgian troops in 1923. By the 1930s, changes in the political climate enabled them to bring to fruition plans developed by Seeckt, most notably the withdrawal from the Military Inter-Allied Commission of Control for Disarmament in January 1927, and the obtaining of equal rights at the Geneva Disarmament Conference in December 1932. In the spring of 1932, before Hitler even came to power, the minister of the Reichswehr, former Lieutenant General Schleicher, created the Umbau Plan, which would transform the German army within five years of April 1, 1933. Approved by Lieutenant General Hammerstein-Equord, at the time the army's commander in chief, the mobilization plan sought to augment the army from seven to twenty-one divisions (from 100,000 to 300,000 men), just as Manstein had proposed when he had been the head of Group One of the *Truppenamt*, and to even set up units provided with equipment prohibited under the Treaty of Versailles (heavy artillery, anti-tank batteries, tank battalions, etc.). Without the Reich having even denounced the military clauses of the peace treaty, its army had thus freed itself from the constraints that defeat had imposed upon it.

With Hitler's arrival to power and while Blomberg was minister of the Reichswehr, one witnessed a change in rhythm with the fulfillment of the Umbau Plan. It goes without saying that from the very beginning, armament and foreign policy were part of an expansionist military logic accepted without reservations by all of the generals, including Manstein. Hitler and the high ranks of the army were in perfect agreement on its implementation: the creation and utilization of military power. But, contrary to an apologetic legend that came about after the Second World War, the composition and significance of the armament was not dictated by Hitler to his military chiefs. The rearmament was conceived and carried out by the general staff of the army, within which Manstein played a crucial role during the decisive years from 1935 to 1938.

The first steps towards a policy of military expansion were undertaken in collaboration with the military command, particularly within the framework of withdrawing Germany from the Geneva Disarmament Conference and the League of Nations on October 14, 1933. From the moment the National Socialist regime was established, the generals advocated a policy of rapid and large-scale rearmament, not restricted by any treaties or agreements. A unilateral and autonomous military policy, such was the path recommended the entire time by the group of senior army officers surrounding Colonel General Blomberg. Quite obviously, they wanted neither a "League of Nations army," nor a militia, but rather a national army based on military service, which would not be subject to any restrictive regulations imposed by international treaties. An offensive military power was the essential instrument needed to achieve a revisionist policy of hegemony in Europe.

Should one be surprised that Blomberg, as minister of the Reichswehr, was responsible for pressuring a hesitant Hitler to withdraw from the Geneva Disarmament Conference and the League of Nations in October 1933, at the point when the generals were beginning to fear that a compromise concerning a limitation of arms could appear at any moment, which would have then prevented Germany from excessively rearming? For the officers, an acceleration in rearmament was essential for Germany to be in a position to prepare for and lead a war of conquest in the shortest amount of time. This mattered all the more, for in their opinion a major European conflict was in any case inevitable in the near future.

Thanks to the commotion during the month of October 1933, the officers, in agreement with the political leadership, were able to amend the Umbau Plan. On December 18, 1933, a new rearmament program was adopted which endeavored to raise by 1939, thus in less than six years, the number of mobilized soldiers to thirty-six divisions during peacetime and to sixty-three in wartime. The rearmament, already clandestinely underway during the Weimar Republic, had to be further accelerated in order to quickly create an instrument of power so strong that any other force attempting to intervene would face incalculable risks. During the same period, in order to intensify the army's expansion, the military chiefs solicited Hitler to introduce a draft and to remilitarize the Rhineland as soon as the international situation would permit it.[46]

In the spring of 1935, with diplomatic circumstances to its advantage, Germany switched from a clandestine to an overt rearmament. On March 10, 1935, Göring, in his position as air minister, announced that the Reich was henceforth equipped with an air force, the Luftwaffe. Then, on March 16, 1935, officially repudiating the military clauses of the Treaty of Versailles, Hitler issued a law on the reconstruction of the army which included the following three points: 1) reinstatement of obligatory military service; 2) a peacetime army of thirty-six divisions; 3) another law for the reorganization of the new army. This last point, published on March 21, 1935, abandoned the term Reichswehr, which was meant to designate a protective force, for the term Wehrmacht, which denoted more appropriately a combined-arms force, though the latter term had been in wide use for some time throughout the political and military circles of the Reich. Almost simultaneously, Hitler announced the restoration of the army general staff as well as the prestigious Berlin *Kriegsakademie*, both of which represented infractions of the Treaty of Versailles.

The replacement of the small Reichswehr with the Wehrmacht and the reinstatement of obligatory military service, which led to the enlistment of 650,000 men in the autumn of 1935, and of 1,200,000 in 1936, occurred to a great extent under the supervision of Major General Manstein and his immediate superiors, Colonel General Fritsch and General Beck. These three men were ardent champions of the new military policy, dedicated partisans of the accelerated rearmament who were unconcerned with foreign reactions, which they left for the diplomats to avoid. Beginning in December 1935, they abandoned the

Umbau Plan's concept of "strategic defense" in favor of an "offensive defense." The objective could not be more clearly defined: to reinforce the offensive military capabilities of the German Army. In June 1936, after having increased the duration of military service from one to two years, they anticipated being in a position of mobilizing an army of 2,680,936 men by 1937–1938. In their estimations, the total number of servicemen should increase to 3,612,673 men by 1940. In the autumn of 1939, the Wehrmacht was able to account for 2,758,000 men in its ranks, divided into 102 divisions—numbers far superior to those of the Kaiser's army which, in the summer of 1914 only included 2,147,000 men in its ranks, divided into 87 divisions. And, by that fall of 1939, this powerful military machine declared itself ready to move into action, for its only objective was to lead a war of aggression.

Clearly, such an accelerated rearmament program would place the Reich's economic resources under an extreme amount of pressure. Military spending represented approximately one quarter of public investment in 1933, and nearly three quarters in 1938. Germany was thus confronted with the possibility of no longer being able to follow its long-term armament plan that she herself had implemented. In August of 1936, Major General Friedrich Fromm, chief of the General Army Office, brought to Colonel General Fritsch's attention the impending dilemma. "By 1940, military spending will have risen to such an extent that an army of this size, ready to intervene at any moment, will no longer be able to be supported by Germany. It will be necessary to either dismantle this army, which is ready for war—making this entire under-taking worthless—or to not hesitate to utilize the Wehrmacht after this period." Yet the army general staff, in which Manstein played a prima-ry role, categorically refused to slow down the rearmament, particular-ly because of the deterioration of the international situation, a conse-quence of its own policies which had provoked the Western powers to take long-term countermeasures by initiating their own rearmament. As a result, the only solution was to utilize the Wehrmacht prematurely. Furthermore, the Führer's memorandum concerning the "four year plan," which was made public at this time, should be considered in rela-tion to this dilemma that one distinctly perceived in the Wehrmacht command. In the memorandum, Hitler demanded that both the econo-my and the Wehrmacht be ready for war within a period of four years.[47]

To this effect, under the leadership of Fritsch, Beck, and above all,

Manstein, the army adopted a new strategy to revitalize the war of operational mobility: a war based on the theories of Major General Heinz Guderian in which there was a concentrated use of armored tanks and combat aircraft. As the creator of German armored warfare, Guderian advocated the use of tanks in massive formations within the framework of panzer divisions (*Panzerdivisionen*), which would in turn be directly reinforced by aerial units. The objective was to take the enemy by storm, and after having capitalized on the effect of surprise, send in rapid, armored, and mechanized units, which would be supported by the air force. Surrounding the opposing armies through a large-scale encirclement operation was meant to result in a quick and decisive victory. Through such a theory of tactical management, which was based on mobility and founded on both surprise and rapidity, breaking through the front was entrusted to the panzer divisions and the Luftwaffe squadrons, while ground occupation was left to the infantry divisions. Complying with the new strategy, Manstein, in agreement with Fritsch and Beck, augmented the thirty-six infantry divisions with three tank divisions, the role of which was to serve as spearheads to the offensives. Commanded by these three generals, the army was thus immediately oriented towards an offensive and mechanized strategy.

In volume two of his *Memoirs*, Manstein credited Guderian with the creation and development of the panzer divisions, but he refuted his accusation that the general staff of the army had been initially reticent with regards to his doctrine of tank warfare. In Manstein's view, the general staff was overwhelmed with planning the rearmament, and the issue of supplying tanks was only one among many challenges presented to the military leadership at this time. Considering that such a tactic had not yet been truly proven, forging ahead with this new weapon was risky, all the more so given its expense, requiring large amounts of steel for its fabrication, and consuming great quantities of fuel during maneuvers. And yet it was precisely the raw materials that were needed for their respective armament programs over which the army, the Kriegsmarine, and the Luftwaffe were fighting. The army general staff nevertheless permitted the development of the armored tank, devoting to it enormous resources, and without too much neglect for the experimentation of other weapons.[48]

In this respect, Manstein made a crucial personal contribution with regards to arms development by proposing in 1935 the concept of the "armored assault gun" (*Sturmgeschutz*), a self-propelled armored vehicle equipped with a low-velocity 75mm artillery cannon capable of firing high-explosive shells and with the ability to support the infantry at close range. Unlike the typical tank, the armored assault gun lacked a turret. Recalling the bloody battles on the Western Front during the Great War, Manstein was determined to restore mobility to the infantry, which represented a substantial portion of the German Army, by providing it with armored support vehicles needed to overcome enemy artillery or machine-gun fire. Such armored vehicles were meant to work closely with the infantry and engage in direct combat against enemy infantry, artillery, or armor. They were thus able to provide immediate cover for the infantry by enhancing the firing capacity of the field artillery.

Initially, Manstein's idea received a rather cold reception from the army's commander in chief and its chief of general staff, both of whom came from the artillery. In addition, the tank and artillery units viewed the armored assault gun as a potential competitor, as much on the level of materials as on the level of funding. The infantry, for its part, was in favor of this new weapon, but insisted on keeping a hand on it. Finally, Manstein succeeded in winning over Fritsch and Beck, who made the armored assault gun a branch of the artillery. Throughout the Second World War, the armored assault gun indisputably proved itself, proving to be the most versatile anti-tank weapon. As a result, it destroyed some 20,000 enemy tanks and provoked the Red Army to copy it and introduce a large number into its own ranks after 1943.[49]

The remilitarization of the Rhineland and Manstein's strategic plans

As chief of the operations office of the general staff, Manstein drafted orders that would call for Wehrmacht troops to enter into the demilitarized zone of the Rhineland. Contrary to opinion occasionally put forth in various historiographies, the operation ordered by Hitler was not executed against the wishes of the military leadership. Quite the opposite, since for the army, the reoccupation and remilitarization of the Rhineland was essential to the rearmament plans put into motion in December 1933, and to the defense of the Western Front. It was largely for these reasons that Hitler, on March 7, 1936, completely restored Reich sovereignty to the demilitarized zone of the Rhineland.

The leaders of the Wehrmacht had been informed of the Führer's intentions to remilitarize the Rhineland several weeks before. For logistical reasons, and out of fear of France's instantaneous and brutal reaction, they had quite simply insisted from the very beginning that the reoccupation take on a symbolic appearance and be limited to no more than three battalions. The absence of railway bridges on the Rhine prevented a rapid transfer of large numbers of enlisted men to the left bank of the river. The force dispatched by Manstein into the demilitarized zone included no more than 30,000 specialist soldiers. Barely 3,000 men were to infiltrate into the heart of the zone, while the rest took their place on the east bank of the Rhine. The advanced troops had to be ready, in the eventuality of a confrontation with the French, to retreat and hold them back before engaging in battle behind the Rhine. But the French leadership was content enough with protesting through the intermediary of the League of Nations.

"Finally at the end of three years, it seems that today Germany's struggle for equal rights can be considered over."[50] These were the words expressed by Hitler to the Reich Chancellery on March 7, 1936, while his troops, defying the Western democracies, were in the process of penetrating the demilitarized territory of the Rhineland according to Manstein's operations plan. Even if the officers' corps, and in particular Manstein himself, occasionally appeared contemptuous of the upstarts who now led the Reich, the Wehrmacht had less reason than anyone to be dissatisfied. Tensions with the SA, which had not only preoccupied the military leaders, but also the majority of high-ranking officers like Manstein, during the first year of the National Socialist regime, had long since passed. The political assassination of the two generals, Schleicher and Bredow, during the sinister "Night of the Long Knives," was nothing more than a modest price to pay for the elimination of the threat that the leader of the SA and his followers represented.

At the same time, Hitler had unreservedly supported them in their objective to reconstruct a powerful Wehrmacht which would be able to recuperate the lost territories and to lay the foundations of German domination of Europe. In March 1935, the officers were pleased with the restoration of the draft, particularly in view of the army's expansion, which now included thirty-six peacetime divisions, despite the interdiction of the Treaty of Versailles. In accordance with the promise that Hitler made to the army leadership on February 3, 1933, the rearmament continued to advance at a rapid pace. With the remilitarization of the Rhineland, which brought to an end the last constraints imposed upon the military sovereignty of the Reich by the Treaty, he had thus fulfilled a desire dear to the leaders of the army well before they had even imagined it possible. Undoubtedly, he did everything they wished to see him do, and even more. Because of this, they hardly had any reason to complain.

A few weeks after the Rhineland remilitarization, at General Beck's request, Major General Manstein worked on plans to increase the thirty-six divisions already in consideration in March 1935, at the time when obligatory military service was re-established, to forty-one divisions. The projections put forth by the army general staff anticipated that by 1940 the army would be larger than the Kaiser's of 1914. Contrary to general opinion, the army leaders were not reacting to pressures applied by Hitler; they were following their own orders. They knew perfectly well that their ambitious rearmament coincided with Hitler's political objectives.[51] By providing for Germany's military power, through a rapid and massive acceleration of the armaments program, and without lending the slightest consideration to the inevitably disastrous consequences for the economy, War Minister Field Marshal Blomberg, Commander in Chief Colonel General Fritsch, Chief of General Staff Colonel General Beck, and Deputy Chief of General Staff Major General Manstein clearly opened wide the path to future expansion.

With an encroaching war in mind, Manstein, as chief of the logistics section of the general staff, went to work on his strategic plans, which were based on the refitting of the 1936 armed forces. His first, named the Red Plan (*Fall Rot*), concerned a strategic concentration of the German troops in the eventuality of a war on two fronts, the most significant battles occurring in the West. In this purely defensive plan, one assumed that the French could launch a surprise attack against the Reich while the Czechs would remain essentially on the defensive, which would require the Germans to utilize the majority of their forces in the West. Manstein's second strategic plan was also crafted within the perspective of two fronts, but this time with the principal battle being fought in the southeastern sector of the European continent, following Germany's surprise attack against Czechoslovakia, in order to fend off an imminent assault from the superior numbers of the enemy coalition.

In such a contingency, the Green Plan (*Fall Grün*) thus envisioned the utilization of a large part of German forces against Czechoslovakia, with the intention of eliminating any possibility of threats to the rear of the Reich, during a subsequent battle against the French Army. It was clarified that the necessary conditions needed to justify preventive action against Czechoslovakia, as much from a political perspective as from international law, had to be settled in advance. Preparations were also made to prevent the restoration of the Austrian monarchy by marching on Vienna. This mobilization plan in which Manstein participated was called the Otto Plan (*Fall Otto*), named after the legitimate successor to the Hapsburg throne.[52]

The reorganization of the Wehrmacht high command: the end of a dream for Manstein

In 1938 commenced the final phase of the Reich's plan to become a great world power through domination of the European continent. If the decision to achieve such expansionist objectives through war only appeared implicit at the beginning of the rearmament, it was nevertheless made explicitly on November 5, 1937, when a secret meeting held at the Reich Chancellery in Berlin was made public through the Führer's adjutant, Colonel Friedrich Hoßbach. In the presence of the commander in chief of the armed forces and the war minister, Field Marshal Blomberg, the commander in chief of the army, Colonel General Fritsch, the commander in chief of the Kriegsmarine, Admiral Raeder, the commander in chief of the Luftwaffe, Colonel General Göring, the Reich's minister of Foreign Policy, Konstantin von Neurath, and his adjutant Colonel Hoßbach, Hitler revealed his intentions to next embark upon the conquest of living space in the East, beginning with the annexation of Austria and Czechoslovakia. Though after the war he denied such allegations, Manstein must have been informed of the Führer's intentions by either Fritsch or Beck, who received a few days later from Hoßbach a copy of the minutes from the clandestine meeting; he perhaps even received it from Blomberg who, at almost the same time, took it upon himself to communicate Hitler's wishes to the senior ranks of the Wehrmacht.[53]

The Führer's presentation alarmed Blomberg, Fritsch, and Neurath, though it was not his objective of territorial expansion that preoccupied them. On this point, there was no disagreeing with Hitler. His well known racial interpretation of a vital living space was of a suitable tone, and was in perfect accord with the strategic military interests for German supremacy in central and eastern Europe. The annexation of Austria and the destruction of Czechoslovakia were similarly accepted. Even Beck, who fervently criticized his Führer's intentions after having read the account a few days later, did not contest the prospects of absorbing Austria into Germany's borders and dissolving Czechoslovakia, if the opportunity presented itself. And even less so Manstein, as his belligerent attitude during the Sudetenland Crisis would demonstrate. What particularly offended Blomberg, Fritsch, Neurath, and Beck was the idea of using force prematurely, and the danger that the Reich would incur if it were to do go to war with Great Britain and France.

Their fears were eased when Hitler, in February 1938, initiated a reorganization of the Wehrmacht high command, which had consequences for Manstein's future career as general staff officer of the army. As Field Marshal Blomberg had just remarried to a secretary of the minister of War, a report documented that the young woman was well known among the police and had been on file for quite some time for being a prostitute. At the same time, from apparently irrefutable testimony, Colonel General Fritsch was accused of being a homosexual, which greatly incensed Manstein, who had nothing but the highest respect for him and considered him to be "a man of great military competence who, through his foresight, his soldierly behavior, and his spirit of camaraderie, won the hearts of his troops."[54]

If the first report was accurate, the second was based on testimony that would soon fall to pieces. The double scandal nevertheless presented the Nazi leadership with a rather serious public relations problem that forced the two military chiefs to retire officially for health reasons. Thus, contrary to the widely accepted idea that Blomberg and Fritsch's dismissal was a consequence of their objections brought forth by Hoßberg to Hitler during the November 5, 1937 meeting, everything indicates that the two senior military chiefs were discharged so that any disclosure of their respective troubles would not seriously damage the regime's prestige.[55]

To conceal the entire history behind a smoke screen, Hitler completely restructured the Wehrmacht leadership on February 4, 1938. In addition to Blomberg and Fritsch, twelve generals were put on the sidelines and forty-six other positions were changed. To the head of the army, Hitler appointed Colonel General Brauchitsch, a pure representative of Prussian traditionalism and a committed National Socialist who enjoyed a good reputation within the officers' corps, which was certainly not the case for General Reichenau, his first choice. As for the position of War minister and commander in chief of the armed forces, Hitler decided to take on their duties, within the framework of the creation of the *Oberkommando der Wehrmacht* (OKW)—the high command of the armed forces—with General Keitel as the chief of general staff, and Major General Alfred Jodl as chief of the operations bureau. Both would prove to be exemplary servants, unconditionally loyal to the Führer, and would remain at their posts until 1945, an exceptional feat among the great chiefs of the Wehrmacht. However, for his limitless devotion to Hitler and his conviction in the infallibility of his leader's genius, Keitel would even merit the nickname "*Lakeitel*" (the lackey).

With the establishment of the OKW—which would manage and coordinate the various military branches less than it would provoke rivalry among them—a level of bureaucracy headed by Blomberg, who was both War minister and chief of the armed forces, disappeared. The Führer now exerted his authority directly and absolutely over the entirety of the Wehrmacht, with its three components, the *Oberkommando des Heeres* (OKH, the high command of the army), the Luftwaffe, and the Kriegsmarine.

Nor was Major General Manstein spared in this grand reorganization. General Keitel, the new OKW chief of staff, who had been jealous of Manstein's exceptional talent ever since they had worked together in the operations sections of the *Truppenamt* at the end 1920s, rid himself of this opponent who had so offended him by dispatching him off to Silesia. In Liegnitz (Legnica), his wife's birthplace, Manstein was made commander of the 18th Infantry Division, a newly created unit. Officially presented as a promotion, the posting was in reality an attempt to keep him out of Keitel's way.[56]

In the second volume of his *Memoirs*, Manstein refutes an opinion occasionally put forward in which Hitler himself had insisted that he be relieved of his post, due to the close relationship that he maintained with Fritsch, his primary mentor, which would have appeared suspicious in the Führer's eyes. In Manstein's view this was unlikely, as Hitler hardly knew him at this time. In fact, according to him, his displacement was more than likely due to the machinations of either Blomberg or Keitel, two Wehrmacht chiefs with whom he was on bad terms. To this effect, he mentioned that Beck would have protested to Keitel, communicating his indignation for not having been previously consulted on the matter of his first assistant's transfer.[57]

That Keitel played a role in Manstein's reassignment is a plausible hypothesis insofar as one takes into equal consideration the tumultuous debates between the War minister and the army general staff concerning the restructuring of the Wehrmacht high command during a time of war. If the chiefs of the War Ministry and the army were largely in agreement on the necessity of establishing a centralized supreme command in order to better lead and coordinate the different branches, as much in the perspective of planning as in the supervision of operations, they nevertheless disagreed on the nature of such a structure.

Field Marshal Blomberg, during the period when he was War minister and commander in chief of the armed forces, and General Keitel, his right arm ever since he had replaced General Reichenau in October 1935, were both of the opinion that the War Ministry should become the central organization of the command system during the next war. In their view, the three branches should be on equal footing, all the while being overseen by a central high command that would ensure the planning and coordination of operations among them. On the other hand, Colonel General Fritsch, when he was commander in chief of the army, Colonel General Beck, chief of general staff, and Major General Manstein, at the time first quartermaster, all asserted that the central authority of the Wehrmacht should be attributed to the high command of the army. They stressed the fact that the army was a particularly critical branch, for Germany was a continental power that had objectives of territorial expansion, especially in Europe. Consequently, it was the army high command that would oversee the planning and coordination of operations among the three branches. As for the War Minister, he would carry out the organizational aspects of the war (planning and utilization of materials and manpower) and would serve as a channel of communication between the National Socialist regime and the German Army, thus as the latter's political representative to Hitler.

Ambition and ego certainly played a role in this debate, for

Blomberg and Keitel were both products of the army and also placed, like Fritsch, Beck, and Manstein, the interests of their branch over those of the Kriegsmarine and the Luftwaffe. Furthermore, Jodl declared to Manstein: "This entire situation is explained by the fact that the strongest personalities are found within the OKH. If Fritsch, Beck, and yourself were in the OKW, you would think differently." Manstein accepted Jodl's remark and admitted that Fritsch, Beck, and himself would most likely react in such a manner if that were indeed the case.[58]

With this being said, it is likely that General Keitel took advantage of the Blomberg-Fritsch crisis and his appointment to be OKW chief of staff to plot Manstein's departure from the OKH, and thus to assure the dominance of the armed forces' high command over that of the army. At the same time, he rid himself of a general whose unparalleled tactical talents within the officers' corps had been an affront to him for many years.

Additionally, Colonel General Brauchitsch, appointed to the position of commander in chief of the OKH following the Blomberg-Fritsch crisis, was certainly not without influence over Manstein's transfer, an officer whom he loathed ever since their difference of opinion during the *Kriegsspiele* led by the former army deputy chief to the general staff in 1936–1937. During these maneuver exercises played out on maps, Manstein contradicted on several occasions the solutions proposed by Brauchitsch, who was at the time commander in chief of an army group. It is thus possible that Brauchitsch, once he was informed of his appointment as commander in chief of the OKH, would have conspired in the removal of Manstein, with whom he hardly had any desire to work because of his strong personality.[59]

Nicolaus von Below, Hitler's Luftwaffe adjutant, suggested in his *Memoirs* a completely different version of the facts relative to Manstein's new appointment. According to Below, Beck himself endeavored, at the end of January 1938, to free the position of first quartermaster, i.e. the chief of the logistics section, for General Franz Halder, upon whom he was hoping he could rely more than on his predecessor, Major General Manstein. It is quite possible that Beck wanted to abandon his assistant who, contrary to him, expressed no reservations regarding Hitler's aggressive intentions, particularly concerning the necessity of annexing Austria and destroying Czechoslovakia, even if such conquests forced the Western powers to declare war on Germany.[60]

Manstein was filled with bitterness upon having to leave his post to Halder, all the more so since his reassignment wiped out any hopes of his one day becoming chief of the army's general staff. "My path within the general staff, which led me from the position of chief of the operations section, to first quartermaster, to the chief of general staff's representative, qualified me to become the next chief of general staff. At the time, everything led me to believe that I would be the successor to [Colonel] General Beck when he would one day renounce his position. [Colonel] General von Hammerstein [-Equord] had already given me this impression and even [Colonel] General Beck had alluded to it during his farewell speech. But this was henceforth in the past. The objective of each general staff officer to have the great honor to be able to occupy one day the position that had once been handed down to the likes of Moltke, Schlieffen, and Beck, was for me now laid to rest."[61]

The resentment was such that when he was handing over the key to the safe that contained his dossiers into the hands of his replacement, General Halder, Manstein abruptly declared to him: "Here, now you can read them. Good-bye." Manstein brusquely turned on his heels and left the room, leaving behind him a completely flabbergasted Halder.[62] From then on, the two generals would harbor an implacable hatred for one another.

The disappointment felt by Manstein was further accentuated when he once again had to leave his hometown of Berlin. Despite several transfers throughout the course of his officer's career, he always considered himself a Berliner. For him, his genuine homeland was in northeast Germany, more precisely Pomerania and Prussia. He particularly appreciated the natural landscapes of this region, with its remote forests, vast plains, extensive lakes, and its imposing brick or gothic cathedrals. After his appointment to the army's general staff, he had expected to settle in the Reich capital for several years. As a result, he had purchased for his family a house in the upscale Thielpark neighborhood. The Mansteins were quite comfortable with their surroundings, living in the company of distinguished families from the upper middle class, who in particular belonged to the worlds of business and media, including cinema. Yet the romance with the surroundings of Berlin would only last a short time, and it was thus that with a certain amount of sadness he had to sell the Berlin house to a businessman.

The Anschluß: Manstein's eleventh-hour occupation plan

Before Manstein could even assume his new responsibilities at Liegnitz, his services were required once again in Berlin. On March 10, 1938, Hitler had initiated the military occupation of Austria in order to pre-empt Chancellor Kurt von Schuschnigg, who, the day before, had ordered a referendum for March 13, through which the people would have the opportunity to declare independence for their country. Schuschnigg knew that he could count on a favorable majority to the solution and was thus hoping to thwart Hitler's plans to carry out the *Anschluß*. But, in order to impede the referendum by force, the Wehrmacht had to enter Austria on March 12. No plan, however, had been provided for such a rapid maneuver. It is hardly surprising that Hitler took his generals by surprise by requesting from them plans for a military intervention.

Regarding this matter, the Nazi dictator summoned Keitel to the Reich Chancellery at 10 a.m. on March 10. However, before rushing to the Führer, the OKW general staff chief conferred with Jodl. The chief of the operations section of the OKW recalled the Otto Plan, which Manstein had created to foil an attempt to restore the Hapsburgs to power. As no other military plan of action against Austria existed at that time, Hitler decided that the latter plan would suffice and ordered Keitel to set it in motion.

General Keitel returned posthaste to Wehrmacht headquarters on the Bendlerstrasse to speak with Colonel General Beck. When he solicited details about the Otto Plan, the OKH general staff chief responded in a desperate tone: "We have nothing prepared, nothing has been done, nothing at all." Beck too, was then called to the Reich Chancellery, around 11 a.m. He quickly alerted Major General Manstein, who was just about to leave Berlin to assume his new position in Silesia, and together they went to the Führer. After he explained to them his intentions, Hitler declared that the army had to be ready to enter Austria on March 12. Neither Beck nor Manstein raised the slightest objection to his plan for military aggression. Only a single point worried the two generals: the difficulty of improvising a military maneuver in such a short amount of time.

Having returned to Bendlerstrasse around 1 p.m., Manstein immediately began drafting orders relative to the anticipated military action.

It was absolutely necessary that the orders go out early in the evening. At 6 p.m. Manstein had finished, after five hours of work. The mobilization orders were immediately sent out to the three army corps and the Luftwaffe. And on March 12, after the Führer transmitted the order, German troops entered Austria, in accordance with the directives of the Otto Plan which had been brought into being by Manstein. On the following day, the *Anschluß* was proclaimed. That same day, Manstein took off for Vienna in order to deal with the integration of Austrian troops into the Wehrmacht. This was his last task in the army's general staff.

After the war, Manstein recounted the conversation he had had with the Führer, the day when he went to the Reich Chancellery with Beck. According to Manstein, the Führer's arguments in favor of a military occupation of Austria were logical and convincing, and his analysis essentially correct. He undoubtedly wanted to justify his crucial role in the preparations relative to the military occupation of a country: "The situation that Hitler had presented to us was founded on arguments that were completely logical and in a perfectly objective tone. It was the first time that I had the opportunity to be in front of him, within the framework of a small group of attendees, before whom he spoke not as a common speaker, but rather as a lucid politician. I must admit that his presentation was absolutely convincing, along with his prognosis, which turned out to be accurate."[63]

The Sudetenland Crisis: Manstein the warmonger!

In April 1938, Manstein finally appeared in Liegnitz to take his post as commander of the 18th Infantry Division. It was from Silesia that he participated in the Czechoslovakian crisis, which developed a few weeks after the military occupation and annexation of Austria by the Third Reich. At that time, Hitler had decided to settle Czechoslovakia's fate. His goal was not just to integrate the Sudetenland, a mountainous region of Bohemia where a German minority of three and a half million lived, into the Reich, but to destroy the Czechoslovakian state. Indeed, on the pretext that the Sudeten Germans were oppressed by the Czech authorities, Hitler laid claim to the incorporation of this region into the Reich. But this was no more than a ruse, for he actually wanted to dissolve the entire state of Czechoslovakia. Of course, the execution of such a plan was tantamount to war with Czechoslovakia and, more than likely, with the Western powers, all the more so since the Führer's foreign policy was going above and beyond any sort of revisionist or national integration plans.

Nearly all of the Wehrmacht generals, including Manstein, as his belligerent attitude in the summer of 1938 would show, approved of Hitler's intentions to lead an offensive war against Czechoslovakia, which was in their view an artificial state born out of the Treaty of Versailles, thrust dangerously into the flanks of the Reich. Behind the general staff's military policy, one recognized the ulterior motives of an aggressive expansionism clearly led against Czechoslovakia, to which Beck remarked at the end of May 1938: "In its current form, its existence is intolerable to Germany. We must find a solution for eliminating her as a source of danger for Germany, and if need be, through war."[64]

Only a lack of preparation and economic risk dissuaded a few of the generals in the spring of 1938 from the idea of a war expanded beyond a local operation against Czechoslovakia. Among them was Colonel General Beck, the OKH chief of general staff, who thought the Führer's temerity could lead to disaster by risking war against the Western powers which Germany, he thought, could not possibly win considering its lack of preparation. Consequently, Beck's opposition did not focus on the use of war, which no one was questioning. His resistance was essentially of a technical nature, for he was no less ready to work on a military attack against Czechoslovakia than subordinates.

On May 28, 1938, Hitler made the irrevocable decision to crush Czechoslovakia through military action in the near future, at the very latest by October 1, 1938, even if Germany had to be led into war against Great Britain and France, though he considered such an eventuality unlikely. Two days later the decision was ratified in the preamble of an updated Green Plan, dated from May 30, 1938. The latter carried the mark of the OKW and took into account the situation created by the incorporation of Austria into the German Reich.

Faced with the Führer's intentions, Beck responded to Brauchitsch on May 5 and 30, June 3, and July 16, through a series of very critical memorandums that insisted on the fact that a German attack against Czechoslovakia would provoke a European war in which Great Britain and France. In such an event Germany, he was convinced, could not win a long war due to a lack of raw materials. However, the colonel general was only just beginning to discover the extent to which he was isolated within the German Army. The personal position of the OKH's chief of general staff and the very strength of his arguments were both appreciably weakened by mid-June, when the results of a *Kriegsspiele* indicated that, contrary to his dire prognosis that banked on a campaign of at least three weeks, Czechoslovakia would probably be defeated in eleven days, which would allow for a rapid deployment of troops to fight on the Western Front should Great Britain and France enter the war.

Even within the high command of the army, Beck was regarded as a kind of Cassandra with all of his excessive warnings. More and more isolated, he went so far as to advocate, during the summer, a collective resignation of military chiefs in order to force Hitler to renounce moving forward with his intentions. But he failed miserably in his attempt, which was intended to win over Colonel General Brauchitsch, the commander in chief of the army, to the idea of giving Hitler an ultimatum from the generals. In fact, almost all of the generals, including Manstein, refused to stand behind him. Even if they agreed with Beck on the fact that a European war could prove to be disastrous for Germany, they did not share his opinion that an invasion of Czechoslovakia would inevitably lead to a confrontation with the Western powers. They most certainly did not deny the possibility of such a confrontation, which Hitler himself even admitted to in his directive of May 30, 1938. But with regards to foreign policy, they had much more confidence in the Führer's judgment than that of their chief of general staff. Furthermore, had Hitler not displayed an exceptional political flair concerning major international issues ever since he came to power?

Beck's opposition is interesting in itself, since it brings to mind the question that must have haunted all of their souls during the Nuremberg trials: for an officer, did there exist a higher authority than that of the Führer? At Nuremberg, the German generals, like Manstein, attempted to find an excuse for their war crimes by responding negatively. Because it was their duty as a soldier, they had to obey orders, so they said. But, on July 16, 1938, Beck held a different opinion, one that he would try to impose until the very end of the war, and almost always without success. There existed, he said, limits to the obedience due to the supreme command when a soldier's conscience, his knowledge of certain facts, and his feeling of responsibility forbade him to obey. The generals of the Wehrmacht, he thought, had reached such limits. If Hitler insisted on waging war, they had to refuse him their services by resigning as a group. In these conditions, he added, the Führer could not conduct a war since there would be no one to lead the armies. By acting in such a way, the generals would avoid the worst for their homeland, i.e. defeat and disaster. "Such exceptional times," he concluded," "demand exceptional actions."[65]

Major General Manstein, commander of the 18th Infantry Division, was not overly concerned with such ethical questions. To the contrary, he advised Beck to rid himself of the burden of these responsibilities, which were actually the responsibility of the political authorities, and to completely devote himself to ensuring the success of the military attack against Czechoslovakia, a state which had, in his opinion, neither legitimacy nor *raison d'être*. In fact, on July 21, 1938 he wrote a letter to Beck in which he insisted on the necessity of wiping Czechoslovakia off the European map, and annexing as quickly as possible the Sudetenland. He also suggested that such a decision fell completely within the Führer's responsibility, since he was in the position to judge whether the international situation required the Reich to intervene in Czechoslovakia as soon as possible. Even though he recognized the possibility that the Western powers might come to the aid of their Czech ally, he asserted that a soldier had to assume the responsibilities for the duties assigned to him and, as a result, not question the primacy of politics over the military. In these exceptional times, he responded to Beck, one needed men of this caliber.[66]

The belligerent attitude demonstrated by Manstein during the summer of 1938 was not the exception, but rather the rule among his peers. He was well assimilated into the officers' corps, which was preparing for war, and he was clearly part of its dominant mindset. One question nevertheless remains unanswered: by adopting such an attitude, did the ambitious Manstein also hope to find favor with Hitler so that the latter would grant him the position of army chief of general staff, since he was fully aware that Beck envisioned resigning from his post as a form of protest regarding the Führer's decisions about Czechoslovakia? Nevertheless, in his letter addressed to Beck, Manstein expressed his perspective on the relation between politics and the military in terms of typical Clausewitzian thought, which he would reiterate on several occasions during the Second World War; in other words a theory which stipulated that a soldier was in service to the politics of the state and that it was his duty to restrict himself to military issues. Such a manner of seeing things would also influence his decision not to join the conspirators of July 20, 1944.

An isolated figure among military officials concerning strategic policy, and unsuccessful at convincing his colleagues of the necessity to oppose Hitler's plans, Beck concluded by submitting his resignation on August 18, 1938. As he stated in his own words several months later: "I warned them, and in the end, I found myself alone." Paradoxically, he had more than anyone else contributed towards providing Hitler the military strength of which he so impatiently wanted to make use. In fact, without his participation in the preparations for the war, it would most certainly not have happened.[67]

It was General Halder who replaced him as OKH chief of general staff chief on September 1, 1938. But Major General Manstein was not to be outdone, for at the height of the Sudetenland Crisis in September 1938, he took over the post of chief of staff of the Twelfth Army. Commanded by General Wilhelm Ritter von Leeb, the Twelfth Army was one of five assigned to invade Czechoslovakia. At the beginning of October, Manstein therefore took part in the Sudetenland occupation, as a result of the Munich Accords. After fulfilling his duties with the general staff of the Twelfth Army, he returned to his command of the 18th Infantry Division at Liegnitz.

The Green Plan had thus not been implemented, and Hitler did not have his "small war." Within the range of concessions put forth by the Western powers during the Munich Conference on September 29–30, 1938, he had to abandon, at least provisionally, the complete destruction of Czechoslovakia. But this would be for another time; the final act would come on March 15, 1939, with the "Prague coup," through which the Wehrmacht would occupy Bohemia-Moravia and dismember what remained of Czechoslovakia in favor of Hungary and a Slovak puppet state.

Summoned to Nuremberg as witnesses, the German generals declared that they were relieved that war had been avoided thanks to the Munich Accords. Among them was Manstein, who had nevertheless taken a rather belligerent position during the summer of 1938. The warmonger, who, during this time did not in the slightest way question the feasibility of a campaign against Czechoslovakia, was asked to respond to the question whether the launches against Austria and the Sudetenland were considered preliminaries to war: "No! Certainly not, for our troops were not fully mobilized. The mobilization of the corps at the time we entered Austria had proven that nothing was prepared enough for us to reasonably execute an operation, and that if the war were to intensify, we would not have been able to effectively defend our western border nor the Polish border. And, without a doubt, if Czechoslovakia had defended itself, we would have remained caught up in its embattlements, for we hardly had the means to take them by force. And so it could not have been a question of testing the military; it was rather a test of nerves."[68]

Of course, through such a deposition, Manstein was attempting to evade the critical role played by the high command of the German Army in the preparations for an invasion of Austria and Czechoslovakia, along with his belligerent attitude during this time. Moreover, he was trying to demonstrate that together the generals had supported Beck in his opposition to Hitler's plan to attack Czechoslovakia. In fact, Manstein's warmongering tendencies were representative of an attitude held by the entire German officers' corps and would become even more pronounced during the time of the Polish crisis.

IV

THE POLISH "LABORATORY"

On April 1, 1939, Manstein was promoted to the rank of lieutenant general. At the same time, he was assigned to the position of chief of general staff of *Arbeitsstab Rundstedt* (Colonel General Gerd von Rundstedt's general staff), the most important of the army groups, along with that of *Heeresgruppenkommando I* (the command of Colonel General Fedor von Bock's Army Group I). With a war against Poland in mind at the end of the summer 1939, Hitler clearly could not do without the brilliant talent of a Manstein, and it is for this reason he appointed him as chief of staff to an army group. From that moment on, the officer in question buckled down to the job of planning the invasion of Poland. Although Manstein played a crucial role in the preparations and supervision of a war of aggression against Poland, almost none of the historical studies focusing on this officer make reference to this role. It would be thus fitting for us to bring to light here his role in the planning of this war and his contribution to the Wehrmacht's stunning victory, along with his attitude in relation to the crimes that he committed during it.

The White Plan: A *product of Manstein's insight?*

In the first volume of his *Memoirs*, Manstein asserts that he was not informed of the White Plan (*Fall Weiß*), the military offensive against Poland prepared under Hitler's order, until the middle of the summer of 1939. According to his remarks, the plan of attack did not yet exist during the previous spring. "Quite to the contrary," he asserts, "all the military arrangements in the East were in place to defend or maintain the security of the border in case of a conflict with other powers." With the OKH having never prepared an offensive plan against Poland prior to the summer of 1939, the conception of the White Plan would thus have appeared, following his argumentation, only a few weeks before the beginning of the German attack. He added, furthermore, that the prolonged support of a defensive military posture in the East prior to the beginning of hostilities was significant of the Reich's desire to proceed above all with a peaceful revision of its borders with Poland.

For his part, the opinion expressed in 1922 by Colonel General Seeckt, who was at the time commander in chief of the army, stated that Poland's existence was intolerable and incompatible with the conditions necessary for Germany's future, and as a result it had to disappear from the map of Europe. Such a theory represented for Manstein an outdated point of view because of changes in the geopolitical situation since the 1920s. The removal of the Polish state was no longer desirable for Germany, he emphasized, for it would have made Bolshevik Russia a new and much more dangerous, unpredictable neighbor. He concludes that "rectifications of the border could be advantageous for the two countries, but a total disappearance of Poland was not desirable for the Reich. Whether it was pleasing to us or not, it would have been better to have her between us and the Soviet Union. Naturally, we were hoping, along with all of our compatriots, that a peaceful revision would return to the Reich territories that were incontestably German."

Despite Hitler's confidence concerning the Polish matter, particularly so during a conference held with his generals at the Berghof—the Führer's residence, located on the side of a mountain (the Obersalzberg) in the Bavarian Alps, overlooking the town of Berchtesgaden—on August 22, 1939, everything led his generals to believe, according to Manstein, that he was resorting to the political ruse that had served him so well during the Sudetenland Crisis. To support such a claim, he points out that two considerations were leading the army leaders to think that a peaceful agreement could be ratified at the last moment, as had been the case at Munich on September 30, 1938.

First of all, the conclusion of the non-aggression pact with the U.S.S.R. on August 23, 1939 would incite Poland to display more flexibility with regards to Berlin. On one side, Great Britain and France, seeing no other way to help their ally than by engaging in a bloody offensive in the West, would doubtlessly urge Warsaw to yield to Hitler's demands in relation to the return of the city of Danzig and the construction of a road and rail link that would cross the Polish corridor to connect Pomerania and East Prussia. On the other side, the Polish "should henceforth expect that by dealing with the Germans, the Soviets, desirous of satisfying their former claims on the eastern part of their country, would possibly intervene to the rear."

Secondly, the convening of Wehrmacht leaders by Hitler at the Berghof, at the most critical moment of the crisis, was an event that did not go unseen from abroad, and was without a doubt the climax of a deliberate political bluff. As Manstein wondered, was Hitler not looking for a compromise, despite the belligerent remarks he had made during the conference? Was it not the conference's objective to exert a final pressure on Poland and its British and French allies? "In any case," declares Manstein, "the OKH had assumed, until the last critical days of August—like us, in Army Group South—that everything would be resolved politically as was the case at Munich."

By offering to us this version of the history concerning the preparations for the Polish campaign, it is clear that Manstein is attempting to conceal not only the responsibility of the Wehrmacht high command at the beginning of the Second World War, but equally so his own. Indeed, it would not be difficult to characterize the cataclysm that would set Europe ablaze in September 1939 as accidental. One could gather through reading Manstein's *Memoirs* that Hitler only determined to wage war at the very last moment, after having come to the conclusion that there was no other hope of arriving at a *modus vivendi* with Warsaw. Concerning the development of a plan of attack against Poland, Manstein would have been kept out of it until he was summoned on August 12, 1939, to fill the role of chief of staff of Army Group South, under Rundstedt's command, where he would have had the task of finalizing the last details of the attack for the army group.[69]

In reality, military preparations had commenced at the beginning of spring 1939, with the intention of bringing the Polish issue to an end. In a strictly confidential directive dating from March 25, meant for the commander in chief of the army, Colonel General Brauchitsch, Hitler revealed his intention of resorting to force against Poland in the event of diplomatic failure. He thus ordered Brauchitsch to initiate as quickly as possible preparations for a military attack.

On April 26 or 27, Brauchitsch presented to Hitler a preliminary sketch of the OKH's operations plan, which was accepted without any major modifications. This preliminary plan had been conceived by General Halder, OKH chief of general staff, and by his adjutants, General Otto von Stülpnagel, chief of the logistics section, and Colonel Hans von Greiffenberg, chief of the operations section.

On May 1, it was submitted for review by the general staffs of the two army groups assigned to the Polish campaign. The staff of Army Group South was composed of members from the *Arbeitsstab Rundstedt*, in which the heads were Colonel General Rundstedt and his chief of staff, Lieutenant General Manstein. As for the general staff of Army Group North, it was formed of the *Heeresgruppenkommando I*, with Colonel General von Bock as commander in chief and General Hans von Salmuth as chief of staff. Both staffs had to submit their own plans based on the general directives proposed in the first sketch of the OKH's plan. The staff of Army Group South presented its operations plan on May 20, while that of Army Group North submitted its own on May 27. After multiple discussions, concerning in particular the plan suggested by Army Group North, which was met with much reluctance, the OKH finally offered its definitive operations plan on June 15.[70]

In its final version, the White Plan largely reflected the research of Army Group South. The overall layout of the situation that constituted the plan for the invasion of Poland was actually the brainchild of Lieutenant General Manstein. Not only was the plan full of imagination and audacity, but other than a few minor modifications, it was his plan that was ultimately implemented. One may thus assert, as do a few other authors, that the White Plan was above all the work of Manstein.[71] Within the *Arbeitsstab Rundstedt*, Manstein received invaluable assistance for the conception of his operations plan from his deputy chief of staff, Colonel Günther Blumentritt, with whom he always had a remarkably close working relationship.

Manstein's operations plan was aimed at catching the Polish army in a pincer movement through East Prussia to the north and Pomerania to the northwest, as well as through Silesia to the southwest and Slovakia to the south. The position of the border allowed them to attack the adversary on both his flanks, which would make the encirclement of the primary Polish armed forces, who were assembled near the borders in order to protect the rich industrial and agricultural regions of Poland, much easier. Divided into two army groups, one to the north, the other to the south, on flanks set greatly apart, the German armed forces had to regroup behind the Vistula so as to take from the rear the main body of the Polish Army, which was deployed to the west of the river. To carry out such an operation, Manstein took the risk of leaving a large breach in the center.

Logically, Manstein had decided that the principal clash would come from Silesia. On the one hand, this was due to the fact that Germany had a rail and road network there, which would allow her to concentrate a considerable number of men more quickly than in Pomerania or in East Prussia. On the other, an attack following the Poznan-Warsaw axis would be less effective, since it would be completely head-on. As a result, Army Group South would be stronger than Army Group North.

The latter, commanded by Colonel General von Bock, included the Third Army of General Georg von Küchler in East Prussia, and the Fourth Army of General Hans von Kluge in Pomerania. The two armies encompassed five army corps and one panzer corps, totalling 17 infantry divisions (nine active and eight newly formed), two panzer divisions, two motorized divisions, and a cavalry brigade, for a total of 21 divisions.

The mission for Bock's army group was to attack from the rear the main body of the enemy armed forces, which was stationed in the great loop of the Vistula, as soon as the link between the Third Army, pushing to the south from East Prussia, and the Fourth Army, pushing to the east from Pomerania, had been established. After the Polish units were eliminated from the corridor, Kluge's formations were to link up with Küchler's in order to attack across the Narew, in the direction of Warsaw, and envelop the Polish right flank.

Commanded by Colonel General Rundstedt, Army Group South was appreciably more powerful. It was composed of Colonel General Wilhelm List's Fourteenth Army, Colonel General Walter von Reichenau's Tenth Army, and Colonel General Johannes Blaskowitz's Eighth Army. These three armies had eight army corps and four panzer corps, totalling 23 infantry divisions (15 active and eight newly formed), four panzer divisions, four "light" divisions, and three mountain divisions, for a total of 36 divisions.

Rundstedt's army group had to advance with the Fourteenth Army across the industrial region of Upper Silesia, the eastern part of

Moravia, and the western region of Slovakia in the direction of Krakow, with the Tenth Army from Upper Silesia in the direction of the Vistula on both sides of the city of Warsaw, and with the Eighth Army from central Silesia in the direction of Lodz. The objective was to beat the enemy forces at the great bend of the Vistula, and in Galicia, and to charge on Warsaw in order to seize as quickly as possible the crossings of the Vistula to annihilate, in liaison with Army Group North, the rest of the Polish Army.

For Lieutenant General Manstein, it was imperative that, on the southern front, the Tenth and Eighth Armies emerging from Silesia manage to maneuver in such a way as to prevent the enemy forces from hiding behind the Vistula-San line. For this, armored units from the Tenth had to rush forward in order to destabilize the adversary's defense, which was set up just behind the border, to reach the Vistula crossings between Warsaw and Deblin before the enemy could retreat there. Additionally, the Fourteenth Army, advancing across Galicia, needed to reach and cross the San as quickly as possible. If the enemy was contemplating putting up a definitive resistance only behind the San and the Vistula, Manstein was intending to foil their intention by ordering the Fourteenth Army to link up with the right flank of Army Group North to the adversary's rear in order to ensure the success of the pincer movement. Army Group South thus had to do its best to force the mass of opposing forces to fight before the Vistula and to destroy them, all the while taking into account the adversary's potential desire of only going into a decisive battle behind the San-Vistula line.[72]

To give the German Army a crushing superiority over that of Poland, the OKH was prepared to take the risk of withdrawing a considerable number of troops from the Western Front. But contrary to prevailing opinion, the military leaders did not fear a war on two fronts. They considered the possibility of an offensive on the Rhine from the Western powers rather improbable, at least for as long as the campaign was to take place on the Eastern Front. They left, therefore, their western borders with little protection so that they could hurl the mass of the armed forces against Poland.

The OKH engaged 57 divisions in the battle against Poland. Among these, 42 were active. They included 24 infantry divisions, 3 mountain divisions, 6 armored divisions, 4 light divisions, 4 motorized divisions, and 1 cavalry brigade. To the active divisions, an additional 15 were sent for mobilization, thus of little value, along with a few regiments of the Waffen SS, most notably the *Leibstandarte Adolph Hitler*. Only 46 divisions, of which 11 were active, were left in the West. Among these, not a single armored or motorized unit was to be found. In front of them, 88 French divisions, of which 51 were active, had been in the process of mobilizing since August 21. Likewise, the bulk of Luftwaffe formations—two out of the three air fleets—was engaged over Polish soil. In other words, 1,929 Luftwaffe aircraft were called to participate in the Poland campaign; their primary task would be to facilitate the advance of 3,600 armored vehicles.

Opposing the Reich, Poland had only 30 infantry divisions at its disposal, along with 11 cavalry brigades, one mountain brigade, and two motorized brigades. Nonetheless, she hoped to be able to mobilize ten supplemental divisions as soon as hostilities were under way. The opposition also possessed an air fleet of approximately 900 aircraft, of which 500 were on the frontline. The equipment and armament of the Polish Amy was, however, dated and technically inferior to that of Germany. Poorly equipped for modern warfare, the Polish army possessed only 750 armored vehicles.[73]

Aggression against Poland: A *war for the generals*?

Contrary to what the German generals purported after the war, Hitler received a warm welcome from the Wehrmacht regarding his intentions of attacking Poland. The senior officers, including Manstein, were dying to fight the Polish, after demonstrating an even more hostile spirit vis-à-vis Czechoslovakia. While some among them had feared that the Western powers would intervene during the Sudetenland Crisis, several generals were now assuming that England and France, in light of their attitude at Munich, would remain inactive, and that it was desirable to let the negotiations with the Polish government concerning Danzig and the corridor fall in favor of military action.

A war against Poland, they asserted, would be just as popular with the army as it would be with the German populace. Moreover, from the very beginning, the leadership of the various branches of the armed forces worked more closely on the preparation of military operations in Poland than they had during the first stages of the Sudetenland Crisis. Despite the guarantee of Polish independence, they continued to place their trust in the Führer and feared less the possibility of Western inter-vention.[74]

This mindset was confirmed during the second half of April 1939, when the OKH chief of general staff, General Halder, presented a broad outline of the objectives to destroy Poland to the army commanders and the staff chiefs assembled at the *Kriegsakademie* in Berlin. His speech paid witness to the major role played by the high command during the commencement of the Second World War.

Before the senior officers of the Wehrmacht, among whom was to be found Lieutenant General Manstein, the principal engineer of the plan against Poland, Halder took obvious pleasure in the notion that a military victory against Poland could be quick and easy, and further envisioned a conflict with the U.S.S.R. and the Western powers. With an obvious display of contempt towards the Polish Army which, in his view, did not in the slightest constitute a serious adversary, he insisted upon the necessity of destroying Poland in record time. Even a British safeguard, he insisted, would not prevent such an accomplishment.

Next, he gave a brief presentation characterizing the German offen-sive, drawing attention to the vital cooperation between the army and the SS units, along with the occupation of the country by the party's paramilitary troops. He thus left no doubt as to the ideological charac-ter that the military campaign in Poland would assume. This would, in effect, be carried out in the purest spirit of National Socialism. The cru-cial objective, he repeated, was not only the destruction of the Polish armed forces, but the complete liquidation of the country, even if Great Britain and France intervened in the West, an intervention that he ulti-mately thought was highly unlikely.

The OKH chief of general staff completed his speech with a glimpse of the future, beyond the Polish conflict: "We must be done with the Polish in three weeks, and if possible, in fifteen days. It will thus be left to the Russians to say whether the Eastern Front will dictate or not the destiny of Europe. In any case, a victorious army, filled with pride from the rewards of glorious victories, will be ready to confront Bolshevism or [...] to launch itself against the West." When all was said and done, not only did Halder envision confronting Poland and risking an armed conflict with the Western powers, but he was also set to attack Bolshevik Russia during the same offensive.[75]

Halder's remarks provoked no opposition among the generals present at the conference, not even from Manstein, which rather illuminated the warlike spirit of the officers' corps and especially its desire to eliminate the Polish state. If a few of them remained skeptical regarding the non-intervention of the Western powers in the case of a German offensive, the majority of them were nevertheless convinced of the necessity of bringing an end once and for all to the Polish situation. It was a prerequisite for pursuing Hitler's expansionist policy in order to solve the problem of German living space.

The aggression against Poland therefore won the practically unanimous praise of all the senior officers against a state and a people they had held in contempt since 1919. After the war, Manstein made reference to what this state represented to the German officers: "Poland was for us nothing but a source of bitterness after being appropriated, thanks to the Treaty of Versailles, from German territory over which they possessed no historical right, or right of self-determination, and for us, the soldiers, it was nothing more than a source of disquiet during a time of weakness for Germany."[76]

Since the time of Seeckt, the military objective concerning Poland had always been the same: recover the former territories in the East through the military destruction of the Polish state, whose existence was judged incompatible with the development of Germany as a great European power. But, with the recovery by the Reich of its military power and the amelioration of its geostrategic position in Europe ever since Hitler's arrival to power, the capture of Poland was nothing more than a stage in the conquest of vital living space at the expense of Bolshevik Russia. Consequently, from the viewpoint of the conquests in the East, Poland was simply a step on the path towards the Soviet Union. For both Hitler and the Wehrmacht generals, the annexation of Danzig from East Prussia, and the Polish part of Upper Silesia, was not an end in itself, but rather a pretext for truly initiating the conquest in the East of territories deemed necessary to ensure the development of the German Reich as a continental, even world, power.

On the eve of the completion of the non-aggression pact that divided the spheres of influence in Eastern Europe between the Germans and the Soviets, Hitler had summoned to the Berghof nearly fifty high ranking officers of the Wehrmacht, among whom was Manstein, to reveal his definitive intentions as to the Polish situation. A few days before the German offensive, which had been set for August 26, the Führer was anxious to ensure that his generals were convinced of the necessity to attack Poland. Hitler addressed himself to rousing his generals' zeal for combat and ensuring that the army could fulfill its duty. According to him, it was rather improbable that the Western powers would enter into war, yet he nevertheless had to accept the risk. He thus demanded unwavering resolve from the high ranks.

That the risk of a world war was minor, the fact that the attack was only to be against Poland, the traditional enemy of Prussia and Germany, and that it had moreover been preceded by the conclusion of a non-aggression pact with Russia, was sufficient enough for Hitler to win the support of the majority of his generals, as the absence of any objection from them during his conference illustrated. A large majority of the Wehrmacht leadership was simply keen on the idea of eradicating the Polish state, whose existence was beholden to the "loathsome" Treaty of Versailles, and of establishing a vital living space in Eastern Europe, which had already been initiated by the *Anschluß* and the dismemberment of Czechoslovakia.

The performance of the army's commander in chief, Colonel General Brauchitsch, furthermore had a significant effect on the critical role of the Wehrmacht in the commencement of the war. Following the signing of the German-Soviet pact, a good number of generals appeared fully satisfied with the situation in which their country found herself, for they were convinced, following Hitler's example, that the West would not attempt to rescue Poland if Germany were to launch an attack against her. And if the Western powers actually did decide to intervene, the non-aggression pact between Germany and Russia would at least eliminate the threat of encirclement and a war on two fronts, while safeguarding the Soviet Union's neutrality.

However, the sudden and unexpected ratification of an alliance between London and Warsaw on August 25, 1939, provoked Hitler to withdraw from such a stance. He immediately gave Brauchitsch orders to retain the Wehrmacht troops at the border, ready to attack on August 26. The OKH commander in chief hastened to execute the orders which he enthusiastically welcomed, not out of a fear of intervention of the Western powers, but for purely logistical reasons. If the attack had begun on August 26, the first day of the mobilization, the Wehrmacht would not have been fully prepared. Conversely, by delaying the offensive to the seventh day of the mobilization, September 1, the Wehrmacht would be in a position to execute the maneuvers more rapidly and efficiently. He stated to Hitler, "Give me seven more days to carefully fulfill the mobilization and the deployment, and I will thus be able to have at my disposition more than 100 divisions," precisely what he was able to achieve.

For Brauchitsch, as for many other generals of the Wehrmacht, if a war with the Western powers had to happen, it was preferable that it occur immediately, while they were still militarily weak, and thus the reason why he wished to attack Poland not on August 26, but rather on September 1, 1939.

Far from being frightened by the Anglo-Polish alliance, the OKH commander in chief instead expressed his enthusiasm to commence the war. And it was for these same reasons that the Führer came to the conclusion once again that it would be better to go to war at a time when the military circumstances were much in the Reich's favor. Delaying the offensive by seven days, as Brauchitsch requested, would permit the Wehrmacht to fully complete its mobilization and deployment on the Eastern Front. And as chief of staff of the army group called to take on the lion's share in the campaign, Manstein could not have been more delighted that measures were being taken that would contribute to the rapid success of an operations plan of which he was the principal author. While the number of armored divisions for the September 1 offensive remained exactly the same as the week before, the Wehrmacht was nonetheless able to count on an additional 21 infantry and two motorized divisions.[77]

As a result, and in light of the letter he had sent to General Beck during the Sudetenland Crisis, which emphasized the necessity to erase Czechoslovakia from the map of Europe, everything leads us to believe that Lieutenant General Manstein's mindset, on the eve of the attack on Poland, was not any different than that of Brauchitsch or Halder. All the more so as, contrary to its standing in the summer of 1938, the Wehrmacht found itself, a year later, in a much better position from the standpoint of military preparations, to hurl itself into a European war. The man who had participated in the conception of the White Plan, and who was insistent with his colleagues on the fact that achieving such a plan would not pose any difficulty for the Wehrmacht, seems to have shared the enthusiasm of the majority of generals for the idea of annihilating once and for all the Polish state.

A return to mobile warfare: A *triumph indebted to Manstein?*

On September 1, 1939, when German troops broke through the Polish border, surprising the adversary's army with the ferocity of their attack, the general staff of Army Group South was positioned at Neisse. It was from here that Manstein closely followed his army group's operations and gave his directives while following the evolution of the campaign. With that said, the question here is defining Manstein's overall contribution to the Wehrmacht's lightening victory in Poland, especially in regard to its planning, as the development of operations are well enough known that we do not particularly need to dwell on them here.

The German *Blitzkrieg* was devastating for the adversary. The Polish Army's losses rose to approximately 70,000 dead, 133,000 wounded, and 700,000 prisoners; while the Wehrmacht hardly counted more than 11,000 killed, 30,000 wounded, and 3,400 missing.[78] The speed and destructive power of Germany's land and aerial operations against Poland astounded foreign observers. In France, the shock was particularly rough. With the bloody trench battles of the First World War still in their memory, the French military leaders had counted on a Polish resistance at least until winter or even spring. But *Blitzkrieg* tactics had allowed the Germans to reinstate the use of mobile warfare, thus making possible a short-term military campaign.

The German advance into Poland was so shocking that General Halder noted on September 5: "The enemy has been practically defeated."[79] He was not wrong, for only two days after the beginning of the offensive, the Polish Air Force was annihilated, the bulk of its 500 front-line aircraft having been destroyed on the ground by German bombardment before they could even take off. On September 3, when Great Britain and France entered the war, the advance of Kluge's Fourth Army had cut off the corridor and reached the lower stretches of the Vistula, completing the junction with Küchler's Third Army, which was for its part exerting pressure on the Narew River. On September 6, Reichenau's Tenth Army had advanced well beyond the Warta River, reaching Lodz and Kielce. On that same day, Krakow, Poland's second city, was taken by List's Fourteenth Army. That evening, the Polish government left Warsaw to take refuge in Lublin. The very next day, Halder, believing the Polish Army to be finished, prepared for the transportation of certain troops to the Western Front, even though no activity had been reported. No later than September 8, Reichenau's advanced units found themselves at the gates of Warsaw after having crossed the Vistula to the south of the capital. They had covered more than 220 kilometers during the first week. List's troops were not to be outdone, for they arrived at the same time at Sandomierz, at the confluence of the Vistula and the San. While Guderian's armored tank corps, the spearhead of Kühler's army, skirted the Bug line and advanced towards Brest-Litovsk, General Ewald von Kleist's panzer corps, on List's front, crossed over the San and reached the city of Lvov on September 12. The day that Soviet forces entered eastern Poland, September 17, Guderian's panzers linked up with the patrol units of List's Fourteenth Army at Wlodawa, 80 kilometers to the south of Brest-Litovsk, closing the claws of the grand pincer movement. The entire Polish Army was thus encircled. On September 27, with its forces entrenched at Warsaw, Poland capitulated.

The campaign came to an end when the last Polish troops, which had not been able to pass into Romania, definitively put down their weapons on October 6. And so Poland, like Austria and Czechoslovakia before her, disappeared from the map of Europe. Yet this time, the Reich had been assisted and encouraged by the Soviet Union. This was Poland's fourth division by Germany and Russia (Austria had participated in the others) and, until the very last day, was by far the most barbaric and ruthless.

While the U.S.S.R. was annexing the Polish regions to the east of the Narew-Bug-San line, Germany was taking much more back than its 1914 border. Its new eastern borders covered territories that had never been part of its former Prussian regions. The Reich borders thus expanded some 150 to 200 kilometers more to the east, with the Germans being the majority population in no other region but Danzig. In the rest of the annexed territories, the proportion of Germans rarely reached more than 10 percent.[80] It was thus no longer a matter of restoration, but rather an imperialistic and criminal invasion to which the senior officers of the Wehrmacht had subscribed.

The Wehrmacht had applied in Poland a revolutionary military doctrine based on the tandem use of tanks and aircraft linked by radio, which represented an indisputable innovation. It was such German military theory that had allowed the army to reinstate the use of mobile warfare. Breaches had thus been gained on narrow fronts by massive tank attacks operating in autonomous divisions. Armored columns had quickly and thoroughly capitalized on these ruptures in order to out-flank the enemy troops and to accomplish their encirclement. The infantry was then in charge of occupying and clearing the area of any pockets of resistance. The deep openings and pincer movements achieved by the panzer divisions had been assisted by the support of the air force, which relentlessly bombarded the enemy lines. But the Luftwaffe's role extended well beyond the front, with the bombardment of the enemy's airfields, headquarters, communication lines, signals, and supplies. And to add to the disorganization of the adversary's command, units of paratroopers had also been dropped behind enemy lines. When all was said and done, it was a resounding demonstration of the new form of warfare foreshadowed by Colonel General Seeckt in the 1920s, one that was immediately called *Blitzkrieg* by the Western press.

The campaign was certainly a personal success for Guderian, cre-ator of the panzer divisions and theorist of mobile warfare, which com-bined armored forces with those of the Luftwaffe. It was as much so for Manstein. It was to latter's credit that he subscribed very early on to Guderian's theories and contributed to those which were accepted as official doctrine within the high command of the army.

Later, Manstein would attribute part of rapid and stunning success of the Poland campaign to the completely innovative use of large armored formations, which operated in an independent manner, and to the support provided by an air force of crushing superiority: "The essen-tial point was nevertheless that this small Reichswehr, despised by so many people, knew how, from the moment of defeat of the First World War, to save and bring back to life the great German tradition of com-mand and formation. The new Wehrmacht, a child of the Reichswehr, had succeeded—and it was the only organization to have achieved this—at escaping from the degeneration of static warfare [...]. In the Wehrmacht, with the help of new methods of combat, one had managed to restore the veritable art of command in the ever-changing manage-ment of operations."[81]

But the astonishing successes of the Wehrmacht in Poland were not only indebted to the form of warfare to which it had recourse. The German military's plan of operations, essentially the product of Manstein's research, was largely responsible for it. Indeed, Manstein the strategist knew how to exploit to the maximum Poland's unfavorable geostrategic situation, which put its flanks at risk to offensives simultaneously launched from East Prussia, Pomerania, Upper Silesia, and Slovakia. Following the application of his plan, Poland became an enormous salient, caught in a pincer movement by the Wehrmacht. Manstein had also perfectly anticipated the adversary's defensive strategy, which consisted of fighting just behind its borders in order to protect the western regions which were Poland's richest, most industrialized, and most populated. Since the bulk of the Polish forces had been deployed to the west of the country, the Wehrmacht's pincer maneuver, through the north, the northwest, the southwest, and the south, took shape from the beginning of the offensive. The encirclement had also been facilitated by the incomplete mobilization of the Polish Army at the moment the German soldiers crossed the border. As a result, only one third of the Polish frontline units were prepared to face the invader on September 1.[82]

The weakness of the Polish position, because of its border and the inferiority of its forces, should have prompted the high command to establish its defense behind the Narew-Vistula-San line. But this would have led to the abandonment of a large part of its principal industrial zone, which was located to the west of the line created by the three rivers. In his *Memoirs*, Manstein calls attention to the issue of the Polish deployment: "From an operational perspective, this was the only appropriate proposal, for it avoided any possibility of envelopment and utilized its rivers as an important obstacle against the German armored tank formations. [...] Yet, accepting this would have led to the abandonment of western Poland where the most precious industrial and agricultural regions of the country were found."[83] Nevertheless, for a long time this had been the strategy proposed by the French high command to the Polish general staff; but the latter had at once refused to forsake a third of its national territory. The economic arguments in favor of attempting to delay the enemy advance in the principal industrial zone of the country were reinforced by national pride and the excessive confidence of the military leaders, as well as by illusions maintained regarding the Western Allies' ability to reduce the pressure of the German troops.

Wanting to protect everything, including the corridor and the developed region of Poznan, the commander in chief of the Polish Army, Marshal Edward Rydz-Smigly, could do nothing but lead his army into defeat. Deploying an army to defend an entire territory and abandon nothing causes it to be weak everywhere and accelerates its defeat, even more so if its forces are inferior to those of the adversary. What was precisely the case for Poland in 1939 would be equally true of Germany between 1943–1944, when Hitler would order Manstein to retain at all cost both the Donetz basin and the Dnieper loop.

By gathering the bulk of its forces to the east of the Narew-Vistula-San line, the Polish general staff would have been in a position to better recognize the primary axis of the German offensive, even if it were able to easily anticipate that the spearhead of the enemy attack would come from Upper Silesia, for reasons previously suggested. On the other hand, one may wonder if the abandonment of the western region to Germany would not have provoked the U.S.S.R. to intervene more quickly in eastern Poland. Whatever the case may be, an established resistance behind the Narew-Vistula-San line would not only have eliminated the threat of encirclement through East Prussia, Pomerania to the north, and Upper Silesia and Slovakia to the south, but would have also won some time for Poland. It was in its interest to keep its army intact as long as possible, hoping that a Western offensive would force Germany to withdraw a large majority of its forces from the Polish theater of operations. It was furthermore Poland's last hope of later recapturing its western regions that had been sacrificed.[84]

Had France and Great Britain let pass a unique opportunity to take advantage of the weakness of German defenses in the West in order to launch an ambitious offensive that could have spelled grave consequences for the Reich? At the very least, it was what several German generals asserted after the war. In his *Memoirs*, Manstein stresses the mistake of the Western powers for not having dared to exploit the very serious risk that the German high command took in the West. "Things would have unquestionably taken an absolutely different turn if the Western Allies had gone on the offensive as quickly as possible."[85]

His claim was somewhat illusory. First of all, France did not have at its disposal an offensive plan against Germany. Its army's strategy had been strictly defensive ever since the middle of the 1920s; her only aim was to defend the territorial integrity of the Hexagon. This strategy was reinforced by the Maginot Line, a system of fortifications on the northeast border, for which construction had commenced at the end of the 1920s. Not even possessing a trained army to conduct operations beyond her borders, France was therefore unable to keep her commitment of assistance that she had contracted out to her allies. Even if she were resigned to launching a widespread offensive, she would not have been able to forestall Poland's destiny, given the slowness of mobilization and the training of her troops, which would have taken a minimum of three weeks. Taking into account the fortifications of the Siegfried Line, which were particularly dense on the northeast border, such an offensive would most likely have been quickly transformed into a battle of attrition, moreover with heavy losses. For its part, the British contribution was much too modest to change anything; the first four divisions of the British Expeditionary Force arrived on French soil only during the first weeks of October.[86]

The deterioration of German military discipline

If there is one aspect of Manstein's career that historians have done little to acknowledge, it is clearly his indulgence concerning the crimes of the Wehrmacht in Poland. After the war the officer asserted with utter surety that the army had never suspected Hitler of actually intending to implement a policy of extermination in Poland. Concerning the military conference held by Hitler on August 22, 1939, he asserted: "What Hitler declared regarding an eventual war against Poland could not be, in my opinion, understood in the sense of a policy of extermination, as the accusation at Nuremberg maintained. If he called for a rapid and merciless destruction of the Polish armed forces, he was only expressing the goal of any great offensive operation. In any case, none of us based our interpretation of his speeches in terms of his later behavior towards this country."[87] Yet the facts not only demonstrate that the high-ranking generals, including Manstein, were perfectly aware of the Nazi regime's policy of extermination in Poland, but that they also willingly participated, which would thus implicate the Wehrmacht in criminal actions against the Jews, prisoners of war, and the political, religious, and intellectual elite of Poland.

Although they did not receive any explicit and formal instruction from the Führer apropos of the cruel policy of perfunctory executions and the displacement of the population led by the *Einsatzgruppen* (SD groups in charge of ethnic cleansing operations in the occupied territories, who followed in the wake of the army), the generals of the Wehrmacht commanding there were nevertheless well informed of the

Nazi criminal program.

The fate prescribed for the population of the vanquished territories was without precedent, even worse than the barbaric subjugations of centuries past. In the minds of its new overlords, the former Poland was no more than a colonial territory from which one could pillage the resources as it pleased, whereas, thanks to modern racial theories concealing old prejudices, its inhabitants were considered members of an inferior race that one could treat as brutally as one judged necessary.

The Polish campaign thus gave rise to particularly ferocious acts of barbarism. In the western region, invaded by the Germans, the *Einsatzgruppen* brought about a reign of terror. Five in number and attached to each of the armies—in compliance with an agreement reached between the SD and the OKH before the beginning of the campaign—the *Eisatzgruppen* were charged with eliminating the nobility, the clergy, the intelligentsia, and above all, the Jews. However, they rather liberally interpreted their mission of executing the enemies of the Reich in order to punish all demonstrations of hostility or to attack any resistance, in other words all those who displayed the smallest sign of active opposition to the occupying forces.

The goals of the Polish campaign were therefore not only limited to military objectives. They equally included actions that were racist and ideological in nature. With the intention of securing living space in Eastern Europe, the western part of occupied Poland had to be purified of its Slavic and Jewish elements, then incorporated into the Reich and repopulated with Germans. The Polish elite, who composed part of the nobility, the middle class, civil servants, and the clergy, would all be exterminated so as to deprive the intelligentsia of any opportunity to form a ruling class. The Polish elements that were considered "useful" from a racial point of view would be systematically Germanized. The other Polish were destined to become non-educated slaves in service to the "race of German lords," creating a labor force in the eastern part of occupied Poland, which was soon known under the name "General Government." As for the Jewish population, a certain number would be decimated, while others would be evacuated into designated ghettos.

Concerning the atrocities committed in Poland, the Wehrmacht was far from having "clean hands." Not only did the ruthless policy of racial purification pursued by the Nazi authorities coincide closely with the anti-Polish and anti-Semitic attitudes of many soldiers and officers of the Wehrmacht, but the latter, in accordance with Hitler's directives, led a brutal and merciless war against the Polish state and its population. And so, from the initial weeks of combat, numerous reports from the army cited instances of pillaging, arbitrary executions, brutalities against unarmed people, rapes, synagogues set ablaze, and massacres of Jews by German soldiers. The OKH was thus well informed of everything that was happening behind the front, not only concerning the activities of the police force and the *Einsatzgruppen*, but also the participation of Wehrmacht units in pogroms and routine executions of enemies of the Reich, most notably the Jews.[88] The German soldiers, therefore, did not wage "a purely military battle" inspired by a "chivalrous temperament," as Manstein claimed after the war.[89]

The Wehrmacht, the police force, and the *Einsatzgruppen* thus perpetrated, on some occasions separately, on others together, the most repugnant of barbaric criminal acts. Under the pretext of reprisals for sabotage, anti-German activities, armed insurrection, or quite simply because the victims were part of the Polish intelligentsia, these organizations committed atrocious massacres against the civilian population. By the end of October, they had carried out 764 massacres during which nearly 20,000 people were killed. The Wehrmacht alone was responsible for 311 of these massacres. On its own initiative, it had also participated in several violent demonstrations against the Jews: humiliations, pillages, forced labor, expulsions, and executions. Although the police force and the *Einsatzgruppen* were primarily responsible for the extermination of the Jews, the army willingly lent its support. Over the course of the single month of September 1939, Wehrmacht soldiers put to death more than 1,200 Jews. By the end of 1939, the German occupying authorities, assisted by units from the Wehrmacht, had executed nearly 7,000 Polish Jews.[90]

The acts of looting, brutalities against civilians, rapes, and massacres of Jews took on such proportions during the campaign that the army leadership felt compelled to take measures to reduce lapses in discipline. Indeed, individual soldiers as well as several units had on their own initiative perpetrated heartless crimes. The leadership of the Wehrmacht attempted in turn to punish those who had disrupted troop discipline by bringing them before military tribunals. But Hitler granted amnesty to the majority of them by a decree on October 4, which justified the German actions as retaliatory measures prompted by atrocities

committed by the Polish. On October 17, through a measure which contributed to the appreciable extension of the SS and the police force's
autonomy, Hitler decided to remove them from the army's jurisdiction.
Two days later, a decree stipulated that the military administration of
Poland, up until this point under the command of Colonel General
Rundstedt's general staff, would cease to exist on October 25, and
would be replaced by a civil authority.

That the army was discharged from responsibilities did not prevent
Colonel General Blaskowitz, commander in chief of the army in Poland,
after the end of his military administration, to denounce the unremitting
and repugnant acts of violence perpetrated by the SS, particularly in a
written report on February 6, 1940, which he addressed to Colonel
General Brauchitsch, head of the OKH. Yet the latter, to prevent soldiers
and officers from gaining the sense that Nazi directives were in contradiction to the army's traditional values, had put forth an order on
October 25, 1939, which explicitly forbade them from criticizing any
actions issued from the state leadership and implemented in the occupied territory. On February 7, 1940, one day after the report from
Blaskowitz, the army's commander in chief returned to the attack, by
justifying for his troops the policy of racial purification: "The fulfillment of tasks dictated by our racial policies, organized by the Führer,
and necessary to secure a vital living space for Germany, necessarily
required that they be fulfilled through harsh measures, which would
otherwise be out of the ordinary, against the Polish population in the
occupied zone. The accelerated nature of such tasks, on account of the
German people's decisive battle, naturally caused a further intensifica-
tion of these measures."[91]

Brauchitsch's reaction to Blaskowitz's protests compromised the
army's position and opened the path to an arrangement between the latter and the SS on the measures of mass extermination that had to be
implemented in the U.S.S.R. in the summer 1941. In fact, Blaskowitz
himself came back in support of the criminal policy of ethnic cleansing
authorized by Hitler. On July 22 1940, Colonel General Küchler, commander of the Eighteenth Army deployed in Poland, issued an order
that only reinforced the Wehrmacht's complicity with the criminal policy of ethnic cleansing of the Hitler regime: "I am insisting on the necessity that all soldiers of the army, particularly the officers, abstain from
all criticism of the battle against the population of the General

Government, for example that which concerns the treatment of Polish minorities, Jews, and matters of the church. The final *völkisch* solution to the ethnic conflict, which has been raging for centuries on the eastern border, demands particularly severe measures."[92]

All things considered, Colonel General Blaskowitz was one of the only ones—with, among others, General Wilhelm Ulex, the commander in chief of the southern section of the front—to rise up against the inhumane treatment meted out to the Polish population of the occupied territories by the German Army. This would cost him dearly, as he fell into disgrace and was not again promoted until the end of the war.[93] Lieutenant General Manstein—who expressed no criticism about the matter—and the large majority of his officer colleagues responded with either complicit silence or overt approval. But one thing is certain: they could not have been unaware of the numerous crimes perpetrated behind the front lines and even less of those committed by the Wehrmacht units; this would perhaps be especially true for Manstein because of his position as chief of staff of Army Group South.

Manstein's complicity in the crimes of the Wehrmacht

Within the framework of his duties, Manstein was aware of several memorandums addressed to his general staff, which reported numerous cases of physical cruelty brought on the Jews and Polish civilians by the police force, the SS, and Wehrmacht units. During the Polish campaign, a memorandum from Colonel General List, commander in chief of the Fourteenth Army operating on the front of Army Group South, referred to "pillaging, arbitrary executions, poor treatment of unarmed people, rapes, and synagogues set on fire" by soldiers of the Wehrmacht. Memorandums from Colonel General Blaskowitz, commander in chief of the Eighth Army deployed in the sector of Army Group South, and from General Ulex, at the head of the 10th Infantry Corps attached to the Eighth Army, made observations similar to those of List, condemning the atrocities committed by units of the Wehrmacht and the moral decline within its ranks. Clearly, Manstein could not have been unaware of the content of such allegations coming from two army commanders and one corps commander belonging to the southern group from which he led his operations.

Many were the reports addressed to him which paid witness to the

German Army's implication in criminal actions committed against the Polish civilian population, in particular the Jews. For example, on September 8, 1939, Major Rudolf Langhaeuser, an officer assigned to the intelligence agency of Rundstedt's general staff, drafted a letter intended for the army commanders in which he condemned the looting and the physical abuses of the Wehrmacht soldiers in Poland, notably at the expense of prisoners of war, which contravened the discipline and honor of the German Army. To remedy the worst abuses, he recommended taking the most severe action against any Wehrmacht soldier who engaged in such acts of violence. But Lieutenant General Manstein, as chief of staff of Army Group South, refused to take any action regarding the letter. In a handwritten note by Major Langhaeuser found at the bottom of his draft, one can read his remark concerning Manstein's refusal to forward it to Colonel General Rundstedt for his signature.[94]

In a report concerning three soldiers who had assaulted a Jewish man, raped his daughter, and committed armed robbery at the house of a Jewish merchant, one finds a note from Manstein asking the following question: "How much time will it take before this situation is brought to an end?" His post-war declarations, notably during the Nuremberg trials, according to which he never had any knowledge during this time of crimes committed against Jews or other Polish civilians, are thus nothing more than deceitful.

Another report brought to Manstein's attention concerned the Blonie massacre in the sector of the Tenth Army, commanded by Colonel General Reichenau. In this small Polish town, located nearly twenty kilometers west of Warsaw, an officer of the SS division *Leibstandarte Adolf Hitler* ordered the execution of 50 Jews during the night of September 18–19, 1939. After Lieutenant General Joachim Lemelsen, commander of the 29th Motorized Division, recommended the arrest of the officer in charge of this slaughter for breach of discipline, Colonel General Rundstedt, as commander in chief of Army Group South, demanded in a letter addressed to Reichenau that he be sentenced. One can assume that Manstein was informed of the matter, for Rundstedt's letter was sent through his general staff.

He was equally aware of the massacre that took place at Konskie a few days earlier, triggered out of retaliation for the death of General Wilhelm Roettig, chief of the German police force in Poland. The latter was killed in combat against regular troops of the Polish Army, though the *Einsatzgruppen* declared that he had been savagely assassinated. To follow up on their allegation, they immediately set up a commission in charge of finding those who were guilty, who, according to them, were most likely to be found among the inhabitants of Konskie. However, this did not prevent them in the meantime from killing 20 civilians who had nothing to do with the death of General Roettig. Nevertheless, to facilitate the search for the guilty, Colonel General Reichenau, chief of the Tenth Army deployed on the front of Army Group South, ordered the arrest of any civilian male eighteen years and older in and around Konskie—some 5,000 people all together—and for them to be taken to a camp near the city for interrogation.

Though they were not injured, 120 people—Jews, Polish, and Polish plain-clothed soldiers—were wearing blood-stained clothes, which made them immediately suspicious, all the more so since they were in possession of Germany currency. In fact, they were declared guilty on the spot and executed straightaway. Numerous Wehrmacht soldiers, called upon to form several execution platoons, participated in the routine killing of the condemned.[95] The events of Konskie thus do not in any way correspond to the version recounted by Manstein in his *Memoirs*. The latter grossly minimized the magnitude of the massacre, leading one to believe instead that it was an incident like any other that occurred in war.[96]

Far from being content with a complicit silence, Manstein even provided his own contribution to the war against the Jews. After the Soviet Union invaded Poland, the OKH issued a deplorable order regarding the Jews that the chief of staff of Army Group South hastened to immediately pass on to his army commanders. Through this order, the Wehrmacht was required to prohibit Jews who had fled the German advance, and who now found themselves in the Polish sector occupied by the Red Army, from crossing the German-Soviet demarcation line in order to return to their homeland. With his army group in mind, Manstein amended the OKH's order with the following sentence: "We must prevent the Jewish refugees, by any means necessary, from returning to Upper Silesia." And as if such a directive did not suffice, Tenth Army's Colonel General Reichenau added the following words to Manstein's sentence: "If necessary, with weapons."[97] Apparently, the fate of the Jews of Poland seems to have left Manstein completely indifferent.

The activities of the *Einsatzgruppen* being carried out to the rear of the Eighth, Tenth, and Fourteenth Armies of the southern group were obviously known to Manstein. Furthermore, the atrocities committed in Poland after the military campaign were brought to his attention and to that of his colleagues deployed in other theaters of operation. And so, on December 19, 1939, in a letter written to Brauchitsch, Colonel General Leeb, commander in chief of Army Group C on the Western Front, characterized the behavior of the police and the SS in Poland as "unworthy of a civilized people."[98] Yet such a denunciation was the only one from a commander attached to an area other than Poland.

As for Lt. General Manstein, he did not express any objection concerning the numerous abuses committed in Poland, neither before nor after his general staff was transferred from the Eastern to the Western Front on October 24, 1939. By refusing to stand up against the excesses of the German Army, and taking upon himself to enforce an order from the OKH against the Jewish refugees, he had already to a great extent compromised himself in this criminal war. He knew very well that he could not make a career for himself in a totalitarian regime without such compromise, eespecially in a regime he had decided to support as an ally, even if he did not approve of all of its policies. Besides, he certainly did not forget that his opposition to the enactment of racial legislation in the Wehrmacht in 1934 had almost cost him a disciplinary sanction which could have damaged his advancement. He had obviously learned his lesson. A brilliant and energetic officer like him, whose ambition was to become chief of the general staff or commander in chief of the army, could not allow himself again to stand in opposition to the political-ideological objectives of the National Socialist regime.

By approving the program of extermination which was at the heart of the barbaric campaign of ethnic purification in Poland, the army's generals had crossed the Rubicon. Indeed, by accepting to be more or less willing accomplices to the criminal policies of the Nazi regime, the leaders of the Wehrmacht proved themselves to be just as guilty. The events that unfolded in the subjugated territories were, certainly, still far from the systematic genocide perpetrated during the Russian campaign. Yet the operation already had genocidal features. It was, so to speak, the testing ground for what was to follow on a larger scale in the Soviet Union: a racial war of extermination.[99]

THE MANSTEIN PLAN

After the campaign in Poland, Manstein would play a crucial role in the formation of an operations plan against the Western Allies, a role that today is still the subject of great debate, particularly with regards to whether he had truly initiated the concept of the *Sichelschnitt* (Sickle Cut) plan, which made possible the lightening victory of the Wehrmacht in the west. The debate over this issue is of primary importance, for it indeed concerns one of the most consequential misunderstandings in German military history.

Manstein isolated from the generals' revolt?

On October 24, 1939, the staff of Colonel General Rundstedt and Lieutenant General Manstein was transferred to the Western Front to take command of Army Group A, which had just been formed. Army Group A was located to the left of Army Group B—which had been entrusted to Colonel General Bock, formerly known as Army Group North, which had fought in Poland before being transferred to the West on October 10—and to the right of Colonel General Leeb's Army Group C, in position since the beginning of the war. It was in Koblenz, at the Riesen-Fürstenhof Hotel, located along the Rhine, where Rundstedt and Manstein's general staff set up its headquarters. No sooner was he transferred to the Western Front than Manstein began to play a major role in the formation of the operations plan.

On October 21, he received orders to appear at OKH's headquarters in Zossen to take delivery of directives intended for his army group. He was informed at that time of the Yellow Plan (*Fall Gelb*) in relation to the offensive in the West, organized by Hitler at the end of the Polish campaign.

On September 8 Hitler had revealed for the first time, to his principal adjutant, Lieutenant Colonel Rudolf Schmundt, his intention to attack the Allies immediately after the Polish campaign. On September 25, he had announced to the OKH his decision to commence a general offensive in the west beginning in the autumn of 1939, while the Franco-British armies were not yet prepared. As for the commanders in chief of the three branches of the Wehrmacht, he had made them aware of his decision on September 27, the day Warsaw capitulated to the Wehrmacht.[100]

On October 10, Hitler summoned his main military leaders to present them the motives for the offensive in the West for which two weeks later he would set the date of November 12. He asserted that it was necessary to defeat the Western powers so that they would no longer be in a position to stand against the strengthening and development of the Reich. In addition, their defeat was absolutely necessary in order to make room for the expansion of the German population in eastern Europe. Since time played to the enemy's favor, he said, Germany had to strike as rapidly as possible, while she still possessed an advantage in armaments. If only for the United States' hostility or the uncertain behavior of the U.S.S.R., the Reich had every interest to take advantage of its brief superiority. He concluded that an attack could nevertheless be diverted if an agreement were to be reached with London and Paris, with the condition that German gains in Poland would not be compromised.

For the Wehrmacht leaders, Hitler's unilateral decision to attack the Western powers seemed irrational, all the more so since it came immediately after the Polish campaign. In fact, the attitude of the German generals had rarely before been as unanimous as it was in the rejection of such an offensive in the West, with the exception of Lieutenant General Manstein, whose views in this matter will later be examined. In a sense, the Führer's intention to attack in the West prompted a revolt on the part of the generals.

Colonel General Brauchitsch, commander in chief of the OKH, and General Halder, chief of the general staff, asserted to Hitler on October 7 that, in spite of his spectacular success, the Poland campaign had revealed serious deficiencies, as much on the level of equipment and training as on the troops' readiness to fight. The armored formations had suffered from a flagrant lack of tanks. The relationship between the panzer divisions and the non-motorized infantry had often been laborious. Furthermore, they claimed that the Wehrmacht would not encounter in the Western theater conditions as favorable as those in Poland, where it had clashed with an army inferior in men and materials, and furthermore, in sheer numbers. Primarily assembled in the region of Poznan, in an extremely unfavorable geostrategic position, the Polish Army was able to be easily encircled by a pincer maneuver from East Prussia and Pomerania in the north, and Upper Silesia and Slovakia to the south. In the West, on the other hand, the Wehrmacht would be confronted with narrow fronts, fortified positions in both France and Belgium, and with adversaries who were completely mobilized and who disposed of large numbers of soldiers and supplies. With the memories of the First World War still in mind, its duration and its bloody trench battles, Brauchitsch and Halder were convinced of the French Army's strength and the quality of its leaders.

Even the tank warfare specialists, such as Generals Guderian and Erich Hoepner, in addition to Colonel General Reichenau, advised against the commencement of an offensive with winter approaching, which would put the troops at risk of getting bogged down in the autumn mud. Field Marshal Göring himself reckoned that apart from the limited number of hours of daylight, the November fog could paralyze the operations of his Luftwaffe. General Stülpnagel, chief of the logistics section of the OKH, claimed for his part that the armored and motorized divisions had been too overworked by the tough battles in Poland to be further utilized in the fall. He considered that because of the time required to compensate for the losses in weapons and supplies, as well as for completing the training of units, an attack in the West would not be possible for two years.

Although the principal leaders of the German Army had closely analyzed the Polish campaign and translated the acquired experiences into training tools, they did not believe that it would likely serve as a point of comparison for a conflict with the Allies. Clearly, the primary adversary of the First World War was still held in the greatest respect. Concerning an offensive in the West, Colonel General Leeb was entirely pessimistic with regards to their chances of victory: "Surprise is not possible. We will have an infinite number of casualties without being able to overcome the French. An attack against France cannot be led like the attack against Poland, for it will be long and give rise to enormous losses."

Like Leeb, other German generals still dreaded an expansion of the conflict. A violation of the Belgian and Dutch neutralities could definitively compromise any possibility of a peaceful resolution. They thus advised to wait. The Wehrmacht should keep on the defensive, reinforce its military potential, renounce taking any initiative, and remain ready to respond to an Allied offensive in 1940 or 1941. This idea of a defensive war in the West was advocated, in particular, by General Halder and his assistants at the OKH.[101]

Halder and his loyal adjutant Stülpnagel even began to envision the idea of a putsch at the end of the month, after Hitler had confirmed his intention to attack on November 12. The chief of the OKH general staff placed his subordinate in charge of discretely polling a few generals on their likely reaction to a coup d'état. The results were hardly encouraging. While being opposed to an offensive, the commanders on the Western Front rejected the idea of a putsch, on one hand out of their duty to obey the head of state, on another out of fear that their troops would not follow them. Even Halder's and Stülpnagel's attempt to create, in reaction against Hitler, a coalition with the commanders in chief of the three army groups failed. Although Rundstedt and Bock had a similar appreciation of the situation, they were unable to come to a resolution concerning active resistance. Only Leeb had been willing to stop at nothing, as were a few generals who were critical of the regime, like Witzleben and Hoepner. As for himself, Leeb tried to convince the commanders in chief of the two other army groups to resign in order to pressure Hitler, though without any success. Not being able to count on a majority of the generals, Halder concluded that the German population also supported Hitler and was consequently not prepared to support a putsch.[102]

On November 5, at the instigation of his army group commanders, the head of the army, Brauchitsch, met with Hitler in order to dissuade him from unleashing an attack that autumn. Accompanied by his chief of general staff, he brought up the list of objections that had already been presented on October 7, to which he added those from the generals on the Western Front: an unfavorable season, the strength of the French Army, and the necessity to rectify the weaknesses of the German forces. However, he was vehemently driven out by an icy Hitler who remained unwavering. After having sharply denounced the "spirit of Zossen," the defeatism expressed at the general headquarters of the OKH, he confirmed once again the date of November 12 for the initiation of the offensive. In fact, it would be postponed 29 times throughout that autumn and winter, essentially for meteorological reasons.

Whatever the case may be, the fact that Hitler spoke about destroying the "spirit of Zossen" left Halder thinking that he had gotten wind of the plot to oust him. Fearing that the Gestapo could appear in Zossen at any moment, he and Stülpnagel hastened, as soon as he returned to his headquarters, to destroy all of the documents related to the conspiracy. Clearly, the Führer's diatribe against the two leaders of the OKH had snuffed out any of their plans, albeit tentative, to overthrow him. Indeed, Halder and Stülpnagel were now resigned to accept the responsibility for an offensive in the West to which they were nonetheless opposed. At any rate, they were well aware that they army was divided. If a few generals were hostile to Hitler, the large majority, including Manstein, supported him. And so, for the military leaders, this was the beginning of the headlong rush, allowing themselves to be completely carried away in preparations for the offensive. If one was unable to prevent a military campaign in the West, it was then at least necessary to win it.[103]

While awaiting that fateful day, the Führer summoned some two hundred high-ranking officers from the Western Front, commanders and staff officers, to the Reich Chancellery on November 23. Among them was Lieutenant General Manstein, chief of staff of Army Group A. On the eve of the great battle, Hitler believed that it was crucial to rouse them to a level of exaltation. In his speech, he essentially raised the same arguments articulated in his memorandum of October 9, which he had read the following day to the chiefs of the OKW, the OKH, the Luftwaffe, and the Kriegsmarine.

Not a single senior officer raised his voice in objection to the Führer's motives and objectives concerning the offensive in the West, or asserted the immorality of such an attack against Belgium and the Netherlands, the borders and neutrality of which the German government had solemnly guaranteed.

Manstein wrote in his *Memoirs* that "the reasons given to explain the fundamental necessity of launching an offensive were well-considered and convincing (except with regards to the matter of the date)."[104]

Indeed, during visits made to the staff of Army Group A in October and the beginning of November by the commander in chief of the OKH and his chief of staff, Manstein essentially brought up the reservations that had already been expressed by these men and the other generals on the Western Front. Unleashing an offensive at the end of autumn, he asserted, would have no chance of achieving a decisive success. The season was quite simply unfavorable for such an undertaking. It hardly permitted the Wehrmacht to fully utilize its armored units and its air force. Because of the brevity of daylight hours, the pace of operations was greatly reduced. In addition to this, the newly formed units had not yet been fully trained. Only the active divisions were truly in a position to take part in a large-scale offensive in the autumn of 1939. The others still lacked cohesion and training. He equally insisted that the army had still not completed the restoration of its armored divisions from the end of the Polish campaign. In order to lead an offensive in the West that autumn, one would have needed to withdraw them from the east much earlier. Moreover, the air force also needed to be replenished before embarking on any new operations. In short, for the chief of staff of Army Group A, the Wehrmacht could not contemplate an attack in the Western theatre before the spring of 1940. And yet, given the prevailing state of affairs, if spring 1940 represented the closest moment, it was also the last opportunity that the Reich could hope to launch a victorious offensive.[105]

Like his fellow officers, Manstein did not believe that Germany would reach an understanding with the Western powers after her victory in Poland.[106] It appeared inconceivable to him that the Reich would accept a restoration of the Polish state, as Great Britain and France were demanding, seeing that it had just led a victorious military campaign there to settle the issue. In any case, it seemed impossible to restore Poland in order to arrive at an agreement with the West, since Russia had already absorbed half the country into its own borders. Manstein and his peers were thus in complete agreement with the proposed compromise offered by Hitler to the Reich Chancellery on October 6, 1939. Its rejection by London and Paris did not surprise them in the least.

However, the chief of staff of Army Group A in no way shared the perspective of certain OKH generals, especially Halder, who advised waiting in hope that the Western powers would decide to attack, thus giving the German high command the opportunity to achieve an out-come through a counter-offensive. According to Manstein, nothing guaranteed that the Western powers would decide to take the offensive. In fact, such an attack appeared to him as rather improbable. How could the Allies reconcile the fact that they had not even dared to attack during the time when the bulk of the German forces were fighting in Poland, now that the Germans' main strength was deployed in the west? The Allies' objectives appeared instead to be aimed at ensuring the impregnability of French territory and, as should be expected, to bring aid to Belgium and the Netherlands if they were attacked. Consequently, one could not project a favorable outcome to the war by remaining in a defensive position. In no case could the Reich allow itself to wait until its adversaries succeeded in making up for their delay in the domain of ground and air forces, or acquired superior military strength with the help of the Americans, which one had to expect; and even less so when the unpredictable behavior of Bolshevik Russian was taken into account. The more the Western powers reinforced themselves militarily, the chief of staff of Army Group A thought, the more precarious Germany's situation would become with the Soviet giant in its rear.[107]

For Manstein, the Reich quite simply did not have a choice; it had to move to the attack so as to force a quick outcome in the West. Furthermore, he confirmed during the Nuremberg trials the point of view he had adopted after the Poland campaign concerning the Führer's intention to attack in the West: "In my opinion, when it turned out that a political union with the Western powers was unattainable through peaceful means, there was no other option than to lead an offensive in the West and thus to finish the war."[108] He therefore appeared res-olutely more aggressive than the generals of the OKH who proposed adopting a defensive strategy. He was, however, of the opinion that the Wehrmacht, if it wanted to achieve a decisive success against the Western powers, absolutely had to opt for a plan of operations other than the one that the OKH had devised.

The Yellow Plan: The operations plan of the OKH

Hitler had distanced himself from the military operations in Poland, as much during the preparations as during the course of the campaign. Yet in the planning of the western offensive he created a precedent by directly intervening for the first time. On October 9, 1939, Hitler delivered to the OKH, by way of the OKW, his directives concerning the offensive in the west. They underscored the necessity of dismantling as much of the French armed forces as possible, along with the Allied armies fighting on their side, and at the same time conquering as much of the territories in the Netherlands, Belgium, and northern France as possible. The conquest of these territories would serve as the base of operations for an air and naval war against Great Britain and as a buffer zone against Allied bombardments of the Ruhr. In accordance with the Führer's general directives, the OKH had the task of preparing a detailed operations plan as quickly as possible.

In the strategy decreed by Hitler, one finds no reference to a lightening war as such. Instead of gambling everything on one card in relation to a single battle that could bring the war to an end, his strategy was aimed at only partially fulfilling the objectives: one had to destroy as much of the Allied armies as possible and conquer as much territory as possible in order to create a base of operations necessary for the continuation of the war. In the mind of the supreme commander of the German forces, who was hindered by a train of thought inherited from the Great War, it was undoubtedly a matter of taking the harbors and airfields, a preliminary condition for a war of attrition that was subsequently and primarily expected to be waged against England.[109]

The OKH's operations plan was completed on October 19. Supervised by the commander in chief of the army, Colonel General Brauchitsch, the plan was the work of his chief of general staff, General Halder, along with his adjutants, General Stülpnagel, chief of the logistics section, and Colonel Greiffenberg, chief of the operations bureau. According to the general directives given by Hitler on October 9, the OKH expected to unleash an attack through the Netherlands and northern Belgium, with a powerful right wing to destroy the Dutch and Belgian forces, along with the Franco-British forces that were coming to their rescue. It was indeed through the right wing that the OKH hoped to gain its victory. Composed of a detachment from Army N and Army Group B, the right wing would gather on the lower stretches of the Rhine and in the northern part of Eifel. Whereas detachment N's (three divisions) mission was to remove the Netherlands from combat through action in the direction of Utrecht, Army Group B, consisting of three armies (37 divisions, including eight armored and two motorized), had

to attack Belgium by way of north and south of Liege in the direction
of Brussels, with the help of its armored units deployed on the frontline.
Army Group A, which was composed of two armies (27 divisions
including 1 armored and 1 motorized), had to shield the operations of
Army Group B to the south, while Army Group C, divided into two
armies (25 divisions), would ensure the defense of the *Westwall* fortifications facing the Maginot Line.[110]

Faced with the obvious dissatisfaction of Hitler and certain high
ranking military leaders, notably Keitel, with respect to the plan of
operations, the OKH introduced a few modifications which were overall relatively minor. On October 29, it sent its second plan of attack to
the Führer and the OKW. Contrary to the first, this plan did not have a
single target in the direction of Brussels, but two simultaneous points,
one in the direction of Brussels, the other in the direction of Namur.

In this second deployment order, the Netherlands was no longer an
issue of concern for the German offensive. Army Group B remained the
most powerful, with 30 infantry divisions and the bulk of the rapid
units, nine armored divisions and four motorized. It was thus a matter
of having almost half of the 102 divisions now available on the Western
Front. Now composed of four armies gathered on the lower stretches of
the Rhine and in the northern part of the Eifel, Army Group B was to
attack in Belgium, on both sides of Liege, in the dual directions of
Brussels and Namur, with two armies on the frontline, the Fourth and
the Sixth, along with two others on the second line, the Second and the
Eighteenth (the reinforced Army Detachment N). The conquest of the
Netherlands was later reactivated and entrusted to the Eighteenth Army.

The mission of Army Group A to the south was to protect Army
Group B, which was in charge of fulfilling the task. Its zone of concentration being in the southern part of Eifel and in the region of Hunsrück
(between the Moselle and the Nahe), it had to advance through southern Belgium and Luxembourg. Divided into two armies, the Twelfth and
the Sixteenth, Army Group A included 22 infantry divisions with not a
single rapid unit. Whereas the Twelfth Army would protect the left flank
of Army Group B during its advance, the Sixteenth Army would branch
off to the south after having crossed through Luxembourg to offer protection to the entirety of the operation. It would take a defensive position on a line extending from the far eastern end of the Maginot Line to
the east of Sedan, between the Meuse and the Saar.

With the strength of two armies and 18 infantry divisions, Army Group C was responsible for the security of the *Westwall*, between the borders of Luxembourg and Switzerland. The OKH left in reserve 17 infantry and two motorized divisions.[111]

Regardless of whether it was the first or the second operations plan, the OKH's objective remained limited. During the first phase of the campaign, the chiefs of the OKH did not anticipate having to remove the French Army from battle, but rather to force it to retreat to the south of the Somme, then to occupy the coast of the English Channel, thus cutting England off from its French ally and at the same time providing air and naval bases from where they could harass and block the British Isles. It was as if they thought that following such a defeat, albeit a limited one, England and France would appear willing to negotiate and leave the Reich free to focus its attention once again on the East.

Manstein's objections concerning the Yellow Plan

Lieutenant General Manstein immediately rejected the OKH's operations plan. His first reaction was to consider it nothing more than a simple repetition of the famous Schlieffen Plan, which was conceived in 1905 and utilized by the German Army in 1914. Following the example of this model, not only was the primary focus of the OKH's offensive concentrated on the right wing, but the principal axis was to cross Belgium and northern France. Even if any resemblance between the two plans stopped there, Manstein still considered General Halder's plan less than satisfactory since it could in no way produce a strategic outcome, contrary to the former Schlieffen Plan. Indeed, if the latter was hoping for a complete strategic victory, the Yellow Plan's objective only provided for a partial success. It would thus be erroneous to presume, as some have occasionally done, that the Yellow Plan constituted a simple re-edition of the Schlieffen Plan.

In his famous 1905 plan, Field Marshal Alfred Graf von Schlieffen, who was chief of general staff of the Imperial Army from 1891 to 1906, expected to defeat the French Army in a single military campaign through a very large pincer maneuver. This was to be executed in two phases by a powerful right wing. To start, a vast encircling maneuver would bring the German right wing across Belgium and northern France, well beyond the Seine, to the west of Paris. Subsequently, this advancing wing, pivoting to the east, south of Paris, would encircle and destroy the French forces that remained, cornered on the Metz-Vosges-Swiss border front. To achieve a complete and definitive outcome over the entire enemy army, Schlieffen was hoping that the French would attack in Alsace-Lorraine from the very beginning of hostilities to retake this region, which was lost during the Franco-Prussian War of 1870–1871; such a move on their part would facilitate a pincer maneuver by the German Army. He thus accepted the risk of suffering initial losses in Alsace-Lorraine, even perhaps temporarily losing this region. Furthermore, he opposed the construction of a powerful line of fortifications in the west precisely because he considered that a French advance in Alsace-Lorraine was not only desirable, but also necessary. In Field Marshal Schlieffen's mind, Alsace-Lorraine had to simultaneously serve as a lure and a trap for the French Army.

On the other hand, General Halder's plan in no way expected a complete and definitive outcome over the enemy forces. He did not envisage his plan from the perspective of total victory. Far from the strategic results sought by Schlieffen, the chief of the OKH general staff only set a partial operational success as his target. In fact, he deemed the possibility of an absolute success in the western theatre as nonexistent. His plan was thus uniquely aimed at a partial victory over the Allied forces encountered in Belgium, and a limited territorial conquest of the English Channel. The acquisition of the Channel would provide a base of operations for the continuation of the war against England and France. Recalling that the German Army, after the failure of its 1914 offensive, had not succeeded in acquiring the bases needed to manage the submarine war against England, the OKH granted an absolute priority to the occupation of the English Channel. He wanted to wait, however, to determine how to continue the offensive and what form to give it, once he had achieved his primary objectives, specifically a partial victory over the Allied forces in Belgium and the occupation of the Channel coast.

But contrary to Schlieffen, Manstein did not believe that the French Army could be completely defeated in a single blow. He judged that a repetition of the 1914 plan was impossible because of the differences in the situation. In the first place, if the German Army had been in a position of expecting to achieve an operational surprise in 1914, it could hardly do so in 1939 or 1940. It was henceforth impossible for the army to conceal from the enemy the build-up of its forces on the northern wing. Based on memories from 1914, the French general staff had, at any rate, to expect a return of the Schlieffen Plan. It undoubtedly expected that the German Army would circumvent the Maginot Line through Belgium, just as she had bypassed in 1914, through this same country, the fortified front of Verdun-Toul-Nancy-Epinal. Next, he asserted, the Germans could not bet on a French strategic initiative. To the contrary, they should instead count on a vigorous counterattack against the southern flank of the German forces committed in Belgium. There was no doubt that the high command of the Allied forces would immediately send significant forces into Belgium to stand against the German advance. He concluded that it was thus not by an offensive depending on a powerful right wing passing through the Netherlands and Belgium that Germany could hope to surprise the enemy.

The OKH's operations plan included other shortcomings. According to Manstein, if one desired, after having obtained the partial results wished by the OKH, to continue the offensive with the idea of completely eliminating the Western forces, it would be necessary to lead the first operation according to this final objective. It had to first guarantee the total destruction of the northern wing of the enemy so as to obtain a decisive superiority, which would permit it to then annihilate the rest of the Allied armies in France from a base of operations which would be favorably positioned for this second undertaking. But the OKH's plan did not at all appear to fulfill these two essential conditions for conducting a second operation aimed at bringing about a total and definitive triumph over the adversary. Neither the balance of power in the right wing nor the terrain in Belgium permitted the Wehrmacht to anticipate such a possibility.

Army Group B, which was on the right wing, had a total of 43 divisions. After its entry into Belgium, it would clash with 20 Belgian divisions and 10 Dutch divisions. Even if the latter were inferior in comparison with German combat formations, they would be able to resort to substantial fortifications and to numerous natural obstacles to resist the invader. Indeed, one could find in Belgium powerful fortifications on both sides of Liege, along the Albert Canal all the way to the Anvers Fortress, and along the Meuse with Namur as its central base, not including the numerous natural obstacles in Holland, such as the streams and canals.

The German troops hardly had the time to break through the resistance of Belgian and Dutch forces before being confronted by the Franco-British armies. The latter, having been deployed along the Franco-Belgian border precisely because their high command was expecting a German attack by way of the Netherlands and Belgium, could oppose Wehrmacht units in Belgian territory from the very first days of battle. The Wehrmacht would then lose numerical superiority on its right wing. Having to conduct a frontal attack, before an adversary of roughly the same strength, perhaps even superior, it would no longer have any possibility of accomplishing a highly intricate surprise pincer maneuver as in 1914. In a situation of frontal attack, the German Army would be forced to seek victory through an offensive of tactical maneuvers and no longer through strategic positioning. As long as the enemy, with its skilled and energetic command, could avoid a defeat in Belgium, such a victory could only be partially achieved. Indeed, if the enemy proved incapable of remaining on the fortified line of Anvers-Liege-Meuse, it could always withdraw its units that were still able to fight behind the lower stretches of the Somme and establish, with reserve formations, a new defensive front.

Meanwhile, the German offensive would have already exceeded its *dénouement*. Army Group B would see its advance halted by the adversary. As for Army Group A, it would not be in a position, because of its deployment and its forces, of preventing the enemy from establishing a new defensive front extending from the lower stretches of the Somme to Sedan. The German Army would thus find itself in a situation analogous to that of 1914, after the Battle of the Marne, i.e. in a war of fixed positions. The only advantage that it would gain would be possession on the coast of a larger base for the continuation of its operations.

A bold and resolute enemy could equally gain from the shortcomings of the OKH's plan, not only by stopping the German offensive in Belgium which it was expecting, but also by launching a counteroffensive against the southern flank of the Wehrmacht's right wing. Even by sending into Belgium soldiers intended to rescue troops from that country and from Holland, it would have a sufficient number of reserves to assemble nearly 50 divisions for such a counterattack. For this, all it needed to do was withdraw units from the Maginot Line. The further Army Group B would advance in the direction of the English Channel or the mouth of the Somme, the more effective the Allied counterattack would be. With only 22 divisions, Army Group A would most likely not be in a position to forestall it.

The chief of staff of Army Group A thus came to the conclusion that the OKH's plan of operations would indeed lead the Wehrmacht into a frontal battle following which it could achieve neither the destruction of the Allied forces encountered in Belgium, and consequently a superiority adequate enough to guarantee the outcome, nor a favorably positioned operational base for a second maneuver intended to destroy the remainder of the enemy armies. The operation conceived by the OKH would lead to nothing more than a partial success. Threatened by a counterattack on the southern flank of its northern wing, the Wehrmacht would probably find itself in a war of fixed positions as during the Great War.[112]

The "Manstein Plan" or the idea of the sickle cut

In light of such considerations, Lieutenant General Manstein decided to communicate his objections to the OKH concerning the plan for the offensive in the West, and at the same time submit a new plan of attack. At the time, he was completely unaware that the plan conceived by Halder and his staff displeased the Führer. He simply considered it a timorous way of approaching a strategic problem that by instinct he judged open to a more daring solution. With the help of his superior, Colonel General von Rundstedt, his chief of the logistics section, Colonel Blumentritt, and his chief of the operations bureau, Lieutenant Colonel Henning von Tresckow, Manstein thus conceived a different operations plan at the end of October 1939.

By October 31, Rundstedt had sent two documents to the OKH which included all of Manstein's fundamental ideas. Whereas the first document set forth the reasons why it was preferable to delay the German offensive until the spring and to adopt an operations plan other than the one proposed by the OKH, the second complemented such considerations by proposing a different method whereby the Wehrmacht should conduct the attack.

Manstein's primary view was that the Wehrmacht's spearhead had to be located on the left wing and not the right. The action anticipated by Army Group B in the OKH's plan would undoubtedly end in a frontal battle with an adversary who was expecting them. It could achieve an initial success, but the frontal shock would at the very most lead to a war of fixed positions on the Somme. By shifting the focus of the offensive's concentration from Army Group B to Army Group A, the Wehrmacht could thus hope to provoke surprise and confusion in the enemy's territory. An advance of Army Group A through the Ardennes, with the bulk of its armored and motorized units, would not fail to take by surprise an enemy who considered this wooded region unsuitable for such an action, expecting instead to encounter him further north in Belgium. After traversing the Ardennes, Army Group A would cross the Meuse, enter Dinant and Sedan, and then focus on the objective of reaching the lower stretches of the Somme in order to cut off from the south the retreating Franco-British forces that had been sent into Belgium. Only through such a method could one annihilate the adversary's northern wing, which would create a situation in which one could hope for a decisive victory in France.

It was possible that the enemy, if maneuvered with skill, would try to avoid a disastrous outcome for itself in Belgium by retreating if need be behind the Somme. A bold and flexible Allied high command would then gather its available forces to launch a counteroffensive against the German southern flank, with the idea of encircling the bulk of the Wehrmacht forces in Belgium or against the lower stretches of the Rhine. If the German offensive across Belgium ended up coming to a halt on the lower stretches of the Somme, the Western powers could succeed in establishing, with their operational reserves, a defensive front extending from the far northwest of the Maginot Line to the east of Sedan, all the way to the English Channel and the length of the Aisne and the Oise. In order to avoid such a scenario, the Wehrmacht had to immediately counter all intervention of enemy forces against its southern flank between the Meuse and the Oise. From the very beginning of the offensive, it was thus necessary for it to destroy the cohesion of the adversary's front in this region so as to allow for the possibility of taking the Maginot Line in the rear.

Since the center of gravity of the entire operation was assigned to the left wing and not to the right, Army Group A had to consist of three armies instead of two. It also had to join together the primary armored, motorized, and rapid units for the offensive through the Ardennes. The first of the three armies would advance through southern Belgium, cross the Meuse, and then charge forward in the direction of the lower

Somme, to attack in the rear the Allied forces engaged against Army Group B in Belgium. The second army would push to the southwest, with the mission of attacking all of the enemy forces gathered for the purpose of counterattacking the southern flank of the German Army in the region west of the Meuse. The third army's directives would be to provide defensive protection of the flank of the overall operation to the north of the Maginot Line, from Sierck to Mousson, east of Sedan.

Shifting the focus of concentration from Army Group B to Army Group A nonetheless presented a problem as to the deployment of the divisions: space. One could introduce a new army into Army Group A only during the development of the offensive. Yet to ensure that the offensive would be quickly executed, it had to be ready from the very beginning.[113] Such were the ideas in the "Manstein Plan," which would later be better known as the "Sickle Cut" (*Sichelschnitt*), which the staff of Army Group A communicated to the OKH.

Manstein's plan: *a perfecting of Schlieffen's operational theories?*

Manstein's operations plan was both brilliant and daring. He was looking to achieve a strategic outcome and not a simple operational success. Instead of a frontal offensive in Belgium, he instead recommended a pincer maneuver around all of the enemy forces deployed to the north of the Somme. For this, he shifted the operation's center of gravity from Army Group B on the northern wing, to Army Group A on the southern wing. As the spearhead of the German offensive, Army Group A had to cross the Ardennes with the bulk of the armored, motorized, and rapid units and then cross the Meuse between Dinant and Sedan, finally to charge forward to the coast of the English Channel by following the axis outlined by the Somme, from Amiens to Abbeville. By means of a pincer maneuver to the south, Army Group A would thus take in the rear the northern Allied armies after their advance into northern Belgium to hold up the progress of Army Group B, whose mission was, to a certain extent, to act as a lure. Certainly, a pincer maneuver against the southern flank of the Allied formations sent into Belgium was more ambitious than a simple frontal maneuver intended to breach the enemy forces. It also had many more chances to take the adversary by surprise, to break up the cohesion of its front, and to destroy the bulk of its forces.

With his strategic clairvoyance, Manstein already had in mind the second phase of the campaign in the west. He considered the idea of trampling the French and her allies with one single pincer operation as unrealistic. This had turned out to be a fatal move in 1914, with the Schlieffen Plan. He preferred to consult Clausewitz, who had explained that during an offensive it was not necessary to try and achieve prematurely the final outcome. He thus proposed to lead the campaign in two large connected operations stemming from a successful penetration near Sedan; one after the other, each half of the Allied front would be encircled and destroyed. The objective of the first operation, named the Yellow Plan (*Fall Gelb*), was to encircle the northern wing of the enemy armies by an armored offensive ranging from Sedan to the coast of the English Channel. As for the second operation, named the Red Plan (*Fall Rot*), it was a matter of encircling the southern wing, from Sedan to the Swiss border. The offensive was to unfold in a manner similar to the Schlieffen Plan and force the French to fight behind the Maginot Line, with a reversal of fronts.

With his plan of attack, Lieutenant General Manstein not only perfected Field Marshal Schlieffen's operational theory, but to a certain extent surpassed it. To the idea of envelopment that had been proposed by the Imperial Army's former chief of general staff, he added the method of breaching, which had been rejected by the latter. The Manstein Plan consisted of two partial operations: a breach in the region of Sedan and a pincer maneuver all the way to the English Channel. In this case, if one were to define the Schlieffen School through the notion of envelopment and the rejection of a breach, the Manstein Plan, which was staked on breaching the line from the Meuse to Sedan, and on the pincer maneuver to the north of the Somme, obviously did not descend from this school of thought. In view of the destructive power of modern firearms, Schlieffen had considered frontal assaults impossible and dismissed the idea of a breach. In other words, he wanted to avoid, during a time when armies of mass numbers and firepower imparted superiority to the defense, a direct shock that would lead to considerable losses without any decisive results. He thus stuck with a strategy of attacking one wing, seeking to outflank, then envelope. Since then, the possibilities offered by the motor, notably the partnership between tanks and aircraft, had permitted Manstein to envision a breach while offering a new method of encirclement and destruction.

His plan was thus divided into two partial operations: in that of the breach, the Meuse line was to be frontally forced in Sedan; in that of the envelopment, one had to charge through the breach and attack to the rear of the enemy.

The premise of both strategies nevertheless remained the same: it was the tactic of enemy envelopment that was the most adaptable on a strategic level. In other words, in order for a battle to achieve decisive results, it was necessary that it be engaged on inverted fronts, that the enemy's lines of retreat be cut, or that the outflanking or rupture of the front provoke the breakup of the adversary's army.

Manstein had analyzed the Schlieffen Plan down to its slightest details, and had especially examined the reasons for its failure, by which he was inspired to elaborate his operational theory. Everything leads us to additionally believe that he had studied, in a more general scope, the theories of the German Army's former chief of general staff, for whom the model *par excellence* of a battle of annihilation through outflanking and encircling the enemy was the Battle of Cannae carried out by Hannibal against Terentius Varron in 216 B.C. The Carthaginian general, with approximately 50,000 men, had encircled and destroyed a Roman army with a strength of almost 80,000 men. The latter had been lured into a retreat from the center towards the funnel that two Carthaginian wings, by cutting across, closed in around Terentius Varron's troops. According to Schlieffen, with the exception of the Franco-Prussian war of 1870–1871, during which Field Marshal Helmuth Graf von Moltke had essentially won the war by surrounding Napoleon III's army during a battle of encirclement at Sedan—the "Cannae of the 19th century"—no other "perfect Cannaes," with a complete encirclement of the enemy, had ever been achieved.[114]

Like Schlieffen, Manstein believed that a decisive victory in the west could only be achieved through a complete encirclement of enemy forces. And similar to Schlieffen, his objective was to repeat the 1870 Battle of Sedan, but this time on a greater scale. Furthermore, to gain acceptance of his operations plan he quoted Moltke, chief of the Prussian Army's general staff from 1858 to 1888, many times in his memos addressed to the OKH. He shared a similar point of view of the famous field marshal, according to whom the ultimate objective of military operations was the complete annihilation of the enemy: "A victory achieved during a key battle is a crucial moment in a war. Only victory breaks the enemy's will and forces him to submit to our desires. It is not the occupation of a part of the territory or the conquest of a fortified area, but the destruction of the enemy armed forces which [...] will bring about an outcome. This, consequently, is the principal objective of operations."[115]

And just like Schlieffen, he completed a systematic examination of envelopment, of attacking the flanks or the rear of the enemy. He thus based his operational theory on the concept of the pincer maneuver, which he considered to be the ultimate art of military strategy, for it was the most likely to bring about a complete victory over the enemy's armed forces. Yet, within the scope of his operations plan, it was first necessary to breach the enemy's front in order to take it from the rear, the rupture being a *sine qua non* of the outflanking and envelopment of the enemy.

Manstein's pincer maneuver involved another distinction with Schlieffen's operational theory. For the latter, a pincer operation was only conceivable through completely overcoming one of the wings of the enemy's army. From here it should then proceed with an encirclement of all of the enemy forces in a single operation. As for himself, the chief of staff of Army Group A envisioned an envelopment maneuver not of the entire body, but of a large portion of the enemy forces. For this, he took the risk of exposing one of the Wehrmacht flanks to a counterattack. Once this large-scale encirclement maneuver had been achieved, he intended to lead a second one of smaller scale, meant to destroy the remainder of enemy troops.

In his *Memoirs*, Manstein underscored the risk taken by Schlieffen in his operations plan: "[...] he had accepted the risk of suffering initial failures in Alsace all while hoping that the enemy would do its best to facilitate the success of the German operation by attacking in the Lorraine."[116] However, the risk that Manstein was taking with his operations plan was not so much about seeing Army Group B suffer initial failures in Belgium or in Holland, but rather about suffering a counterattack against the southern flank of Army Group A. For, if the Franco-British troops remained stationed on the border, they could withdraw in time behind the Somme. And if they were ever to create a breach to the south, it was the German envelopment wing that risked another "Cannae" along the coast of the English Channel. However, Manstein's judgment of the enemy's likely actions would later be proven correct.

One of the reasons for the failure of the Schlieffen Plan was that his successor as the head of the general staff, General Helmuth von Moltke, "the Younger," nephew of the victor of Sedan, did not appear inclined to expose the left wing of the German Army to a powerful French attack and to accept, through the very fact of the situation, the risk of temporarily losing Alsace-Lorraine at the beginning of the Great War. Chief of the German Army's general staff from 1906 to 1914, Moltke the Younger did not possess the audacity of his predecessor, who had been opposed to the construction of a powerful line of fortifications in the West precisely because he considered an advance of the enemy forces into Alsace-Lorraine as being absolutely essential for the accomplishment of a pincer maneuver by the German northern wing.

The distribution foreseen by the Schlieffen Plan of 1905 was for 10 divisions to the east, 62 to the west, including 54 on the right wing between Aix-la-Chapelle and Metz, and 8 on the left wing in Alsace-Lorraine. The ratio of forces between the right wing, mobile and offensive, and the left wing, static and defensive, was nearly 7 to 1. In 1914, Moltke the Younger had use of eight more divisions than Schlieffen had anticipated in 1905. Wanting to reduce the risks of a deep advance of the French into Alsace-Lorraine, a move that would have threatened regions that were economically significant, he did not commit any to the right wing, preferring rather to utilize all of them on the left wing to double the number of divisions from 8 to 16. By acting in such a manner, he unfortunately altered the ratio of forces from 3 to 1. The French Army having also been noticeably reinforced since 1905, the Schlieffen Plan thus lost all of its operational advantage.

Moreover, during the first days of the German offensive in August 1914, just before the Battle of the Marne, Moltke the Younger modified once again the original intentions of the Schlieffen Plan. He withdrew two army corps from the Second Army, deployed to the left of the First Army which was situated to the far north of the principal endeavors of the wheeling flank, to redeploy them to East Prussia in order to reinforce the front against the Russians, while no demand for reinforcements had been expressed for this purpose. When they arrived, the situation had already been restored by the victory at Tannenberg. In his *Memoirs*, the chief of general staff admitted that this decision had been his most serious error.

By reinforcing the fronts of Alsace-Lorraine and East Prussia instead of providing a maximum number of forces to his wheeling flank in Belgium and northern France, Moltke the Younger denied the latter any second line divisions which were absolutely necessary to relieve the frontline divisions once they had achieved their best impact. Situated on the second line, these divisions could have created a second strike force and enabled the continuation of the offensive. Such a strategic error led to defeat during the Battle of the Marne, after which Moltke the Younger was relieved of his command. The advance of the wheeling flank in France came to an immediate end. A war of fixed positions was thus substituted for a mobile war.

Yet in reality, the decisive error did not lie so much in the weakening of the right wing than in the reinforcement of the left wing. By doubling the number of divisions on the left, Moltke the Younger virtually removed from Alsace-Lorraine it's role of serving as both lure and trap for the French forces, one of the Schlieffen plan's prerequisites for success. The formations committed to the left wing had acquired such a combat strength that the attacking French were no longer in a position, as Schlieffen at the time had wished, to advance as deeply into Alsace-Lorraine. To the contrary, instead of pulling the enemy troops deeply into Alsace-Lorraine, by remaining stationed on the defensive, the Germans of the left wing launched a spontaneous counterattack that succeeded in pushing back the French, who had willingly rushed into this zone to recapture its lost regions. Although it came to an end on the French fortified borders, the counterattack from the German left wing prevented the enemy from falling into the trap originally set by Schlieffen. The counterattack was in serious contradiction with the Schlieffen plan. How could the German Army accomplish its pincer maneuver through the north and west if the French had been pushed to the south from Alsace-Lorraine? Moltke the Younger seems not to have understood that the latter would thus become available for a counterattack against the southern flank of the right wing of his army. He also does not seem to have understood that the enemy could only recapture Alsace-Lorraine through a frontal battle. The enormous losses which would have resulted from such a battle would have considerably weakened the French, an action that would have favored an attack to their rear by the German right wing.[117]

An analysis of the causes for the failure of the Schlieffen Plan further reinforced Manstein's conviction that the success of a pincer maneuver within his own operations plan depended precisely on the strength of the army group assigned this mission and the effectiveness of the trap placed before the enemy forces. But, if his plan of attack were to be accepted by the OKH, it would be critical to move forward with a massive reinforcement of Army Group A. The latter would then not only be able to successfully conclude its pincer maneuver, but also oppose any counteroffensive on its southern flank.

A first step in the direction of Manstein's concept

The general staff of Army Group A received no official response from the OKH concerning the two documents of Manstein's operations plan sent on October 31. After being informed of the plan on November 1, Halder declared, with a certain amount of condescension, that the plan contained not a single positive element.[118]

However, a visit from Brauchitsch and Halder to Army Group A on November 3 would provide Manstein an opportunity to give a more detailed presentation of his plan via Rundstedt. If the latter were to put all his influence behind his chief of staff's operational concept, it was not so much because he believed in it than because the plan in question called for assigning his army group a key role in the offensive. The head of the OKH and his chief of staff, however, rejected the plan under the pretext that they did not have the necessary forces to grant Army Group A a third entire army, as well as powerful armored and motorized forces. They were quite simply opposed to the idea of shifting the offensive's focus from Army Group B to Army Group A.

Three days later, the commander in chief of Army Group A used an invitation from the OKH to present his intentions, within the framework of the directives that had been sent to him, to revive his chief of staff's proposals.[119] Just like the October 31 presentation, he received no response to his new memo, dated November 6.

On November 11, however, to their great surprise, the staff of Army Group A received a message from the OKH announcing the allocation of an armored corps to be pulled from Army Group B. On the Führer's orders, the OKH granted Army Group A General Guderian's 19th Panzer Corps which consisted of two panzer divisions (the 2nd and 10th), one motorized division, and two elite independent regiments (*Grossdeutschland* and SS *Leibstandarte Adolf Hitler*). The armored corps' directive was to defeat the enemy mobile units engaged in southern Belgium and to thus facilitate the mission of the Twelfth and Sixteenth Armies. Its mission was also to seize by surprise the western banks of the Meuse at Sedan after crossing the Ardennes. It would thus be in the position of creating favorable conditions for the continuation of operations, in case the armored units of the Fourth and Sixth Armies of Army Group B were not successful at breaking into northern Belgium.

And so, at Hitler's instigation, the fateful name Sedan appeared for the first time in the operations plan, in the search for an alternative solution and an eventual breach of the French center. But this meant the addition of a third target to the two that had already been defined in the second deployment order, which thus further diminished the Wehrmacht's strike force. Clearly, Hitler did not dare place all his bets on a single card, and because of this, infringed upon one of the fundamental principles of lightening warfare: that of concentrating forces on one precise point. To justify his decision, the Führer explained that the target should only be established during the course of the operation, by supporting any opportunity that would arise.[120]

His directive to the OKH nevertheless created a first step, albeit tentative, in the direction of the ideas proposed by Manstein. Already on October 25, in the presence of the OKH chiefs, the commanders of the army groups, and the army commanders of the Western Front, he had wondered if it were not preferable to launch the principal assault to the south of Liege to cut off the Allied armies deployed in Belgium, by turning, once west of Namur, towards the coast of the English Channel.

After the war, Halder himself took responsibility for having made this suggestion to Hitler at the end of September 1939. His assertion, however, has not been corroborated by any convincing document. If this had been the case, then why, when he had the opportunity, did he not make any comments with respect to the Führer's proposal? That the chief of the OKH general staff himself proposed such an operational concept would be, to say the least, surprising, not only because of his condescending remark from November 1 apropos of Manstein's first memo, but also because of the one he would write in his diary on December 19, 1939, concerning Manstein's sixth memo—dated from the day before—that Colonel Walter Buhl, Stülpnagel's adjutant, had delivered to him: "Buhle brought to me Army Group A's idiotic proposal." Far from being the innovator of the Sickle Cut, such as he maintained after the war, Halder was one of its most determined adversaries before joining in only after Hitler had imposed it on him in February 1940.[121]

With that being said, Hitler did indeed instruct the generals of the OKH to examine the idea. They deemed, however, the operation too risky, as it required the army to cross the difficult and wooded terrain of the Ardennes, which presented obvious problems for the tanks. Apparently, Hitler was not truly convinced himself, for he spoke no more of it. On the very next day, he mentioned that one should no longer expect for the time being any major amendments to the operations plan in effect. The primary focus of the German offensive should still be carried out to the north and south of Liege.[122]

One thus cannot consider the idea of an attack focused to the south of Liege, put forth by Hitler on October 25, on the same level as Manstein's carefully thought out and rigorously based theories found in his memo addressed to the OKH on October 31. It was much more a question of the dictator's sudden, and immediately fleeting, intuitions. Concerning this, Halder remarked: "This is a typical 'idea' from Hitler, indeed even a good idea. But his interventions during the course of the operation, subsequently demonstrated the extent to which he was incapable of translating the idea to a tactical level." Later, General Hermann Hoth asserted that this was no more than one of the many "brutal intuitions" of Hitler. He thus warned against the temptation of seeing in this idea, hastily launched on October 25 and abandoned the following day, a prelude to the Sickle Cut.[123]

The addition of an armored corps was not satisfactory to Lieutenant General Manstein. In his estimation, it could only lead to the dispersion of the German armored forces and make the task of breaching the adversary's front all the more arduous. General Guderian completely shared Manstein's opinion. According to the armored warfare specialist, it would perhaps be better to ram the adversary at a single point with the entire panzer force. And so, when Manstein presented to him the major points of his plan and his attempt to shift the center of gravity from the northern wing to the southern wing, demonstrating to him the effectiveness of taking the adversary in the rear at the mouth of the Somme, Guderian expressed his eager enthusiasm. As Manstein recounted after the war, Guderian was at once "burning with enthusiasm." The armored specialist, who had participated in the crossing of the Ardennes in 1914, confirmed to him that the idea of leading an offensive through the forested region, with the armored formations on the frontline, was entirely possible despite the hilly terrain. Furthermore, Guderian insisted upon the necessity of mobilizing a sufficient number of armored and motorized divisions, and if possible the entirety of them, in order to ensure the success of this daring plan.[124]

On November 21, the OKH held a conference in Koblenz gathering together the generals from Army Groups A and B. Colonel General Brauchitsch wished to hear from the commanders of both army groups and armies what their intentions or arrangements were in relation to the OKH's directives. However, when it came time for the generals of Army Group A to speak, after those of Army Group B, Brauchitsch declared that hearing from the army commanders would suffice. Clearly, he did not want to grant Rundstedt and Manstein the opportunity to present their divergent plan. There remained nothing more for them to do other than present it once again in writing, in a third memo, hardly different from the first two, addressed to the OKH.[125]

A possible change in the area of concentration for the offensive?

In the meantime, Hitler apparently took charge of attaching the 19th Panzer Corps to Army Group A, wondering if it were necessary to eventually add other forces, in case the tanks gathered on the front of Army Group B could not manage to act effectively in Belgium and as a result, to achieve the expected rapid success. On November 20, he sent directives to the OKH charging it with finalizing the measures necessary for a rapid shift of the operation's focal point in favor of Rundstedt's army group, in the event that it could achieve a more rapid success than Bock's group. It was obviously in application of these directives that the OKH transferred at the end of November the 14th Motorized Corps to the right bank of the Rhine, behind Army Group A's zone of concentration. This corps, however, remained in the OKH's reserve, for it wanted the ability to post it to either of the two army groups depending on how the situation developed.

It is possible that the Führer wanted, by the end of November, to have the possibility of putting in effect a transfer of the center of gravity from Army Group B to Army Group A during the course of the offensive. As far as one knows, such a decision did not indicate that he had abandoned the OKH's plan currently in effect, nor had he adopted the main ideas of Manstein's operational concept. Quite the opposite, for all the directives given by the OKH to the commanders of the army groups and the army remained valid, despite the transfer of the 14th Motorized Corps behind Army Group A's assembly area, where it was held in OKH reserve. As was previously the case, Army Group B was entrusted with the mission of leading the principal offensive assault, whereas Army Group A was assigned the role of covering the entire operation. However, if the success did not achieve the desired scale in the zone of Bock's armies, or if the situation appeared to be more critical in that of Rundstedt's armies, Hitler reserved for himself the power to change the offensive's center of gravity.

This became clear in a response (the first) made by Halder to a new memo (the fourth) from the general staff of Army Group A, dated November 30, still in relation to the operations plan in the West proposed by Manstein.[126] The chief of general staff of the OKH confirmed that a second center of gravity was indeed projected for Army Group A. If the breach through the Ardennes turned out to be successful, this second center of gravity would lead to an expansion of the objective and to the conduct of operations in terms of Army Group A's proposals. Moreover, the majority of them, asserted Halder, would fully coincide with those of the OKH. But he had received from Hitler the formal order of maintaining the center of gravity with Army Group B, all while remaining prepared for the possibility of shifting it during the course of the offensive.

Unsatisfied by this response, Manstein had another memo sent on December 6 to the chief of the OKH general staff in which he expressed once again all the factors in favor of his operations plan.[127] On December 15, not having received a response, he telephoned Halder to ask him how much longer the OKH intended to remain silent with respect to his proposals. Halder hastened to assure him that his ideas were shared by the OKH, but that the Führer had given him a formal order to keep the center of gravity in Army Group B. In this case, retorted Manstein, why had Hitler ordered the transfer of Guderian's armored corps? Because the Führer, responded Halder, wanted to keep the option of shifting the offensive's center of gravity from the northern wing to the southern wing if justified by the way the campaign unfolded.[128]

At first glance, one could thus assume that the OKH had adopted Manstein's proposals and had communicated them to Hitler in one form or another. The latter however, not being inclined to accept them in their entirety, the OKH found itself forced to implement the current operations plan. However, shortly thereafter, Manstein learned from Colonel Walter Warlimont, Jodl's adjutant at the OKW, and from Lieutenant Colonel Bernhard von Loßberg, an officer in the operations bureau of the OKW, that the OKH had never intervened with Hitler on behalf of his proposals. Not only had Brauchitsch and Halder never revealed to Hitler Manstein's operational concept, but they had never taken it into consideration. In addition to finding it too risky, they only saw in it a maneuver from the commander of Army Group A and his chief of staff to gain for themselves the key role in the execution of the Yellow Plan. It is true that, in the second half of December, Manstein's operations plan was the object of examination within the OKH. But nothing leads one to assume that the chiefs had informed Hitler. Apparently Brauchitsch had not forwarded to Hitler a single one of the memos in which Manstein presented his operations plan. It thus seems clear that Hitler was only made aware of Manstein's ideas concerning the offensive in the West at the moment of their personal meeting on February 17, 1940, or a few days before, through the intermediary of Lieutenant Colonel Schmundt, his principal adjutant.[129]

The idea of transferring the center of gravity from the northern to the southern wing only during the course of the offensive did not correspond in any way to Manstein's operational concept. It could not be a question of waiting for the operations to unfold in order to know if it would be necessary to transfer the center of gravity, for Army Group A's plan was based above all on the idea of surprising the enemy. To shift the center of gravity according to turns of events was to provide the adversary a golden opportunity to attack the German Army's southern flank with its powerful operational reserves, and at the same time to relinquish the possibility of destroying the Allied forces in the northern Belgium by encircling them from the south. For the chief of staff of Army Group A, the idea of waiting to shift the center of gravity came under Field Marshal Moltke's principle according to which "an error committed in the initial deployment can no longer be recovered."[130]

His memo from December 6 not having obtained the desired effect, he presented to Rundstedt on December 18 a new memo that, once approved, was immediately sent to the OKH. By presenting his theories relative to the western offensive in a manner that was more concrete than his previous attempt, he was hoping that the OKH would decide to accept them.[131] But his sixth memo met the same fate as the preceding ones, with Brauchitsch and Halder refusing to pursue it.

Not being able to know if Hitler had been made aware of his theories during this time, Manstein decided to prepare a new memo which would permit him to resolve the issue. On January 12, 1940, he sent a seventh and final memo to the OKH in which he presented once again his ideas on the management of the offensive in the west.[132] He additionally asked that they be forwarded to Hitler. Signed by Rundstedt, this note ran counter to German military tradition. According to the memo, only the commander in chief, or on his behalf, the chief of general staff, were qualified to present proposals to the supreme leader of the armed forces. However, if the OKH was to a great extent in agreement with Manstein's ideas, as it had already asserted to him on several occasions, it could still take his plan and present it to Hitler under its own name.

But the chief of staff of Army Group A did not receive the response he was expecting, for the OKH refused to forward his memo to Hitler. In fact, and in light of its response, the OKH was clearly not inclined to propose Manstein's alternative solution to the plan they had already put in effect.

The "yellow plan" falls into enemy hands

Meanwhile, an unfortunate setback occurred for the high command of the Wehrmacht. On January 10, a liaison plane made a forced landing in Mechelen-sur-Meuse in Belgium. Aside from the pilot, aboard was the deputy chief of staff of the 7th Division of the Luftwaffe, who was carrying with him the documents for the OKH's operations plan. Having left from Münster, the liaison officer was required to go to Bonn in order to discuss with the air force command certain details of the invasion plan. Flying through foggy and windy conditions, the pilot lost his way above the frozen and snow-covered Rhine and inadvertently entered Belgian territory where he was forced to land. The liaison officer was unable to completely burn the documents of the Yellow Plan and a portion of them were taken into Belgian hands. The German military attaché in Holland thus learned that the documents seized were sufficient to compromise the secrecy of the plan's operations.

This regrettable hitch had, according to numerous opinions expressed after the war, a decisive effect on the modification of the plan of attack in terms of what Manstein had proposed. The adjutant to the chief of the operations bureau at the OKW, Colonel Warlimont, claimed that the Führer decided to change the plan of attack on January 16, and that such a decision was primarily motivated by the plane crash.[133] However, there are many indications that it did not influence serious modifications in the plan, even as it may have left Hitler more open to Manstein's alternative proposals.

At the January 25 military conference, the first since the forced landing of the liaison plane, there was absolutely no question of making any significant changes to the operations plan in effect, for the three spearheads of the attack—those that had been envisioned from November 11, 1939—were preserved. At the meeting were gathered the chiefs of the OKH, those of Army Groups A and B, and their high ranking officers. Only the mission of Bock's group was expanded, the Eighteenth Army henceforth being charged with occupying all of Holland and no longer, as was the case up to this point, only the region located outside of "Fortress Holland" (*Vesting Holland*). As for the mission of Rundstedt's group, it remained unchanged. The 2nd Infantry Corps was now established in its zone of concentration, but it remained, like the 14th Motorized Corps, at the OKH's disposal. These few modifications were transmitted to the armies through the OKH's third operations plan dating from January 30.[134]

Lieutenant General Manstein took advantage of the opportunity to emphasize to Colonel General Brauchitsch that committing only the 19th Panzer Corps in the Ardennes would not guarantee success at Sedan, for the adversary in the interim had brought new forces to the Meuse. But the commander in chief of the OKH declared to him that it was impossible for him to position the 14th Motorized Corps and the 2nd Infantry Corps under the command of his army group. Clearly, such a response demonstrated that the OKH still maintained that any transferral of the center of gravity was subject to the unfolding of the offensive. Plainly, the forced landing incident in Belgium had in no way encouraged the army high command to significantly modify its directives.[135]

The period of adverse winter weather that followed provided an opportunity to re-examine from top to bottom the planning of operations. Hitler denounced the OKH's operations plans, stating that they appeared to be the "ideas of a student soldier." He was deeply concerned by the lack of new ideas capable of producing an effect of surprise.[136] All the solutions proposed up to this point by the army high command could only lead to partial tactical, or at best, operational successes. Meanwhile, an officer on the sidelines of the OKH general staff who was responsible for the planning of operations had developed a theory that would allow for such an effect of surprise and to grasp a decisive victory. Yet Hitler had still not been informed of it.

VI

DISGRACE AND A DRAMATIC
TURN OF EVENTS

While Lieutenant General Manstein had been the author of the Sickle Cut plan, he was also its first victim, as it was due to his obstinate desire to impose such an idea, deemed as idiotic by the OKH, that the latter relieved him of his duties as chief of staff of Army Group A. However, his operational theory ended up being adopted at the behest of Hitler, even though the leaders of the OKH had rejected it.

Manstein's dismissal

Exasperated by Lieutenant General Manstein's insistence at having his operations plan accepted in place of theirs, Colonel General Brauchitsch and General Halder decided to remove him from his post of chief of staff of Army Group A and send him to command an infantry unit. There he would be less burdensome and inconveniently positioned to promote his ideas. With Brauchitsch's approval, Halder thus succeed at "putting on the shelf" the stubborn and undesirable officer through a personal political maneuver. He knew how to persuade Colonel General Rundstedt that one must not forget Manstein when it came time to promote personnel, for Lieutenant General Georg-Hans Reinhardt, with less seniority, had already been named commander of an armored corps in Army Group A. Halder thus suggested also granting an army corps to Manstein. When on January 27 the latter was informed of his appointment as commander of the 38th Infantry Corps being formed in Stettin, Pomerania, a city far away from the Western Front, he was not overjoyed. Lieutenant General Georg von Sodenstern would replace him as chief of staff of Army Group A.[137]

119

It was thus a matter of elegantly removing a troublesome officer. Indeed, through such a transfer disguised as a promotion, Halder's desire to push him aside was fulfilled. For Manstein, the appointment appeared as a disgrace, all the more so since he was henceforth diverted from the principal theater. If such a procedure could appear as normal, he later asserted, the reassignment of a chief of staff on the eve of a great offensive was still suspicious. According to him, the issue of seniority stated as the pretext by the OKH could have been resolved another way. There was no doubt in his mind that "the OKH wanted to rid itself of someone who stood in its way and who had dared propose a plan in opposition to theirs."[138] The OKH even refused him the command of a panzer corps under the pretext that he lacked the necessary experience to undertake such a duty, a decision which made him even more annoyed about his fate. For the second time in his career, Manstein was put out to pasture.

As Halder's former rival for the position of chief of OKH general staff, Manstein took the rap for the antipathy that the latter had demonstrated toward him ever since. Presumptuous and arrogant, notably because of the position he held within the army, Halder—and it was the same for Brauchitsch—desired in no way to have a subordinate officer offend him, and even less so when such an officer was already recognized as one of the best operational minds of the Wehrmacht. The animosity that he demonstrated towards Manstein was coupled with jealousy of his talents on the operational level.

Furthermore, the enormous prestige that the success of the French campaign ultimately conferred on Manstein infuriated Halder and Brauchitsch to such an extent that they in turn sought to be rid, once and for all, of the one man in the Wehrmacht who offended them. For this, they attempted to dismiss him to a secondary theater of operations, first in Norway, then in Africa. And so, in February 1941, they made the decision to entrust to him the command of the *Afrika Korps*, the German expeditionary corps that had just been created in order to restore the situation in Northern Africa, following the Italian Army's failure in the region against Great Britain. Only the intervention of the Führer, who preferred to grant the leadership of the *Afrika Korps* to Erwin Rommel, spared Manstein from having to take a command on the Mediterranean front.[139]

At the time, in the circle of German generals, Halder appeared to be an exceptional officer in terms of intellect. However, in Manstein, a younger, ambitious man in search of promotion, appeared a rival who a good number of generals respected for his superior abilities. A great deal differentiated the Bavarian Halder from the Prussian Manstein when it came to making decisions, as much from the point of view of their nature as from their intellect. Because of his methodical and systematic thought, Halder ruminated for nights, imagined every possibility, and consulted several colleagues before making an important decision. Conversely, Manstein was a man of quick decisions, made without any outside opinions. He trusted his intuition rather than any methodical or systematic thought process. It would perhaps only be because of his surprising prescience which he demonstrated in the sphere of strategy that Manstein clearly distinguished himself as the most brilliant general of the Wehrmacht.

From the time that he was chief of general staff of the army, Colonel General Beck had become quickly interested in the operational talents of this young prodigy. It was due to his assistance that Manstein owed his appointment as chief of the logistics section to the army's general staff in October 1936. Thus, despite his relatively young age, he became Beck's representative as chief of general staff and, as a result, was considered his successor. But Beck, who was later to become one of the leaders of the military resistance, was at this time no longer in favor with Hitler. Consequently, following the Blomberg-Fritsch crisis, it was not him who became the commander in chief of the army—which would have made Manstein almost automatically the new chief of general staff—but Brauchitsch, who was deemed more manageable. Manstein had then been sent to Liegnitz to command a division while Brauchitsch replaced him with Halder. A few months later, Beck resigned in protest against Hitler's intention to attack Czechoslovakia. On September 1, 1938, Halder succeeded him. The tense relationship between Halder and Manstein can thus only be understood if one takes into account their shared background.[140]

In this rivalry, Halder had a double advantage at Manstein's expense. In the military hierarchy, as a general, he was one rank superior to Manstein, who was only a lieutenant general. Moreover, he was truly a staff officer by training, having completed his coursework at the Bavarian staff school, whereas Manstein had been unable to complete his training at the Prussian *Kriegsakademie*, which would have provided him with a staff officer certificate, because of the commencement of the First World War. Despite this, Manstein had been assigned to several key posts within various staffs ever since the Great War, even rising to the general staff of the army before Halder. At the moment of his departure to command the Liegnitz division, it had moreover been mentioned within the officers' corps that Beck had forced Halder on Brauchitsch. In a way, it was for all of these reasons that Halder had such a deep hatred for Manstein. As for Brauchitsch, he did not have much more affection for this officer, who was moreover a protégé of Rundstedt, with whom he was not in the slightest way on good terms ever since the latter had criticized him in 1938 for having done nothing with regards to clearing Fritsch's name.[141]

Manstein did not have a high opinion of Brauchitsch, describing him in his *Memoirs* thus: "The future Field Marshal von Brauchitsch was a very able officer. While not belonging to quite the same class as von Fritsch, Beck, von Rundstedt, von Bock, and von Leeb, he certainly ranked immediately after them and, as events have shown, also possessed the requisite qualities of a commander in chief of the army. As far as [his] character is concerned, his standards of personal behavior were quite unassailable. Neither would I dispute his willpower, even though it tended in my own experience to be manifested in a somewhat negative inflexibility rather than in creative resolve. He preferred to have decisions suggested to him rather than to take and impose them on his own initiative. Indeed, he frequently evaded decision in the hope of being spared a struggle to which he did not feel equal."

He then added the following severe remarks about him: "At bottom, however, he was no fighter. He was never really the sort of man to get his way by sheer force of personality. [...] Just as he lacked the aggressiveness that commands an opponent's respect, or at least compels him to act warily, so did he fail to impress one as a forceful, productive personality. The general effect was one of coolness and reserve [...]. Admittedly, General von Seeckt had been far colder, even to the extent of being unapproachable. But in his case everyone had sensed the inner fire that inspired him and the iron will which made him a leader of men. Neither quality had fallen to the share of von Brauchitsch, nor had he been blessed with that soldierly boldness which—apart from his great qualities as a commander—had won von Fritsch the hearts of his troops."

Concerning Halder, his judgment was not quite as severe. "Like most of the officers who had begun their careers on the Bavarian general staff, Halder had a remarkable grasp of every aspect of staff duties and was a tireless worker in the bargain. A saying of Moltke's, 'Genius is diligence,' might well have been his motto. Yet this man hardly glowed with the sacred fire that is said to inspire truly great soldiers. While it speaks for his high sense of responsibility that he prepared for the Russian campaign by having an operations plan 'drawn up' [by General Pauls] on the basis of studies made by the chiefs-of-staff of the Army Groups, the fact remains that the basic concept of a campaign plan should be born in the mind of the man who has to direct that campaign. In his outward bearing Halder had not the elegance of von Brauchitsch."[142]

The fateful Hitler-Manstein meeting

On February 7, two days before Manstein's departure from Koblenz to Stettin, his operations plan was able to be the subject of a map exercise, directed by himself. Halder, the OKH's chief of staff, was present at this *Kriegsspiel* expressed his skepticism regarding the possibility of the armored and motorized divisions easily crossing the Ardennes and quickly reaching the Meuse. With all of their winding, narrow, and steep-sided roads, he claimed, the forests of the Ardennes did not lend themselves well to the passage of armored and motorized columns. Regarding the Meuse, he added, it presents a powerful anti-tank obstacle, over which the crossing seemed extremely risky, especially since the French troops had been positioned there since September 1939. Consulted on the remark, General Guderian firmly believed that it was possible to cross the river from the fifth, or even the fourth day of the campaign. This was a claim that General Halder judged insane. In fact, according to him, exploiting the breach of the adversary's front along the Meuse at Sedan was only possible, at the earliest, on the ninth day of the offensive, and more realistically, on the tenth day.[143]

In an irony of history, the OKH's conclusions were similar to those of French staff officers, for whom the Ardennes was considered impenetrable by tanks and the Meuse was thought to be uncrossable. Indeed, they had calculated that for an enemy offensive through the Ardennes it was necessary to count on a minimum of five days, but realistically nine.

But as events proved, the first German tanks reached the Meuse at the end of two-and-a-half days. The French had also believed that the attacker would need around seven additional days to deliver artillery, stockpile munitions, etc. To their great surprise, hardly a day later the German troops were already engaging in an attack on their heels, with the intention of crossing the Meuse. In fact, exactly as Guderian had anticipated, it was on the fourth day of the offensive that the Germans succeeded in crossing the Meuse at Sedan. They in fact arrived there a few hours before the approaching French reserves.[144]

Sickle Cut could only succeed if one were to bet everything on the single card of mobile armored warfare. The Meuse had to be crossed by the fifth day at the very latest, otherwise the French, once they had a clear understanding of what the plan entailed, would still have time to shift their reserves close to the river. After having crossed the Meuse, the panzer divisions had to charge towards the mouth of the Somme as quickly as possible, without concern for their exposed flanks, or else the Allies would still have time to escape from the trap that had been set for them. However, with Manstein scarcely out of his post, the staff of Army Group A, alarmed by his audacity, wanted to plan a "slow-moving *Blitzkrieg*," by having the infantry divisions, not the armored divisions, lead the attack. In fact, several generals from Army Group A's staff were skeptical about the possibility of crossing the Meuse with armored units.

For example, Lieutenant General Sodenstern, Lieutenant General Manstein's successor to the position of Army Group A's chief of staff, did not consider it possible to cross the Meuse in the face of the enemy with tanks. "I am convinced that we will not be able to force our way across the Meuse with motorized forces. In order to achieve this, we must instead resort to the infantry. [...] Despite all the respect that the success of the armored force in Poland deserves, it is necessary to recognize that, faced with such a defense, one can only give them very little or next to no chances at all for success." Colonel Blumentritt, in charge of supervising operations at the general staff of Army Group A recommended "[...] that one leave the motorized units to the rear, lead the battle with infantry divisions, and bring into play the armored forces only once the tactical breach has been achieved and the freedom of operational action acquired."[145]

On February 9, Manstein left Koblenz to take up his new position in Stettin. Despite this, however, the lieutenant general would finally have the opportunity to present his ideas directly to the Führer. Protocol demanded that all new army corps chiefs pay their respects to the chief of state. On February 17, Manstein was thus summoned to Berlin to be presented to Hitler, together with all of the generals newly appointed to command of army corps. Normally the ceremony should have been a simple formality. But Colonel Schmundt, Hitler's primary military assistant, had organized for the occasion a private meeting between the new commander of the 38th Infantry Corps and the Führer.

On January 30, Schmundt had been sent to Koblenz to verify for himself the state of Army Group A's military preparations. Upon his arrival, he first met two of Manstein's close colleagues, Colonel Blumentritt and Major Tresckow, whom he knew very well since the time they had served together in the 9th Infantry Regiment in Potsdam. Blumentritt and Tresckow were shocked by the way their superior had been pushed aside, and so they seized the opportunity to inform Schmundt that their army group had forwarded to the high command an operations plan conceived by Manstein. In their opinion, the plan was superior to the one in effect, but the OKH would not give it any consideration, and even refused to forward it to the OKW. Puzzled by what he had just heard, Schmundt immediately asked to be introduced to Manstein so that he could hear an outline of his plan. He was later surprised to discover from Manstein, though in a much more elaborate and precise form, a plan closely resembling the one that the Führer had already elaborated before him.

On February 4, 1940, Major Gerhard Engel, the Führer's adjutant to the Luftwaffe, noted in his diary: "Schmundt went to Koblenz and [...] returned highly impressed by a long conversation that he had had with Manstein. The latter expressed serious reservations against the operations plan proposed by the army high command. Schmundt, who was very excited, recounted to me that Manstein mentioned the same ideas regarding the principal effort of the armed forces that the Führer was continually expressing, but in a much clearer form."

At Schmundt's request, Rundstedt sent to him, a few days later, a memo drafted by Manstein concerning his theories on conducting an offensive in the West. One does not know with any certainty if it was shown to Hitler or only to the chief of the OKH operations bureau, Lieutenant General Jodl. Everything leads to one believe however, that

Hitler would have no doubt been informed by Schmundt of Manstein's operations plan. For, beginning on February 13, 1940, Hitler reported to Jodl his intention to employ the bulk of the armored and motorized forces on the southern wing in the direction of Sedan, where the adversary would not expect to receive the main impact of the German offensive. Jodl immediately informed the OKH of this and invited it to submit proposals consistent with the plan.

Schmundt was therefore very impressed by his interview with the chief of staff of Army Group A. Considered a fervent admirer of Manstein, he found that the OKH had behaved poorly with regards to him. He thus eagerly accepted the request from his friend Tresckow to provide an opportunity for Manstein to present his ideas directly to Hitler without rousing any suspicion from Halder and Brauchitsch. The meeting would take place at the Reich Chancellery in Berlin on February 17, following the formal ceremony.[146]

After the lunch that followed the presentation of the new army corps commanders, Hitler asked Manstein, who was about to leave, to follow him into his office, and there invited him to present his ideas on the offensive in the West.[147] No one else except Lieutenant General Jodl and Colonel Schmundt were present at the discussion. Whereas Hitler had the disagreeable habit of interrupting his generals' presentations after a short amount of time to launch into one of his interminable monologues, this time he listened in silence to Manstein's analysis. He found in the lieutenant general's way of thinking arguments that he had missed and, moreover, that were formulated in a remarkable manner. Impressed by his presentation, he even succeeded at hiding the personal aversion that he ordinarily harbored against this type of general, a typical representative of the officer caste of "old Prussia" that he rejected, finding them reactionary. Furthermore, after their conversation, Hitler mentioned of Manstein: "He certainly has a particularly intelligent mind and a great operational talent, but I do not trust him."[148] He nevertheless left the meeting enthusiastic about his conversation with Manstein and approved of his conclusions, including putting into action considerable armored forces. The die was thus cast, and the idea of the Sickle Cut would be set in motion.

Manstein did not know if or to what extent the Führer had already been informed by his adjutant, Schmundt. Whatever the case may be, he was surprised at how promptly and completely Hitler adhered to his operational concept that combined both audacity and originality. In turn, Hitler benefited from hearing ideas from a professional strategist that were developed in precise terms, and which corresponded to certain intuitions that he had already had. He finally had the alternative plan he had been picturing since the airplane crash on January 10. A plan that, contrary to the previous one, would have the effect of surprising and annihilating the adversary.

Hitler was won over by the brazen, even rash, ideas proposed by Manstein. Like him, Hitler thought that the only chance of succeeding was by taking risks. If the armored forces were sent through the Ardennes, they would reach the Allies right where they expected it the least, for their generals, like the majority of the German generals, most likely considered this undulating and wooded region hardly favorable for combat tanks. An initial trap set by the German right wing would undoubtedly cause the Franco-British armies to rush into Belgium. Thus, by creating a breach in the Allied front between Dinant and Sedan, and by heading for the English Channel, along the right bank of the Somme, the Wehrmacht would trap the bulk of the Allied forces.

The acceptance of the Manstein Plan and the redeployment of troops on the Western Front

On February 20, Hitler, supported by the OKW, forced on the OKH a complete revision of the operations plan according to Manstein's ideas. The result was the fourth deployment order presented on February 24, 1940. This would definitively transfer the center of gravity from the right wing to the left wing. The breach of the French front would occur near the Ardennes, despite the difficulties presented by a wooded and mountainous terrain, covered by winding and narrow roads plus a sizeable unknown, the crossing of the Meuse, which represented a tremendous anti-tank obstacle. The operation would take place in the direction of the English Channel, so as to trap the Allied armies that had entered into Belgium.

By virtue of such a fundamental modification, Army Group A, upon whom fell the responsibility of the principal maneuver, was henceforth equipped with 45 divisions, including seven armored and three motorized. Its mission was to cross the Ardennes, establish solid bridgeheads in order to cross the Meuse between Dinant and Sedan, and to charge forward in the direction of Abbeville on the lower Somme. It then had to block off behind the river the line of retreat of the enemy forces engaged in northern Belgium against Colonel General Bock's armies. Likewise, it was to stand up against any counterattack launched against its southern flank.

As for Army Group B, which was meant to play a secondary role, it found itself reduced to 29 divisions, including three armored and two motorized. With the participation of the airborne troops, its directives were to shatter Dutch resistance and to overcome the Belgian fortifications on the Albert Canal and the Meuse. Once this task was accomplished, it had to thrust forward in order to drive back the enemy troops it encountered in northern Belgium, and to facilitate through this action the pincer maneuver to be carried out by Colonel General Rundstedt's armies attacking from the south. With the intention of monopolizing the adversary's attention during the first fateful days of the offensive and thus to permit Army Group A to cross the Ardennes and to cross the Meuse as quickly as possible, Army Group B had to appear to the adversary as the German Army's spearhead. Its principal objective was thus to act as a lure and attract a maximum number of Allied troops into Belgium so as to prepare for the encirclement. As well, it was still required to protect the right flank of Army Group A.

For its part, Army Group C had to confine itself to a kind of static war. Composed of only 19 divisions and denied any armored or motorized units, it would ensure the security of the *Westwall* between the borders of Luxembourg and Switzerland. It also had the mandate of holding back as many adversary formations as possible on the front of this sector, along the Maginot Line[149].

Nevertheless, the Sickle Cut strategy was neither more nor less than that of a hammer and anvil; the role of the hammer being played by Army Group A with its armored divisions, and that of the anvil by Army Group B with its infantry divisions. The more the enemy advanced towards the anvil, the more violent the hammer strike would be on their rear. One can also compare it to a bullfight. Army Group B, on the right wing, would represent the red cape of the bullfighter who was required to provoke the enemy so that it would rush forward, like an angry bull, into the arena. Acting as the sword for the bullfighter, Army Group A, on the left wing, could thus thrust into the unprotected flank, the armored units representing the point of the sword.

After a few final hesitations, the OKH ended up yielding to the Führer's pressures, as well as to those of Keitel and Jodl, and modified the operations plan in accordance with the directives of February 20. If Brauchitsch and Halder only reluctantly converted, they nevertheless began to work relentlessly on the new version of the plan. The latter was thus completed on February 24, and the generals on the Western Front received the order to redeploy their troops on March 7.

Of the ten armored divisions of the Wehrmacht, seven were attached to Army Group A, with the entirety of the heavy and medium tanks. Contrary to Rundstedt's armies, those of Bock would hardly have to encounter any enormous tank formations in the Netherlands and northern Belgium. Consequently, the three panzer divisions granted to Army Group B were mainly composed of light vehicles. A large majority of the motorized divisions, three out of five, were assigned to Army Group A as well.

Just as Manstein had proposed, General Guderian's 19th Panzer Corps and General Gustav von Wietersheim's 14th Motorized Corps were brought together as a single armored group, newly created under the command of General Kleist. Better still, this armored group was augmented with another panzer corps, General Reinhardt's 41st. General Kleist's panzer group therefore formed Army Group A's spearhead. With Guderian's 19th and Reinhardt's 41st Panzer Corps, they gathered a force of 1,222 tanks, which is to say half of the Wehrmacht's armored forces.[150] Moreover, the Second Army was attached to Colonel General Rundstedt's group and gathered together with other units in order to create a third army. It was to be integrated as soon as the Sixteenth Army, branching off to the southwest, had expanded the army group's attack front. Even the Fourth Army of Army Group B was dependent on Army Group A for procuring it the necessary space for mobility in the direction of the lower Somme.

Displeased with his secondary role, Colonel General Bock submitted to the OKH chief of general staff a critical analysis of the new operations plan, which he judged unnecessarily risky. He begged him to abandon such an absurd plan and criticized him for gambling with Germany's future: "You are going to take your breach flank within 15 kilometers of the Maginot line while trying to conceal yourself and you hope that the French will notice without doing anything. You pile up the bulk of the tanks on the narrow roads of the Ardennes Mountains, as if aerial forces did not exist! And afterwards, you hope to lead an operation all the way to the coast with an exposed southern flank stretching for 320 kilometers, with the mass of the French Army right next to you. This goes beyond the limits of reason!"

The warning given by the commander in chief of Army Group B reminded the officers of his generation of the last exposed flank operation of the German Army in 1914, which came to an end with the Battle of Marne. If he was correct in thinking that the Wehrmacht risked getting stuck in a static war in the west if the Manstein Plan failed, he was wrong, however, to assume that it could fail in the same manner as the Schlieffen Plan.

On the one hand, contrary to the 1914 fortified line of Verdun-Toul-Nancy-Épinal, the Maginot Line was not a fortress from where it was possible to launch a sudden counterattack on the enemy's flank. It had been conceived in such a way that its garrison was stationary and reduced to a purely defensive role against a frontal attack that the Wehrmacht was in any case not intending to deliver. On the other hand, the armies under Rundstedt's command were not going to advance along the length of the Maginot Line. After having traversed the Ardennes and crossed the Meuse, they would progress at a rate of 50 to 60 kilometers per day, just as they had done in Poland. But the French Army did not possess the necessary mobility to oppose this type of maneuver. As for the French Air Force, it was quite inferior to the Luftwaffe, in terms of both quality and tactics.

This was at the very least what the majority of the generals were thinking. Indeed, more and more of them were beginning to believe in the success of the offensive, the very daring nature of which ended up filling them with enthusiasm. Even Colonel General Brauchitsch and General Halder were henceforth convinced of the validity of the Sickle Cut, and feverishly labored over its preparations. After having been the most resolved adversary of this plan, Halder responded to Bock: "Even if the operation has no more than a ten percent chance of success, I will support it. For it alone will lead to the annihilation of the adversary."[151]

The Dyle Plan: The Allied operations plan

The generals' confidence in the Manstein Plan was strengthened by the German intelligence service, which was in the position of deciphering the French signals code. Consequently, the Wehrmacht was very well informed of the Allies' planned march into Belgium, as well as the structure of their armies, in case of a German attack.

In fact, the Allied response was summarized in the Dyle Plan, which had been passed by the Allied Supreme Council in Paris on November 17, 1939. According to the plan, the First, Second, and Ninth French Armies and the British Expeditionary Force were to advance into Belgium, take position along the line of Anvers-Dyle-Louvain-Wavre-Namur-Meuse, and gather the Belgian divisions that would have delayed the German advance on the Albert Canal and the Meuse. With the assistance of the Seventh French Army, the plan anticipated extending the line of defense to Breda, in the south of the Netherlands, in the event that that country was also attacked by Germany. Such a strategy was credited with safeguarding the security of the ports along the coast of the English Channel, which provided the necessary link between Great Britain and France, as well as bases for the Royal Air Force. It would also ensure the protection of the key industrial region of the French northeast.[152]

The concept of the Dyle Plan was based on the certainty that the German Army would utilize a revised edition of the Schlieffen Plan. Due to the existence of the Maginot Line, constructed on the northeastern border, the French were convinced that the Germans would try to circumvent it through Belgium and also perhaps through the Netherlands. Cleverly conceived as an obstacle upon which the country could rely to overcome the German advantage in manpower, and to gain enough time to complete a counterattack in Belgium, the fortified system was also intended to spare France from the terrible losses incurred during the 1914–1918 war, and to prevent the northern industrial region of France from once again becoming the theater of confrontation.

After the war, few commanders were as criticized as General Maurice Gamelin for the defeat of May-June 1940, resulting from the failure of the Dyle Plan. Nevertheless, from his point of view, his decision to march into Belgium in case of a German attack was to be considered justified and logical. The right flank of the French frontline was protected by the Maginot Line, which the French generals quite simply deemed impregnable. To the center, the Meuse and the Ardennes created a two-fold obstruction. "The Ardennes are impregnable to tanks and the Meuse is impassable!" as one used to say in the French and British general staffs. Gamelin could thus concentrate his best units on the left wing. Everything, therefore, led one to believe that the Germans would attack again, according to the Schlieffen Plan, with the focus on the right, but this time with tanks. Moreover, these were precisely the original intentions of the general staff of the OKH.

The premise that tanks would not be able to traverse the Ardennes and that the Meuse was impassable was acknowledged as dogma in the French and English general staffs after the First World War. The fact that an authority like Marshal Philippe Pétain, the victor of Verdun, characterized the Ardennes as "impenetrable" certainly contributed to this. Likewise, the French commander in chief, General Gamelin, had reckoned that the Meuse represented "the best anti-tank obstacle that existed in Europe." Actually, the double geographic obstacle of the Ardennes and the Meuse appeared as a strategic barrier that one could certainly circumvent, but one that would be additionally difficult for armored units. And so, as the area of Sedan was considered safe from attack, the French neglected to construct any fortifications there, in favor of other areas of the front, and had stationed there only secondary troops. Furthermore, it was believed that, even in the case of a German offensive through the Ardennes, there would be a sufficient amount of time to bring in reinforcements.

During the interwar period, there had nevertheless been no shortage of warnings that brought into question the myth of the "impenetrable" Ardennes. In 1928, the British military theorist Basil Henry Liddell Hart visited the region and was surprised by the illusory belief on the part of the French high command that the Ardennes was impassable for assault tanks. Liddell Hart's expertise as a specialist of armored warfare had been recognized when the British Ministry of War organized more significant armored formations in 1933. It had been vital to know how, in case of a possible war, to be able to make the best use of armored forces. He suggested an Allied counteroffensive across the Ardennes using powerful armored forces should a German invasion in France occur. He received the response that this wooded region was impassable for tanks, to which he replied that in light of a personal examination of the terrain he considered such a theory an illusion, as he had already suggested in several books since the end of the Great War.[153]

Within the French Army during the 1930s, studies were also conducted to determine the actual level of difficulty that the Ardennes would present. In May-June 1938, General André Gaston Prételat, at the time commander in chief of the Second Army, led a map exercise. The scenario that was described was amazingly like that of Guderian's armored offensive in May 1940. To the surprise of his superiors, Prételat arrived at the conclusion that the Germans were in a position to reach the Meuse in sixty hours and to cross it in a single day. In fact, he was off by only three hours, for the first German tanks reached the Meuse within fifty-seven hours. Informed of the alarming results of the exercise, Gamelin accused Prételat of pessimism. Having himself directed a similar map exercise in 1939, he was convinced that, even given the hypothesis of a successful German offensive crossing the Meuse, the French Army would be completely able to resolve the crisis by engaging its reserves.[154]

Because he did not believe in the possibility of a massive attack through the Ardennes, Gamelin was of the opinion that it was hardly worth preparing for such an eventuality. His inaction meant that the surprise would only be greater. As insane as it could be, the idea of launching the bulk of Germany's tanks into the middle of the Ardennes in a way reminded one of Hannibal's elephants crossing the Alps. Gamelin's decision to order a counterattack in Belgium, i.e. right in the very middle of the trap, thus provided the prerequisite conditions for the German envelopment. By setting into motion the Dyle Plan, he was behaving as the Roman war chief Terentius Varron did at the beginning of the Battle of Cannae. With all eyes turned on Flanders, he had lost sight of the Meuse and the Ardennes.[155]

Yet the plane crash of January 10 should have prompted the Allied high command to modify its operations plan, or at the very least to take the precaution of confronting the probability of a transfer of the weight of the attack that the German supreme command would not fail to do if the confiscated plans were authentic. But, rather than benefiting from the information that had fallen into its possession, the Allied high command interpreted it as an attempt to mislead them. Such a reaction was absurd, for it would have been a rather dangerous deception to run the risk of putting Brussels on her guard and pushing Belgium into a closer collaboration with Paris and London. The Belgian government could just as well have decided to open its borders to the Franco-British armies in order to reinforce its defenses before the German offensive was put into action.[156] The decision of the Franco-British military leaders not to grant validity to the confiscated documents would thus prove to be most harmful for their armies.

The author of the Sickle Cut Plan: Manstein or Hitler?

While Manstein was the designer of the Sickle Cut Plan, he was also its first victim, as it was due to his supposedly absurd idea that he was dismissed from his post. However, his operations plan was eventually accepted, even though the majority of generals had rejected it. In fact, he had only succeeded at getting Hitler to accept his theories in relation to the offensive in the West despite initial opposition from the leaders of the OKH. Thanks to his position as supreme commander of the Wehrmacht, the Führer was able to override the army high command's decision regarding the plan. But the personal animosity and the professional jealousy on the part of Brauchitsch and Halder with respect to Manstein had led them to relieve him of his position as chief of staff of Army Group A, and to appoint him as commander of an infantry corps.

That the designer of one the shrewdest and most daring strategic war plans only played a secondary role in its implementation is certainly one of the greatest ironies in military history. That the most gifted of the Wehrmacht officers was kept in the background of the military campaign, while the decisive and expeditious victory achieved was in large part owed to him, still remains remarkable to this day. Indeed, it was only during the second phase of the offensive, when victory was assured, that the most brilliant operational mind of all the general staff officers of the Wehrmacht would enter onto the scene in the role of an army corps commander. It was all the more ironic that he was placed at the head of an infantry corps, even though he understood better than anyone else, with the exception of Guderian, how to exploit the potential of the armored branch in a mobile war.

It was altogether characteristic of Hitler to have claimed that he himself had conceived the Sickle Cut plan as soon as he had adopted it. He only acknowledged Manstein for the credit of having agreed with him. "Among all the generals I talked to about the new plan in the west, Manstein was the only one who understood me."[157] Considering himself a military genius, the Führer ended up believing that it was his own plan. At any rate, sharing the credit with Manstein would come back, as it were, to offend his claim of being the supreme strategist of the

Wehrmacht. Furthermore, after Germany's military victory over France, German propaganda took charge of presenting the Führer as the author of the plan of attack in the west.

The assertion that he would have found, instinctively, and as a result of intuitive considerations, the same operational solution as Manstein, which was based on his calculations at the level of the general staff, does not at all correspond to reality; and even less so the opinion that he was the principal author. The Sickle Cut plan was exclusively Manstein's idea.

To be convinced, one only has to wonder if Hitler and Manstein were truly thinking the same thing when, with their finger on the map, they pointed in the direction of Sedan. And yet, the way in which the campaign would later unfold clearly demonstrates that the dictator was not capable of grasping the operational scope of this idea. However, after the victorious campaign, his madness led him to believe that he was indeed the author of the plan, the pioneer of the idea of the Sickle Cut which was a testament to his genius as supreme leader of the German armed forces.

Hitler had certainly juggled with the idea of shifting the offensive's center of gravity from the right wing to the left wing. But this was only one of his intuitive and erratic ideas to be abandoned the very next day. He had in fact pointed to Sedan on the map, but it was only a tactical operational concept aimed at crossing the Meuse, and not a strategic one, with the objective of reaching the English Channel and thus taking from the rear the spearhead of the Franco-British armies. It had never been a question for him of completely shifting the center of gravity towards the south, on the Meuse between Dinant and Sedan, and even less a question of pursuing the attack towards the English Channel while following the Saint-Quentin-Amiens-Abbeville axis. The limited understanding that Hitler had of the operational dimension of modern warfare did not allow him to expand the idea of a tactical breach on the Meuse into a strategic operation that would bring about a complete resolution. While for Hitler the breakthrough was to stop on the right back of the Meuse, for Manstein, it was to instead terminate at the mouth of the Somme.[158]

In other words, the ideas that Hitler associated with Sedan were of a solely tactical nature. As Manstein later mentioned, he had only recognized "that it was around Sedan that one could cross the Meuse the easiest."[159] But, as someone who was self-taught on military matters, he was not in a position of pushing the idea right to the end. It was the strategic issue, to the contrary, which was occupying Manstein's mind, as he was searching for a way to achieve total success. Whereas Hitler's thoughts stopped on the eastern banks of the Meuse, Manstein's went all the way to the coast of the English Channel. It was here, on the lower stretches of the Somme, he estimated, that a total victory was possible, but on the condition that one succeeded at advancing quickly enough to encircle the Allied armies gathered in the north. When the panzer divisions, after their breach at Sedan, advanced at top speed to the coastline of the English Channel, exactly as Manstein had wanted it, Hitler was panic-stricken. And so, how could the dictator have thought of and planned the idea of the Sickle Cut, when, at the moment when it was about to succeed, coming close to a nervous breakdown, he called a halt to the advance of the panzers?[160]

Thus, the basic reflections of an amateur could hardly come close to the brilliant meditations of a professional strategist. Far from being the fruit of convergent ideas between Hitler and Manstein, the Sickle Cut plan was exclusively the work of the latter. It is thus not the "Hitler Plan," but rather the Manstein Plan, that one should speak of in reference to the definitive version of *Case Gelb*.

"The guiding principle of the campaign came from Manstein," was the postwar assertion of General Hoth, who had played a key role during the French campaign as commander of the 15th Panzer Corps operating within Army Group A. He then added the following remarks: "Hitler's role in the formulation of the operations plan is that since he was convinced of the relevance of Manstein's ideas, he ordered the appropriate directives to the army high command. He is credited for having implemented Manstein's ideas in his deployment directives of February 24, 1940." Having later become colonel general, Johann Adolf Graf von Kielmansegg, captain and chief of the logistics section of the 1st Panzer Division during the western campaign, unequivocally asserted with regards to the plan: "The idea was incontestably and entirely Manstein's."[161]

Within the officers' corps of the Wehrmacht, one generally admitted that the author of the plan for the offensive in the West was no doubt Manstein. Among them were men who also claimed that Manstein—following the adoption of his operational concept by Hitler—should have logically become Halder's successor. After the clear-cut success of the French campaign, Manstein would acquire a reputation that would make him a legendary figure within the circle of officers of the general staff. Furthermore, he acquired the honorable nickname "Schlieffen of the Second World War."[162] And such a legendary reputation would not cease to gain momentum later on with his successes and military feats in the U.S.S.R., particularly in the Baltic region, in the Crimea, and in the Ukraine.

His extraordinary strategic and tactical sense was due to, among other things, a method of working differently from that of the majority of other general staff officers. Lieutenant Colonel Adolf Heusinger, deputy chief of operations of the OKH, made the following observation after the war: "From 1930 onward, I served immediately under Manstein, Jodl and then for four years under Halder. The methods of the Prussian [Manstein] and the two Bavarians [Halder and Jodl] were fundamentally different. Manstein's tactical decisions sprang largely from intuition. The task of his assistants was to determine to what extent this intuition could be put into practice. Halder and Jodl, on the other hand, spent long hours of work at night on the military ground-work, before they managed to reach a decision." Manstein clearly had an innate strategic sense.[163]

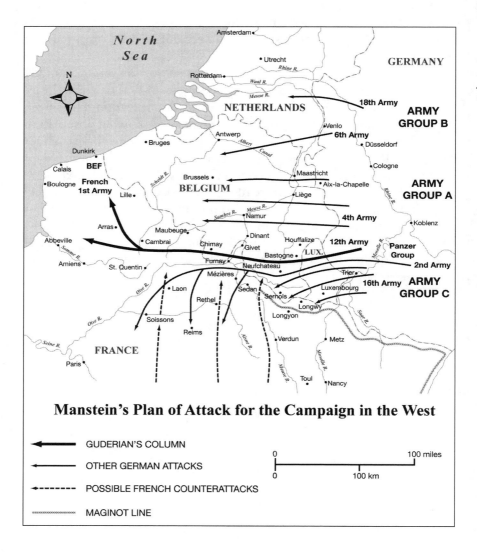

Manstein's Plan of Attack for the Campaign in the West

GUDERIAN'S COLUMN

OTHER GERMAN ATTACKS

POSSIBLE FRENCH COUNTERATTACKS

MAGINOT LINE

VII

THE INCOMPLETE VICTORY
OF THE SICKLE CUT

During the course of the western campaign, the operational concept of the Manstein Plan was not implemented by the German high command to its fullest extent. Furthermore, its tentative and inconsistent adaptation of the bold idea of the Sickle Cut could have led to a sort of "slow-moving" *Blitzkrieg*. Yet, thanks to the individual actions of a few generals at the head of the panzer forces, the operation followed another course and ended by achieving the success expected by Manstein. However, by not anticipating the "miracle of Dunkirk," out of its own fault, the German military leadership transformed the complete strategic victory intended by Manstein into little more than a simple, if spectacular, operational victory.

The opposing forces at the beginning of the offensive

Contrary to the generally accepted opinion explaining the success of the Manstein Plan during the Battle of France, the Wehrmacht did not have at its disposal a superior number of ground forces over its adversaries in terms of divisions, artillery, or tanks.

Concerning the number of divisions, the German Army had 157 on May 10, 1940. Of this number, 135 were destined for the offensive in the west, including 42 reserve divisions. And furthermore, among these, a few had just been formed and were hardly organized. At the beginning of the campaign, only 93 divisions participated in the assault. Opposing them, the French Army had 117 divisions at its disposal, of which 104 were located on the northeastern front, including 11 reserve divisions. On the day of the German offensive, the British Expeditionary Force consisted of 13 divisions, of which three were not fully formed. Two other divisions, including the 1st Armoured, were also brought onto the continent by the end of May. To the Allied contingent, one can add 22 Belgian and 10 Dutch divisions. In May 1940, facing the 135 German divisions, among which were 42 in reserve, were a total of 151 Allied divisions.

On the level of artillery, the Allied superiority over Germany was crushing. France alone had the use of more than 10,700 cannons, to which one could add 1,280 pieces of artillery from the British Army, 1,338 from the Belgian Army, and 656 from the Dutch Army. Thus the Western armies were able to commit nearly 14,000 heavy weapons, whereas the Wehrmacht had only 7,378.

As for tanks, the assertion that the Allied armies were the victims of a humiliating superiority of German panzers is no more than a legend. In May 1940, the 2,439 Wehrmacht tanks were opposed by 4,204 tanks from the Western forces. The French Army included in its ranks 4,111 tanks, without counting the 250 that were stationed in the colonies. On the northeastern front, there were no less than 3,254 tanks placed on the line on May 10, 1940. On this day alone, the British Expeditionary Force committed 310 tanks onto the continent. But one must also take into account the 330 assault tanks of the 1st Armoured Division that were transported across the Channel, arriving by the end of May. The Belgian Army had use of some 270 tanks, whereas the Dutch Army placed approximately 40 on the line.

If Germany had a numerical superiority, it was exclusively on the level of aviation. At the beginning of the offensive in the west, the Luftwaffe had 3,864 combat aircraft, among which only 2,756 were operational or at hand. And by deducting the minimum number of contingents deployed to Norway, there remained only 2,589 combat aircraft available for the offensive out of a total of 3,578. Against this force, the Allies countered with 1,453 operational combat aircraft (bombers and fighters) on the Western Front on May 10, 1940. Out of 3,562 French combat aircraft, some 3,097 were stationed within the Hexagon, including 1,410 on the northeastern front. Among these, only 879 were operational. The British air forces (bombers and fighters) engaged on the continent rose to a number of 1,150 aircraft, of which 384 were concentrated on the French northeastern front. Belgium had 118 bombers and fighters ready to intervene out of a total of 140, whereas the Dutch Air Force deployed 72 out of its 82 total aircraft.[164]

The crossing of the Meuse and the "second Battle of Sedan"

Just as Manstein had anticipated in his operations plan, the bulk of the Allied armies were sent into Belgium according to the Dyle Plan at the very beginning of the German offensive. As the Maginot Line was able to doom to failure any frontal attack, the Allied high command was expecting that the adversary would revise the maneuvers of the Schlieffen Plan. The Franco-British troops thus massively penetrated into Belgium so that they could resist the onslaught of Army Group B. Believing that the mass of the Wehrmacht's primary spearhead was located on the right wing, the Allied high command fell into the trap, since they executed precisely the movement that provided for the success of the Manstein Plan, as Army Group A approached through the Ardennes.

In their advance, General Küchler's Eighteenth Army and Colonel General Reichenau's Sixth Army, brought together under the command of General Bock, benefited from the operations of the Luftwaffe which, during the first three days, voluntarily kept itself at a distance from the true direction of the primary attack. The Stukas relentlessly bombed enemy positions, railways, and the major roads, as well as the command posts and airfields of the enemy. The rapid successes of the German right wing captured the attention of the Allies and distracted them for several days from the principal attack that had been launched on the southern wing through the wooded hills of the Ardennes.

All the diversionary measures achieved the result that Manstein had counted on in his operations plan: the French and British generals kept their eyes riveted towards the north. They did not see the mortal danger that was threatening them on their right flank. While the best Allied troops were marching to the north, toward Belgium, next to them, on their right, the armored and motorized columns of Army Group A were advancing in the opposite direction, to the southwest, across the Ardennes. They only clashed with weak resistance so that by the end of the afternoon on May 12, their vanguards were already reaching the Meuse at Dinant, Monthermé, and Sedan. They accomplished this without provoking any particular alarm within the Allied high command, who were still convinced that the offensive's center of gravity was situated in the Netherlands and Belgium, particularly between Maastricht and Liège.

However, the surprise was unveiled on May 13, with the crossing of the Meuse, not after a powerful artillery preparation, but after a massive Luftwaffe attack, following the scenario imagined by Manstein and Guderian during a *Kriegsspiel* at Koblenz, held on February 7, 1940. An entire Luftflotte, nearly half of the combat aircraft available in the West, was concentrated in this region.

The first crossings occurred at the end of the day of May 12 in Dinant, on the front of General Hoth's 15th Panzer Corps. Infantry units from Major General Rommel's 7th Panzer Division traversed the Meuse and immediately created a bridgehead after having fought a tough battle against troops that had been installed in secure positions for several months. During the middle of the night on May 13, the first tanks were already passing onto the right bank. The following day, the bridgehead had been expanded to a distance of more than twenty kilometers, thus facilitating the crossing of combat tanks. Further to the south, General Reinhardt's 41st Panzer Corps succeeded in grabbing a foothold on the left bank of the Meuse at Monthermé, thanks to General Kempf's 6th Panzer Division. But its further advance was blocked by fierce French resistance in this area. The most crucial crossing occurred at Sedan with the 1st, 2nd, and 10th Panzer Divisions of General Guderian's 19th Panzer Corps. After the infantry had cleared the crossings of the Meuse on May 13, and the bridgehead had been reinforced and secured to a distance of some 20 kilometers, the tanks followed them the very next morning.

By the afternoon of May 14, nearly 570 German tanks had already reached the left bank of the Meuse. By pushing forward in the direction of Charleville-Mézières, Guderian's panzer units allowed those of Reinhardt to extricate themselves from Monthermé. Following closely behind the 19th and 41st Panzer Corps was Wietersheim's 14th Motorized Corps. During the evening of that same day, a breach of 70 kilometers was taking shape on the front of Army Group A.[165]

On the third day of the offensive, armored and motorized columns congested more than 250 kilometers from the Meuse to the Rhine, crossing the territories of France, Belgium, Luxembourg, and Germany. Kleist's panzer group alone, composed of the 19th and 41st Panzer Corps and the 14th Motorized Corps, with its 41,120 vehicles and 1,222 tanks, were squeezed into a narrow corridor which had only a total of four routes, thus causing a monstrous traffic jam. This presented the Allied air forces with the unique opportunity of annihilating the German armored and motorized vehicles that had been marking time all the way from the Ardennes. But to the Germans' great surprise, not a single French or British plane appeared in the clear sky on this particular day. The Allied air forces were mainly intervening in northern Belgium, where the Luftwaffe was also engaged. At noon, the latter had abruptly disappeared in order to concentrate nearly all of its forces against the area around Sedan, the true center of gravity of the German offensive.

Being aware that this area of the front represented the Germans' Achilles heel, the Allies quickly improvised on May 14 an operation designed to destroy the Sedan bridgehead. Of the 402 Allied bombers and fighters gathered for this mission, 167 were shot down, a veritable slaughter. Not only were they confronted with 1,470 Luftwaffe bombers, Stukas, and fighters, but also with the intense fire of some 303 anti-aircraft batteries assembled by Guderian in this sector of operations. The defeat was complete in the Allied camp, as the German columns were virtually unaffected and able to continue the river crossing without serious interruption. After the air battle of Sedan on May 14, the Stukas continued to bombard the French infantry positions and artillery batteries which were located on the left bank of the Meuse without encountering the slightest amount of opposition in the sky.

The operation of the 19th Panzer Corps, having forced a breach of the front at Sedan under the framework of Sickle Cut, is often called the "Second Battle of Sedan," in reference to the famous 1870 battle of encirclement, itself often being called the "Cannae of the 19th century." Nevertheless, a major difference exists between Field Marshal Moltke's pincer maneuver and that of Lieutenant General Manstein's regarding the size of the operations. Whereas in 1870 the assembly point of the two armies which formed the pincer was located nine kilometers from Illy Hill, where Moltke was acting as chief of general staff, the 1940 operation represented a gigantic pincer movement, with a length of almost 400 kilometers, extending out in the form of a sickle from the Ardennes to the coast of the English Channel.

If in 1870 the Germans had succeeded in encircling in Sedan a French Army of 120,000 men, in 1940 it would now be close to 1.7 million Allied soldiers who would fall into the trap set by Manstein. With the rupture of the front at Sedan by Guderian's panzer units, the French defeat was becoming inevitable, since the Allied armies of the North were already in place in Belgium.[166]

An uninterrupted advance of panzer units all the way to the English Channel?

The breakthroughs at Dinant, Monthermé, and Sedan were made possible above all by the audacity of the commanders of the armored units, such as General Guderian, who had known how to make perfect use of the principle of "forward command." They had rushed towards the coast of the English Channel while going beyond their orders, which not only presented the Allies, but equally so the leadership of the German military, with a *fait accompli*. In fact, the OKH had not adopted Lieutenant General Manstein's operational theories to their fullest scope and extent when it had proceeded with the revision of his offensive plan on February 24. The latter was no more than a weak, half-hearted imitation of the bold Sickle Cut plan. This watered-down version of the original theory could have led to a failure to achieve complete success against France. Yet, thanks to the individual actions of a few generals, Manstein's original intentions were fulfilled.[167]

Reinforced by the approval of a tank specialist of Guderian's caliber, Manstein had originally conceived the drive through the Ardennes, the crossing of the Meuse, and the advance to the Channel as a single uninterrupted operation. The panzer divisions were to charge forward at great speed and without stopping from the Ardennes all the way to the Channel. Without this, the northern wing of the Allied armies would have had time to retreat behind the Somme and escape the trap set in Belgium by Bock's army group. As for the armored units of Rundstedt's group, it was thus a question of advancing to the rear of the enemy in complete isolation, without worrying about their flanks being exposed.

Hitler and several high ranking generals, such as Rundstedt, Kleist, and Ernst Busch, the commander of the Sixteenth Army, were nevertheless skeptical with respect to the possibility of rapidly crossing the Meuse, despite the arguments provided by Manstein and Guderian. They were even more doubtful about Manstein's conception, supported not only by Guderian, but also by Halder, of a single uninterrupted operation by the armored divisions. Instead of a single advance to the Channel, as proposed by the "progressive" generals, the "traditional" generals, or those of the "old school," rather had the intention of calling for a halt at Dinant, Monthermé, and Sedan, thus at the halfway point. The panzer units had to be content with establishing secure bridgeheads and waiting on the left bank for the arrival of the motorized divisions and the infantry. The actual rupture and exploitation would only occur several days after the crossing of the Meuse, once the infantry was in a position to protect the flanks of the armored divisions.

Guderian had sharply protested against such an intention on the part of the Führer and certain senior officers of the military, for a halt would grant a sufficient amount of time for the Allies to withdraw behind the Somme and construct a new line of defense to the west of the Meuse. According to Guderian, it was necessary to maintain Manstein's idea and charge quickly towards the lower Somme, following the Saint-Quentin-Amiens-Abbeville axis, without even stopping a single moment after having crossed the Meuse. Otherwise, one would run the risk of missing the great opportunity of a complete encirclement of the Allied northern wing, thus a strategic victory, instead of a mere victory on the operational level.

It was at that moment when one of the most decisive episodes of the France campaign occurred. Instead of ordering his panzer divisions to wait at the bridgehead a few more days until the motorized divisions and the infantry were also able to cross the Meuse, General Guderian launched his 1st and 2nd Panzer Divisions onward to the west, in the direction of the Oise and Saint-Quentin, leaving the 10th Panzer Division and the motorized regiment *Grossdeutschland* the responsibility of ensuring the protection of its left flank. In so doing, he unleashed an avalanche, as the other armored divisions followed him. The advance to the west of two of his three panzer divisions from the Sedan bridgehead converged rapidly with that of Reinhardt's two panzer divisions coming from Monthermé, along with that of Hoth's two panzer divisions from the outskirts of Dinant. The operation thus gained an appropriate dynamic, evolving according to Manstein's wishes.[168]

The first halt-order and the panzer advance to the Channel

By May 16, the French front had been fully ruptured through its center. The panzer divisions surged forward through a breach of more than 100 kilometers. The German maneuver finally took shape as Manstein had forecast in his operations plan. However, the tank advance took on the form of a thin scythe, due to the lack of protection on its flanks. From this came the postwar term of "sickle cut," (*Sichelschnitt*), Winston Churchill being the author.[169] On the sixth day of the offensive, the push towards the west had advanced more than 120 kilometers from the Meuse in the direction of the English Channel, and it had already reached the Oise.

Another golden opportunity thus seemed to present itself to the Allies. A gap clearly observed by French reconnaissance aircraft had opened between the armored divisions and the German infantry who were trying their best to keep up with them. The panzers were progressing through a narrow corridor approximately 60 kilometers wide, and the infantry units were posting a delay of three to four days, at a distance of 100 to 125 kilometers. The 10th Panzer Division, attempting to join with the 1st and 2nd Panzer Divisions of Guderian's corps, was spread out across nearly 100 kilometers.

The situation provoked great apprehension in Hitler, Colonel General Rundstedt, at the head of Army Group A, and General Kleist, chief of the panzer group. Guderian's tank advance was conducted in such a way that they dreaded a French counterattack on its left flank. Within the high echelons of the German high command, there was fear of a repetition of the "miracle of the Marne," which had led to the failure of the Schlieffen Plan in September 1914. The void that continued to grow between the tanks and the infantry provoked serious tensions between Guderian and his immediate chiefs.

Already on May 15, Kleist, worried about the lightning-fast push of the 19th Panzer Corps with its flanks exposed, had ordered Guderian to pause in order to allow the infantry to catch up to his panzers. Guderian had refused to obey such an order, which, in his opinion, amounted to abandoning the aspect of surprise and all his initial successes. After a heated discussion over the phone, Kleist authorized him to pursue his advance for twenty-four hours before implementing a break allowing his infantry divisions to regroup at the Sedan bridgehead. Having fully decided to take advantage of the depth of the rupture of the enemy front, the commander of the 19th Panzer Corps nevertheless continued his advance well beyond what had been permitted him.

But Hitler ended up letting his nerves get the best of him. The dictator was convinced that the French were mounting a significant counterattack from the south to cut off the armored spearheads from the rear. During their conversation at dawn on May 17, Rundstedt offered Hitler his support, informing him of his fears regarding a surprise counterattack from the French troops in the region of Verdun and Châlons-sur-Marne. Hitler then asked him to put the breaks on Guderian's advance, which had already reached the Oise. The latter was thus requested to halt for two days in order to permit the infantry to join with the armor and ensure the protection of its left flank along the Aisne.

This halt-order (*Haltbefehl*), the first of the campaign, which Brauchitsch and Halder emphatically opposed, was forwarded to Guderian by Kleist, who had requested his presence at the Montcornet airfield at 7 A.M. An extremely turbulent discussion ensued between the two men. Convinced by aerial reconnaissance that no threat was hanging over his left flank, Guderian immediately presented his resignation, which Kleist all too eagerly accepted. Notified of the situation, Rundstedt rushed to find a compromise. The next evening at 6 P.M., Guderian returned to his command and was authorized to pursue a "reconnaissance in force" towards the English Channel while leaving behind his headquarters. Hitler would accept such a compromise only once Halder had assured him that the infantry would gradually arrive at the Aisne in order to form a shield.[170]

Before the campaign, Hitler had asserted on several occasions that France would fall like a house of cards. Now that the prediction was materializing, he had a difficult time believing it. However, the danger coming from the left flank turned out to be illusory. Not a single argument, even Halder's which relied upon clear and precise reports from the intelligence office, truly succeeded in relieving Hitler of his instinctive fear of having the flanks exposed. As Manstein observed ironically, Hitler had right before him the "ghost" of a menace to the rear. In the same breath, he also noted the fact that it was the dictator who carried the responsibility for the absurd interruption of the operation.[171] Yet Rundstedt and Kleist also had their share of responsibility in this timid halt order.

Friedrich-Wilhelm von Mellenthin, future lieutenant general, estimated that only two major mistakes had been committed in the western campaign: the halt order of Montcornet and the halt order of Dunkirk. Some, like the staff officer Kielmansegg, even inferred that if the

German attack had not come to a halt on May 17–18, the "miracle of Dunkirk" would have had little chance of occurring.[172] Whatever the case may be, Guderian was correct in wanting to take full advantage of his advance towards the sea, since the Allies were not in any sort of position to launch a full-scale counteroffensive on the southern flank of his armored corps. Halder too had the right assumption; the French quite simply did not have the necessary forces to mount a counterattack from the south.

Guderian asked for nothing more. His panzer corps resumed its advance, uninterrupted, towards the English Channel. On May 18, he crossed the Oise and occupied Saint-Quentin. Two days later, he seized Amiens and reached, that very same evening, Abbeville right next to the sea, cutting off the lines of communication of the Allied left wing in Belgium. The operational objective intended by Manstein had thus been achieved. Throughout its blazing advance, Guderian's armored corps had established bridgeheads on the Somme, in Péronne, Amiens, and in Abbeville, which the Allies, despite the deployment of significant forces, were unable to forestall. Shielded behind a defense line established along the Aisne and the Somme, Guderian's 19th Panzer Corps drove shortly after to the north and surrounded Boulogne on May 22, and Calais on the following day.

The decisive phase of Manstein's Sickle Cut operation thus ended in success. The German tanks had pushed through part of the Allied front and trapped the entirety of the northern wing against the coast of the English Channel. Not only was the Belgian Army caught in this enormous net 200 kilometers in length and 140 kilometers deep, but also the British Expeditionary Force, the First and Seventh French Armies, and scattered elements of the French Ninth Army. Caught in the trap, the Allied northern wing appeared to be finished once and for all.

The second halt-order and the "miracle of Dunkirk"

On the morning of May 24, the Germans were no more than 15 kilometers from Dunkirk, the last port on the English Channel still available to the Allies. The first units of Guderian's armored corps had already crossed the Aa Canal, between Gravelines and Saint-Omer, the last natural obstacle, after having established five bridgeheads. There were no longer any troops of notable size between the German tanks and

Dunkirk. It was thus only a matter of hours before the only remaining Allied port on the English Channel would fall into the hands of the Germans. As soon as this port was closed off, nearly a million Belgian, British, and French soldiers would be trapped. The majority of them were still located some 100 kilometers from Dunkirk. Battling against Army Group B, they had absolutely no chance of reacting to the deadly threat that was taking shape behind them. It was at that moment that one of the most remarkable episodes in military history occurred: the "miracle of Dunkirk." The Allied soldiers realized with astonishment that the formidable German tanks were no longer moving.

Why this decision to halt the tanks, when they were on the verge of gaining the greatest German victory of the campaign? This second halt order of the campaign has been the cause of interminable controversies since the end of the war. According to the most thorough studies, Hitler issued the order for military reasons and on advice from his military chiefs. As such he did nothing but confirm the directives of Rundstedt, Keitel, Jodl, and Göring. His decision would have been principally inspired by three motives: the desire to retain the panzers for the second part of the offensive; the fear that they would get stuck in the marshes of Flanders; and Göring's arguments in favor of the Luftwaffe.

On the morning of May 24, Hitler paid a visit to the headquarters of Army Group A, which was then located in Charleville, approximately 100 kilometers from the English Channel, to discuss with Rundstedt the military situation. Considering the victory achieved in northern France, Rundstedt, one of the generals in whom Hitler had the most trust, proposed to halt the advance of the armored divisions beyond the Aa, in proximity of the Dunkirk pocket, until he had brought more infantry. Exhausted by an uninterrupted advance of two weeks, the panzer units, he estimated, were in need of rest to recuperate. It would also be necessary to hold them in reserve in order to regroup them for the prospect of a counterattack emerging from the south, and especially for the ultimate offensive to the south of the Somme and the Aisne, under the framework of the Red Plan, conceived to eliminate the remaining French forces.

Hitler at once approved Rundstedt's suggestion, especially since they strengthened the conclusions to which Keitel, Jodl, and himself had previously come. For Hitler and the two chiefs of the OKW, the terrain did not lend itself to armored attack, due to the fact that Flanders was such a swampy region. Likewise, such an attack, which was intended to eliminate the Dunkirk pocket, would lead to severe panzer losses and would weaken the impending offensive in the south of France.

Moreover, Göring supported Hitler in his decision to halt the tank advance. He persuaded him that the Luftwaffe alone was capable of dealing a deathblow to the encircled Allied armies around Dunkirk, thus eliminating the necessity of employing armored formations for this operation. Undoubtedly wanting to provide his air force with the opportunity of fighting a decisive battle and granting it the glory of success, Göring impressed upon Hitler the advantage of dissolving the pocket without the slightest sacrifice of tanks and, as a result, without delaying the second part of the offensive in France.

It was at 12:45 P.M. that the famous Dunkirk halt order was issued. It is clear that Hitler's idea, suggested by Rundstedt, Keitel, Jodl, and Göring, yet emphatically opposed by Brauchitsch and Halder, was to let the Luftwaffe and Army Group B eliminate the enemy troops captured in the pocket. For its part, Army Group A, with the bulk of the armored units, would stand its ground and maintain the encirclement, all while ensuring the protection of the southern flank.[173]

On the following morning of May 25, when Brauchitsch demanded to engage the tanks on the Dunkirk plains, the Führer stood up against him, explaining to him that the region of Flanders was not favorable to armored units and that the risk of losing any tanks for the offensive in the south was too great. He nonetheless left the final decision to Rundstedt, who chose not to deploy the tanks against Dunkirk, because he needed to regroup them for the intended operation in the south. Brauchitsch and Halder were appalled. They had to put up with a supreme chief of the Wehrmacht who was intervening more and more directly in the conduct of operations.

It turned out very quickly that halting the panzer divisions had been a grotesque and consequential error. Neither Göring's Luftwaffe nor Bock's army group proved capable of fulfilling their mission. The Luftwaffe, which still only had available distant airfields, was impaired by the onset of bad weather and especially by the massive intervention of British fighter squadrons that were operating very close to the south of England. As for Army Group B, its advance was too slow, due to a lack of sufficient armored and motorized units. It was only on May 26, after it was too late, that Rundstedt, little by little, began to doubt the viability of the halt order. He went to the front to see Kleist and Hoth, who together vehemently insisted that freedom of mobility be returned to them. There remained nothing more for him to do than update Hitler on the turn of events, following which the latter repealed at 1:30 P.M. the halt order. Meanwhile, the tanks were either resting, in the process of reorganizing, or busy making repairs. As a result, the offensive was only able to reconvene on May 27 at 8 A.M. The panzer divisions thus remained motionless before Dunkirk for a total of three days and eight hours.

During the delay, the Allies had the time to construct an exhaustive defensive position spread out around Dunkirk and to hastily assemble an evacuation fleet under the codename Operation Dynamo, in order to proceed with the embarkation of the soldiers for England. Guderian's armored corps clashed with a well organized resistance which he was unable to break through in any significant way. Deprived of steady and massive support from the Luftwaffe, either grounded by the poor weather or overwhelmed by the unexpected opposition of British fighter planes, he had to witness, impotently, the evacuation of Allied troops. Operation Dynamo, from May 26 to June 4, the last day of the Battle of Dunkirk, permitted the Allies to save 338,682 men by sending them to England. In total, with some 28,000 soldiers previously evacuated from various ports on the Channel, and some 4,000 British that had escaped through the other French ports, the total number reached nearly 370,000 men. Among them were approximately 247,000 British and 123,000 French.

Nevertheless, 80,000 French soldiers were unable to evacuate in time from Dunkirk and it was necessary to add to them the surrender of 35,000 men, which was all that remained of the First Army encircled in the region of Lille. In spite of the setback that it suffered at Dunkirk, its first since the beginning of the war, the Wehrmacht could nevertheless claim responsibility, in less than three weeks of fighting, for the capitulation of the Dutch and Belgian forces, respectively on May 15 and 28, the destruction of three French armies and the expulsion of the British Expeditionary Force from the continent. France had already lost 250,000 soldiers, among which were her best troops, 930 tanks, and the important economic and industrial region of the Northeast. On Britain's side, despite the repatriation of most of the BEF, the losses were equally severe: 68,000 soldiers and a little more than 100 tanks, plus the loss of nearly all its artillery.[174] Its ground forces could be considered defeated, since only one Canadian division possessed heavy weapons on British soil.

The first phase of the campaign: A simple operational victory

Brauchitsch and Halder could hardly contain their anger. In their opinion, if Guderian's 19th Panzer Corps had not been forced to halt for more than three days, it could have dissolved the pocket and prevented a massive evacuation of the Allied troops to England. The latter's troops would have never had the time necessary to institute an organized resistance around Dunkirk.

Even though the terrain of the Flanders region, crisscrossed by canals, ditches, and marshes, was not suitable for the tanks, Guderian's armored corps had no less built five bridgeheads on the Aa, between Gravelines and Saint-Omer, by the time of the May 24 halt order. On that particular day, there was only a single British battalion to hold the some 30 kilometers of the Aa between Gravelines and Saint-Omer. The Germans thus had no difficulty constructing the bridgeheads on the other side of the river. Furthermore, the river was, according to General Lord Gort, commander in chief of the British Expeditionary Force, the only anti-tank obstacle for the Allied troops trapped in the Dunkirk pocket. Once the Aa was crossed, nothing could have stopped Guderian's panzers, or have prevented them from barricading the line of retreat of the BEF, the bulk of whose troops were not yet assembled at the port. Nothing could have prevented them from dealing the fatal blow that would have hammered the Allied armies of the north on the anvil of Bock's Sixth and Eighteenth Armies arriving from the northeast, except for Hitler's order demanding that they halt.

Even if it was only sustained for three days, the halt allowed Lord Gort to deploy against Guderian's panzer units three infantry divisions along with substantial artillery support.[175] This turned out to be sufficient. As soon as they were on their way, the 19th Panzer Corps was incapable of achieving any significant breach in the enemy's defense system in place around Dunkirk, and even less so of preventing the evacuation of the majority of the troops trapped in the pocket. By the panzer halt order of May 24, Hitler had compromised the success of the Sickle Cut plan. And this "perfect Cannae" that the Schlieffen School had hoped to reproduce did not take place. To the contrary, the British Expeditionary Force's embarkation for England reduced Manstein's intended complete strategic victory to a simple, if spectacular, operational victory. All things considered, the campaign in the West was nothing other than, to make reference to the first volume of Manstein's *Memoirs*, a "lost victory." It was, one might say, his first "lost victory" of the war.[176]

After the war, the majority of the German generals, including Manstein, Guderian, and Halder, put the blame exclusively on Hitler. Even Rundstedt placed the fault on Hitler, even though he had exerted a decisive influence over the latter's decision to stop the panzers before Dunkirk. No doubt to protect the image of an exceptional and remarkable military high command on an operational level, which only fell victim to the Führer's incessant interventions and amateurishness, Manstein, Guderian, and Halder thus spared Rundstedt, Kleist, Keitel, and Jodl of any blame.

Manstein even gave an exaggerated account of the consequences at Dunkirk: "[…] the fact that the evacuation of Dunkirk was allowed represents one of Hitler's most critical mistakes. It prevented him from later attempting the invasion of England and consequently allowed the British to pursue the war in Africa or Italy."[177] If the retreat of the British Expeditionary Force indeed permitted the English to pursue the war in Northern Africa after the fall of France, it is false to assume, as Manstein did in his *Memoirs*, that it prevented the Wehrmacht from attempting an invasion of England. If there was no invasion, it was quite simply because the OKH decided to turn once again to the East, this time against the U.S.S.R.; and the result of the Battle of Britain in no way influenced a decision made before its commencement.

If Hitler had not ordered the halt of his armored divisions before Dunkirk, and if they had been able to prevent the evacuation of the Allied troops trapped in the pocket, thus gaining the strategic success sought by Manstein, would Great Britain have capitulated? For some, if the British Expeditionary Force had been defeated, it would have been almost impossible for Churchill to survive the increasing pressures of those who, in his country, wanted to come to an arrangement with Hitler.[178]

In any case, the Battle of Cannae itself was a classic paradigm of a victory of annihilation on a battlefield which did not necessarily bring about a political outcome. Despite a brilliantly orchestrated pincer maneuver at the Romans' expense, the victory won by Hannibal at Cannae nevertheless did not lead to a strategic result. To the contrary, for the winners of this battle would finally lose the Second Punic War (218–201 B.C.).[179]

Manstein's 38th Infantry Corps on the defensive

After having taken the command of the 38th Infantry Corps, Lieutenant General Manstein was busy organizing his general staff in Stettin and supervising the training of newly formed divisions. His abrupt removal from the general staff of Army Group A, even though he was the designer of the operations plan in the West, hardly delighted him: "While the others were developing the ideas that I had defended for so long, I mainly had the modest task of organizing my general staff in Stettin and inspecting from time to time the divisions being formed in Pomerania and in Poznan. On May 10, 1940, I learned about the beginning of the offensive from the radio in Liegnitz, where I was on leave for forty-eight hours. It goes without saying that during the following days all my thoughts and prayers were with our units moving into the Ardennes. [...] But one will also understand that it was not exactly pleasant for me to be so far to the rear, while the others were implementing the plan for which I fought so long and so fiercely."[180]

On the evening of May 10, he received orders to transfer his army corps' headquarters from Stettin to Brunswick. Three days later, the 38th Infantry Corps came under the command of Army Group B before being attached, on May 16, to Army Group A. Within this group, it had to integrate itself into the Twelfth Army, which was located between the Fourth in the north and the Sixteenth in the south. The Twelfth Army was responsible for following the attack to the west, while the Second, positioned to the southwest, was to be inserted between the Twelfth and the Sixteenth.

However, on May 17, the Twelfth Army received instructions to turn to the southwest, placing itself on the defensive. The Second positioned itself between the Fourth and the Twelfth in order to continue the attack in the direction of the west. These new directives were coming from the high command's decision, made on Hitler's initiative with the support of Rundstedt and Kleist, to halt the advance of Guderian's 19th

Panzer Corps before the Oise. He wanted to avoid at all costs a German setback, even a temporary one, which could have rekindled the morale of the French troops who were already near the end of their tether. In fact, he feared a reversal of this order if the Twelfth Army, continuing as planned in the direction of the lower Somme, were attacked on its southern flank to the west of the Meuse. But the Allies appeared to be incapable of launching a large-scale counterattack in this region.

On the one hand, it was clear that halting Guderian's armored corps risked compromising the decisive victory over the enemy forces engaged in Belgium, which he was supposed to take in the rear. On the other hand, the order given to the Twelfth Army to place itself on the defensive was equivalent to forsaking the initiative between the Meuse and the Oise; in other words, it amounted to abandoning the idea proposed by Manstein in his operations plan with regards to covering the southern flank by an offensive. By limiting itself to the defensive, instead of attacking to the southwest between the Meuse and the Oise, the Twelfth Army allowed the adversary to establish a new front on the Aisne, which could only be breached through tough battles during the second phase of the offensive. The Twelfth Army thus lost the possibility of preventing, through an offensive action, the creation of the front at this critical point. Such an offensive action represented, however, one of the essential ideas of the Manstein Plan, in addition to the encirclement of the Allied forces engaged in Belgium.

The May 17 decision revealed that neither Hitler nor Rundstedt and Kleist possessed the necessary audacity to accept a temporary risk on the southern flank. "This example shows one more time that an operations plan can never be executed just as it was conceived by its author if the execution is incumbent upon someone other than himself, even if there appears to be no other reason to step away from it," declared Manstein after the war.

In his *Memoirs*, he recognized that the Führer "possessed a certain instinct for strategic matters. But he lacked the training of a genuine military officer which would allow him to even accept a high risk during the course of an operation while knowing that he will be able to gain control of it." In the context of the offensive in the West, he added: "Hitler clearly adopted Army Group A's idea of cutting off the enemy forces engaged in northern Belgium by attacking through the Ardennes and pushing all the way to the sea, and he faithfully followed it at least until right before Dunkirk. But he did not completely understand the other idea, which consisted in creating through the first phase a situation that would favor the implementation of the second. The German command was satisfied, during the advance of Army Group A's rapid units towards the coast, with covering the movement against an anticipated enemy counterattack on both sides of the Meuse, while spreading out defensively the divisions that followed like a pearl necklace along the threatened southern flank. It appeared too risky for him to destroy in advance any attempts from the adversary to launch the counteroffensive, by attacking to the south, west of the Meuse, in order to thus definitively drive the enemy front between the Meuse and the Oise."[181] Challenging Manstein's reckless concept, Hitler therefore preferred to play it safe and opt for a defensive cover for the first act of the German offensive in France.

On May 25, Manstein's staff received orders to replace the 14th Motorized Corps which Kleist had left, along with the 9th Panzer Division and the 2nd Motorized Division, in the Abbeville-Amiens sector to cover the rear of his two panzer groups along the lower Somme. On May 27, the 38th Infantry Corps took position and henceforth confined itself to monitoring the river. More precisely, his mission consisted in safeguarding the bridgeheads at Abbeville and Amiens.

Lieutenant General Manstein suggested to the commander in chief of the Fourth Army, Colonel General Kluge, to whom his corps was now subordinate, to try to gain initiative through maneuver in this region rather than remaining on the defensive. The defensive task assigned to his corps would doubtlessly offer the adversary the chance to firmly create a new defensive front. Additionally, sustaining the two bridgeheads would become difficult if the enemy were to bring in new forces with the intention of launching a full attack. By remaining in place, the 38th Infantry Corps and the two rapid divisions attached to it would only be able to intervene if the enemy were to take over the bridgeheads and come out onto the northern banks of the Somme. Consequently, it would be necessary to cross the river by surprise between the two bridgeheads with the two rapid divisions, to take action against the flank of the forces attacking Abbeville and Amiens, and to rout them. Next, it was necessary to engage the army corps in a mobile battle to the south of the Somme until the battle in northern Belgium reached an end, all while awaiting the arrival of the German northern wing on the lower Somme in order to support its exposed flanks and to prevent the adversary from developing a solid front. As long as it remained alone to the south of the river, the 38th Infantry Corps would find itself in a perilous situation. But it had to accept the risk in the interest of the second part of the offensive in order not to have to fight such arduous battles against a soundly established enemy front in the interim.

Most likely at Hitler and Rundstedt's instigation, Kluge rejected Manstein's suggestion, which enabled the Allied troops to create an uninterrupted front on the southern banks of the Somme between the bridgeheads of Abbeville and Amiens. The high command obviously desired to avoid any risks until operations in Belgium came to an end, at which time it would then be able to concentrate all its forces against the newly formed front. After having previously abandoned the initiative between the Oise and the Meuse, thus permitting the establishment of a front on the Aisne, it now relinquished the idea of retaining maneuverability to the south of the Somme, which then led to the creation of a French front south of the river. In fact, it left the adversary the time to create a defensive line to the far northwest of the Maginot Line at the mouth of the Somme.[182]

The march towards the Seine and the Loire

It was during the second phase of the campaign, under the framework of the Red Plan, that Lieutenant General Manstein, promoted on June 1 to the rank of General of Infantry, would finally play an active role in France. Participating in the June 5 attack under General Kluge's Fourth Army, the mission of his 38th Infantry Corps was to cross the Somme at Picquigny, approximately ten kilometers to the northwest of Amiens. The initial assault was to be led by the 27th and 46th Infantry Divisions, while the 6th Infantry Division would be held in reserve. Opposing Manstein's army corps were two French divisions which enjoyed the advantage of favorable terrain. The northern banks were formed in this area by a plateau that gradually descended into the Somme, without any woods to provide the 38th Infantry Corps with cover. On the other hand, the southern banks were very steep, affording the French divisions a very clear view of Manstein's troops. The latter, as a consequence, ordered his infantry to prepare the rafts, dinghies, and gang-boards for the crossing of the Somme during the night. The men went into action at dawn on June 5, without the benefit of artillery preparation. Such action was necessary in order to provide an element of surprise to the German attack.

Despite significant losses, the crossing of the Somme by the 38th Infantry Corps was a complete success. The heights of the southern banks were already taken by the end of the day. The French artillery, in spite of superiority in numbers, proved to be ineffective, due to its lack of adaptability on the battlefield.

Once the enemy resistance was overcome on the southern banks of the Somme, the 38th Infantry Corps continued its advance to the Seine. The mission assigned by the OKH to the Fourth Army was to construct bridgeheads to the south of this river. In light of the development of the previous days' battles, it was clear that the French troops could no longer present a serious opposition. Everything indicated that they would try to create a defensive front behind the Seine by calling up their reserves. The Germans were thus required to force their way across the river before the French had time to organize themselves.

On June 8, nearly 70 kilometers from the Seine, Manstein received orders not only to have his motorized units to the river by the following day, but also to cross it. The infantry and its harnessed artillery would rapidly follow in order to reach it by the following day. For this, he positioned the 6th and 46th Infantry Divisions respectively towards Les Andelys and Vernon, two key positions on the Seine between Paris and Rouen. As for the 27th Infantry Division, it was brought back to the second line. On June 9, Manstein's two frontline divisions arrived at the river, but they had been unable to prevent the enemy from destroying the bridges at Les Andelys and Vernon. The units of the 6th were nevertheless in a position to cross the river on the evening of June 9. On the other hand, the 46th would not be able to cross until the next morning. The 38th Infantry Corps was the first German contingent to set foot south of the Seine.[183]

Convinced of the necessity of maintaining the initiative in the region so that the enemy would not have time to organize its defense or to mount a counteroffensive, Manstein asked Kluge for permission to attack as soon as his army corps' artillery had crossed the river, instead of maintaining the defense of the bridgeheads in Les Andelys and Vernon, as planned. In the meantime, the bridgeheads were expanded all the way to the Eure. Moreover, the 27th Infantry Division had also arrived on the southern banks of the Seine. Manstein's proposal was met with a refusal. The counterattack that the 46th Infantry Division had to resist on June 11–12, not without suffering significant losses, confirmed the judgment of the situation by the 38th Infantry Corps' commander.

On June 16, Manstein received instructions from Kluge sending him in the direction of Le Mans-Anger, to the southwest of Paris. He was required to achieve this objective, however, without the 46th Infantry Division, which had been placed under the command of the 1st Infantry Corps deployed to his left. On that same day, his army corps once again came into conflict with organized resistance on the Ferté-Vidame-Senonche-Châteauneuf line, which had been breached during the night. On June 19, he crossed Le Mans and on June 22, the day that the Franco-German armistice was signed, the 6th and 27th Infantry Divisions both arrived on the southern banks of the Loire, after reaching the Angers sector.

As commander of the 38th Infantry Corps, Manstein demonstrated great tactical sense on the battlefield. The lightening advance of nearly 400 kilometers past the Somme to the Loire by his army corps was a testament to his capability of leading and maneuvering his infantry divisions as if they were mobile troops. Daring and imaginative, he took the initiative at a time when the situation demanded it, and demonstrated flexibility at preparing for the unforeseen. On more than one occasion, he positioned himself at frontline command posts in order to better evaluate the situation. In short, he had demonstrated the qualities of a true leader on the battlefield. Furthermore, the blazing push of his army corps from the Somme to the Loire in fourteen days earned him the Knight's Cross of the Iron Cross.

The Manstein Plan, or the six-week war

On August 3, 1914, at the time of the unleashing of the offensive in the West, the German high command was believed to be in position to conquer the French Army in six weeks. However, the failure of the Schlieffen Plan transformed the conflict into a static war lasting four long years in which the Kaiser's army never succeeded at decisively breaching the adversary's front. On the eve of the offensive on May 10, 1940, the chiefs of the OKH and the OKW had envisaged a rapid victory in the Western Theater. But never, even in their wildest dreams, did they seriously expect an outcome in six weeks, or even less so a breach of the adversary's front in only three days. The offensive had progressed at a staggering rate, which left everyone in the Wehrmacht stunned. Even Hitler had hardly dared to hope for a success of such magnitude.

However, emerging from the forests of the Ardennes on the fourth day, the armored and motorized columns were able to take advantage of the breakthrough that was created the previous day on the Meuse, between Sedan and Dinant, and roll over in a single movement the rear of the enemy front in the direction of the Channel, thus closing off the northern Allies in an enormous pincer movement. Ten days after the commencement of the offensive, the German troops had already covered 240 kilometers and reached the coast of the English Channel. Manstein's sickle cut worked perfectly. The Allied forces were cut in two; a large majority of them were thus trapped between the coast and the arriving German divisions. In less than two weeks, the French campaign had been decided. At the point where the Schlieffen Plan had failed, the Manstein Plan had succeeded. All things considered, the Sickle Cut operation represents the most gigantic envelopment maneuver in military history.

The disparity in the death toll reflects the extent of the victory. The French losses rose to 92,000 soldiers killed, 200,000 wounded, and close to two million taken prisoner; the rest of the Allies counted 80,000 soldiers killed, of which nearly 70,000 were British. For their part, the Germans suffered 27,000 soldiers killed, 15,000 missing in action, and 111,000 wounded.[184]

After the western campaign, General Manstein would acquire the reputation of a military genius, even gaining legendary status in officer circles.[185] There is no doubt that without his Sickle Cut plan, full of imagination and daring, a *Blitzkrieg* against France would have hardly been conceivable and difficult to attain.

Manstein immediately denounced the restricted objectives and the absence of surprise of the OKH's initial operations plan. Instead of the partial success sought by the OKH, his aims had been set from the very beginning on a decisive victory on the battlefield. Rather than the destruction of the largest possible number of Allied armies in Belgium and the conquest of the shores of the English Channel, he proposed the complete annihilation of the Allied armies in the west and control of the entire Atlantic coast in France, Belgium, and Holland. Instead of a primary offensive through Belgium, as put forth in the Schlieffen Plan, which the Allies were expecting, he suggested a massive attack through the Ardennes, which was considered uncrossable terrain for tanks. Rather than launching a frontal offensive in Belgium, which risked coming to a standstill on the Somme and giving way to a static war analogous to that of 1914–1918, he advocated a bold solution which consisted of charging towards the English Channel from Sedan and thus taking in the rear the main enemy forces deployed in Belgium.

The results of the campaign were equally indebted to Guderian and his theories on the joint use of tanks and aircraft, which Manstein had not only supported early on, but had fought to have adopted by the army high command. Their revolutionary tactical conception called for an element of surprise, a massive number of troops, and swift implementation. The traversing of the Ardennes and the crossing of the Meuse between Sedan and Dinant by the bulk of the German armored and motorized units had permitted the breach of the front at the very place where the adversary was expecting it the least, thus ensuring a strategic surprise. The exploitation of this center breach in the direction of the Channel occurred as a result of the expeditious action of the panzer and motorized units acting in close relation to the air force.

The Allied armies were only able to respond to the Wehrmacht's rapidity, maneuverability, and concentration of forces with the preconceived notion of dispersing their forces along a solid front, with a slow and methodical advance. During the course of the battle, the Franco-British high command was unable to free itself from an outdated military doctrine inherited from the preceding conflict, and in absolutely no way were prepared for the new mobile form of warfare imposed by the German general staff. After the disaster of Sedan, General Maxime Weygand, who had been appointed commander in chief of the French Army in place of General Gamelin on May 19, rightly declared: "We have gone to war with an army of 1918 against a German Army of 1939. It is sheer madness."[186]

Promotions and gifts from the Führer

In the euphoria of victory, the German generals recognized Hitler's personal role in the success of the Wehrmacht. When the demand for an

armistice with France was announced, Colonel General Keitel proclaimed him the "greatest army leader of all times." After the definitive
suspension of hostilities, Colonel General Brauchitsch additionally characterized him as the "premier soldier of the German Reich," an hon-
orific title around which the soldiers enthusiastically rallied.[187] For the
Germans who had lived through the trying experience of the First World
War, and who had been saddled with defeat, a victory over the French
represented a reversal of the humiliation of November 1918; an intolerable shame brought about by the legend of being stabbed in the back
which the soldiers had attempted, as a matter of honor, to alleviate. The
German Army had now recaptured the honor that it had once lost. The
alliance between the generals and Hitler could not have been stronger.

Moreover, on July 19 during a gathering at the Reich Chancellery,
the Führer presented a field marshal's baton to twelve colonel generals,
and a special baton, which resembled a scepter, to Göring, who was promoted to the newly created rank of Reichsmarshal, which placed him,
in terms of military hierarchy, above all the others. He was also awarded the Grand Cross of the Iron Cross—the fifth and highest mark of dignity conferred by the kings of Prussia to Blücher, Moltke, and Hindenburg—and he was the only one to receive it throughout the war.

Among the twelve colonel generals who were promoted to the rank
of field marshal, nine came from the army: the three army group commanders, Bock, Leeb, and Rundstedt, the commander in chief of the
OKH, Brauchitsch, the chief of general staff of the OKW, Keitel, four of
the most distinguished colonel generals, Kluge, List, Reichenau, and
Witzleben; and three from the Luftwaffe: Erhard Milch, Albert
Kesselring, and Hugo Sperrle. If the Kriegsmarine had been forgotten, it
was because Raeder, its commander in chief, had already been promoted to grand admiral—the naval equivalent to the rank of field marshal—on April 1, 1939. Halder, who had led two brilliant military campaigns as chief of the OKH's general staff, climbed only one rank, from
general to colonel general. As for Manstein, the designer of the operations plan in the West and the principal author of the plan in Poland, he
was completely forgotten during this promotions ceremony. He thus
remained at the rank of infantry general.

The extent of the promotions leads one to conclude that the Führer
considered the war, as it were, already won. But if attributing such honors to the leaders of the war for their courageous efforts during a cam-

paign or a battle was completely natural, Manstein nevertheless considered the degree to which they were handed out excessive. It was an opinion that, in his view, was shared by his comrades-in-arms. As he wrote in his *Memoirs*, by creating twelve field marshals in addition to one Reichsmarshal, Hitler did nothing but diminish the merit of Germany's highest military rank. He explained his viewpoint thus: "Up until this point, in order to be appointed [this rank], it was necessary (with the exception of a few field marshals nominated in times of peace by Kaiser Wilhelm II) to have independently led a campaign, won a battle, or conquered a fortress. After the Polish campaign, where the commander in chief of the army and the two army group commanders had fulfilled their obligations, Hitler had not judged it necessary to express his gratitude by promoting them to field marshals. Yet, he was now creating a dozen, among whom, next to the commander in chief who had led two brilliant campaigns, was the chief of the OKW, who had neither led a command nor filled the duties of a chief of general staff, and the secretary of state to the Air [Ministry] who—whatever his merits as an organizer—could not be placed on the same footing as the commander in chief of the army."

If it is true that certain promotions were not justified, like those of Göring, Keitel, and Milch, Manstein's assertion that only a few field marshals had been promoted to this rank in peacetime by Kaiser Wilhelm II is nevertheless unfounded. During the time of the Kaiser, no fewer than 25 generals had been appointed to field marshal, and the majority of them during times of peace. The number of generals who had been elevated to the rank of field marshal in the past was equally more significant than Manstein had implied: by Frederick Wilhelm I: 10; Frederick the Great: 21; Frederick Wilhelm II: 4; Frederick Wilhelm III: 12; Frederick Wilhelm IV: 5; Wilhelm I: 8. In addition, those who had received their field marshal baton during the First World War had not all earned it through satisfying one of the three criteria set forth by Manstein. Should one deduce that Manstein was expressing his bitterness, or perhaps even his jealousy, for not having himself been promoted at the end of the French campaign, even though he had been the author of the operations plan? Did he rather want to attach more credit to his nomination as field marshal which occurred after his conquest of the Sevastopol fortress in the summer 1942?

Moreover, Manstein claimed to be outraged by Göring's promotion to the rank of Reichsmarshal. Such a promotion placed the latter above all the commander in chiefs of the army and navy, as well as being the only one decorated with the Grand Cross of the Iron Cross. "The gesture," mentioned Manstein, "could only be interpreted as a deliberate demotion of the chief of the army and fully expressed Hitler's state of mind with respect to the OKH."[188] In fact, all Hitler was quite simply intending to do from the very beginning was to thank his old fellow traveler and faithful accomplice.

By granting so many promotions, he nevertheless undermined the highest military rank in Germany, especially if one considers that the Kaiser had only appointed five field marshals during the course of the First World War and that Ludendorff had not even been promoted to that rank. By acting in such a manner, Hitler not only wanted to reward the contribution of his primary war chiefs, but also to reinforce his hold over them by further heightening their loyalty. In his postwar account, Joachim Wieder, as a Wehrmacht soldier who fought during the Battle of Stalingrad, described the partisan loyalty, the unconditional submission and obedience sought by Hitler through the granting of such promotions to his military elite: "After the French campaign, new field marshal appointments and countless spectacular promotions fueled an increase in ambition and a devotion promising glory on the part of the great army chiefs who particularly felt indebted vis-à-vis the Führer."[189]

The distribution of honors or gifts by political powers was already standard practice in the Middle Ages. The king granted to his elites titles of nobility, estates, or lands as a form of gratitude for their services during a victorious war. By rewarding the duty and loyalty of his subjects, the king clearly sought to further increase their dependence and loyalty with regards to his person. The granting of rewards by the king to his elites continued beyond the reign of Napoleon I. Furthermore, the practice was customary under the King of Prussia and the German Kaiser Wilhelm I: Field Marshal Moltke and Chancellor of the Reich Otto von Bismarck had both received sums of money that were considerable for the time, as well as estates and titles of nobility for raising the German nation to the level of a great power following the wars of unification.

By bestowing a profusion of promotions and honors, Hitler was thus only continuing an old practice which essentially consisted in corrupting the elite. Just like the kings or emperors, he sought nothing less than increasing their allegiance. Through these acts of generosity, the high ranking generals found themselves further connected, regardless of their political ideas, by their oath of allegiance to Hitler, to whom they owed these promotions and honors.

When he presented his twelve field marshals with their baton, the total value of which rose to 72,000 RM—Göring's, more elaborate because of his rank of Reichsmarshal, cost an additional sum of 22,750 RM—Hitler asserted the importance that he attached to the unconditional loyalty of his commanders. The new Field Marshal Bock noted in his diary: "The Führer presented us in the Chancellery of the Reich with the field marshal baton. He insisted upon the necessity that the German people be united [...] and upon the absolute necessity that the Wehrmacht declare itself in perfect harmony with National Socialist thought." During the ceremony, Colonel General Blaskowitz's absence was conspicuous. His protests against German atrocities committed in the occupied territories of Poland had cost him in May 1940 the command of the army which he had led in that country since October 1939. He was thus the only colonel general not to be promoted to the rank of field marshal. Even if subsequently he would assume various commands on the Western Front, he would never again be promoted. The message could not have been any clearer. The senior officers who blindly obeyed orders would as a result be rewarded, whereas those who demonstrated a rebellious spirit would see their careers stagnate.[190]

In addition to granting promotions to the high leaders of the Wehrmacht, Hitler would allocate to them, beginning on August 8, 1940, through the intervention of his minister of the Reich Chancellery, Hans Heinrich Lammers, a tax-free monthly stipend—paid directly into their bank account—better known under the name of *Aufwandsentschädigungen* (expense account). From then on, the field marshals and grand admirals received 4,000 RM per month, while the colonel generals and the admirals received a monthly sum of 2,000 RM. To such gifts, it was necessary to add another monthly amount granted as a supplement to the generals since November 10, 1939, according to the type of command they held: 250 RM for an army group or an army; 150 RM for an army corps; and 50 RM for a division. Obviously, Manstein, who would benefit from these tax-free stipends for the rest of the war, made practically no mention of it in his *Memoirs*.

All such bonus amounts were added to their annual salary. From April 1, 1939 to April 1, 1942, the commanders in chief of the three branches and that of the OKW earned 26,550 RM per year, whereas the field marshals, grand admirals, colonel generals, and admirals received annually 24,000 RM. From April 1, 1942 until the end of the war, the commanders in chief of the three branches and that of the OKW, as well as the field marshals and the grand admirals received an annual salary of 26,550 RM; the colonel generals and the admirals 25,500 RM; the generals and the vice admirals 24,000 RM. By receiving a monthly tax-free bonus of 4,000 RM, the field marshals and the grand admirals tripled their annual salary, while the colonel generals and the admirals, by collecting each month a tax-free sum of 2,000 RM, doubled theirs. For example, in 1943, Manstein, then field marshal, received a tax-free sum of 48,000 RM which supplemented his annual salary of 26,550 RM, whereas Guderian, at the time colonel general, enhanced his annual salary of 25,500 RM by a tax-free amount of 24,000 RM. In the two cases, this represented a staggering amount, especially if one takes into account the fact that the weekly salary of an unskilled worker under the Third Reich was approximately 28 RM, hardly 1,500 RM per year.

The profound mistrust that he felt towards his generals explains why Hitler resorted to such measures even though the war was not yet concluded. Despite the oath of allegiance that his officers took for him in August 1934, they inspired in him nothing but mistrust. His public declaration in February 1938, which remarked the Wehrmacht's full devotion to the National Socialist state and asserted its blind loyalty and obedience, concealed a genuine suspicion with respect to the high military command.

Such mistrust is explained in part by the reluctance of the Prussian conservative and aristocratic officers to accept without question the strategic decisions of a man whom Field Marshal Rundstedt was still characterizing in private in 1944 as a "Bohemian corporal." The dismissal of Field Marshal Blomberg and Colonel General Fritsch in the winter of 1938, as well as the removal of Colonel General Beck in the summer of that same year, only served to augment the Führer's suspicion of his senior officers, just as did the negative reaction of several of them concerning his intention to launch an offensive in the west in autumn 1939. Another part of his mistrust was explained by the refusal of a few generals to support the criminal policies of the Nazi regime in the occupied territories since the beginning of the war. Colonel General Blaskowitz's objections to the German atrocities committed in Poland did not fail to provoke Hitler's anger. His conviction that Blaskowitz was speaking on behalf of his colleagues prompted him to denounce the "childish attitudes" of the army leadership and to assert that one could not win the war "with the methods of the Salvation Army." It was thus in this context, when the outcome of the war was still uncertain, that Hitler decided to implement a system of coercion based on bribing the generals in order to ensure the unconditional obedience and staunch loyalty of his military elite.

By accepting large sums of money which were being granted to them through the intermediary of a secret system coming from a special fund of the Reich, the high ranking generals allowed themselves to be coerced, thus becoming accomplices to Hitler and his regime. Furthermore, the message to the senior officers who were receiving these sums of money was very clear: anyone who opposed the criminal policies of the National Socialist regime, like the elimination of the Jews and the intelligentsia in Poland, which had been occurring since autumn 1939, would see his tax-free monthly bonus come to an end.[191]

By achieving the rank of colonel general or field marshal, the officer immediately notified Lammers, who would inform him of the amount of tax-free money that he would receive each month. The conditions for payment were clearly explained to him: it was contingent upon his exemplary performance. Concerning this matter, the minister of the Reich Chancellery explained to him that the money came from the Führer's fund and not the military budget. Consequently, the tax-free monthly stipend could be revoked at any moment. It was in this manner that the transfer of funds into Field Marshal Friedrich Paulus' bank account was terminated in April 1943; not because of his capture in Stalingrad two months earlier, but because of his relations with the Soviets during which he charged Hitler with the responsibility of the destruction of the Sixth Army. It was clearly a similar case for Field Marshal Witzleben, for his participation in the conspiracy on July 20, 1944, against Hitler.

However, the stipend paid to the officers of the two highest ranks was not exclusively reserved for those who were active. In actuality, an agreement reached in March 1943 between Lammers and Keitel stipulated that any new posting or leave of absence would not lead to a stop in payments, which was not the case for a resignation or a retirement. All those who were relieved of their command during the war thus continued to receive their monthly tax-free bonus. For example, the future Field Marshal Manstein would receive a monthly sum of 4,000 RM from April 1944 to April 1945, a period during which he was nevertheless inactive due to Hitler placing him on reserve on March 30, 1944.

Despite the absence of any documents regarding the beneficiaries' reaction, all indications are that they eagerly accepted the monthly checks from the Führer, for which the conditions of cashing them amounted to signing one's name on what could appear to be a second oath of allegiance. Like the majority of his peers, Manstein would take advantage of this system without feeling the slightest amount of remorse. It appears, in fact, that the beneficiaries considered such sums of money as a legitimate payment that obviously went to all the field marshals and colonel generals. However, the simple fact that the amounts were significant for the time and moreover free from taxation, and that the money was secretly paid to them, all of which was dependent upon their performance, should have been amply sufficient to make them realize that it was in no way legitimate and even less so a demonstration of the Führer's gratitude for services provided to Germany.

As a beneficiary of the monthly tax-free bonus for commanding an army corps (150 RM per month from February 1940 to September 1941), Manstein would later be paid sums relative to the rank of colonel general (2,000 RM per month from February 1942 to June 1942), field marshal (4,000 RM per month from July 1942 to April 1945), as well as sums for his army commands (250 per month from September 1941 to November 1942) and his army group (250 RM per month from November 1942 to March 1944). After his dismissal in March 1944, he would continue to receive a monthly stipend of 4,000 RM in accordance with his rank of field marshal, until the end of April 1945, the last month that the Führer's system of endowments was in effect.

In the spring of 1945, when the noose around Germany was becoming tighter and tighter, and hundreds of German soldiers were being executed for desertion, some of the senior officers, whose monthly stipend had been deposited up to that point in a bank located in regions under enemy fire, transferred their accounts to banks in more secure areas. In other words, the money could be withdrawn, but not the troops! The following field marshals were included among the names of the officers: Erich von Manstein, Georg von Küchler, Wilhelm List, and Maximilian von Weichs.[192]

VIII

BETWEEN TWO CAMPAIGNS

Shortly after the end of the French campaign, General Manstein learned that a new posting was planned for his general staff. It would to be transferred to the coast of the English Channel in order to prepare for the invasion of England. But the abandonment of this plan at the end of summer 1940 provoked great disappointment for this senior officer who, like others within of the Wehrmacht, believed in the operation's success and pushed most vigorously for its preparation. However, despite the virulent criticisms expressed in his *Memoirs* concerning the reasons that led to invasion's abandonment, he no less justified Hitler's decision to instead invade Bolshevik Russia out of strategic considerations, even speaking of it in terms of a preventative war. Clearly, by taking into account the Nazi rhetoric on the war of aggression, he found his own ideological objectives enacted, particularly the destruction of the Jewish Bolshevik system and the elimination of its representatives, a criminal mission for which the Wehrmacht needed to commit nearly all of its forces.

Operation Sea Lion (Seelöwe)

By bringing down France and taking her out of the conflict, Hitler was hoping to induce England into a peace compromise with Germany, which would in turn free him from a conflict with the West he had not wished for, and which he believed he could avoid by signing a pact of non-aggression with Stalin. On June 25, 1940, at the time when the armistice with France came into effect, he confided to his entourage: "The war in the west is over. France has been defeated and before long

I will find common ground with England. All that remains is to settle our score with the East. But this is a task that opens global problems, such as relations with Japan and the power struggle in the Pacific, problems which we will not be in a position of addressing before ten years. Our hands will be busy for years managing and strengthening what we have won in Europe."[193]

With the prospect of a compromise with England, which was to bring the war in the west to an end, at the end of May he had already ordered, even before the conclusion of the French campaign, a reduction in ground forces. These would decrease by 35 divisions, thus from 155 to 120. The number of mobile divisions would nevertheless be doubled from 10 to 20 panzer and from 5 to 10 motorized divisions.[194]

But Hitler's enthusiasm over the prospect of a compromise soon gave way to skepticism with the failure of diplomatic efforts undertaken through the intermediaries of Sweden, Switzerland, and the Vatican. His idea that Great Britain, following the French defeat and the offer of "reasonable" conditions, would resign herself to the inevitable, in her own interest, would prove to be erroneous.

On July 19, without much conviction, Hitler described to the Reich Chancellery his last peace proposal to England in hopes of bring an end to the war. In his proposal, he appeared prepared to spare the British Empire as long as she accepted that the Reich had free reign over the continent. Despite London's negative response to his proposed peace compromise, Hitler was not overly surprised, all the more so since he had recently begun to envision a landing in England.

By June 30, Lieutenant General Jodl had already delivered to Hitler a memorandum which suggested various actions to take in case England were to refuse a compromise with Germany. The OKW followed the memorandum up with delivery of its own directive on July 2, which called for the three branches to initiate preparations for an eventual landing. Then, on July 16, Hitler gave consent to the preparations for a landing operation against England. In the plan, the Royal Air Force had to be eliminated so that it could not interfere with the transport of troops across the Channel. The operation's code name was "Sea Lion" (Seelöwe) and its preparations had to be completed by mid-August.

The very next day, the OKH formulated a detailed landing plan on an expansive sector of the southern coast of England. It sent 13 elite infantry divisions to the Channel coast, near departure points for the first wave of invasion. Like the Battle of France, the primary responsibility for the invasion was entrusted to Field Marshal von Rundstedt and his Army Group A, which consisted of the Sixteenth and Ninth Armies. Six divisions from Colonel General Busch's Sixteenth Army were to embark at Pas-de-Calais and reach the beaches of southeastern England between Ramsgate and Bexhill. Four divisions of General Adolf Strauß's Ninth Army would cross the Channel from various ports located between Caen and Dieppe, in the region of Havre, and land on the southern English coast between Brighton and Portsmouth. Further to the west, Field Marshal Bock's Army Group B, with three divisions from Field Marshal Reichenau's Sixth Army, casting off from the Cotentin peninsula at Cherbourg, would come up alongside Lyme Bay on the southwestern English coast on both sides of Weymouth. In all, 90,000 men would be landed during this first wave, for which the transportation across the Channel required the utilization of 155 ships, representing some 700,000 tons, and more than 3,000 boats of lesser tonnage (1,720 barges, 470 tug boats, and 1,160 motor boats).

The second invasion wave would be composed of an operational mobile force of six armored divisions and three motorized divisions distributed among three army corps. This wave would be followed by a third consisting of 17 infantry divisions. After this third day of invasions, the OKH expected to have landed a total of 260,000 men organized in 39 divisions, which included six panzer and three motorized, in addition to two airborne divisions.

According to the OKH's prediction, the campaign would last at the very most four weeks. Such an esetimate corresponded in every point to the view of the Führer, who insisted that the operation be concluded around September 15. The 41 German divisions were deemed sufficient to crush the enemy resistance in a single month. At the beginning of July, the OKH estimated that the English forces had a "combat worth" of 15 to 20 divisions. In reality, there were at this particular time 29 divisions in England, but hardly more than a half dozen were "combat worthy," for they possessed practically no combat tanks nor heavy artillery, having lost so much equipment in France.[195]

On July 19, General Manstein was informed that the 38th Infantry Corps which he was commanding was to participate in the first wave of invasion. Two infantry divisions, the 24th and the 36th, would be under his control.[196] His staff headquarters would be immediately established at the harbor town of Le Touquet, nearly 20 kilometers to the south of Boulogne. It was from this locale that he had to finalize the last details of the invasion for his army corps and supervise his troops' embarkation and debarkation drills with the assistance of the navy. Placed under the command of Busch's Sixteenth Army, Manstein's corps was to leave from Boulogne-Étaples and land at Bexhill. Conscious of the risks that such an operation entailed, Manstein was no less convinced of its success, and it was with the greatest zeal that he pushed forward his preparations.

However, Grand Admiral Raeder, commander in chief of the Kriegsmarine, appeared skeptical from the very beginning. He voiced serious objections concerning the fulfillment of such a large-scale operation in such a short amount of time. In his opinion, an amphibious operation on such a scale and on such an expansive front, which extended over 300 kilometers from Ramsgate to Lyme Bay, exceeded the capabilities of the German Navy to provide convoys and protect them. Faced with the difficult task of transporting a strong army from the other side of the Channel, and confronted with a far superior British Navy and an enemy air force which appeared ever more active and effective, he insisted that a landing only be envisioned as a last resort. And furthermore, it was necessary that the Luftwaffe gain air superiority above the Channel and southeastern England.

The leaders of the army also expressed apprehension regarding the risks their troops faced by crossing the sea on such short notice. As the OKH had neither anticipated nor studied an invasion of England prior to or during the French campaign, the troops had received no appropriate training, and nothing had been done to construct the necessary landing flotilla. Lacking a proper landing flotilla composed of barges adapted for the transportation of personnel and supplies, they would be required to assemble in the Channel ports an ill-assorted armada of tugboats, coastal vessels, and Rhine barges, as well as have the troops carry out seafaring drills. In addition, the chiefs of the OKH hardly had any confidence in the ability of the Kriegsmarine or the Luftwaffe to ensure the protection of the convoys. This was why they desired to execute the invasion on a wide front, from Ramsgate to Lyme Bay, in order to force the adversary to scatter its forces and thus enable a rapid exploitation of the interior beginning with areas that were barely defended.

On July 31, Grand Admiral Raeder was summoned by Hitler to the

Berghof to provide him with a definitive presentation of his views. September 15, Raeder declared, would be the closest possible date to undertake Operation Sea Lion, and only then under the condition that "no unforeseen circumstances due to the weather or the enemy were to occur." With the exception of the first two weeks of October, the weather, he explained, was generally poor on the Channel, with periods of light fog in the middle and thick fog at the end. But this was only part of the problem, for the operation could only be carried out if the sea were calm. If it were rough, the barges would sink and even the big ships would be useless, as they would not be able to provide supplies. The grand admiral was appearing more pessimistic as he continued to list all of the difficulties: "Even if the first wave were to succeed at crossing with favorable meteorological conditions, there would be no guarantee that such auspicious weather would last for the second and third waves [...]. In reality, we must admit that not a single vessel worthy of its name would be able to cross for several days, until certain ports were able to be utilized." In accordance with considerations related to both weather and logistics, he concluded, "The best period for the operation would be in May 1941."

But Hitler did not want to wait so long, for the British Army would be able to take advantage of such a postponement to build itself up again to 30–35 effective divisions, a considerable force in the planned invasion zone. He thus decided to make Operation Sea Lion dependent upon the results of the aerial Battle of Britain set for mid-August. If on the one hand, the Luftwaffe were to succeed at completely eliminating the Royal Air Force from the skies over the Channel and the southern coast of England, and on the other hand overpower the British Navy or at least keep it at bay, an amphibious operation could then be executed in autumn 1940.[197]

Despite this decision, Hitler was becoming more and more resistant to the idea of proceeding with Operation Sea Lion, which he considered to be extremely risky. In fact, his thoughts were now mainly reserved for the Russian issue. Pressured by Field Marshal Brauchitsch and Colonel General Halder ever since July 21 to undertake an attack against Bolshevik Russia, Hitler made the decision to return his attentions to the East on July 29. Raeder's July 31 presentation on the difficulties of landing in England only served to further support his inclination. Even if the aerial offensive above England would still occur, it was henceforth the planning of military operations against the U.S.S.R. that captured the attention of Hitler and the OKH chiefs.

Finally, on September 17, Hitler postponed *sine die* Operation Sea Lion. Despite its best effort, the Luftwaffe had proved to be incapable of gaining air superiority over the Royal Air Force during the Battle of Britain, which had been taking place for a month.

The abandonment of Sea Lion incited bitter disappointment in General Manstein, who represented the part of the army that believed in the success of the operation and pushed forcefully for its preparation. In fact, he would have preferred to settle the matter of England before taking on that of Russia. In his view, the military high command should have done everything possible to conclude as quickly as possible the war with Great Britain. In fact, it was because of the latent threat that the Soviet Union was posing in Germany's rear that it seemed to him more than necessary to reach a final outcome in the west without delay. Once England was forced into peace through force, he asserted, Stalin would find himself at the mercy of the goodwill of the German Reich, for whom the Western Front would have been definitively secured.

After the war, he lamented the absence of any previous preparations for the plan to invade England. The Wehrmacht was thus unable to take immediate advantage of the adversary's momentary weakness and let pass the most favorable moment to execute a landing. "The preparations were undertaken straightaway," he affirmed, "but they took so much time that the success of a landing became problematic merely because of the weather conditions."[198] In fact, only the weakness and the momentary disorganization of the British forces, after the loss of the majority of their weapons and equipment in France, could have given such a hasty landing operation an opportunity for success.

Manstein's strategic considerations on the continuation of the war

According to Manstein, three options could have been available to Hitler and the military high command if they had been ready to launch a full attack against England.

The first would have consisted in cutting off the shipping channels and thus England's imports, which would have forced them to surrender. At first glance, he asserted, the conditions would have been most favorable for Germany to undertake such a task. She had the entire coastline of Norway, the Netherlands, Belgium, and France at her disposal to establish air and submarine bases. However, he recognized that the naval and aerial means were seriously lacking for her to achieve this goal. The Kriegsmarine did not possess a sufficient number of submarines and even fewer large ships, in particular aircraft carriers, to collaborate with them. As the Battle of Britain had demonstrated, the Luftwaffe was not yet powerful enough to gain control of the skies, or at the very least to prevent the RAF from intervening against the German submarines. Given the still limited number of bombers and the lack of fighter aircraft with sufficient range at their disposal, it was impossible for the Luftwaffe to quickly eliminate the RAF and destroy its sources of armament. Being incapable of paralyzing the majority of ports by destroying them, the Luftwaffe was even less prepared to work closely together with the submarines in their fight against the enemy's maritime supply lines.

In Manstein's view, to proceed with this option would have demanded a significant increase of naval and air fleets in order to ensure success. For this, in order to free up the work force, a reduction in the army would have been inevitable. It would have thus been necessary to prepare for a long war. But, he added, a reduction in the number of ground forces and a sustained focus on aerial operations against Great Britain could have tempted Moscow into political blackmail, or even to enter into war. If one were able to predict with any amount of certainty how the U.S.S.R. would behave in the eventuality of such a merciless war between Germany and England, it was nevertheless highly likely, he assured, that the United States would have intervened to save her last ally in Europe from defeat. With a prolonged operation she would at least have the time for this, whereas in the case of an outright invasion of Britain, she would have arrived too late.

Even though this was not the solution he would have recommended, Manstein stated the following opinion: "[Germany] could have judged it possible to move in such a direction with the firm prospect of success, still excluding a Soviet or American intervention, under the condition of strictly limiting herself to achieving the destruction of the British Air Force and then a complete blockade of naval communications. Any infringement of this rule, in the vague hope of crushing the morale of the enemy nation through attacking its cities, would only decrease its chances of success."[199]

Judicious in itself, Manstein's analysis of the ins and outs of this strategic question demonstrated a certain proclivity to overestimate the abilities of the Wehrmacht. There is no doubt that control of the Atlantic French coast would provide the Reich an operational platform that would further increase its chances of success in a blockade against the British Isles. In this case, it was absolutely necessary to concentrate its war efforts on the navy and air force in order to increase considerably their respective fleets.

Yet, even if such a concentrated war effort in favor of the Kriegsmarine and the Luftwaffe had been implemented, and that no secondary war theater emerged in the meantime, the Reich could not have expected to lay siege to Great Britain with any success before 1942, or even before 1943, according to Admiral Karl Dönitz. It would still be necessary to sink more ships than were actually coming out of the British shipyards, and to avoid, for as long as possible, the United States' entry into the war; at the very least it was necessary to restrict as much as possible the level of American aid to England. For his part, Grand Admiral Raeder estimated that it would be necessary to send to the bottom at least a million tons of merchant ships per month in order for the siege to achieve a decisive conclusion. Such a number was significant, as the *U-Boots'* record of sinkings was 63 ships in October 1940, for a total of 352,407 tons. A war against British lines of communication was thus unable to guarantee an immediate success and even less so a long-term one, for it was almost certain that the United States would react with an increased effort to save England from defeat if she were to be further threatened.[200]

The second option would have consisted in the seizure of strategic positions from Great Britain in the Mediterranean. By cutting off British lines of communication with India and the Middle East, the Wehrmacht could seriously compromise its supply line, particularly for petroleum. However, Manstein did not believe that this would have been sufficient to force a peace compromise. In his opinion, it would have still been possible to reach the Far and Middle East by way of the Cape of Good Hope, which could not be cut off, except for a narrow blockade of the British Isles that could only be achieved by the Kriegsmarine and the Luftwaffe, which would be a return to the first option. Such a blockade would have exhausted all the resources of the navy and the air force, leaving nothing for the Mediterranean battle.

In order to remove England from the Mediterranean theater, he surmised, it would be necessary to capture Gibraltar and Malta, and in case troops had been positioned in Egypt or Greece, to drive them out of these two locales. Manstein did not doubt that the Wehrmacht would have been militarily capable of accomplishing such as task. However, a significant part of its forces would need to be committed there. To gain control of Gibraltar, it would be necessary to either come to an agreement with Spain, which Hitler was not in a position of achieving, or to exert pressure over the country, which in a way amounted to occupying it. The Reich thus would be forced, either in agreement or against the wishes of Madrid and Lisbon, to take responsibility for the coasts of the Iberian Peninsula. It would have also been crucial to occupy French North Africa so as to prevent British from gaining any more of a foothold in the Mediterranean.

If only because of the necessity to cut off the petroleum supply to England, the Wehrmacht would have been forced to commit itself in the Middle East. It has often been stated that the possession of a base in the Middle East would have provided Germany with two advantages: on the one hand, the possibility of threatening India, and on the other hand, the acquisition of a position on the southern flank on the U.S.S.R, which would have restrained the latter from attacking the Reich. For Manstein, such an argument was completely erroneous. Without taking into account the long-term effect that German occupation would have on the attitude of the people of that region, he raised two challenges. In the first place, he argued: "If not for the issue of supply lines, one could have undertaken operations against India or against Russia from the Middle East, with sufficient forces to ensure a veritable success." Given the long supply line, however, British naval power would have been highly troublesome. In addition he added: "Germany's appearance in the Middle East would not have prevented the Soviet Union from attacking, but would have to the contrary provoked it into battle."

In his opinion, Great Britain's loss of positions in the Mediterranean theater would probably not bring about a peace agreement. To the contrary, a battle in this region would tie up, in the long run, such a significant number of German forces that the temptation for Bolshevik Russia to intervene would have been heightened in order to protect its interests in the Balkans and especially in the Middle East. He thus drew the following conclusion: "Moving through the Mediterranean in order to take down England would be taking a roundabout path analogous to the one that Napoleon had imagined would fatally wound England in the Indies via Egypt. In the long run, it would commit German forces in an indecisive direction, thus allowing the British homeland to rearm herself, and would provide the Soviet Union with its best chance against the Reich. In reality, it would have meant *evading* the decision we felt unable to achieve against the British motherland itself."[201]

Manstein was probably not wrong in asserting that the Reich could not have forced England into a peace agreement simply by seizing her strategic positions in the Mediterranean. However, he does not seem to have correctly recognized all the advantages his country could have gained from a limited offensive in the Mediterranean and from the acquisition of key strategic points like Gibraltar, Malta, and the Suez Canal. The advantages were the following: securing the southern flank of the Axis powers, considered to be the "soft underbelly of Europe"; rendering impossible any attempt for England to establish a second front through an intervention in the Balkans or elsewhere; avoiding a subsequent division of Wehrmacht divisions; making use of an ideal springboard in order to seize, if necessary, the principal bases of Vichy France in Northern Africa, such as Dakar and Casablanca; acquiring access to the Middle East's sources of petroleum which would in turn significantly reinforce the German war economy.

Such a strategy was precisely what Grand Admiral Raeder, the commander in chief of the Kriegsmarine, was suggesting. In September 1940 he had written two memorandums for Hitler's attention in which he strongly advocated a strategy aimed at destroying British forces in the Mediterranean and the Middle East. According to Raeder, it would be necessary to capture Gibraltar and the Suez Canal before pushing towards Palestine and Syria all the way to the Turkish border. Bases in Dakar, Casablanca, and the Azores would reinforce the presence of the Reich in the Atlantic.

As for domination of the Mediterranean, it would deny Great Britain her primary strategic center and expel her from the Middle East. At the same time, it would permit Italy's ascendency in eastern Africa, all the while preventing the United States from acquiring bases in northwestern Africa prior to entering the war. With England being isolated and perhaps even forced to come to an agreement, Germany would be in such a powerful position that she would have nothing more to fear from the United States. To convince his Führer, Raeder then played his last card. If Turkey were under German influence, the Soviet threat would be reduced. "It would then be doubtful," he concluded, "that it would still be necessary to attack the Russians from the north."[202]

After the French campaign of May–June 1940, Great Britain had the use of only a single armored division to provide for the defense of Egypt and the Suez Canal. Germany, on the other hand, had at its disposal a dozen panzer divisions. If she had decided to utilize only four of these to seize Egypt and the Suez Canal, the Royal Navy would have been forced to retreat to the Red Sea, no longer being able to count on adequate resupply via convoys through the Mediterranean. The Reich would have only had to seize Malta and Gibraltar to secure full control of the Mediterranean and thus block the Royal Navy from its last access to the sea. The German armed forces would have then had the use of an ideal springboard to occupy, if circumstances demanded it, the colonies of Vichy France in North Africa—Morocco, Algeria, and Tunisia—as well as take control of the base in Dakar, on the west African coast of Senegal, from which German submarines and aircraft would be able to control the principal maritime routes of the southern Atlantic.

Once Germany had gained control of the Suez Canal, the way would have been opened for her to undertake military operations in Palestine, Syria, Iraq, and Iran. This would have permitted her to not only have access to the Middle East's sources of petroleum, but also to isolate Turkey, threaten the British hold on India, and situate armored divisions in reach of the Soviet oil fields of the Caucasus. In this context, it was highly likely that Turkey would have been forced to either align herself with the Reich or grant it's armed forces the right of passage through its territory. Great Britain, for her part, would have in all likelihood been compelled to deploy additional forces in India in order to increase the protection of this jewel of her colonial empire. As for the Soviet Union, it would have had every interest in safeguarding more than ever its peace with Germany, due to the perilous position in which it would find itself, henceforth threatened by the Wehrmacht as much on its southern flank as its western.

If, for logistical and supply reasons, an operation against India could not be undertaken with enough forces to ensure success, this was not necessarily the case for an operation against the U.S.S.R through the Caucasus. With direct access to the Iraqi oilfields providing a sufficient quantity of fuel, a few armored and motorized units would have been able to rapidly advance across the Caucasus and join with a German army group emerging from the Ukraine. The latter's route would have been facilitated by the fact that the German troops attacking through the Caucasus would have tied down a number of enemy divisions. In case Hitler and the Wehrmacht leaders decided not to attack the U.S.S.R., the presence alone of German forces on its southern flank would have further prompted it not to attack the Reich and to appear benevolent towards them, particularly with regard to the delivery of foodstuffs and raw materials, in accordance with trade agreements included in the German-Soviet non-aggression pact.

Germany would also be placed in a much more favorable position to confront political and military developments in the Balkans in the spring of 1941. In fact, Yugoslavia and Greece would most likely be forced to come to an agreement with her. With the support of Hungary, Romania, and Bulgaria, the Third Reich would thus be able to enforce its hegemony over southeastern Europe, without even having to deploy a single soldier. In such circumstances, it could have avoided postponing Operation Barbarossa—the attack against the Soviet Union—from May 15 to June 22, 1941, thus ensuring another month of good campaigning weather.

By imposing its hegemony over Europe, with the exception of Great Britain and the U.S.S.R., as well as North Africa and the Middle East, and by making use of an almost completely intact powerful armed forces and a war economy in the position of exploiting the resources of three continents, Germany would become practically invincible in terms of her military. The British resistance on the periphery of Europe would have thus become progressively less significant and the United States would have no longer had any genuine hope of undertaking, with any success, an invasion of the European continent.[203]

In many respects, this second strategic option appeared to be much more suitable than Manstein had once thought. If he were to claim otherwise, it was without a doubt because he sought, as we will later see, to justify the invasion of the Soviet Union by raising the argument that Germany would have been forced to lead a preventive war as a result of Stalin's aggressive policies and the concentration of Soviet forces threatening the eastern border of the Reich.

The third option brought up by Manstein would have consisted of a landing on the English coast, just as Operation Sea Lion had envisioned. In his opinion, "an invasion represented the *quickest* way to crush England," whereas the two other options "would only be able to work *in the long run*." The conquest of the English homeland would have removed from the adversary the base essential for her to attack the European continent from the sea. Even if the Churchill government were to decide to pursue the struggle from Canada, and the United States were to enter the war, they would not be able to plan an invasion of the European continent across the Atlantic without the use of the British Isles as a springboard. The occupation of Great Britain, which would have led to the elimination of the Royal Air Force, the repression of the rest of the naval fleet on the other side of the Atlantic, and the suppression of any military potential of the homeland would doubtless have allowed the Reich to settle the situation in the Mediterranean theater. From a military point of view alone, he asserted, "The invasion of England, *if it had any chance of succeeding*, was undeniably the right solution."

Of course, Manstein was fully aware of the enormous risk of such a military operation across the Channel. However, he still considered it attainable in the summer of 1940. The comparison with the massive technical capabilities implemented by the Allies at the time of the Normandy landings in June 1944, he argued in retrospect, was alone not enough to conclude that an invasion attempt executed with such poorly adapted methods of transportation that the Germans had in the summer of 1940 was necessarily doomed to failure. It was the same concerning the control of air and sea space, regardless of its decisive importance in 1944.

In the summer of 1940, Germany possessed a major advantage according to Manstein: she did not have to count on, at least for the time being, "an organized defense of the British coast by troops that were sufficiently well armed, trained, and commanded." In fact, he explained, England appeared vulnerable to an invasion and would have been even more so "if Hitler had not let the expeditionary corps escape from Dunkirk."

In his eyes, the success of a landing in England in the summer of 1940 depended on two factors: "1) executing [the operation] as quickly as possible in order to capture the country at a moment when she was still incapable of defending herself on the ground and to take advantage of favorable weather conditions. (In front of us, the Channel was almost always smooth as a mirror in July, August, and the beginning of September.); 2) the possibility of preventing, *to a sufficient extent*, the British air force and naval fleet from intervening in the landing zone during the period of crossing and the time needed after it." The unpredictability of the weather and the impossibility of ensuring that the Luftwaffe would be in a position of gaining air superiority above the Channel and to the south of England would confer upon Operation Sea Lion a considerable degree of risk. It was precisely because of this risk that the undertaking had been viewed by Hitler and his military leaders, from the very beginning, with a large amount of concern.

According to Manstein, the Führer had finally given up on the idea of undertaking a landing for two main reasons. First, because the preparations had been extended to such an extent that the crossing of the first wave could not be expected before the end of September, thus at the time when the Germans were no longer confident of having a long enough period of good weather to lead successively and unremittingly the three waves of invasion. Second, the Luftwaffe was not in a position, at that time, to gain air control above the Channel and the south of England. It was self-evident, he insisted, that this second reason was more critical that the first one.

In his opinion, the first pitfall could have been avoided if a plan of invasion had already existed. And so, a significant part of the preparations could have been undertaken even before the end of the French campaign. The execution date would not have had to be delayed until autumn if Hitler and the Wehrmacht leaders had made the decision to invade England at the very latest when France capitulated, in other words in the middle of June and not in the middle of July. If such a decision had been made four weeks earlier, it would have allowed the date of the operation to be set for the middle of August.

As for the second reason, he added, the military high command had made an error of judgment in its attempt to gain control of the skies above the Channel and England through an isolated aerial battle, beginning well before the first date planned for the invasion. By achieving aerial superiority in this sector before the landing, the military leadership had clearly wanted to guarantee the success of the operation. However, it had succeeded in doing little more than squandering the Luftwaffe forces in conditions that were completely unfavorable to it.

Taking into consideration the balance of power alone, according to Manstein, would have led the Luftwaffe's high command to notice that its methods were neither sufficient nor appropriate to achieve success over the British air force and its centers of armament. On one side, it underestimated the power of the enemy's fighters; on the other, it over-estimated the effect of its own bombers. In addition, it was surprised by the existence of a radar system already in a position of functioning effec-tively. The high command should have known that the range of its bombers, and especially its fighters, was insufficient to wage a long-dis-tance operation. The German fighters would only have minutes over enemy objectives, while the bombers would be hugely vulnerable as soon as their fighter protection left the area. British fighters, of course, would be flying from nearby bases and have plenty of fuel, and in the event of being shot down, both their aircraft and pilots could often be retrieved. Finally, they made the mistake of modifying, during the Battle of Britain, the objectives of the aerial offense. While the Luftwaffe was on the verge of gaining control of the skies above Kent and Sussex, fol-lowing the attacks against the aviation industries and the airfields, they shifted the center of gravity of the offensive to London, an objective which henceforth no longer had any relation with the operation in terms of preparing for the invasion.

Given such considerations, Manstein explained, Göring's staff should have sought a "decisive battle only in conditions that were equal to the British Air Force, in other words above the Channel or the coast, thus in close operational liaison with the landing itself:" He added: "[...] Even though it is always desirable to gain control of the skies even before the beginning of the landing operation, a lucid examination of all the elements would have led the German command to only engage deci-sively its air force in close liaison with the landing."

Manstein recognized that the Luftwaffe would have thus had sever-al missions to fulfill, such as the attack of the air bases in the south of England, the protection of embarkations in the French ports, the pro-tection of the transport fleet during the crossing of the Channel, the sup-port of the first waves when they arrived on the beaches, and opposi-tion to an intervention by the British fleet, in collaboration with the Kriegsmarine and coastal artillery. But with such missions being required to follow in rapid succession, it would nevertheless not have had the time to achieve all of them simultaneously.

In his mind, the outcome would have probably depended on a decisive aerial battle waged above the Channel or southern England, beginning from the time the Army and Kriegsmarine commenced the operation. Moreover, the Luftwaffe would have found the conditions appreciably more favorable in this battle than in attacks inside the country. He was of the opinion that this "clearly equaled gambling everything on a single card. It was nevertheless the cost of playing if, in the present circumstances, one were to decide to attempt the invasion."

Hitler found himself confronted with a military undertaking which undoubtedly involved very serious risks, of which Manstein was well aware. If the invasion were to fail, the Führer would lose the army and navy forces engaged in the operation, as well as a part of the air force. Without suffering irreparable damage, from a military point of view alone, the Wehrmacht would not come out of this battle without being seriously tested. The political consequences would however, be even more serious. The willpower of British resistance would certainly be strengthened, whereas the incentive for the United States and the U.S.S.R. to enter the war would be greater than ever. Also, such a failure would not fail to compromise the prestige of the dictator, as much in Germany as internationally.

To the two military considerations previously put forth to explain the abandonment of the Sea Lion plan, Manstein would provide a third, political in nature. According to him, Hitler had always sought to avoid a fight with Great Britain and its empire on account of his political ideas. On more than one occasion, he had asserted that it was not in the Third Reich's interest to destroy this empire, for its overseas possessions would not fall to Germany, but into the hands of the United States, Japan, or the Soviet Union. Consequently, he had neither wanted nor expected war with Great Britain. If at all possible, he had wished to avoid a critical battle with an empire that he admired as a political and civilizing achievement.

Rather than conquer this power with weapons, he had decided to convince her of the necessity of an agreement while bringing down Soviet Russia, which seemed to be her last hope on the continent to continue a fight against Germany. "Such backpedaling in front of an obviously very high military and political risk caused Hitler to commit," as Manstein declared, "his greatest mistake in judgment." If he feared waging a critical battle against England at a most favorable time for her,

"Germany would sooner or later find herself in an untenable situation." The longer a war with England continued, the greater the Soviet Union's position could become threatening for the Reich. But if he finally refused to wield a decisive blow in the summer of 1940 by allowing to pass an opportunity which would never appear again, continued Manstein, Hitler was unable to confine himself to a wait-and-see attitude. "He was forced to eliminate the Soviet Union as an adversary, through a preventive war, as long as a dangerous enemy did not yet exist on the continent in the west."[204]

The abandonment of the plans for the invasion of England thus represented a bitter disappointment for Manstein. Despite its high risks, it had, in his opinion, a genuine chance of success if it were executed in the summer of 1940. He believed that it was a question of adopting the best solution for the continuation of the war, as the remark that he made in his *Memoirs* demonstrates: "In reality, Hitler backed away from facing the risk that an invasion of England entailed, accepting the much larger one of a war on two fronts."[205]

There was no doubt that Manstein was right to claim that an invasion represented the quickest way to drive England to defeat. But due to the extreme risks of such an invasion, it nevertheless appeared wise on the part of Hitler and his Wehrmacht chiefs to make the plan dependent upon the results of the Battle of Britain. For Operation Sea Lion, the Kriegsmarine did not have a sufficient amount of ships to ensure simultaneously the transport of troops and their protection. Since it did not possess the appropriate landing flotilla, it would have been necessary to have an exceptionally long period of calm weather conditions in order to attempt the invasion. It was also necessary that the Luftwaffe be in a position to overpower the enemy air force above the Channel and the southern coast of England during the crossings and the landings, all the while simultaneously intervening against the British fleet to compensate for the inferiority of the Kriegsmarine.

Moreover, Manstein's criticism that the high command displayed a lack of foresight by neglecting to prepare for an invasion of England before the end of the French campaign was greatly exaggerated. Not only did an amphibious operation across the Channel represent a considerable risk, but preparing for such an operation before the conclusion of military operations in France would have imposed a large handicap on the Wehrmacht forces, which were almost all still deployed against the French. At this time, there did not remain a sufficient amount of forces available to undertake preparations for an invasion of England. Even if it were possible to assemble all the necessary boats, declared Raeder to Hitler in the summer of 1940, the German economy would be ruined, for to remove so many barges and tug boats would destroy the country's entire system of domestic river navigation, upon which her economic life largely depended.[206]

As well as turning out to be extremely risky, an invasion of England proved, as it were, almost impossible to execute, even at the end of the French campaign. With the backpedaling, the strategic option that appeared to be wisest was thus the second, in other words the one that consisted in seizing Great Britain's strategic positions in the Mediterranean. Of the three options, it was this one that could be executed and achieved the most easily, that held the least number of risks, and that could reap the most appreciable geopolitical, geostrategic, and economic gains.

The Russian campaign: a preventive or aggressive war?

Despite his disappointment concerning the abandonment of Operation Sea Lion, Manstein justified no less Hitler's decision to attack the Soviet Union. On more than one occasion in his *Memoirs*, he underscores the latent menace that the U.S.S.R. represented for Germany, even for Europe altogether. He portrays Bolshevik Russia as a power that was "devoted to the idea of universal revolution" and that sought to "exploit the dissensions among the European people in order to achieve its policy of expansion."

According to Manstein, Germany was susceptible to this latent threat of an intervention from the Soviets since "ominous concentrations of Soviet forces on the eastern border of the Reich were inevitably arousing suspicions regarding the Kremlin's future posture." Certainly, he declares, one could not say "if the decision to attack the Soviet Union was not unavoidable for political reasons. In any case, the concentrations of troops on our borders and on those of Hungary and Romania were nevertheless threatening." He could not, however, say if Stalin was preparing to attack Hitler in the near future: "To tell the truth, the Soviet Union—having become the Reich's neighbor—represented a latent danger in the East despite the Treaty of Moscow [the pact of non-aggression], but one could not assume that it would take an aggressive attitude, *in the immediate future*, after the German victories over Poland and France." This in turn led him to further clarify his thought: "Judging by the number of units assembled in the west of the country, and by the massive concentration of tanks in the region of Bialystok as well as around Lvov, he must have been dreaming of attacking us sooner or later—an idea that was in any case a pretext for Hitler to justify his action. However, the dispositions of Soviet forces on June 22 did not reveal any aggressive intention, *for the time being*."

When the German troops advanced onto Soviet soil on June 22, 1941, he clarifies, the forces of the Red Army were spread so far apart that they could only wage, in their current positions, nothing more than a defensive battle. "One would without a doubt be very close to the truth in declaring that the system in place, in the expansive regions annexed by the Russians in eastern Poland, in Bessarabia, and in the Baltic countries, represented 'a deployment covering all possibilities'." But the Soviet defensive system would have been able to take on an offensive character rather quickly: "The Red Army—of which each army group was superior in number if not in merit, to its corresponding German [army group]—could organize itself in a very short amount of time to move to the offensive. In fact, such a deployment represented a latent threat." As such, it provided an additional rationale that amounted to defending, though in quite vague terms, the thesis of a preventive war: "Assuredly, in the summer of 1941, Stalin would have still preferred to avoid a conflict with Germany. But if the developments of the situation had led the Soviet leadership to think it could exert political pressure, or more precisely a military threat, the system was in a position of taking on an aggressive character very quickly."[207]

In reality, the chiefs of the Wehrmacht and Hitler never feared being attacked by the Soviet Union. The same could be said for the German military attachés and diplomats in Moscow. Not only did they judge the intentions of the Soviet high command as purely defensive, but the possibility of an attack from the Red Army appeared to them as rather improbable. According to them, if Stalin had ordered a massive concentration of troops near the western border of the U.S.S.R., it was quite simply with the goal of securing the territories that it had recently annexed. In no case, they thought, would the head of state of the Soviet Union take the risk of launching an attack against the Reich when the

Red Army had not yet achieved its military reforms and the Wehrmacht appeared to be at the pinnacle of its art. To the contrary, everything indicated to them that Stalin would even be ready to make sacrifices in order to maintain peace, showing the Germans that a war against Russia would not be to their advantage. Stalin, they concluded, would thus pursue his objectives without threatening German interests.[208]

All things considered, the theory of a preventive war, in which Operation Barbarossa would have been, by its very nature, a preventive offensive imposed upon Germany by a Red Army military stance that was both offensive and threatening, had been advanced by Hitler and his minister of propaganda, Joseph Goebbels, at the moment when the German attack was unleashed to justify the Wehrmacht's venture against a supposed "Bolshevik threat." Later taken up by former Wehrmacht officers in light of the repercussions of the war, the theory has once again been suggested by a few military historians, who were unable to succeed at convincing the majority of their specialist colleagues.

The Otto Plan: Precursor to Barbarossa

By attributing the intention to attack the Soviet Union exclusively to Hitler, Manstein seems once again to have passed over in silence the central role played by the OKH in the preparations for the invasion. A recent study of documents from the Soviet archives has reported the existence of the Otto Plan, a precursor to the Barbarossa Plan. In light of such a discovery, it is now clear that the OKH did not hesitate, after the French campaign, to push a hesitant Führer to undertake an attack against the U.S.S.R.

Already, from the end of May 1940, when Germany's victory over France left no doubt, General Halder, chief of the army general staff, was contemplating preparations for a war in the East. In mid-June, even before the conclusion of the French campaign, he was elaborating the Otto Plan, with the assistance of officers from his general staff. Completed on June 19, the plan postulated a *Blitzkrieg* in the U.S.S.R. from the end of the summer of 1940, with 80 divisions and 400,000 men placed in reserve. Halder planned a military campaign of nine weeks at the very most, during which the Wehrmacht would occupy, before the beginning of the fall muddy season, the Baltic states, White

Russia, and the Ukraine. Even if it were a question of a limited campaign, the OKH chief of general staff still estimated that the Wehrmacht would be in a position to seize Moscow, Leningrad, and Kharkov.

At Halder's instigation, Colonel General Brauchitsch, commander in chief of the army, began on June 25 the redeployment of the Eighteenth Army in East Prussia (Königsberg and Danzig, today Kaliningrad and Gdansk) and in the eastern part of annexed Poland (Posen and Breslau, today Poznan and Wroclaw). With 15 active infantry divisions divided into six army corps, General Küchler's Eighteenth Army was the most powerful of the Wehrmacht armies, even more so since the OKH had placed General Guderian's panzer group at its disposal. Deployed in two armored corps in the regions of Berlin and Breslau, Guderian's panzer group, which included six rapid divisions of four armored and two motorized, was the most formidable of the Wehrmacht. To these forces transferred to the East, it was necessary to add the seven infantry divisions that the OKH had maintained in Poland during the French campaign. Thus, on July 4, Küchler's staff was already assuming the command of the Eighteenth Army in Bydgoszcz in Poland, while the bulk of the formations would take position on the Eastern Front at the end of July. In all, 600,000 men were deployed in the east, where they were to be at the immediate disposal of the OKH under the framework of the Otto Plan. Two groups were established: one was to attack in the direction of Bialystok, and the other in the direction of Lvov.

Such heavy preparations for a military aggression involved in the Otto Plan had commenced without the Führer's knowledge, as he was only informed on July 21, which is to say one month after the conception of the plan and the execution of Eighteenth Army's redeployment. On this very day, after having summoned to Berlin the commanders in chief of the three branches of the Wehrmacht in order to finalize the preparations for Operation Sea Lion, Hitler was brought up to date on the existence of the Otto Plan by his OKH commander.

Thunderstruck, the Führer next learned from Brauchitsch that the OKH had already prepared for a military campaign against Bolshevik Russia. According to the new field marshal, 80 frontline divisions and 20 reserve divisions would suffice for the operation. The Russians, he asserted, were only in possession of 50 to 75 good divisions, as reports from the intelligence office concerning the Red Army indicated. For the time being, he proudly asserted to Hitler, his chief of general staff had at his disposal on the Eastern Front numbers that could be increased up to 60 divisions (42 infantry and 18 rapid). The preparations for the deployment having begun on June 19, he mentioned to Hitler that the Wehrmacht could undertake a lightening war against the U.S.S.R four or six weeks later, thus near the end of the summer 1940. The objective of military operations was to conquer the Red Army in such a way that it would enable the Wehrmacht to occupy the Baltic countries, White Russia, and the Ukraine before the beginning of the muddy fall season. He was thus counting on an expeditious campaign of two months at the very most. Neither Hitler, who was supreme commander of the armed forces, nor Field Marshal Keitel, chief of the OKW general staff, nor General Jodl, chief of the OKW operations bureau, and even less so the leaders of the Luftwaffe and the Kriegsmarine, had been informed of the existence of the Otto Plan before this fateful meeting of July 21 in Berlin.[209]

As much for Halder as for Brauchitsch, the war with the lifelong ideological enemy, Bolshevik Russia, had to happen sooner or later. Consequently, it was preferable to strike before it had completed its military reforms. The Red Army, they estimated, was in no way prepared to attack Germany in 1941, or even in 1942. On the path to becoming a powerful instrument of modern warfare, notably on the level of armaments, she was nevertheless not yet capable of launching a large-scale offensive war, because of her organizational and command deficiencies. For this reason, it was necessary to take advantage of the opportunity while all of the Soviet state's military measures were defensive in nature, while the Wehrmacht was militarily superior, and while it was still possible for her to attack the East with all of its forces. This confirms the post-war allegations of Curt Siewert, a staff officer in the OKH, according to which Brauchitsch strongly pushed an indecisive Hitler to launch an offensive against the Soviet Union as soon as possible.

For Halder and Brauchitsch, as for Hitler and a good number of Wehrmacht generals, the supreme objective was to conquer for the German people *Lebensraum* (living space) in the East, by dismembering the Soviet state and pushing Russia as far away as possible from the European continent, putting in place a quarantine line composed of satellite states beholden to Germany. The attack on the Soviet Union was integrated into the old German policy of the "march to the East"

(*Drang nach Osten*), which had been set in place during the Middle Ages by the religious and military order of the Teutonic Knights. Such a policy had been applied at the end of the First World War by the high command of Hindenburg and Ludendorff, particularly with the Brest-Litovsk Treaty of March 1918, which permitted the Reich to extend its influence over the Baltic States, White Russia, the Ukraine, the Crimea, and even the region of Kuban. Just as during the 1914–1918 war, it was thus once again a question of creating, in conformity with spirit of Brest-Litovsk, a confederation of Baltic states, Belorussian states, and Ukraine under German domination.

With the conquest of a vast space in the East, Germany would thus be able to make use of foodstuffs and raw materials deemed inexhaustible there, and necessary for her development as a great continental, even global, power. By becoming an autarchic continental empire able to withstand any blockades, she could thus spread her hegemony over all of Europe. It would be possible for her, as a result, to create a United States of Europe by unifying the various nations of the continent under her domination. Indeed, the dream was of a Europe organized according to the model of the former Bismarck Reich: in other words a unified Europe, composed of states of which one, a National Socialist Germany, would play a preeminent role by exerting the same role which Prussia had fulfilled domestically in imperial Germany. The idea was to construct a German Europe through gaining the resources of the vast spaces of Eurasia.

On July 29, after several days of consideration, Hitler decided to attack the U.S.S.R. as Brauchitsch was pushing him to do. Then, two days later, he summoned his military chiefs to the Berghof to announce to them his official decision. However, instead of the campaign planned by Halder, which was limited to 80 frontline divisions 20 reserve divisions, Hitler preferred a larger-scale military operation in which 120 frontline divisions and 20 reserve divisions would be committed to operations on the Eastern Front. Nearly 40 others, held on the Western Front, would provide its deep reserve. However, for logistical and operational reasons, due in particular to the unfavorable conditions of the fall season, the increase in numbers from 100 to 140 divisions, the enormous difficulties of transferring the bulk of the army from the West to the East, and the poor state of the transportation routes in Poland, the projected offensive in Soviet Russia was postponed until the spring of

1941. Instead of nine weeks, the Wehrmacht would take nine months to complete its preparations.[210]

The failure of Operation Barbarossa: Hitler's mistake, or his military leaders?

After the war, Manstein blamed Hitler alone for underestimating the strength of the Soviet regime, the country's sources of power, and the merits of the Red Army. Yet such an allegation is fallacious insofar as the final attack plan had been essentially the fruit of studies by the OKH and not the result of the Führer's wishes, as Manstein leads one to believe in his *Memoirs*.

Once the July 31 meeting at the Berghof was concluded, Halder, recently promoted to colonel general, enthusiastically got down to work, in the company of members of his staff with whom he immediately revised his plan of attack according to the Führer's directives. Even though he claimed in both his *Memoirs* and his post-war declarations to have opposed such an attack and characterized it as mad, remarks discovered in his diary reveal his enthusiasm for his new task at this time. At no moment did he inform his closest colleagues of the slightest doubt regarding the logic or the feasibility of a military operation in Russia. In fact, he anticipated Hitler's desires by working, from mid-June, on the preparations for a military intervention aimed at forcing the Russians to recognize Germany's domination over Europe.[211]

Contrary to the autumn of 1939 when Hitler's decision to undertake a military campaign in the west had given rise to worries, the senior leadership of the Wehrmacht was hardly alarmed in the summer of 1940 by the prospect of jumping into preparations for a war against Bolshevik Russia.

Following Hitler's example, they considerably underestimated Russia's military potential. Such an underestimation was not merely explained by the military factor. Their disdain of the Slavs easily coincided with their contempt for what Bolshevism represented. The generals of the Red Army, with whom they had been in contact during the dividing of Poland, did not make a strong impression on them. The disappointing performance of Soviet forces in Finland, where, contrary to all expectations, the underequipped Finnish Army had inflicted heavy losses on the Soviets at the beginning of the Winter War of 1939–40, did not improve the Red Army's image in their eyes. And above all, Stalin's purges of 1937–1938, had decimated the Soviet officers' corps. For all of these reasons, the German military leadership judged the Red Army incapable of leading large-scale operations appropriate to a modern mobile war based on liaison between tanks and aircraft. Although an invasion of England remained a dangerous enterprise, an offensive against the Soviet Union did not inspire any fear. One was expecting to lead there a genuine *Blitzkrieg*.

Intoxicated by their lightening victory over France, Germany's "hereditary enemy"—and its toughest opponent in the Great War—they began to consider the Wehrmacht invincible, and to believe in the infallibility of their command. Convinced of possessing a clear advantage over their adversary, as much from the perspective of the quality of their armament and training as of their command skills or even their military doctrine, they were certain of being able to conquer the Red Army in two or three months at the most.

In comparison with the French Army, which the Wehrmacht had crushed with relative ease, the Red Army seemed to be easy prey. For the military chiefs, the Russia campaign was to be nothing more than a simple military map exercise—a *Kriegsspiel*—in comparison with the French campaign. Therefore, they could not but agree with the intentions of their Führer who, from the time of France's capitulation, had declared to Jodl and Keitel that "a campaign against Russia would be child's play" compared to what had been accomplished in the West.[212] After all, during the Great War, had the Reich not conquered Russia in the east, even while still having to fight France in the west?

Thus, in the minds of the German generals, there was no doubt that a rapid Wehrmacht victory over the Red Army could be achieved in a single campaign, all the more so since their convictions relative to the superiority of Germanic culture over that of the Slavic world was profoundly marked by a latent and virulent anti-Marxism and anti-Semitism. It was indeed the same for Manstein. After the war, however, he led one to believe otherwise—as one would expect—since a retrospective view permitted him to support such a position. By taking into account the ratio of forces and the expanse of the theater, he declared, the high command should have envisioned in advance "the possibility of destroying the Soviet armed forces in *two* campaigns."[213] However, during the war in the East, he himself had many times underestimated the adversary, for example during the Battle of Kursk in the summer of 1943.

The definitive version of the OKH's plan for the assault against Bolshevik Russia was presented to Hitler on December 5, 1940 by Field Marshal Brauchitsch and Colonel General Halder. It was a result of studies that the latter ordered the chief of staff of the Eighteenth Army, Major General Erich Marcks, and the new OKH deputy chief of general staff, Lieutenant General Friedrich Paulus, to complete. At no time during their respective planning did Marcks and Paulus allow a single doubt to remain as to the chances of success of a military campaign in Russia. To the contrary, they both estimated that only eight to eleven weeks of battle would suffice for the Wehrmacht to knock the Red Army out of action.[214]

After having required a few modifications of the plan concerning strategic objectives, Hitler put forth on December 18 his directives for the invasion of the Soviet Union under the code name "Barbarossa," the plan formerly called "Otto" having slipped into history's dustbin. Initially anticipated for May 15, 1941, Operation Barbarossa would finally be unleashed on June 22, 1941, after a postponement following the German attack against Yugoslavia and Greece in April 1941.

Taking command of the 56th Panzer Corps and the German operations plan

In mid-February 1941, General Manstein was recalled to Germany to take command of the 56th Panzer Corps, which had just been created. His constant desire to command a rapid corps was finally achieved. However, just as in the Polish and French campaigns, he would not play any role, due to his new duties, in the drafting of the operations plan for the offensive. He thus only received marching orders for his armored corps in May 1941, a few weeks before the launching of the attack.

On the other hand, it is difficult to believe that he would not have been informed of the Führer's intentions to attack their neighbor to the east until the spring of 1941. In his *Memoirs*, he recalls the situation: "At the end of September 1940, when Operation Sea Lion was cancelled, the 38th Infantry Corps returned to the job of training as normal. The means of transportation that had been assembled for us were withdrawn from the Channel ports, having already been threatened by the British Air Force. But nothing transpired from Hitler's intentions with respect to the Soviet Union, which furthermore he decided to attack only much later. The first indications of what was being prepared only came to me in the spring of 1941, when I was called to the new post of [commander of the 56th Panzer Corps]."[215]

Manstein and his officer colleagues were focused on the intentions of the Führer and the OKH from November 1940. On the eve of a visit from the Soviet Minster of Foreign Affairs, Viatcheslav Molotov, planned for November 12, Hitler announced to his generals his firm decision to attack Bolshevik Russia at all costs: "Political discussions will take place with the intention of clarifying the Soviet Union's attitude. [...] Irrespective of their results, the decisions that I have made about Russia and which I have already verbally communicated, will be executed."[216] On November 11, it was thus clear that Hitler could not be dissuaded from launching an offensive in the East, despite the conciliatory attitude which Molotov was demonstrating towards Germany.

Even if he had not participated in the elaboration of the operations plan, Manstein nevertheless expressed in his *Memoirs* the differences between Hitler and the OKH apropos of the strategic conception. Such deviations sprang up not only during the preparation of the campaign, but equally so during its execution. As Manstein explained: "Hitler's strategic aims were based primarily on *political* and *economic* considerations. These were: (1) the capture of *Leningrad* (a city he regarded as the cradle of Bolshevism), by which he proposed to join up with the Finns and dominate the Baltic; and (b) possession of the raw material regions of the *Ukraine*, the armaments centres of the *Donetz Basin*, and later the *Caucasus oilfields*." He was thus expecting to paralyze the war economy of the Soviets.

However, most high-ranking officers of the Army took a different view. The OKH claimed, and justifiably so, that the conquest of these regions, though undoubtedly of great strategic importance, involved one prerequisite: taking the Red Army out of action. Yet, it was on the road to Moscow that one was to find the bulk of their army (a hypothesis which was nevertheless not entirely confirmed by the distribution of Soviet forces), as the city represented for the regime a power center it could not risk losing. This was on the one hand because—contrary to the situation in 1812—Moscow was the political capital, on the other because the occupation of its industrial region had at the very least significant repercussions on the country's war economy. Its fall would have practically cut in two the Soviet resistance and rendered the Russian command incapable of organizing a unified operation. From a strategic point of view, such a divergence can be expressed in such a way: Hitler desired to seek a military outcome *on the two wings* (for which the German means were not sufficient due to the ratio of forces and the expanse of space), while the OKH desired it in the *center*."

According to Manstein, the OKH had thus bet on a good strategic conception. But its choice was ruined by Hitler who sought to impose on it his own plan, whose objectives were quite simply excessive on an operational level. "It was over this difference in ideas that the German command finally failed. [...] The dissension with regards to the operational objectives persisted during the entire campaign. There could have only been one result: Hitler did not achieve his goals, which were moreover too far apart from one another, all while spoiling the OKH's idea."

Even if the extraordinary military successes achieved by the Wehrmacht during the first months of the campaign brought the Red Army to the brink of defeat, such formidable exploits, he concluded, were only expedients, for want of an operations plan that should have been fully formed from the very beginning: "But such a formula could in no way replace an operations plan based on the idea and execution upon which one should have been unanimously agreed within the high command, an operations plan which, taking into account the amount of forces and the size of the theater, had to figure in advance the possibility of destroying the Soviet armed forces in *two* campaigns."

On the other hand, he acknowledged, Hitler "approved the division of forces proposed by the OKH, according to which the bulk of the army was to be engaged in two groups to the north of the Pripyat marshes and in only a single group to the south."[217] Operation Barbarossa thus put into play three army groups. Under the command of Field Marshal Leeb, Army Group North was composed of two armies (Colonel General Küchler's Eighteenth and Colonel General Busch's Sixteenth) and one panzer group (Colonel General Hoepner's 4th, to which Manstein's 56th Corps was attached), for a total of 26 divisions, of which three were armored and three were motorized.

In addition, he was supported by fourteen Finnish divisions. Army Group Center, commanded by Field Marshal Bock, was by far the strongest. He assembled together two armies (the Ninth of Colonel

General Strauß and the Fourth of Field Marshal Kluge) and two panzer groups (Colonel General Hoth's 3rd and Colonel General Guderian's 2nd), altogether 50 divisions, including nine armored and six motorized. As for Army Group South, commanded by Field Marshal Rundstedt, he brought together three armies (Field Marshal Reichenau's Sixth, General Stülpnagel's Seventeenth, and Colonel General Schobert's Eleventh), and one panzer group (Colonel General Kleist's 1st). In all, he had at his disposal 41 divisions, which included five armored, four motorized, as well as the equivalent of 14 Romanian brigades.

Taking into account the approximately thirty divisions placed in reserve, the Wehrmacht committed 153 divisions at the commencement of the offensive, for a total of 3,200,000 men. It gathered on the Eastern Front 17 of its 21 panzer divisions—two were located in Libya and two were being re-built—for a total of 3,350 tanks, in other words almost one thousand more than during the French campaign, plus 250 assault guns. It also placed on the frontline its 13 motorized divisions and 7,146 pieces of artillery. Such an assemblage is, however, rather deceptive. With 153 divisions, the Wehrmacht only had at its disposal 12 more divisions than during the French campaign. If it were counting on the additional seven panzer divisions and the seven motorized divisions, it nevertheless had two fewer infantry divisions and a significantly inferior number of aircraft. With having to leave a third of its formations in Scandinavia, on the coasts of the English Channel, and on the Mediterranean, for a total of 1,766 aircraft, the Luftwaffe deployed only 2,510 aircraft on the Eastern Front, slightly fewer than had been on the Western Front the previous year.[218]

Enormously underestimating the numbers of the Red Army, the OKH thought it had a completely adequate number of forces to defeat the adversary in a single campaign. On the eve of the invasion, its intelligence service evaluated the numbers of the Red Army deployed in the European region of the Soviet Union at 226 divisions, of which 10 were armored and 37 motorized. Of these 226 large units, only 187 were mobilized, including 8 armored and 32 motorized. In addition, it estimated that the Soviets possessed 10,000 tanks and 8,000 aircraft.

In reality, the Red Army deployed 198 divisions in the western region of Russia, including 28 divisions placed in reserve, out of a total of 303 divisions. If one were to add to the 198 deployed divisions on the Western Front, the 60 others in the process of being mobilized or transported to the front, the Soviet high command would be able to count on 258 divisions to counter the Wehrmacht aggression during the first weeks of Operation Barbarossa. Of the 170 frontline divisions, 36 were armored and 19 motorized. Several others were placed in reserve or deployed in Asia, for the U.S.S.R. had use of some 60 large armored units and an additional 30 motorized divisions. In short, the Red Army placed on the Western Front 2.9 million men out of a total number of 5 million, nearly 15,000 tanks out of 24,000, some 9,000 aircraft out of 23,000, and close to 35,000 pieces of artillery out of 148,000.[219]

That the OKH underestimated the opposing forces to such an extent not only stems from a worldview based on racial ideology, but also on the blatant failure of its intelligence service. Yet the Germans were not the only ones to underestimate Soviet power. At the time the Wehrmacht entered into the U.S.S.R. on June 22, the British and American authorities were expecting an extremely easy German victory over the Red Army. Their evaluations of the duration of Soviet resistance varied between ten days and three months. This demonstrated the failure of the intelligence services of the Anglo-Saxon powers, as well, to obtain any solid information on the Red Army.[220]

Authorized barbarism: The criminal orders of the Wehrmacht

In Manstein's opinion, it was unrealistic to believe that Germany was capable of defeating the U.S.S.R. in a single campaign. "For this," he asserted after the war, "it would have been necessary to cause simultaneously the collapse of the regime from the interior." Yet, he adds, the brutal policy that Hitler applied in the occupied territories by the SS and the SD, contrary to the aspirations of the military chiefs, was only able to produce the opposite effect. "Thus disappeared," he concluded, "the unique opportunity to win a rapid victory which had perhaps [once] existed."[221]

However, it turned out that the Wehrmacht chiefs became accomplices of the Hitler regime in his policy of extermination in the East by willingly participating in the drafting and execution of criminal orders aimed at the elimination of Jews, political commissars of the Red Army, partisans, and Soviet prisoners of war. Manstein himself gave orders that encouraged his troops to commit criminal actions against the representatives of Jewish Bolshevism. In fact, the conquest of living space in the East, the economic exploitation of occupied territories, and the extermination of Jewish Bolshevism formed an integral whole, not only for the high military command, but also for the majority of the senior officers, including Manstein, as we will later see. Because National Socialist ideological convictions were imbued with anti-Bolshevism, anti-Semitism, and anti-Slavism, which they shared in various degrees, the large majority of generals could not envision a fight against the U.S.S.R. any differently than in the form of a war of destruction and annihilation.

The "new order" that the National Socialist leaders desired was guided by the following principal objective: a Europe governed by Germany, for which the resources would be exploited to the Reich's advantage, for which the inhabitants would become slaves to the German race, the "race of the lords" *par excellence*, and of which the "undesirable elements"—the Jews primarily, but equally a large number of Slavs in the East—in particular their political, intellectual, and religious elites—would be exterminated. In the eyes of the Nazi elites, the Jews and the Slavic people were nothing other than inferior beings (*Untermenschen*). Consequently, they did not have the right to live, with the exception of those among the Slavs who were needed to labor in the fields or work in the mines, as simple slaves, on behalf of their German masters.

As a racially-obsessed community, the Third Reich thus fought against racially inferior nations with the goal of conquest, exploiting mineral and agricultural resources, reducing the populations to slavery, and sending German colonists in order to better dominate, administer, and exploit the territories. The substitution of a racial state in place of a traditional state, which Manstein seems to have never fully understood, logically led to the racist behavior of the war. As a result, the Wehrmacht would lead in the Soviet Union a criminal war of extermination and annihilation, thus breaking the most elementary rules of war.

The decision to attack the U.S.S.R. thus proceeded simultaneously from strategic, political, military, economic, and ideological considerations. The program of expansion in the East, the destruction of Bolshevism, and the extermination of the Jews were, in short, concepts inextricably linked together. The necessity to destroy once and for all Jewish Bolshevism resulted at the same time from the necessity of obtaining the security required for *Lebensraum* and ensuring for the

Third Reich its political and military domination over the European continent. However, it was only in March 1941 that the Führer began to insist on the priority of the ideological objectives of Operation Barbarossa.[222]

The role that Hitler assigned to the Wehrmacht during the preparations for the invasion in spring 1941 leaves no doubt as to the army's implication in the crimes committed by Nazi Germany. On March 3, the remarks of General Jodl, chief of the OKW operations bureau, on the directives of Operation Barbarossa, which had been given him by Hitler on February 26, for the purposes of revision, could not have been any clearer: "All of the Bolshevik leaders or commissars must be immediately eliminated." On March 31, the revised version of Field Marshal Keitel, as chief of OKW general staff, indicated that *Reichsführer-SS* Himmler had received from the Führer certain special missions inside the army's zone of operations. Such a limitation of military jurisdiction brought about no protest within the army high command.[223]

On March 26, Lieutenant General Eduard Wagner, chief of the supply corps within the OKH and *SS-Gruppenführer* Reinhardt Heydrich, chief of the police force and the SD, laid the foundations for an agreement between the Wehrmacht and the SD tracing the demarcation line between the areas of responsibility of the two organizations in the elimination of enemies of National Socialism. The next day, Field Marshal Brauchitsch, addressing his commanders of the Eastern campaign, brought to their attention the completely distinctive nature of the war against the Soviet Union: "The troops have to realize that this struggle is being waged by one race against another, and proceed with the necessary harshness." From that moment, the Wehrmacht was already in complete adherence to the ideological objectives of the Nazi regime: to eradicate and annihilate without pity the Jewish Bolshevik foundations of the Soviet regime.[224]

Following such a declaration from the commander in chief of the OKH, General Manstein could not be unaware that it was a looming battle between two ideologies, between two racial conceptions, which excluded all chivalrous forms of warfare. If he nevertheless still had any doubts, they could only have been dispelled by the Führer's speech at the Reich Chancellery on March 30, which he attended. Before more than 250 senior officers commanding the units which were preparing to invade the U.S.S.R., Hitler presented, in the clearest of terms, his vision of the imminent war with the Jewish Bolshevik enemy, and explained what he expected from the Wehrmacht. It was not a question of speaking about strategy and tactics, but of presenting to his generals the nature of the conflict in which they were going to engage: a racial war of extermination. This discourse is of major historical importance, for by guaranteeing the proposals that the Führer set forth, thus by accepting to prepare and lead a racial war of annihilation in the East, the generals definitively sealed the ideological alliance between Hitler and the Wehrmacht.

The ideological goals of the war presented by Hitler to his high-ranking generals were transcribed by Halder: "*Class of two ideologies*: Crushing denunciation of Bolshevism, identified with asocial criminality. Communism is an enormous danger for our future. We must forget the concept of comradeship between soldiers. A Communist is no comrade before nor after the battle. This is a war of extermination. If we do not grasp this, we shall still beat the enemy, but 30 years later we shall again have to fight the Communist foe. We do not wage war to preserve the enemy. *War against Russia*: Extermination of the Bolshevik commissars and of the Communist intelligentsia. [...] We must fight against the poison of disintegration. This is no job for military courts. The individual troop commanders must realize the issues at stake. They must be leaders in this fight. [...] Commissars and GPU men are criminals and must be dealt with as such. [...] Commanders must make the sacrifice of overcoming their personal scruples." The war in the East was thus going to be very different from the one in the West.

After the Führer's discourse and his numerous other remarks made in private associating Bolshevism with "Jewry," after measures taken by the Reich since 1933 against these enemies of National Socialism, and especially after the murders perpetrated on a large scale in Poland at the expense of the Polish intelligentsia and the Jews, there could remain no more doubt on the part of the generals, including Manstein, that the leading Communist class and the Jews of the Soviet occupied territories would also be exterminated.[225]

Even though his notion of an ideological war against Bolshevism had been familiar to the generals for quite some time through his numerous public and private remarks, Hitler nevertheless called upon them for specific actions against the representatives of Bolshevism, in other words against the civil servants to the state and the Communist

Party, and the political commissars of the Red Army. He denied them any military status and demanded that they be treated as criminals. His formula with regards to the "poison of disintegration" surely conjured up memories among his audience of the disintegration of the Kaiser's army in the autumn of 1918, which Nazi propaganda attributed to Bolshevik agitation.

As the principal representatives of Bolshevism, the "Jewry" had transmitted to the soldiers the ferment of the Bolshevik revolution, thus leading to the subsequent disintegration of the armed forces and the overthrowing of the Bismarck Reich. Such an interpretation of the causes of the fall of imperial Germany was widely accepted and deeply internalized by the generals, notably Manstein, as we have previously seen. It goes without saying that the correlation between the interior enemy of the Reich at the time and the exterior enemy of the new Reich—specifically the Soviet Union or, in its more simplistic form, Jewish Bolshevism—encountered fertile ground. And so, for a good number of officers, it appeared normal that the war against the leading Jewish Bolshevik class would not be waged according to the rules of international law and military traditions; and so Hitler succeeded at leading the army, beyond its strictly military tasks, into a war of annihilation against an ideology and its representatives.[226]

In the weeks that followed Hitler's March 30 speech, the supreme commanders of the Wehrmacht and the army willingly and enthusiastically drafted orders that were in close conformity with the extremist perspective of the war to come. If the inspiration came from Hitler, the implementation of this series of orders on how the war in the East would be waged was clearly the doing of the military chiefs—and their legal counsellors—all impatient to fulfill his desires.

The first order to enter directly into the framework defined by Hitler at the time of his March 30 speech concerned the fate reserved to segments of the Soviet population organized under the category of enemies of the Reich, and the determination of the respective areas of responsibility for the SS and the German Army. The meeting that occurred on April 16, 1941, between Lieutenant General Wagner and *SS-Gruppenführer* Heydrich was expressed through an order designed by Field Marshal Brauchitsch on April 28, 1941, and had the name "agreement on the intervention of the police force and the SD in the army units" (*Regelung des Einsatzes der Sicherheitspolizei und des SD im Verbande des Heeres*). It ordered the Wehrmacht officers to collaborate logistically and operationally with the *Einsatzgruppen*, special forces of the SD in charge of eliminating the Jews and the Bolshevik intelligentsia behind the front.

Furthermore, an agreement between the OKH and the SD set the number of *Einsatzgruppen* that would go into action and advance in the footsteps of the Wehrmacht to four. *Einsatzgruppe A* was posted to Army Group North in the Baltic region; *Einsatzgruppe B* to Army Group Center in Belorussia; *Einsatzgruppe C* to Army Group South in central and northern Ukraine; and *Einsatzgruppe D* to the Eleventh Army in Bessarabia, southern Ukraine, and in the Crimea. Thus an *Einsatzgruppe* was to be appointed to each army group and to the Eleventh Army. In turn, the army group and the Eleventh Army were to dispatch the *Einsatzkommandos* or *Sonderkommandos*—special units of an *Einsatzgruppe*—next to each of the armies (or divisions in the case of the Eleventh Army). In addition, the agreement stipulated that the three army groups and the Eleventh Army would be responsible for the movement and resupply of the *Einsatzgruppen*, but that the orders concerning their activities would come from the chiefs of the SD. Even though the SD were the only ones to have the right to give orders to the *Einsatzgruppen* regarding their activities, there existed a general agreement, in terms of which the OKH also had the right to issue them directives if the course of operations demanded it.[227]

The second order was the "decree on the exercise of the war in the 'Barbarossa' zone" (*Erlaß über die Ausübung des Kriegsgerichtsbarkeit im Gebiet "Barbarossa"*), more commonly termed the "Barbarossa decree." Drafted by the legal branch of the OKW on May 13, 1941, it defined the application of the military code within the framework of Operation Barbarossa. Any reprehensible acts committed by civilians were excluded from the jurisdiction of military tribunals. In other words, the decree authorized troops to take the law into their own hands for all hostile acts on the part of civilians. Those who participated in guerilla warfare were to be executed without any form of trial. In cases where guilty individuals could not readily be identified, collective retaliations against entire communities were to be ordered. As for crimes against civilians or enemy prisoners, they would only be court martialed in case there was a breach of military discipline in battle.

Such a limitation in the area of application of martial law in the

U.S.S.R. followed, as it were, the Führer's decree of amnesty of October 4, 1939 in Poland. However, the execution of civilians suspected of guerilla activities or sabotage was clearly illegal. Even the accusation of threatening the security of the troops could not serve as a pretext to abandon the most fundamental of human rights. In fact, the "Barbarossa decree" granted to the German soldiers a veritable permit to kill. Field Marshal Bock, commander in chief of Army Group Center, was not wrong to assert that the decree gave every soldier the right to execute any civilian that he suspected of guerilla warfare or sabotage. The "Barbarossa decree" thus constituted not only an indisputable perversion of traditional military values, but also a patent violation of the rules of war.

The "Barbarossa decree" was followed by the "directives on the conduct of troops in Russia" (*Richtlinien für das Verhalten der Truppe in Rußland*) drafted by the OKH on May 19, 1941. They presented Jewish Bolshevism as "the mortal enemy of the German National Socialist people" and demanded "swift and merciless actions against the Bolshevik agitators, partisans, saboteurs, and Jews, as well as the complete elimination of any active or passive resistance." In short, they ordered the soldiers to act brutally and mercilessly against resistance fighters and Jews.

Finally, the "directives for the treatment of political commissars" (*Richtlinien für die Behandlung politischer Kommissare*) of June 6, 1941, more commonly known as the Commissar Order (*Kommissarbefehl*), denied political commissars, even though they were fully committed members of the Red Army, the status of combatant and, as a result, the right to request protection for themselves under the Hague Convention. In fact, the directives ordered their immediate execution on the battlefield on the premise that in ideological terms the political commissar presented a formidable threat to the security of the Wehrmacht and the pacification of the occupied territories. The order had its roots in precedents and it was the OKH that was both the instigator and the author.[228]

The supreme commanders of the Wehrmacht and the army both realized that the systematic elimination of the political cadres of the Red Army constituted a flagrant infraction of international law, all the more so since the actual motives of their obligatory execution was based less on simple presuppositions of guerilla activities or resistance to the

Wehrmacht than on the official duties that they occupied within the governmental apparatus. It was for this reason that, to legitimize such severe actions, they insisted upon the necessity of resorting to preventive reprisals against the agents of Bolshevism within the Red Army who, according to them, were not genuine soldiers and represented a most serious danger to the security of the Wehrmacht and the pacification of the territories.

The indulgence and complicity with which the military leaders accepted Hitler's directives inviting them to conduct a criminal war in the East was not in the least surprising, given their attitude in Poland which, a year-and-a-half earlier, had practically pushed the army into a criminal landslide. Far from being obliged to force his will on the Wehrmacht, Hitler, to the contrary, could count on the enthusiastic collaboration of his military chiefs. Indeed, not only did the majority of the senior generals accept Hitler's ideological theories of the war in the East, they were even keen to the idea of waging a crusade against Jewish Bolshevism. The ideological symbiosis between the Wehrmacht and the Nazi regime had never before reached such a degree of intimacy.

Two examples pay witness to the high level of the generals' affinity with the Führer's ideological concepts. First, Colonel General Küchler, commander of the Eighteenth Army, defined for his subordinates on April 25 the real issues of the war in the East. He at once declared to them that peace could only be achieved on a long-term basis in Europe if the German people occupied territory that would assure it, and other European states, of fresh resources. But this was inconceivable without a confrontation with the Soviet Union. In terms hardly different than those pronounced by Hitler during his March 30 speech, he continued: "We are separated from Russia, ideologically and racially, by a deep abyss. R[ussia] is, if only by the mass of her territory, an Asian state. [...] If Germany wishes to live in peace for generations, safe from the threatening danger in the east, this cannot be a case of pushing R[ussia] back a little—or even hundreds of kilometers—but the aim must be to annihilate European Russia, to dissolve the Russ[ian] state in Europe. [...] The political commissars and the GPU people are criminals. They are the people who enslave the population. [...] They are to be put before a court martial and sentenced on the strength of the testimony of the inhabitants. [...] It will save us German blood and we shall make headway faster."

Next, the operational orders given to the 4th Panzer Group—to which Manstein's 56th Panzer Corps was attached—by its commander in chief, Colonel General Hoepner, on May 2, even before the drafting of the Commissar Order, was even more categorical: "The war against Russia is an essential phase in the German nation's struggle for existence. It is the ancient struggle of the Germanic peoples against Slavdom, the defense of European culture against the Muscovite-Asiatic tide, the repulse of Jewish Bolshevism. That struggle must have as its aim the shattering of present-day Russia and must therefore be waged with unprecedented hardness. Every combat action must be inspired, in concept and execution, by an iron determination to ensure the merciless, total annihilation of the enemy. In particular, there must be no sparing the exponents of the present Russian Bolshevik system."[229]

As a significant and meaningful fact, General Manstein, commander of the 56th Panzer Corps, would himself issue, before the beginning of Operation Barbarossa, an order to his troops which corresponded in every respect to the idea of the war (*Weltanschauungskrieg*) in the East that Hitler promoted, and which made him complicit as a criminal war. On June 12, 1941, he set forth the following directive to his men: "This fight demands ruthless and forceful measures against the Bolshevik agitators, the mavericks, the partisans, and the Jews."[230] The necessity to annihilate the Jewish Bolshevik enemy could not have been expressed more clearly.

In addition, in light of his actions on the Eastern Front, General Manstein seems to have been part of the circle of German officers who did not consider the political commissars of the Red Army as officers, but rather as paramilitary civil servants who supervised the command of the actual officers and tried to rouse the enthusiasm of the troops in combat. Clearly, in his *Memoirs* he takes care to qualify his opinion concerning the status of political commissars of the Red Army, placing it midway between those of soldiers and noncombatants. Yet he considers the commissars as nothing less than criminals, most certainly to implicitly legitimize the treatment that was reserved for them by the Wehrmacht and his own troops: "With good reason, one could harbor doubts as to the status of the commissars within international law. They were assuredly not soldiers, but one could neither attribute them the status of noncombatant [...]. They were, furthermore without being soldiers, fanatical combatants whose activity, in the traditional sense, could be considered nothing more than illegal. Their role was not only to monitor the military chiefs from a political point of view, but to breathe the most violent hatred into battle by giving it a character absolutely contrary to normal ideas. In fact, they were the first to be held responsible for such combat methods and the treatment of prisoners, which so overtly violated the Hague conventions."[231]

In fact, Lieutenant Colonel Tresckow, deputy chief of staff of Army Group Center, was one of the only ones to have expressed any reservations regarding the planned violation of the rules of war. "If international law is to be infringed," he observed on May 10, 1941, "it should be done by the Russians and not by us." As his remark proves, it was evident that the Commissar Order contravened international law. However, it was precisely because the large majority of senior officers did not share Tresckow's viewpoint that the Führer was able to suspend so easily the fundamental principles of the law of war.[232]

The complicity of the majority of generals was inscribed in the very manner in which they had been raised and educated, in their way of thinking. They were in favor of the creation of a Greater German Reich in central and eastern Europe which would dominate the entire continent. Contempt for the Slavs was profoundly rooted within the officers' corps. The visceral hatred of Bolshevism was rife in all of the senior ranks of the Wehrmacht, and anti-Semitism was also widespread among them, although rarely in Hitler's radical form. Such an ideological relationship with the Nazi leaders thus explains somewhat better why the generals had no difficulty in engaging their troops in a war of conquest and annihilation in the East. One can thus not cite the officers' obedience or even their subservience as an explanation of their behavior in the U.S.S.R.

By expressing the Führer's ideological intentions in the East in the form of military orders, the chiefs of the OKW and the OKH thus contributed to transforming the Wehrmacht into an instrument perfectly adapted to the war of annihilation against the encroaching Jewish Bolshevism. They had become full participants in Hitler's game, which consisted of transferring onto the Wehrmacht the horrible deeds of the provocative and incendiary madness of the National Socialist regime. Yet they no less judged the collaboration of their units with those of the SD as being essential to achieving a lasting hold on the conquered territories. For this, the Wehrmacht was inevitably required to assist the

Einsatzgruppen in their common fight against the deadly Jewish Bolshevik enemy by eliminating the political commissars of the Red Army, the civil servants of the Communist Party, the Jews, the partisans, and any civilian suspected of guerilla warfare or sabotage. The military battle for the conquest of *Lebensraum* in the East, the criminal political measures for its pacification, and its economic exploitation were thus various facets of a great war of annihilation against the Soviet Union and its population.[233]

Contrary to what has been suggested after the war, Manstein and his fellow generals were in absolutely no way soldiers who had been deceived or victims of fanatical political leaders. They were rather fully committed accomplices to the Hitler regime and entirely guilty of actions in violation of the rules of war which they more or less actively ordered or tolerated. There existed a completely natural sense of community between the Nazi leadership and that of the Wehrmacht. Far from being simple accomplices, they in fact formed a genuine alliance. The two organizations shared similar preoccupations and a completely compatible world vision, particularly concerning the political, ideological, and strategic objectives in the East. Consequently, the Wehrmacht was not an entity separate from the Nazi apparatus, but truly an instrument that voluntarily placed itself at the service of the regime.

The war in the East, which would decide the future of the European continent, was clearly more than "Hitler's war." It was not imposed by an all-powerful dictator upon a recalcitrant military elite. Far from it. They rallied behind it with indulgence and enthusiasm. Like ordinary Germans, they adopted the theme that Nazi propaganda was applying to the conflict: "a crusade against Bolshevism." Indeed, they would accept without any difficulty the idea of a preventive war in order to keep the "hordes of Asiatic Bolsheviks" from destroying Western culture. As a result, they believed more than ever that Europe would not be free as long as Jewish Bolshevism had not been eradicated. A legacy of more than two decades of visceral, often fanatical hatred of Bolshevism, often profoundly accompanied by anti-Semitism, was about to emerge into a genocidal war, particularly into the Jewish Holocaust.[234]

IX

THE CONQUEST OF THE CRIMEA

As commander of the 56th Panzer Corps, General Manstein gained an extraordinary reputation in the summer of 1941 by advancing into Soviet territory more rapidly than anyone else at the head of a large rapid unit, and moreover in a region that was hardly suitable for tank maneuvers. He demonstrated that he was, along with Colonel General Guderian, an officer who thoroughly understood the demands of mobile warfare in the era of motorization.

For the offensive, General Manstein's 56th Panzer Corps was incorporated into Colonel General Hoepner's 4th Panzer Group, which was part of Field Marshal Leeb's Army Group North. On June 26, 1941, Manstein's troops seized Dünaburg (Daugavpils). In four days, they had already advanced 300 kilometers inside Soviet territory, an average of 75 kilometers per day. Leningrad was located no more than approximately 550 kilometers away. Such success was due to the fact that Manstein did not hesitate to rapidly charge forward without regard to flank cover. Moreover, the 41st Panzer Corps and the Sixteenth Army of Army Group North were located 100 to 150 kilometers to his rear. In order to avoid a Soviet attack on the exposed flanks of Manstein's armored corps, the German high command forced him to halt for six days on the Dvina River, time enough for the Sixteenth Army and the 41st Panzer Corps to catch up with him.

He was disappointed when he received orders to await the arrival of the other formations. Without disregarding the possibility of a counterattack from the enemy, he nevertheless thought that if permitted to continue his advance, the appearance of his armored corps so far behind enemy lines would doubtless have provoked enormous confusion in the Soviets' rear. The farther his corps advanced, he asserted, the less the adversary would be in a position to systematically deploy superior forces ahead of him. He recalled his understanding of the situation as such: "Of course, the risks increased as the corps or the armored group plunged deep into Soviet territory. But the security of a large rapid unit, operating behind enemy lines, rests above all on its mobility. If it stops, it is immediately attacked by the opposing reserves."

The six-day halt permitted the Soviets to create new lines of defense. If not for the pause, Manstein believed that he would have been capable of quickly seizing Leningrad. Such a stunning raid would inevitably provoke confusion and panic among the civilians, destroy lines of communication, and render the enemy almost incapable of reacting in a coordinated way. Yet by stopping for six days on the Dvina, he asserted, the 56th Panzer Corps had definitively lost such an advantage.[235] And so, during the following weeks, he had to engage in numerous battles between Lakes Ilmen and Peipus in order to repel the enemy's repeated counterattacks.

On September 12, Manstein received orders from the OKH to set off immediately for Army Group South in order to take command of the Eleventh Army. It was with joy that he received the announcement of such a great promotion in his military career. His new appointment was an indication of the more and more dominant role played by Hitler in military matters for, not being in the good graces of the OKH, it cannot be said that without the Führer's intervention he would have been assigned to lead the Eleventh Army, despite his remarkable performance in the Baltic region.[236]

The Crimean campaign would permit Manstein to distinguish himself as commander in chief of an army. With the capture of the fortress of Sevastopol, recognized as the strongest in the world, he would receive his field marshal baton, which represented in his eyes the crowning achievement of his military career. From that point on, this virtuoso of mobile warfare would be considered by his Führer as a master in the art of laying siege to a city or a fortress, indeed even as a sort of "secret weapon" for perilous missions.

The situation when Manstein took command of the Eleventh Army

On September 17, General Manstein arrived at the headquarters of the Eleventh Army, positioned at the military port of Nikolaev, at the mouth of the Bug, then, beginning on September 21, at Askania Nova. His predecessor, Colonel General Eugen Ritter von Schobert, had been killed on September 2, after his plane made a forced landing into a minefield during one of his regular visits to the front.

The staff of the Eleventh Army, from which a nucleus of officers would later successively form the staffs of Army Groups Don and South, would prove to be excellent. In the first volume of his *Memoirs*, Manstein made reference to the staff that was to remain with him for two-and-a-half years of extremely difficult warfare. In his eyes, the group was composed almost entirely of highly valued officers. Among them, there was his chief of staff, Colonel Otto Wohler, "whose unshakeable composure," he recalls, "was of priceless assistance to me at those times of crisis during the Crimea campaign," and above all his chief of operations, Lieutenant Colonel Theodor Busse, who would go on to be appointed chief of staff of Army Group South and remain with it until the very end. "During all of these difficult years," writes Manstein with respect to Busse, "he was my most invaluable advisor, not only because he was a man of good judgment, but also because he was a man of tireless activity who never once lost control of his nerves in critical situations. In addition, he became my most loyal friend. After the war, he sacrificed more than a year [...] to remain at my side in order to contribute to my defense during my trial."[237]

General Manstein had two army corps under his command plus one mountain corps and one Romanian army, lent by Marshal Ion Atonescu, head of the Romanian state. On the southern wing, General Hans von Salmuth's 30th Infantry Corps joined together the 22nd and 72nd Infantry Divisions and the motorized SS division *Leibstandarte Adolf Hitler*. The latter was the only mobile unit of the Eleventh Army. On the northern wing, General Ludwig Kübler's 49th Mountain Corps was composed of the 170th Infantry Division, as well as the 1st and 4th Mountain Divisions. These two groups had pursued the defeated enemy across the Dnieper River, and were approaching the axis defined by Melitopol and the Dnieper bend to the south of Zaporojie. Another army corps, General Christian Hansen's 54th, was advancing with the 46th and 73rd Infantry Divisions towards the Perekop Isthmus. The 50th Infantry Division, partly under the command of the Fourth Romanian Army, remained in front of Odessa and cleared the coast of the Black Sea. The Third Romanian Army, whose combat merit was far below that of comparable German units, included a mountain corps (1st, 2nd, and 4th Brigades) and a cavalry corps (5th, 6th, and 8th Brigades), and was still to the west of the Dnieper.

The OKH had assigned the Eleventh Army a double mission which was to lead it in two opposing directions. First, while advancing on the right wing of Army Group South, it was to pursue the enemy troops retreating to the east. For this, it was necessary to pass alongside the northern coast of the Azov Sea and take hold of Rostov-on-Don, a vital crossing point near the mouth of the Don. Second, it had to capture the Crimea, particularly the military port of Sevastopol. This would exert a favorable influence over Turkey, which had long vied with Russia in the region; eliminate Soviet air bases that constituted a threat to the Romanian oilfield regions which were of vital significance to the Reich's war economy; and eliminate the threat that existed on the right flank of Army Group South's offensive. After the conquest of the Crimean peninsula, the mountain corps would cross the Kerch Strait toward the Caucasus, eventually to pursue an offensive beyond Rostov-on-Don.

However, the Eleventh Army was incapable of fulfilling this double mission with the forces made available to it. It could only accomplish one mission at a time. But which of the two should it favor? For Manstein, the priority should be granted to the Crimea. With the enemy retaining control of the Black Sea, the peninsula represented a danger to the Eleventh Army's southern flank, without mentioning the aerial threat over regions of the Romanian oilfields. As a result, the advance on Rostov-on-Don quite simply had to be postponed.

The Crimea was largely separated from the continent by the Sea of Sivach. The surrounding marshes were impassable by infantry, since accompanying artillery and supply vehicles could not get through. In fact, only two land routes led to the Crimea: to the west, the Perekop Isthmus; to the east, the Arabat strip, which was too narrow for any sort of offensive. Only seven kilometers wide, the Perekop Isthmus would only allow for a frontal attack across land that had absolutely no cover. It offered no possibility of a flanking maneuver. Additionally, the Red Army had organized a solid defense line across its entire width. After having surmounted this line, the Germans would confront another, the Isthmus of Ichoun, around which salt lakes reduced its width to between three and four kilometers.

While taking into consideration the enemy's ground and aerial superiority, nothing guaranteed that the 54th Infantry Corps, after having eventually taken the Perekop Isthmus, would remain strong enough to take that of Ichoun. Two divisions would certainly not suffice to capture the Crimea, including Sevastopol. To quickly succeed, it would be necessary to remove units engaged in the pursuit of the enemy around the Melitopol-Dnieper bend line and postpone the advance on Rostov-on-Don. Manstein thus handed over to the 54th Corps all of the Eleventh Army's artillery, engineers, and anti-aircraft units. He also called upon the 50th Infantry Division, still far to the rear, for the forcing of the Isthmus of Ichoun, and the 49th Mountain Corps for the rapid taking of the peninsula after crossing each isthmus.

According to the OKH's orders, the corps was then to cross the Kerch Strait in order to advance towards the Caucasus. It would meantime be of great use to occupy the southern mountainous region of the Crimea. In addition, the motorized SS division *Leibstandarte Adolf Hitler* would be utilized for the capture of Sevastopol. In order to compensate for the weakening of Army Group South's flank, the Third Romanian Army and the 22nd Infantry Division were summoned forward.[238]

The forcing of the Perekop Isthmus and the Battle of the Sea of Azov

On September 24, General Hansen's 54th Corps launched its attack on the Perekop Isthmus. The Red Army had organized its defenses fifteen kilometers deep and fiercely defended each trench, each base of operations. The corps, driving back violent counterattacks, nevertheless succeeded in taking Perekop on September 26. In spite of the severity of the battles and the enemy's ground and aerial superiority, it broke through the fortified zone at the end of three more days. The enemy was forced to retreat to the Ichoun Isthmus after having suffered severe losses, and leaving 10,000 prisoners, 112 tanks, and 135 pieces of artillery in German hands.[239]

But the corps was unable to take advantage of the situation by definitively breaking all the way through to the Crimea. The ratio of forces in favor of the enemy and the severe losses that the corps had suffered prevented it from immediately taking the Ichoun Isthmus. Manstein's intention to bring up fresh units—the 49th Mountain Corps and the *Leibstandarte Adolf Hitler*—was on the other hand thwarted by the enemy. On September 26, the Soviets launched a counterattack with two armies, the Ninth and the Eighteenth, composed of twelve divisions, on the right flank of Army Group South. While it was held back in the sector of the 30th Corps, this was not true in the area of the Third Romanian Army, where the Russians opened a breach of fifteen kilometers and threatened to push the invaders all the way back to the Dnieper. The commander in chief of the Eleventh Army thus lost his bet: that of accepting the risk of a Soviet counteroffensive on the eastern flank of his troops near Melitopol, to the north of the Azov Sea, in order to quickly seize the Crimea through a concentration of the largest possible number of units on the Perekop front.

To restore the situation, he did not have a choice. He had to order the German mountain corps to make an about-face, the OKH having withdrawn his only rapid unit, the *Leibstandarte Adolf Hitler*, to employ it in the direction of Rostov-on-Don. Forced to send it back to mainland, Manstein was thus unable to use it to capitalize on the Perekop success. In this case, it was as much about taking advantage of the opportunity offered by the enemy who, because of his counterattack, was no longer able to dispose of operational reserves to guard against a crossing of the Dnieper at Zaporojie and Dniepropetrovsk, from where Colonel General Kleist's 1st Panzer Group could attack on its northern flank and the Eleventh Army on its southern flank. Manstein proposed this joint operation to Field Marshal Rundstedt, commander in chief of Army Group South, and it was thus ordered on October 1.

The pressure from the armored group was quickly felt, since on the very next day the Russian units beat a retreat towards the east. The 30th Corps, the 49th Mountain Corps, and the Third Romanian Army immediately moved in pursuit of the enemy. On October 6, Melitopol was taken and elements of the 49th Mountain Corps and the 1st Panzer Group joined together to the south of the town of Orechov. During the following four days, the Ninth and Eighteenth Soviet Armies were encircled and then destroyed in the Tokmak-Mariupol-Berdiansk zone by the 1st Panzer Group, the *Leibstandarte Adolf Hitler*, elements of the 30th Corps, the 49th Mountain Corps, and the Third Romanian Army.

At the end of the battle of the Sea of Azov, which ended on October 10, the Eleventh Army had captured 27,000 prisoners, 64 tanks, and 130 pieces of artillery. The joint captures of the Eleventh Army and the

1st Panzer Group were 106,362 prisoners, 212 tanks, and 672 cannon.[240] Such a clear-cut success was indebted to Manstein, who knew how to employ both force and daring by seizing the occasion to crush the enemy counterattack with the assistance of Kleist's panzers, even despite the critical situation in which his own army found itself.

The forcing of the Ichoun Isthmus and the pursuit of the enemy in the Crimea

Following the battle of the Sea of Azov, the OKH proceeded with a reorganization of the southern wing of the Eastern Front. It had clearly recognized that a single army could not simultaneously lead an operation towards Rostov-on-Don and another into the Crimea. The first was thus entrusted to Kleist's 1st Panzer Group, to which the Eleventh Army was to yield the 49th Mountain Corps and the SS *Leibstandarte*. To compensate, the Eleventh Army received from the OKH Lieutenant General Hans Graf von Sponeck's 42nd Infantry Corps, consisting of the 24th, 42nd, and 132nd Infantry Divisions. Besides this corps, Manstein also had the use of two others: the 30th (the 22nd, 72nd, and 120th Infantry Divisions) and the 54th (the 46th, 73rd, and 50th Infantry Divisions, a third of the latter remaining positioned before Odessa). As for the Third Romanian Army, which was returning under the orders of the marshal and Romanian head of state Antonescu, it was in charge of ensuring the protection of the shores of the Black Sea and the Sea of Azov. At Manstein's request, Antonescu accepted, however, to leave him his mountain corps, with one cavalry brigade and another mountain brigade to guard the eastern coast of the Crimea.

Despite the Eleventh Army's reinforcement, the opposing enemy still possessed a numerical superiority. To the nine German infantry divisions, the Russians would soon oppose eight infantry divisions and four cavalry divisions, after having evacuated Odessa on October 16 and transporting their units into the Crimea. In addition to coastal batteries, the Russians disposed of tanks, which the Eleventh Army was totally lacking. However, the Germany artillery was superior to its rival.[241]

Relieved of the responsibility of protecting its eastern flank to the north of the Sesa of Azov ever since the advance towards Rostov-on-Don had been entrusted to Kleist's 1st Panzer Group, Manstein's Eleventh Army could now concentrate its primary forces on capturing the Crimea. With the Perekop Isthmus having already been crossed, the following task was to breach the Ichoun Isthmus. The nature of the terrain did not permit, however, any sort of flanking maneuver. The attack could only be frontal and occur along three strips of narrow land, cut apart by lakes, with the Gulf of Karkinit to the west and the Sea of Sivach to the east. The width of these strips only allowed the three divisions of the 54th Corps to engage at the start of the attack; the 30th Corps could take part only once the Germans had gained enough space to the south.

With the steppe not providing the assailants the slightest amount of cover, the advance of the 54th Corps was difficult and its losses considerable, even more so since it did not have the use of any armor to break quickly through the powerful enemy defenses. To add to the difficulties of its attack, the air space was largely dominated by the Soviet Air Force. Faced with the slowness of his troops' progress, visibly exhausted by the severity of battles and the significant losses, Manstein requested an armored corps from Army Group South—with at least two armored divisions and one motorized division—in order to force the enemies' defenses, along with Luftwaffe reinforcements to be able to contest the Soviet air superiority and also reduce the opposing artillery batteries established behind solid fortified positions. However, not having a single armored formation in reserve, Army Group South could only send him air reinforcements, which nevertheless proved to be sufficient. Success was finally achieved with the help of units from the 4th Air Fleet of Colonel Werner Mölders, who had been transferred from another sector of Army Group South's front. On October 28, on the tenth day of the attack, the Soviet resistance finally crumbled.

After the battle, the German captures amounted to 15,700 prisoners, 30 tanks, and 109 pieces of artillery. The Eleventh Army's losses were 1,195 killed, 5,588 wounded, and 249 missing in action. Since the September 24 attack against the Perekop Isthmus, Manstein's troops had already captured 53,175 prisoners.[242]

The Eleventh Army then went in pursuit of the enemy in the Crimea. On November 26, the entire peninsula, with the exception of the Sevastopol fortress, was in the hands of Manstein's men. There was no question of taking the fortress by surprise with infantry divisions, as it would have been necessary to have a fast armored or motorized division. "By granting this to us," commented Manstein after the war, "we would have been spared a great deal of blood, difficult winter battles, and a future assault of the fortress; we would also have soon had available an additional army for the other operations on the Eastern Front." All of his efforts to gain, in place of the motorized SS division *Leibstandarte Adolf Hitler*, the 60th Motorized Infantry Division, then incorporated into the First Army, were in vain, as Hitler was keen on seizing as quickly as possible Rostov-on-Don.

This was of little importance, for the Eleventh Army had almost completely annihilated the enemy in the open country. It had defeated two armies including a total of twelve infantry and four cavalry divisions. Out of approximately 200,000 men, the enemy had suffered considerable losses: 25,000 killed, 100,000 prisoners, 160 tanks, and 700 cannon. Only small remnants, without heavy weapons, had been able to cross the Kerch Strait or make it to the Sevastopol fortress. Through naval transport of personnel and supplies, these armies could however be quickly rehabilitated to a state of combat readiness.[243]

The Eleventh Army was nevertheless unable to make the most of the chase to seize through a raid the last enemy bastion in the Crimea. To conclude the assault on the Sevastopol fortress, it had to act quickly so as to deny the enemy time to organize itself and mount an intervention from the sea. It was equally necessary for it to concentrate the largest number of forces possible, even if it meant allowing the Russians to land at any favorable point on the inadequately defended coast. According to Manstein, it was better to accept extreme risks while clearing out the rest of the Crimea, in particular the Kerch Peninsula, than to compromise the success of the attack by executing it with too few forces.

In consideration of the time required for the deployment of troops and their resupply of munitions, the date for the commencement of operations was postponed to November 27. But the Russian winter, which was slowing down the most advanced elements of Army Group Center before Moscow, was also felt in the Crimea. Incessant rainfall beat down upon them, transforming into a nasty impassable quagmire the majority of the roads and paralyzing the supply convoys. Preparations for the attack were drawn out to such an extent that it could only begin on December 17. The enemy clearly took advantage of this delay of three weeks to reinforce its defenses and to prepare for an intervention from the sea.

At the end of December, while units of the Eleventh Army were engaged in heavy fighting against Sevastopol, with the exception of one German division and two Romanian brigades, the Soviets landed troops in Kerch, then in Feodosiya. The necessity to send reinforcements to the threatened areas as quickly as possible thus became most urgent.[244]

The failure of Operation Barbarossa: Manstein as commander of the German Army?

In the turmoil of the crisis during the winter of 1941–42, marked by the failure of Operation Barbarossa, several high-ranking officers were relieved of their command, in particular Field Marshal Brauchitsch, commander in chief of the OKH. An opportunity for General Manstein to succeed him thus presented itself, all the more so since certain generals wished that he take the position. But it was still necessary for the Führer to express his own desire for him to occupy this post.

The failure of Operation Barbarossa was recognized on December 5. While the Germans believed that Soviet resistance had reached a critical point, General Zhukov launched a powerful counteroffensive on the central front, on either side of Moscow, and inflicted upon the Wehrmacht its first great defeat. The myth of the German Army's invincibility was thus overturned. For the first time since September 1, 1939, the Wehrmacht found itself forced into a defensive position, the initiative having shifted, for a while, to the enemy camp. Panic stricken, several German generals ordered retreats that were conducted under the worst conditions, with the almost total abandonment of heavy weapons, tanks, trucks, and artillery.

Faced with the threat of collapse, Hitler issued to his troops on December 16 his famous *Haltbefehl*, a halt-order that this time was not meant to pause an advance but to stop a withdrawal. Forbidding any further retreats, he instructed the troops to "stand and fight." Even though certain generals contested it, the Führer's incredible stubbornness in demanding that his troops stand firm, regardless of the danger and losses, most certainly saved the German Army from collapse, sparing it from suffering the same fate as Napoleon's army.[245]

Emerging from the crisis of that winter, no fewer than 35 generals were dismissed for their retreats, albeit even minimal at times. On November 30, Field Marshal Rundstedt was relieved of his command of Army Group South after he abandoned Rostov-on-Don, despite the

Führer's formal order not to evacuate the town. He was replaced by Field Marshal Reichenau, who had until then been at the head of the Sixth Army. On December 18, Field Marshal Bock relinquished leadership of Army Group Center to Field Marshal Kluge, commander of the Fourth Army. On January 15, Field Marshal Leeb was unable to avoid his own turn in the purge that was scouring the high command. Colonel General Küchler, commander of the Sixteenth Army, succeeded him in command of Army Group North. Colonel Generals Guderian and Hoepner were dismissed, respectively, on December 26 and January 8 for each having ordered in turn a retreat of their panzer groups before Moscow without the Führer's prerequisite authorization.

The most significant dismissal, however, occurred on December 19. On this particular day, Hitler accepted the resignation of Field Marshal Brauchitsch, who was on the brink of a nervous breakdown and was having a difficult recovery from a heart attack he had suffered in November, and assumed command of the army himself. Hitler nevertheless retained Halder as chief of the army's general staff. The latter was apparently pleased by this turn of events. Far from rising up against what appeared to be a final blow to the army's independence from political power, to the contrary, he put up with the new situation rather well. It was a period of enthusiasm for him, thinking that he would thus be in direct contact with the Führer to make decisions, which would permit him to exert even greater influence. He also believed that he could work with Hitler better than with Brauchitsch.

With Brauchitsch having been placed on the sidelines more and more often as the crisis worsened, the change was in a way not as critical as it appeared. In the eyes of those who saw the disdain with which Hitler had been treating him for several weeks, his dismissal was hardly surprising. Placing the burden of responsibility for the winter crisis on him, Hitler displayed nothing but contempt for his former army commander in chief, who he treated as a coward and an incompetent. As for the latter, he was anxious to resign and tried to do so right after the Soviet counteroffensive during the first week of December, thinking of Field Marshal Kluge or General Manstein as possible successors.

At the time, Hitler confided hypocritically to his entourage that he did not have the slightest idea who could replace Brauchitsch, even though a number of people had been mentioning Manstein's and Kesselring's names for quite some time. As for Field Marshal Albert

Kesselring, known to be a tough and capable organizer, as well as an eternal optimist, he had just been appointed—on December 2, 1941—as commander in chief of the Mediterranean theater. During the night of December 16–17, at the instigation of Colonel Schmundt, his principal adjutant, Hitler finally made the decision to assume supreme command of the army himself.

At the height of the crisis, which ended with the "stand and fight" order, Hitler was convinced that taking charge of the army was nothing more than a "little matter of operational command [...] that anyone can do." In addition, he felt as if he had been failed by his military chiefs, even though they had pushed him, in the summer of 1940, to undertake the conquest of the U.S.S.R., assuring him that it would be defeated in less than three months. He was also of the opinion that his commanders were fainthearted, that they had not been tough enough during the winter crisis, and that only his willpower and determination had prevented the collapse of the army.

Slightly earlier during the day of December 16, General Jodl had discussed the critical situation on the Eastern Front with his old friend, Lieutenant Colonel Loßberg. For the latter, the strategic direction of the war had to be assigned to a "distinguished soldier" who would know how make himself understood by the Führer. He thus suggested Manstein's name, but Jodl remained evasive. If he acquiesced to the idea that a general must take the command and that Manstein was probably the best candidate, he nevertheless maintained that Hitler would never approve such a nomination.[246]

There were many generals in the German Army, particularly among the youngest, who were precisely hoping to see Manstein succeed Brauchitsch as commander in chief of the OKH. They quite simply considered him the best strategist of the Wehrmacht. But Hitler wanted this post for himself. On the other hand, though, he had thought for some time about appointing him as chief of the OKH general staff. But at the last moment he decided otherwise, fearing that his personality was not as conciliatory as Halder's. To those closest to him, he justified his decision not to entrust to Manstein the position of chief of army general staff, declaring that he certainly had "the brain of a genius, but a personality that was too independent."[247] If he recognized in him a great talent for operational matters, on the other hand he obviously barely trusted him.

Henceforth, Hitler occupied the duties of head of state, supreme commander of the Wehrmacht, and commander in chief of the army. In the latter role, it goes without saying that he was expecting to play a crucial role in the conduct of operations. Far from being an institution strictly concerned about operational matters independent of the political sphere—such was at least how Fritsch, Beck, and Manstein had envisaged it—the OKH found itself henceforth directly subordinate to Hitler, and restricted to only the theater of operations on the Eastern Front, with the OKW being granted oversight of the other fronts. The chief of the OKH general staff did not possess the slightest influence over the distribution of forces between the various theaters of operations, nor even, as was often the case, sufficient knowledge of the numbers and supplies that were in other theaters. An opposition between the OKW and the OKH was thus inevitable in such conditions, but it corresponded to Hitler's principles, for it gave him the last word on all matters. Instead of uniting the two command structures—the OKH and the OKW—in order to simplify operations, Hitler was moving in the opposite direction.

The Soviet landings in Kerch and Feodosiya, and the Sponeck affair

Apart from his role in the war crimes of the Eleventh Army in the Crimea, few things have given rise to so much controversy in Manstein's military career as the Sponeck affair, named for the Lieutenant General who was commanding the 46th Infantry Division on the Kerch Peninsula during the Soviet landings in that region and in Feodosiya. For having evacuated the Kerch peninsula in order to stave off dangers which were threatening his units from the Soviet seaborne landings, and despite formal orders from General Manstein forbidding him, Sponeck was dismissed of his duties. Later court martialed for his disobedience, on the insistence of Field Marshal Reichenau and the Führer, he was sentenced to death by Reichsmarshal Göring, who was acting as presiding judge of the court. The sentence was commuted by Hitler to seven years in prison; however, Sponeck was then executed in July 1944 by the men of *Reichsführer-SS* Himmler, following the conspiracy against Hitler in which he had not in any way participated. Sponeck's tragic fate, beginning as a result of his dismissal by Manstein, is occasionally attributed, at least in part, to the latter.

On December 26, two Soviet divisions crossed the strait and landed on both sides of the town of Kerch. The commander of the 42nd Corps, Lieutenant General Sponeck, only had the 46th Infantry Division at his disposal. He thus requested authorization from his superior to evacuate the Kerch Peninsula with the intention of blockading it from the Parpatch Isthmus. But General Manstein categorically refused. If the enemy were to succeed in gaining solid ground at Kerch, he explained to Sponeck, it would result in the creation of a second front and an extremely threatening situation for the Eleventh Army, which would find itself divided between the forces at Sevastopol and Kerch. He thus ordered him to drive the enemy back into the sea before they were able to establish solid bridgeheads. In order to allow him to utilize all the forces of the 46th Infantry Division, he dispatched to Feodosiya the 4th Romanian Mountain Brigade, stationed around Simferopol, and the 8th Romanian Cavalry Brigade, which would defend the eastern coast in order to prevent a new landing at that critical point. Likewise, the last regiment of the 73rd Infantry Division, at the time advancing towards Rostov-on-Don under orders from Army Group South, was brought back from Genitchek to Feodosiya. By December 28, the 46th Infantry Division had succeeded in reducing the landings from the north and south of Kerch to a small bridgehead on the northern coast. Sponeck nevertheless requested once again to evacuate the peninsula, but Manstein formally prohibited him from doing this.

On December 29, six Soviet divisions landed at Feodosiya. The forces stationed in the port, limited to an engineer battalion and a few coastal batteries, were unable to oppose them (the two Romanian brigades only arrived on the following day). A radio message sent by the 42nd Corps informed Manstein's staff that Sponeck had ordered the immediate evacuation of the Kertch Peninsula out of fear of an encirclement of his troops. Manstein hastened to send an immediate counterorder, but it was not received by the army corps which, before beating a retreat, had dismantled the radio station of its command post. For the commander in chief of the Eleventh Army, a rapid retreat would in no way improve the situation, for the enemy, having landed in Kerch, would pursue the 42nd Corps, which, upon arriving at the Parpatch Isthmus, would find itself in a crossfire, given that it would also be confronted with the troops landed at Feodosiya.

To restore the situation, he ordered the two Romanian brigades that had arrived in Feodosiya, and the German regiment, which was en route to the town, to push back to the sea the Soviets that had just landed. If they could not be deceived by the offensive strength of the Romanian units, the Soviets had as yet only been able to deploy a small number of forces on the ground. An immediate and forceful action would still provide a chance at success, and at the least enable the enemy to be contained in a narrow bridgehead until the arrival of the German forces. However, not only did the Romanians fail in their attack, they were pushed all the way back to Staryi Krym. During this time, the 46th Infantry Division quickly reached the Parpatch Strait, not without having abandoned a large portion of its artillery. Moreover, it was completely exhausted by the effort. The situation was all the more critical since, by the night of December 31, the Soviets had already landed 40,519 men, 43 tanks, and 236 cannon on the Kerch Peninsula and in Feodosiya.

Fortunately for the Germans, the Russians did not know how to take advantage of the golden opportunity that had been offered to them. If they had exploited the situation by pursuing the 46th Infantry Division and the two Romanian brigades, the Eleventh Army's situation in the Crimea could have become extremely precarious. By driving steadfastly on to Djankoi, they could have fully intercepted the Eleventh Army's supply by cutting off the Djankoy-Simferopol rail line. With the German forces in front of Sevastopol, the 170th and 132nd Infantry Divisions, having been removed, they would not be able to intervene in the west or southwest of Feodosiya before two weeks. Instead of this, the Soviet formations were satisfied with advancing to the west or northwest of Staryi Krym and to place themselves on the defensive in order to strengthen their bridgehead. They were clearly only seeking a tactical success on the peninsula, disregarding the strategic goal which would have created an interruption in Eleventh Army's communications.[248]

Despite this, Lieutenant General Sponeck was dismissed from his duties by General Manstein. For the latter, the evacuation of the Kerch Peninsula and the manner in which it had been conducted, clearly demonstrated that Sponeck was not the right man to overcome the crisis which his army corps was facing. He was thus replaced with Lieutenant General Franz Mattenklott, who had just been appointed to the head of the 30th Corps.

After the war, Manstein maintained that he dismissed Sponeck from his command because he did not consider him capable of remedying a situation as critical as the one that existed at this particular moment on the Kerch Peninsula. And so, it was apparently not for having disobeyed the formal order of his commander which forbade any retreat that Sponeck was discharged. After the Soviet landings in Kerch on December 26, Manstein had prohibited him, on two occasions, from evacuating the Kerch Peninsula, despite the critical situation in which his army corps was found. Nevertheless, after the Soviet landing in Feodosiya on December 29, Sponeck had judged the situation untenable and demanding a quick reaction. Without obtaining the prerequisite authorization from Manstein, he ordered a retreat all the way back to the Parpatch Isthmus, believing that such a solution was the only one that would save his division. One is confronted here with the classic conflict between an officer's duty to obey and that of his conscience or his personal interpretation of the evolution of the situation on the battlefield. Yet by dismissing Sponeck from his command, Manstein clearly gave his preference to obedience.

According to Manstein, Sponeck knew the risks that he was running by acting in such a way. By announcing to the Eleventh Army's headquarters that the evacuation had already been ordered, the 42nd Corps presented it as a fait accompli, all the more so since they had prevented the possibility of receiving a counter-order by dismantling the radio station. In addition, the retreat was so hasty that it provoked panic among the ranks of the 46th Infantry Division, causing it to leave behind most of its heavy artillery. At the time when the German division reached the outskirts of Feodosiya on December 31, its troops, close to exhaustion, were no longer in condition to launch an attack against the Soviet bridgehead. If the enemy that had landed in Feodosiya had immediately pursued them, claimed Manstein, it would have had no difficulty in crushing the division's resistance and, as a result, cutting the Djankoy-Simferopol supply line, the vital artery of the entire Eleventh Army in the Crimea.[249]

The order given by Sponeck to his army corps to evacuate the Kertch Peninsula on December 29, 1941, created for the Eleventh Army a crisis which to this day remains controversial. Even though it dramatically influenced the rest of his career, Sponeck's dismissal should not, *a priori*, only be analyzed under such circumstances. What later happened to him was a result of unforeseeable, tragic circumstances during the winter of 1941–42.

After having been relieved of the command of the 42nd Corps, Sponeck was temporarily appointed to the head of the 30th Corps to replace Mattenklott. But he never had time to assume this new duty, for he was immediately replaced by Lieutenant General Maximilian Fretter-Pico. Considering himself to have been the victim of wrongful actions, he called for an investigation in order to assert his point of view on the reasons that had compelled him to evacuate the Kerch Peninsula. Consumed on all sides by the crisis with which the Eleventh Army was confronted at this particular moment, Manstein deemed it impossible for him to conduct an investigation into the matter.

On January 4, Field Marshal Reichenau, commander of Army Group South, informed Hitler of his indignation concerning the retreat of the 46th Infantry Division. According to him, Lieutenant General Sponeck should be reprimanded, for there was no doubt that his insubordination represented "a significant wrong and a danger to Germany's security." Considering the retreat a direct violation of his December 16 order of "no withdrawal," Hitler demanded an immediate court martial at his headquarters in East Prussia in order to try Sponeck for disobeying orders.

The trial took place at the beginning of February. Given that Manstein was unable to leave the front to appear in court, his initial report to Army Group South on the situation in the Kerch Peninsula was used as testimony against the former commander of the 42nd Corps. Presided over by Reichsmarshal Göring, the court rendered its verdict on February 16. Charged guilty of military indiscipline, Sponeck was sentenced to death, a sentence that shocked not only General Manstein, but equally so Field Marshal Bock, who had been commander in chief of Army Group South since January 19, 1942, following the death of Field Marshal Reichenau, who had died from a heart attack two days earlier. In fact, it seems that the large majority of the officers' corps was deeply scandalized by the outcome of this affair.[250]

In his *Memoirs*, Manstein asserts that the severity of the verdict could only be explained by Göring's role as presiding judge of the court martial. He was probably not incorrect, because Göring and Sponeck had suffered a deadly hatred of one another ever since the latter had agreed to appear in court as a defense witness during the trial of the former army commander, Colonel General Fritsch, which was held in 1938 and presided over by Hitler's *prince*. Sponeck's deposition before the tribunal, aimed at preserving Fritsch's honor, had been interrupted at the time by Göring.[251]

Sponeck's insubordination clearly did not justify such a severe sentence, particularly considering his exemplary command of the 22nd Infantry Division in Rotterdam during the French campaign and at the Berislav bridgehead on the Dnieper during the first months of Operation Barbarossa. Furthermore, certain high-ranking officers had supported Sponeck's initiative to evacuate the Kertch Peninsula. On December 30, 1941, in a message intended for Army Group South, Colonel General Halder, chief of the OKH general staff, mentioned that the critical situation caused by the Soviet landing in Feodosiya could not be restored by the 46th Infantry Division alone, unless it was sent immediate reinforcements. In his opinion, Lieutenant General Sponeck's decision to evacuate the Kertch Peninsula was fully justified. On the following day, General Sodenstern, chief of staff of Army Group South, expressed the opinion that the commander's withdrawal of the 42nd Corps could be justified because of the significant number of Soviet formations that had landed in Feodosiya, and because of the difficulty in restoring the situation that would arise were they to lose the 46th Infantry. All things considered, like Guderian and Hoepner in front of Moscow, Sponeck had ordered the withdrawal of his troops after having considered that the current military situation had left him hardly any choice.

In retrospect, Manstein himself considered that Sponeck had perhaps been correct. On February 10, 1942, in a second report on the evacuation of the Kertch Peninsula written for Army Group South and later communicated to the OKH through Bock, the commander of the Eleventh Army claimed that the retreat of the 46th Infantry Division was justified for three reasons. First, the collapse of the Romanian forces permitted the troops of the Red Army that had landed in Feodosiya to advance to the north, all the more so since bad weather had held up German reinforcements for a week. Consequently, it would have been impossible for the 46th Division to hold the Parpatch front and avoid encirclement. Second, Sponeck's troops, who found themselves critically short of supplies, could not have held on until the arrival of reinforcements. Third, because of poor weather conditions, the Luftwaffe would not have been able to drive back the Soviet formations or resupply the 46th Division. In such circumstances, concluded Manstein, Sponeck's decision to evacuate the Kerch Peninsula was justified. But Manstein's intervention in favor of Sponeck was met with Keitel's refusal.

Nevertheless, Sponeck's death sentence was not executed. Hitler commuted the sentence to a modest seven years imprisonment. Despite the repeated efforts of Bock and Manstein, Sponeck was, however, not reinstated. In fact, he would meet a tragic end after the assassination attempt on the Führer on July 20, 1944, being executed by the SS under orders from Himmler. And yet he had in no way participated in the conspiracy. It appears, rather, that the chief of the SS had acted at Göring's instigation. Not only was Sponeck executed under Himmler's orders on July 22, 1944, but his fortune was confiscated and his widow was sent to a concentration camp.[252]

At the end of the war, some blamed Manstein for being responsible, at least in part, for Sponeck's death, particularly for having relieved him of his command. However, it cannot be said that in such circumstances another commander would have acted differently, as Reichenau's comments to Hitler regarding the matter at the beginning of January demonstrated. Furthermore, if Sponeck had not called for an investigation concerning Manstein's decision, he would have perhaps met a different fate. His execution was due to Göring, who had seized the opportunity offered by the purging of the officers' corps, which Hitler had ordered Himmler to complete out of revenge for the July assassination plot, in order to settle the score with an old enemy.

With Sponeck's dismissal having occurred shortly after Brauchitsch's discharge and Hitler's "no withdrawal" order, it is tempting to consider it, to a certain extent, as Manstein's attempt to enter into the Führer's good graces. In a more general context, the Sponeck affair represented above all a punitive example, the objective of which was to discipline the officers' corps as well as the members of the Wehrmacht. The Nazi regime desired to make an impression on the soldiers by taking aim at not only a general, but also his family. This type of action, arbitrary and cruel, had its effect and was not forgotten for the remainder of the war.

The counterattack before Feodosiya

With only its own forces, the Eleventh Army could hardly hope to successfully lead the assault on the Sevastopol fortress, all while trying
simultaneously to drive back to the sea the enemy forces that had landed in Kerch and Feodosiya. The attack on Sevastopol thus had to be
temporarily postponed. On December 30, 1941, Manstein gave the
orders to suspend the offensive against the fortress, convinced that there
was no longer any hope of success under such circumstances. Not being
able to count on significant reinforcements from Army Group South, he
was forced to remove the 30th Corps from the forces that were laying
siege to the fortress in order to send it into the sector of the 42nd Corps.
He was well aware that Lieutenant General Mattenklott, Sponeck's
replacement, could in no way clear the eastern region of the Crimean
peninsula with only his 46th Infantry Division, which was not only
exhausted, but also lacking the heavy artillery it had left behind in
Kerch during its retreat.

The Eleventh Army did not even have time to launch its planned
counteroffensive in Kerch and Feodosiya before the enemy struck a new
blow. On January 5, another landing, supported by naval units,
occurred at the port of Eupatoria, nearly 75 kilometers to the north of
Sevastopol. General Manstein decided to divert the 105th Infantry
Regiment, a unit taken from the sector of Army Group South and which
had been en route to Feodosiya, to Eupatoria. With the reconnaissance
detachment of the 22nd Infantry Division, a few artillery batteries, and
the 70th Engineer Battalion, which were already at the scene, the 105th
Infantry succeeded at taking over Eupatoria on January 7.

During this time, the Feodosiya front continued to see heavy fighting. The Soviets had landed other troops there and brought even more
from Kerch. The two German divisions coming from Sevastopol could
not intervene for another week. In order to lead the counterattack envisioned against the town, Manstein designated the 30th Corps, without
which his forces at Sevastopol would have difficulty sustaining themselves. Incessant Soviet attacks made matters worse on the Sevastopol
front, at the time held by only four German divisions and a Romanian
mountain brigade.

On January 15, 1942, the 30th and 42nd Infantry Corps were finally able to launch their counterattack outside of Feodosiya. In spite of the

ratio of forces of nearly three to one in favor of the enemy (3.5 German divisions and one Romanian mountain brigade against 8 Soviet divisions and 2 brigades), the city was taken by January 17. But because of the limited number of forces at his disposal, the commander of the Eleventh Army was unable to immediately take advantage of the Feodosiya success to completely drive the enemy off the Kerch peninsula. The army settled for driving the Soviets back to the narrow Parpatch Isthmus. During the course of the battle the Soviets lost 6,700 killed, 10,655 prisoners, 177 cannons, and 85 tanks.[253] In recognition of the successes gained by Manstein, Hitler promoted him to the rank of colonel general on February 1, 1942.

The capture of the Kerch peninsula

In the spring of 1942, the OKH worked relentlessly on preparations for the great summer offensive planned for the southern region of the Eastern Front. According to its directives, the Blue Plan (*Fall Blau*) was to be unleashed after the definitive expulsion of Russian forces from the Crimea, including from Sevastopol. For this, Hitler summoned Manstein to his Rastenburg headquarters in East Prussia on April 16 to inform him of his intentions regarding the mission that was awaiting him. It was the first time that Manstein had met with Hitler since February 1940, when he had presented his ideas concerning the offensive in the West. According to the Colonel General, the Eleventh Army had to first capture the Kerch Peninsula and destroy the enemy forces stationed there before attempting once again to conquer Sevastopol. If it wanted to be able to concentrate all of its forces for the capture of the fortress, it was first necessary to ensure the security of its rear. Not only were the Germans unable to forecast the amount of time necessary to seize Sevastopol, but the Kerch Peninsula was the one area where the adversary would be able to bring in its forces most quickly, which made this a most dangerous front for the Eleventh Army.

In his *Memoirs*, Manstein described his discussion with the Führer: "It was the first time that I would meet him, now as army commander, since February 1940, when I had presented to him my ideas on the offensive in the West. Once again, I had the impression that he was not only perfectly informed about all details of the previous battles, but he demonstrated a great deal of understanding of the plans that one presented to him. He listened to me attentively and approved of my intentions for the two operations. At no moment did he try to interrupt me, nor launch into an interminable enumeration of production numbers as was so frequently the case."[254]

Hitler approved without reservation Colonel General Manstein's ideas concerning the two successive offensives that he was planning in the Crimea. Clearly, he was fully confident in the man who already had a reputation for being the most talented general on the operational level, a reputation that he himself considered in private as being completely accurate. At the same time, he formally announced to him his intention to utilize the Eleventh Army next in the Kuban, once it had crossed the Kerch Strait, to either cut off the retreating enemy forces driven back from the Don towards the Caucasus or to build up a reserve for the southern wing, intentions which the commander of the Eleventh Army by no means opposed.

The ratio of forces on the Kerch Peninsula was largely to the advantage of the Soviets. They had the use of their Forty-fourth and Fifty-first Armies, which included a total of 17 divisions, 3 mobile brigades, 2 cavalry divisions, and 4 armored brigades. On this front, the Eleventh Army was only able to oppose 5 German infantry divisions and the 22nd Panzer Division, which had been recently formed and placed at Manstein's disposal by the OKH. It would be necessary to add the 7th Romanian army corps, which included the 10th and 19th Infantry Divisions and the 8th Cavalry Brigade. In all, 6 German divisions and 3 Romanian (roughly counting the cavalry brigade as a division) were to confront 26 large Soviet units. The ratio of forces was thus approximately three to one in favor of the Russians.

According to Manstein, the attack across the Parpatch Isthmus inevitably had to be frontal, for its span of 18 kilometers prohibited any encirclement maneuver. Nevertheless, the objective of destroying the two Soviet armies could not be achieved by driving them back frontally, or even through a simple breach. If they were to succeed at confronting them from a position more to the rear, they would have to start all over again. Since the peninsula expanded from 18 to 40 kilometers in width after the isthmus, the Soviets would thus be in a position to deploy all of their forces and make use of their numerical superiority. It was thus necessary not only to burst through the Parpatch front and then advance rapidly, but to destroy the bulk of the enemy forces during the very first breakthrough. The way in which the Soviet command had made use of its forces offered precisely an opportunity to achieve this. According to German reconnaissance, the enemy had massed together two thirds of its forces in the northern sector, where the terrain was more suitable for an attack, and the remainder in the southern sector. The commander of the Eleventh Army thus decided, logically, to deliver a decisive blow in the southern sector, along the coast of the Black Sea, in other words in an area where the adversary was least expecting it.

The principal attack fell to the 30th Corps and the 22nd Panzer Division, the recently arrived 28th Light Division, and the 50th and 132nd Infantry Divisions. The 170th Infantry Division, which remained primarily in the northern sector to deceive the adversary, later had to take action in the southern sector. According to Manstein's plan, the army corps, with three infantry divisions, would puncture the Parpatch position and then take primary control of the area to the east, along the Black Sea, just beyond the deep anti-tank ditches, in order to allow the tanks to cross over them. Next, the corps would bear to the northeast with the 22nd Panzer, towards the Sea of Azov, then to the north, to attack the flank and rear of the bulk of enemy forces stationed in the northern sector, and then encircle them, in liaison with the 42nd Corps and the 7th Romanian Corps, in order to drive them back to the coast. Such a movement would be covered to the east, against any forces capable of coming from Kerch, by the Groddek brigade, a mobile unit composed of German and Romanian motorized elements. In order to facilitate the breach, an operation of assault boats would transport at dawn, to the rear of the Parpatch front, a battalion leaving from Feodosiya. Finally, in the northern sector of the front, the 42nd Corps and the 7th Romanian Corps would execute a diversionary attack to immobilize the enemy forces and then complete their encirclement started by the 30th Corps.[255]

The entire operation would be supported by a powerful array of artillery, and above all by the 8th Air Fleet of Colonel General Wolfram Freiherr von Richthofen, without a doubt the greatest Luftwaffe chief of the Second World War. Due to the inferior number of his forces, Colonel General Manstein estimated that the success of the operation would be based in part on the close cooperation of the German land and air forces, particularly for the breach of the front and its thorough exploitation, necessary conditions to cut off the enemy lines and to attack its forces on the flank and rear. In fact, the cooperation between Manstein's Eleventh Army and Richthofen's 8th Air Fleet would prove to be, at the level of the joint-branch commands, an example of coordination rarely matched during the war.[256]

Initially planned for May 5, the battle of the Kerch Peninsula did not finally begin, because of poor weather conditions, until three days later. It nevertheless unfolded according to the broad lines of Manstein's plan. After four days of difficult battles, the mass of Soviet forces in the northern sector were encircled and annihilated. On May 16, Kerch itself was taken. But five additional days of battle were necessary to destroy the enemy elements that managed to reach the eastern coast. The battle thus drew to a close on May 21, after thirteen days of fighting. The success was complete. The 26 large Soviet units were eliminated. The Soviet losses were considerable: 169,198 prisoners, 1,133 pieces of artillery, 258 tanks, 3,800 motorized vehicles, and 300 aircraft. The German losses only amounted to 7,588 men. Some 120,000 Soviets had, however, escaped capture, having succeeded in crossing the Kerch Strait and reaching the Taman Peninsula.[257]

Launching the bulk of German forces deep behind enemy lines to the south of the front, in the most weakly defended area, in order to take from the flank and rear the mass of Soviet forces concentrated to the north, immobilized by a few diversionary troops, this attack is today still considered a classic battle of encirclement and annihilation.[258] Such a decisive and stunning success of the Eleventh Army against an enemy by far superior in numbers is largely indebted to the operational talent of its commander, Colonel General Manstein. Conversely, it was also the result of the adversary's poor deployment, and inability to discern the Germans' true intentions. In fact, a prudent command would have spread out its forces more thoroughly so that it could have applied its operational reserves to the precise area where the attacker had revealed himself. Even if could not have repelled the attack, the Red Army could have at least considerably slowed down the swiftness of its execution.[259]

Capturing the strongest fortress in the world: Sevastopol

There remained nothing more for Colonel General Manstein's troops to do other than capture the fortress of Sevastopol, recognized as the most formidable in the world. Given the general offensive planned by Army Group South in the direction of the Volga and the Caucasus, was it really advisable to tie up the Eleventh Army for an indeterminate amount of time in the attack of Sevastopol, particularly when the Kerch victory had eliminated any danger in the Crimea? In his *Memoirs*, Manstein mentions that this matter had not been discussed in principle during his meeting with Hitler in mid-April 1941. "This question was clearly brought up by the high command and not us. For my part, I was at the time convinced, and I still am today, that it was advisable first to take Sevastopol. Even if I were content with besieging it, it would have been necessary to leave there three or four German divisions, in other words half of the Eleventh Army, in addition to the Romanian units."[260]

The strength of the fortress resided in the extraordinary difficulty of the terrain, cut apart by ravines, mountains, forests, and rivers, and in the multiplicity of fortified positions, minefields, entanglements of barbed wire, and anti-tank ditches. The defenders had created three lines of principal resistance, in which the most powerful strongpoints consisted of concrete defenses equipped with batteries that the Germans had nicknamed Stalin, Volga, Donetz, Gorki, Molotov, the GPU, Siberia, the Urals, the Tcheka, and Lenin.

In order to reinforce their system of fortifications at Sevastopol, the Soviets had taken advantage of the five-month break in the Eleventh Army's assault against the fortress since the end of December. During this period, they had also called upon reinforcements dispatched across the Black Sea—which was still under the Soviet Navy's control—from the Kuban and the Caucasus. From mid-November 1941 to the beginning of June 1942, the number of troops in the fortress had doubled, increasing from 52,000 to 106,625 men. The Red Army thus had at its disposal seven rifle divisions, one cavalry division, and four navy brigades. It also possessed 606 pieces of artillery, 2,000 mortars, 38 tanks, and 109 fighter aircraft. Colonel General Manstein was expecting to confront a much more bitter resistance than during the previous winter, which further complicated his task of "cleansing" the Crimea as quickly as possible in order to permit Operation Blue to commence shortly thereafter.

Just like the previous winter, the commander of the Eleventh Army and his staff came to the conclusion that it was preferable to attack with the bulk of their forces from the north and the northeast, rather than from the south. If the defenses were more powerful and numerous in the northern zone, the terrain presented fewer difficulties, all the more so since the artillery and the air force were able to take action there more easily, rather than in the mountains of the south. However, it was also necessary to attack from the south, primarily to divide the opposing forces and also because one would expect that the enemy, even after having lost the area to the north of the Severnaya Bay, would try to keep their footing in the town and on the Chersonese Peninsula. But it was no longer as crucial as the previous winter to gain control of the port so quickly for, with the participation of the 8th Air Fleet, the enemy was unable to resupply itself from the sea as freely as before.

The offensive was thus deployed on two axes. To the north, the 54th Corps, with the 22nd, 24th, 50th, and 132nd Infantry Divisions, along with the 213th infantry regiment, would attack from the Belbek valley in the direction of Severnaya Bay. It was here where they focused their main efforts. To the south, the 30th Corps, with the 72nd and 170th Infantry Divisions and the 28th Light Division, would advance in the direction of Mount Sapoun and the Chersonese Peninsula. In the central area of the front, which was covered with forest, the Romanian mountain corps was assigned the mission of pinning down the Soviet forces. Some 204,000 Germans were deployed on the Sevastopol front, which extended 35 kilometers.

The task of ensuring the security of the Kerch Peninsula and the southern Crimean coast was assigned to the 42nd Corps (the 46th Infantry Division) and the 7th Romanian Corps (the 10th and 19th Infantry Divisions, the 4th Mountain Division, and the 8th Cavalry Brigade). As for the 22nd Panzer Division, it was to be returned to Army Group South.

In order to facilitate the infantry's advance, Manstein ordered the air force and artillery to embark upon an intensive bombardment of the opposing positions for five days preceding the commencement of the attack. Richthofen's 8th Air Fleet would attack the town, port, armament installations, supply lines, and airfields without respite, while the artillery would target the enemy's batteries and advanced positions.

The heavy artillery included batteries of 190mm and a few of 305mm, 350mm, and 420mm guns. In addition, there were also two 600mm cannon and another, named Dora, with a caliber of 800mm. She was originally intended to be used against the Maginot Line. The barrel of the cannon reached almost 30 meters and the carriage was the height of a two-story house. The cannon launched five-ton projectiles a distance of 50 kilometers and seven-ton projectiles 40 kilometers. It required 60 locomotives to bring her into position on special rails. Two anti-aircraft defense battalions ensured her permanent protection. As well, Manstein called upon several anti-aircraft regiments of the 8th Air Fleet for ground combat. The 88mm anti-aircraft guns would prove effective against pillboxes and enemy armor. In all, the Eleventh Army aligned on its front a powerful artillery array of 1,300 pieces, more than double that of its adversary entrenched in the fortress.

No other operation of the Wehrmacht throughout the war achieved a similar concentration of artillery. Without counting the batteries of the anti-aircraft regiment, the Eleventh Army was able to make use of 208 batteries at Sevastopol on a front of 35 kilometers, thus 6 batteries per kilometer, a ratio that was obviously much higher in the northern sector, the principal assault front. Such a concentration was nevertheless minimal if one considers that the Russians, in 1945, utilized up to 250 pieces of artillery per kilometer. Whatever the case may be, asserted Manstein in retrospect, the results gained by the shelling of the fortress did not fully justify such a concentrated effort of batteries and even less so the deployment of Dora.[261]

The commander of the Eleventh Army estimated that the second offensive against the Sevastopol fortress would last just under two weeks. It would actually last one month. The attack began on June 2 with an intensive bombardment from the Luftwaffe and the artillery. The objective was to prepare for the infantry's assault, which was to commence five days later. Despite considerable damage, the shelling did not appreciably weaken the enemy's defenses. Consequently, the infantry did not succeed at achieving any significant breach. Its advance was slow and its gains negligible. After two weeks of violent fighting, the assailants succeeded, not without taking heavy losses, at driving through to the fortified zone of the northern sector and reaching the northern coast of the Severnaya Bay, and penetrating the defenses of the southern sector, before the hills of Sapoun. On June 26, they were in possession of almost all of the frontline positions of the fortress. The enemy had been driven back into the zone formed by the southern cliffs of Severnaya Bay and the hills of Sapoun, which joined with those of Balaklava.

From that moment on, a double problem confronted Manstein. How could the 54th Corps cross Severnaya Bay with its artillery before the fortified hills of the southern banks? How could the 30th Corps capture the powerful fortified positions of Sapoun with only the forces it had available to it? It thus appeared advisable to transfer the center of gravity of the offensive from the northern wing to the southern wing. But this proved to be impossible. Just to transport there the divisions coming from the north would require several days, a delay that would give more time to the enemy and which would hinder even more the commencement of the Operation Blue, the code name for the 1942 summer campaign. Moreover, the only road that existed between the two sectors in no way lent itself to the movement of artillery. The commander of Eleventh Army thus resigned himself to accepting the risk which involved crossing Severnaya Bay. It was precisely because such an amphibious operation seemed to have no chance at success, he thought, that it would create such a surprise, which could quite possibly be the key to victory. Despite objections expressed by his subordinates, he held firm to his foolhardy plan.[262]

At dawn on June 29, the 54th Corps crossed Severnaya Bay at the same moment that the 30th Corps began its assault on the Sapoun line. Aboard the assault craft, the first wave, composed of the 22nd and 24th Infantry Divisions, succeeded in grabbing a foothold on the southern banks before the opposing defense even had the time to move into action. With the massive support of the 8th Air Fleet and the artillery, the 54th Corps was able to quickly take hold of the plateau and seize, as a result, the formidable position of Sapoun. The advance of the 30th Corps was thus made easier.

Once this first objective was achieved, the divisions of the 54th Corps burst into the defense belt surrounding the town of Sevastopol itself, and penetrated it on July 1. And so was concluded a siege that had lasted 250 days. For their part, the divisions of the 30th Corps fanned out from the springboard created in the hills of Sapoun to conquer the Chersonese Peninsula, which fell into their hands on July 4. The Crimea was henceforth entirely in the possession of the Germans. During this last operation, the Eleventh Army had captured 95,000 prisoners and an impressive cache of war supplies: 467 pieces of artillery, 758 mortars, 155 anti-aircraft guns, 26 tanks, and 141 aircraft. The German losses were also significant, as they rose to 24,000 men killed and wounded.[263]

On July 1, the day that Russia's strongest fortress was taken, Colonel General Manstein received the following message from the Führer: "In reward for your exceptional merits during the victorious battles of the Crimea, which were crowned in the annihilating battle of Kerch and the taking of the Sevastopol fortress, powerfully fortified by nature and skill, I name you Field Marshal. I pay homage to you before all the German people with this promotion, and the creation of a special badge for all of the combatants of the Crimea for the heroic exploits of the troops placed under your orders."[264] The field marshal baton represented unquestionably the crowning moment of Manstein's military career.

Thus for the capture of the Sevastopol fortress on July 1, 1942, Manstein was awarded the rank of field marshal, just as Rommel had received it for his seizure of the fortress of Tobruk on June 21, 1942. The granting of the field marshal baton for the taking of a fortress had only occurred three times in the history of the German Army. Before Rommel and Manstein, there was only the prince and Colonel General Friedrich-Karl von Preußen, who had earned this honor during the Franco-Prussian war of 1870, after seizing the fortress of Metz.[265]

As commander of the Eleventh Army in the Crimea, Manstein had led the operations with a degree of autonomy superior to any other army commander on the Eastern Front. The geographic situation of the peninsula offered an explanation. Although subordinate to Army Group South, the Eleventh Army was not in direct contact with the other German formations except during the first half of October 1941 during which it had led, in conjunction with Kleist's 1st Panzer Group, a counterattack in the area of Melitopol, to the north of the Sea of Azov. Clearly, the OKH and the Führer had closely followed the unfolding of the Crimean campaign, but never intervened in Manstein's decisions. Hitler had even approved without reservation his intentions from mid-April 1942 concerning the two offensives that he was planning for the taking of the Kerch Peninsula and the siege of the Sevastopol fortress.

During the Crimean campaign, Manstein demonstrated qualities that contributed to his reputation as the most brilliant German war strategist and tactician: vigor, flexibility, and imagination. The destruction of Soviet forces on the Kerch Peninsula in May 1942 was conceived and executed in an exceptional manner. At a disadvantage in terms of numbers and the terrain, Manstein nevertheless succeeded at deceiving the adversary about the *Schwerpunkt* of his offensive and at achieving a classic battle of annihilation. The planning and execution of the crossing of Severnaya Bay during the final offensive against Sevastopol demonstrated his senses of initiative and audacity. The fall of the fortress was in the end indebted to his determination, tenacity, and his unrelenting desire to conquer. Credit was also given to him for having confronted the numerous crises that afflicted his army throughout the winter. It was with a rare composure that he skillfully shifted his forces from one point to another in order to contain, then eliminate, each of the Soviet counteroffensives.

After Sevastopol, on to Leningrad?

Under the original concept of Operation Blue, Field Marshal Manstein's Eleventh Army, once the Crimea was completely conquered, was to cross the Kerch Strait and seize the Kuban peninsula in order to eliminate the primary Soviet naval bases on the eastern coast of the Black Sea, such as Novorossisk, and to cut off the retreat of enemy forces driven from the Don towards the Caucasus. Alternatively, it was to act as an operational reserve for Army Group A, advancing as the latter's second line in the direction of the Caucasus with the intention of seizing the oil fields around Maykop and Grozny. But Hitler, who as always tried to do several things at once, abandoned the original idea of utilizing the Eleventh Army in this framework.

While his staff was preparing the crossing of the Kerch Strait which would allow the army to participate in that summer's general offensive, Manstein received new instructions from the OKH. Only the 42nd Corps, with the 46th Infantry Division along with a few Romanian units, would cross the strait. As for the rest of Eleventh Army, the 54th and 30th Corps, with the 24th, 132nd, and 170th Infantry Divisions and the 28th Light Division (thus only four divisions) were to participate in the seizure of Leningrad, while being followed by the bulk of the heavy artillery. Three other infantry divisions were removed from Eleventh Army. The 50th was to remain in the Crimea in order to ensure its defense. The 22nd Infantry would be transformed into an airborne division and sent to Crete, where it would remain more or less idle until the end of the war; and the 72nd Infantry would be attached to Army Group Center to fill in a gap in that sector.[266]

The capture of Sevastopol, a remarkable success in itself because of the terrain, the strength of the fortifications, and the enemy's determination to fight until the very end, had prompted Hitler to abandon the initial plan to use Eleventh Army in the Kuban in favor of a new mission which would henceforth send it north, with the objective of taking Leningrad. After the siege of Sevastopol, Hitler considered Field Marshal Manstein as a master in the art of laying siege to a town or fortress, even as a sort of "secret weapon" for dangerous missions. He thus appeared to him as altogether suited to seize the stronghold of Leningrad. Hitler's thinking was supported by Jodl, who ardently suggested entrusting the next assault on Leningrad to Field Marshal Manstein and not Field Marshal Küchler, given that the latter seemed to lack strength of character. On August 21, Hitler thus delegated to Manstein complete responsibility for the operations required for this mission. Because of this, Manstein relegated Küchler, who was nevertheless his superior as commander in chief of Army Group North, to a subordinate role.[267]

However, for Manstein, it was not exactly an opportune time to remove Eleventh Army from the southern wing of the Eastern Front in order to commit it to the northern wing, because Leningrad, when all was said and done, was an objective of minor significance since it was in the southern area of the front that the high command was seeking a decisive strategic outcome. The Wehrmacht could never be too strong for the decisive thrust, thought Manstein, all the more so since the southern offensive, according to the goals sought by Hitler, had to move in two directions—Stalingrad and the Caucasus—and, while advancing to the east, leave its northern flank increasingly exposed. The presence of the Eleventh Army on the southern wing was well advised, for by crossing the Kerch Strait it would be able to cut off the Soviet forces retreating towards the Caucasus, or it could at least act as a vital reserve for Army Group South. All available forces thus should have been focused on the principal sector of that year's offensive.

Manstein discussed the matter with Colonel General Halder when he arrived at the OKH's headquarters at Vinnitsa in the Ukraine, to examine his new mission. The chief of general staff did not conceal from him that he disapproved of Hitler's desire to seize Leningrad while the southern offensive was still in progress. But he was unable to convince him to change his opinion. Halder nevertheless believed that the southern wing could do without Eleventh Army for the time being, a point on which the commander of that army remained skeptical.[268] Field Marshal Manstein had no alternative but to get to work on his new mission.

Surround Leningrad and let its population die of hunger

On August 27, after a journey of nearly 2,000 kilometers from the Crimea, the general staff of the Eleventh Army arrived on the Leningrad front, intending to attack in the sector of General Georg Lindemann's Eighteenth Army. It was expected that Field Marshal Manstein's army would relieve Lindemann's in the northern area of his front, leaving for him the eastern area, on the Volkhov. The front of Eleventh Army was located in the sector of the Neva, running from Lake Ladoga all the way to the southeast of Leningrad. The attack front was situated to the south of the city and extended to Oranienbaum, on the southern coast of the Gulf of Finland.

In addition to the enormous artillery brought from Sevastopol, which included the famous 800mm Dora, two 600mm, two 420mm, and six 400mm cannon, Manstein was to take under his command thirteen divisions plus an SS brigade, his command including the Spanish "Blue Division," plus an armored and a mountain division. But two divisions each would remain on the Neva and Oranienbaum fronts, so that he only had nine and a half divisions for the offensive. Facing him, the enemy had 19 divisions, a rifle brigade, a frontier guard brigade, and one or two armored brigades.

Like Field Marshal Küchler, commander in chief of Army Group North, and Colonel General von Richthofen, commander of the 8th Air Fleet assigned to participate in the operations against Leningrad, Field Marshal Manstein doubted, in light of his experience at Sevastopol, that bombardments by artillery and the air force would prove to be as effective as Hitler was expecting. He did not share the Führer's opinion that terror attacks alone would be capable of forcing Leningrad to surrender. "It would be preferable," he declared to Küchler, "to encircle the city and let the defenders as well as the inhabitants die of hunger." He thus noted in his diary: "I am proposing an attack to take over the mouth of the Volkhov so as to reduce the city to famine and so leave aside the difficult attack of the fortress."[269]

In light of such an assertion, one could believe, at first glance, that the preoccupations of the generals responsible for the planning of the assault against Leningrad appeared above all to limit themselves to operational aspects. Yet Manstein, Küchler, Halder, Keitel, and Jodl in no way stood up against Hitler's request demanding the complete destruction of the former Czarist capital and its population.[270] The Führer's decision to raze Leningrad to the ground—as well as Moscow—had been expressed on several occasions since the beginning of the war against Bolshevik Russia, and in particular, during the course of long conversations with Küchler and Manstein on August 23 and 24, 1942.

"The attack against Leningrad," asserted Hitler to Küchler, "must be executed with the intention of destroying the city. It would thus be desirable to include the destruction of the city in the preparations." The instructions given to Manstein were no less explicit: "Phase 1: encircle Leningrad and create a liaison with the Finns. Phase 2: occupy Leningrad and raze it to the ground."[271]

The Battle of Lake Ladoga

Field Marshal Manstein prepared to fulfill his mission under the code name "Northern Lights" (*Nordlicht*). The city was protected by a dense system of fortifications covering the countryside. Given a breakthrough of this defensive belt, the German units were in absolutely no case to allow themselves to be led into battle inside the city itself, which would result in heavy losses. They were thus required to breach the defenses to the south of the city, with three corps, along with the massive support of the artillery and the Luftwaffe, but then halt at its border. During this time, two other corps would attack from the east to cross by surprise the Neva to the southeast of Leningrad, destroy the forces stationed between the city and Lake Ladoga, cut off the supply from the lake, and closely surround the city from that side. In this way, thought Manstein, the Eleventh Army would obtain the capitulation of the city, as had previously been achieved at Warsaw—quickly enough and without difficult street fights.

However the enemy succeeded in thwarting his intentions. On August 27, the Soviets launched a new offensive against the Eighteenth Army on the Volkhov front. It was a large-scale attack intended to ward off the German offensive planned for September 14. The Soviet forces succeeded at creating a breach eight kilometers wide and twelve kilometers deep to the south of Lake Ladoga. On September 4, dissatisfied with the performance of Küchler to that point, Hitler entrusted responsibility for containing the offensive to Manstein. An immediate intervention, he said to him over the telephone, was essential on the Volkhov front in order to avoid a complete disaster. It would thus be necessary for him to adroitly take command so as to restore the situation. Instead of the planned attack against Leningrad, Manstein engaged instead in a battle to the south of Lake Ladoga.

After violent battles, the Eleventh Army succeeded at sealing off the breach during the following days, and then moved to counterattack. From September 21, it was successful at cutting the enemy penetration off from its lines of communication. However, the Germans immediately had to drive back powerful new attacks designed to extricate the encircled forces, as well as another assault consisting of eight Soviet divisions launched from Leningrad. The battle concluded on October 2 with the complete elimination of the pocket in which the enemy had been trapped. In all, seven divisions and six rifle brigades, as well as four armored brigades, were obliterated there. The number of prisoners rose to 12,000, though Soviet dead numbered much higher. More than 300 pieces of artillery, 500 mortars, and 244 tanks had either been captured or destroyed. The battle was, however, not without repercussions for the Germans who, on their side, counted 26,000 dead and wounded.[272]

If the situation had been restored, there was nevertheless no longer a possibility of taking Leningrad and destroying it. The last chance to achieve this had vanished for good. Not only had the Eleventh Army suffered heavy losses, but it had consumed a significant portion of its munitions intended for the attack on the city. Hitler was reluctant to abandon the idea, but on the other hand failed to recommend more limited objectives of which Eleventh Army was still capable. Manstein pointed out that scaling down the task would not in any way bring about a solution to the Leningrad front, the ultimate objective. He asserted that no undertaking against the city should be attempted without the assistance of fresh forces, and above all not with insufficient forces.[273] The following weeks were thus taken up by discussion and the preparation of new plans.

Manstein and the command of the Eleventh Army

On October 25, Manstein flew to the Führer's headquarters in order to receive his field marshal baton. After having thanked him for the results obtained by the soldiers of the Eleventh Army in the battle of Lake Ladoga, Hitler informed Manstein that he was transferring him to Army Group Center, in the region of Vitebsk, where the enemy was preparing a large offensive. To counter this, Manstein was to launch a pre-emptive attack. He was also informed that Hitler intended to assign him to the command of Army Group A, deployed in the Caucasus, which Hitler was leading himself since relieving Field Marshal List a few weeks earlier. The Führer then declared that he was planning, the following year, to cross the Caucasus with a motorized army group to penetrate the Middle East. For Manstein, this demonstrated "the extent to which he was still deluding himself on the general situation and on operational feasibility."

On November 20, after Eleventh Army's transfer to the Vitebsk region, Manstein received orders to take immediate command of a new Army Group Don, which was in the process of being formed in the Stalingrad sector. As weather conditions did not permit the use of aircraft, he had to leave Vitebsk by train, though he was held up on two occasions by partisan-laid mines. On November 24, his fifty-fifth birthday, he arrived at the headquarters of Army Group B, which was still commanding over his future sector, even as its main component, the Sixth Army, had just been surrounded by the Soviets at Stalingrad.

In his role as army commander, Manstein had demonstrated on more than one occasion his operational genius, as the conquest of the Kerch peninsula and the reduction of the Sevastopol fortress revealed, with forces inferior in number to those of his adversary and in a territory where the lay of the land clearly provided a defensive advantage. Such military successes had contributed to his considerable increase in popularity with his troops, but also throughout the Wehrmacht and Germany. His presence alone at frontline outposts had sufficed to motivate his troops, exhausted by long and difficult battles, and provide them the additional push necessary to overcome the enemy.

Like the majority of other commanders, he would read military reports morning and night and would be present on the front during the

afternoon to visit and inspect his troops. If he hated all of the paper-
work which kept him from his men, he no less kept a firm control over
his staff. Furthermore, upon his initial arrival at the head of Eleventh
Army, he had been examined under a magnifying glass by his subordinates and harshly compared to his predecessor. Bavarian, accommodat-
ing, and relatively cordial, Colonel General Schobert had been more a
soldier than a man of the general staff. Under his command, he had left
the planning of operations to his chief of staff, Colonel Wöhler, and to
his deputy chief of staff, Lieutenant Colonel Busse. A Prussian who was
severe and rather cold, Field Marshal Manstein was a staff officer at
heart who took pleasure in exerting complete control over operations,
to the great displeasure of Wöhler and Busse. For the troops of southern Germany, who formed the majority of the Eleventh Army, Manstein
thus represented all the qualities they disliked in a Prussian officer. Even
if he could at times be charming, certain officers of his staff were hardly pleased with him, at least initially, due to his arrogant, proud, and
pretentious personality, as well as his rather Spartan style of command.
But the majority of his subordinates quickly learned how to overlook
his faults, and were gradually able to appreciate his great qualities as a
military leader.

According to Mellenthin, a German staff officer during the war,
Manstein would have been even more popular within his officers' corps
if he had been more relaxed and cordial in his interactions with colleagues. For the officers and soldiers who did not know him well,
Manstein gave the impression of being a cold and distant man. "He did
not appear to be very sociable," recalled Hans-Adolf von Blumröder, an
officer who served on Manstein's staff in 1943 and 1944. He was also
perceived by his peers as a self-important officer who was all too aware
of his immense talent. "Manstein liked to let the others know that he
was more intelligent than them," declared Kielmansegg, a staff officer
in the operations section. His daughter Gisela explained the reason why
her father gave others such an impression: "He was a quiet man, even
reserved and timid. He was not a man who liked being in large crowds.
Yet with men whom he knew well, he was calm and relaxed." He was
indeed generally on good terms with his staff officers, even developing
friendships with some of them which would last well beyond the war.[274]

Field Marshal Erich von Manstein.
National Archives

A September 1939 visit by Hitler to Army Group South in Poland where he was surrounded by an array of Third Reich luminaries, some of whom had yet to become famous. Pictured from left (near the plane's front propellor) are Halder, Bormann, Rundstedt, Brauchitsch, Keitel, Hitler, Rommel, Reichenau, Paulus, Manstein, and Schmundt.

Bundesarchiv, Bild 1011-013-0060-20 / photo: Falk

General von Manstein celebrates the 1st anniversary of Command Headquarters among his officers and men, 2/4/1941.
National Archives

In July 1941, during the onset of Operation Barbarossa, Manstein consults a map with General Brandenberger, commander of the 8th Panzer Division.
Bundesarchiv, Bild 101I-209-0086-12 / photo: Koch

In May 1942 in the Crimea, Manstein views enemy positions while the Luftwaffe's Wolfram von Richthofen (peaked cap) looks on.
Bundesarchiv, Bild 141-0227 / photo: o.Ang.

In the summer of 1942 in Russia, Manstein admires the soup of Hermann
Hoth, commander of 4th Panzer Army.
Bundesarchiv, Bild 101I-218-0543-10 / photo: o.Ang.

After the completion of his successful Kharkov counteroffensive, Manstein
is warmly greeted by Hitler in March 1943. At right is W. von Richthofen.
Bundesarchiv, Bild 146-1995-041-23A / photo: o.Ang.

A seemingly agitated Manstein during the defensive battles of early fall
1943, together with Army Group South's chief of staff, Hans Speidel.
Bundesarchiv, Bild 101I-705-0262-06 / photo: Mahia

Field Marshal von Manstein (left) at an unknown location in
southern Russia during the summer of 1943.
Bundesarchiv, Bild 101I-022-2927-30 / photo: Mittelstaedt, Heinz

X

THE WEHRMACHT AND THE GENOCIDAL WAR IN RUSSIA

Called to testify at the Nuremberg trials in August 1946, Field Marshal Manstein took the stand as the representative of a chivalrous notion of war, which thus required a duty to defend the honor and integrity of the Wehrmacht during the Second World War. He vehemently denied any accusations which characterized the military high command as a criminal organization comparable to the branches of Hitler's regime such as the Nazi Party, the SS, or the SD: "I have been a soldier for forty years. I belong to a family of soldiers and was raised on the concept of duty. . . . As young officers, we naturally considered military fame as something great. I do not want to deny that I was proud that an army had been entrusted to me during this war. But our goal—and also that of my colleagues—was not in the conducting of the war in itself, but to the contrary, in the education of our youth in order to make of them honorable men and brave soldiers. And it was this youth, numbering in the millions, who were devoted to the death under our command."

He then added a personal note: "My eldest son died as an infantry lieutenant at the age of nineteen; two of my sons-in-law, raised in my house, died as young officers; my best friends during this war, my young adjutant and my young chauffeur, and almost all the sons of my brothers and sisters, have died. That we senior soldiers have led our youth, who we hold dear to our hearts, into a criminal war would be beyond anyone's wildest imagination in assuming man capable of committing such base acts. It is possible for one man alone, without family and tradition, who is possessed by a fanatical belief in a mission of grave impact, to go beyond the limits of human justice. We soldiers, from a purely humane point of view, would have been incapable of doing this.

We were incapable of leading our youth in such crimes."[275]

However, it was a completely different reality. Not only was Manstein knowledgeable of the nature of war crimes in the East perpetrated by the Wehrmacht, but he also willingly participated in them. In his role as commander in chief of the 56th Panzer Corps on the Baltic front, then with the Eleventh Army in the Crimea, his responsibility in the execution of Jews, political commissars, and Soviet prisoners of war, as well as in the delivery to the SD, police, or *Einsatzgruppen* of "elements deemed undesirable" by the National Socialist regime, is manifest. Like the large majority of his fellow generals, Manstein engaged in a veritable criminal war in Bolshevik Russia, thus rendering himself guilty of actions contrary to the laws of war.

The Wehrmacht and the Holocaust

That the war in the East led to genocide was not accidental, for the invasion of the Soviet Union was deliberately conceived as a war meant to exterminate Jewish Bolshevism, its system, and its representatives. The eradication of Jewish Bolshevism was in fact a central objective closely linked to the military campaign. In other words, the conquest of *Lebensraum*, the extermination of Bolshevism, and the annihilation of the Jews were objectives inextricably joined together, elements of a war of extermination that was one and the same. The Russia campaign was thus a war in search of territory, a clash of ideologies, and a racial struggle. From the very first days of the invasion, with the criminal and murderous operations of the *Einsatzgruppen*, shouldered effectively and vigorously by the Wehrmacht, the horrific character of the conflict was already taking shape. It would very quickly take on the proportions of an enormous, systematic program of genocide.[276]

Incommensurable with the precedent of the Poland campaign, the close cooperation between the SS and the army leadership in the preparation of Operation Barbarossa allowed for the barbarism of the *Einsatzgruppen* to explode into proportions never before seen. The generals of the Wehrmacht quite simply made use of ideological fervor for the fight against Jewish Bolshevism. And so they willingly collaborated with the SD, providing it with essential assistance without which the *Einsatzgruppen* would not have been able to effectively fulfill their mission on such a large scale. Furthermore, in the summer of 1941, reports from the various *Einsatzgruppen* concerning their interactions with the Wehrmacht described a harmonious relationship, and particularly an excellent understanding among the generals with respect to the necessity of merciless actions against the Jews. "Above all," as one report indicated, "one observes in the circles of the Wehrmacht a relentless growth in interest and understanding concerning the jobs and activities of the SD. This is particularly evident during the executions."[277]

During the first weeks of Operation Barbarossa, the actions undertaken by the *Einsatzgruppen* were above all aimed at male Jews. Yet beginning in August 1941, following verbal instructions given by *Reichsführer-SS* Himmler, then by the commanders of various execution platoons, women and children were generally to be included in the massacres under the pretext that they could possibly commit acts of vengeance. And thus, *Einsatzkommando 3*, which operated within *Einsatzgruppe A* following in the wake of Army Group North, under the framework which Manstein's 56th Panzer Corps was fighting in the summer of 1941, eliminated 4,239 Jews including 135 women in July, but 26,243 women and 15,112 children out of a total of 56,459 Jews executed in September 1941. Overall, the four *Einsatzgruppen* killed approximately 50,000 Jews before mid-August 1941. The extent of the murders in Russia was much more significant than those committed in Poland two years earlier. But it was still only a tenth of the some 500,000 Jews who died during the following four to seven months. During the war, 2.2 million Jews were executed by the *Einsatzgruppen*, the SD, and the police force.[278]

If the majority of the murderous actions against the Jews of the occupied Soviet territories were carried out by the four *Einsatzgruppen* operating to the immediate rear of the front, the Wehrmacht found itself implicated on various levels. Not only were the generals most certainly informed of the crimes committed by the execution platoons, but the latter received from the army vital logistical assistance. The number of men initially engaged in the actions of the *Einsatzgruppen*, totaling nearly 3,000, would have been insufficient to assemble and execute the Jews in such a proportion, when all was said and done, to implement a genocidal program, without the full cooperation of units from the Wehrmacht.[279]

The application by the Wehrmacht of criminal orders drafted by the OKW and the OKH as well as its support of the *Einsatzgruppen*, ren-

dered it just as responsible as the latter groups for carrying out the genocide of the Jews in Eastern Europe. The horrific strategy of extermination against the Jewish population was fully accepted and even encouraged by the military authorities. From July 1941, the *Einsatzgruppen*
were the subject of numerous solicitations on the part of the army in
order to lead the "cleansing actions" necessary for the pacification of
the occupied territories. Far from having been ignored or rebutted, the
lethal actions of the *Einsatzgruppen* were, to the contrary, solicited and
encouraged by the majority of high-ranking officials of the army—
including Manstein, as we will later see—who desired having the for-
midably effective auxiliary units apply repression behind the front.
Furthermore, Colonel General Halder never stopped singing the praises
of the *Einsatzgruppen*: "For us, these men are worth their weight in
gold."[280]

Soviet prisoners of war

Manstein's deposition at Nuremburg entailed other aspects: "In what
concerns the treatment of war prisoners, inasmuch as they were brought
to our attention, it is necessary for me to clarify above all that we only
felt, as soldiers, respect vis-à-vis for the valiant adversary, and that otherwise, as we knew from the First World War, that any mistreatment of
foreign prisoners leads, in the end, to repercussions against our own soldiers. We have thus treated, as a matter of policy, the prisoners of war
as we had been taught to as soldiers, and as we were required to do,
which was conveyed to us according to the stipulations of martial
law."[281] This obviously in no way corresponded to the reality at hand.

The inhumane character of the Wehrmacht in the war against the
Jewish Bolshevik enemy was also demonstrated in the fate reserved for
the Soviet prisoners of war. With the exception of the Jews, Soviet
POWs suffered the worst destiny among all the victims of Nazi
Germany. Throughout the Russian campaign, the Wehrmacht captured
more than 5.7 million Red Army soldiers, of which 3.3 million (57.9
percent) died in captivity. Of the 3,350,000 Soviets imprisoned during
the year 1941, 1.4 million had already died by December 1941. By
February 1, 1942, 2 million of these 3,350,000 had perished, thus
600,000 in December 1941 alone, for a death rate of approximately 60
percent. The horrifying character of the fate of Soviet prisoners of war

achieves its full effect when one considers that of the 232,000 English and American soldiers who fell into German hands during the war, only 8,348 perished, thus 3.6 percent.[282] In fact, in the autumn of 1941, no fewer than 8,348 Soviet prisoners would die each day.

Such an unprecedented death rate among Soviet prisoners of war was the result of the German plans for a war of extermination, which had been drafted since March 1941. The soldiers of the Red Army captured by the Wehrmacht were not treated as comrades-in-arms. In this war in the East, the Hague Conventions were deemed inapplicable and political commissars were executed without any form of trial, while the civilian population was subject to the cruelest retaliatory measures. The death of Red Army soldiers who became prisoners under the Wehrmacht was thus explained by the ideological conceptions of the war of extermination led against Bolshevik Russia.

After the war, the officers indicted at Nuremberg explained that such an appalling slaughter of Soviet prisoners was a regrettable but inevitable tragedy. In their view, the military administration would have been overwhelmed by the arrival of numerous and successive waves of prisoners following the enormous successes of the German military in the summer and autumn of 1941. Not having expected that the mass of prisoners could take on such proportions, they asserted, it would have been impossible to properly feed them.[283] Called to testify at Nuremberg, Manstein declared that during the great battles of encirclement of 1941, it had been impossible for the German armies to carry with them provisions necessary to ensure the subsistence of several hundreds of thousand prisoners.[284]

Taking on a considerable number of prisoners was, however, foreseeable, if only for the reason of the lightening warfare strategy implemented against the U.S.S.R. But the food rations granted to the prisoners was well below the minimum levels needed to sustain life. Despite the proliferation of reports on the horrific conditions pervasive in the prisoner camps, on October 21, 1941, Lieutenant General Eduard Wagner, Halder's chief of supply, ordered a reduction in the amount of rations provided to prisoners detained in the occupied territories directly controlled by the Wehrmacht. The Soviet soldiers held by the German Army were thus deliberately reduced to famine and left out in the open, without any shelter, condemned to die during the terrible icy and snowy winter of 1941–42. In fact, at the end of exhausting transfers back toward the home front, during which they risked being shot along the road if they did not succeed at keeping up, or even dying from the cold when they were transported on uncovered wagons in the middle of winter, the Soviet prisoners were penned up in camps that were often nothing but simple plots of land surrounded with barbed wire and exposed to the sky. Malnourished and directly exposed to the bad autumnal weather, then to the harsh winter, they were overwhelmingly dying from hunger, cold, or illnesses such as dysentery or typhoid. Their terrible fate was nevertheless knowingly accepted by the military leadership.

To say that the Wehrmacht was not prepared to receive the mass extent of prisoners it seized is thus to miss the essential point. If no measures had been taken into account, it was because of the two choices available to them: that of giving absolute priority to getting fresh supplies to the Reich, and that of not involving, for political and racial reasons, the prisoners of the Red Army in the German economy. Such a two-fold choice condemned a large portion of the captives to death. However, the decision to terminate the second choice at the end of autumn 1941, as the continuation of the war made the utilization of every bit of manpower essential, noticeably enhanced the chances of survival for the prisoners of war capable of working. It goes without saying, however, that such criminal treatment reserved for the Soviet prisoners of war by the large majority of Wehrmacht units very likely contributed to the development of the atmosphere in which the "final solution" against the Jews became possible.[285]

The Commissar Order

An even more flagrant violation of international law was the execution of Red Army political commissars, not because they were suspected of acts of resistance, but rather due to their duties as representatives of the Communist Party within the ranks of the army. According to exhaustive studies on the matter, not only was the Commissar Order not ignored, contrary to what Manstein and a good number of his fellow generals maintained after the war, but it was zealously applied by all of the Wehrmacht units.[286] Just like the Führer, as a whole the officers did not consider the political commissars as true soldiers and thought it was necessary to eliminate them because they were the ones carrying out the will of the Communist Party within the Red Army, and thus were the representatives of the Jewish-Bolshevik worldview.

Recognizable by a special insignia on their uniform, many political commissars were executed during the first weeks of Operation Barbarossa. After having been informed of the actions being aimed against them, the commissars quickly removed their insignia. On July 17, 1941, the OKH authorized the *Einsatzgruppen*, the SD, and the police force to penetrate into camps located in Germany, occupied Poland, and in the conquered Soviet territories in order to select among the prisoners the "undesirable political elements" to execute. Expanded three months later on October 7, to zones controlled by the army, such measures had the objective of facilitating the identification of the commissars. However, the procedures of selection in the prisoner camps was not only limited to members of the party, but applied to all Jews. It is thus likely that the majority of the political commissars were not executed at the front, but in various prisoner camps.

Between June 1941 and May 1944, 580,000 to 600,000 prisoners were immediately handed over to the SD, the *Einsatzgruppen*, or the police and were executed on the spot. Those who survived the initial selection were condemned to later succumb to hunger, exhaustion, cold, or epidemics. An indeterminate, though most likely considerable, number of Red Army soldiers were executed by Wehrmacht soldiers after their capture, even before being designated as prisoners. In addition to the murders of the prisoners, political and biological enemies of the Reich were also executed, as they were characterized for the most part as "partisans," without much effort at distinguishing the true partisans from the political suspects or the Jews. Such euphemisms actually assisted in concealing the enormous massacres of unarmed soldiers and defenseless civilians.[287]

It is hardly surprising that Manstein claims in his *Memoirs*, like many of his Wehrmacht comrades-in-arms, to have refused to implement the Commissar Order: "But, if one had doubts of their status, the idea of executing them without any form of trial after having captured them was no less loathsome in the opinion of all the soldiers. Such an order was contrary to the military mindset. Not only would its implementation taint the honor of the troop, but it would also compromise its morale. I thus found myself forced to inform my superiors that it would not be enforced under my command. On that point I was in perfect agreement with my senior subordinates and so it was clearly not put in place. It goes without saying that my superiors shared my sentiments."[288]

Nevertheless, the execution of the Commissar Order was one of the crimes for which Manstein, in his role as commander in chief of the 56th Panzer Corps and then the Eleventh Army, was declared guilty at his trial. Soon after the first moments of Operation Barbarossa, Franz Walter Stahlecker, chief of *Einsatzgruppe A*, which was operating in the wake of Field Marshal Leeb's Army Group North, remarked on his "harmonious relationship" with Colonel General Hoepner's 4th Panzer Group, to which was attached General Manstein's 56th and General Reinhardt's 41st Panzer Corps. On July 10, 1941, the 4th Panzer Group reported the execution of 101 political commissars during the period June 22 to July 8. Nearly two weeks later it announced that 172 commissars had been executed by July 19. Other similar reports began to pile up throughout the following weeks. Furthermore, the implementation of the Commissar Order by Army Group North, particularly by the 4th Panzer Group, was clearly demonstrated at Nuremberg.[289]

Quite obviously, Manstein's armored corps behaved no differently than the other units of the Wehrmacht. And the situation hardly changed after Manstein took command of the Eleventh Army in the Crimea, where frequent executions of Red Army political commissars took place.[290] In his *Memoirs*, he claims that the Commissar Order was not enforced by the Eleventh Army during the period he was in command. He nevertheless felt obliged to clarify that "the few commissars who were indeed executed had not been taken in battle, but on the home front where they were chiefs or partisan organizers. They were then treated according to the laws of war."[291] Of course, such an assertion was pure fantasy, for it is in no way consistent with the reality.

It is important to clarify that neither Manstein nor any other commander on the Eastern Front were realistically able to forbid their troops from implementing an order descending directly from the Führer. They could certainly express their displeasure to the high command regarding Hitler's directive, and make known to their subordinates their desire that it not be applied; but they were hardly able to formally prohibit it. Consequently, whether or not he agreed with the Commissar Order, Manstein was required to communicate it to his troops.

Having said this, everything indicates that he was totally indifferent to the fate of the political commissars, if only because of his visceral hatred of the Soviet system. Likewise, he knew very well that he would not be able to have a career within a totalitarian regime without compromising his political beliefs. And so, the fact that he satisfied his duty to obey by transmitting such an order hardly concerned him. For fear of being relieved of his post, he thus preferred to close his eyes to the elimination of political commissars and to focus strictly on military issues.[292]

At Nuremberg, General Wöhler, the Eleventh Army's chief of staff, was asked what measures had been taken by Field Marshal Manstein, his commander, to prevent the implementation of the Commissar Order by his subordinates and units under his control: "Whatever actions he took, I do not know. To tell the truth, I did not come across any actions in this area, for the issue concerning the Commissar Order was first and foremost a matter that unquestionably came under the commander and not the chief [of staff]. If I were led to do something, which I cannot remember, I then did it under orders from the commander in chief. But I know nothing else."[293]

In light of Wöhler's response, one could venture to say that Manstein indeed did not take any action to prevent the execution of political commissars in the operational zone coming under his command. In any case, the principle of the chain of command did not allow resorting to measures that would forbid the application of an order coming from the superior ranks. Knowing that the OKH was simultaneously the author and instigator of the Commissar Order, and that it received consent from the supreme leader of the Wehrmacht, i.e. Hitler himself, any firm opposition could earn a commander his displacement or even his discharge.

Manstein's order of November 20, 1941, on the eradication of Jewish Bolshevism

During Operation Barbarossa, several key army commanders, such as Reichenau, Hoth, and Manstein, instead of trying to curb the brutality of their soldiers, decided that they were showing too much leniency with respect to the enemy. They thus endeavored to instill a better understanding of the policy of radical repression into them, considering it essential to victory in a war between two antagonistic ideologies. To achieve this, they made a particular effort at getting the troops to understand that resistance was primarily due to the Jews and the Bolsheviks, and that it was suitable to treat them with the greatest severity. Indeed, according to them, the growth of partisan actions—which were in fact a direct consequence of the Wehrmacht's criminal policies—demanded brutal and merciless measures against the Jews and the Bolsheviks, whom they considered as the principal instigators of Soviet resistance. And so, during the months of autumn 1941, they put forth decrees that directly echoed the Führer's orders from March 30, 1941, and which revealed once again the ideological union between the leadership of the Wehrmacht and the National Socialist regime.[294]

On September 12, 1941, the chief of the OKW general staff, Field Marshal Keitel, issued the following directive: "The fight against Bolshevism demands harsh, implacable, and swift action, especially against the Jews, the principal harbingers of Bolshevism."[295] Other high-ranking military leaders would go even further in their exhortations, indicating that they thought Keitel's directive was not firm enough.

On October 10, 1941, the ultra-Nazi Field Marshal Reichenau, commander of the Sixth Army, which was operating on the front of Army Group South, gave his troops an order worded in the following terms: "There remain many confused ideas concerning the troops' conduct with regard to the Bolshevik system. The primary goal of the campaign against the Jewish Bolshevik system is the total destruction of its instruments of domination and the elimination of the Asian influence over the European sphere. It entails for the soldiers obligations which go beyond traditional military behavior in the strict sense. In the East, the soldier is not only a combatant according to the rules of warfare, but also the representative of a rigid national idea and the avenger of all the savagery inflicted upon the German people and those allied to her. As a result, the soldier must have a perfect understanding of the necessity of inflicting a severe but just chastisement on the subhuman Jews. Such a punishment also has the goal of choking off rebellions to the rear of the Wehrmacht which are always prepared by the Jews as experience has shown." And Reichenau concluded: "It is only in this way that we will accomplish our historic duty, which is to liberate, once and for all, the German people from the Judeo-Asian threat."[296]

Far from being an isolated case within the officers' corps, Reichenau was expressing an ideological vision of the war in the East that was shared by the majority of his colleagues. Furthermore, many senior officers not only agreed with the terms of his order, but hastened to immediately communicate it to their own troops. Thus, the order from the commander of the Sixth Army was soon known by all of the units deployed on the Eastern Front. In addition, barely one week after it was signed, Field Marshal Rundstedt, commander in chief of Army Group South, broadcast the order to General Manstein's Eleventh Army, Colonel General Hoth's Seventeenth Army, Colonel General Kleist's 1st Panzer Group, and to all of the reserve units in Army Group South. He appended a cover letter in which he suggested that his commanders circulate directives analogous to Reichenau's, of which he entirely approved. Indeed, not only did Rundstedt distribute Reichenau's order, but he also wrote on the document: "I fully subscribe to its contents." On October 28, 1941, the chief of supply within the OKH, Lieutenant General Wagner, informed all of the army group commanders of Reichenau's order and requested each of them to put forth similar instructions. The order from the Sixth Army's commander thus served as a model for several other Wehrmacht generals. It was also particularly appreciated by Hitler himself, who characterized Reichenau's initiative as "excellent."

At the beginning of November 1941, however, a visit from Reichenau to his units convinced him that his order concerning the "conduct of troops in the East" had still not been made sufficiently clear to his men. He then assigned his subordinates the responsibility of verifying that every soldier understands well what it entails and that they especially know "why the measures that are being taken in the East are not applicable in civilized countries." Historians thus have full reason to bring attention to the difference between the way the Germans conducted the war in the East as opposed to the West.

Among the reasons that could be purported as an explanation of the order given by Reichenau to his troops was that there had been a deterioration of the Wehrmacht's operational base since the beginning of the campaign and an increase in partisan activity subsequent to the war of extermination, enslavement, and pillaging by the Wehrmacht on Soviet soil. But the deciding factor for issuing this order was the almost unanimous acceptance within the officers' corps of the concept of an ideological war against Jewish Bolshevism. The physical destruction of the Eastern European Jews was thus justified as a punitive measure. In this context, the presumed connection between "Jewry" and the partisans simply provided an additional justification.[297]

Having replaced General Stülpnagel as the head of the Seventeenth Army on October 5, 1941, Colonel General Hoth was persuaded that the campaign in the East had to be carried out in a manner that was quite different than the one conducted in France. In an order on "the conduct of German soldiers in the East," issued on November 17, 1941, he would go even further than Reichenau by presenting a much more detailed analysis of the historic and ideological context of the war. He nevertheless arrived at the same conclusion: it is only by exterminating the enemies of inferior race, who were moreover "morally depraved," that the Wehrmacht would save European, and in particular German, culture, threatened by the "Asian barbarism" embodied by Jewish Bolshevism.

He was thus speaking of two ideologies irreconcilable by their very nature: "It has appeared to us more and more clearly this summer that here, in the East, two profoundly incompatible visions have come face to face: a feeling of honor for the race of the Germans, and a secular military tradition (*Soldatentum*), against an eastern way of thinking and primitive instincts, provoked by a small number of intellectuals, for the most part Jews: the fear of the knout, the contempt for moral values, the leveling down, the disdain for individual life deemed worthless. More than ever are we occupied by the thought of a new era, in which the leadership of Europe is entrusted to the German people by virtue of the superiority of her race and her accomplishments. Our mission is evident: to save European culture from the advance of eastern barbarism. We now know that we must fight against a fierce and tenacious adversary. This fight can only end by the destruction of either of the combatants; there is no compromise."

He continued by clarifying that "the Red Army had brutally assassinated German soldiers." Consequently, any "sympathy and indulgence with respect to the population was completely supplanted." And because of this, he called upon the soldiers to understand "the necessity for severe actions against elements alien to the nation and the race." In a more resolute manner than Reichenau, Hoth justified the measures for the extermination of the Jews by insisting upon their culpability in Germany's fate after the First World War. The annihilation of the Jews, who the commander of the Seventeenth Army described as "the spiritual support of Bolshevism, the representatives of their murderous organization, the assistants to the partisans," responded to the rule of "self-preservation." And he concluded in these terms: "Russia is not a European state, but rather an Asian one. Each step that we take in this miserable country, reduced to servitude, shows us this difference. Europe, and in particular Germany, must be forever liberated from this pressure and the destructive forces of Bolshevism."[298]

On November 20, 1941, General Manstein, commander in chief of the Eleventh Army, equally felt the necessity to explain in greater detail to his troops the objectives of the war against the Soviet Union, as well as inform them of their position with respect to the annihilation of the Jews of Eastern Europe. Repeating parts of Reichenau's argument, he offered a personal perspective of the situation, yet in much more radical terms: "Since June 22, the German people have been fighting a battle to the death against the Bolshevik system. This war, and only this war, against the Soviet armed forces, has not been waged according to the norms established by the rules of European warfare. Even behind the front, the battle continues and plain-clothed partisans and snipers, are attacking isolated soldiers and small units; they are trying to cut off our supply through sabotage, mines, and bombs."

He continued by inferring that the responsibility for the war of extermination occurring in the East fell upon a Soviet regime dominated by Jews: "The Jewry is thus acting as an intermediary between the enemy within the country and the rest of the Red Army forces who are still fighting. Even more strongly than in Europe, it occupied all of the key positions in the leadership in the areas of politics, administration, business, and local industry, and forms the nucleus of all possible troubles and riots." He then described the objective of the war in the East: "The Jewish Bolshevik regime must be removed once and for all. It must never again intervene in our European territory. This is why the German soldier has the duty not only to crush the military potential of the regime, but must also stand up in defense of a racial concept and avenge all the cruelties that have been perpetrated against him and the German people." The double mission that he assigned to his soldiers was thus approximately the same as the one previously set forth by Reichenau and Hoth to their troops.

The commander of the Eleventh Army next criticized his troops for their lack of confidence, even their negligence with respect to the fight being waged by the Bolsheviks behind the front, along with the distribution of foodstuffs to Soviets who had not been placed in the service of the Wehrmacht: "The fight behind the lines has not yet been led seriously enough. The active cooperation of every soldier must be demanded in order to disarm the population, for the control and arrest of prowlers, both civilian and enlisted, and the removal of the Bolshevik symbol. All sabotage must be immediately punished by the most severe measures and all signs of this will have to be exposed. The situation of the homeland demands that the troop must live off, to the greatest extent, the country's resources, and also so that large amounts of provisions can be made available to the homeland. Above all, a large part of the population in the enemy cities will have to suffer from hunger. In spite of everything, nothing that the homeland offers, while denying herself, must be distributed to the prison population, unless they are at the service of the Wehrmacht."

Like Reichenau and Hoth, Manstein urged his soldiers to understand the necessity of the severe punishment inflicted upon the Jews: "The soldier must be conscious of the tough expiation imposed upon Judaism, the spiritual guardian of the Bolshevik terror. It is also essential in order to choke off all the riots, which are, for the most part, due to the Jews. It will be up to officers of all ranks to keep alive the significance of the present fight. We will have every reason to prevent, through lack of initiative, the Bolshevik struggle from being made any easier behind the front."

Finally, he demanded that his troops treat fairly the non-Bolshevik elements of the population. But if they were to refuse to participate in the fight against Bolshevism, they must be compelled through appropriate methods: "Concerning the Ukrainians, the Russians, and the Tartars who are not Bolshevik, it will be necessary that they be won over to the new order. The passivity of numerous so-called anti-Bolshevik elements must give way to an unequivocal resolve to actively collaborate against Bolshevism. If this is not demonstrated, it must be forcefully obtained through adequate measures."[299]

Within the concept of a battle against the partisans, Manstein and his comrades-in-arms Reichenau and Hoth thus played, on their own initiative, a major role in the implementation of the genocide of the Jews in Eastern Europe—a major role framed in the context of the war of extermination planned by the Hitler state and to which the Wehrmacht was party. As key commanders on the Eastern Front, Manstein, Reichenau, and Hoth brought up the war against the partisans in order to justify the ruthless fate reserved for the Jews. By conflating the Jews with the partisans or by seeing them as their principal support, they thus charged their troops to resort to brutal and implacable measures against them. In other words, they motivated their troops to eliminate the Jews in the occupied territories, whom they held responsible for all demonstrations of resistance. "Where there's a partisan, there's a Jew; where there's a Jew, there's a partisan," was the attitude as much in the Wehrmacht as in the SD to legitimize the extermination of the Jews in the occupied territories. Therefore, the term "partisan" served to designate all civilians deemed unworthy of living by the German Army, whether it was because of their acts of resistance or their political or racial identity.[300]

General Hans Röttinger, chief of staff of the Fourth Army, then of the Fourth Panzer Army on the Eastern Front between 1942–1943, confirmed this assertion by declaring at Nuremberg in November 1945 that he understood that the war against the partisans in the occupied territories had been utilized by the German authorities as a pretext in favor of "a merciless elimination of the Jews and any other undesirable elements."[301]

And so Manstein, Reichenau, Hoth, and several other high-ranking officers were not just satisfied with safeguarding the program of elimination of individuals who belonged to the political and racial categories undesirable to the German Reich, they also vigorously encouraged it. The central element that one finds in the arguments of these generals was that the attack on Bolshevik Russia had been nothing more than a preventive measure destined to thwart the imminent invasion of the "Asian barbarism" led by Jewish Bolshevism, the objective of which was to ravage Europe and to destroy her civilization. It was due to this terrible threat that the most ruthless actions were taken to remove the pillar of Soviet rule, in other words the Communists and the Jews. The logic of such argumentation thus consisted in shouldering the responsibility of Germany's criminal policy in the East on her victims.[302]

It goes without saying that the belief in a global conspiracy led by the Jews was widespread within the officers' corps of the Wehrmacht and many among them expressed their approval towards the Führer, who had known how to launch just in time the great battle against the

Jewish Bolshevik enemy accused of threatening Germany's existence. The respective decrees of Reichenau, Hoth, and Manstein are good examples of this. Until the final months of the war, Hitler appears to have benefited from significant credibility with his senior officers.

Hatred of the Jews was already present within the Kaiser's army. Indeed, the imperial high command, led by Field Marshal Hindenburg and General Ludendorff, had not hesitated to organize in October 1916, right in the middle of a world war, a registration of every Jew serving as a recruit. It next conceived of certain plans during the same period in which the Jews were to be displaced (*verpflanzt*) and detained in a large border zone separating Polish Russia from the German Reich.

However, studies demonstrate that the German Jews were patriots no less ardent than other Germans. During the years 1914–1918, nearly 500,000 Jewish citizens lived in Germany. Among those, some 100,000 fought in the ranks of the German Army as soldiers, non-commissioned officers, or officers, and 12,000 died in battle. It is without doubt that they demonstrated bravery, courage, and a sacrificial spirit, as 35,000 among them received military decorations, from the Iron Cross to the highest of distinctions, the Pour le Mérite. Despite this, anti-Semitism remained profoundly anchored in the army and was based on prejudices which associated the Jews with pacifism, socialism, communism, and internationalism, elements that were clearly in opposition to the worldview of the Prussian officers' corps, whose foundations rested on anti-liberal and anti-democratic values, those of the Prussian monarchy, militarism, authoritarianism, and a longstanding conservative nationalism.

The anti-Semitism of many officers was fueled by the trauma of the difficult post-war years during which the imagined world of Jewish Bolshevism had taken on the strength of dogma. Military defeat, the fall of the Hohenzollern Empire, the arrival of the Weimar Republic, and the Communist revolutions of the Spartacist movement were all attributed to the Jews, a conviction reinforced by the legend that Germany had been stabbed in the back. That the democrat Matthias Erzberger, accused of being a Jew by extremist nationalists, signed in the name of his country the Rethondes Armistice, then accepted the Treaty of Versailles, only strengthened such a legend.

Violently anti-Semitic and blindly believing in the notion of an international Jewish conspiracy aspiring to global domination by way of revolutionary coups d'état, as in Russia in 1917, or in Germany between 1918–19, General Ludendorff warned the Germans against "the defeatist, pacifist, and internationalist thought of the Jewry and the Vatican," which sought to "destroy the racial heritage and national character of the Germans." In this respect, Ludendorff's anti-Semitism was hardly different than that exhibited by Hitler. Also, it was not accidental that the former general in chief of the First World War was connected to Hitler when the latter attempted to overthrow the Weimar Republic on November 9, 1932, by a putsch in Munich. In a book that he published that same year under the title *Conducting War and Politics* (*Kriegführung und Politik*), Ludendorff mentioned that Germany must make herself Jewish-free (*Judenrein*) before undertaking the next war. Hitler's racial policy from 1933 to 1939 would thus move closer to the anti-Semitic ideas presented by Ludendorff and shared by a good number of senior officers of the Wehrmacht.

The anti-Semitic policy of the Nazi regime had therefore hardly aroused negative reactions within the officers' corps; in fact, quite to the contrary. Many generals were pleased at the purge of Jewish elements in the army. That the prohibition of marriage with non-Aryan women only provoked rare protests demonstrated how much the development of anti-Semitism within the army, after Hitler's ascent to power, was as much a result of an indigenous process as the internalization of the anti-Semitic policy implemented by the Hitler regime.[303]

A man such as Colonel General Fritsch, for whom Manstein and several other officers had an enormous amount of esteem, was a fanatical anti-Semite in the tradition of a Ludendorff. Less than a year after having been discharged from his duties as commander in chief of the army because of base slanders, and only a few weeks after the pogrom of *Kristallnacht*, he wrote: "It is very odd that so many men were looking to the future with such increasing worry, despite the indisputable successes achieved by the Führer throughout the past years. [...]. Shortly after the [First] World War, I arrived at the conclusion that it was necessary for us to win three battles if Germany were to regain its power: 1. the battle against the working class—Hitler won it; 2. against the Catholic church, or perhaps better said, against the ultra-montagnards; 3. against the Jews. We are right in the middle of these battles, with the struggle against the Jews being the most difficult. I hope that everyone will see clearly see the difficulties of such an endeavor."[304]

Such remarks would have easily won the approval of numerous officers and undoubtedly of Manstein himself. In fact, had Fritsch not been, in some way, a spiritual father for Manstein and many other officers who had served directly under his command within the army high command?

Even more interesting is the point of view on the position and significance of the Jews in the U.S.S.R. that Manstein held during his trial held in Hamburg in 1949. He justified there the preventive measures taken by the Wehrmacht against the Jews which he associated, in line with Nazi rhetoric, with the partisan groups: "I was of the opinion that there was a direct relation between the Bolshevik system and the Jewry. One found large numbers of Jews in important positions, not only in political or economic circles. On my occasional [pre-war] visits paid to the Red Army in Russia, I recall having met Jews in the highest ranks and command positions. The Jews were numerous among the groups of partisans and saboteurs. [...] I do not deny that the National Socialist policy had provoked the Jews to revolt against us. However, it was natural for us to take preventive measures in order to keep them from transforming their hatred into action."[305]

Without being as violently anti-Semitic as Blomberg, Fritsch, Brauchitsch, Halder, Küchler, Hoepner, or Reichenau, for example, Manstein was no less convinced of the necessity of inflicting severe punishment on the Jews, as the primary representatives of Bolshevik terror, the main supporters of the partisans in the occupied territories, and as responsible for all the post-Versailles misfortunes suffered by the German people. And so one was able to detect, as much in his own decree as in that of Reichenau or Hoth, the national trauma of the November 1918 revolution for which Jewish Bolshevism was held responsible. Quite obviously, Manstein was a product of the Prussian officers' corps, which held anti-parliamentarism, anti-Marxism, anti-Slavism, and anti-Semitism at the heart of its worldview. Not only had he been exposed to such a view his entire life, but he had clearly made it his own.

Such a context allows us to better understand the motivations that led to the criminal behavior of an entire military caste on the Eastern Front. The multiplicity of criminal orders formulated as much by the OKH or the OKW as at the level of the armies or divisions, was less a matter of concessions to the current climate than a reflection of deeply rooted anti-Slavic, anti-Semitic, and anti-Bolshevik racist convictions. Racial contempt for the Jewish Bolshevik enemy was unquestionably the foundation of the German officers' attitude in the U.S.S.R. It goes without saying that the archaic conditions of the lands that were crossed—unpaved roads, lack of electricity, running water or sewers, extreme poverty in the country—further confirmed their prejudices according to which the Slavs and Jews were dirty, subhuman races, brutal and incapable of social organization.[306]

It is nevertheless interesting to note that, like the majority of high-ranking officers in the Wehrmacht, Manstein made a clear distinction between the Jews of Eastern Europe and the Germans who had at least one Jewish grandparent—the *Mischlinge* (Métis). Furthermore, in 1934, did he not defend German enlisted men of Jewish descent, thus standing up against the Aryan measures introduced into the army? Even though he was a declared supporter of the Führer, the National Socialist regime, and its racial policies, Field Marshal Reichenau was himself no less sympathetic to the cause of the *Mischlinge* serving within the German Army, even coming to the aid of some of them during the years preceding the Second World War.

Like the large majority of generals, Manstein and Reichenau did not place on equal footing the *Mischlinge* and the Jews. For them, to rid Germany of the Jews, as Colonel General Fritsch stated in December 1938, was a crucial objective. However, they were inclined to make exceptions for the *Mischlinge*, whom they simply considered comrades-in-arms. Neither Manstein, after not having received any response to his 1934 protest against the Aryan measures, nor Reichenau, after one last effort in 1938 to help a *Mischling*, made any other attempts to prevent the persecution of *Mischlinge*. To the contrary, their respective decrees from autumn 1941 contributed rather to sanctioning the death of thousands of innocent Jews, the very fact of which diminished the impact of their benevolent actions towards a few *Mischlinge* during the 1930s. If they were of the opinion that certain *Mischlinge* should be saved, at least those wearing the uniform of the German Army, they were nevertheless in agreement on the fact that Jews in general had to be exterminated, notably those of Eastern Europe who were Communists, Slavs, or Asians.

One must not lose sight of the fact that the Führer himself came to the aid of the *Mischlinge*, and this at the very moment when he was ordering the "Final Solution." After all, some 150,000 *Mischlinge* served in the Wehrmacht during the war. Within the various high commands, there were no less than 77 high-ranking officers, including 25 generals, who were declared "Aryan" by Hitler himself. Among them was no doubt one of the most well known, Field Marshal Milch, inspector general and head of development of the Luftwaffe, who was quite simply considered essential.[307]

If the decrees put forth by high-ranking generals such as Manstein, Reichenau, and Hoth were influential over their troops, there were still others who differed. Even if they were rare and did not receive any support in the army, a few commanders issued orders significantly different than those disseminated by the three aforementioned. One of them, General Eberhard von Mackensen, commander of the 3rd Motorized Corps, demanded on November 24, 1941 that his soldiers resort to brutal and ruthless measures towards the resistance, but to avoid engaging in, as much as possible, arbitrary actions against the civilian population, which would only inspire resistance against the occupying forces all the more.[308] Clearly, Mackensen's action remains in the minority, an isolated case, for at no time did the superior ranks of the military hierarchy envision the slightest softening of the policy adopted against the occupied civilian population.

The ideological and racist concept of the war in the East promoted by Manstein in his decree tends to brand him a veritable Nazi officer, for there was nothing to stop him from putting forth an order similar to Mackensen's. The argument claiming that Manstein would not have had the choice to promulgate an order notifying his troops to resort to the most rigorous measures against the Jews and the Bolshevik elements, because the OKH had demanded its commanders of the Eastern Front to issue directives similar to those of Reichenau, does not hold water. Just as Mackensen was not sanctioned, Manstein could not have been unaware that his order gave his troops carte blanche to assassinate all the elements deemed undesirable by the Reich. Given that analogous orders had already been introduced by other high-ranking generals, the impression of German soldiers that they henceforth possessed a permit to arbitrarily kill could only be reinforced.

In Nuremberg, when he was interrogated about Reichenau's order from October 10, 1941, Manstein gave his version of the facts: "Such an order, upon Hitler's desire, was sent to us, as it were, as a model; I myself refused it and never made use of it to transmit my own. I am unaware if any other commander in chief took it into consideration." He was then asked what he had done when it was suggested to him to introduce an order analogous to Reichenau's. "It was not proposed to me; we received it only as issued from Hitler, as a model. I completely disregarded it and considered such orders as absolutely out of place. I wanted to continue to fight like a soldier and not otherwise." The prosecution then presented a document dated from November 20, 1941, signed by Manstein himself, which undeniably proved that the latter really had distributed to his troops an anti-Semite manifesto very similar to the one previously introduced by Reichenau.

Manstein half-heartedly asserted that he had absolutely no memory of this document, but recognized that it bore his signature. His credibility was just smashed to pieces: "I have to say that this order has completely escaped from my memory. According to the signature [...] I must admit that the order is accurate and that I issued it." It would be surprising, to say the least, that he forgot an order of such importance, if only because of his extensive memory which he demonstrated in his autobiography, notably for the vivid retelling of the events of the war. "But I would like to affirm that if it is stated here: 'the regime must be annihilated...' this signifies the extermination of the Bolshevik system and not that of its men." One can nevertheless doubt that his soldiers truly understood such subtlety. When he was asked if it were not accurate that his order was drafted with the intention that his troops would follow it, and that they expressed sympathy for the task of the *Einsatzkommandos* who had been assigned to exterminate the Jews, Manstein was hardly more convincing: "No, there is absolutely no way that I ever, even between the lines, desired to encourage my troop to cooperate in such methods."[309]

Beyond his radically ideological and racist worldview of the war in the East, it is also quite possible that his order of November 20, 1941, was motivated, to a certain extent, by a desire to gain the favor of the Führer. During this period he knew well that the war in the East would continue well beyond 1941. In addition, he was not unaware that the days of Field Marshal Brauchitsch as commander in chief of the OKH were numbered, because of his patent failure during Operation Barbarossa and his incessant altercations with the Führer regarding the conduct of military operations. He also had to suspect that Colonel

General Halder, chief of the OKH general staff, would also find himself, for the same reasons as Brauchitsch, in a rather precarious position. And so, by enthusiastically demonstrating a National Socialist world-view of the war in the East, he was perhaps hoping that the Führer would call upon him for his services as commander in chief or as army chief of staff. It was perhaps in such a way that he was hoping to achieve the ultimate dream of his entire military career, that of being appointed head of the German Army.

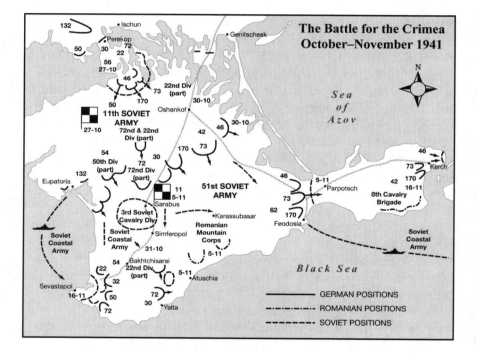

XI

MANSTEIN, THE ELEVENTH ARMY IN THE CRIMEA, AND THE FINAL SOLUTION

At his trial held in Hamburg in 1949, Manstein was declared not guilty in relation to the issue of the extermination of the Jews. However, his order from November 20, 1941 was enough evidence to prove his guilt.[310] In addition, the arguments that he presented in his defense were grossly erroneous. For example, he declared that he knew practically nothing, during the course of the war, of the *Einsatzgruppen*, apart from the fact that they had a political mission that concerned, among other things, surveillance of the population in the occupied territories. Such an assertion was hardly different from his testimony at Nuremberg, three years earlier, on the same subject: "Concerning the duties of the *Einsatzgruppen*, I only knew that they were assigned to prepare the political administration, which is to say through a political surveillance of the population of the occupied territories of the East which they were accomplishing according to Himmler's special instructions and under his leadership. [...] This organization of *Einsatzgruppen*, such as it appears clearly to me today, was not in the very least clear during this period. Its missions even less so."

Concerning the intention and order to exterminate the Jews and other elements of the population, Manstein claimed never to have heard any discussion of this, responding quite briefly: "No, I did not know about it." To the question whether he had ever been advised of the killings of Jews, he responded in way that was just as categorical: "I received absolutely no news relative to the execution of the Jews. I only heard talk of rumors." When asked again if he was claiming before the tribunal that he did not know that one of the most important missions of the *Einsatzgruppen* was to exterminate the political commissars and

267

the Jews, he remained consistent with his previous responses: "No, I did not know about it."[311]

Yet, Manstein was incapable of not knowing what was occurring behind the front, and even less so behind the army's operational zone which fell directly under his command. It is entirely impossible that he was unaware of the *Einsatzgruppen* activities. According to the March 26, 1941 agreement, reached between Lieutenant General Wagner and *SS-Gruppenführer* Heydrich, the *Einsatzgruppen* were to be placed under the control of the armies concerning their movement and resupply, and were moreover required to inform the army commanders of their operations on a regular basis. Consequently, Manstein and all the other army commanders on the Eastern front must have logically been informed of the activities of the *Einsatzgruppen*. In this respect, *SS-Obergruppenführer* Eric von dem Bach-Zelewski asserted at Nuremberg that all the generals of the Eastern Front were fully aware of the actual job of the *Einsatzgruppen*.[312]

Einsatzgruppe D in the footsteps of Eleventh Army in the Crimea

At Nuremberg, *SS-Oberführer* Otto Ohlendorf, chief of *Einsatzgruppe D*, which was operating behind the Eleventh Army in the southern Ukraine and later in the Crimea, presented one of the most enlightening testimonies concerning the relationship between the army and the *Einsatzgruppen*. At the trial of the major war criminals, this twisted intellectual, with university degrees in both law and political economy, and a former professor at the Institute of Applied Economics, in no way sought to exonerate the Wehrmacht generals and even less so himself. Indeed, far from attempting to dispute the facts of which the commanders of the Eastern Front and himself had been accused, he appeared rather proud, which reinforced all the more the credibility of his testimony.

He first mentioned that the zone of action of his *Einsatzgruppe* was determined from the fact that it was attached to a specific army group or to the Eleventh Army, and as a result advanced with either of the two, whereas the zone of operations for specific *Einsatzkommandos* was defined by the military commanders. He then recalled that, if the chiefs of the SD and the police force were the only ones authorized to issue orders to the *Einsatzgruppen*, there nevertheless existed an agreement under the terms of which the army group or Eleventh Army had the right to give orders to their *Einsatzgruppe* if the progress of operations demanded it. For this purpose, there was a liaison officer between the army group command or the Eleventh Army and the SD.

Even more interesting was his assertion that the commanders in chief of the army groups were not only informed of the orders to eliminate the Jews and Soviet civil servants, but that they had received orders to assist the SD units in their respective zones of operation so that they could properly accomplish the extermination. And without this instruction to the Wehrmacht commanders, as Ohlendorf rightly clarified, "the activities of the *Einsatzgruppen* would not have been possible."

Regarding the Eleventh Army, the chief of *Einsatzgruppe D* declared that he received marching orders from Field Marshal Manstein and his chief of staff: "[...] during the discussion on how things were progressing, personal conversations took place between von Manstein, his chief of staff, and myself." In addition, he specified that Manstein was aware of the extermination operations of *Einsatzgruppe D*. To the question whether he could say in what way the commander in chief of the Eleventh Army was leading or monitoring *Einsatzgruppe D* in the fulfillment of its extermination activities, Ohlendorf implicated Manstein: "In Nikolaiev, the Eleventh Army sent the order to commence the extermination only within a radius of 200 kilometers around the commander in chief's headquarters." He then recalled another case: "In Simferopol, the commander of the army requested the *Einsatzkommandos* that were involved to expedite the elimination, because famine was imminent and the lack of housing would be seriously felt." Then, when he was asked if he knew how many people were killed by *Einsatzgruppe D* during the period when he was in command of the sector located just south of the Ukraine and attached to the Eleventh Army, Ohlendorf shrugged his shoulders and responded, with a slight hesitation: "During the year extending from June 1941 to June 1942, the *Einsatzkommandos* accounted for the elimination of approximately 90,000 people."[313]

Ohlendorf's testimony leaves no doubt about the fact that Manstein was perfectly aware of the criminal mission of the *Einsatzgruppen* and, in particular of *Einsatzgruppe D*, which was marching in the wake of the Eleventh Army that he was commanding. His assertion that he did not know what was occurring behind the front is quite simply unbelievable. At the time he was in the Crimea, Manstein received numerous accounts of the criminal activities of *Einsatzgruppe D*, which were actively supported by units of the Eleventh Army. Indeed, the army provided troops and supplies to *Einsatzgruppe D* in order to facilitate its job.

The Field Marshal's participation in the genocide of the Jews was thus not only passive, but also active. If he appears not to have given much attention to the reports and briefings on the extermination of the Jews that were presented to him, he did place units from the Eleventh Army at the disposal of *Einsatzgruppe D*, notably in Simferopol, where 11,000 Jews were executed. Everything leads one to believe that *Einsatzgruppe D* was operating in the military zone of the Eleventh Army, benefiting not only from Manstein's agreement—who was very well informed of its criminal activities—but also from his support.[314]

From the time when Colonel General Schobert commanded the Eleventh Army, *SS-Oberführer* Ohlendorf was making note in his reports of the excellent relationship between this army and *Einsatzgruppe D*. Far from disintegrating with Schobert's replacement by Manstein, the collaboration between Eleventh Army and *Einsatzgruppe D* continued to become closer and more harmonious. And the activities of *Einsatzgruppe D* continued to be reported to Eleventh Army directly or through the command located to the rear of the army's zone of operations, better known as *Korück 553*. In the end, Ohlendorf characterized as "excellent" the rapport between *Einsatzgruppe D,* which he was leading, and the Eleventh Army that Manstein was commanding.[315]

At Nuremberg, within the scope of the trial against the *Einsatzgruppen*, Ohlendorf shed light on the legal framework in which the extermination program in the Crimea had taken place. "Such activity fell under the responsibility of the commander in chief. He was the only one who held executive authority and controlled life and death. And such responsibility was never restricted." This declaration was followed by another from Ohlendorf, just as revelatory, on Manstein's responsibility for the genocide of the Jews in the Crimea: "The units [of *Einsatzgruppe D*] fell within the domain of the army regarding tactical intervention. They were held accountable respectively to the army, the army corps, and the divisions for all measures taken. In every case, my activity as chief of *Einsatzgruppe D* was at every moment under the complete jurisdiction of the commander in chief of my army. And for each action that I had to execute, I had to take into consideration the full sovereignty of the commander in chief."

Such remarks from *SS-Oberführer* Ohlendorf, which spoke volumes on Manstein's responsibility in the war of extermination led by the Wehrmacht in the U.S.S.R., have been confirmed by documentary evidence. Furthermore, the judgment delivered at the trial of the *Einsatzgruppen* concluded that the Eleventh Army had actively participated in the genocide of the Jews in the Crimea.[316] The Eleventh Army had thus in no way remained loyal to the German tradition of chivalry, as Manstein claims fallaciously in his *Memoirs*.[317]

Quite to the contrary. The surrender of Soviet prisoners of war to the SD in the Eleventh Army's zone of operations occurred without a hitch. The selection of political commissars and Jews among the prisoners, and their execution, took place in the most routine manner. As soon as they were selected among the gathered prisoners, the Jews and the commissars were shot on the spot. Likewise, the Eleventh Army neglected to furnish its prisoners with the provisions and clothing necessary to keep them alive. Many thus died from hunger and cold during the winter of 1941–1942. Between December 1941 and August 1942, Eleventh Army handed 3,311 Red Army soldiers over to the SD. During the same period, 7,504 others were reported as either dead or executed by Wehrmacht guards.[318]

Manstein and the war crimes of Eleventh Army in the Crimea

There are numerous archival documents that attest to Eleventh Army's implication in the extermination of the Jews, whether during the time it was commanded by Schobert or Manstein. Even though certain reports only use the term "partisan," one should not lose sight of the fact that the expressions "commissar," "Jew," and "partisan" were generally used haphazardly, and often interchangeably. In this context, the struggle against the partisans served as a pretext to justify the handing over of the Communists and the Jews to the SD, and subsequently their execution. An analysis of the choice of words used in the orders of the high-ranking officers of the Wehrmacht, and in the reports of the *Einsatzgruppen*, clearly demonstrates that one equated the terms "Bolshevik," "partisan," and "Jew" with one another.

From the very beginning of the campaign in Russia, an intimate collaboration was created between the Eleventh Army and *Einsatzgruppe D*. On July 3, 1941, while it was still under the command of Colonel General Schobert, Eleventh Army issued the following directive, signed by its chief of staff, General Wöhler: "*Einsatzgruppe D* of the police force, approximately 470 men strong, will be placed under the orders of the high command of the Eleventh Army for its actions, lodging, and provisions."[319] On the same day, the chief of staff of Eleventh Army gave a strike order to *Sonderkommando 11b*, which was attached to *Einsatzgruppe D*: "[...] the capture of the politically unreliable elements in Kishinev will be assigned to a *Sonderkommando* of the (motorized) police force, with a total of 50 men [...]. For its orders, lodging, and its provisions, the *Sonderkommando* will be placed under the command [of Eleventh Army]. The *Sonderkommando* will work under orders of the chief of the police force and will be his own responsibility. Any measures taken must be reported to the high command of Eleventh Army [...]. After the execution of its assignments, within the framework of the unit to which it is attached, the [*Sonder*]*kommando* will be once again placed at the disposal of the Eleventh Army and will receive from it other directives."[320]

On July 9, 1941, the chief of the police force and the SD informed Army Group South's headquarters of its activities in the military zone of Eleventh Army: "On the 8th of this month, a significant action was conducted during which the leading Jewish class was fully stopped. On the following day, approximately 100 Communist Jews [...] were executed. [...] In all, more than 500 Jews have been executed by the Wehrmacht and the police during the 8th and 9th of this month."[321]

On August 3, 1941, *Sonderkommando 10a* reported to *Einsatzgruppe D*, to which it was attached, the following news: "In Kodyma [...] the command of the XXX Army Corps placed 400 soldiers at the disposal of the [*Sonder*]*kommando* in order to raid the Jewish quarter. On this occasion, the use of weapons was necessary. [...] 97 Jews were killed [...]. The execution [of the Jews] has been left to, within the framework of a joint intervention, 24 men from the Wehrmacht and 12 from the police force [...]."[322]

Four days later, the high command of Eleventh Army received a report from the secret military police force 647 describing the execution of 98 Jews in Kodyma.[323] On close to the same date, it was informed by

Sonderkommando 11a, the unit dispatched by *Einsatzgruppe D*, of its activities in Kischinev. The latter indicated that it had executed 68 Jews due to Communist activity and 6 others for arson.[324]

On September 8, 1941, *Sonderkommando 11a* sent to *Einsatzgruppe D* an activity report in which it underscored its collaboration with units of the Eleventh Army in actions against elements deemed undesirable by the Reich authorities: "In collaboration with units from the Wehrmacht, the [*Sonder*]*kommando* set into motion a few investigations from Nikolaiev to Kherson which concluded in the capture of several partisans. [...] During the march on Nikolaiev, seven political officials of the Communist Party were identified and executed. [...] The comments and complaints of the senior authorities of the Wehrmacht, according to which acts of violence by the Jews have been on the increase, have been taken into account. [...] Expiatory measures will occur through the execution of 227 hostages. [...] 122 Jews will be executed in Kherson."[325]

Barely a few days after taking command of Eleventh Army, Manstein, still a general at the time, was informed of the execution of Jews in the military zone falling under his authority. On September 12, 1941, *Einsatzgruppe D* sent to the high command of Eleventh Army a report concerning the activities of *Sonderkommando 11a* in Kherson during the period August 22 to September 10. It was received on September 14, three days before Manstein assumed command. On the 26th it was presented to Manstein and he signed it. The report, which represents one of the charges filed against Manstein during his trial, described the situation in the following terms: "The Jewish issue is, for the moment, partially resolved. The order had already been given on August 23, 1941, calling upon all Jews for mandatory registration and wearing of the yellow star. [...] The commando has completed the following executions: 400 male Jews and 10 female Jews have been shot as a punitive measure for acts of sabotage or for having been connected to intelligence. [...]. Having been informed of the events, the commander of the 72nd Infantry Division has expressed to the command his recognition and gratitude. The army had placed units at its disposition [...]."[326]

At his trial, Manstein had to explain why his signature was found on this report concerning the activities of *Einsatzgruppe D* in Kherson. In an unconvincing way, Manstein asserted that he had not read it, otherwise he would have demanded that its contents be explained. He then added this completely implausible response: "I never received a report from the SD in which was mentioned the execution of Jews."[327] However, in the report in question, dated from September 12, 1941, *Einsatzgruppe D* precisely indicated that it had slaughtered 410 Jews.

In October 1941, *Sonderkommando 10a* committed a massacre on the outskirts of the town of Genitchesk, in which soldiers from the 22nd Infantry Division belonging to the Eleventh Army participated. In a memo from October 6, addressed to *Einsatzgruppe D*, the chief of staff of Eleventh Army pointed out that *Sonderkommando 10a* was in the combat zone of the 22nd Infantry Division when it carried out a massive series of executions: "They should have first waited until all the measures, in particular the public executions in the town of Genitchesk [...] had received the agreement of the general staff of the division."[328]

On October 10, 1941, General Wöhler, in his role as Eleventh Army's chief of staff, signed an order concerning civilian resistance: "[...] the partisan groups are being incessantly reinforced by the Jews. The troop as well as the police and the army's instruments of security (the secret military police, the local police, and the police force of the SD) will be utilized."[329]

Three days later, the commander of Melitopol sent to *Korück 553* an activity report in which he mentions the execution of 2,000 Jews by the SD: "Melitopol and the villages of Peschanov and Kisejar, which have been incorporated into it, included approximately 85,000 inhabitants. Among them, 45 percent were Russian, 40 percent Jewish, and 2 percent of German descent. During the city's occupation by the Wehrmacht, nearly 40,000 inhabitants remained there. All of the Jews (2,000) were executed by the SD."[330] On October 28, 1941, a report provided a statement of the situation in Melitopol since the town's occupation by the German Army. The report confirmed the fate of the 2,000 Jews who were living there. "The administration and the instruments of the [Communist] Party fled on September 28, 1941; one [soldier] of the Red Army, 24 suspects, and 2,000 Jews have been handed over to the SD."[331]

On October 20, 1941, the commander of Kachowka addressed a report to *Korück 553* noting the ethnic cleansing taking place in the town: "13,000 inhabitants, among whom 30 percent are Jews. The purging of the area of Jewish and Communist elements has already been carried out by the police force in liaison with the Ukrainian militia."[332]

On October 29, 1941, the commander of Mariupol reported to *Korück 553* an operation undertaken in the town: "8,000 Jews have been executed by the SD."[333] On November 30, 1941, the commander of Armjansk informed *Korück 553* and Eleventh Army of the execution of 14 male and female Jews in the town on November 26, actions taken in order to reinforce the security of the combatant units.[334]

Eight days earlier, on November 22, the commander of Kertch had sent to *Korück 553* the following message: "The registration of the Jewish population living in Kertch has not yet been achieved. The elimination of the Jews will soon be implemented, due to the problems brought on by the alimentary situation in the town."[335] On December 7, 1941, he forwarded this memo to the same addressee: "The execution of the Jews, close to 2,500, occurred from December 1–3, 1941. Other subsequent executions are planned, for part of the Jewish population has fled or is still in hiding [...]."[336]

Even more significant was the operation conducted in Simferopol in mid-November 1941, which resulted in the death of 11,000 Jews. Demanding that the town be purged of all its Jewish elements before Christmas, the high command of Eleventh Army placed a few of its units at the disposal of the SD. The zealousness of Manstein's general staff to move forward with the execution of the Jews of Simferopol before December 25 was explained not by religious reasons, but rather by military motives related to the offensive planned against the fortress of Sevastopol. Since the town of Simferopol was located at the crossroads of communication routes in the Crimea, its pacification was judged essential to ensuring complete safety for the resupplying of Eleventh Army whenever it carried out its Sevastopol offensive. For this, they called for the execution of the Jews, who were considered the principal instigators of resistance activity. In other words, a preventive action, or rather revenge, against the Simferopol Jews was requested in order to secure the occupied territories of the Crimea.[337]

At Nuremberg, Ohlendorf described the demands of the Eleventh Army in minute detail: "The high command demanded that the elimination of the Jews in Simferopol be put into action before Christmas. This directive from the army was communicated to me by a liaison officer. Dr. Werner Braune [chief of *Sonderkommando 11b*] later negotiated with the army, for we did not have the prerequisite conditions in order to move forward with the extermination. And so, once an agreement had been reached, the army committed itself to fulfilling the prerequisite conditions. This is what took place and the extermination was able to happen before Christmas 1941. [...] The army placed at our disposal trucks to transport the Jews, drivers, gas, and local police for the roadblock."

He next explained the reasons that led Manstein's staff to formulate such a request: "In Simferopol, a request to accelerate the extermination was submitted by the high command of the army to the appropriate *Einsatzkommandos* according to the justification that this region would be threatened with famine and an enormous lack of lodging." To the question asking him if Manstein had disseminated an order enjoining the extermination of the Jews of Simferopol, Ohlendorf once again placed the responsibility on the commander in chief of the Eleventh Army: "No, I cannot say it, but it is obvious, in accordance with the chain of command, that the first quartermaster cannot do such a thing without the agreement of his commander in chief."[338]

In a report from the commander of Simferopol dating from November 14, 1941, addressed to *Korück 553* with a copy addressed to the high command of the Eleventh Army, appeared the following comment: "Simferopol had around 156,000 inhabitants [...] about 120,000 remained there. Among these, 70,000 were Russian, 20,000 Ukrainian, 20,000 Tartar, 20,000 Jews, with the remainder being divided among the various peoples, which included barely 100 of German descent [...]. The 11,000 Jews who remain will be executed by the SD."[339]

The help provided by the units of the Eleventh Army to *Einsatzgruppe D* in actions against the Jews of Simferopol has been proven by numerous documents.[340] At Nuremberg, Manstein contested Ohlendorf's testimony according to which the Wehrmacht soldiers would have participated in the execution of the Simferopol Jews. He gave his word as a Prussian officer: "That soldiers from my army participated in the execution of Jews, I consider this as absolutely impossible. [...] If a unit or an officer from my army had participated in such acts, that would have been the end of him."[341]

During his trial, General Wöhler, Manstein's chief of staff, wondered for his part if the 50 men from *Sonderkommando 11b* had alone gathered, led, and executed the 11,000 Jews from Simferopol, or if they had received assistance from the Wehrmacht. His response was most evasive: "I do not know [...] how they did it. I cannot understand it."

To the question asking him if it were possible that 50 men could bring in, assemble, and shoot 11,000 people, he responded quite simply: "I am not able to tell, for I have not thought about it [...]." Obliged to explain next how he had been able to be kept in the dark regarding the execution of 11,000 Jews in Simferopol, as he himself claimed, while the headquarters of the Eleventh Army was located at this time in Sarabus, 30 kilometers away, he made this unconvincing declaration: "Fine, I cannot explain it. I can only explain it with the arguments or the reasons that I have already given, which is to say, because of the secret character of the SD."

He even had the audacity to go so far as to claim that he knew nothing regarding the extermination of the Jews: "That National Socialism fundamentally desired to kill the Jews because they were Jewish, we were not aware of it." As to this response, the tribunal made the following statement: "The massacre of 90,000 people by police units unquestionably could not have occurred under such circumstances without the chief of staff of this army being aware. In such a case, he would be proven exceptionally incompetent. Actually, the behavior of the charged has not given us the impression of any incompetence on his part, and the opinion expressed towards him by his various chiefs refutes such a hypothesis."[342]

There was, however, no doubt as to Wöhler's anti-Semitism. In his role as commander in chief of the Eighth Army, he declared at the end of May 1944: "I ordered the arrest of these creatures (Jews). In short: the Jews must disappear." When he learned, during the same period, that German soldiers were maintaining relationships with Jewish families he expressed his anger thus: "[...] shameful and impudent behavior of the German soldiers [...]. He who gets together with Jews [...] does not deserve to be a German soldier."[343]

During his trial, General Wöhler even explained the origins of the animosity he felt towards the Jews: "In Germany, we have endured enough the Jewish Bolshevik system during the first years following the First World War. The fall of the Hohenzollern Empire, the control over the soldiers, the peace treaty, and all the anguish of the officers' corps left its mark." In thinly disguised terms, he thus designated the Jews as responsible for the ordeals experienced by Germany at the end of the Great War and at the beginning of the 1920s. It therefore appeared justifiable to him to take revenge upon them, in conformity with Field

Marshal Manstein's order from November 20, which called for severe punishment to be inflicted upon the Jews, the spiritual representatives of the Bolshevik terror. For the chief of staff of the Eleventh Army, it was necessary at all costs to spare German troops from being once again stabbed in the back. To this end, he could count on *SS-Oberführer* Ohlendorf's *Einsatzgruppe D*.[344]

Following the Simferopol operation, *Einsatzgruppe D* presented an account of its activities since the beginning of the Russian campaign: "The total number of executions is at 75,881." It also painted a broad picture of its operations aimed at exterminating "undesirable elements" during the period November 11 to December 11, 1941: 17,645 Jews, 2,504 *Krimtschaken* (an ethnic group with distant Jewish origins who had been living in the Crimea for a long time), 824 Tzigans, 212 Communists and partisans.[345] Concerning its actions subsequently undertaken in the surroundings of Simferopol, *Einsatzgruppe D* presented the results on January 9, 1942: "The area of activity of the *Kommando* groups, especially in the small villages, has been purged of Jews (*Judenfrei gemacht*). In one report [...] 3,176 Jews, 85 partisans, 12 thieves, and 122 Communist officials have been shot."[346] On the following day, the commander of Simferopol reported to *Korück 553* and the high command of the Eleventh Army that soldiers had handed over to the SD three political commissars who it immediately took care of, as well as twelve people arrested for possession of weapons.[347]

There were no fewer than 2,400 soldiers from Manstein's Eleventh Army who jointly participated with Ohlendorf's *Einsatzgruppe D* in genocidal operations in Simferopol and its surroundings between mid-November 1941 and mid-January 1942.[348] In a strike order from *Sonderkommando 11b*, signed by *SS-Sturmbannführer* Dr. Braune on January 12, 1942, it was indicated that more than 2,300 soldiers from Eleventh Army had been placed at the SD's disposal, with the intended action against the Simferopol Jews outlined in directives from the army's high command: "Under orders from the high command of the Eleventh Army [...] swift action will be implemented on January 12, 1942, at 11:00 A.M. in order to halt the untrustworthy elements (partisans, saboteurs, eventual enemy troops, plain-clothed paratroopers, Jews, key Communists, etc.) The high command of the Eleventh Army [...] assigned *Einsatzgruppe D—Sonderkommando 11b—*, the police force, and the SD to go through [Simferopol] with a fine-tooth comb. [...]

Forces on the order of 2,300 men [from the Wehrmacht], as well as 55 men from the local police, and 20 men from the secret military police will be placed at the disposal of *Sonderkommando 11b* [...]."[349]

After the Simferopol massacre, the Eleventh Army was wrestling with a shortage of watches and exerted pressure to equip its troops in order to better coordinate the forthcoming operations. To this effect, an exchange of letters followed between Ohlendorf and Wöhler. One of the letters from the chief of *Einsatzgruppe D* was signed by the commander of the Eleventh Army and his chief of staff. The two letters are dated from February 12, 1942.

The first, signed by Ohlendorf, concerned the requisition of watches taken from the Jews during the extermination operation: "The commandeered watches, following an action against the Jews, are in good shape. Watches of any value (watches in gold or silver) will be sent, in accordance with the directives, to the State Treasury in Berlin. The other watches of little value [...] will be given to the members of the Wehrmacht (offers and troops) and to the members of *Einsatzgruppe D*. [...] As experience proves, almost only the old watches have been found and are for the most part unusable. For the moment, there are a number of watches that have been repaired and are still available, and which can be handed over to the aforementioned staff."[350]

At the head of the second letter, also signed by Ohlendorf, were found the signatures of Wöhler and Manstein. It pointed out the request from the Eleventh Army's commander to obtain for his troops the available watches collected during actions against the Jews: "After a telephone call from the commander of Simferopol, I learned that *Herr* commander in chief had demanded for the army, for professional use, the watches that were available after having been collected during action against the Jews. I hereby forward 120 watches to the army, which have since been repaired and are in working order. There are still 50 other watches which are being repaired, a portion of which will be back in working order. If the army needs any more watches, please inform me of it."[351]

Manstein had to explain at his trial why he signed this letter. As was to be expected, his declaration was ambiguous: "Yes, I signed the letter [...]. I believe that it is easy to explain the situation. I asked the responsible officer to procure for me more watches and to speak to the mayor of Simferopol. Simferopol was the largest city of the Crimea and there were naturally watch stores and repair studios." He was then asked if he had read the letter and he responded that even if he had read it, it would never have occurred to him that the watches had been stolen following the execution of the Jews. It is, however, inconceivable that he did not read the contents of the letter which was only four sentences long.[352]

In his defense during Manstein's trial at Hamburg in 1949, the British lawyer Reginald Paget asserted that his client had believed that the commandeered watches were of Swiss fabrication. Such a supposition, claiming that the watches sold in the stores of Simferopol could originally be from Switzerland, especially at this time, was pure fantasy. However, when he had been called to testify at Nuremberg three years earlier, Manstein expressed a completely different view. He claimed to have believed that the watches were of German fabrication and that they had been sent directly from Germany.[353] Such a contradiction can only leave us perplexed as to Manstein's supposed lack of knowledge of the fact that the watches belonged to the executed Jews.

After the war, Wöhler tried to evade his own responsibility in the matter by condemning Manstein, his former superior. He disputed having made the decision himself to commandeer the watches stolen from the Jews. According to his remarks, such a decision would only have been made under orders of the commander of the Eleventh Army. To the question that was posed to him by the court asking if he knew that the requisitioned watches came from the assassinated Jews, Wöhler attempted once again to evade the issue by replying in the negative. He then added that if he had known it, he would never have taken the watches. When he was next asked if the watches had truly been handed over to the Eleventh Army, he responded unconvincingly: "It's possible."[354]

To counter acts of sabotage or attacks against German occupying forces, Eleventh Army resorted to brutal and arbitrary measures towards innocent civilians. On November 16, 1941, the commander of Simferopol decreed that, for every act of sabotage perpetrated or attempted against the Germans, 100 inhabitants from the region would be executed in retaliation. For example, on November 29, 50 people were shot in Simferopol to avenge a German soldier killed by a mine on November 22, and a German non-commissioned officer shot down by a partisan during the night of November 27–28.[355] Even though the number of people executed was half of what was called for in the November 16 decree, this took nothing away from the arbitrary nature of such an act of vengeance.

On December 15, 1941, Major Stephanus, the official in charge of the fight against the partisans at the general staff of Eleventh Army, issued a directive to his units which stipulated that: "[...] when there exists the slightest suspicion that the population is not standing up in opposition against the demands of the partisans with enough force [...] one should proceed with the most severe actions against the people (executing hostages [...] burning villages) [...]. The Jews must be handed over to the SD [...]. The partisans who have run rampant will, however, be hanged."[356] Two weeks earlier, this same Stephanus forwarded a memo to Manstein, dated from November 29, apropos of what was needed to defeat the partisans: "The annihilation of numerous identified partisan groups, the prevention of the formation of other groups, and the securing of the supply lines constitutes a significant condition for the definitive purification [...] of the Crimea. All the units of Eleventh Army, in particular the reserves and supply troops, must participate in this task."[357]

On December 3, 1941, Major Stephanus was thus in a position to announce the results of a week's worth of combating the resistance in the southern Crimea since November 25, 1941: "The systematic battle against the partisans in the Crimea has provided, so far, the following success: 470 partisans killed, 490 arrested."[358] Such numbers correspond precisely to those that had been released on the preceding day by Major Hans Riesen, from the department of the *Abwehr* within the staff of the Eleventh Army. In addition, Riesen indicated in his report that the German and Romanian losses during the anti-partisan operations were: 45 killed, 72 wounded, and 1 missing in action from the German side; 29 killed, 30 wounded, and 1 missing from the Romanian side. Finally, he underscored in particular the contributions of the XXXth Infantry Corps and the 132nd Infantry Division in the operations, as well as the execution of 62 Jews and Communists by *Einsatzgruppe D*, in retaliation for an attack against Wehrmacht soldiers.[359]

Previously, on November 24, 1941, Riesen had reported the participation of troops from the Eleventh Army in the elimination of elements that were considered undesirable by the Reich: "On November 22, 17 Jews, who, according to testimony from the civilian population, were involved with the partisans, were shot in Yalta by the 72nd Infantry Division."[360]

On December 16, 1941, Stephanus notified his superiors in the Eleventh Army: "Through December 15, 1941, 950 partisans have been killed and 641 taken prisoner."[361] These numbers were corroborated by Riesen's report from December 15, 1941, in which Wehrmacht losses in the fight against the partisans were listed as: 80 killed, 126 wounded, and 1 missing in action from the German side; 54 killed, 57 wounded, and 1 missing among the Romanians.[362] Five weeks later, on January 23, 1942, Stephanus provided the following account: "Since the beginning of the battle against the partisans on November 25, 1941, through today, January 23, 1942. [...] 748 partisans have been arrested, 1,435 partisans killed, and 21 paramilitary killed."[363]

However, the battle against the partisans assumed a genuinely anti-Semitic character in the port of Eupatoria. On January 5, 1942, a Red Army landing, supported by naval units, occurred at Eupatoria. Simultaneously, a revolt broke out in the city, in which a portion of the population participated. The small number of German forces that were deployed in the area could neither prevent the landing nor hold back the insurrection. After reinforcements were sent in, the Germans succeeded in recapturing the Crimean city. Under Manstein's order, the German occupiers then unleashed on Eupatoria a particularly terrible and gratuitous vengeance: 1,200 civilians, of whom many naturally were Jews, were shot on January 7, 1942.[364]

Such vengeance unfolded under the direction of Major Riesen, an officer of the *Abwehr* on the staff of Eleventh Army. This officer was in charge of the battle against the partisans in the army's zone of operations, according to an order from the high command of Eleventh Army signed by General Wöhler. All the news concerning the partisans was required to be communicated to Riesen, whose responsibility it was, moreover, to call upon army units to support those of *Einsatzgruppe D* when the need presented itself.[365] On January 11, Riesen made note of the retaliatory measures in Eupatoria in a report addressed to his superiors in Eleventh Army: "As an expiatory measure against the behavior [...] of the population in Eupatoria during the Russian landing attempt, nearly 1,200 civilians were shot on January 7, 1942."[366]

As much in his *Memoirs* as during his trial, Manstein laconically asserted that the 1,200 people shot in Eupatoria were armed partisans.

Obliged to provide further explanation regarding this matter, he denied having given any sort of order to Riesen to resort to retaliatory measures. Furthermore, he mentioned that he was hardly troubled by the context in which the executions occurred: "One did not report to me if these partisans had been shot during combat with their weapons in hand or if they had been arrested with their weapons in hand and then later shot. At the moment, it made no difference; our situation was much too serious to think about minor differences such as this."[367]

However, Riesen presented at Nuremberg a completely different version of the facts concerning the massacre in Eupatoria. He declared having been assigned by Manstein himself to execute, as a retaliatory measure, all those who were caught carrying weapons: "I had carried out the retaliatory action under the commander in chief's order. Dr. Braune was also present [...] 1,184 men were chosen and shot."[368] Ninety soldiers from the Eleventh Army participated in this killing. Apparently, Major Riesen had wanted to entrust the operation to *SS-Sturmbannführer* Dr. Braune, but *SS-Oberführer* Ohlendorf was opposed to it, irritated by the fact that, in his opinion, Wehrmacht officers were constantly looking to pass off onto the *Einsatzgruppen* military jobs of this type. Dr. Braune revealed, for his part, that the executions in Eupatoria had been ordered by Manstein himself, which confirms Riesen's remarks regarding the full responsibility of the Eleventh Army's commander in the massacre of innocent civilians. Even Ohlendorf corroborated the statements of Riesen and Dr. Braune, averring that it was truly Manstein who had demanded retaliatory measures in Eupatoria by the execution of all those who were carrying weapons.[369]

After the retaliatory measures conducted in Eupatoria, numerous actions of a lesser scale were undertaken against Jews in the surrounding area. For example, on January 17, 1942, Eleventh Army was informed of the execution of 23 partisans and Jews 15 kilometers to the northwest of Eupatoria.[370] On January 30, 1942, in the small village of Sarabus, where Manstein's headquarters was located, a document attested to the arrest of Jews, partisans, and other suspects, then of their execution by the SD.[371] On February 14, 1942, a report from the commander of Karasubasar, addressed to *Korück 553*, indicated that two Jews, who were hiding in the town, had been handed over to the SD.[372] Yet *Einsatzgruppe D* had already announced in an activities report dated from January 2, 1942 that this town had already been purged of Jewish elements (*Karasubasar "Judenfrei" war*) since the end of 1941.[373] On February 28, 1942, *Korück 553* reported the elimination by the SD of 90 Jews from the town of Bachtschissaraj, an operation that occurred on December 31, 1941: "In Bachtschissaraj, 90 Jews. The SD executed the Jews on December 31, 1941."[374] On February 28, 1942, the commander of Bachtschissaraj addressed to *Korück 553* the following memo: "From a political perspective, calm rules over the city, which has been completely purged of Jews [*ist vollkommen Judenfrei*]. A resistance movement from the population is not to be expected."[375]

Even more significant is the report from *Einsatzgruppe D* on the assessment of its activities in northern Crimea for the first half of February, 1942: "From February 1 to 15, 1,451 people have been executed, including 920 Jews, 45 partisans, and 12 pillagers, saboteurs, and social misfits, for a present total of 86,632."[376] As for the battle that *Einsatzgruppe D* was waging against groups of partisans, Major Riesen noted the elimination of 255 partisans during the period from February 4 to 24, 1942.[377]

According to a report concerning its activities in the town of Feodosiya, *Einsatzgruppe D* disclosed on January 2, 1942 that it had cleansed it of all Jewish elements (*Feodossia "Judenfrei" gemacht*).[378] But a few Jews had succeeded in hiding themselves, as an activities report from the commander of the town addressed to the attention of *Korück 553* attests on February 28, 1942. In this report, there was mention of the elimination in Feodosiya of Jews, members of the NKVD, and partisans, an operation led in conjunction with soldiers from Eleventh Army and members of the SD: "Through February 15, 1942, 36 Jews, 16 members of the NKVD, 12 partisans, and 12 youth were shot by the [*Sonderkommando 10b*]. [...] German soldiers are working in collaboration with the German police."[379]

Another report, dated this time from March 27, 1942, mentioned that the town of Feodosiya had been scoured thoroughly by the Wehrmacht: "The observations that have been made following the work of the police force from *Sonderkommando 10b* leads one to conclude that there still remain many untrustworthy and hostile elements in the region of the town of Feodosiya. The first raid took place on March 5, 1942. [...] Nearly 380 soldiers were at the disposal" of *Sonderkommando 10b* "to move through with a fine-tooth comb" the first district of the town and to "cordon off" the untrustworthy and hostile elements: "[...] 13 people, including four women, were incarcerated [...]. The 13 people who were arrested were as follows: four Jews, among whom two had fake passports [...]; three female Jews, among whom two had fake passports [...]; one partisan; one member of the NKVD; one man who was caring for and illegally hiding partisans; one woman who was caring for and illegally hiding partisans; one member of the Communist Party [...]; one man who had killed a German soldier [...]. In all, 13 people were later executed. The man who had killed the soldier was hanged in public in the main square."

"The second raid occurred on March 9, 1942. [...] 360 members of the Wehrmacht were placed at the disposal" of *Sonderkommando 10b* "to pass through with a fine-tooth comb" the town's second district: "[...]. 15 people, including five women [...] were incarcerated. The 15 people arrested were as follows: six Jews, of which three had fake passports from the NKVD; three female Jews; one woman who had pillaged to a large extent goods from the Wehrmacht; one plain-clothed Red Army lieutenant (probably a stray partisan); two members of the NKVD; one spy [...]; one member of the Communist Party [...]. These 15 people were shot after a long interrogation."

"The third raid took place on March 13, 1942. [...] The raid was led with key units from the Wehrmacht [...]. Approximately 350 men from the Wehrmacht were at the disposal" of *Sonderkommando 10b* to scour the city's third district: "[...] 17 people were incarcerated [...]. These 17 people were as follows: three male Jews; eight female Jews; one *Politruk* (political officer) (plain-clothed—a stray); three members of the NKVD; two men who took part in pillaging. Of these 17 people, 15 were later executed and two were released, for it was not proven that they had taken part in the pillaging."

"On March 20, 1942, the fourth and last district was passed through with a fine-tooth comb" by *Sonderkommando 10b* with "approximately 350 soldiers. [...] Seven people were incarcerated. These seven arrested people were as follows: three Jews, three Communists [...]; one key member of the NKVD. In all, seven people were executed after long interrogations." The job that consisted in "passing through the town of Feodosiya with a fine-tooth comb has been completed. Overall, the result can be characterized as satisfactory."[380]

In an activities report for the period April 16–30, 1942, addressed to *Korück 553*, the commander of Feodosiya announced: "Two people suspected of hostile actions have been handed over to the SD, as well as a member of the Red Army and a female Jew for other reasons." He also included this clarification: "During the second half of April 1942, 43 people have been executed, among whom were 22 Jews."[381]

In another report dated from March 20, 1942, Major Riesen provided an assessment of the battle against the partisans in the area around Karasubasar for the period March 13–15, 1942: 353 partisans killed, of whom three were political commissars and eleven were women.[382] Three weeks later, on April 12, 1942, he reported within the context of the battle against the partisans the elimination of 491 people by *Einsatzgruppe D* for the period ranging from February 25 to March 31, 1942.[383] On April 14, 1942, a report from the secret military police 703 indicated that 255 people connected to groups of partisans had been arrested and then executed in Eupatoria, among whom were 51 partisans, 49 spies, 44 Communists, and 5 Jews.[384]

Two days later, *Einsatzgruppe D* informed the command of Eleventh Army, in a report on its activities since February 1, 1942, that the Jews in the Crimea had all been eliminated: "*The Crimea is purged of Jews [Von Juden ist die Krim freigemacht]*. Only occasionally do small groups appear, particularly in the regions of the north. There where they can disguise themselves by using fake identity cards, they will sooner or later be recognized, as experience has demonstrated [...]."[385]

A report from *Einsatzgruppe D*, dated April 8, 1942, specified that 91,678 Jews had been executed. According to the most reliable studies on the genocide of the Jews, the total number of people assassinated by *Einsatzgruppe D* in the wake of the Eleventh Army in southern Ukraine and in the Crimea surpassed 100,000. Of the total number of Jews executed by *Einsatzgruppe D*, approximately 33,000 were killed when Field Marshal Manstein was commanding the Eleventh Army, which signifies that approximately two-thirds lost their life during the period when the army was led by Colonel General Schobert.[386]

The massive executions of Jews, political commissars, partisans, and other elements deemed undesirable by the German authorites continued throughout the following months in the military zone of Eleventh Army. On May 14, 1942, Major Riesen observed the final operations of *Einsatzgruppe D* against the partisans: "During the period from April 1–30, 1942, 191 partisans [...] were shot."[387] Thirteen days later, he described the battle led by *Einsatzgruppe D* against the partisans in the Crimea for the period from November 15, 1941 to May 19, 1942: 4,020 partisans killed and 1,290 incarcerated. Within the scope of the operations against the partisans, the Germans counted 150 among their dead and 148 wounded, whereas the Romanians listed 90 dead and 121 wounded.[388] On June 19, 1942, Riesen reported the elimination by *Einsatzgruppe D* of 278 partisans from May 1–30, 1942.[389]

On June 26, 1942, a few days prior to the fall of Sevastopol, a report from the secret military police 647, focusing on its activities for the month of June 1942 and addressed to the attention of the Eleventh Army's high command, made note of the arrest of 132 people, among whom 58 were killed, primarily partisans and saboteurs.[390] The following month, the secret military police 647 submitted a new report to Eleventh Army about its activities, this time for the month of July. The report informed the high command that they had proceeded with the arrest of 133 people and the execution of 29 among them, mainly partisans, but also a few Jews and political commissars.[391] In its activity report for the month of August 1942, addressed to the attention of Eleventh Army's high command, dating from August 25, 1942, the secret military police 647 announced the arrest of 238 people, among whom 116 were shot, essentially partisans, but also a few Jews and political commissars.[392] Four days later, Riesen provided an account of the fight against the partisans from November 15, 1941 to August 25, 1942: 5,165 partisans killed and 1,329 incarcerated. The losses of the Wehrmacht during those operations were as follows: 170 killed and 163 wounded on the German side; 136 killed and 201 wounded on the Romanian side.[393] Finally, on September 26, 1942, the secret military police 647 sent to the high command of Eleventh Army a report regarding its activities on the Leningrad front during the month of September 1942. It stated that 12 people had been executed, primarily partisans but also several Jews, in Eleventh Army's zone of operations.[394]

Manstein's responsibility in the extermination of the Jews

The documents found in military archives give a clear image of the widespread activity of *Einsatzgruppe D* following in the tracks of the Eleventh Army in southern Ukraine and the Crimea. They also contribute toward an understanding of Field Marshal's responsibility in his role as commander in chief of the Eleventh Army in this area. Not only did he support the extermination operations against Jews and Communists in the military zone falling under his authority, he occasionally placed at the disposal of *Einsatzgruppe D* units from his own army when they were required to successfully conclude the elimination of those elements deemed undesirable by the National Socialist regime. And so, by abetting these policies and operations, he was fully complicit in a criminal regime.

At the time Manstein took command, Eleventh Army was already greatly implicated in the criminal activities of the units of *Einsatzgruppe D*. By taking leadership of the army in mid-September 1941, he thus inherited staff officers and unit commanders who had been fighting in the southern sector of the Soviet front and collaborating with *Einsatzgruppe D* since the beginning of Operation Barbarossa.

According to Wehrmacht's military jurisdictions, the commander in chief of an army is the expression of executive authority and responsible for order in the military zone falling under his leadership. The destiny of the local population located in this military zone also came under the responsibility of the commander in chief. Consequently, it does not take much to prove Manstein's responsibility in the theater of operations of the Eleventh Army.[395] At Nuremberg, Manstein claimed that his duties as commander of the Eleventh Army had not permitted him to learn what was happening to the Jews of the Crimea: "No, I was not presented with the opportunity to learn this, for during the year I found myself successively at twelve or thirteen command posts always out in the field of operations. [...] One must take into account the fact that a commander in chief was so absorbed by concerns of the battle and that, rightly so, only the most important of facts of secondary importance were communicated to him." He next maintained that he had never tolerated the slightest violation against martial law: "In my military sector, I did not tolerate such things, and whatever was happening on the ideological level outside of that, we knew nothing about. This was outside our area of control and knowledge. We had neither the power nor the right to prevent anything, disregarding the fact that we were never aware of all of the atrocities presenting themselves."[396]

The pretext referred to by the field marshal according to which his duties as commander in chief of an army had prevented him from being aware of the fate of the Jews finding themselves in territories occupied by his troops, notably because of his worries and preoccupations about the battle, is totally absurd due to the fact that he was spending a large part of his evenings playing chess or bridge, his favorite pastimes, with his adjutant, Lieutenant Alexander Stahlberg. According to the latter, together they had probably played more than a thousand chess games in less than three years. And this does not take into account, still according to Stahlberg, the time that Manstein devoted to listening to his favorite records on a portable gramophone, primarily the music of Mozart.[397]

In the autumn of 1942, Manstein went to Hitler's headquarters in order to receive the field marshal's baton that his capture of the Sevastopol fortress had earned him. At breakfast, he asked his Führer what was to become of the Jews. During this period, hundreds of thousands of Jews had already been killed by the *Einsatzgruppen* and the Wehrmacht. Likewise, the gas chambers of Aushwitz-Birkenau were running at full capacity. Hitler replied that Germany must create a state for the Jews. He had first thought of Palestine, then of the island of Madagascar. But he had realized that a Jewish state would have to be controlled by the Germans. As a result, he had decided that it would be from within Lublin's Polish government that the Germans would control the Jewish state. Hitler did not say a single word about the extermination of the Jews. The field marshal, who knew well that the main job of the *Einsatzgruppen* consisted of the elimination of all the Jews and the cadres of the Communist Party, was satisfied with his Führer's response, and insisted no more.[398] Was it his intention, through this conversation, to create for himself an alibi, in case he would have to later answer for his actions?

During his trial at Hamburg, Manstein's lawyers did not contest that numerous briefings on the criminal activities of *Einsatzgruppe D* could have been regularly reported to the high command of the Eleventh Army, either directly by *Einsatzgruppe D* or through the intermediary of *Korück 553*. But they claimed that their client did not have a single moment of time to read them, all the more so since his staff did not want to weigh him down with such news which could have provoked him to abandon his command.[399]

Whether or not he was aware of all of *Einsatzgruppe D*'s criminal activities, this does not in any way detract from his responsibility, for because of the authority he carried in his military zone as commander in chief of Eleventh Army, it was his duty to be knowledgeable of every-thing that occurred there. Clearly, in no way could he prohibit the activities of the *Einsatzgruppe* that were attached to his army, but he nevertheless had the authority to be informed as much as possible about the extent of their operations, even to limit their reach. Nevertheless, because of his excessive ambition to one day become the German Army's commander in chief or chief of general staff, he not only preferred to close his eyes to the horrible massacres committed by *Einsatzgruppe D* behind his front, he also consented to providing it with troops whenever the need presented itself.

One thus understands better why the high command of Eleventh Army, apropos of the Nikolaiev case, gave instructions to *Einsatzgruppe D* to move forward with the elimination of the Jews at least 200 kilometers away from the commander in chief's headquarters. However, *SS-Oberführer* Ohlendorf departed from this rule on at least two occasions: first in Simferopol, where the executions took place 30 kilometers from Manstein's headquarters established in Sarabus; then in a small town, where they took place practically in front of the field marshal's door, which was not soundproofed.[400] Quite obviously, the fate of the Jews in the occupied territories left Manstein completely indifferent.

When his adjutant, Lieutenant Stahlberg, spoke to him in the spring of 1943 about reports of the massive executions of Jews in the occupied territories which his friend Colonel Hans Oster, from the intelligence service of the *Abwehr*, had shown him during a visit to the latter's office in Berlin, Manstein, then commander in chief of Army Group South, remained silent, preferring to make no comment.

In the autumn of 1943, Stahlberg also reported to Manstein a conversation he had had in private with his friend Eberhard Finckh, first quartermaster of Army Group South. The latter had informed him of the remarks of two staff officers who had by chance participated in a mass execution of Jews which had occurred in the forested region behind the front under the military jurisdiction of Army Group South. Perpetrated by men who were wearing SS or SD uniforms, the slaughter had clearly been well organized. The two witnesses had also revealed to Finckh that, according to an SS officer, the number of Jews assassinated at this time rose to more than 100,000.

Manstein's reaction to Finckh's statements, which Stahlberg had reported to him, was lively and sudden. In his eyes, that 100,000 Jews had been killed was something absolutely unbelievable. If 100,000 Jews had truly been executed in a forested region, then how, he wondered, had they been able to get rid of the bodies? The impracticality of it proved, in his opinion, that Finckh and himself had been the victims of vile propaganda aimed at undermining the Germans' morale. He recalled, furthermore, that he himself had experienced the enemy's propaganda as a young officer during the war of 1914–18. Consequently, he added, it was important to protect oneself against insidious assertions or any sort of brainwashing by the enemy. Since they had both participated in the opening ceremonies of the 1936 Olympic games in Berlin, where more than 100,000 people filled the stadium, Manstein asked Stahlberg to visualize such a mass of people and to then tell him where 100,000 Jewish bodies could have been dispersed. He then suggested to him to tell his friend Finckh to dismiss such fantastical stories.[401]

In the archives, there is nothing to confirm a mass execution of 100,000 Jews in a single day in the wooded region located to the rear of Army Group South's zone of operations. In 1987, Rüdiger von Manstein called upon the expertise of the Institute of Eastern Europe in Munich (*Osteuropa-Institut in München*) to look into the veracity of the testimony in question. After the analysis he concluded: "The murder of such a large number of Jewish inhabitants from the U.S.S.R. in a forest can be dismissed with certainty [...]." But this does not so much signify that Manstein was in no way knowledgeable of the fate of the Jews. He quite simply did not want to believe that which appeared to him unimaginable.[402]

After the war, witnesses claimed that Manstein had participated in a conference held by the high authorities of the Nazi regime in Poznan on January 25, 1944. During this, *Reichsführer-SS* Himmler spoke, for the first time, to 300 field marshals and generals on the matter of the extermination of the Jews, even referring to the elimination of millions among them. In fact, according to Stahlberg, Manstein was actually not in Poznan, but at his Proskurov headquarters. He had left his headquarters on the following day for Liegnitz in order to spend the day with his family before going to the Führer's headquarters in Rastenburg on January 27, where he and his fellow officers had been summoned by Hitler, who was in a hurry to once again be assured of their unfailing loyalty.[403]

At the time when he was at the head of the Eleventh Army in the Crimea, Manstein had been informed by one of his staff officers, Captain Ulrich Gunzert, of a massive execution of Jews in which the latter had participated. Gunzert reported to him the following events: "In a deep ditch, were lying several layers of cadavers. After each round of firing, the men of the SD went down into the ditch and shot in the head all those who were still alive. It was a public massacre. I will never forget the faces of these people, who, on an embankment overlooking the ditch, were waiting to be executed. When I tried to intervene against this, a man from the SS prevented me from doing so: 'Get out of here, this does not concern you'!"

Manstein's reaction was typical of his behavior with regard to the regime's genocidal policy ever since the Poland campaign. Gunzert wrote: "I suggested to Manstein to carry out something against this. But he refused, for he carried no influence in this backcountry region. Besides, he had many other worries. Manstein took refuge behind his military duties and ordered me not to speak of this with anyone else. It was a question of fleeing from his responsibilities, a moral failure."[404]

Manstein's declaration at his trial that during the war he had not received any information on the extermination of the Jews was thus a complete lie, all the more so since he had even been informed of what was occurring in the concentration camps by his assistant, Lieutenant Stahlberg. When, in autumn 1943, the latter specifically informed him of the concentration camps, notably that of Auschwitz, Manstein at first remained silent, then considered the news of Auschwitz and the other extermination camps as being so implausible that he refused to believe it.[405] However, at Nuremberg, he claimed never to have been informed of the Jewish genocide that was taking place inside the camps: "[...] I knew as little as the German people and even less, for when one is engaged in a battle a thousand miles from Germany, one never hears talk of such things. I learned before the war of the existence of two concentration camps: Oranienburg and Dachau. An officer who had been invited to visit such a camp recounted to me that there was a veritable collection of criminal figures there, with political detainees, and that they were furthermore, according to what he had seen, severely but appropriately treated."[406]

That he was totally indifferent to the fate of the Jews in the occupied territories is clear. The advancement of his career, the promotions, and honors obviously counted more for him. For this, he had to close his eyes to the regime's criminal policies, even actively participate in them. Although he clearly did not possess in any way a criminal instinct, Manstein shared no less the prejudices of his contemporaries with respect to the Jews, particularly those of Eastern Europe. And that was enough for him—as well as for his fellow officers—to accept a war of extermination in the U.S.S.R.

When he was transferred from the Baltic region to the area of the Black Sea, Manstein found himself from that moment on in an area inhabited by many Jews. For racial and ideological reasons, all motivated out of a consideration for security and pacification, he felt compelled to contribute to their extermination. One can thus wonder what his fate would have been had he received the command of the *AfrikaKorps* instead of Field Marshal Rommel. When the *AfrikaKorps* was created, Hitler had juggled the idea of entrusting its leadership to Manstein. Not only would Manstein have had as much success as Rommel on a military level, but he would have felt beholden, like the latter, to conduct a "proper" war, focusing on more traditional politico-military objectives.[407]

Could the fact that he most certainly had Jewish origins, however distant, have influenced Manstein's attitude regarding the fate reserved for the Jews by the Third Reich? Was his performance when confronted with the Jewish issue a deliberate or subconscious result of some sort of denial of his possible Jewish roots? For some, the very suspicion that he probably had Jewish ancestors must have certainly had an influence over his attitude towards National Socialism.[408] In no way did Manstein conceal from those closest to him that he perhaps had Jewish roots and that it was furthermore as a Jew that he was harshly judged by several leading members of the Nazi regime, such as *Reichsführer-SS* Himmler and Minister of Propaganda Goebbels. Like the majority of his fellow officers, Manstein quite simply shared the anti-Semitic prejudices that were circulating as much within the army as in German society since the end of the First World War, and which had been taken to their extreme under the Hitler Reich, particularly in the context of a ruthless racial and ideological struggle led in Bolshevik Russia.

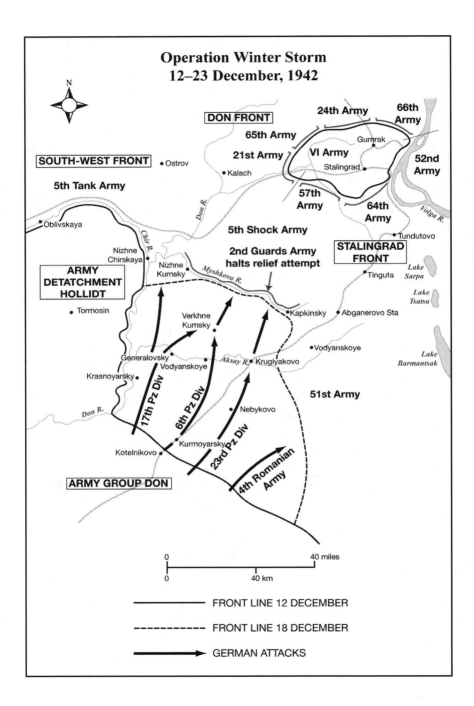

Operation Winter Storm
12–23 December, 1942

N

DON FRONT

SOUTH-WEST FRONT

• Ostrov

24th Army

66th Army

65th Army

Gumrak

21st Army

VI Army

52nd Army

5th Tank Army

• Kalach

Stalingrad •

57th Army

Obliskaya

Don R.

5th Shock Army

64th Army

Volga R.

Nizhne Chirskaya

Chir R.

2nd Guards Army halts relief attempt

• Tundutovo

ARMY DETATCHMENT HOLLIDT

Nizhne Kumsky

Myshkova R.

STALINGRAD FRONT

Lake Sarpa

• Tinguta

Lake Tsatsa

• Tormosin

Verkhne Kumsky

• Kapkinsky

• Abganerovo Sta

Generalovsky

Aksay R. • Krugiyakovo

• Vodyanskoye

Vodyanskoye

Lake Barmantsak

Krasnoyarsky

17th Pz Div

6th Pz Div

51st Army

Don R.

• Nebykovo

23rd Pz Div

Kurmoyarsky

Kotelnikovo

4th Romanian Army

ARMY GROUP DON

| 0 | | 40 miles |
| 0 | 40 km | |

———— FRONT LINE 12 DECEMBER

- - - - - FRONT LINE 18 DECEMBER

———▶ GERMAN ATTACKS

THE WINDS OF BEREZINA: THE STALINGRAD TRAGEDY

Following the encirclement of the German Sixth Army in Stalingrad, Field Marshal Manstein received orders to take command of the newly formed Army Group Don, which was in the process of being positioned on either side of the city. Its mission: to stop enemy attacks and recapture territory lost since the beginning of the Soviet counteroffensive. Such a task proved, however, impossible to carry out with the forces and reserves placed at its disposal. As for the destruction of Sixth Army, did Manstein have to assume part of the responsibility, particularly for not having been in a position to extricate it from the Soviet hold? Was the failure a result, at least in part, of his decision to accept the sacrifice of Sixth Army, which was holding back the bulk of Soviet troops in the region, in order to facilitate the strategic withdrawal of his army group, itself threatened with encirclement throughout the winter of 1942–43? Before we focus on the command of Army Group Don in the context of the Stalingrad tragedy, it would be appropriate for us to first retrace the progression of the tragedy in order to better evaluate Manstein's subsequent decisions, some of which remain controversial to this day.

Manstein's analysis of the causes that led to the Stalingrad tragedy

After a glorification of the heroic efforts of the German soldier on the Volga, Manstein presents in his *Memoirs* a penetrating analysis and evaluation of the operations which, since the German offensive of summer 1942, led to an encirclement of Sixth Army and to disaster during the following winter. He also assesses the situation as it stood when he took command of Army Group Don.

He assigns straightaway, and furthermore rightly so—as we will later see—the responsibility of the Sixth Army's destruction to Hitler: "The destruction of the Sixth Army is of course due to Hitler's refusal—inspired above all by his desire for prestige—to willingly evacuate Stalingrad. Yet if it found itself in such a situation, it was due to the operational mistakes made by the high command in the preparation and conducting of the 1942 offensive, especially in setting the terms of its objectives."

He then raises points that had a decisive significance on the fate of the Sixth Army. First of all, because of the objectives dictated in consideration of the war economy, Hitler committed the German offensive in southern Russia on two widely divergent axes of attack: in the direction of Stalingrad and towards the Caucasus. When the offensive came to a halt, the OKH inherited an overextended front which its available forces were incapable of holding. After having transferred the Eleventh Army to the Leningrad front, Hitler no longer had at his disposal an operational reserve in the sectors of Stalingrad and the Caucasus. According to Manstein, the high command thus committed a catastrophic error by removing the Eleventh Army from the Crimea in order to utilize it in Leningrad and to patch up the rest of the front. If not for this mistake, he asserted, the Stalingrad tragedy would have been avoided: "If—as it was initially planned—one had made [the Eleventh Army] cross the Kertch Strait to cut off in Kuban the retreating the enemy forces driven back from the Don to the Caucasus by Army Group A or, if it was too late, to serve as a reserve for the southern wing, the Stalingrad tragedy would have without a doubt been avoided."[409] It would clearly not be an exaggeration to assert that the Eleventh Army's support in the southern sector of the front would have prevented, or at least greatly mitigated the tragedy of the Sixth Army in Stalingrad.[410]

Nevertheless, continued Manstein, "Army Group A was positioned to the south, between the Black and Caspian Seas, while Army Group B held, facing to the east and northeast, a front that was organized on the Volga to the south of Stalingrad, sweeping over towards the midpoint of the Don to the north of the city, and followed this river all the way to Voronezh." The two army groups' forces were insufficient to defend such extensive fronts, all the more so since the southern wing of the enemy forces had not been decisively defeated and had succeeded at eluding annihilation. In fact, the U.S.S.R. still possessed rather significant operational reserves behind other sectors of the front and further inside the country. Finally, there existed between Army Groups A and B a gap of 300 kilometers on the Kalmuk steppe, which a single division, the 16th Motorized stationed in Elista, attempted to fill.

Apart from errors made in the preparation and the conduct of the summer offensive, Manstein underscores three other mistakes of serious consequence that were to lead the Sixth Army into its desperate situation at the end of November 1942. The first was the attempt to hold at all costs an overextended front. The second, even more grave, was the order given by the Führer to Army Group B to engage the Sixth Army and the Fourth Panzer Army—in other words the bulk of its offensive forces—in and around Stalingrad. The security of the northern flank of this group along the Don was in turn entrusted to three satellite armies: the Third Romanian Army, the Eighth Italian, and the Second Hungarian, and in the sector of Voronezh, to the German Second Army, possessing units that were much too weak. According to Manstein, Hitler should have known that these allied contingents were in absolutely no position to confront, even behind the Don, a powerful Soviet counteroffensive. And he makes the same remark apropos of the Fourth Romanian Army, to which Hitler had delegated the mission of covering the completely exposed right flank of the Fourth Panzer Army. The third mistake was the organization of the command on the German southern wing, which Manstein characterized as "truly ridiculous," since Army Group A did not have its own chief, being commanded indirectly by Hitler.

Manstein recognized that one must occasionally accept risks in order to win. But in his opinion, the German high command should have never accepted the risk to which it exposed itself at the end of autumn 1942, by situating the primary forces of Army Group B in the Stalingrad sector for too long and by being satisfied with defending the Don front with units whose readiness to fight was relatively weak: "With Stalingrad having only been partially captured in the first assault, the decision to seize it with a concentrated attack, in order to ensure control of the Volga, was justified so long as they limited themselves to a very short space of time. On the other hand, engaging Army Group B's primary forces in the city for several weeks with its flanks insufficiently protected, represented a decisive mistake. It was to relinquish the initiative to the adversary, to give it a formal invitation to seize the opportunity to encircle the Sixth Army which was thus offered it to it."

He concludes his analysis by mentioning the risk that the German high command should have accepted after the summer offensive had gained a large expanse of territory, but not the decisive defeat of the southern wing of the Soviet front: "It should have consisted in recommencing a mobile war between the Caucasus and the middle reaches of the Don, while taking advantage of the operational possibilities provided by the great bend of the Don, in order not to hand the initiative over to the adversary. But it was not in Hitler's character to manage risks in such a way. He did not draw any conclusions from the fact that his offensive came to a halt without producing any decisive results, and thus prepared the way for the Stalingrad tragedy."[411]

Manstein's point of view clearly pays witness to a certain overestimation of the possibilities that were available to the Wehrmacht at this time. With the benefit of hindsight, it is now evident that at the beginning of September the Wehrmacht had already lost the strategic and operational initiative on the Eastern Front, even if the battle of Stalingrad was only then entering its decisive phase. At this time, it was no longer in a position of achieving the initial objectives that it had targeted for the Caucasus front, particularly concerning the capture of the Grozny oilfields. It was only in the Stalingrad sector that it was still able to achieve a partial success. Indeed, the capture of this city would have liberated the operational reserves. But it is quite doubtful that they would have been sufficient enough to reinforce significantly the approximately 550 kilometers of the front between Voronezh and Stalingrad, on the upper reaches of the Don, that the Romanian, Italian, and Hungarian forces were holding, and on which in view of the weak combat capability of those units, the Soviets had built several bridgeheads.

Considering the limited number of operational reserves, the weakness of the allied contingents, and the problems of supplying fuel and weaponry, it would have been preferable to proceed with a thorough strategic withdrawal of the two army groups on the frontline extending from Voronezh to Rostov-on-Don or, even better, on the line from June 28, from where the Blue Plan had commenced. By contracting the frontline, the Germans could have thus freed numerous operational reserves necessary for stabilizing their positions and to drive back the Red Army's counteroffensive which was expected at the beginning of winter. Admittedly, this would have signified the abandonment of the strategic triumphs achieved throughout the summer, but it was the price to pay in order to avoid the Stalingrad tragedy and the collapse of the southern wing of the front.[412]

But Hitler was not inclined to agree to the slightest strategic withdrawal. Furthermore, at the pinnacle of the summer campaign, conflicts within the high command became more and more frequent, particularly between Hitler and Halder. The chief of the general staff was striving to get Hitler to understand that Army Group South did not possess the necessary strength to conduct two huge offensives of similar scale in two opposing directions. The assault against Stalingrad was more than enough to swallow up all the available forces. But Hitler refused to listen to reason, convinced that the Russians were finished. For the chief of the OKH general staff, the blind underestimation of the enemy's resources by the Führer, and his complete inability to embrace the situation and its consequences considerably increased the risks of a military debacle. Halder was keen on being the operational brain of the army. Hitler nevertheless insisted on the superiority of his own ideas. The intolerable situation led to Halder's discharge on September 24.

The latter was replaced by General Kurt Zeitzler, chief of staff for Field Marshal Rundstedt, who was commander in chief of the Western Front. At 47 years old, he was eleven years younger than Halder and was of relatively low rank in the military hierarchy: only a major general since April 1942, Hitler had promoted him two ranks after having appointed him chief of the OKH general staff. Recognized as a fervent follower of the Führer, he had been recommended by his personal friend, Lieutenant General Schmundt, Hitler's liaison officer with the army, and also by Göring. Hitler thus rejected Keitel's proposal according to which Manstein or Paulus would be better qualified than Zeitzler to assume the duties of chief of the OKH general staff. Once again, Manstein saw his dream of becoming army chief of staff fly away. His exceedingly strong personality could hardly be pleasing to a man like Hitler, who preferred to surround himself with obedient officers.[413]

The state of affairs when Manstein took command of Army Group Don

The telegram that Field Marshal Manstein received in the region of Vitebsk on November 21 requested him to take command of Army Group Don—composed of the Sixth Army, the Fourth Panzer Army, and the Third Romanian Army—in order to ensure the coordination of defensive operations north and south of Stalingrad. He was given the mission, for that matter impossible to execute with the existing forces and reserves, of restoring the situation on the fronts of the Don and the Volga. In fact, in a way he was assigned the responsibilities of Colonel General Weichs, commander in chief of Army Group B, somewhat similar to his being assigned those of Field Marshal Küchler in the Leningrad sector a few months earlier. To assume his new duties, he was assisted by General Friedrich Schulz, his chief of staff and his closest colleague since the end of the Crimean campaign, as well as by Colonel Theodor Busse, his deputy chief of staff since the day he had taken command of Eleventh Army in the Crimea.

Manstein's remarkable operational and strategic talent made him the ideal candidate to assume this new command specifically created to restore the situation on the Stalingrad front. Besides, at the time of his nomination, Manstein's reputation was such that mention of his name alone was enough to inspire the German troops.[414]

The field marshal was able to have a precise idea of the events that occurred during the previous days and of the current situation only once he arrived at the headquarters of the new Army Group B—formed of the Second German Army, the Second Hungarian Army, and the Eighth Italian Army—in Starobielsk on November 24, 1942, the day of his 55th birthday. Showing Manstein the duly updated operations map, Colonel General Weichs and General Sodenstern, his chief of staff, did not hide from him the gravity of the situation over which he was about to assume responsibility.

On November 19, 1942, the Soviets had unleashed at dawn, in a blizzard, Operation Uranus, for which the preparations had commenced two months earlier under the supervision of Generals Georgi Zhukov and Alexander Vassilevski, respectively commander in chief and chief of general staff of the Red Army. After an extremely powerful artillery preparation, the Soviet tanks, in a massive formation, had breached the lines of the Romanian Third Army to the northwest of Stalingrad, advancing in the direction of the Don bend. On the following day, to the south of the city, other powerful columns broke through the Romanian Fourth Army and charged towards the Don. The two Romanian armies were quickly smashed and the tough Soviet armored units immediately tore through the breaches. By November 22, the two branches of the pincer movement had come together at Kalatch, at the tip of the Don bend, 60 kilometers to the west of Stalingrad. The trap thus closed around Colonel General Paulus' Sixth Army and parts of the German and Romanian units from Colonel General Hoth's Fourth Panzer Army, thus 21 German divisions and 2 Romanian, for a total of approximately 250,000 men. Even worse, the Kalatch bridge, which controlled the Sixth Army's supply route, fell completely intact into Soviet hands. Encircled in a pocket 40 to 50 kilometers wide, Paulus' troops were henceforth only able to be resupplied through an airlift.

As soon as General Zeitzler, chief of the OKH general staff, realized that the Soviet maneuvers were aimed at isolating Stalingrad, he implored Hitler to order the retreat of the Sixth Army back into the Don bend where the breached front could still be reconstituted. But Hitler refused to issue such an order. In his view, a retreat would amount to recognizing the failure of the 1942 campaign, and he was not ready to admit to this. On November 21, he himself ordered Colonel General Paulus to stand firm, reiterating this formal order the following day, after the complete encirclement of the Sixth Army in Stalingrad. The Führer believed that the situation could be remedied. In his eyes, it was possible to extricate the Sixth Army by employing a powerful armored counterattack. Such an operation could be attempted in approximately ten days, time enough to gather the necessary reinforcements. In the meantime, the Luftwaffe would ensure the resupply of Paulus' troops.

It was a calculated risk, but Reichsmarshal Göring, head of the Luftwaffe, guaranteed Hitler that it was possible. Colonel General Hans Jeschonnek, his chief of staff, was careful not to contradict him, despite Zeitzler's vehement protests. Even within the Luftwaffe, Colonel General Richthofen, commander in chief of the Fourth Luftflotte, raised strong objections because of the winter weather conditions and the lack of enough equipment to deal with such an undertaking. Hitler chose to believe his faithful and loyal Göring.

On November 23, Paulus, with the support of the majority of his corps and division chiefs, requested authorization to break out to the southwest, citing his limited reserves of provisions, equipment, munitions, and fuel to ensure the defense of Sixth Army's positions. Weichs and Zeitzler approved it without any reservations, seeing it as the only realistic option. Hitler nevertheless remained steadfast. He maintained his decision to resupply Paulus' Sixth Army by air before being able to send it any reinforcements. Such an irrevocable decision on the part of the Führer would definitely seal the fate of 250,000 men.[415]

On November 24, the situation thus presented itself for Field Marshal Manstein, commander in chief of the new Army Group Don:

Colonel General Paulus' Sixth Army was encircled around Stalingrad, in a pocket of some fifty kilometers from east to west, and approximately forty from north to south, with 21 German divisions and 2 Romanian. Colonel General Hoth's Fourth Panzer Army had nothing more at its disposal in terms of intact units than the Romanian 18th Infantry Division on the northern wing, and the German 16th Motorized Division, spread out on the Kalmuks steppe on either side of Elista, more than 250 kilometers to the south of Stalingrad. But it could not be withdrawn from the steppe, where it represented the only cover for Army Group A's left flank, deeply committed in the Caucasus. Whatever remained of the Fourth Romanian Army had been placed under Hoth's command. Of the Third Romanian Army, there remained barely more than three infantry divisions, which had not been struck by the Soviet counteroffensive and were located on the Don next to the Italian contingents.

On the enemy's side, 24 units had moved through the southern breach and 24 others through the northern breach, both wings advancing all the way to Kalatch. Further to the west, 23 units were reported marching to the southwest, towards the Chir River. To these it would be necessary to add the Stalingrad forces which had held Sixth Army in check to this point, and which were being reinforced from across the Volga, plus those that remained on the northern front, between the Volga and the Don. In all, by November 28, the Red Army was able to deploy 143 large units against the new Army Group Don.[416]

Thus, apart from the Sixth Army, out of action from an operational point of view, Army Group Don only had the use of small fragments of units, those of the Fourth Panzer Army and two Romanian armies, within which only a German motorized division and four Romanian infantry divisions were still intact. Clearly, one could not be under any illusion as to their ability to curtail the Soviet counteroffensive.

Manstein's evaluation of the situation and his strategic considerations

Manstein's first decision was to call upon reinforcements from the

OKH. On November 21, in a message addressed to the OKH chief of staff, General Zeitzler, he described the clear impossibility of accomplishing the mission that fell upon his army group, given the forces brought into play by the enemy. To restore the situation, reinforcements reaching the magnitude of an army would be necessary, capable of moving as quickly as possible to the counteroffensive after their assembly had been completed. On the following day, he received Zeitzler's reply announcing to him the arrival, at the beginning of December, of the 3rd Mountain Division, the 306th Infantry Division, and the 17th Panzer Division.

But unlike Paulus, Weichs, and Zeitzler, Manstein was not in favor of an attack from out of the pocket by the Sixth Army before the arrival of reinforcements. On November 24, he presented his argument by telephone to Zeitzler. From an operational point of view, he stated, it was preferable to await the intervention of expected relief troops, at least for as long as Sixth Army could be sufficiently resupplied by airlift. An operation designed to extricate it could be undertaken once the new units had arrived at the beginning of December. Yet it was absolutely necessary to continuously reinforce them in order to counter the powerful support that the enemy was itself to receive in the interim. An isolated breakout from the Sixth Army would only become necessary if pressure from the enemy prevented Army Group Don from deploying its new forces. Through his optimism regarding the possibility of the Luftwaffe establishing an airlift in order to support the resistance of the troops encircled in Stalingrad, Manstein thus supported Hitler in his decision not to abandon the city.[417]

In fact, the field marshal was of the opinion that the favorable moment for a breakout by the Sixth Army had clearly passed. It could have only avoided an encirclement by attempting, from the very beginning of the Soviet counteroffensive, to retreat either towards the west, by crossing the Don, or towards the southwest, by remaining to the east of the river. Of course, it was up to the high command to give him the order. But Paulus should have himself made the decision to retreat from Stalingrad, even if he was not as informed as the OKH on the situation of the neighboring armies. When he proposed on November 23 to drive towards the southwest, the decisive moment had by then definitively passed.

A breakout attempt towards the southwest, in the direction of what remained of the Fourth Panzer Army to the east of the Don, approximately 120 kilometers away, entailed enormous risks. The Sixth Army could not count at this moment on the intervention of any German force capable of bringing it aid, even if it succeeded at breaking through the encirclement. When it tried to cross the Don, it would have on its heels the Soviet forces which, to this point, were pressing the army from the east, north, and west. The Soviets would pursue it towards the south in order to prevent it from crossing the river. Left to its own devices, which were limited to 150 tanks, the Sixth Army would be fighting with the enemy on the steppe, without any munitions, fuel, or provisions. If certain units nevertheless succeed at escaping, the armored units in particular, the rest would probably all be doomed, which is not to mention the fate of the army's sick and wounded. And a breakout to the west, in the direction of Kalatch, approximately 70 kilometers away, had even less chance of succeeding. Even if it managed to break the ring around Stalingrad, the Sixth Army would have to cross the Don, with its munitions almost entirely spent, in the face of powerful Soviet forces marching towards the Chir.

After the war, Manstein claimed that Paulus should have known that the Führer would have never accepted evacuating the city. He should have quite simply presented him with a *fait accompli*, which would have been much easier than the OKH not submitting any precise directive during the first two days of the Soviet counterattack. But Manstein recognized that this would have probably cost him his command: "One can nevertheless think that it was this consideration that prevented Paulus from acting as he saw fit. It was without a doubt his loyalty to Hitler that prompted him to solicit the breakout authorization, all the more so since he stayed in radio communication with the OKH. In addition, […] he most likely did not have a sufficiently clear perspective of the general situation. The decision to act independently must have been even more difficult to make at this time, on account of the fact that the Sixth Army was running more risks by trying to break out than by remaining around Stalingrad."[418]

On November 24, during a meeting with his chief and deputy chief of staff, General Schulz and Colonel Busse, Field Marshal Manstein came to the conclusion that the Red Army was going to make every effort to destroy the encircled Sixth Army. Moreover, he envisioned the likely possibility that it would try to take advantage of the collapse of the Third Romanian Army by moving forward with rapid units into the great bend of the Don, in the direction of Rostov. It could then not only cut off the lines of communication from Army Group Don, but those of Army Group A, which was engaged to the south in the Caucasus. He believed that the forces the Red Army had at its disposal, and which would most certainly increase through the arrival of reinforcements, would permit it to pursue these two objectives simultaneously.

From November 24, thus before even arriving at his new headquarters in Novotcherkassk on November 27, the day when he took actual command of Army Group Don, Manstein had already correctly evaluated the strategic situation on the southern wing of the Eastern Front. It was not a question of the fate of a single army, but of the entire German southern wing in Russia and, finally, of the fate of the entire front. If the Red Army were to succeed at gaining control of Rostov-on-Don, it would cut off the communications (aside from Sixth Army) of Army Groups Don and A, in other words of the Fourth and First Panzer Armies, the Seventeenth Army, and fragments of the Fourth Romanian Army, altogether an approximate total of 1.5 million men. Consequently, the disaster would be considerably larger than that of Stalingrad. Such an eventuality was all the more foreseeable since the Soviet forces marching towards the Chir were only approximately 300 kilometers from Rostov-on-Don, whereas the First Panzer Army, which represented the left wing of Army Group A engaged in the Caucasus, was located some 600 kilometers from the city.

Furthermore, this was not to be the last time that Manstein would precisely anticipate the Soviet intentions in his role as commander in chief of Army Group Don. Such an evaluation of the strategic stakes was also the first rational analysis of the general situation on the southern wing of the front since the Soviet counteroffensive on November 19. And for that matter, it would motivate all the subsequent operations of Army Group Don. Indeed, from his taking command at the end of November 1942 to the Fourth Panzer Army's counteroffensive at the end of February 1943, Manstein would never lose sight of the fact that the Red Army was focusing its main efforts against Army Group Don, with the objective of cutting the southern flank off from the rest of the German front. All of the field marshal's operational decisions would be based on this premise, despite the attempts of the Soviet high command to deceive him as to its actual intentions by particularly trying to divert his attention towards other areas of the front. It was Manstein's ability not to allow himself to become distracted by the adversary that would permit him to restore and eventually stabilize the situation on the southern wing.

On November 27, when Field Marshal Manstein finally arrived at his headquarters in Novotcherkassk, the situation that had just come to light three days earlier had hardly changed. The enemy was apparently dedicating its main forces to the encirclement of the Sixth Army. Out of 143 large units reported in the sector of Army Group Don, approximately 60 were assigned to this undertaking, thus a total of seven armies.[419]

Manstein was charged with a double mission: "It was above all necessary to extricate and save the Sixth Army. This was the most pressing endeavor, the most important, not only from a humane point of view, but also from an operational perspective for, if this were not accomplished, we would risk no longer being able to restore the situation on the southern wing and, as a result, compromise the entire front. But it was also necessary not to lose sight of the fact that the entire southern wing of the Eastern Front ran the risk of being annihilated, an event which, in all likelihood, would have been decisive and would have led to losing the war. If the Russians were to succeed at tearing down the thin curtain of protection hastily established between the rear of Army Group A and whatever remained of the Don front, it would not only be necessary to abandon all hope of saving the Sixth Army, but to realize the worst fears for all of Army Group A."[420]

The credit for forestalling this fate went to the Fourth Panzer Army and the Third Romanian Army, who struggled to fill in the enormous breaches and thus prevented the Soviet high command from quickly exploiting the situation. If the latter had been successful at immediately launching its rapid units in the direction of Rostov-on-Don, Army Group Don and Army Group A, in addition to the Sixth Army, would have most likely been destroyed. The entire German front would have then collapsed, doubtlessly bringing with it the end of the war.

From the moment he took command, Field Marshal Manstein worked with Colonel General Richthofen, commander in chief of the Fourth Luftflotte in charge of providing supplies to the Sixth Army. The latter had convinced him that, given the present terrible weather conditions, a satisfactory airlift would be impossible. Even if the weather improved, it would be impossible to maintain aerial resupply for a substantial amount of time. It was thus obvious that the assurances given to Hitler by Göring were fallacious. Because of the inadequacy and the precariousness of the airlift, it was crucial to gather as quickly as possible the relief units intended to free Paulus' troops.

On November 28, the commander of Army Group Don sent to Hitler a detailed report on the situation of the enemy forces, as well as on the state of Sixth Army. He emphasized that the latter would soon lose its firepower and mobility, given that its munitions and fuel were almost exhausted. Taking into account the limited reinforcements that the OKH had promised him, all that he could hope for was to open a corridor that would allow him to resupply the Sixth Army so that it could regain its mobility. It would, however, be immediately necessary to pull it out of the pocket, he added, for it would not be able to hold its position for the entire winter on the steppe. Finally, he insisted, it was strategically dangerous to pin the German forces down to fixed positions while the enemy retained its freedom of action on a front several hundred kilometers long. Maneuverability had to be regained at all cost and as quickly as possible.

He received his response by December 3. Hitler declared that he was in agreement with the majority of his ideas. But he did not want to draw in the front to the north of Stalingrad in order to free up forces for other endeavors. Clearly, he in no way envisioned withdrawing Sixth Army from the Stalingrad pocket should it occur that Army Group Don were to succeed at restoring communication with it, and even less so of commanding a general retreat so as to restore and stabilize the southern wing of the front. A few days earlier, on November 29 or 30, Hitler had furthermore stated to Manstein during a telephone conversation that he could not acquiesce to his proposal of pulling Sixth Army from the pocket in which it found itself surrounded in Stalingrad. "The Sixth Army will remain in Stalingrad, he declared. It has entrenched itself under my orders and will defend the fortress!"[421]

The operations plan to extricate the Sixth Army

Meanwhile, the OKH had informed Manstein that it would provide other forces for Army Group Don's mission. Two panzer divisions (the 6th and the 23rd) and a Luftwaffe field division (the 15th), would be attached to Colonel General Hoth's Fourth Panzer Army, whereas two panzer divisions (the 11th and the 22nd), three infantry (the 62nd, 294th, and the 336th) and two Luftwaffe field divisions (the 7th and the 8th), would form General Karl Adolf Hollidt's newly created army detachment. But out of the seven divisions anticipated for the latter, one panzer (the 22nd) and two infantry (the 62nd and the 294th) had to be rushed immediately to the front of the Third Romanian Army to fill in the breaches. Moreover, of the three divisions promised by the OKH on November 22, none were able to partaicipate in the attempt to cut through to Sixth Army. The 3rd Mountain Division did not even arrive. Its units had been dispersed between Army Group A and Army Group Center in order to deal with local crises. As for the 17th Panzer and the 306th Infantry Division, they arrived too late to participate at the decisive moment. Considering that the Luftwaffe's field divisions could only be employed for defensive missions, for example the protection of the flanks of the assault groups, only two panzer divisions remained in the Fourth Panzer Army for the extrication operation, and only one panzer and one infantry division in Army Detachment Hollidt.

Despite the inadequacy of his reinforcements, Manstein put forth on December 1 his directives concerning Operation Winter Storm (*Wintergewitter*). Hoth's Fourth Panzer Army would attack, with the bulk of its forces, from the region of Kotelnikovo, which was approximately 120 kilometers to the southeast of the Sixth Army encircled in Stalingrad. After having breached the enemy's defenses, it would have the job of breaking through the Soviet siege front at Stalingrad from the south or west, counting on Sixth Army's cooperation by exerting pressure from inside the pocket at the decisive point.

During this time, Army Detachment Hollidt would also attack, launching from the Nijne Tchirskaya bridgehead on the middle reaches of the Chir in the direction of Kalatch, to disrupt the adversary's lines of communication and to create a crossing on the Don for Sixth Army. The latter was to break out, on a date that would be set later depending on the results obtained by Fourth Panzer Army, to the southwest in the direction of the Donskaya Tsaritsa River, in order to connect with Hoth's panzers, and to the west, to coordinate with Hollidt's divisions in crossing the Don at Kalatch. However, under the Führer's formal order, it was required to maintain its positions in the Stalingrad region, thus making its mission all the more difficult. Protection of the right and left flanks of the offensive would be provided, respectively, by what remained of the Fourth Romanian Army (now integrated into the Fourth Panzer Army) and by the Third Romanian Army along with certain units from Army Detachment Hollidt. That some of the forces in charge of covering the offensive had themselves collapsed a few weeks earlier during the powerful Soviet counterattack of November 19, demonstrated just how desperate the situation was for Army Group Don.[422]

At the beginning of December, the Red Army launched attacks not only against the Sixth Army in Stalingrad, but also on the Chir front and in the region of Kotelnikovo, thus in the sectors where the rescue efforts were being undertaken. Field Marshal Manstein had then to postpone the commencement date of Operation Winter Storm, originally set for December 3, first to the 8th, and finally to the 12th.

Following the Soviet attacks in the sectors of the Chir and Kotelnikovo, Manstein started to fear more and more the possibility of a large-scale offensive against the fronts of the Third Romanian Army and the Fourth Panzer Army, the objective of which would clearly be to reach Rostov-on-Don. As a result, he was henceforth no longer certain as to how to conduct the operations once communication had been restored with Sixth Army. Up until that point, he had always advocated that the army break out once the corridor was opened, as it was an essential component to stabilizing the situation on the southern wing of the front.

But now, he wondered if it were not preferable for Sixth Army to maintain its position in Stalingrad, even if an extrication operation were to restore its communications. In other words, despite the urgent need for troops to reinforce Army Group Don in its mission aimed at restoring the situation on the southern wing of the German front, Manstein believed that the Sixth Army would perhaps play a more useful role by holding Soviet forces down around the Stalingrad pocket. And yet a successful rescue operation would without a doubt contribute more to the restoration and stabilization of the entire German southern front. On the other hand, he thought, if Sixth Army were to succeed at escaping from the Stalingrad pocket, the encirclement forces would immediately become available for a large-scale offensive in the direction of Rostov-on-Don, with the intention of cutting off both Army Groups Don and A. It would in turn result in the destruction of the entire southern wing of the front and the probable end of the war.[423] It would thus be better for Sixth Army to remain in Stalingrad after the arrival of relief and not to try and free itself.

Operations Winter Storm and Thunderbolt

While Hoth's Fourth Panzer Army was building its concentration to the east of the Don, around Kotelnikovo, the Red Army attacked once again on December 10, this time to the west of the Don, on the front of the lower Chir. Every hope of engaging Army Detachment Hollidt from the Nijne Tchirskaya bridgehead on the Chir and the Don in conjunction with Fourth Panzer Army just melted away. Hollidt had his hands full simply to maintain his position, while Fourth Panzer Army now had to rely solely on its own forces to restore contact with Sixth Army. But it clearly could not reach the Stalingrad pocket with only two divisions (the 6th and 23rd Panzer Divisions), for a total of 232 assault tanks. The commander in chief of Army Group Don thus demanded the immediate dispatch of the 3rd Panzer Corps and the First Panzer Army engaged in the Caucasus Mountains, and the 16th Motorized Division deployed around Elista. Hitler denied him the armored corps, for Army Group A would then be required to evacuate a very advanced position in the Caucasus, and the motorized division, which represented the latter's only form of flank cover.[424]

Operation Winter Storm, as it were, seemed doomed for failure from the very beginning. It was basically a desperate act that, given the operational strength and mobility demonstrated by the adversary, carried within it the seeds of failure. This was all the more so since the Russians had expanded the number of their large units deployed on the front of Army Group Don between November 28 and December 9 from 143 to 185.   The commander in chief of Army Group Don nevertheless believed that he could still take this questionable undertaking upon himself. This was of course the result of his self-confidence, smugness, and a feeling of superiority as a commander, intoxicated by the great victories pulled off since autumn 1939. Yet, beyond Manstein's refined expertise, an underestimation of the enemy, which would have serious repercussions, was also most likely in play.[425]

On December 12, after artillery preparation, Hoth's armored units were able to attack the Stalingrad front at the weakest point of the

Soviet encirclement. Despite its inferior resources, Fourth Panzer Army succeeded in driving back the Fifty-First Soviet Army and to force its way across the Aksai River on December 17. The Soviet high command immediately rounded up its armored and motorized units to confront the threat that had emerged from the south. Not limiting itself to the defensive, it relentlessly launched counterattacks in an attempt to either regain the ground captured by Hoth's tank army or to encircle parts of the latter. In spite of the violent battles, Hoth continued to advance, and on December 19 he reached the Myshkoya River, behind which Soviet forces were holding an even stronger line. The Fourth Panzer Army was at that point no more than 48 kilometers from the besieged Sixth Army.

Inside the pocket in Stalingrad, the soldiers of the Sixth Army listened, full of hope, to the growing sound of battles being fought in the distance. A great clamor was heard among the ranks of the besieged troops: "Manstein is coming!" For those loyal to Hitler, the blasts of the cannons and guns from afar was even more proof that the Führer was still keeping his promises. He was going to pull them out of this. Hitler, however, did not have the slightest intention of withdrawing the Sixth Army from Stalingrad. He declared to Colonel General Zeitzler that it was impossible to retreat from the city, for that would amount to repudiating the "whole meaning of the campaign." He added that too much blood had been spilled for them to abandon Stalingrad.[426]

Joachim Wieder, a soldier of the Sixth Army, recalled after the war the hope that Manstein's attack had aroused: "During the second week of December, one knew, first in the general staffs, that Army Group Don, under the command of Field Marshal von Manstein, had commenced the rescue operation that had been hoped for so long. Soon, the good news was also known in the ranks. The great news spread with lightening speed, which renewed our morale [...]: 'Manstein is here!' Our hope rocketed again. A new *joie de vivre*, a new confidence, a new spirit of enterprise began to emerge. And so, the suffering and the sacrifices were not in vain! Now, salvation was before us. The Führer was holding true to his promise. And he was surely offering his word out of generosity. [...] Outside help was approaching. 'The Führer will pull us out of here!' One was firmly counting on the fact that it was possibly a large-scale rescue operation, the success of which one might say was certain. The fact that the mission to liberate our army was entrusted precisely to Field Marshal von Manstein filled us with an exceptional satisfaction. The remarkable strategic abilities of this war chief about whom one spoke in our staff with the greatest respect reinforced our confidence and seemed to at first sight guarantee the positive outcome of the future operation."[427]

But such hopes were in vain. After extremely violent battles and serious losses, Fourth Panzer Army's vanguards temporarily captured a weak bridgehead, but it was immediately threatened on all sides in the sector of Myshkoya. The panzer troops, exhausted, were forced onto the defensive and the initiative switched to the superior enemy forces. The rescue operation had already failed. The situation even worsened in the meantime because of new enemy offensives on the Chir. The Red Army had redoubled its efforts on the western banks of the Don to break through the Chir front and to seize the bridgehead of Nijne Tchirskaya, held by the Germans at the confluence of the two rivers. It was thus against the latter that it launched its attack on December 12. Two days later, the bridgehead was lost, after being hastily destroyed by the Germans in order to prevent the complete collapse of the Chir front. At the same time, a new danger presented itself on the left wing of Army Group Don.

On December 16, from the great bend of the Don, the Soviets unleashed an offensive that struck Army Detachment Hollidt, the Third Romanian Army, and the Eighth Italian Army in the sector of Army Group B. Before the total meltdown of Army Group Don's left flank, the key problem for Manstein became the defense of the Donetz basin and the corridor of Rostov-on-Don, the only retreat route available for Army Group A, still engaged around the Caucasus. The high command of the Red Army had just set into motion Operation Saturn. Army Detachment Hollidt had succeeded, for better or worse, at creating a new front level with that of the Third Romanian Army to protect its flank and also to cover at all costs the air bases of Morosovski and Tajinskaya, which were essential for resupplying the Sixth Army. But it was clear that such a situation could not be maintained for many more days, all the more so since Soviet forces were henceforth occupying the entire left bank of the Chir.

Given the critical situation on the Chir front and the left wing of Army Group Don, the Germans could only pursue the rescue attempt initiated to the east of the Don for a very limited amount of time. Manstein strongly doubted that Fourth Panzer Army could reach the

Stalingrad pocket, as the enemy appeared to be relentlessly opposing it with new forces. All things considered, the reinforcements proved to be essential to relaunching the attack. Hitler finally decided to grant the 16th Motorized Division, which was to be relieved by units from Army Group A, to the Fourth Panzer Army. But the movement demanded ten days, a delay much too long for it to be able to intervene at the opportune moment. And furthermore, Manstein had asked for this precisely ten days earlier. As for the 3rd Panzer Corps of the First Panzer Army, the Führer was still refusing to remove it from the Caucasus region. Hoth's forces alone, meantime, continued to remain inadequate to save the Sixth Army.[428]

Consequently, at noon on December 19, Manstein sent a message to Hitler advising him that the Fourth Panzer Army could not, in all likelihood, restore contact with Sixth Army, and even less so maintain it. For this, Paulus' army would need to attempt to break through to the southwest in order to link up with Hoth's armored units coming to its aid. In this event it would have to transfer its forces to the southwest of the pocket, abandoning the northern sector of the Stalingrad region.

By 6:00 P.M., having received no response, Manstein asked Paulus to prepare to carry out a desperate breakout in the direction of the Fourth Panzer Army, which, on its side, would attempt one last forward thrust.[429] His idea was not so much a gradual evacuation of the Stalingrad region as the expansion of the pocket to the southwest so as to permit the opening of a corridor through which the Fourth Panzer Army could supply the Sixth Army with fuel, munitions, and provisions necessary to continue its resistance.

Within the scope of Operation Winter Storm, Sixth Army had already received the order to prepare for this breakout towards the southwest, in the direction of the Donskaya Tsaritsa River, to restore contact with Fourth Panzer Army. However, it was instructed to also hold down the other fronts around Stalingrad, in accordance with the Führer's formal order. But in the army's current state, it was physically impossible for it to hold the entire front around Stalingrad while making every effort to break through to the southwest. Consequently, Manstein envisioned henceforth, in accordance to instructions issued to Paulus under the code name "Thunderbolt" (*Donnerschlag*), the abandonment of several of the Sixth Army's positions, at least those to the north, in order to permit the expansion of the pocket towards the southwest. In other words, it was question of the latter gradually shifting its blockaded front, depending on the progress achieved in the breach attempt, in order to restore contact with the Fourth Panzer Army and to allow entry to the supply convoys.

On December 19, Field Marshal Manstein sent his intelligence officer, Major Hans Eismann, into the pocket by air. The commander in chief of Army Group Don was to assert after the war that the major's mission consisted of asking Colonel General Paulus and Major General Arthur Schmidt, his chief of staff, to prepare Sixth Army with Operation Thunderbolt in mind. Various versions were given from conversations and remarks made by different officers, so much so that it is difficult to come to any clear conclusion. What is clear, however, is that Manstein refused to take responsibility for disobeying the Führer's orders. He quite obviously did not provide any truly precise instructions to the commander of the Sixth Army and refused, for perfectly legitimate security reasons, to go into the pocket himself to discuss the situation with Paulus face to face. Yet Manstein must have known for quite some time that Paulus, always respectful of official command channels, would never make a move without a formal order having come from the supreme command of the army, i.e. from Hitler.[430]

On the evening of December 23, Manstein and Paulus discussed the situation during a conference held by way of a teleprinter. The commander in chief of Army Group Don emphasized that the Fourth Panzer Army has been confronted with very strong opposition and that, on the northern flank, the Italian troops had caved in. Paulus asked if the Sixth Army was now authorized to attempt a breakout. Manstein replied that he had not yet received the supreme commander's agreement. The field marshal believed at the time that it was appropriate not to go into detail. If the colonel general had been given more information, he would have been able to see that Sixth Army could no longer be rescued. Did he make this request out of desperation?

Stahlberg, at this particular moment in the antechamber, was able to hear clearly the conversation. "*Herr* field marshal," implored Paulus, "I am begging you to give the order for the breakout!" There was hardly any hesitation to Manstein's response: "Paulus, I cannot give you the order. But if you make the decision independently, I will do all that is in my power to help you and to justify your decision."[431] Obviously, Manstein was refusing to forge ahead and take responsibility for a personal action in opposition to the Führer's will. He feared that such an initiative could lead Hitler to counter his order, then to dismiss him from his command, a consequence which would at the same time bring his dream of one day becoming commander of the German army or its chief of staff to an end.

In any case, the Sixth Army was already no longer in a position to accomplish a breakout which, when all was said and done, entailed many difficulties and enormous risks. The army needed, it was estimated, six days to prepare for a breakout, a length of time Manstein deemed much too long. The onset of the crisis on the Chir front and, more precisely, on the left wing of Army Group Don, no longer permitted him to wait for six days. In addition, the substantial reduction in the Sixth Army's strength and the decrease in its mobility, resulting from a lack of fuel and the slaughtering of many of its horses, made even more perilous an undertaking that was to be executed in the harsh conditions of winter.

The critical situation with regards to fuel was such that the tanks of Sixth Army, of which hardly a hundred were still in operation, could not advance any farther than 30 kilometers. In order to execute the breakout, it would thus be necessary either to provide an adequate supply of fuel or have Hoth's panzers approach at least 30 kilometers closer to the Stalingrad pocket. However, the latter was still located 48 kilometers away. Likewise, Army Group Don could absolutely not wait for the Sixth Army to be sufficiently refueled by airlift, which would mean the delivery of about 4,000 tons. For the Luftwaffe it was physically impossible, so there was nothing to suggest that air supply would ameliorate the situation. When all was said and done, the commander of the Sixth Army described the breakout attempt, especially if it had to be accomplished without outside assistance, as "a catastrophic solution."

Hitler approved an attack from the Sixth Army to the southwest in order to restore contact with the Fourth Panzer Army. However, he insisted that the former absolutely continue to hold down the front around Stalingrad. He was still hoping to be able to open a corridor which would allow for the movement of supplies, but without having to abandon the slightest plot of land to the enemy. He thus asked the commander of Sixth Army exactly how far he thought he could advance to the southwest if the other fronts were to be held. The response was clear: because of the fuel issue, it was not only impossible to execute the breakout, but even to prepare for it. Without delay, Hitler decided to abandon the idea. On December 21, Manstein nevertheless made one last effort to persuade him to approve Operation Thunderbolt. The Führer immediately replied that there was no possibility of Sixth Army expanding the pocket to the southwest due to a lack of fuel: "What exactly do you want? Paulus has only enough fuel for 20 kilometers, 30 at the most. He is unable to break through, as he himself declares."[432]

However, it is likely that with his impressive intelligence, Manstein had understood that any breakout attempt was obviously doomed to fail. Even before the bulk of the Second Guards Army had been deployed ahead of it, Hoth's Fourth Panzer Army had been blocked on the Myshkoya River. Paulus' Sixth Army, with its exhausted troops and barely a hundred fuel-starved tanks, had no chance of breaking through the besieged front. Even more importantly, Manstein had known since December 16 that Operation Saturn, which launched three additional Russian armies to his rear, had cast a new light on everything. Yet he probably felt that, in consideration of how history would remember him, as well as his Wehrmacht colleagues, he had to appear as a commander who had attempted everything in his power to rescue the troops at Stalingrad, even if he believed that the only true chance for Sixth Army to free itself had vanished almost a month earlier. His apparent guilty conscience after the war was likely due to the fact that, given Hitler's refusal to pull out of the Caucasus, he had utilized the Sixth Army to hold down the seven armies of the Red Army that were encircling Stalingrad. And furthermore, even if Paulus had been able to break through the blockaded front, there would have remained too few Sixth Army men, in too poor a state, to be of the slightest combat use in later operations.[433]

In his postwar account, Manstein gave the impression that the decisive order to break out of Stalingrad, against Hitler's wishes, had in fact been issued by Army Group Don, whereas Paulus, because of his much too conscientious analysis of the risks and his obedience to the supreme command of the Wehrmacht, had refused to execute it. He thus charged Paulus with the responsibility for not having attempted the breakout, despite the fact that he had issued the order.

In his *Memoirs*, Manstein appears quite critical towards Paulus: "If I have presented in such great detail the reasons that led the chief of the Sixth Army to abandon the last chance of saving it, it was because I attributed the responsibility of this decision to him, without taking into account his personality nor his future attitude. Such reasons, as I have stated, cannot be dismissed. But once again, it was a matter of the one and only chance at salvation. To not seize it—while accepting the inevitable risks—was to be resigned to losing the army. To seize it, however, was to place all of one's money on one card. Our opinion at the command of Army Group Don was that this needed to be done.

It is easy to criticize the attitude that the future Field Marshal Paulus had during these decisive days. But, his blind obedience to Hitler does not, in any case, explain it. He most certainly suffered a serious conflict of interest, with the operation requiring him to abandon Stalingrad, contrary to desires formally expressed by Hitler. Such an abandonment was nevertheless justified by the invincible pressure from the enemy. On the other hand, Army Group Don assumed all responsibility for having ordered him. [...] If [Colonel] General Paulus did not seize this last opportunity, if he hesitated, and finally abandoned the idea of taking the risk, it was quite certainly out of the feeling for the responsibility that was weighing upon his shoulders, a responsibility that the army group command had tried to take by issuing its order, but from which Paulus believed incapable of freeing himself in view of Hitler or himself."[434]

Had Manstein actually issued the decisive order to launch Operation Thunderbolt, thus relieving Paulus of the responsibility of a personal act of disobedience against the supreme command of the Wehrmacht? In actuality, the archives refute such an allegation.[435] From Paulus' *Memoirs* clearly emerges the claim that Sixth Army never received such an order. As we have seen earlier, when, on the evening of December 23, 1942, Paulus pressured him to launch Operation Thunderbolt, Manstein urged him to be patient, telling him that he could not yet issue the order. It is thus not surprising that Paulus expressed a rather caustic criticism after the war against Manstein: "He who did not believe at the time that he was able to issue me the order or authorization for a breakout does not have the right today to write that he had wished for my breakout and that he had covered it."[436]

Whatever the case may be, on December 21, 1942, Manstein could not continue to ignore the general situation of Army Group Don, which could no longer support the Fourth Panzer Army to the east of the Don, particularly because of the scale of the offensive being unleashed by the Red Army since December 16. Henceforth, the fate of the Sixth Army was no longer the only concern. The future of Army Group Don and Army Group A were also at stake, as the enemy was threatening more than ever to cut off their lines of communication. Indeed, there existed a danger of seeing the enemy take advantage of the breakthrough in the Italian sector to advance, through the crossings on the Donetz which were now open before it, towards Rostov-on-Don and the vital artery of the entire southern wing. The enemy clearly had the intention of preparing a "super-Stalingrad" for the entire German southern front. The priority was now to hold down the left flank in order to prevent a catastrophe even worse than the loss of Sixth Army. From this point on, Manstein no longer had a choice: if he wanted to avoid the collapse of the entire southern wing of the German front, he absolutely had to sacrifice the Sixth Army. The salvation of the *Ostheer* quite simply meant safeguarding Army Groups Don and A, which between them numbered approximately 1.5 million men.[437]

The crisis in the sector of Army Detachment Hollidt was now at its height. Soviet armored and motorized units drove deeply into the breach that had been created by the collapse of the Eighth Italian Army. Some were already approaching the airfields of Morosovski and Tajinskaya, while others had reached the rear of some of Hollidt's units, which were still fighting on the middle and upper reaches of the Chir. On December 23, Manstein had to withdraw the armored division from the Third Romanian Army in order to restore the situation on the left wing. In order to compensate for this loss, it was necessary for him to order Fourth Panzer Army to send the 6th Panzer Division to the lower Chir, without which the front could not have been maintained. As a result, Hoth had to pull back his weakened tank army. On Christmas Eve, it was attacked on the Myshkoya River by forces that were greatly superior in number and continually increasing, and driven back onto the Aksai River.

Facing an enemy that had just thrown into battle two armies (the Fifty-First and the Second Guards), and its intention to envelop it from the east and west, Fourth Panzer Army had to retreat during the following days back to Kotelnikovo, from where it had launched its offensive on December 12.[438] The endeavor to break through to Stalingrad had thus failed. And the fate of the Sixth Army was thus definitively sealed.

A hero's death? The sacrifice of the Sixth Army

From this point on, Sixth Army was on the verge of death. After Paulus rejected, under the Führer's order, a call to surrender on January 8, the Russians launched their last attack which would destroy Sixth Army two days later. Despite the inequality of forces, fighting continued for more than three weeks. Worn out, short on munitions, famished, and frozen to the bone, the Germans were driven back into the ruins of Stalingrad. To bring to an end the unspeakable suffering of his men, Paulus requested from Hitler on January 22 an authorization to surrender. Hitler refused and ordered, to the contrary, the troops to fight until the very end. On the following day, the Sixth Army started to disintegrate. It was cut in half by Soviet troops that had linked up from the south and the west of the city. Three days later, the scission of Sixth Army was complete. On January 31, Paulus was promoted to field marshal, as Hitler was doubtlessly expecting that he would die the death of a hero, for the idea that a German army could capitulate was intolerable to him. Nevertheless, on that very same evening, the new field marshal surrendered. Two days later, on February 2, the last units in the northern sector of the city were overwhelmed. The battle of Stalingrad was over. Out of 250,000 men of the Sixth Army, 25,000 were able to be evacuated by plane, 112,000 were dead, and 113,000 were taken prisoner. On the Soviet side, the losses incurred for having encircled the German forces were even more severe: 155,000 killed and 331,000 wounded.[439]

After the failure of the rescue effort led by the Fourth Panzer Army, an immediate capitulation by the Sixth Army could have certainly diminished its losses and shortened its suffering. By fighting to the very end, it nevertheless prevented the enemy from achieving the complete destruction of the southern German wing which was within its reach. Indeed, if it had stopped resisting not at the beginning of February, but seven weeks earlier when the situation obviously became hopeless, the Soviets would have probably succeeded in crushing the entire southern wing. Germany would have then experienced a military disaster on a much far larger scale than that of Stalingrad. Field Marshal Manstein's forces would not have been able to resist the Soviet wave that would have unfurled along the Don all the way to Rostov, while those in the

Caucasus region would have been isolated. Both Army Groups Don and A would have most likely been lost if Sixth Army had abandoned its position, either through an earlier surrender or by escaping the encirclement and retreating to the west.

Even though Sixth Army's resistance during the second half of January was not strong enough to prevent the Soviets from sending significant forces in the direction of Rostov-on-Don, it did, however, hold back enough of their units in order to give the German armies in the Caucasus an opportunity to reach Rostov in time to slip away. All in all, by fighting on until it had exhausted all of its means, the Sixth Army, through its heroic sacrifice, decisively contributed to the restoration of the German front.[440] Hitler and Manstein were not wrong when they declared, by way of consolation, that the sacrifice of the army in Stalingrad had given the German high command the time and opportunity to take measures upon which the fate of the entire Eastern Front depended.

And so, when the Führer enjoined Paulus to reject the offer of capitulation presented on January 8 by the Soviet high command, Manstein appeared to be in full agreement with this decision. At this particular moment, he was of the opinion that Sixth Army's resistance was still necessary for the survival of the entire southern wing of the German front. After the war, he made the following statement regarding this: "I am not of the purely military view according to which an army must never capitulate as long as it is in a position to fight. To abandon such a principle, however, would be to extinguish the military spirit. As long as there will be soldiers, it will be maintained. Even if the fight appears impossible to resolve, this does not justify capitulating. If every chief who deemed their situation hopeless decided to capitulate, no war could ever be won.

In any case, concerning [Colonel] General Paulus, it was his duty to reject the capitulation. His army still had a crucial role to play within the scope of the general situation. It had to hold back for as long as possible the enemy forces before it." In the same breath he added: "The army must always fight, even if it has nothing to expect for itself. Each day won by it is of decisive importance for the fate of the entire German front. That is not to say, with the war having been finally lost, that it would have been better to accelerate the end to spare useless suffering. That would be the wisdom of hindsight. During this time, it was not in the least certain that Germany would lose, militarily that is. A peace compromise was still in the realm of possibility, but for that, it was necessary to restore the situation on this part of the front, which was finally accomplished. To achieve this result, it was essential that the Sixth Army continue to hold back the enemy forces before it for as long as it could. The harsh necessity of war required the high command to call upon this ultimate sacrifice on the part of the valiant troops. Whether it was responsible for having led the army into this situation is another question."[441]

There is no doubt that Sixth Army's sacrifice permitted the entire southern wing of the German front to be saved, while allowing Army Group Don and Army Group A to escape the encirclement. At the end of November, of the 143 large Soviet units in opposition to Army Group Don, approximately 60 participated in the siege of Stalingrad. The Fourth Panzer Army's offensive forced it to shift some of its units from there for some length of time. But others arrived to replace them so that, by mid-January, out of the 259 large units deployed in the sector of Army Group Don, 90 were in front of the Sixth Army.[442] It is thus easy to see what would have occurred if Paulus had surrendered on January 8, letting loose another torrent of Soviet forces to attack the rest of the German front.

Indeed, the general situation had greatly deteriorated in the meantime since the Red Army had pushed through the front held by the Second Hungarian Army, which, as it were, sent Army Group B into retreat. The Soviets had thus succeeded at opening an enormous breach that extended from Vorochilovgrad on the Donetz, to Voronej on the Don, in other words a distance of approximately 320 kilometers. The very existence of Army Group Don and Army Group A in the region of the Caucasus was threatened more than ever. Based on the necessity of continuing to hold back the enemy units before Stalingrad, the Führer's decision—supported by Manstein—to refuse the Sixth Army's surrender was judicious in itself, despite the enormous sacrifice that was demanded of it.

Moreover, in spite of the loss of the Sixth Army, it was not predetermined that the war on the Eastern Front, and consequently the war itself, was irreparably lost—far from it. A compromise solution with Stalin appeared possible, in the eyes of the German generals, if Hitler wanted it and sought it. But this was not the case. In his ideological war against Jewish Bolshevism, the Nazi dictator was a fanatic and determined extremist. On this point, Manstein thus harbored illusions.

However, he did have the opportunity to fully dispute Hitler's determination to fight until the very end when on January 22 the latter refused Paulus' request to enter into negotiations with capitulation in mind. On that same day, Manstein begged the Führer to authorize the surrender of Sixth Army, believing that it had completely fulfilled its mission of holding back for as long as possible the bulk of enemy forces before Stalingrad. His solicitation was based on the fact that for several days, the German pocket had contracted to such an extent that Sixth Army was no longer holding down significant enemy mobile forces. But, just like Paulus' request, his own was rejected out of hand. For Hitler, there could be no question of capitulation, for it was a point of honor.[443]

The loss of the Sixth Army: Was Manstein partially responsible?

When he recalled the battle of Stalingrad after the war, Manstein attributed the primary responsibility for the debacle to Hitler, but also, to a certain extent, to Göring, for having assured his Führer, unrealistically, that the Luftwaffe could supply Sixth Army from the air, as well as to Paulus, for the error of not having attempted to break through the encirclement when there was still enough time to do so. As for Hitler, his disastrous leadership and his overwhelming guilt were undeniable. Furthermore, he himself recognized his responsibility, during a conversation with Manstein on February 6, 1943: "For Stalingrad, I am the only one who carries responsibility. I could perhaps say that Göring provided me with an inexact portrayal of the Luftwaffe's possibilities concerning aerial resupply, and in which case it would thus be possible for me to throw part of the responsibility onto him. But I myself designated him to succeed me; consequently I have to take complete responsibility."[444]

For some, Manstein would also carry part of the responsibility, particularly for not having advocated a breakout by the Sixth Army before the arrival of reinforcements, or for having undertaken too late, and with inadequate forces, the rescue offensive. To make such a judgment, however, is to forget that when he took actual command of Army Group Don on November 27, five days after the encirclement of the

Sixth Army in Stalingrad, it was already too late for the latter to attempt an isolated breakout without outside assistance. If it had nevertheless decided to make the endeavor, one has the right to assume that only a few fragments could have joined the Fourth Panzer Army. Not only would the Sixth Army have lost its operational capacity, but it would have freed the Soviet forces which it had been holding back up until that point. The destruction of the entire southern wing of the German front would have most likely have resulted from this, and by that very fact, the end of the war.

As for the criticism that Manstein undertook too late, and with inadequate forces, his rescue efforts, how could one blame him for having attempted in desperation an operation aimed at saving his comrades-in-arms? If he had been unable to launch his counterattack sooner and with sufficient forces, it was because of the incessant pressure from the enemy in other areas of the front, which was threatening to collapse at any moment, and the miserly and late arrival of reinforcements to his army group.

Still, others have blamed him for having launched his rescue operation from the Kotelnikovo region, located approximately 120 kilometers from Stalingrad, instead of from the Chir front, at only about 70 kilometers. They have claimed that if he had gathered the forces of Fourth Panzer Army in this sector, he would have perhaps succeeded at extricating Sixth Army. Had not Hoth's tanks arrived to within some 50 kilometers of the Stalingrad pocket, precisely after having advanced 70 kilometers? To propose such an argument, however, is to ignore the fact that the enemy forces on the Chir front were three times as large as those at Kotelnikovo and that the enemy high command was apparently expecting a rescue operation from the Chir sector. Clearly, if Hoth's tank army had won a few initial successes from its departure point in Kotelnikovo, it was because of the relative weakness of the enemy forces that it had met on there and from the fact that it did not have to cross the obstacle of the Don.

For these various reasons, Field Marshal Manstein must not be held responsible for the Stalingrad tragedy.

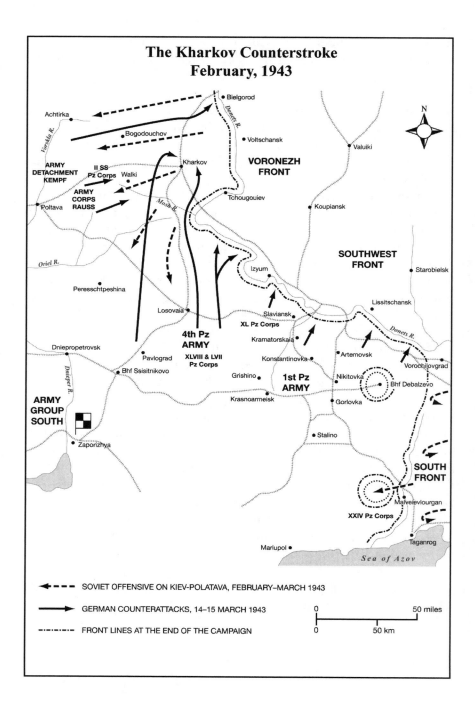

The Kharkov Counterstroke
February, 1943

Achtirka

Bielgorod

Voltschansk

Valuiki

Bogodouchov

ARMY
DETACHMENT
KEMPF

II SS
Pz Corps   Walki

Kharkov

VORONEZH
FRONT

ARMY
CORPS
RAUSS

Poltava

Tchougouiev

Koupiansk

Oriel R.

Peresschtpeshina

Izyum

SOUTHWEST
FRONT

Starobielsk

Losovaia

Slaviansk

XL Pz Corps

Lissitschansk

Dniepropetrovsk

4th Pz
ARMY

XLVIII & LVII
Pz Corps

Kramatorskaia

Artemovsk

Vorochilovgrad

Pavlograd

Konstantinovka

Nikitovka

Bhf Ssisitnikovo

Grishino

1st Pz
ARMY

Bhf Debalzevo

ARMY
GROUP
SOUTH

Krasnoarmeisk

Gorlovka

Zaporizhya

Stalino

SOUTH
FRONT

Malveievlourgan

XXIV Pz Corps

Taganrog

Mariupol

Sea of Azov

N

SOVIET OFFENSIVE ON KIEV-POLATAVA, FEBRUARY–MARCH 1943

GERMAN COUNTERATTACKS, 14–15 MARCH 1943

FRONT LINES AT THE END OF THE CAMPAIGN

0   50 miles

0   50 km

XIII

FROM RETREAT TO BACKLASH

After having failed in its mission to extricate Sixth Army from the Stalingrad pocket, all that remained for Army Group Don to accomplish was to save the entire southern wing to the German front. The latter was not only the theater of operations for Army Group Don, but also for Army Groups A and B. Since the commencement of the Soviets' Operation Saturn in mid-December, the situation on this particular front had become considerably worse, notably in the sector of the Eighth Italian Army. The question was thus to know if the Red Army was going to succeed at encircling the southern wing of the *Ostheer* and achieve a decisive step towards a final victory or if the German high command would succeed at intercepting such a catastrophe. The battles of winter 1943 would thus prove to be decisive for the continuation of the war. And it was while leading them that Field Marshal Manstein would achieve his most exceptional military feats, by succeeding at restoring and stabilizing the Eastern Front after his counter-attack in the Kharkov sector, by means of a bypass which remains today a classic of its kind.

The Caucasus army groups and the threat of a second Stalingrad

By November 24, 1942, Field Marshal Manstein had understood that the Red Army's powerful counteroffensive of November 19 not only had the objective of destroying the encircled Sixth Army in Stalingrad, but also to exploit the collapse of the Third Romanian Army by charging forward with rapid units into the great bend of the Don in the direction of Rostov. This city, located at the northern tip of the Sea of Azov,

325

was the key to controlling communications between the Ukraine and points farther east. Its possession by the Soviets would cut off not only Army Group Don but Army Group A, which was still engaged hundreds of kilometers to the southeast in the Caucasus. The encirclement and the destruction of these two army groups, in addition to the loss of Sixth Army, would thus seal the fate of the entire Eastern Front.

In order to grasp the scope of the danger that the situation presented for the Germans and the opportunities it offered to the Soviets, it would suffice to understand that between the sector where the Third Romanian Army had been overrun on November 19 and Rostov-on-Don went the lines of communication for all of Army Group A (First Panzer Army and Seventeenth Army), as well as those for the Fourth Romanian Army and the Fourth Panzer Army. The left wing of Army Group A, in the region of the Caucasus, was located some 600 kilometers from the city, and the Fourth Panzer Army, deployed to the south of Stalingrad, was approximately 400 kilometers away. Further to the rear, the lines of communication for the southern wing of the German Army crossed the Dnieper in Zaporoje and in Dniepropetrovsk. Yet these essential crossing points were approximately 700 kilometers from the Sixth Army in Stalingrad and 900 kilometers from First Panzer Army in the Caucasus.

On the other hand, on the middle reaches of the Don, the enemy was no more than 420 kilometers away. After the war, Manstein explained more precisely what was going through his mind: "I knew too well, through my own experience, what such a situation could mean. In the summer of 1941, with the 56th Panzer Corps, I had covered in four days 300 kilometers separating Tilsit from Dünaberg, against resistance far superior to what the Romanian, Italian, and Hungarian armies of the Don were capable of putting up against the Russians. In addition, [the Soviets] disposed of, behind their front, much greater reserves than what we possessed in the winter of 1942."[445]

Already, on November 29 or 30, 1942, during a telephone conversation, Manstein had requested from Hitler permission to place Army Group A under his command and to give him complete operational liberty over the two army groups. There was hardly any hesitation in the Führer's response: "This is not possible, Field Marshal!" Far from acknowledging defeat, Manstein asked that he at least be given the First Panzer Army. If Army Group A absolutely had to retain its acquired positions in the Caucasus, he stated, it could accomplish this with only one of its two armies, the Seventeenth. But Hitler remained inflexible. Exasperated, Manstein posed to him this crucial question: "My Führer, tell me please, what is Army Group A supposed to be doing in the Caucasus?" Hitler sharply replied: "That is a question relative to the possession of Baku, Field Marshal. Unless we can gain petroleum from Baku, the war is lost. [...] If I cannot procure for you the fuel for your operations, you will be incapable of doing anything." Retorting that he had no doubt as to the importance of the petroleum from Baku, Manstein nevertheless asserted that priority must be granted to Sixth Army in Stalingrad and not to the petroleum of Baku. "Place the entire Army Group A under my command and give me complete operational freedom and I will deliver a decisive battle in southern Russia, after which you will be able to obtain all the petroleum that you desire."

The commander in chief of Army Group Don then put forth other arguments: the enemy forces in the region of Stalingrad, the numerical superiority of the Russians, the signs that clearly pointed, in his opinion, to the fact that the Russians at this moment were seeking to gain a final victory in the south of their country. "My Führer, the Russians have learned from us. Instead of simply pushing forward, they have resorted to strategy. They have started to have confidence in themselves." Hitler did not react. After a silence, he abruptly ended the conversation: "Field Marshal, I have to remind you of something that I have already said to you on several occasions: we have to march on the Caucasus next spring. And I am thinking of placing you in command of the spring offensive. You will then link up in Palestine with Field Marshal Rommel's army, which will come to meet you in Egypt. We will next march with joined forces towards India, where we will seal our final victory over England."[446]

Shortly before the commencement of Operation Winter Storm, Manstein was still advocating for a retreat of the armies from the Caucasus, while asking for the transfer of the 3rd Panzer Corps from the First Panzer Army to the Fourth Panzer Army for his attack in the direction of Stalingrad. In his eyes, if the Wehrmacht were not successful at extricating the Sixth Army or at restoring the situation on the Don front, it could no longer be a question of maintaining Army Group A in the Caucasus. In any case, as soon as the breakthrough on the right wing of Army Group B opened up the way to Rostov-on-Don to the

Soviets, it became quite evident to him that the German high command could no longer, in any way, think of holding on to the Caucasus front.

On December 20, the day when the collapse of the Italian Eighth Army exposed the flank of Army Detachment Hollidt and opened up to the Red Army the way to the Donetz crossings, Manstein informed the chief of the OKH general staff, Kurt Zeitzler, that the enemy would probably drive forward in the direction of Rostov-on-Don in order to encircle Army Group Don and Army Group A. On December 24, he mentioned once again to Zeitzler that the Soviet offensive in the sector of Army Group B had the objective, while following the Millerovo axis to Rostov-on-Don, of cutting off the lines of communication of Army Group Don and Army Group A. Consequently, he urged him to withdraw the latter from the Caucasus and to reinforce the former, which was attempting, for better or worse, to free the Sixth Army and to restore the northern wing of its front.

Faced with Manstein's and Zeitzler's insistence, Hitler finally decided on December 28 to withdraw the First Panzer Army, which was highly exposed on the eastern wing of Army Group A, back onto the Kuma River, between Piatigorsk and Praskoveya, in other words approximately 100 kilometers from the position that it was holding to the south of Mozdok. But the Führer was in no way thinking of abandoning the Caucasus front. By this strategic removal, he was hoping at the very most to allow Army Group A to move towards the Manytch, stabilize the situation between that river and the Don, particularly the great bend of the river, and simultaneously secure the lines of communication for the southern wing of the front, specifically along the lower Dnieper. He was thus not intending to abolish, but rather reduce the "balcony" that the front had formed in autumn which had extended all the way to the Volga and the Caucasus, and which was at the heart of the critical situation in which the Wehrmacht found itself since November 19, 1942. Such an intention was utopian insofar as the OKH did not have at its disposal reserves to compensate for the loss of the two Romanian armies, the Italian Army, and shortly after, the Hungarian Army. Consequently, Hitler would sooner or later have to decide to evacuate the entire Caucasus.

Due to a lack of fuel, First Panzer Army could not commence its retreat until January 2, 1943. The movement occurred as slowly as possible in order to conserve its supplies. As a result, not a single unit was quickly available. Finally, it was only at the end of twenty-five days that the entire army reached its new position on the Kuma.[447]

A retreat maneuver followed by a flank attack, or a shift of forces from east to west?

After the situation took a seriously threatening turn because of Hitler's obstinacy, it was necessary to find as favorable a solution as possible under the circumstances. For Manstein, the ideal next step, after the failure to rescue Sixth Army, was to abandon the ground captured during the summer offensive, territory which could in any case no longer be held. For this, it was necessary to withdraw the forces from Army Groups Don and A, first behind the lower Don and the Donetz, then to the lower Dnieper. Such an operation was without a doubt most difficult to achieve without provoking a large-scale collapse.

In the meantime, it was necessary to assemble, in the Kharkov region, as many units as possible, including those of the two army groups now available following the contraction of the front, and have them attack the flank of the huge stream of enemy units that was pursuing the two army groups or attempting to cut off the Don crossings. The idea was thus to transform a massive retreat operation into a counterattack with the intention of driving the adversary back to the sea and destroying it there.

The commander of Army Group Don proposed this solution to the OKH after the Russian breakthrough in the Italian sector, when it became clear that Army Group A could no longer remain in the Caucasus. But Hitler was in no way willing to support an operation which required abandoning the gains made during the summer of 1942, and which unquestionably entailed considerable operational risk. At any rate, to carry out such a withdrawal followed by a strategic counterstrike, the commander of Army Group Don did not possess the necessary authority. He would need to have control over the entire southern wing of the German front, from Voronezh to the Caucasus, and to have free rein over the operational reserves of the OKH.

For the moment he could only be concerned, within the scope of his abilities, to avoiding a catastrophe even larger than the one of Sixth Army: the encirclement of the entire German southern wing. The operational reserves which the OKH had at its disposal nevertheless proved inadequate to ensure the communications security of the armies on the lower Don and the Dnieper. It was thus essential for Manstein's army group to withdraw its eastern wing and to regroup the liberated forces to the west. Obviously such an operation had to occur as quickly as possible so that the transferred units could fend off the enemy's pincer maneuver which was extending more and more to the west, a mission all the more difficult since Army Group B found itself on the verge of collapse due to the frantic retreat of the allied armies. On the other hand, this displacement of forces could not have adequate strength without also removing units from Army Group A, which was not under Manstein's command.

The idea of staving off an enemy pincer movement by shifting forces from the east to the west was the simplest solution under such circumstances. However, it had to be implemented soon, which is to say before the threat of encirclement had reached a critical phase. The only way to immediately perform the bypass proposed by Manstein was to bring back in a single breath the Fourth Panzer Army to Rostov in order to have it defend the southern flank and the lines of communication to the west of Army Group Don, and to withdraw back onto the Donetz the Mieth Group—named after the general who had taken command of the former sector of Third Romanian Army—and Army Detachment Hollidt, which was still fighting in the great bend of the Don.

However, the order given to Colonel General Kleist, commander of Army Group A since the end of November, to retain his positions in the Caucasus rendered such a solution impossible, for it would have meant completely vacating his rear. But the mission of Manstein's army group was not only to cover the rear of the armies in the Caucasus, but also to ensure their lines of communication which went through Rostov-on-Don. The idea of a maneuver that involved transferring Manstein's center of gravity to the west in order to intercept an encirclement of the southern wing of the German armies was thus not immediately possible. Despite the worsening threat on their western flank, the armies commanded by Manstein were forced to carry out a desperate battle to protect the rear of the armies in the Caucasus. Hitler was still guided by the principle of keeping a strict hold on territory, whereas Manstein thought that the way to inflict serious setbacks on the enemy was through mobile operations.[448]

The battle between the Don and the Dnieper for the communications of the southern wing

Instead of fending off the threat of encirclement through displacing its center of gravity to the west, as the situation was demanding, Manstein's army group was to fight under increasingly more critical conditions in order to gain more time. To the south of the lower Don, Fourth Panzer Army was to cover Army Group A's rear, while keeping its lines of communication, which passed through Rostov, open. On the great bend of the Don, between that river and the Donetz, Army Detachment Hollidt had to slow down the enemy's advance to the lower Don enough to prevent it from cutting off the supply lines of Hoth's tanks, as well as those of Kleist's armies. At the same time, it was necessary for Hollidt to prevent a Soviet crossing of the Donetz in the Vorochilovgrad sector, and as a result an approach to Rostov from the north. Finally, together with any OKH reserves that might appear, Hollidt had to find a way of keeping open the lines of communication with the west, along the lower Dnieper.

It was Fourth Panzer Army that had to fulfill the mission of protecting the rear of Army Group A. On the one hand, it had to prevent the enemy from advancing into the rear of First Panzer Army as long as the latter did not occupy a front facing east. On the other hand, it was necessary to prevent a breakthrough on the lower reaches of the Don that would expose Rostov, the key communications chokepoint of not only Fourth Panzer Army but all of Army Group A. It was matter of a double mission, which Hoth's tank army was clearly not in a position to fulfill, for it did not have adequate forces at its disposal to create a barrier between the lower reaches of the Don and the foothills of the Caucasus while confronting greatly superior enemy units. After the loss of the Romanians, it consisted only of the 57th Panzer Corps, among which two divisions (the 17th and the 23rd Panzer) were already considerably weakened, and the 15th Field Division of the Luftwaffe, which was not yet ready to go into action. The only reinforcements that OKH could provide were the 16th Motorized Division and the SS *Wiking* Division, both released from Army Group A.

Even before being able to reconstruct its forces, the Fourth Panzer Army had been driven back to the west of Kotelnikovo by three Soviet

Armies (the Twenty-Eighth, the Fifty-First, and the Second Guards), by the beginning of January. On the 9th of the month, it engaged in difficult battles between the Manytch and the Sal rivers. The enemy was clearly intending to envelop it from the north and the south. The Second Guards Army was located in Konstantinovsk, on the Don, and was advancing towards Proletarsk to the southeast, to reach the rear of Hoth's forces, while the Twenty-Eighth Army, having recently come out of the Kalmuks steppe, attempted to encircle the latter along the Manytch.

Rather than attempt an inadequate resistance on an overextended frontline, Manstein decided that the Fourth Panzer Army had to keep its forces concentrated, which would be the only way to present a truly strong resistance at a significant point. For this, it had to temporarily evacuate certain sectors. In any case, the means at its disposal only permitted it, at the very most, to execute only one of its two missions. Consequently, it decided to give priority to covering First Panzer Army while it changed fronts. Such a decision certainly increased the threat against Rostov. But if the enemy were to succeed in encircling First Panzer Army, holding this city would no longer have any use, the fate of Army Group A having been sealed. On the other hand, if First Panzer Army were to succeed in switching its front, a crisis at Rostov could still be averted.

Despite repeated armored thrusts by the Russians, Colonel General Hoth succeeded at realigning his tank army, along with that of Army Group A, which completed its change of fronts on January 14. With its left wing, the First Panzer Army occupied henceforth the Tcherkessk-Petrovskoie line facing the east, which permitted it a certain operational coordination with the Fourth Panzer Army. The latter had thus fulfilled its first mission. Only the second remained for it to complete: cover the lines of communication of Kleist's army group which went through Rostov-on-Don.

In the meantime, Army Detachment Hollidt had to prevent the enemy, coming down from the north, from advancing on the lower reaches of the Don, i.e. to the rear of Fourth Panzer Army, and above all prohibit it from breaching Rostov. Likewise, it had to defend the crossings of the Donetz in the Vorochilovgrad sector. To accomplish this double task on a front approximately 200 kilometers, extending from Nijne Tchirskaya on the Don to Kamensk-Chakhtinski on the Donetz, it disposed of the Mieth Group (now under its authority), with four weary, battleworn infantry divisions (the 62nd, 294th, 336th, and 387th), plus the 6th and 11th Panzer Divisions, as well as the newly arrived 7th Panzer. Also at its disposal were ad hoc units formed from supply and rear-echelon troops, and some Flak units that were not only valuable against Soviet aircraft but could be used in an anti-tank role. The two Luftwaffe field divisions placed under Hollidt's command were not yet ready for combat, while the 22nd Panzer Division, having already suffered too much, had to be disbanded.

Army Detachment Hollidt found itself quickly outflanked by three Soviet Armies (the Fifth Shock Army, the Fifth Tank, and the Third Guards) on both its flanks: to the west, following the loss of the Italian Army, in place of which the Fretter-Pico Group—named after the lieutenant general who had taken command—slowly retreated while fighting from Millerovo towards the Donetz; and to the east, after the defection of the Romanian armies, when several enemy units crossed the Don at Potemkinskaya, then at Tsymlianskaya. After harsh and violent battles, the army detachment finally succeeded in stopping the adversary's advance on the Donetz, and as a result prevented the lines of communication of the Fourth Panzer Army and Army Group A from being cut.[449]

In mid-January, at the time when First Panzer Army reached the Tcherkessk-Petrovskoie line, thus creating a front facing east, the situation on the front of Army Detachment Hollidt worsened. The enemy succeeded at creating a breach in the direction of the Donetz with its rapid units south of Millerovo, in the Fretter-Pico Group's zone. Its objective was to cross the river on both sides of Kamensk-Chakhtinski, while at the same time other rapid units surged into the sector formed by the Sal, the Don, and the Manytch, thus between Army Detachment Hollidt and Fourth Panzer Army, which was still covering the northern flank of First Panzer Army, ahead of Salsk. Such forces could cross the Don to seize Rostov, or even advance into the rear of Army Detachment Hollidt. Their actual intention became clear on January 20, when they attacked on the lower reaches of the Manytch in the direction of Rostov-on-Don. Armored units even reached the city's airfield. Simultaneously, the enemy continued its assaults on the front of Army Detachment Hollidt with the rather obvious intention of holding it in place until the moment when the capture of Rostov would permit the enemy to encircle it.

Once again, Field Marshal Manstein was required to decide which threat to fend off first. The risk to Rostov-on-Don appeared to be much more pressing and immediate in his view. He thus ordered not only the Fourth Panzer Army, but also the First Panzer Army to retreat back onto the city. It was the only solution. If not, one would have to abandon all hopes of transferring adequate forces to the west in order to intercept the encirclement of the entire southern wing of the German front. If Hitler was willing to grant Fourth Panzer Army complete mobility by releasing it from its duty of covering the northern flank of First Panzer Army, he nevertheless still appeared hesitant about approving the latter's retreat back to Rostov.

By delaying his decision concerning Manstein's proposed shift of forces, Hitler was clearly giving an advantage to the enemy. Since January 19, a breach triggered by the collapse of the Eighth Italian Army and then the Second Hungarian Army occurred in the interim, opening up a distance of approximately 320 kilometers from Vorochilovgrad on the Donetz, to Voronej on the Don. The enemy had time to exploit the rupture of the Italian and Hungarian sectors and propel forward significant forces which Army Group Don was incapable, for the time being, of opposing. The Red Army therefore had the opportunity to launch units directly towards Rostov or to envelop the western wing of Army Detachment Hollidt from Vorochilovgrad. At the same time, Sixth Army's resistance in Stalingrad began to breathe its last. Manstein could thus expect to see a multitude of Soviet units, heretofore held up before the Sixth Army, let loose in the region of Starobielsk, i.e. in the expansive breach between Army Groups B and Don.

On January 22, Hitler finally decided to allow the withdrawal of the northern wing of First Panzer Army back to Rostov, thus in the area where the decisive battle was occurring, and to place it under the command of Army Group Don. As for the southern wing, including the 13th Panzer Division, it would be incorporated into the Seventeenth Army, which was to move back to the Kuban peninsula, where he hoped to retain a bridgehead for a new drive into the Caucasus later in the year. From that moment on, Hitler agreed to accelerate the maneuver in order to transfer as quickly as possible the Fourth Panzer Army to the west. Two days later, the northern wing of Army Group A was in Belya Glina and further to the south, to the east of Armavir, thus 150 and 250 kilometers from Rostov-on-Don. While Fourth Panzer Army was desperately fighting in the southeast and right next to Rostov in order to keep open the Don crossing for the northern wing of First Panzer Army, Army Detachment Hollidt was defending, for better or worse, the Donetz. But it was clear that the latter could not contain for much longer the considerably superior enemy forces.[450]

By the end of the month, Army Group A's retreat was altogether achieved. On January 29, First Panzer Army was operating in conjunction with Fourth Panzer Army and, three days later, it reached Rostov-on-Don. As for the Seventeenth Army, it took position in the Kuban bridgehead on February 2. After an exhaustive withdrawal of 500 to 600 kilometers in occasionally dreadful winter conditions, without any air support, and confronting an enemy that was far superior in numbers and supplies, it was nothing less than an extraordinary performance in operational terms that Army Group A had achieved. However, it was not only Hitler's dream of a later operation in the Middle East against British positions that had just been smashed to pieces, but also the entire *raison d'être* of the campaign of the summer of 1942. Even if Hitler was hoping to launch a new offensive into the Caucasus from the Kuban bridgehead in the summer of 1943, there were no guarantees that he would be capable of achieving this.[451]

Manstein as supreme commander in the East?

On January 12, 1943, Field Marshal Manstein had transferred his head-quarters to Taganrog, and then on January 29 he moved to Donetsk (Stalino), while the center of gravity of his forces was shifting from the Don towards the Donetz. Having successfully achieved his second mission, for which the immediate objective was to cover the evacuation from the Caucasus of Army Group A, the question now at hand for Army Group Don was to see if it would be able to maintain the Donetz basin, an industrial region that had played a crucial role in Hitler's strategic considerations since 1941.

At the beginning of February, the enemy launched new forces against Army Group Don. Consequently, it was exerting even greater pressure on the latter's right wing, particularly on the Fourth Panzer Army, which was covering the movement of the First Panzer Army from Rostov towards the middle reaches of the Donetz. It was expected that the Soviets would launch a large-scale attack against Rostov from both sides of Novotcherkassk. On Army Group Don's left wing, Russian units had crossed the Donetz, and because of the quick retreat of the Italians, had reached to the east of Vorochilovgrad. The enemy was henceforth in front of Slaviansk and had taken Izium. It was clearly seeking to prevent the retreat of Army Detachment Hollidt back to its position on the Mius River. The threat of envelopment of the entire southern wing of the German front was looming high on the horizon.

Faced with the worsening situation, Manstein asked for the evacuation of the eastern region of the Donetz basin through an immediate retreat of his army group's right wing. However, Hitler had absolutely no intention of approving such a maneuver. Despite his objection, the necessity of arriving at a mutually agreeable solution had never been more urgent. Manstein was thus called to the Führer's headquarters in Rastenburg, East Prussia, on February 6, 1943. The discussion focused on two points: conducting operations in the sector of Army Group Don and the issue of the high command.

Hitler began by declaring that he alone was responsible for the tragic end of the Sixth Army, which had occurred a few days earlier. Given Hitler's chastened mood, Field Marshal Manstein took advantage of the Führer's confiding in him to challenge the high command itself, i.e., the manner in which Hitler was controlling it since the departure of Field Marshal Brauchitsch. Knowing full well that it was impossible for a dictator like Hitler to abandon his self-appointed responsibility without losing face, he tried to find an acceptable solution that would not infringe upon his prestige, but would ensure a more effective management of military operations. Manstein suggested that the Führer choose, all the while remaining as nominal supreme commander, a single chief of staff for the three branches of the Wehrmacht in whom he had complete trust, and to whom he would delegate his powers and responsibility related to them. In other words, he attempted to persuade him to step down from commanding the army and to appoint a responsible supreme leader who, having his complete confidence, would have full authority over conducting operations in all of the theaters or, at the very least, on the Eastern Front.

But Hitler was not inclined to take this matter seriously into consideration. He continually shifted the discussion to personal matters, speaking about the disappointments that the former War, Field Marshal Blomberg, as well as the former commander in chief of the army, Field

Marshal Brauchitsch, had caused him. It was also not possible, he added, to designate a chief of staff to whom Göring would be almost completely subordinate. Given that the latter was his *prince* and the only Reichsmarshal of Germany, never would he accept such subordination, even if the chief of staff were to speak in Hitler's name. Never would Göring agree to submit to anyone's authority other than Hitler's own and to only be an equal with the generals of the OKW and OKH. The Führer was perhaps correct apropos of Göring's self-importance, but he was probably also bringing it up as a pretext to avoid discussing the true reasons that motivated his refusal.[452]

Field Marshal Manstein was the natural candidate for the position of "supreme commander in the East." There is no doubt that he was thinking of himself when he made this suggestion to Hitler. Not only did he consider himself the most appropriate officer for this duty, but he was hoping to be the one who would be designated by the Führer. In addition, he knew full well that several army leaders wished to see him assigned the position of chief of staff or *generalissimo* of the three branches of the Wehrmacht. Even within the Luftwaffe, leading senior officers, such as Colonel General Richthofen and Field Marshal Milch, agreed that the Führer should appoint a commander in chief on the Eastern Front, and that this should be Field Marshal Manstein.[453]

However, Hitler did not want to elevate Manstein to this degree, even if he did consider him as the best of his commanders. He knew of no man, he added, to whom he could entrust such a command. His viewpoint was supported by Göring, extremely jealous of the prestige which Manstein enjoyed within the officers' corps and with the troops. Moreover, Colonel General Guderian was probably right to worry that Manstein had too independent of a spirit and was too outspoken in the eyes of the Führer. After the bitter arguments and conflicts of the preceding months, the latter preferred the servility of a Keitel or a Jodl to potentially vehement objections from a man like Manstein, even if the result were to further weaken the military effectiveness of the Wehrmacht.

Furthermore, during the following days, Hitler even toyed with the idea of relieving Manstein of his own command. He was apparently annoyed by the views the Field Marshal had expressed with regards to the manner in which he was fulfilling the supreme command. Until then, no one had ever presented to the Führer in such a way the inadequacies of his military leadership. If in the end he decided to retain Manstein in his duties, it was most likely because he came to the conclusion that, in this extremely critical moment of the war, the professional expertise of the field marshal was absolutely essential for him to restore and stabilize the situation on the southern wing of the German front. In Hitler's words, Field Marshal Manstein was quite simply "the best brain that the general staff has produced."[454]

With the meeting remaining fruitless up to this point, the two engaged in a long and obstinate discussion on the operational situation on the southern wing. In order to get his ideas approved, Manstein insisted that the forces of his army group were in no way adequate to hold the Don-Donetz salient. Whatever significance this region held, he declared, it was simply a matter of knowing if it were necessary to attempt to maintain it while at the same time taking the risk of losing Army Group Don, and as a result of that, Army Group A, or if it was agreeable to sacrifice a portion of the Donetz region in order to escape disaster. According to him, if Army Group Don were to remain in the salient, the enemy would have a free hand to encircle the entire southern wing on the lower Dnieper or on the coast of the Sea of Azov with significant forces, having taken into account the almost complete elimination of Army Group B. And, he asserted, the entire fate of the war in the East depended on the outcome of the southern wing of the front.

In order to achieve the encirclement of the southern wing, the Soviets were able to call upon powerful operational reserves, notably those freed from fighting at Stalingrad. With the enemy being strong enough to execute this large-scale maneuver while still being able to cover its flank facing the west in the region of Kharkov, a counterattack from the II SS Panzer Corps, which had recently arrived in the area, would not be adequate to stem the tide, no more than the entirety of the remaining operational reserves.

It was thus essential, insisted Manstein, to have First Panzer Army, which was marching towards the mid-point of the Donetz, follow close behind the Fourth Panzer Army in order to fend off the threat of envelopment which was taking shape between the Donetz and the Dnieper. If such an action were conducted, it would then become possible, with the aid of reinforcements currently en route, to restore the situation on the southern front. But for this, it would be absolutely necessary to withdraw Fourth Panzer Army from the lower Don, which would require the evacuation of the Don-Donetz salient owing to a retreat behind the Mius. There was not a day to lose, said Manstein, for it was in no way certain that Army Detachment Hollidt could succeed in retreating in time before it was overwhelmed. The field marshal was thus forced to request authorization to abandon the entire area of the Donetz region located to the east of the river.

Hitler reiterated his habitual repugnance at willingly abandoning conquered territory, even though, he stated, there were no guarantees that an evacuation of the Donetz basin, even a partial one, would necessarily restore the situation. But faced with the tenacity with which Manstein held to his ideas, he finally agreed to a retreat back to the Mius, thus concluding the far-ranging conversation that had lasted for four hours.[455]

The retreat behind the Mius

On February 7, upon his return to Army Group Don's headquarters, Field Marshal Manstein ordered Army Detachment Hollidt to evacuate its position in the Donetz bend and to retreat behind the Mius in order to create a line of defense there extending from Taganrog on the coast of the Azov Sea, to Krasnyi Luch on the mid-point of the Donetz. But, before reaching this new position, he first had to pull back to the Novotcherkassk-Kamensk-Chakhtinski line, for given that the enemy was already to the south of the Donetz in Vorochilovgrad, to the rear of his left wing, there were no guarantees that he would be able to retreat in a single movement back to the Mius, nor that the First Panzer Army would be able to hold or restore the front on the middle reaches of the Donetz. The situation was further complicated with the imminent collapse of the Kharkov front, in the sector of Army Group B which had, for the most part, vanished into thin air. The Russians could then not only make a push for the crossings on the Dnieper, and thus cut off the lines of communication of Army Group Don and Army Group A, but also advance up the river, cross it, and take from the rear the entire southern wing of the German front. Colonel General Hoth's Fourth Panzer Army was therefore required to "leap-frog" as quickly as possible from the eastern flank to the western flank but, because of the distance and the condition of the routes, the maneuver took approximately two weeks.

Despite such measures, new crises arose in Rostov and in Vorochilovgrad, where the Russians were advancing. The critical position in which Army Detachment Hollidt found itself was further hindered by the inability of Colonel General Mackensen's First Panzer Army to prevent the enemy from crossing the Donetz, from Kissichansk to Slaviansk. On February 9, Red Army units seized Bielgorod and Kursk, to the north of Kharkov, in the sector of Army Group B. Other units, emerging from the Donetz bend at Izium, advanced to the west. General Hubert Lanz's army detachment, newly situated around Kharkov, and Army Group B's Second Army, greatly worn out, were practically the only forces that remained in the breach between the Dnieper and the right wing of Army Group Center, which began to the far north of Kursk.

On February 12, the commander in chief of Army Group Don sent to the OKH a report on the still-festering situation. Despite the arrival of a series of new divisions, the ratio of forces was still 8 to 1 in favor of the enemy in the theater of operations for the southern wing, whereas it was only 4 to 1 in the enemy's favor for Army Groups Center and North. This indicated that the Red Army, following up its success at Stalingrad, was clearly seeking an outcome by trying to destroy the southern wing of the front. Moreever, Army Groups Don and B had been fighting vigorously and relentlessly for several months in open country, which was not the case for the two other army groups who were driving back sporadic attacks from dug-in entrenchments. Consequently, the armies of the southern wing of the front could not be left for much longer in such a numerically unfavorable situation. In order to improve the ratio of forces on this wing, it would be necessary to agree to withdrawals from other sectors of the Eastern Front or other theaters.

Manstein received a response from the OKH on the same day. Army Group Don, which had transferred its headquarters to Zaporojie to be closer to the area where the decisive combats would take place, received the designation of "Army Group South." Moreover, a new army would be deployed on the Poltava-Dniepropetrovsk line, and another to the southwest of Orel, thus to the rear of the southern wing of the Second Army. The objective was to commit them to battle by the end of February; but such measures did not achieve the desired effect. Second Army did indeed receive a few reinforcements, but they were withdrawn from those already promised to Army Group South. As for the "army" that was to take position on the Poltava-Dniepropetrovsk line, it was finally revealed to be Army Detachment Lanz, already in place around Kharkov. It would subsequently be subordinated to Army Group South at the same time as Army Group B's sector near Bielgorod. The Second Army was incorporated into Army Group Center, whereas Army Group B was removed from the table of organization on the Eastern Front its surviving components placed under other commands.

If he had been unable to convince Hitler to name him supreme commander on the Eastern Front, Field Marshal Manstein had at least gained control of the entire southern wing. Henceforth, he disposed of 32 divisions deployed on a front of 700 kilometers extending from the Sea of Azov to Bielgorod.[456] Even if a number of their formations were inferior to German divisions, no fewer than 342 large Soviet units were deployed in front of Army Group South. The removal of Army Group B nevertheless gave Manstein the opportunity of commanding alone at the decisive point where that winter's primary campaign was taking place.

The Kharkov sector was, however, a new source of worry. Hitler had ordered Army Detachment Lanz to hold this city at all cost. In addition, the SS panzer corps, which represented its nucleus, was to attack in the direction of Lozovaya in order to free the left flank of Army Group South. Given that only two of the three divisions of the SS corps had arrived, specifically the *Das Reich* and the *Leibstandarte Adolf Hitler*, Army Detachment Lanz was unable to simultaneously execute these two missions. Manstein then suggested to Hitler to abandon the city in order to eliminate the Soviet forces (the Sixth Army) to the south of it and to avert the danger of seeing them cross the Dnieper on either side of Kremenchug. He also proposed to halt the Soviet armored units (the Twenty-Fifth Tank Army and the 1st Guards Armored Corps) which were advancing on Zaporojie and Dniepropetrovsk through the intervention of the Fourth Panzer Army. If Army Detachment Lanz were to fight the enemy to the south of Kharkov, it would eventually be able to recapture the city. But, as was his habit, Hitler was in no way inclined to adopt a solution that required the abandonment of territory, in this case the city of Kharkov.

Fortunately for Manstein, the circumstances outweighed Hitler's desire to retain the city at all costs. Threatened with encirclement, the

SS panzer corps evacuated the city on February 15, contrary to General Lanz's orders. The SS commander, Lieutenant General Paul Hausser, appeared to be more forceful than Field Marshal Paulus had been when he found himself faced with another Stalingrad. If the abandonment of Kharkov, occupied by the enemy the very next day, had been ordered by an army general, Hitler would have most likely court martialed him, but since it was an SS officer, nothing transpired. Furthermore, this initiative was later approved by Manstein and Zeitzler. General Lanz was the one whose head had to roll, as he was replaced a few days later, under the pretext that he was a mountain troop specialist, by Werner Kempf, a specialist of armored units. Hitler once again considered relieving Field Marshal Manstein of his command, precisely because of the abandonment of Kharkov by the SS corps, in spite of his formal order to hold this town until the last German soldier. But, due to the worsening situation, he once again decided otherwise at the last minute.[457]

On February 16, as Manstein had been expecting for quite some time, advanced units of the Sixth Soviet Army marched towards Pavlograd and Dniepropetrovsk. If they were to reach the Lozovaya or even the Pavlograd rail junction, the rail line coming from Poltava would be cut. The situation became so critical that the Führer decided to go to Manstein's headquarters in Zaporojie to discuss the latter's further intentions.

The east-west bypass and the counterattack between the Dnieper and the Donetz

When Hitler arrived on February 17, Manstein hastened to present to him a detailed account of the situation. Army Detachment Hollidt had reached the Mius position that very day, though closely pursued by the enemy. First Panzer Army had halted the enemy in the region of Krasnoarmeisk-Grichnino, but proved incapable of eliminating it. As for Army Detachment Lanz, it had evacuated Kharkov and retreated to the southwest, behind the Moch River.

The commander of Army Group South then explained to Hitler his intention to withdraw the SS corps from the Kharkov region, leaving only the other units of Army Detachment Lanz. Departing from the area of Krasnograd, the SS would attack to the southwest, in the direction of Pavlograd, to establish contact with Fourth Panzer Army coming from the south. The common mission of these forces was to cut off and destroy the enemy forces that had rushed into a huge breach, 160 kilometers wide, between First Panzer Army and Army Detachment Lanz. The results obtained, and the danger of seeing Army Detachment Hollidt and Mackensen's tank army encircled thus being averted, it would next be a matter of recapturing Kharkov.

As was to be expected, Hitler refused to take action on Manstein's operational concept. Not only did he not want to believe that significant forces were present between First Panzer Army and Army Detachment Hollidt, but he speculated that a recent thaw would halt all operations planned between the Dnieper and the Donetz. But the primary motivation for his refusal stemmed from his desire to retake Kharkov as quickly as possible, as soon as the SS panzer corps had received its third division, the *Totenkopf*.

What he did not appear to realize, however, was that the elimination of the threat to the Dnieper crossings represented the key condition for an attack on Kharkov. The recapture of this town would be of no use if the lines of communication of the First Panzer Army and Army Detachment Hollidt were cut. In addition, the collaboration of the Fourth Panzer Army remained essential, for the forces of the SS corps alone would not be adequate for such an undertaking. Finally, the thaw would realistically interrupt the operations between the Donetz and the Dnieper well before those around Kharkov, further to the north. Consequently, it was still reasonable to hope to attack the town after having eliminated the Soviet forces between Mackensen's First Panzer Army and Army Detachment Lanz.

It was only after two days of discussions, on February 19, that Manstein succeeded in convincing Hitler of the necessity of drawing up almost all of the armored divisions of Army Group South to launch a counterattack on its western wing in order to secure its lines of communication. To this end, he took advantage of the worsening situation during the past twenty-four hours. Not only had the Russian troops reached Sinelnikovo, thus cutting off the main supply line from the center and right wings of Army Group South, but they were no more than 60 kilometers from its headquarters, where the Führer was still located. Finally realizing the risk of encirclement that the southern wing of the Eastern Front was running at this particular moment, the latter ordered Army Group A to yield all of the units it could spare. He had obviously abandoned the idea of acting offensively from the Kuban bridgehead. Moreover, he agreed to Manstein's proposal of deploying Hoth's tank army with the intention of an attack against the enemy forces that were located on the Perechtchepino-Pavlograd-Grichino line.[458]

It would be necessary to act quickly, for the Russians were squeezing Army Detachment Hollidt against its Mius position, seeking a rupture in three areas, and trying to breach the still very weak front of Army Detachment Kempf (named after the general who had replaced Lanz) to the southwest and west of Kharkov, to envelop it on its northern flank. In spite of this desperate situation, Field Marshal Manstein sought to restore the German front and regain a strategic initiative through offensive action. Despite all their successes, the Soviets were now extending their own supply lines, dozens of large units rushing headlong toward the great bend of the Dnieper. Manstein's intention was to exploit the risky situation of the Red Army by launching a counterattack against the barely protected and overextended flanks of the Soviet armored columns.

With this goal in mind, Fourth Panzer Army had to quickly defeat the enemy engaged between First Panzer Army and Army Detachment Kempf in order to maintain the lines of communication with the crossings of the Dnieper. Next, in conjunction with Mackensen's tanks, Hoth's tanks would attack the Soviet forces that were in the Krasnoarmeisk-Grichino sector. During this time, Army Detachment Kempf would restrict itself to putting up fierce resistance in order to prevent the enemy from reaching either Dniepropetrovsk through Krasnograd, or Kremenchug through Poltava, while Army Detachment Hollidt would hold the Mius front at all cost.

The following days brought with them the hoped-for success of the counterattack executed by Fourth Panzer Army, and thus returned the initiative to the Wehrmacht. For his counteroffensive, Manstein benefited from the support of Richthofen's Fourth Luftflotte, which, with its 950 aircraft, carried out more than 1,000 sorties each day starting on February 20, in comparison to the 350 sorties each day of the preceding month. In fact, the Luftwaffe would be in a position, for the last time on the Eastern Front, of gaining aerial superiority over the ground units of the *Ostheer* during a large-scale operation. The Fourth Panzer Army, which had the II SS Panzer Corps at its disposal, first defeated the enemy forces that were advancing towards the Dnieper crossings around Pavlograd. Four corps were involved: two armored, one infantry, and one cavalry. Then, in liaison with the First Panzer Army, it destroyed the four armored or motorized corps halted on the latter's front. Meanwhile, the Mius front had remained firm. One Soviet cavalry corps, encircled at Debaltsevo, was destroyed. Likewise, an armored corps that had created a breach in Matvaiev Kugan, was enveloped and forced to surrender.

After this victory, Manstein decided to take advantage of the newly gained initiative to launch an attack on the Voronej front, thus where Soviet forces had positioned themselves around Kharkov in opposition to Army Detachment Kempf. Initially, his intention was to take from the rear the enemy which was squeezing Army Detachment Kempf in the region of Achtyrka and Poltava, in order to engage it in a battle on inverted fronts. For this, the Fourth Panzer Army would have to cross the Donetz, downstream from Kharkov, then cut across to the west, to get to the rear of the forces stationed in this city and to its west. The ice had nevertheless become too fragile. This was regrettable for the Germans, for if they had been able to cross the Donetz quickly and position themselves in the rear of the Russian armies which were advancing to the west, they would probably have inflicted upon the Soviets a disaster comparable to the one that they had suffered themselves in Stalingrad. Manstein thus chose to confront the enemy forces on their southern flank in order to drive them from Kharkov and later take them in the rear from the north and northeast. The objective was not so much to recapture Kharkov as it was to destroy the forces to the southwest of the town before they had received reinforcements and the thaw prevented any offensive action.

On March 5, the Fourth Panzer Army and the SS panzer corps, which had received its third division, the *Totenkopf*, in the interim, destroyed the Soviet forces in position on the Berestovaya, to the southwest of Karkov, which permitted an attack to the north while departing from the area of Krasnograd. Army Detachment Kempf was to join the offensive as soon as the adversary started showing signs of weakness on its front. By cutting off the enemy forces located in front of Army Detachment Kempf, Manstein was hoping to be able to capture Kharkov in a *coup de main*. He was quite determined to prevent at all cost turning the city into a second Stalingrad, with slow and brutal street fighting. He thus had to forcefully intervene in order to prevent

SS Lieutenant General Hausser from executing a frontal attack, from getting caught there, and from allowing the enemy units west of the town to escape. He finally succeeded at having him bypass Kharkov to the north and northeast. On March 14, the town fell into the hands of the SS *Leibstandarte Adolf Hitler*, which was able to cut off the retreat to the Donetz of significant Soviet forces. Army Detachment Kempf recaptured the town of Bielgorod, which had fallen to the Soviets five weeks earlier, and reached the midpoint of the Donetz. On March 23, Soviet resistance to the west of the river was definitively eliminated.[459]

Manstein's offensive that retook Kharkov and reached the Donetz was an extremely vital success. In one month of combat, Army Group South had destroyed three Soviet Armies (Sixth Army, the Third Tank Army, and Army Group Popov), and had pushed back three others with heavy casualties (the First Guards, the Fortieth and Sixtieth Armies). In all, the Red Army suffered 46,000 killed, 14,000 prisoners, and 600 tanks and 1,200 artillery pieces destroyed or seized.[460]

The recapture of Kharkov and Bielgorod brought Army Group South's second counterattack of February–March 1943 to an end. The thawing ground no longer permitted mobile operations. Consequently, Manstein's intention of reducing the expansive Soviet salient established around Kursk could not be achieved, all the more so since Army Group Center believed it was incapable of making a substantial contribution. Army Group South could only hold onto its restored front, from Bielgorod to the Sea of Azov, where the German troops had spent the terrible winter months of 1941–1942 and from where they had commenced Plan Blue at the beginning of summer 1942.

Despite the enormous sacrifices incurred in its numerous offensives during the winter of 1942–1943, the Red Army did not succeed at achieving its principal objective, which was to encircle the entire southern wing of the German front by pinning it back to the Azov or Black Sea. In the euphoria of its victory at Stalingrad, it had evidently overestimated its operational abilities and underestimated the remaining combat worth of the *Ostheer,* and above all the strategic and operational talent of Field Marshal Manstein. Expecting to pursue the German retreat to the Dnieper, it was completely caught off guard by Manstein's counteroffensives of February–March 1943, all the more so since it had made the gaffe of scattering its forces over a large front and neglecting their long and exposed flanks.[461]

However, after the ordeal by fire of a first year of war marked by stinging failures, Soviet armament, training, and command had considerably improved. The high command had effectively learned from its enemy in relation to large operations, mobility, offensive mindset, and the rational use of forces at the appropriate focal points. But what it had learned most from the beginning of hostilities concerned the organization and employment of armored units. The masses of tanks, which it had not known how to engage autonomously in 1941, now represented a formidable armored corps which knew how to thoroughly apply German breakthrough tactics, and whose advances were massively supported by the air force.

The use of such doctrine did not, however, permit the high command of the Red Army to envelop the entire southern wing of the German front. It had been clearly incapable of arriving quickly enough at the decisive area and with enough forces. It thus not only allowed Kleist's army group enough time to evacuate the Caucasus, but also Manstein's group to engage in battle at the decisive point, thanks to the transfer of forces that he carried out from his eastern wing to his western wing.

For Germany, the two counterattacks between the Dnieper and the Donetz represented "a veritable victory of the Marne."[462] To commemorate such an exploit, Hitler decorated Field Marshal Manstein by conferring upon him the Knight's Cross with oak leaves. The operational success of Manstein's army group contributed to the restoration and stabilization of the southern sector of the Eastern Front, and forced Stalin to realize that the *Ostheer* still disposed of sufficient reserves to launch powerful counterattacks, even after its defeat in Stalingrad. But if the Germany Army had succeeded at restoring the front, it had still lost all of its new conquests of summer 1942. It had certainly regained the strategic initiative by inflicting two defeats on the enemy, but its losses no longer allowed it to truly achieve a military victory. Even more worrisome for the *Ostheer* was the ratio of forces increasingly in favor of the Red Army. As of April 1, 1943, while the latter was able to place on the line 5,792,000 soldiers distributed among 500 divisions and supported by more than 6,000 tanks and 20,000 pieces of artillery, the German Army deployed on the Eastern Front no more than 2,732,000 men distributed among 147 divisions, supported by 1,336 tanks and 6,360 guns.[463]

Hitler, however, had regained his confidence. Witnessing the extent of Soviet losses between February and March, he had deduced once again that Stalin's reserves had to be on the point of utter exhaustion. As remarked by Major General Warlimont, deputy chief of staff for the OKW, the Führer left Vinnitsa in mid-March to return to Rastenburg "with the air of a victorious warlord, clearly considering himself and *his* leadership primarily responsible for the favorable turn of events in the East which had temporarily ended the withdrawal after Stalingrad." To his press chief, Otto Dietrich, Hitler furthermore declared: "I am the one who recaptured Kharkov, and not *Herr* von Manstein!"[464]

Manstein: a master in the art of the backlash, or second strike

The recapture of Kharkov and Bielgorod, and as a result the restoration of Army Group South's front on the mid-point of the Donetz, marked the end of the winter campaign of 1942–1943. In four weeks, Field Marshal Manstein's counteroffensive had accomplished what had seemed inconceivable after the encirclement of Sixth Army in Stalingrad on November 22, 1942: it had prevented the Red Army from achieving a "gigantic Stalingrad," in other words, the encirclement of the entire southern wing of the German front. It gave Hitler his last victory in the East, and to Manstein, it provided certainty that he could overcome any extremely critical military situation by resorting, on a completely fluid battlefield, to the concept of mobile warfare.

Shortly before the German counterattack between the Dnieper and the Donetz, the Soviet high command had sought to achieve an operational concept that closely resembled Manstein's Sickle Cut Plan. Within the scope of the offensive in the West, the German Army had placed its primary efforts in the direction of the mouth of the Somme, with the objective of reaching the rear of the Anglo-French forces north of the river and pushing them back to the English Channel. In February 1943, the center of gravity of the Soviet offensive was towards the lower reaches of the Dnieper with the intention of encircling the German southern wing and pinning it against the Sea of Azov or the Black Sea. Caught in the trap, Army Groups South and A would not have been able to repeat the Dunkirk miracle from the Crimean peninsula, if only because of the inferior number of German ships on the Black Sea and the control that the Soviet naval fleet had over it.

Field Marshal Manstein thus decided to transform an enormous retreat operation into a brilliant counterattack between the Dnieper and the Donetz in order to counter a massive pincer maneuver executed by the enemy. As the author of the Sickle Cut Plan, the most ingenious pincer maneuver of the Second World War, Manstein was also a master in the art of the backlash, or second strike, i.e. a counterattack in the context of strategic defense. Such a tactic consisted in deliberately letting the enemy advance as deeply as possible in order to launch a counterattack, at the appropriate moment, on its overextended flanks. In February-March 1943, he thus took advantage of the exposed position of the Red Army in order to strike the Soviet armored columns on their poorly protected and thinly spread flanks, which were advancing in the direction of the great bend of the Dnieper. For this, he first waited for the Soviet offensive to reach its climax, in accordance with Clausewitzian principles. The idea was that the further the armored columns advanced to the west, the more devastating would be the trap Manstein could set for them.

Manstein's operational plan was based on a static eastern wing and a mobile western wing. As he did not dispose of an adequate number of operational reserves to intercept the enemy's pincer maneuver between the Donetz and the Dnieper, he removed forces from Army Group South's eastern wing to regroup them to the west, in the area where the decisive battle was occurring. But for this, he had to draw in the front of his own army group. By ordering the evacuation of the Don-Donetz salient for a retreat back to the Mius, he could thus have the First Panzer Army, marching towards the midpoint of the Donetz, followed by the Fourth Panzer Army. He next instructed Army Detachment Hollidt to hold at all costs the Mius front, while Hoth's tanks would attack, in conjunction with Mackensen's, the enemy engaged between the latter two and Army Detachment Kempf, in order to maintain the lines of communication with the Dnieper crossings. Once this mission was accomplished, Hoth could launch an attack in the direction of Kharkov and drive back the Soviet forces beyond the Donetz. It was thus by implementing a shift from the east to the west that Manstein was able to succeed at transforming an enormous retreat into a brilliant counterattack that took the enemy in the rear and completely by surprise, since the latter was expecting at that point to pursue the Germans all the way to the Dnieper.

During the winter battles of 1942–43, Manstein demonstrated all the qualities of a true military genius: energy, determination, audacity, foresight, and the acceptance of risk. Indeed, after a retreat of more than 600 kilometers in three months, he succeeded in bringing it to a halt by launching a counterattack that permitted the elimination of numerous Soviet forces and the recapture of substantial territory. He not only never lost sight of the fact that the primary objective of the Red Army's high command was to encircle the entire German southern wing, but he was still able to anticipate its maneuvers, which allowed him to launch, at the right place and at the right time, his reverse counterattack which some still consider to this day as a veritable masterpiece of strategy.[465]

By avoiding the destruction of the southern wing of the German front through a well organized and methodical retreat, and by succeeding at regaining the strategic initiative by means of a powerful counterattack, he demonstrated that mobile warfare was the most appropriate tactic against an enemy largely superior in number, on a territory as expansive as that of the Soviet Union. Like Field Marshal Rommel in the Cyrenian Desert, he proved that it was possible to transform a retreat into an unexpected military victory through the use of armored and motorized units on favorable terrain such as that of the Soviet steppes. It was thus obvious that the Führer's desire to fight for every inch of land, within the framework of a static war aimed at holding the front at all cost, could hardly be profitable for the German Army.

Pursuing the war in the East to reach a peace agreement?

With surprising naivety, Field Marshal Manstein, in his account of the winter campaign of 1942–1943, came to the following conclusion: "At the end of this winter campaign, the initiative was in the hands of the Germans. The two defeats inflicted by them over their adversaries were not, it is true, decisive in nature, but allowed them to stabilize their front and opened the possibility for them to continue the war in the East with the idea of reaching a peace agreement. All hopes of launching a decisive offensive during the summer of 1943 were dashed. Quite obviously, the high command should have reached the conclusion that it was necessary for it, at all cost, to seek an agreement with at least one of its adversaries and understand that henceforth, on the Eastern Front, it would be necessary to pursue a single objective: spare its forces, avoid in particular the loss of entire armies like in Stalingrad, while trying to exhaust the offensive strength of the Russians. Deliberately abandoning all secondary objectives meant transferring onto this front the center of gravity of German forces for as long as the western adversary was not in a position of landing in France or carrying out a decisive blow from the Mediterranean."[466]

If there existed an opportunity for Germany to reach a peace agreement with one of its adversaries, this would be found in Moscow. From autumn 1942 to summer 1943, the Soviet government actually appeared inclined to commence negotiations in this direction, establishing as a condition a return to the borders of June 22, 1941. But Hitler was in no way willing to abandon all the occupied territories and retreat to his original borders. After two years of bloody effort on the Eastern Front, such conditions appeared inacceptable to him. In any case, because of his "all or nothing" temperament, he was unable to imagine the idea of a peace agreement with a lifelong ideological enemy which he had attacked with the intention of eradicating Jewish Bolshevism and conquering *Lebensraum* necessary for the survival and development of the German Reich as a continental, even global, power.

The principle of unconditional surrender adopted by Churchill and Roosevelt at the Casablanca Conference, which took place January 14–24, 1943, was in perfect harmony with the Walhalla mentality characteristic of the Führer. For him, such a decision only served to confirm that he had the right to be intransigent. As he revealed to his entourage at the beginning of February, he now felt freed from all efforts undertaken to persuade the Soviets to seek a negotiated peace. Just as he had always asserted, it would be victory or destruction.[467] As a result, Manstein was mistaken to think that the Führer could be tempted into playing the political card in the East.

Yet he refused at this time to dismiss such an eventuality, preferring to believe that the Führer would sooner or later decide to come to an agreement with Stalin, to give the Reich the prospect of a victorious defense on the Western Front. Indeed, the landing of Western forces in North Africa in November 1942 foreshadowed the end of operations in that theater and the commencement of a second front in Europe in the near future. The time granted to Germany to conquer Bolshevik Russia before the Anglo-Americans were able wield a decisive blow in Europe seemed for the most part to have passed. According to Manstein, the

Casablanca declaration left hardly any other possibility than to seek the opportunity to reach a compromise solution in the East, for on this front all that the Wehrmacht could hope for, in military terms, was to reach a tie. For this, it nevertheless had to act judiciously. It had to deal new military setbacks to the Red Army, a necessary condition to persuade Stalin to propose a solution acceptable to Hitler.

In his *Memoirs*, Manstein attempts to explain his reasoning at the time: "There existed no other possibility to act decisively against the Western [powers] ever since Hitler had prematurely abandoned his attack against England in order to take action against Russia. Furthermore, the Casablanca declaration left nothing to doubt as to their desire to destroy not only Hitler and his regime, but Germany herself. There was no hope of negotiating peace with them except—perhaps—after having driven back an eventual landing or fought the forces that succeeded in landing. But, in both cases, it was first necessary to withdraw a significant number of forces from the Eastern Front. The first question to ask was thus to know if it were still possible to reach a solution that was acceptable in the East at this time. Evidently, not in the sense of a complete victory over the Soviet power. But could one not hope to reach a compromise, opening the Reich up to the prospect of successfully getting along? One could say today that it was nothing more than a fanciful dream, though this was not certain at the time. Was an agreement with the Soviet Union politically possible in the spring of 1943? We, the soldiers, were unable to judge, but nor could we completely dismiss such a possibility—provided of course that Hitler was inclined to it."

He then continued his thought: "On the one hand, we were convinced, in the high command of Army Group Don (which in the meantime was named Army Group South), that on a strategic level, we could end up in a tie [*Remis*] on the Eastern Front, by acting judiciously. The enemy, to advance from Stalingrad all the way to the Donetz, had to endure heavy sacrifices without reaching its strategic objective. We had regained the initiative. The merit of our troops and their command was again affirmed in every combat of this winter campaign. Stalingrad, of course, cost us dearly, but, according to reliable estimates made to the OKH, the enemy had already lost eleven million men since the beginning of the war, in irrecoverable prisoners, dead, and wounded! Russian offensive power would itself clearly end in collapse! In any case, it was in this manner that we judged the strategic situation in Army Group South, influenced perhaps by the fact that we had succeeded at totally crushing [them]. Furthermore, what good would it have done us in any case, to consider the war lost, in the way that so many critics judged after the fact? Our mission was to keep away from the German borders an enemy whom we would eventually be able to lead to a compromise solution only by striking it several new blows. On the other hand, the Casablanca declaration left us with hardly any other possibility than to seek to reach such a solution in the East."[468]

Manstein's assertion that the Casablanca declaration left no doubt as to the willingness of the Western Allies not only to destroy Hitler and his regime, but also Germany herself, explains his reasoning. However, he does not mention the decisive role of the OKH chiefs in the decision to abandon an invasion of England in preference of an attack against the U.S.S.R., while attributing responsibility of the latter to the sole person of Hitler. Even more interesting is the fact that Manstein, despite his great intelligence on military matters, only took into account the extent of the losses in prisoners, the dead, and wounded, in order to judge the condition of the enemy forces, whereas its available operational reserves were a much more decisive factor for the continuation of the war.

To reach a tie with the Soviet Union, it would be necessary to fulfill three conditions according to Manstein. First, Germany must leave no sign of weakness visible to the enemy, notably on the level of domestic policy. Second, the entire German war effort must be temporarily concentrated on the Soviet front, which would require accepting risks in other theaters of operations. Third, Hitler must listen to reason with regards to the direction of military operations by giving responsibility to a single chief of staff for the three branches of the Wehrmacht or, at the very least, to a single commander in chief of the Eastern Front.[469]

Of course, Manstein thought that he was the best candidate among all the German generals to assume the duties of chief of staff of the Wehrmacht, or Eastern Front commander. And he was clearly hoping to be the one who Hitler would designate to fill such duties should the latter finally decide to relinquish leadership of military operations. In addition, Manstein was convinced that, if the Führer were to give him full reign in conducting the war, he could then stabilize the strategic situation on the entire Eastern Front in a way that would force the Soviets to sit down at the negotiation table to sign a peace agreement.

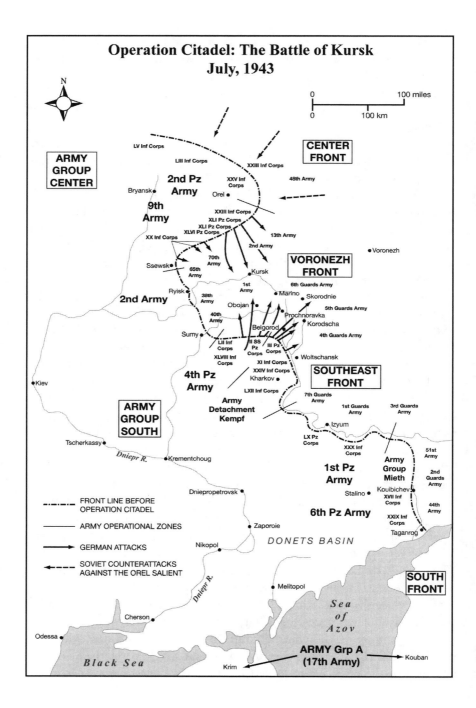

Operation Citadel: The Battle of Kursk
July, 1943

N

| 0 | | 100 miles |
| 0 | 100 km | |

ARMY GROUP CENTER

CENTER FRONT

LV Inf Corps

LIII Inf Corps

XXIII Inf Corps

2nd Pz Army

XXV Inf Corps

48th Army

Bryansk

Orel

9th Army

XXIII Inf Corps
XLI Pz Corps
XLI Pz Corps
XLVI Pz Corps

XX Inf Corps

13th Army

70th Army

2nd Army

Voronezh

Ssewsk

65th Army

Kursk

VORONEZH FRONT

Ryisk

2nd Army

38th Army

1st Army

Marino

6th Guards Army

Skorodnie

Obojan

40th Army

Prochnoravka

5th Guards Army

Korodscha

Sumy

Belgorod

4th Guards Army

LII Inf Corps

II SS Pz Corps

III Pz Corps

XLVIII Inf Corps

XI Inf Corps

Woltschansk

XXIV Inf Corps

4th Pz Army

Kharkov

LXII Inf Corps

SOUTHEAST FRONT

ARMY GROUP SOUTH

Army Detachment Kempf

7th Guards Army

1st Guards Army

3rd Guards Army

Kiev

Izyum

LX Pz Corps

XXX Inf Corps

Army Group Mieth

51st Army

Tscherkassy

Dniepr R.

Krementchoug

1st Pz Army

Stalino

Koulbichev

2nd Guards Army

Dniepropetrovsk

XVII Inf Corps

6th Pz Army

XXIX Inf Corps

44th Army

Zaporoie

Taganrog

DONETS BASIN

Nikopol

- - - · - · - FRONT LINE BEFORE OPERATION CITADEL

———— ARMY OPERATIONAL ZONES

——▶ GERMAN ATTACKS

◀- - - SOVIET COUNTERATTACKS AGAINST THE OREL SALIENT

Dniepr R.

Melitopol

SOUTH FRONT

Cherson

Sea of Azov

Odessa

Black Sea

ARMY Grp A (17th Army)

Krim

Kouban

XIV

CLASH OF TITANS:
THE BATTLE OF KURSK

Spring and summer 1943 were devoted to preparing for and implementing Operation Citadel (*Zitadelle*), the Wehrmacht's final attempt to
maintain the strategic initiative in the East and impose its will over the
Red Army. When it ended in glaring failure, the strategic initiative
moved definitively to the Soviet camp for the remainder of the war. In
this sense, even if it did not represent a decisive turning point of the war,
from which the Wehrmacht could no longer hope to achieve victory, it
nevertheless represented a major step towards the military defeat of the
Reich in the East. With Field Marshal Manstein having played a key
role in preparing and conducting the operation, it would be appropriate
to present here the strategic principles that guided him, as well as the
reasons for his final failure. It is also a question of evaluating Manstein's
share of the responsibility for the failure which had irreversible consequences for the Reich so that we may shed light on a stage of his military career which remains controversial to this day.

Manstein and Hitler: Two different strategic theories
for conducting the war?

Ever since he had been appointed commander of Army Group Don,
Field Marshal Manstein had many opportunities to assess Hitler's practice of military leadership. Indeed, his new posting had placed him, for
the first time, under the direct orders of the Führer, in his capacity as
commander in chief of the OKW and the OKH. He respected, most certainly, his ability to judge operational possibilities, as well as his knowl-

edge and surprising memory for technical matters and problems relative to armament. He also acknowledged Hitler's awareness of the casualties and hardships suffered by the frontline troops. But he denounced the Führer's propensity to stubbornly believe in the superiority of his judgment and intuition, and his view of personal willpower as a decisive element in modern warfare. In addition to his amateurish character, he condemned Hitler's more and more frequent interventions in the actions of his subordinates and his refusal to reorganize the military high command in the interest of a more rational and effective supervision of the war.

It is undeniable that the Führer possessed certain qualities essential for a military leader: a strong will, control of his nerves in moments of crisis, an indisputable intelligence, and, in addition to a certain talent in the area of operations, the faculty to recognize possibilities created through technology. However, he lacked the skills acquired by every professional staff officer. Regarding this, Manstein wrote in his *Memoirs*: "But all in all, what he lacked, were *the military skills based on experience* that his 'intuition' could in no way replace. If he possessed [...] a certain 'flair' for operational possibilities and opportunities or if he quickly noticed them when someone showed them to him, he did not know how to evaluate the conditions and possibilities of execution. He did not understand the relationships that could exist between the set objective, the scope of the operation, and the necessities of time and forces to deploy. Nor did he understand all the contingencies that derived from the issues of resupply."[470]

And so, he appeared not to take into account the fact that every offensive with a massive objective must be constantly supplied with new forces which are added to those necessary for the initial assault, the breach, and the pursuit. His conduct of the summer 1942 offensive vividly illustrated this, just as the unrealistic idea that he expressed to Manstein on several occasions that autumn to push, the following year, after the conquest of the Caucasus, into the Middle East and all the way into India.

What he most lacked was military experience in the area of organization, deployment, and supplying the armies. Not only was he incapable of determining what could be accomplished according to human resources and available supplies, but he did not understand that the strategic goal of every war must be the destruction of the enemy's armed forces, and that this necessitates the highest concentration of forces at the decisive point, and not their dispersal in pursuit of several simultaneous objectives. The separation of operations during the 1942 campaign into two simultaneous offensives along two different axes, and the refusal to withdraw troops from secondary fronts in favor of the one where success had to be achieved, was the most obvious demonstration of this. In addition, he did not understand that victory alone permitted set political and economic objectives to be achieved. The annihilation of the enemy's military forces allowed for the occupation and retention of a territory, whereas the opposite is not necessarily true.

Such deficiencies became even more obvious once the Führer started to continually intervene in the various levels of military command. Manstein had not yet experienced this when Field Marshal Gunther von Kluge gave him a foretaste during a discussion at the Orsha train station, on the Vitebsk-Rostov route on November 21, 1942. The commander in chief of Army Group Center presented him with a dismal description of the situation since the Soviet counteroffensive on the Stalingrad front and told him: "You will find it impossible to move any formation larger than a battalion without first referring back to the Führer."[471] Though this prophecy did not turn out to be strictly true in Manstein's case, a great number of arguments with Hitler had indeed been in store.

Ever since the failure of Operation Barbarossa at the end of autumn 1941, Hitler no longer trusted his generals, who had pressured him in the summer of 1940 to undertake the conquest of the U.S.S.R., while assuring him that the latter would be easily defeated in less than three months. From that time forward, not only did he grant himself credit for the military victories of the first years, but equally so for having overcome a triple handicap in the winter of 1941–42: the force of the Red Army's counteroffensive, the confusion of his own high command, and the ghost of Napoleon's Grand Army of 1812. Convinced more than ever of his genius, Hitler listened to almost no one. However, if he had been superior to the foreign political leaders when he led diplomatic efforts, for which demands were drawn from their ideas, he was clearly inferior to his generals, to the professionals, and to the products of the general staff as soon as he attempted to combine all the powers of a Frederick the Great or a Napoleon by leading his armies at the same time as conducting the war.[472]

MANSTEIN: HITLER'S MASTER STRATEGIST

MANSTEIN: HITLER'S MASTER STRATEGIST

358 MANSTEIN: HITLER'S MASTER STRATEGIST

While Stalin had learned lessons from 1941 to leave military questions more and more often to the specialists, Hitler's old habit of getting
involved in tactical details as well as in grand strategy, due to his
increasingly chronic mistrust of his generals, had profoundly harmful
effects. By delving into ever-smaller details, Hitler accumulated responsibilities that greatly exceeded his abilities. Furthermore, no other head
of state in the war was to be involved to such an extent in the details of
military matters. This included Stalin who, after tremendous initial
defeats, restrained himself from intervening directly in the tactics of the
Red Army.

After the war, Manstein's view of Hitler's military leadership was
severe, but enlightening: "In the military domain [...] Hitler lacked a
sense of the real. His mind, extremely active, grabbed hold of every
objective that seemed appealing to him, and what resulted was a scattering of German forces simultaneously engaged in several directions or
in various theaters of operations. He never truly accepted the rule that
one could not be too strong at a decisive point, that it is necessary to
know how to abandon secondary fronts or accept the risk of temporarily weakening them in order to achieve major results [elsewhere]. [...]
Concerning his objectives—at the very least in the fight against the
Soviet Union—they were above all determined by political and economic considerations. [...] Indeed, such considerations, especially the
economic, had to play a role in our operations. But what he did not see
was that in order to achieve, and above all to maintain, the territorial
objective, it was necessary to defeat decisively the enemy military forces.
While this result was not obtained—as the war against Russia demonstrated—it was becoming problematic to conquer regions of great economic significance, and as a result, to achieve the territorial objectives,
and impossible to maintain them in the long run."

He then came to the following conclusion, in complete Clausewitz
style: "If strategy has to be the handmaiden to political leadership, the
latter must not forget, to the extent that Hitler did, the strategic goal of
the entire war: crush the enemy's military resistance. Only victory will
open the path for political and economic goals." Lastly he said of Hitler:
"He wanted to be a Napoleon, who had only tolerated men under him
who would obediently carry out his will. Unfortunately he had neither
Napoleon's military training nor his military genius."[473]

A faithful heir to Clausewitz's thoughts concerning military strategy, Manstein—as well as a large majority of German generals—beleived that the main objective of a battle was the destruction or annihilation of enemy forces. In military jargon, these two words did not necessarily imply the slaughter of opposing soldiers, but eliminating the combat effectiveness of enemy armies. Likewise, he considered that only the destruction or the annihilation of the enemy's armed forces would permit the occupation of a territory, while the opposite would not: the occupation of a region would guarantee neither the elimination of the armies nor the capitulation of the enemy state. He thus advocated a war of maneuver, insofar as this would allow the Germans to gain the upper hand on the basis of their own initiative and to wage battle in conditions that would provide them with decisive results.

Despite the references to Clausewitz's great strategic principles, Manstein—and it was likewise for his colleagues in the Wehrmacht officers' corps—was hardly influenced by his political theories of warfare, with the exception of the premise that stipulated the primacy of politics over the military in conducting a war. Indeed, the German generals were immersed more in the writings of Schlieffen. After the war, Colonel General Kleist provided an explanation: "For my generation, Clausewitz's teachings were out of fashion, even when I was at the war school and the general staff. One was still referring to them, but one no longer gave them too much attention. His writings, one thought, originated more in military philosophy than in practical instruction. One was much more interested in Schlieffen's books, which seemed more useful since they analyzed the following problem: how could an army of a strength inferior to that of its allied adversaries—which was the case for Germany—conquer its adversaries on two fronts? Nevertheless, Clausewitz's thoughts were still valid, especially his doctrine: war is a continuation of politics through other means. One inferred through this that political factors are more important than military factors. Germany's mistake was to believe that military success could solve its political problems. So much so that, under the Nazis, we had almost overturned Clausewitz's maxim and came to consider peace as a continuation of the war. Clausewitz also professed a correct assumption by predicting the difficulty of conquering Russia."[474]

In spite of generally accepted opinion, the German generals had become, even before 1914, disciples of Schlieffen much more than of Clausewitz or Moltke. And everything leads one to believe that

Manstein was hardly an exception to this rule. As Kleist said, the German generals were speculating on the methods of how to decisively defeat a coalition that had superior resources available to it, thanks to a masterful operational plan.

Furthermore, at the end of winter 1942–43, he believed, albeit naively, that there was still a chance to continue the war in the East with the intention of arriving at a peace agreement. Aware of the fact that the ratio of forces no longer allowed the *Ostheer* to launch large-scale offensives as during the preceding years, he logically recommended resorting to a strategic defensive. He was unable to accept that Germany forego the possibilities offered through mobile warfare for two reasons.

First, no one could say during the spring of 1943 whether the Red Army would resume the offensive at the end of the *rasputitsa*. It could easily remain in waiting, while reinforcing itself until the Western powers had managed to open a second front on the continent. Such a strategy would clearly give them the opportunity to engage in small, local attacks to prevent the withdrawal of German forces from the Eastern Front. If such a scenario were to occur, the Wehrmacht would then have to fight against fully equipped adversaries on two fronts. For this reason, the OKH was unable to resort to a static defensive, appreciably taking the form of a war of fixed positions.

Second, the number of German divisions available in the East simply did not permit the adoption of a static defensive. The front, from the Gulf of Finland to the Sea of Azov, was much too long for the *Ostheer* to be able to put up a contiguous defensive front. This was all the more true in Army Group South's theater of operations, where 32 divisions had to defend a front of 750 kilometers, from Taganrog on the Azov Sea to the southeast of Sumy. Given the ratio of forces largely in favor of the Russians, the latter would still have had the opportunity to achieve crushing concentrations in various areas of the front to later break through it. From this, either the encirclement of the sectors where the German troops were positioned or a retreat would result.

Manstein thus advised adopting not a static defensive, but a strategic defensive, by making use of the superiorities the Germans still disposed over the enemy: a better and more flexible command, the combat merit of the troops, and their greater skill at mobility. He thus explained his point of view: "[…] it was necessary to deal *partial, but vigorous, blows*, not only to inflict bloody losses on the enemy, but also to take many prisoners with the general goal of persuading them to accept a peace agreement. We had to continue, within the scope of this defensive strategy, to execute mobile operations where we were superior, either by taking advantage of the possibilities that the adversary's attacks provided us, or by taking the initiative."[475] It was with this concept in mind that he played a vital planning role with the OKH and Hitler himself from the beginning of February 1943.

The elastic defense proposed by Manstein called for a mobile war that, beginning in 1943, was obviously only possible by voluntarily abandoning, though temporarily, a number of conquered regions. But the Führer held firm on a rigid defense of every inch of ground, a concept inherited from the Great War. After the German troops succeeded at containing the enemy during the winter of 1941–42, Hitler was persuaded that only his intervention to forbid the abandonment of the slightest square foot had prevented the Wehrmacht from suffering the fate of Napoleon's Grand Army in 1812. When he was faced with a new crisis at the end of autumn 1942 in Stalingrad and in the Caucasus, he still believed capable of remediating the situation by ordering resistance at all costs. In spite of the Stalingrad disaster, he almost never strayed from the idea, even if it went against the principle of mobility to which the German Army owed its victories from 1939 to 1942.

According to Clausewitzian theory, defense represents the most powerful form of combat. But this is true only if it is organized effectively enough so that the enemy wears himself out against the defensive front. For this, one must absolutely not find oneself in a situation of overwhelmingly inferior numbers. In Russia this was a constant danger, as the number of available German divisions was not adequate to organize a continuous defense. Having an enormous numerical superiority available, the enemy had the opportunity, by massing its forces at specific points, to implement breaches across a very long and poorly defended front, with some of the German units being encircled.

Later, Hans-Georg Krebs, a captain on Manstein's staff, described the long and bitter discussions between his chief and Hitler concerning the conduct of the war: "Manstein was naturally presenting the idea that it was necessary to relinquish strict hold on territory, for if one wanted to spare the troops and achieve success, one had to conduct mobile operations. During this, Hitler would frequently interrupt him and state: 'Do not speak of this anymore!' This was often successful, as

Manstein become silent. When he realized that he was not going to make any significant gains, he quite simply stopped talking. It was not in Manstein's interest to say nothing whenever he held someone as irresponsible. For him, Hitler was the ignorant corporal of the First World War who thought he knew it all." After an analysis of the situation during which Hitler had once again imposed his will, Krebs heard Manstein exclaim: "My God, is he a fool?"[476] Despite this, Manstein was never dismissed from his position, being considered essential to the Wehrmacht.

The great worth of the German officers' corps and troops was undeniable. However, they could only achieve decisive results with mobile operations, through which the *Ostheer* could perhaps inflict massive defeats on the enemy. As a result, the strategic defensive proposed by Manstein proved to be much more appropriate than the static defensive propounded by Hitler.

A counterattack or a direct attack?

The exchange of ideas within the German high command as to which strategy to adopt on the Eastern Front at the end of the *rasputitsa* lasted until the end of March 1943. Overall, they were leaning towards two alternatives. Should the Wehrmacht try and keep the initiative and launch a preventive attack before the adversary had the chance to fully recover from the consequences of the winter campaign? Or, should it leave the initiative to the Red Army, await its attack, and then, after having restored the situation and created favorable conditions, launch its own counteroffensive? The response quite obviously depended on the enemy's intentions, the second of the two solutions only being possible if the Soviets reassumed the offensive immediately after the muddy season.

Without excluding the possibility that the Soviets could passively await the opening of a second front by the Western Allies, Manstein and his staff were nevertheless of the opinion that they would retake the offensive. The great victory in Stalingrad, they thought, had given their high command new confidence. From a psychological point of view, Stalin was hardly able to pause during the "great patriotic war" destined to liberate the Russian territory. And he also had an incentive to reach eastern Europe before the Allies, especially the Balkans, a region relentlessly sought by Russia since the time of the Czars. This conviction and the arguments used to support it were shared by the OKH.

From that moment on, the enemy's numerical superiority provided it with many possibilities. It could try to breach the southern wing of Army Group North in order to drive it to the Baltic coast and encircle it. It could also attempt to reduce the salient created around Orel on Army Group Center's front, by attacking it with a pincer maneuver. However, it was in the sector of Army Group South where it had its best opportunities, as much from an operational point of view as from a political and economic perspective. The German front in this area took on the form of a "balcony" extending well to the east. By attacking to the east, on the Mius, and to the north, on the Donetz, it could hope to drive back to the coast of the Sea of Azov or Black Sea the armies positioned there and to destroy them. By completing such an operation through an offensive in the Kharkov region, in the direction of the Dnieper downstream from Kiev, it could still achieve the objective that it had missed during the preceding winter, i.e. the encirclement of the southern wing of the German front, including not only Army Group South, but also Army Group A, positioned on the Kuban bridgehead with its Seventeenth Army. A victory in this sector would permit it to recuperate the metallurgic basin of the Donetz, as well as the "wheat basket" of the Ukraine, and would open up for it the route to the Balkans and the Romanian oilfields. Finally, such a victory would have a strong influence on the political attitude of the Turkish government.

All things considered, the distribution of their forces did not leave the slightest doubt of the fact that, if the Russians retook the offensive, their center of gravity would be located on the southern wing of the Eastern Front, with the quite obvious intention of seeking a victory over Army Group South. Consequently, Manstein was expecting an enemy attack against the Donetz "balcony," on the Mius, and on the midpoint of the Donetz, to hold back the German units positioned there, and to push them towards the coast. Such an attack would be completed through a large-scale offensive commencing from the Kharkov region in the direction of the Dnieper. This was exactly what the Red Army high command did in the latter half of the summer of 1943.[477]

Thereupon, Manstein explained to Hitler that the German Army could in no way hope to contain the enemy through a purely defensive strategy. Its forces were inadequate to defend such an expansive front, especially facing an adversary that was superior in number. Their only chance, he declared, was to use the skill and flexibility of his command, as well as the greater combat quality and mobility of his troops, in an elastic defensive strategy. In the framework of such a strategy, Manstein proposed two solutions for conducting operations in 1943, after the end of the muddy season.

The first consisted in keeping the initiative by launching an offensive destined at pre-empting a Soviet attack. Of course, this would be a "direct attack," but nevertheless falling within the concept of a strategic defensive. In this case, it had to be unleashed as soon as possible, in other words, immediately at the end of the *rasputitsa*, before the Red Army had the chance to reconstruct its forces, notably its armored and motorized units. With the reforming of German forces in all likelihood being completed earlier, an extremely favorable opportunity was presented to the Wehrmacht. And the Soviet-held salient around Kursk seemed to be the obvious target where a major defeat could be inflicted on the enemy.

If the two victories earned by Manstein at the end of winter had permitted the restoration of the front all the way to Bielgorod along the Mius and the Donetz, there remained a Soviet salient to the north of Bielgorod, between Army Groups Center and South. Forming an arc around Kursk, it extended from Sumy and Rylsk, to the south of Orel, stretching along the front approximately 500 kilometers and containing a considerable number of forces. In addition to cutting off the railroads going from the sector of Kluge's armies in Kharkov, it represented a departure point for an attack against the southern flank of Army Group Center and against the northern flank of Army Group South. In March, Manstein had the idea of attacking the Kursk salient after the recapture of Kharkov. But the sudden thaw and the inability of Army Group Center to collaborate, which was essential, had prevented him from achieving this.

Such a salient quite naturally represented an inviting target for a direct attack, with the hope of improving the German defensive positions and the liaison between Manstein's and Kluge's army groups, in addition to encircling relatively significant forces and freeing a substantial number of German units. In order to maintain itself in this sector of major operational importance, the enemy would most certainly place into battle the operational reserves at its disposal at the seam between

Army Groups Center and South. After having destroyed these armored reserves, the *Ostheer* would once again be in a position to attack on the Donetz front.

The other solution—the best in Manstein's view—consisted of leaving the initiative to the Russians by allowing them to attack first, before counterattacking their risk-taking armies in order to inflict upon them a decisive defeat. By February, he had already presented to Hitler on several occasions this idea of a "backhand," as opposed to "forehand," attack. Faced with the likely prospect of a Soviet offensive against the southern wing of the German front, it was a matter of Army Group South retreating while fighting in order to lead the assailing armies to the area of Melitopol-Dniepropetrovsk, all while gathering powerful forces behind its northern wing. By letting the enemy advance all the way to the lower Dnieper, the panzer units concentrated in the Kharkov region could then launch a powerful counterattack against the right flank of the Soviet offensive, then, pushing to the southeast or south, driving them back against the coast in order to destroy them. It was, in a way, repeating the type of maneuver executed by Manstein during the counterattacks of February–March 1943.

The principle of this operation differed radically from that of the German offensive in the summer of 1942, for it was about attacking from the rear an enemy that would have largely expended its assault forces. Contrary to the Blue Plan, the objective was not so much the conquest of territory as the destruction of Soviet forces. To prevent them from slipping away to the east, as in 1942, the Germans would offer the enemy a lure they would not know how to resist: opening the way towards the lower Dnieper. If the operation were to prove a success, Army Group South could perhaps then strike a second blow, this time farther north, in the central sector of the front.

Such a maneuver could have been attempted in other sectors, but it could not have achieved a victory as significant as on the southern wing of the front, where the adversary was obviously seeking an outcome, and where the sea would facilitate an encirclement. It was no less a highly daring operation requiring the fulfillment of two conditions.

First, to ensure the success of the operation in mind, it was necessary to significantly reinforce the northern wing of Manstein's army group, which was charged with the principal maneuver. For this, it was absolutely essential to withdraw troops from secondary theaters, even if it meant creating difficulties there, and to remove units from Army Groups Center and North, or at a minimum, form operational reserves while carrying out new modifications on the Eastern Front, particularly by evacuating the difficult-to-defend Orel salient. Second, it was necessary to temporarily abandon the Donetz basin in order to ensure the necessary freedom of action while executing a methodical retreat. The counterattack, if successful, would then allow its recapture.

But as was to be expected, Hitler was not willing to agree to any of these steps. Despite the insistence with which Manstein presented the necessity to concentrate the principal war effort in the East, specifically on the southern wing, he was flatly unable to persuade him to move the center of gravity of the German forces to the south, to yield the Orel salient, and even less so the Donetz basin, a region to which Hitler attributed a capital importance for the German war economy. This was not only due to his reluctance to give up territory, albeit temporarily, but also to his inability to anticipate the enemy's probable action. Hitler's refusal to pursue the idea of a backhand attack had the result of completely denying Manstein the freedom of action that would have been crucial for him to carry out a serious blow against the enemy, by denying him adequate forces on the northern wing of his army group.[478]

Hitler was, however, not alone in demonstrating little enthusiasm with respect to Manstein's preferred solution, which, in a way, consisted of "taking one step backwards, two steps forward." Colonel General Zeitzler was also opposed to it. The idea of definitively beating the Soviet southern wing through a willing retreat instead of a purely offensive action was no more appealing to Zeitzler than to Hitler. They both preferred to take advantage of the temporary weakness of the enemy following its latest defeats in order to strike it a harsh blow before it could regroup its forces. This way, they would not have to evacuate the Orel salient or the Donetz basin.

The preferred strategy of Hitler and the chief of staff of the OKH was an operation entailing the envelopment and destruction of the largest possible number of Soviet divisions in the Kursk salient. Five Soviet armies were located in the salient, which was 200 kilometers wide and 120 kilometers deep. If victorious, the operation would seriously weaken the enemy's potential offensive capability. In addition to the destruction of approximately 60 Soviet divisions, it would allow the release of German forces to other fronts or theaters of operations.[479]

Disagreements among the generals on the Citadel timetable

On April 15, Hitler confirmed the order, issued on March 13 by the OKH, which would become Operation Citadel, which called for a combined pincer attack by Manstein's army group from the south and Kluge's army group from the north, in order to envelop the Soviet troops in the Kursk salient. The operational details of the plan were crafted by Zeitzler.

In Army Group Center, Colonel General Walter Model's Ninth Army was responsible for executing the attack. With the intention of creating a breach in the direction of Kursk, it had three armored corps at its disposal, comprising a total of six armored divisions, two motorized divisions, and seven infantry divisions. These three corps would attack on a front of 50 kilometers, and OKH was hoping to expand this front by engaging, if possible, two infantry corps on either side, so that each could protect the flanks.

For Army Group South, the operation involved five corps, including eleven armored divisions and seven infantry divisions, for it was expected that the enemy would immediately engage its operational reserves, whose destruction was considered as important as the reduction of the Kursk salient itself. The Fourth Panzer Army, under Colonel General Hoth's command, had the mission of implementing a breakthrough to join hands with the Ninth Army, then to destroy the encircled forces to the west of Kursk. For this, it had two armored corps at its disposal, for a total of six armored divisions and one infantry division, whereas another infantry corps of three divisions would participate in the assault on its western flank. Army Detachment Kempf, with one armored corps and one infantry corps of three divisions each, was to cover the breakthrough operation in the direction of Kursk, facing to the east and northeast. Another armored corps, consisting of two divisions, initially held in reserve, would be placed at its disposal as soon as it gained enough space and freedom of mobility. Moreover, with one infantry corps, it had to ensure the defense of the Donetz front, from the southeast of Kharkov all the way up to Voltchansk.

Finally, the Second Army which, with nine weakened infantry divisions, occupied 200 kilometers of the salient to the west of Kursk, had to try and hold back the forces that were confronting it in order to ensure their encirclement. Regarding air support for the attack, it was to be assigned to the Fourth and Sixth Luftflotten. Operating *en masse*, the latter two were charged with clearing the route for the tanks.[480]

The attack carried a significant risk for the two army groups. In Kluge's sector, it was to jump off from the southern flank of the Orel salient, which would give the enemy the possibility of counterattacking into the salient to cut Ninth Army off from behind. In Manstein's sector, there existed an analogous danger, since the Donetz basin had to be retained at all costs, and the enemy was able to assault it from two sides with superior forces. In order to fend off this threat, it was imperative, from the side of the Germans, to complete preparations for their offensive as quickly as possible, for the more time they were to grant to the Russians to reconstruct their units, the more their risks would increase.

For this reason it was expected that Operation Citadel would commence as soon as possible. Manstein and Kluge were urging the OKH to carry it out at the beginning of May, if the muddy season ended by then. In fact, its beginning had been set for mid-May. But significant delays would spoil its chances of success, resulting from disagreements on the timetable of the offensive among the primary generals concerned. On May 4 Hitler gathered them in Munich to discuss the upcoming operation.

Field Marshals Manstein and Kluge, and Colonel General Jeschonneck, chief of staff of the Luftwaffe, supported advancing as quickly as possible, in the middle, or at the very latest, two thirds into May. According to them, this was the only opportunity to inflict heavy losses on the enemy. Otherwise, they argued, it would be better to cancel the operation. They greatly dreaded losing the advantage of surprise and allowing the Russians to reinforce their positions around Kursk if it were to be postponed. As well, they asserted, any delay would considerably increase the risks of Soviet attacks on other sectors of the front, such as the Orel or Kharkov salients, the midpoint of the Donetz, or the Mius. This danger was all the more obvious since the Soviets had placed armored reserves near all of these sensitive positions. If the adversary could not yet move to the offensive, they argued, this would not necessarily be the case in June. In a more general context, Manstein personally added, a delay in the start of the operation risked having it coincide with an attack by the Western Allies on the continent, as Germany was about to lose Tunisia, thus freeing up considerable enemy forces.

On the other hand, the severe defeat at Stalingrad and the weakness of the German southern wing dissuaded other generals from rushing as quickly into a large-scale offensive. Colonel General Model, recognized as a particularly tough and able commander, recommended a postponement until reinforcements were made available. Underscoring the difficulties his attack would face because of the powerful organization of the Russian lines and, in particular, the strengthening of their anti-tank defense, he judged it essential to reinforce his armored units in order to achieve a breakthrough. As a result, he was of Colonel General Zeitzler's conviction, also very much Hitler's, that the new Tiger tanks (56 tons, with an 88mm barrel) and Panther tanks (43 tons, with a 75mm barrel), which had just come out of production, would permit the Wehrmacht to accomplish the rapid breach necessary to carry out a successful encirclement. Hitler equally had great hopes in these two new tanks and gave his support to Model. He then envisioned almost doubling the number of tanks for the operation, which could be launched by June 10 in his estimation.

Manstein equivocated. The additional tanks that were envisioned, he declared, would in all likelihood be offset by an influx of tanks from the Soviet side. Kluge, for his part, allowed himself to be convinced by the idea of reinforcing the armored units. Colonel General Guderian, recently appointed inspector general of the armored forces, supported by Albert Speer, at the head of the armament industry, expressed strong reservations about the premature use of new tanks, all while opposing Zeitzler's operations plan. He observed that it was impossible to solve the initial technical problems of the Panther before the offensive, and that it was necessary to use sparingly the reserves in view of the priority of driving back the invasion that would not fail to occur the following year in the West. Consequently, he asserted that an offensive in the East was unnecessary in 1943.[481]

Guderian's objections made such a strong impression on Hitler who, without dismissing the principle of the operation, refused to commit to it with a precise date. In fact, the Führer's hesitations continued for several weeks. He thus let pass the second and third weeks of May, a period considered as the most favorable by Manstein and Kluge. But the month of June also drifted by without him being able to make the decision to commence the operation. There was no lack of reasons for the postponement. Hitler remained above all preoccupied by the situation in the Mediterranean theater since the loss of Tunisia on May 13, and feared an Allied landing in Italy or the Balkans. He also remained determined to reinforce his panzer divisions by the addition of a substantial number of Tiger and Panther tanks.

During this time, Manstein proposed an alternative to the operation against the Kursk salient, by appealing to an idea that bore little resemblance to traditional theories of military strategy. He suggested reducing the salient not through a concentric attack, i.e. through a pincer maneuver from the north and the south, but rather through an attack precisely where the adversary was expecting it the least, directly from the west. Thus, rather than attacking the northern and southern sides of the salient where one would expect to meet a wall of prepared defenses, he advised an elliptical attack against the western side which, after having smashed open the salient, would split into two wings, one branching off to the northeast, the other to the southeast, reaching the enemy's rear and then encircling his forces which would have remained in position to the west of the pocket. It was thus a matter of an elliptical pincer maneuver and not a classic concentric envelopment maneuver. Such a daring operational concept aroused Hitler's interest, but not Zeitzler's, who clearly preferred to stick with his original plan. At any rate, a complete redeployment of units, in view of Manstein's new operations plan, would have demanded too much time.[482]

On July 1, at his headquarters in Rastenburg, East Prussia, Hitler gathered Manstein, Kluge, and all the commanders of the large units required to participate in Operation Citadel, to announce to them his decision to commence the operation on July 5. Despite the delay, which made the attack more difficult and considerably increased the danger to the Orel salient and the southern flank, especially in the sector formed by the Donetz "balcony," Manstein—and likewise Zeitzler, Kluge, and Model—nevertheless remained convinced the operation would succeed. Manstein was persuaded that Germany could not indefinitely wait for a Russian offensive, which would perhaps only occur in winter or after the opening of the second front.

After the war, he justified his stance: "One can be inclined to believe that, after the fact, we should have point-blank declared the operation impossible, for it was planned to take advantage of the enemy's temporary weakness, a weakness that had disappeared after all of these delays. I did not do it (which could have been a mistake) for the following reasons. First, to abandon Citadel would have led to new circumstances with all of the dangers they would bring, in view of the eventual opening of a second front. One could think that the Russians would indeed wait for this in order to move to the offensive. Second, we were convinced of the success, in any case within the high command of Army Group South, despite the difficulties, even though we were worried about the consequences of a Soviet attack in the Donetz region. A victory at Kursk would have allowed us to fend off a crisis in this region, and perhaps even to achieve an even greater victory."

He was hoping, apparently, and with a certain naivety, that the destruction of the best armies and a significant portion of the enemy's operational reserves in the Kursk salient would open the path to a compromise solution on the Eastern Front, all the more since it would also allow him to quickly gain control over any crises that might arise on the Donetz front. In addition, he still believed in the possibility, in case it was necessary, of a withdrawal from the lower Donetz in order to recommence, after a victory at Kursk, his former idea of a backhand attack. "Such a possibility, of course, would not have won Hitler's praise," he thought, "but a success would have returned the Donetz basin to him."[483]

The largest tank battle of the Second World War

As was to be expected, the Red Army took advantage of the months of May and June in order to amass a large part of its elite armored and mechanized forces in the Kursk salient. They established three primary lines of defense, positioning them in parallel more than 40 kilometers deep, while constructing minefields and anti-tank ditches, and fortifying the villages.

The Soviets also concentrated new types of weapons, like the T-34/85 tank (35 tons, with an 85mm barrel) and the SU-76 assault gun (29 tons, with a 76mm barrel). They were thus ready and waiting when the Germans decided to attack. Indeed, from April 12, three days before Hitler's confirmation of Operation Citadel, the Soviet high command came to the conclusion that the Germans would most likely attack the Kursk salient with a concentric pincer maneuver from the Orel sector in the north, and from Bielgorod in the south. Moreover, shortly after the Führer's military conference on July 1, it was warned by its intelligence service of the approximate date of the offensive: between July 4 and 6.

At dawn on July 5, Soviet batteries opened fire on concentrations of German troops, forestalling the German artillery preparation and delaying for a few hours the offensive. This formidable barrage of Soviet artillery, together with pre-emptive air attacks, gave the Germans a clear sign that the Red Army had been informed of the timeline of Operation Citadel. At least 3,000 tanks and assault guns and 2,900 aircraft had been mobilized to defend Kursk. Facing them were 2,700 *Ostheer* panzers and assault guns and 1,800 Luftwaffe aircraft. Approximately 50 percent of all of the Red Army's armored forces and 64 percent of the Wehrmacht's were deployed in the Kursk sector. Clearly, it was the most extensive concentration of forces ever seen on the Eastern Front in such a limited space. The largest and most intense clash of armor in the Second World War would thus rage for more than a week.[484]

Model's Ninth Army, with its 1,200 panzers and assault guns, did not succeed, despite enormous sacrifices, at thrusting through the Soviet defense system. On the very next day, it was to come under more and more violent counterattacks against its front and flanks. After heavy losses, it was nevertheless able to continue in the direction of Kursk, but only one painstaking mile at a time. It succeeded in forcing the first line of enemy resistance and to even cut into the second. On July 9, it was definitively stopped, before the surrounding fortified hills of Olkhovatka, and then gradually pushed back by the enemy who had thrown its operational reserves into the mix.

By this time Ninth Army had already exhausted its offensive capacity. Its penetration had not reached beyond a depth of approximately ten kilometers. Model nevertheless envisioned resuming the offensive around July 12, in order to complete the breach after having pushed back the counterattacks and shifting the center of gravity of his effort by committing his own operational reserves. But he was not able to realize this intention. On July 12, from the east and northeast, the Russians attacked the Second Army which was holding the Orel salient, located to the rear of Ninth Army. The development of the situation forced Kluge to halt his army's push in order to remove forces to have them intervene in the sector of the Second Panzer Army.

To the south, the results gained by Manstein's armies were more encouraging, without, however, being decisive. The Fourth Panzer Army and Army Detachment Kempf, with a total of 1,500 tanks and assault guns, succeeded in advancing approximately 30 and 10 kilometers respectively. After enormous efforts, Hoth's panzers burst through the first and second enemy lines, fighting tough battles during the first two days. On July 7, they even succeeded at bursting through the third Soviet line of resistance and advancing into free territory, in the direction of Obojan, after having inflicted severe losses on the enemy. But they immediately had to push back powerful counterattacks launched from the northeast, north, and the west, which significantly slowed down their pace.

On July 12, they were once again counterattacked, near Prokhorovka, by the Fifth Guards Tank Army, which had been held in reserve up until this point. The tank battle that followed was the largest of the entire war. Some 450 tanks of the 1st, 2nd, and 3rd SS Panzer Divisions (the *Leibstandardte*, *Das Reich*, and *Totenkopf*) and nearly 1,000 Soviet tanks confronted each other in a ruthless battle that raged the entire day. By that night, more than 300 German tanks, among which were 70 of the 100 Tigers, had been disabled. More than half of the Soviet tanks had suffered the same fate. Since the Germans held the field they were able to retrieve and repair some of their damaged panzers while the Soviets had to write off their losses. Nevertheless, significantly weakened, Hoth's offensive was temporarily halted. Manstein was no less resolved to continue the still uncertain battle, convinced of having beaten the essential Russian reserves on his front. He had at his disposal the 24th Panzer Corps (two armored divisions) in reserve and, risking his all, he wanted to commit it to renew the battle.[485]

But on July 13, Hitler called Manstein and Kluge to his headquarters, where he declared to them that the situation had become very serious in Sicily, where the Anglo-Americans had landed on July 10. The island would most likely be lost and the Western Allies would then be able to utilize it as a springboard for landings in southern Italy or in the Balkans. It was thus urgent to create new armies in these regions. For this, it was absolutely necessary to remove forces from the Eastern Front, and thus bring to an end Operation Citadel. This was exactly what Manstein had anticipated in Munich on May 4, if the *Ostheer* were to delay its offensive.

Kluge asserted that the Ninth Army was incapable of retaking the offensive, having already lost more than 20,000 men. In addition, he was forced to withdraw his rapid units in order to fill in the deeply exposed breaches on the front of Second Army in the Orel salient. For these reasons alone, Model's army had to interrupt its attack in the direction of Kursk and was not in a position of recommencing it.

For his part, Manstein supported a continuation of Operation Citadel. The battle, he argued to Hitler, had reached its decisive climax. Thinking that he had destroyed almost all of the Soviet reserves, taken 24,000 prisoners, destroyed or captured 1,800 tanks, 267 pieces of artillery, and 1,080 anti-tank guns, he estimated that victory was within his reach. In his opinion, Ninth Army could, at the very least, hold back the enemy forces that were confronting it and eventually resume its attack, while the Fourth Panzer Army would try to decisively defeat the remaining Soviet units in its path. Immediately after, it would cut across to the north, cross the Psel to the east of Obojan, then turn back to the west in order to force the enemy units that remained in the Kursk salient to go into battle on inverted fronts. But for this, he added, it was necessary to attach as quickly as possible the 24th Panzer Corps to Army Detachment Kempf in order to allow it to cover this operation to the north and east. If the Ninth Army was no longer in a position to intervene, even after the situation had been restored in the Orel salient, it was nevertheless necessary to try to eliminate the enemy forces against which Hoth's and Kempf's troops were engaged. Otherwise, he asserted, the Germans could expect crises in the Donetz basin and also in the Kursk sector.

Kluge, ruling out the possibility of a renewed offensive by Model's army, even requested that the latter be allowed to retreat back to its start-line. The Führer then ordered the conclusion of Operation Citadel in order to make available forces for the Mediterranean theater. He refused Manstein the free disposal of the 24th Panzer Corps due to the threat that was looming on the Donetz front, but authorized the continued efforts of his armies to defeat the Soviet reserves they had encountered so as to allow for the possibility of withdrawing units from the operation.[486]

The recommencement of the offensive in the southern sector of the Kursk salient was, however, not to be realized. On July 17, two new developments brought the operation to a definitive end. The Soviets launched major attacks on the Mius line and the middle Donetz, compelling the OKH to transfer the 24th Panzer Corps to the south to help restore the situation. At the same time, it ordered Hoth to place his army's SS Panzer Corps at OKH's disposal for transfer to Italy. (As it turned out, the *Totenkopf* Division remained in the East.) Faced with this deterioration of his resources, Manstein was forced to abandon his offensive near Kursk, to disengage his forces, evacuate the painstakingly conquered territory, and to withdraw his armies back to their start lines.

The result of the battle of Kursk was an undeniable success for the Red Army. In a week-and-a-half of ferocious combat, the Germans suffered more than 40,000 casualties. Among the ranks of the two armies commanded by Manstein, the losses rose to 20,720 men, among whom 3,330 were dead. On the Soviet Side, the number of prisoners rose to 34,000 and deaths to 17,000, so that, assuming twice as many wounded as dead, the enemy lost approximately 85,000 men.[487] Most important, for the first time in the war, the Red Army had been able to withstand a full-strength, good-weather offensive by the Germans.

Manstein and his share of the responsibility in the failure of the battle of Kursk

The battle desired by Zeitzler, Manstein, Kluge, and Model had led to a costly military failure. The generals were clearly overconfident and had underestimated the strength of their adversary. Despite the risks incurred by the postponement of the offensive by almost two months, the generals had remained in favor of its commencement. They had even persuaded the Führer that they could not wait indefinitely for a Soviet offensive, which would perhaps not occur until winter or the opening of a second front in Europe. In his *Memoirs*, Manstein tried to mitigate his responsibility: "With the Russians having waited until the middle of July to move to the offensive, our idea of taking the initiative was not in any way erroneous."[488]

The fact remained, however, that the German offensive ended in failure. If Manstein, Kluge, Zeitzler, and Model had made the decision in June to call off Operation Citadel, the Wehrmacht could have saved crucial forces on the Eastern Front which it had just set in position. While keeping the initiative against the Red Army, a significant portion of the units engaged at Kursk would thus have been available to participate on other fronts or theaters of operations. But by losing the battle in which it had placed the bulk of its armored formations, laboriously re-formed and reinforced, the initiative moved definitively into the enemy camp. Henceforth, it could no longer be a question of a political solution in the East, such as Manstein had sought. The Kursk defeat had actually buried the last chance for a peace agreement on this front.[489]

It was thus rightly so that the Führer placed the primary blame for the defeat on his generals: "This is the last time I will listen to the council of my general staff," he declared to his confidents after the meeting with Manstein and Kluge he had convened on July 13 to order them to terminate the operation.[490] Concerning the term "general staff," this was obviously not only aimed at Zeitzler, but also Manstein, Kluge, and Model, who supported forging ahead at all costs, regardless of the delay.

The failure of Operation Citadel was attributable to several reasons, chief of which was its inability to achieve surprise. No amount of camouflage could deceive the enemy for very long, even as the Soviet intelligence network kept apprised of the German plans. By delaying the commencement of the offensive from mid-May to the beginning of July, the Germans allowed the Russians to stockpile forces and reserves inside the Kursk salient, and to build a strong series of fortified lines. At the same time, they lost the opportunity to hold on to their operational reserves before forces needed to be redeployed in the Mediterranean theater due to the Allied offensive.

Would the result have been different had the offensive occurred in May, as Manstein and Kluge had initially wished? This was at least what Manstein claimed after the war: "By executing 'Citadel' at the end of May or, at the very latest, in the beginning of June, it was certain that it would not coincide with a landing from the West on the continent, and we would have struck before the enemy had the time to rebuild its forces. Even by deciding not to increase the number of our tanks, we would have had a superiority capable of ensuring victory. The failure of 'Citadel' was thus due to the fact that the German command tried to avoid a risk that it should have accepted in order to guarantee the success of the last of our great offensive operations on the Eastern Front."

Likewise, he suggested that a few more divisions would have sufficed to ensure the success of the Ninth Army, to facilitate the first breakthroughs of Army Group South, and to accelerate the outcome. It would have also been adequate, he added, to reinforce the front of the Second Panzer Army so that the enemy could not carry out there a rapid success to threaten the Ninth Army in its rear. In his view, the OKH could have obtained these additional forces from the OKW's theaters of operations, yet while accepting such considerable risks in Norway, France, the Balkans, and evacuating in time North Africa, for which resupply could no longer be provided.[491]

However, nothing allows for the confirmation of such claims. In May, the Russian defenses were without a doubt weaker, and their preparations less advanced. But at this time, Army Group South, for example, disposed of only some 850 tanks and assault guns against 1,500 two months later, and it is certain that the new tanks, despite their teething pains, allowed the Germans to thrust forward into certain parts of the Soviet positions. There were no guarantees for a German victory in the spring. Nothing would have prevented the Red Army high command from adopting delay tactics that would have at least worn down the German armored forces and led to a simple shrinking of the front.[492]

Moreover, Manstein was exaggerating when he asserted that Hitler prematurely interrupted the fight on the brink of a decisive victory, and that, if he had authorized him to engage the 24th Panzer Corps in the battle, a decisive success could have been won.[493] In fact, the counteroffensive from the Russians in the Orel sector, as well as on the Mius and middle Donetz, and the landing of the Anglo-Americans in Sicily left no other option than to bring Operation Citadel to an end. It was thus imperative to disengage the Fourth Panzer Army to allow its armor to deal with the new crises. In any case, because of their weak numbers, the German infantry divisions proved incapable of effectively providing protection of the armored units' flanks. As for the latter, they were not in a position to decisively breach the enemy defense lines that were thoroughly spread out before them. In this head-on fight, the battle of one fierce army against another, it was clearly the Red Army's superiority in numbers of men and materiel that was in the end decisive on the battlefield.

After the interruption of Operation Citadel, the strategic initiative in the East passed once and for all to the Russian camp. From this point on, they were able to attack wherever and whenever they wished by utilizing their crushing numerical superiority. Because of its failure, the offensive against the Kursk salient did not provide the Germans with the respite they so hoped for, since they succeeded at neither encircling a significant number of forces in the pocket nor overcoming the operational reserves of the enemy.

Despite its losses, the Soviet high command still possessed a sufficient amount of operational reserves to allow it to continue its preparations for an offensive on the entire front. The attack against the Orel salient was not a simple diversion intended to relieve the Kursk front, but rather the departure point for a series of uninterrupted offensives that were to continue through the summer, autumn, and even winter, and lead the Russian forces from the plains of Ukraine to the foothills of the Carpathians. As was to be expected, the commander in chief of the Red Army, Marshal Zhukov, and his deputy chief of general staff, Marshal Vassilevski, continued throughout this period the objective that had escaped them in the winter of 1942–43: the destruction of the southern wing of the German front. Field Marshal Manstein would nevertheless thwart the enemy's intentions, thanks to a brilliantly orchestrated retreat, one of the most beautiful military achievements of his career, and by this means he would delay the final outcome of the war.

XV

MANSTEIN AND THE MILITARY RESISTANCE TO HITLER

The capitulation of the Sixth Army in Stalingrad had the result of relaunching the conspiracy against Hitler and the National Socialist regime. Field Marshal Manstein refused to take part in any way in Colonel Claus Graf Schenk von Stauffenberg's conspiracy, which led to a failed putsch on July 20, 1944. Given that of the 3,500 generals and admirals who constituted the ranks of the Wehrmacht on the evening of July 20, 1944, only five had vigorously supported Stauffenberg in his assassination attempt against Hitler, and that only fifteen had more or less sympathized with him, one can surmise that Field Marshal Manstein's attitude with respect to the military resistance against Hitler was the rule and not the exception.[494]

Clearly, like almost all of the high-ranking officers, he remained consistent and loyal to the allegiance that tied the army to the regime, all the more so since the oath of allegiance that he and his fellow officers had sworn to Hitler in the summer of 1934 was a form of deliberate submission by the Wehrmacht to the Führer. Furthermore, those who, like Field Marshal Manstein, were invested and engaged within the criminal regime and had burned their bridges along with him, judged that it was perhaps more in their interest to remain tied to the Führer. By refusing to join the conspiracy, they continued to stand as safeguards for the Nazi regime and its crimes.

Manstein's attitude towards the conspiracy: The rule, not the exception

In a letter published on January 10, 1988, in the German daily *Frankfurter Allgemeine Zeitung*, Rüdiger von Manstein, the field marshal's son, succinctly presented his father's five arguments against a coup d'état: 1. In order to come out of the military impasse, it was necessary to reach a tie on the Eastern Front, in other words arrive at a peace agreement with the Soviet Union. For this, it was essential that the political leadership not show any sort of weakness or division; 2. A coup d'état, in the precarious military situation of 1943, would have led to a short-term collapse; 3. Hitler remained the only man who enjoyed the confidence of the people and the soldiers, even more so since they believed in him; 4. A responsible military leader could not demand of his soldiers, for years, such a high degree of involvement and sacrifice, only to then precipitate defeat by his own hand; 5. A coup d'état would have changed nothing in terms of the Western Allies, who were demanding an unconditional surrender.[495]

Manstein's first argument is legitimate insofar as the Wehrmacht could no longer hope to achieve a decisive military victory on the Eastern Front. Only a political solution with the U.S.S.R could permit the Reich to bring itself out of a military impasse in which it was inexorably condemned to defeat in more or less the long term, due to the Red Army's crushing superiority in force and armaments. However, Manstein seems not to have understood that the main obstacle to such a peace agreement was clearly Hitler himself, an adherent of fighting the war to the very end, for which the outcome could only be—according to the Nazi dictator's own terms—total victory or the complete destruction of Germany. By standing against the idea of a coup d'état, Manstein could only contribute towards pushing further away the notion of a peace agreement.

Moreover, the opportunity to reach a tie in the East only became possible in the spring of 1943. Manstein's victorious counterattack in the Kharkov sector had at the time permitted the Wehrmacht to restore and stabilize the southern wing of the Eastern Front that had been threatened with complete collapse consecutively with the Stalingrad military disaster. Following the failure of the Battle of Kursk in the summer of 1943, it could no longer be a question of a tie, but only a peace agreement in favor of the enemy, for the German Army was no longer in a position to launch new offensives on the Eastern Front for the remainder of the war.

However, in the summer of 1943 after the Red Army's counterattack in the Kursk sector and the Anglo-American landings in Sicily,

Manstein still insisted upon believing in the possibility of a draw, not only on the Eastern Front but in the Mediterranean theater. In his *Memoirs*, Lieutenant Stahlberg, the field marshal's adjutant, reports a conversation the two of them had regarding this matter in the spring of 1943: "I considered the idea of a tie rather unrealistic. [...] If I understood correctly [...], I put forth, he was assuming that Hitler would be placed in a situation where he would be able to sit at a table with Stalin, Churchill, and Roosevelt to negotiate a great compromise. Manstein raised his head in agreement. In simplified terms, this was his opinion. I replied that this was an illusion. One had to take into consideration that at the party's public gatherings broadcast over the radio, Hitler had characterized Winston Churchill as a drunk and the president of the United States a paralytic. Because of this alone, Hitler had irrevocably destroyed any chances for political dialogue. Moreover, even before the beginning of the war, Hitler had violated treaties that he himself had previously negotiated. Because of this, he was no longer qualified, in my eyes, to negotiate, and even less so to settle a treaty. And finally, in the territories that we were occupying, actions had been committed on the German side since the beginning of the war that were incompatible with international law."

After he gave his opinion, Manstein attempted to defend his point of view, notably by invoking once again his highly limited concept of the role of the soldier. According to Stahlberg: "Manstein let me speak without contradicting me. But, as soon as I stopped, he declared that I was wrong, even though he did not contest my arguments. In politics, such arguments were in the end insignificant. And above all, it was not the soldier's job to argue about political morality. Germany had in its possession many more useful cards that had not yet been played. For example, not a single Allied soldier had landed up to this point on the European continent. Of course, he was now envisioning that the Americans and the British would land in the near future in Italy, the Balkans, or on the Atlantic coast. At this particular moment, we, the Germans, could, if necessary, withdraw into the Alps, which could be defended with our highly limited forces. We still possessed reserves that had gone unsuspected. But the reserves were only useful if they were used in the appropriate area and only if the strategic plans were developed at the right moment. [...] It would be to Hitler's advantage to leave the planning and the operations to him, Manstein. It was only if things unfolded as miserably as had recently been the case that the situation could one day become critical. But we have not yet reached that point."[496]

Manstein's argument was extremely naïve. How could he believe in the possibility of a peace agreement at a time when the *Ostheer* was beating a retreat before the Red Army after the defeat suffered at Kursk, when Anglo-American troops were landing in southern Italy after having defeated the *Afrika Korps*, and with Churchill having refused to negotiate with Hitler even in the summer of 1940, when the military strength of the Reich appeared invincible following its victory over France, and when England was isolated more than ever? While maintaining this illusion, he would continue to believe in the possibility of achieving a draw, then a peace agreement, even after the summer of 1944, which is to say after the success of the Allied invasion in Normandy in June 1944, the debacle of Army Group Center on the Eastern Front in 1944, and the coup d'état against Hitler on July 20, 1944.[497]

Judging from Manstein's second argument, it is completely possible that a successful putsch, in the difficult military situation of 1943, could have provoked a collapse of the front. However, at this particular moment, the war had already been irrevocably lost for the Wehrmacht and its continuation could only lead to further losses of human lives and the destruction of Germany's cities. The following numbers of German soldiers and civilians killed before and after July 20, 1944 demonstrate well the absurdity of a war waged until the very end. From September 1, 1939, to July 20, 1944, 2,335,000 enlisted men and 500,000 civilians lost their lives, for a total of 2,835,000 people, an average of 1,588 deaths per day. From July 20, 1944, to May 6, 1945, 1,976,000 enlisted men and 2,850,000 civilians died, for a total of 4,826,000 people, an average of 16,641 deaths per day. For the entire duration of the war, thus from September 1, 1939, to May 6, 1945, 4,311,000 enlisted men and 3,350,000 civilians perished, for a total of 7,661,000 people, an average of 3,692 deaths per day. In this respect, Manstein's fourth argument does not take into account the responsibility of every military leader to avoid useless losses when the strategic situation becomes hopeless. Clearly, the field marshal appeared to have been indifferent to the loss of human lives, whether they were military or civilian.[498]

In his *Memoirs*, Manstein furthermore shows no amount of regret for the hundreds of thousands of German soldiers who fell on the battlefield for a desperate cause. To the contrary, in his eyes, "the decisive element was the devotion, bravura, loyalty, and sense of duty of the German soldier, as well as the love of responsibility and knowledge from the chiefs of every rank. They alone allowed us to confront the crushing superiority of our adversaries."[499]

The third argument concerning the confidence of the German people in their Führer without a doubt corresponds to reality. On the other hand, history has often demonstrated that a population could quickly end its allegiance to the head of state or a regime. For example, the announcement of the removal of Mussolini and his fascist regime on July 25, 1943 induced euphoria in almost all of Italy, which was weary of the war and of the dictator's failed policies.

Finally, the field marshal's fifth argument cannot be more accurate. Most of the time, every demand for surrender called for unconditional terms, with the victor dictating its own demands to the defeated who is forced to accept them under the threat of continued battles.[500]

Unfortunately, in the first volume of his autobiography concerning the war years, Manstein hardly broached the issue of overthrowing the National Socialist regime, or the attempt made to that effect on July 20, 1944. In one passage, he made this brief commentary: "I would like to state that I did not believe, in my role as leader and military chief, that I could support the idea of a coup d'état which, in my opinion, would have led to a rapid collapse of the front and, in all likelihood, led Germany into chaos. Not to mention of course the issue of the oath, nor the legitimacy and right to commit murder for political reasons. Just as I declared at my trial: 'One cannot request of a military chief, who has called upon his soldiers, for years, to sacrifice their lives for victory, to subsequently precipitate defeat with his own hands.' On the other hand, it was already clear that a coup d'état would have changed nothing as to the determination of the Allies to demand from Germany an unconditional capitulation. At the time when I was overseeing my command, we were not yet, in my opinion, at the point where this solution appeared to be the only one possible."

Shortly after, he made a declaration along the same lines: "But a military chief cannot step down from his duties like a politician if things go bad or if he does not like the government policy. He is a soldier, thus he must fight just as he is ordered." Finally, further down, he summarizes his thoughts on this sensitive issue: "But I also understood that every attempt to gain the changes essential [to a revision of the military high command] would lead to the collapse of the front. The thought that the Russians would invade Germany, as well as the demand for unconditional surrender drafted by the Anglo-Saxons, ruled out for me recourse to this path."[501]

The fear that a coup d'état could lead Germany into chaos and induce the Bolsheviks to seize power in Berlin was very present among the majority of the generals and field marshals of the Wehrmacht. It could furthermore explain the refusal of most of them to participate in an assassination attempt against Hitler. It was at least what the future Colonel General Kielmansegg, who served in the operational branch of the OKH before being arrested by the Gestapo on August 8, 1944, and then imprisoned for his complicity in the July 20 plot, was thinking. "They were afraid of Bolshevism," he later stated. "Manstein's thought was the following: if we begin a civil war against Hitler now, then everything will collapse, and we will have the Bolsheviks in Berlin." Manstein and the majority of his fellow officers found themselves confronted with a situation in which they considered only two possible parties: National Socialism or Bolshevism; Hitler or Stalin. Fearing that an assassination attempt against the Führer could result in a civil war that would transform Germany into a Bolshevik state, they did not see any other solution than to continue the war under Hitler's leadership and the National Socialist regime.[502]

In the second volume of his *Memoirs*, Manstein provides another explanation to justify his refusal to participate in a plot against Hitler: "The conditions for a coup d'état would have [required] [...] the support of the entirety of the Wehrmacht and the backing of the majority of the population. These two conditions did not exist during the peacetime of the Third Reich nor during the war (with the exception of perhaps the very last months)." After the war, Guderian himself also made similar remarks to explain his decision not to join the ranks of the conspiracy when the war appeared to be lost: "At that time—the fact seems undeniable—most of the German people still believed in Adolf Hitler and were convinced that by killing him his assassin would have eliminated the only man still capable of bringing the war to a favorable conclusion." After the war, Blumentritt, who had not participated in the conspiracy, estimated that at least "half of the civilian population was indignant that German generals had taken part in an attempt to over-throw Hitler, and demonstrated a sharp bitterness towards them—and the army had displayed the same sentiment."[503]

In addition to this argument, Manstein also claimed that the German generals had been prevented from rebelling because their tradition was that of a "fully selfless devotion in service to the state, the Reich, and the nation."[504] They could have only fulfilled their duties by obeying orders, in accordance with the supposed apolitical tradition of the German Army. This myth of a military tradition dismissing any participation in political matters was furthermore a leitmotif present in numerous defensive post-war writings to justify the behavior of the officers with respect to Hitler and his criminal regime. However, such an argument is inaccurate, insofar as the Reichswehr was far from being apolitical, interfering rather frequently in politics in order to defend its own interests. The multiple concessions that it made to Hitler were, as a result, motivated through political calculations, with the intention of exerting an even greater influence within the Nazi regime. To gain the privilege of being the only organization of the Reich to have the right to carry arms, it appeared ready to abandon certain fundamental principles of the German military tradition. The complicit silence of the military leaders on the assassinations of Röhm, Schleicher, and Bredow during the "night of the long knives," or their haste in proposing to Hitler that all soldiers of the army offer to him their oath of allegiance, are only a few examples.[505]

Finally, Manstein suggests in the first volume of his *Memoirs* another argument to explain his refusal to act as guarantor of a coup d'état: he did not have knowledge of the atrocities committed by the National Socialist regime: "I would like to state—concerning the general character of this matter—that, absorbed for years by my difficult duties at the front, I did not have the opportunity to recognize that the regime was sliding downhill, nor Hitler's true nature, with all of the clarity that seems obvious to us today. The rumors that were circulating in the country were hardly reaching the front, and perhaps on ours even less so. The anxieties and preoccupations of battle did not allow us the time to reflect on general issues. In this matter, we found ourselves in a radically different situation than that of the soldiers or politicians residing in our homeland or in the occupied countries where one was not fighting."[506]

Of course, Manstein could not have been oblivious to what was actually occurring behind the front, with the special units of the SS or the SD and those of the Wehrmacht having most often worked in close collaboration, particularly in the Crimea, a sector of operations that was directly under his responsibility. As to the existence of the concentration camps, he had been informed by several close colleagues, particularly his assistant Stahlberg.

From a military perspective, one can wonder why Manstein persisted in remaining at his post so long, despite the fact that Hitler was rejecting most of his proposals while refusing to recognize the most unavoidable necessities. In his *Memoirs*, he implies that, more than the desire to avoid an even more rapid military collapse, it was concern for not abandoning his subordinates which had guided him: "From a personal point of view, I quite often had the desire to step down from my duties. I frequently said to the chief of general staff that Hitler could find a replacement for me since he rejected my proposals or tried to interfere in the duties of my command. What prevented me from retiring—in addition to the pleas of my direct collaborators—could not be expressed by simply stating that I wanted to 'avoid the worst.' It was rather the conviction that no other staff, as united as ours was by the toughest experiences, would be in a position to fulfill the missions that were arising in our sector, which was the most decisive one. My departure would have represented more than a changing of the person of the chief. It was the sentiment that I could not abandon the troops who had faith in me, unless, and rightly so, the request to be relieved of my duties represented a last effort that would entice Hitler into providing for their salvation."[507]

Despite the numerous reservations and criticisms he held with regard to Hitler's conduct of the war, Field Marshal Manstein decided to serve the Third Reich until the very end. He remained consistent and loyal to the allegiance that linked the Wehrmacht to the National Socialist regime, and he only partially detached himself from it after the war. As far as politics was concerned, he thought, it was a soldier's duty to restrict himself to military matters. Not only did he thus choose to respect his oath of allegiance to the Führer, but he hoped, until the very end of the war, that the latter would sooner or later decide to call upon his services as chief of general staff over all of the theaters of operations, or as commander in chief of the Eastern Front, to save Germany from a military disaster that had nevertheless become inevitable. But Hitler was never inclined to reform the military high command, and even less so to entrust the leadership of military operations to Manstein.

Manstein called upon to play the role of Yorck von Wartenburg?

After the failure of Operation Barbarossa, the Führer's relations with his generals continued to deteriorate. He nullified their decisions, ignored their opinions, treated them as cowards, forced them to execute orders which they judged impossible to fulfill, and dismissed them when they did not achieve them. His criticisms with regard to the officers' corps were directed at its conservatism and its pessimistic attitude—in short, its lack of National Socialist fervor in combat. Quite obviously, for Hitler, the combative National Socialist mindset was equivalent to eagerness to execute his orders without hesitating or considering their cost. Nevertheless, the large majority of generals continued to implement the Führer's orders, to lead battles for him in spite of his continual interference, and to accept titles, decorations, and gifts that he granted to them.

However, there were a small number of officers, mostly below the rank of general, who sought to free Germany of Hitler, whom they held responsible for the catastrophic military situation in which their country was found. One of the most important was Colonel Tresckow, the deputy chief of staff of Field Marshal Kluge's Army Group Center, who utilized his position to organize officers who shared his ideas. Born into an old aristocratic Prussian family steeped in military tradition, Tresckow, like many of the officers who joined the resistance, was at first enthusiastic about the new National Socialist regime which, in his eyes, had liberated Germany from contemptible democracy, the Bolshevik threat, and the constraints of the Treaty of Versailles.

From 1930, three years before Hitler came to power, Tresckow revealed his political convictions by demanding that the army be trained and educated in the most pure spirit of National Socialism.[508] An admirer of Hitler for as long as he garnered success upon success before the war, and after that the lightening victories he carried out at the beginning, he then transformed into a determined opponent when he became aware that the direction of military operations was leading the Reich directly towards defeat. He even came to despise the general staff of the army for its obsequious submission to the Führer, but he neverthe-less recognized that the officers' corps remained the only group capable of standing up against the Nazi regime.

Among those whom Tresckow was able to gather at Army Group Center, there was Captain Fabian von Schlabrendorff, who became his adjutant, and Lieutenant Colonel Rudolf-Christoph Freiherr von Gersdorff, chief of the army group's intelligence section. However, these officers were not successful at winning Kluge's clear commitment. Concerned about sitting on the fence, the commander in chief of Army Group Center wished to keep all of his options open so that he could support in the end the victorious party: the regime or the putschists. If nothing was expected on his part, the members of the opposition would nevertheless keep the illusion that the field marshal was at heart on their side. As for the hope to see Manstein join the ranks of the conspiracy, he was quickly disappointed.

Tresckow was thinking that a coup d'état could provoke a beneficial reaction within the Wehrmacht if it resulted in the use of a highly respected chief in a key position. With Field Marshal Manstein inevitably benefiting from the necessary respect, Tresckow, as soon as the opportunity presented itself, appointed his young cousin to assist him: this was Lieutenant Stahlberg, who until then had served with the 12th Panzer Division on the Leningrad and Volkhov fronts. Stahlberg took up his post on November 18, 1942, three days before Manstein was designated by Hitler to command the new Army Group Don.

If the intelligence and military qualities of the field marshal were undeniable, his political sentiments were much more difficult to read. Most certainly, he despised Reich Field Marshal Göring and detested Hitler, whom he considered an upstart. To those in whom he had complete trust, he even admitted having Jewish ancestry. He even liked to ridicule Hitler; not only was he in the habit, in the presence of his most loyal associates, of calling him *Effendi*—a former title of Turkish civil or religious dignitaries—but he had also trained his dog Knirps to raise his paw at the command "*Heil Hitler!*" His wife, on the other hand, was a great admirer of the Führer and a highly involved member of the Nazi party. She surely must have exerted a certain amount of influence over her husband's attitude with respect to the conspirators, all the more so since her confidence in Hitler apparently lasted until the very end of the war.

It took six days by train to cross the snow-covered Russian countryside, from Eleventh Army's headquarters in Vitebsk to the new headquarters of Army Group Don in Novotcherkassk. During the trip, Manstein and his new assistant Stahlberg played chess or bridge, discussed music, common relationships, and literature, but they only broached the subject of politics through allusions. Learning that Field Marshal Manstein was related to the deceased field marshal and president of the Reich, Hindenburg, Lieutenant Stahlberg took the opportunity to ask him, almost daringly, which of the young field marshals of this new war could become, in his view, the "savior of the homeland" in the event of a total defeat. "Certainly not me," Manstein sharply replied.[509] It goes without saying that, in his mind, there was absolutely no question of losing the war.

His optimism was, however, not shared by Colonel General Paulus, whose Sixth Army was at that time encircled in Stalingrad. The conspirators tried to win him over to their side, thinking that he undoubtedly had to feel a bitter disillusion with regards to the Führer, who had made this disaster possible. In fact, they were hoping that Paulus would rebel and thus unleash a reaction throughout the army. In order to incite him to act thusly, they brought up the attitude of the Prussian general Hans Graf Yorck von Wartenburg, who refused at Tauroggen on December 30, 1812, to continue to fight under the King of Prussia who was allied with Napoleon, thus provoking a wave of patriotism in all of the German states would lead to the wars of liberation. Apparently, General Walther von Seydlitz-Kurzback, commander in chief of the LI Army Corps that was encircled in Stalingrad, remarked on this during a conversation with Paulus, while endeavoring to convince him to attempt a breakout, despite formal orders from the Führer. Colonel Herbert Selle, in charge of engineering for the Sixth Army, did likewise. Paulus' response to Selle was not only negative, but fraught with an indisputable fatalism: "I know," Paulus stated to him, "that the history of the war has already given its verdict against me."

Likewise, Paulus was not wrong to reject the comparison between his situation and that of Yorck von Wartenburg in Tauroggen. Without any means of communication, the latter could claim to be speaking in the name of the King of Prussia and retain his command. But during a period when every headquarters was in permanent contact by radio or telephone with the supreme command, a repudiation and an order to place under arrest the rebellious chief would immediately occur. In fact, as Tresckow had already determined, the only actor in the drama capable of playing the role of Yorck von Wartenburg was Manstein. But it did not take him long to understand that the latter had absolutely no intention of accepting such a dangerous role.[510]

The Stauffenberg-Manstein meeting

Called upon to become the leader of the conspiracy against Hitler, Claus von Stauffenberg was a staff officer born into an aristocratic family from Swabia. Like a good number of young officers, he had been seduced by National Socialism, particularly by its insistence on the merits of a powerful armed forces and on a foreign policy in opposition to the Treaty of Versailles. On the other hand, he rejected its racial anti-Semitism. However, when he had served in Poland, he did not conceal his contempt for the Polish and had approved the colonization of the country, all while being enthusiastic about the Third Reich's victory. He rejoiced even more after the stunning successes of the French campaign and those of the first months of Operation Barbarossa. But, when he realized that the war could only result in a catastrophe, he was convinced that it was necessary to act before it was too late.

On January 26, 1943, a few days before the Sixth Army's capitulation in Stalingrad, Stauffenberg, at the time a major, was sent by Colonel-General Zeitzler to the headquarters of Army Group Don in Taganrog in order to meet Field Marshal Manstein. In his role as officer in the organizational section of the OKH, Stauffenberg was to discuss with Manstein the enlistment of volunteer Cossack units. The field marshal did not know the major personally. He had nevertheless been informed of his arrival, while also being told that he was one of the most talented young officers of the army's general staff. As for Stauffenberg, the meeting with the commander in chief of Army Group Don was a golden opportunity to convince him to join the ranks of the conspiracy.

The discussion took place in private, in Manstein's office. His assistant, Lieutenant Stahlberg, drove Stauffenberg there and immediately returned to the waiting room, where his own office was located, while leaving the door that adjoined the field marshal's office partly opened, which allowed him to report the key elements of the conversation in his autobiography. This was not out of the ordinary, his primary task being to listen and note the points that he considered important. Unfortunately, Manstein did not believe that it was worthwhile recounting this conversation of some forty-five minutes with Stauffenberg in his *Memoirs*.

After completing his presentation on the enlistment of volunteer Cossack units and briefly addressing Army Group Don's military situation, including Sixth Army at Stalingrad, and Army Group A, which had still not completed its retreat from the Caucasus, Stauffenberg asked permission to carry on the conversation, to which Manstein agreed. The major continued by asserting that he could not accept that the Sixth Army was the victim of nothing other than foolish strategic errors. In fact, in his view, the entire Russian campaign was nothing other than a series of errors. The field marshal agreed, while insisting upon the fact that the offensive against Russia had clearly been a mistake since the beginning. If one had asked him to draft an operations plan before the commencement of the attack against the U.S.S.R., Manstein stated, it would have been very different from the OKH's. But, he added, it was not the time to discuss what his own plan would have been for a campaign in the East, except to say that he would not have carried out such a constant dispersion of German forces.

"One must learn how to deal with the facts such as they are; in the present case with the fact that Sixth Army in Stalingrad is lost," resumed Stauffenberg. He continued by mentioning that he could hardly be resigned to the idea that hundreds of thousands of German soldiers had been sacrificed for a battle for which the purpose was pointless. The tone of the conversation then became rather tense. Manstein explained to Stauffenberg that the duty of an officer in times of war was to accept the loss of a a battle, adding: "Name for me a victorious war in military history during which a battle was not lost?" The major hardly took any time to reply: "This does not convince me. Up until now, *Herr* Field Marshal, we agree that the Russia campaign [...] was nothing more than a series of errors from the beginning until the end. Who can guarantee that the same scenario will not recur in the future? Since the failure of our offensive in the autumn of 1941, we have moved from one crisis to another; several times our armies have been on the verge of collapse. And now, in the south of Russia, I believe that we are solely indebted to the incredible talent of a certain Field Marshal von

Manstein for the fact that the front has not completely collapsed."

In fact, Stauffenberg did not share Manstein's opinion according to which Stalingrad was indeed no more than a lost battle. In his view, Stalingrad could prove to be the beginning of the end of a lost war, unless one decided to find a solution for the cause of all of the mistakes. Yet, these were above all the work of the supreme command. Manstein agreed and underscored that changes were necessary in the structure of the military high command of the army, and even of the Wehrmacht. In his opinion, a commander in chief who was militarily qualified was needed in order to assume leadership of operations on the Eastern Front and, in order to encourage such a change, he was willing to do his utmost. Unsatisfied by this response, Stauffenberg argued that it was unlikely that the Führer would decide to abdicate his military command. He then hastened to add these words: "*Herr* Field Marshal, you are the one who is predestined, through his talent and rank, to take the military command." Considering that it was actually the position to which he was aspiring for quite some time, Manstein was probably flattered by such an affirmation.

Somehow or another, continued the major, it was necessary to force the outcome of things in this direction. However, it was a threshold that the field marshal refused to cross. He stated that he was prepared to discuss the issue of the high command with the Führer at the first opportunity, but asserted that he was in no way willing to take part, whether directly or indirectly, in any sort of illegal undertaking. Stauffenberg's reply was short-tempered: "If no one takes the initiative, everything will continue like before, which signifies that we will eventually slide into a major catastrophe." Manstein vehemently refuted such remarks, claiming that it was not his intentions, but rather Stauffenberg's, that would lead to a catastrophe, particularly a collapse of the fronts and a civil war. "A war is not truly lost as long as it is not considered as being lost," he asserted. In his view, it was quite possible that the Reich had not yet overcome its greatest military crisis, but if such were the case, then the Führer would not hesitate to understand it and would thus call upon someone who was militarily qualified to stabilize the situation. In the meantime, it was necessary to prove one's faith and wait.

Stauffenberg then mentioned the word "Tauroggen." After a pause, Manstein indignantly shouted that Tauroggen had absolutely nothing to do with the present situation and urged him to be so kind as to desist from suggesting such ideas. But the major returned to the attack. Believing that the field marshal had not understood him well, he explained that his allusion to Tauroggen did not mean that he was expecting an overturning of allegiance to the Russians, but quite simply the possibility of forming a *fait accompli*. "Tauroggen also entails an extreme loyalty," declared the major. With the discussion becoming more and more turbulent, Manstein decided to conclude it, while assuring Stauffenberg that he appreciated the conversation. "What good would a staff be," asked the field marshal, "if the staff officers could no longer speak in complete freedom?" He then unexpectedly cited the following quotation: "Criticism is the salt of obedience." He then asked the major if he knew the author of these words. "Clausewitz? Or the elder Moltke perhaps?" responded Stauffenberg. Manstein smiled and admitted that he did not know either. And so came to an end the discussion between the two officers. At dinner, Manstein invited Stauffenberg to sit next to him, but the two officers did not engage in any actual conversation.[511]

Did Manstein's quotation spontaneously come from his lips? Perhaps he had wanted to reassure Stauffenberg, by making him understand that he did not have to fear being exposed by him? The conversation could have caused him serious problems after July 20, 1944. But, through a spirit of camaraderie, he preferred to keep secret the contents of the discussion and thus protect someone whom Zeitzler considered one of the most gifted, and perhaps even the most talented of all the young staff officers who worked at his elbow at the OKH. Stahlberg asked Manstein his impressions of Stauffenberg, to which he responded: "He is very intelligent. It was a brilliant and very interesting conversation. But he tried to get me to accept that the war was lost. This, I did not accept." Regarding his meeting with Stauffenberg, Manstein wrote to his wife: "I enjoyed it very much. He is pleasant and intelligent. To tell the truth, he is quite simply too intelligent for these difficult times, for he sees the dangers [...] as being insurmountable. I also see them all, but I overcome them."[512]

On the following day, January 27, 1943, during a telephone conversation, Zeitzler asked Manstein, once their discussion of the military status of the southern wing of the Eastern Front was completed, his opinion concerning Stauffenberg. Thinking of promoting the career of this young talented officer, the chief of the OKH general staff was intending on giving great significance to Manstein's point of view. The commander of Army Group Don stated that he agreed with Zeitzler's judgment, even asserting that Stauffenberg had an "extraordinary personality." According to him, there was no doubt that the officer in question possessed all the qualities required to enjoy a remarkable military career. However, it was clear, in his eyes, that Stauffenberg had spent too much time in the OKH, for he had the tendency to worry about problems that in no way concerned him. Because of this, Manstein thought that it was time to transfer him to the front for a certain period of time. After a brief silence, Zeitzler responded: "Very well *Herr* Field Marshal, I will think about it."

A few days later, on February 7, 1943, Major Stauffenberg left the OKH for Field Marshal Rommel's *Afrika Korps*. Since the temporary appointment of a young staff officer to a combat unit at the front was common practice, it is possible that Stauffenberg's had been planned for some time. It remains, however, that Manstein recommended to Zeitzler Stauffenberg's transfer on January 27, 1943, eleven days before it occurred.[513]

Stauffenberg came out of his meeting with Manstein obviously disappointed. In his eyes, it had become clear that the resistance could not count on the support of one of the most gifted field marshals of the Wehrmacht. He wrote to his wife: "Manstein's response was not that of a field marshal." Later, he even asserted to someone close to him that Manstein would have threatened to have him arrested on the spot if he did not immediately abandon the idea of committing an assassination attempt against Hitler. Manstein supposedly declared to him, "If you do not put an end to such things right away, I will have you arrested." However, such an assertion seems unlikely, if only because of Manstein's friendly remarks towards Stauffenberg at the end of their conversation, then his invitation to dine next to him. In fact, Manstein's post-war version regarding this seems more plausible: "That I threatened to have Stauffenberg arrested is totally inaccurate. I endeavored to help this young friend of great merit by listening to his legitimate worries. At the very most, it would be possible that I advised him, in his interest, to demonstrate prudence in his remarks, for there were probably few commanders in chief who would appear, like me, willing to listen to such criticisms towards the Führer."[514]

Contrary to Manstein's position, the Prussian military tradition in relation to the concept of loyalty must not be, according to Stauffenberg, reduced to simple unconditional obedience. The latter actually considered that disobedience could reveal a completely honorable sense of duty if it were to be devoted to serving national interest. In this sense, his allusion to the Prussian general Yorck von Wartenburg's insubordination was completely appropriate. If, at first glance, the insubordination of the latter in Tauroggen on December 30, 1812 could appear as an illegitimate act, it no less represented a form of loyalty in a profound sense of the term; Yorck von Wartenburg had placed the imperative of freeing the German people from the Napoleonic yoke above any obligation of loyalty to the King of Prussia. Consequently, the concept of absolute obedience in the Prussian military tradition for which Manstein and several other high ranking generals of the Wehrmacht claimed responsibility in order to justify their refusal to participate in a coup d'état against Hitler was, so to speak, nothing less than a perversion of Prussian thought."[515]

The Tresckow-Manstein meeting

Shortly after the Major Stauffenberg episode, Colonel Tresckow paid his own visit to Field Marshal Manstein, who, due to the retreat of his army group, had transferred his headquarters from Taganrog to Donetsk on January 29, 1943. In his role as Field Marshal Kluge's deputy chief of staff, Tresckow regularly telephoned Manstein's headquarters, because of the necessity to coordinate the military operations of Army Groups Center and Don. It was Stahlberg who, as Manstein's adjutant, was the first to take the calls, which gave him from time to time the opportunity to talk with his friend Tresckow. One night, during a conversation with the latter, Stahlberg informed him of General Schulz's promotion to the head of a unit at the front and of the possibility of seeing Colonel Busse, the deputy chief of staff, succeeding him. Tresckow let him immediately know that he would try to obtain the post of chief of staff of Army Group Don, since no official decision had yet been made.

Such an appointment would have been logical in Tresckow's career, considering that he had already worked closely with Manstein—as chief of the operations bureau while the latter was chief of staff—within Rundstedt's army group in the autumn of 1939 and the winter of 1940.

The famous operations plan of the French campaign was a result of their fruitful collaboration. Furthermore, it was from Tresckow's friendship with Schmundt, the Führer's principal adjutant, that Manstein owed his fateful meeting with Hitler in mid-February 1940, during which he had been able to present his Sickle Cut Plan. Later, when Manstein had become commander, first of an armored corps, then of an army, he had asked for Tresckow as his chief of staff. He had been refused each time under the pretext, at the very least strange, that he "did not need such an intelligent chief of staff." Manstein had informed Stahlberg on several occasions of the excellent working relationship he had developed with his cousin.[516] All things considered, there existed between Manstein and Tresckow a friendship and camaraderie, as well as a mutual respect that dated back several years.

The day after his conversation with Stahlberg, Tresckow rushed from Smolensk to Donetsk in order to meet with Manstein. With the discussion between the two men taking place behind closed doors, Stahlberg could not hear what was being said. But when he was required to enter the room on two occasions to update the operations map, each time he found Manstein in a state of restlessness that he had never before seen, while Tresckow had tears of desperation in his eyes. He thus had the impression that the conversation was a continuation of the one with Stauffenberg in Taganrog, but this time it was a much more turbulent scene.[517]

It is regrettable that Manstein did not believe it was worthy to report this conversation in his *Memoirs*. However, in an explanatory post-war letter, he disputed having discussed political issues with Tresckow during this meeting.[518] That the latter did not allude to his intentions to overthrow Hitler is highly doubtful, all the more so since he had placed Stahlberg, a few months earlier, on the field marshal's staff precisely for political motivations.

Furthermore, shortly after his conversation with Manstein, Tresckow revealed to Stahlberg that the field marshal had refused to take him on as chief of staff due to his ideas that he considered too distressing. And so, for primarily political motivations, Manstein preferred to grant this position to Busse. Indeed, like Tresckow, Busse was recognized as a dynamic and capable officer who possessed a talent above the majority of German staff officers. But unlike Tresckow, who was counted among the most critical opponents of the Nazi regime, the new chief of staff of Army Group Don seemed to be an apolitical soldier, during a time when the term "apolitical" quite simply meant an absolute obedience to the powers at hand. Not only was Manstein accustomed to Busse's presence by his side, but he was certain that he would not present any sort of problems for him, contrary to Tresckow, who, because of his involvement in the resistance, could have proven to be a rather unaccommodating colleague. Moreover, Busse was the brother-in-law of General Wilhelm Burgdorf, one of Hitler's adjutants, having married the sister of the latter's wife. Generally recognized as a committed National Socialist, Burgdorf always appeared ready to serve the regime with the utmost willingness.[519] As a result, Busse had become the logical choice for Manstein, who was anxious to demonstrate his loyalty towards the Führer and not to let him believe he could be tempted to align himself with conspirators. This was especially important in the event the plotters were ever arrested by the Gestapo, then forced to divulge all of their activities as well as the people with whom they had been in contact.

In his *Memoirs*, Manstein defends himself for not having chosen Tresckow as chief of staff, citing purely military reasons: "In the spring of 1943, when I was chief of an army group, he was proposed to me, but I could not then distance myself from General Busse who had been collaborating with me for quite some time [...]. The rumor was spread that I did not want Tresckow because he was not a good National Socialist. Whoever knows me knows that I have never chosen my colleagues according to such consideration."[520] However, in a letter addressed to his wife, Manstein gave a completely different explanation: "Tresckow was unable to catch his flight yesterday and stayed here until the evening. One can always have a pleasant conversation with him. In the past, I thought on several occasions of taking him on as chief of staff. But now I do not believe that it would be a judicious choice. Even if I value him a lot and that he is [...] intelligent [...], he sees difficulties and dangers much too severely and negatively. I see them all myself, but I am able to move past them. One needs someone who sees everything clearly, but who does not lose his optimism, for otherwise he could become a burden."[521]

Schlabrendorff asserts in his *Memoirs* that Manstein had confided in Schmundt, the Führer's primary adjutant, that he rejected Tresckow because of his negative opinions concerning National Socialism.[522] Such an assertion, which has been refuted by several authors, seems quite unlikely insofar as such a repudiation on Manstein's part could have brought the military career of Tresckow, an officer who he greatly esteemed, to an end. In fact, not only did Tresckow continue until his death his excellent career as a chief of staff, but he was promoted to the rank of major general and attained the position of chief of staff of the Second Army on the Eastern Front. In a letter addressed to Schlabrendorff after the war, Manstein gave his version of the facts: "My interactions with Tresckow were based on deep mutual respect and on friendship, despite longstanding differences in personality. It would have been childish of me to reject my most loyal supporter for such a reason, for in spite of his friendship with Schmundt, it would not have been without any repercussions for him."[523] If Manstein's remarks seem credible, it is nevertheless doubtful that Tresckow remained his most loyal supporter after their meeting at the headquarters of Army Group Don in Donetsk.

Despite the failure of his request, Tresckow nevertheless succeeded at placing near Manstein, as a successor to Busse in the position of deputy chief of staff, one of his closest colleagues and friends, and one the most sympathetic to his cause, Colonel Georg Schulze-Büttger. Tresckow's disappointment was nevertheless great. Shortly after, when Stahlberg informed him of Manstein's belief that Hitler would end up giving him the supreme command once he realized that it was the only solution to prevent Germany's defeat, Tresckow declared: "This is one of Manstein's typical illusions. Besides, it will not be long before Manstein himself will no longer be in a position to avoid the worst."[524]

The Schulenburg-Manstein meeting and the Beck-Manstein correspondence

Tresckow's failure to convince Manstein to join a movement aimed at removing Hitler from power was not only similar to Stauffenberg's, but also to efforts initiated by Fritz-Dietlof Graf von der Schulenburg and Colonel General Beck.

The first of the conspirators to have approached Field Marshal Manstein was Schulenburg, Germany's former ambassador to Moscow. In the summer of 1942, Schulenburg visited him on the Crimean peninsula. To win him over to his cause, he pulled out of his pocket docu-

ments that testified to the crimes committed by Hitler. The commander
in chief of Eleventh Army rejected them, asserting that he had no need
to have knowledge of them, for he already knew that the Führer was a
criminal. "So, can we count on you, *Herr* Field Marshal? –No, Graf
Schulenburg. –And why not? –Who will give me assurance of its success? –What? –Do you not understand that it is a matter of life and
death for me and the army?" With such a response, Manstein demonstrated once again that his worldview remained that of a soldier at the
service of politics and confined, consequently, only to military issues.[525]
His reply is also proof that he lied in his *Memoirs*, by writing, for example, that he did not have "the chance to recognize that the regime was
sliding downhill, nor Hitler's true nature," because of his difficult duties
at the front.

The second high-ranking individual who tried to convince the field
marshal to join the ranks of the conspiracy was Beck, the former chief
of the army's general staff. Even though the battle of Stalingrad had not
yet reached its conclusion, Beck wrote a letter to Manstein in which he
emphasized that the war was lost and that it was absolutely necessary
to do something in order to avoid catastrophe. In his view, it was insane
to want to continue the war. All that mattered from this point on was
to ensure the existence of the Reich: "It will only be possible to secure
the borders and to maintain domestic order with intact troops." It was
thus necessary to avoid recommitting the 1918 mistake. In his response
addressed to his former mentor, Manstein replied, "A war is not lost so
long as one does not recognize it as lost."[526] This written exchange was
unfortunately not reported by Manstein in his *Memoirs*. After the war,
on February 5, 1968, he nevertheless wrote to the editor of the newspaper *Alte Kameraden* concerning this episode. If he confirmed the
remarks that he made in his response, he nevertheless denied, though
rather unconvincingly, that Beck alluded to a coup d'état in his letter.[527]

Hopes to see Manstein stand behind the cause of the conspirators
had almost all vanished by the end of winter 1943. Shortly before the
Sixth Army's surrender in Stalingrad, Lieutenant General Bernhard
Klamroth had warned Captain Winrich Behr to be cautious with
Manstein on this matter. "When he is quietly at the table," he declared
to him, "Manstein appears very hostile to Hitler, but these are just
superfluous words. If Hitler were to order him to turn left or to turn
right, he would immediately obey."

Klamroth's remarks were completely justified. Despite the disrespect he expressed towards the Führer in private, particularly in the presence of colleagues whom he trusted, Manstein in no way wanted to risk compromising his position, his career, and his ambition of becoming the chief of general staff of the Wehrmacht or the commander in chief of the Eastern Front. On several occasions, he justified his attitude by asserting that an assassination attempt against Hitler would lead to an immediate collapse of the front and chaos within the country. Clearly, he was from the generation of officers for whom anti-Bolshevik sentiments had been forever forged by the revolts and turmoil of 1918–19.

The fear that Hitler inspired in him could sometimes appear obvious. The discussions among his officers on the factors involved in the Stalingrad tragedy disturbed him so much by their candor that he sent a memo to his chief of staff declaring that "discussions about who was responsible for the recent events" must cease, for they cannot "change any of the facts and only undermine confidence." It was also strictly prohibited for the officers to discuss "the causes of the destruction of the Sixth Army" in their personal correspondence.[528]

The Gersdorff-Manstein meeting

In the spring of 1943, Colonel Tresckow kept up his persuasive efforts with Field Marshal Kluge to the degree that he came to tolerate the conspirators' activities within his immediate entourage. His Smolensk headquarters would quickly become the main center of the conspiracy. As the military situation gradually deteriorated, the commander in chief of Army Group Center appeared more willing to discuss the elimination of the Führer and the removal of the regime. Even though he still hesitated to actively engage in the resistance, he henceforth gave his tacit agreement.

During the summer of 1943, he contacted Colonel General Beck and other leaders of the opposition, such as Carl Goerdeler, former mayor of Leipzig, and Johannes Popitz, Prussian Minister of Finance. At Colonel Tresckow's instigation, he even tried to win the support of military commanders, particularly by sending Lieutenant Colonel Gersdorff to Field Marshal Manstein with hopes of persuading him to join the conspiracy and assume the duties of chief of general staff of the Wehrmacht, following a successful coup d'état.

On August 8, 1943, Gersdorff thus went to the headquarters of Army Group South in Zaporojie in order to meet Manstein. He carried in his pockets letters from Goerdeler and Popitz which were to be presented to the field marshal only if the discussion proved profitable, for he was not to place their authors in danger. With Tresckow being in contact with Colonel Schulze-Büttger, chief of the operations bureau, and Lieutenant Stahlberg, Manstein's adjutant, in Zaporojie, the meeting between the latter and Gersdorff could be well prepared. In the presence of Major General Busse, Manstein's chief of staff, Gersdorff was only to discuss military issues. But Manstein did not insist that his chief of staff be present, which allowed Gersdorff to speak frankly with him. If the field marshal did not recount in his *Memoirs* his conversation with the lieutenant colonel, the latter, on the other hand, reported its key points in his autobiography.

Without delay, Gersdorff declared that Field Marshal Kluge was quite worried about the continuation of the war. Due to antagonism between the OKW and the OKH, as well as Hitler's more and more blatant amateurishness as supreme commander of the Wehrmacht, the collapse of the Eastern Front was only a matter of time. For this reason, one had to make Hitler understand that he was leading Germany directly to disaster. In regard to Kluge's concerns, Manstein responded: "I completely agree. But I am not the right person to state this to Hitler. Even though it is in no way the case, enemy propaganda has described me as a man eager to seize power from Hitler. The latter is thus now suspicious of me. Only Rundstedt and Kluge can take on such a mission." To which Gersdorff replied: "Perhaps all the field marshals should go together to see the Führer and hold a gun to his chest." But such remarks hardly pleased Manstein, who hastened to respond in a confident and resolved tone: "Prussian field marshals do not revolt."

A rebel, the lieutenant colonel challenged the field marshal's assertion: "In Prussian history, there are plenty of examples of high ranking generals who have acted against the desires and orders of their king. One need only remember Seydlitz and Yorck. In any case, Prussian field marshals have never been in a position like the one they are in today. Unprecedented situations require unprecedented methods. But we, in addition, no longer believe that a common action from the field marshals would have the slightest chance of success. In Army Group Center, we have been convinced for some time that every means must be taken in order to save Germany from disaster." Dismayed by what he had just heard, Manstein retorted: "So you want to kill him?" Gersdorff said, "Yes, *Herr* Field Marshal, like a mad dog!" This response caused the field marshal to leap out of his chair and nervously walk into his office. He then shouted: "Do not count on me! This will lead to the collapse of the army!"

Remaining calm, Gersdorff emphasized the contradiction in Manstein's remarks: "*Herr* Field Marshal, you said earlier that Germany would collapse if nothing were done to stop him. It is not the army, but Germany and the German people that are the priorities." The field marshal then defended his view of things from a strictly military perspective: "I am a soldier who is on the front line. You do not know the front as well as I do. Every day, I speak with my senior and subordinate officers, and above all with my young officers. I see the enthusiasm in their eyes when they speak about the Führer. They would thus not understand taking action against him. Such a thing would certainly lead to a civil war within the army." The lieutenant colonel went back on the attack: "I also am often at the front and I speak with the young officers. I admit that the majority are still enthusiastic with regard to Hitler. But I also know many others who are of a completely different opinion. I am above all convinced that the officers' corps and the troops will remain behind their military leaders according to the principle of absolute obedience, and that each order issued to them will be executed. After Hitler's removal, there will be in all likelihood be no one who will talk about him."

However, Manstein was not the type who would allow himself to be convinced so easily. Firmly entrenched in his position, he reaffirmed his refusal to participate in a venture that, in his opinion, could only lead to the collapse of the army. Realizing that he could not succeed at changing his opinion, Gersdorff thus decided not to hand Goerdeler's and Popitz's letters to him. Before concluding their discussion, Gersdorff nevertheless informed him of Kluge's request: "Field Marshal von Kluge wanted me to ask if you would be prepared to become the chief of general staff of the Wehrmacht after a successful coup d'état." Manstein leaned slightly forward, then declared: "Tell Field Marshal von Kluge that I thank him for the confidence that he has in me. Field Marshal von Manstein will always be a loyal servant to the legally constituted government."[529]

Through such a response, Manstein was remaining faithful to the traditional attitude according to which the soldier must restrict himself exclusively to military matters. Far from demonstrating any sort of wait-and-see character, he instead recalled that he was an apolitical soldier, having loyally served each legitimate government, from the Bismarck Reich to the Third Reich, including during the Weimar Republic, and this without allowing himself to be influenced by his own political opinions.

And yet, even if his military education stipulated that he obey orders, there was no way that he could not realize that Germany was heading directly towards a military disaster. According to Beck, Manstein's attitude was explained more by his character than by his supposed conviction that everything must be done to prevent the Russians from invading Germany, and that, should a coup d'état occur, this would become even more difficult, if not impossible. In fact, the surest way to guarantee that the Russian armies would reach German territory was to prolong the war. And this was precisely what would happen if nothing was done to overthrow Hitler and the National Socialist regime.

Clearly, the discussion between Manstein and Gersdorff revealed two completely divergent views as to a soldier's duty in times of war. Paradoxically, the two both found their roots in Prussian military tradition. For Manstein, what was most important was the integrity of the army and absolute loyalty to the supreme commander of the Wehrmacht and the head of state, meaning Hitler. As for Gersdorff, it was the survival of Germany and the German people that counted more than anything else.[530]

Manstein's personal diary nowhere mentions that Gersdorff spoke to him about a possible assassination attempt against Hitler. It would have been, quite obviously, very dangerous for him and his family to leave any words regarding this matter. The risk that his diary could one day be found in the hands of the SS or the SD was much too great. Indeed, anyone who dared to criticize the military command exposed himself to considerable risks, as this remark from Keitel demonstrates: "I allow the officers who criticize the Führer or who express their doubts of victory to be shot."

And so, concerning his conversation with Gersdorff, Manstein reported the matter as an issue relating to the high command, weighing his words carefully: "There is no doubt that the consequences of the current situation are the result of errors from the command. But one must absolutely dismiss the idea of Hitler abandoning his duties as commander in chief. Instead, one must convince the Führer of the necessity to proceed with an effective reorganization of the command. The Führer should work with a chief of general staff of the Wehrmacht, or equally assume the role of commander in chief of the Luftwaffe and the navy, and then work with the three chiefs of general staff, but with a command structure in which the dominant position would fall to the army. At the same time, the Führer must be made to understand that he has to listen to his advisers and no longer try to direct everything himself. His job, as the Führer and supreme commander, consists above all in directing the foreign policy of the war, including policies in the occupied regions, and in the management of arms and the economy. On the level of the military, his role should, however, be limited to basic political and military decisions. It is Kluge's job to present this issue of military command to Hitler. I cannot do it myself, because of the enemy propaganda that is characterizing me as a man who wants to take supreme command."

Concerning a potential peace agreement, Manstein also noted that he had let Gersdorff know that every opportunity for negotiation should be utilized, but the subject should be left exclusively to the Führer's domain: "The army has strictly nothing to do with such matters. It took an oath of allegiance and, as a result, it has a duty to obey. It will thus be the institution that will always remain faithful. Any notion that the military leadership is involved in issues of political leadership would signify that it had abandoned the principle of military subordination, something to which it is constantly opposed. In any case, Hitler is the only man who has the trust of the people and the soldiers, and they believe in him. No one else could have the advantage of such confidence. Nor is there anyone else who could replace him if he were to become ill, for example."[531]

Manstein was clearly a soldier and wanted to be nothing else. Educated in the purest military tradition of the Prussian officers' corps, he was held to loyalty and obedience in relation to the legal direction of the state, as well as in relation to Hitler, the only man who, in his view, had the trust of the people and the German soldiers. Between his obligations to conscience and to obedience, he had thus chosen the second.[532]

The Rommel-Kluge-Manstein meeting

A few weeks earlier, on July 13, 1943, Field Marshals Manstein, Kluge, and Rommel had been summoned by Hitler to his Rastenburg head-quarters in East Prussia. In the company of Colonel General Zeitzler, the army's chief of staff, the Führer wanted to review the situation pertaining to Operation Citadel, which had commenced on July 5, 1943, and the Anglo-American landings in Sicily, which had taken place five days later.

After the meeting, Manstein, Kluge, and Rommel went to the living room of the guest house to have drinks and eat dinner. The three field marshals again discussed the military situation, but they did not agree on conclusions drawn from the battle of Kursk and the Allied amphibious operation in Italy. Contrary to Kluge and Rommel, who were witnessing the approach of military defeat on the horizon, Manstein still believed in the possibility of achieving a tie on the Eastern Front, thereupon freeing up forces to fend off a large-scale invasion by the Anglo-Americans in Western Europe.

When Kluge rose to go to bed, he issued some final words: "Manstein, the end will be disastrous. And I will reiterate what I have already said to you earlier: I am prepared to serve under your orders." In his courteous way, Manstein kindly thanked him for what he considered to be a fine compliment, but did not pursue it any more.

In the living room, Rommel, Manstein, and his adjutant Stahlberg were the only ones who remained. Finishing his glass of wine, Rommel all of a sudden leveled with Manstein: "The end of the war will be a total catastrophe. If the Allies were also to land in the Balkans, and in the end on the Atlantic coast, the entire house would then collapse." But Manstein replied that they had not yet gotten to that dramatic point. Indeed, he assured Rommel that the Führer would willingly abandon the supreme command of military operations before it became too late. In his unrelenting way, Rommel hurled back: "He will never voluntarily step down from the supreme command. Clearly, I know him much better than you, *Herr* von Manstein." Manstein rose to wish Rommel a good night, and the famous "Desert Fox" did the same, before adding: "I am also ready to serve under your orders." "Good night," responded Manstein while heading towards the hall. At the same time, Rommel grabbed Stahlberg's sleeve and declared to him: "Your field marshal is a fine strategist. I admire him, but he is deluded. See to it that he does not forget what I just said to him."[533]

Contrary to Manstein, the conspirators and their sympathizers were not full of illusions. For them, the war had been lost since the Wehrmacht's defeat before Moscow in December 1941, or at least at Stalingrad in the winter of 1942–43, and they believed Hitler would never willingly give up the supreme military command, even less so political power. But Manstein would naively hope, until the very end of the war, that Hitler would call upon his services, entrusting to him the entire responsibility of conducting military operations to save Germany from an otherwise inevitable defeat. His assumption of the supreme military command was precisely, in his mind, the prerequisite to snatch from the hands of the Soviets a drawn war and thus a peace agreement. Such ambition to become Germany's savior and to enter into history as such was testimony to his enormous self-confidence and exceptional pride in his tactical and strategic abilities. It was an assurance that was doubtless reinforced by the fact that field marshals of the caliber of Kluge and Rommel, senior to him, were ready to serve under his orders.

Manstein: Supreme commander in the East or generalissimo of all the theaters of operations?

Rommel was not incorrect to assert that Manstein was deluded to think that the Führer would decide either sooner or later to voluntarily give up the supreme command of the Wehrmacht. On two other occasions, in the summer of 1943 and the winter of 1944, Manstein would ask Hitler, in vain, to hand over the supervision of operations, or at least those on the Eastern Front. Despite Hitler's categorical refusal each time, Manstein would continue to hope, with disconcerting naivety, that the latter would end up changing his mind as soon as the military situation left him with no other logical choice.

On September 3, 1943, following the critical worsening of the situation on the Eastern Front, Manstein went by plane, in the company of Field Marshal Kluge, to Hitler's East Prussia headquarters in order to emphasize to the Führer the necessity of creating a single high command, which would thus eliminate the duality of the OKW (the Western, Scandinavian, and Mediterranean Fronts) and the OKH (the Eastern Front).

Upon his arrival in Rastenburg, Manstein, supported by Kluge, asked Hitler to entrust the leadership of military operations of all the theaters to a chief of general staff who would answer to him, and to appoint a commander in chief specifically for the Eastern Front. Even if he were to remain, by virtue of this proposal, nominally supreme commander, Hitler was hardly willing to create a single high command that would be overseen by a chief of general staff. He was in no way inclined to give up direct supervision of operations, not even on the Eastern Front, by appointing another man to do it.

By once again trying to convince Hitler of the need to turn the conduct of military operations over to a professional general who was qualified in the subject, Manstein, this particular time, did not conceal his ambition to assume such duties. Without beating around the bush, he proposed himself as a candidate to occupy the position of overall commander in the East: "My Führer, if you were to think of me, I guarantee to you that I would succeed [...] in stabilizing the front." Hitler responded that he alone had the determination necessary to overcome such a series of crises. Once again, the field marshal suffered a bitter disappointment in view of the Führer's refusal.[534] Yet he did not become overly discouraged.

On January 4, 1944, when Manstein went to the Führer's headquarters to describe the rapid deterioration of the situation of Army Group South, he asked to speak to Hitler privately, along with Zeitzler, chief of the OKH general staff. Reluctantly, as if he did not know what he was in for, Hitler accepted. As soon as the room was empty, Manstein explained to him that the unfortunate position of the *Ostheer* did not result solely from the enemy's unquestionable superiority, but also from the way in which it was led. Already cold, Hitler quickly turned icy, piercing the field marshal with an intense stare. Persevering, without letting himself be intimidated by the volatile atmosphere, Manstein declared that the Wehrmacht's method of command could no longer be sustained, and that it was necessary for him to revive his proposal, already presented on two occasions, according to which the Führer needed a genuinely responsible chief of general staff upon whose advice he could rely for the conduct of military operations. As a result, he needed to appoint to the Eastern Front, as was already the case for Italy and the West, a commander in chief who had absolute authority over the general management of the war.

As in the request that he had already presented twice to Hitler, Manstein did not conceal his ambition to have himself designated commander in the East with a free hand to act within the scope of the general strategic objectives, like Field Marshal Rundstedt in the West and Field Marshal Kesselring in Italy. By having full responsibility over military operations on the Soviet front, Manstein was hoping to be able to maneuver in such a way to achieve a draw with the enemy, which would permit Hitler to negotiate a peace agreement with Stalin. For this, Hitler nevertheless had to agree to abandon his military command in order to hand it over to Manstein.

But Hitler did not want to hear such talk. He regarded himself as the only one qualified to hold in his hands all the powers of the German Reich and, because of this, the ability to effectively lead the war. Likewise, he was the only one in a position to determine which forces to utilize in the various theaters of operations and to assign the appropriate operations. In addition, he emphasized that Göring would never accept orders from someone else. Regarding the matter of appointing a commander in chief on the Eastern Front, he responded to Manstein that no one else could have the same authority as he already held: "I cannot even get the field marshals to obey me! Can you imagine that they would perhaps obey you more willingly?" On the verge of insolence, Manstein retorted that no one would ever disobey his orders. Upon which Hitler, containing his anger all while being clearly affected by his field marshal's insubordination, brought the discussion to an end.[535]

Once again, Manstein had failed in his attempt to persuade the Führer to modify the system of the military high command. Not only did he not have any chance of being appointed commander in chief of the Eastern theater of operations, his outspokenness and personal ambitions had aroused doubts in Hitler's mind as to the necessity of his overseeing the leadership of Army Group South. Meanwhile, Hitler's order to Manstein could not have been any clearer: there was no question of implementing the slightest tactical retreat.

The last Tresckow-Manstein meeting

The conspirators were unable to pull into their ranks any of the active field marshals. There was of course Field Marshal Witzleben, former commander in chief in France and one of the first conspirators, but he was on leave and did not have any troops under his command. Field Marshal Rundstedt, commander in chief of the Western Front, was invited to join the conspirators, but he refused to abandon his oath of allegiance to the Führer. Like Field Marshal Kluge, the very popular Field Marshal Rommel lent an ear to the conspirators, but without really being won over by them. As to the idea that Field Marshal Manstein could have been taken part in the resistance, it was wiped out in the autumn of 1943.

On November 25, 1943, arriving at the Second Army's headquarters, to which he had just been appointed chief of staff with the rank of major general, Tresckow took the opportunity, while on his way, to visit Manstein. If he could hardly count on the field marshal's active participation in the plot against Hitler and his regime, he nevertheless hoped to gain his moral support, which he deemed essential to ensure order among the troops in case the coup d'état was successful. But Manstein was in no way convinced. In his opinion, a coup d'état would weaken the morale of the troops and destroy any opportunity for the Reich to reach a peace agreement. In short, an assassination of the head of state would only provoke a collapse of the front and the occupation of Germany by the Russians. Convinced that the Führer would yield to him sooner or later the supervision of operations in the East, he ended the discussion by calling Tresckow a defeatist. Witnessing the conversation, staff officer Blumröder understood Manstein to say to Tresckow: "Tresckow, stop bothering me with your stupid peace politics."

Tresckow's visit with Manstein was the final attempt by the conspiracy to win the greatest commander of the Wehrmacht over to its cause. The latter would obviously not support in any way a coup d'état. Even if those in the Wehrmacht had come to terms with the idea, the disappointment among the ranks of the opposition was great. When the field marshal was dismissed from his duties by Hitler on March 30, 1944, Beck made the following comment: "Even though I held him in high esteem for a very long time, I do not at all regret Manstein's discharge."[536]

The Manstein case was broached once again in the spring of 1944, when Lieutenant Stahlberg paid a social visit to his friend, Major General Hans Oster at Bendlerstrasse, in Berlin. During the course of their conversation, the chief of the *Abwehr* intelligence service spoke in contempt of the field marshals who, in his view, had enslaved themselves to a corporal, to the detriment of their better judgment, out of sole concern for their careers. Stahlberg, however, did not see his chief this way. In his eyes, Manstein had the temperament of a Moltke and was unable to resign himself to admitting that his expertise and military talents had been taken advantage of by Hitler. In fact, he was biding his time, declared his adjutant. When Oster asked him if the field marshal had been informed of the extent of the massive extermination of the Jews, Stahlberg responded that Manstein considered the briefings on Auschwitz and the other concentration camps as being so improbable that he quite simply refused to believe it.

A few days later, Stahlberg had a similar discussion with Tresckow, on leave at his Babelsberg residence. They spoke of Manstein's loyalty and obedience with respect to Hitler, as well as his inability to recognize that the latter was not only a poor strategist, but also a man completely lacking in scruples and conscience. When Tresckow asked Stahlberg who Manstein would side with if Hitler were killed, he stated that the field marshal would be wherever the law required him to be. Like Oster, Tresckow also asked him if Manstein had been informed of the magnitude of the extermination of the Jews, to which he responded yes, before adding that his chief refused to take into consideration news that he considered as unlikely.[537]

"So it will be, my Führer!" Manstein's declaration of loyalty to Hitler

Far from being seduced by the conspirators' plans, Field Marshal Manstein would reconfirm his unconditional loyalty to the Führer on two occasions during the winter of 1944, the first time on January 27, and the second on March 19.

On January 27, Hitler convened at his headquarters one hundred of his military chiefs, including all the army group commanders of the Eastern Front. He spoke to them for quite some time about the necessity to inculcate the army with the spirit of National Socialism, all the while ensuring them that he could never harbor such a lowly idea as surrender. He thus demanded from his generals not only their loyalty, but absolute support. At the climax of his long-winded speech, he declared: "If, in the worst case, I would ever be abandoned as supreme chief, I must have around me, as a last line of defense, the entire officers' corps, swords drawn, creating a blockade at my side." At which time he was interrupted, which had not happened to him since the Munich beer halls. "So it will be, my Führer!" exclaimed Field Marshal Manstein, who was in the very first row. Visibly disconcerted by such an unexpected reply, Hitler lost his chain of thought. He threw him an icy glance while commenting: "Very well. If this is the case, it will be impossible for us to lose this war; never, whatever happens. For the nation will then go to war with the necessary vigor. I will take note of it with great pleasure, Field Marshal von Manstein!" He immediately regained his composure, asserting all the same the necessity of completing the National Socialist education of the officers' corps.[538]

Taken literally, Manstein's exclamation could be perceived as a sign of fanatical submission towards Hitler. However, as the field marshal himself indicated after the war, his implicit sense was much more critical. It was because he had had the feeling that the Führer had undermined his honor and that of his fellow officers by insinuating that their loyalty could be challenged. "This exclamation naturally had nothing to do with our personal sentiment regarding National Socialist training or Hitler himself," he wrote in his *Memoirs*. "It was simply meant to show that we did not need to be given a moral lesson, even by him."[539]

Hitler, for his part, was hoping that the field marshal had wanted to reassure him of his loyalty. But Martin Bormann, chief of the Reich Chancellery, and his adjutants said to him that the generals had interpreted it otherwise. At the worst, the Führer understood Manstein's interruption as a way of criticizing his mistrust towards the generals. The meeting that he had with him on the preceding January 4 still weighed heavily upon him. He had not pardoned his criticism of the military high command and thus his own method of leading operations. Nor had he appreciated the memo that Manstein had subsequently sent him in which he did not mince words regarding his command. Still stunned, he summoned Manstein a few minutes after his speech and, in Field Marshal Keitel's presence, forbade him from such outbursts in the future. "*Herr* Field Marshal, I will not stand for your interrupting me when I am speaking to the generals. You would not tolerate it from one of your subordinates." Clearly irritated, he added a gratuitous insult: "Furthermore, you sent me a memo on the situation a few days ago. It will be without a doubt useful, recorded in the archives, to vindicate you before history." Cut to the quick, the commander in chief of Army

Group South replied: "The letters that I personally sent to you are, quite obviously, are not recorded in our archives. This memo was sent through the mail directly to the chief of general staff. Once more, forgive me for using an English expression. Faced with the interpretation which you are implying, I will merely say that I *myself* am a gentleman."[540] After a long silence, Hitler thanked Manstein and ended the meeting on this discordant note. Manstein's days were clearly numbered.

In his diary, on January 27, 1944, General Schmundt noted: "The Führer gave a very serious speech before his field marshals and generals of the three branches of the Wehrmacht at the conclusion of a meeting of National Socialist leaders. During the talk, Field Marshal von Manstein took the liberty of intervening. Following this interruption and the various recent tensions, the question of replacing Field Marshal von Manstein in his role as commander will be reassessed."[541]

Even though the situation of the Wehrmacht on the Eastern Front was critical, the field marshals from every branch were summoned to the Berghof at the end of the winter. Among them were Manstein, Kleist, Weichs, Busch, and Rommel. Within the context of a curious, small ceremony held on March 19, the men were witness to the presentation to Hitler by their most senior member, Field Marshal Rundstedt, of a declaration of loyalty that they had all signed. It was General Schmundt, the Führer's primary adjutant, who had gathered their signatures while making his rounds to the various theaters of operations.

The idea of thus reinforcing Hitler's trust in the Wehrmacht had come from Goebbels and was discretely achieved by Schmundt without the Führer's prior knowledge. He had been prompted by the subversive propaganda coming out of Moscow by General Walther von Seydlitz-Kurzbach and other officers taken prisoner by the Russians in Stalingrad. Even if such propaganda only had a limited effect, Goebbels' and Schmundt's intention was to dispel Hitler's mistrust of his field marshals and to rekindle relations which the January 27 conference in Rastenburg, interrupted by Manstein, had revealed as icy. That, at the height of the war, the military leaders believed it worthwhile to sign a declaration of loyalty to their supreme commander and head of state was not only surprising, but remarkable in itself.

Such reasoning did little to conceal a certain uneasiness. This was most likely what Field Marshal Manstein was thinking, when he became the last to place his signature on the document in question. As he stated to Schmundt, he had the feeling that such a declaration was entirely superfluous coming from a soldier who had already offered his oath of allegiance to the Führer in August 1934, after the death of the elder Field Marshal Hindenburg. But with the other field marshals having signed it, he had no other choice but to imitate them, for a refusal would have equated to acknowledging sympathy for the propaganda of Seydlitz-Kurzbach. In any case, Hitler appeared touched by the ceremony and was particularly satisfied to see that Manstein, the most critical of his field marshals, had signed the declaration. Concerning this declaration of loyalty, Goebbels indicated to his Führer that he was "quite categorically, very explicitly, and totally National Socialist." This was clearly one of those rare moments of harmony in Hitler's relations with his most senior military chiefs after the summer of 1941.[542]

Manstein's dismissal

Less than a week later, on March 25, Field Marshal Manstein was back at the Berghof. The First Panzer Army was being threatened with encirclement by Soviet troops that had broken through from Ternopol towards the Dniester River. Its situation was so critical that a Russian tank army had cut off its lines of communication to the west, while another army was already advancing on the western banks of the Dniester. To the commander in chief of Army Group South, First Panzer Army had to force a breakthrough to the west, to restore its lines of communication with the Fourth Panzer Army north of the Carpathians. Perhaps it could then succeed at cutting off the resupply of the two Soviet tank armies that had broken through to its rear.

But there could be no question of withdrawing it to the south, beyond the Dniester, as General Hans Valentin Hube, its commander, suggested. Manstein recognized that this was the easiest path at this time. To the west, it would be necessary to open a path through two Soviet tank armies, while to the south it could still escape without meeting any resistance. However, it was considered absolutely essential that the army regain contact with General Erhard Raus' Fourth Panzer Army to the west. Otherwise, the enemy would be able to break through towards the Galicia River, to the north of the Carpathians. Moreover, by marching towards the Dniester, it would be on the road to ruin, for it did not possess the necessary supplies in order to cross the river on such a wide front. While trying to cross on the few remaining permanent bridges, it would lose the greater portion of its heavy materials to Soviet air attacks. Since the enemy was itself already advancing to the south of the Dniester, First Panzer Army would sooner or later find itself crushed between these two units and the two tank armies that had outflanked it. A maneuver to the south would likely end in a new encirclement, and in turn the destruction, of Hube's panzer army. For these various reasons, Manstein thus ordered a breakout to the west. But for such a maneuver to be successful, Fourth Panzer Army had to also pressure the Soviets, and as a result had to be quickly reinforced. For this, the Führer's agreement was essential, for the reinforcements that he needed to assist the First Panzer Army could only be removed from another section of the front.

Hitler refused to grant his field marshal's request. It was impossible for him, he asserted, to remove units from other sectors of the Russian front, and even less so from the West, so long as there remained the threat of an invasion. It was equally impossible for him, for political reasons, to draw from forces stationed at that time in Hungary. Furthermore, he declared, if First Panzer Army tried to reconnect with other German forces in the west, it was still absolutely not allowed to abandon the front that it was holding to the east. A vigorous discussion then began between the two men in which the Führer held Manstein personally responsible for the unfortunate position of his army group. The field marshal replied that if he had immediately been allocated the reinforcements he had been requesting for such a long time for his northern wing, or if he had been granted complete freedom of action on his southern wing, his army group would not be in this situation. The noon military conference thus came to an end and the continuation of deliberations was postponed until the evening. Exasperated, Manstein informed General Schmundt, the Führer's adjutant, of his intention to resign from his command if Hitler did not approve his proposals.

At that night's military meeting, when the discussion recommenced, Hitler, contrary to all expectations, expressed a change of opinion. For what reason? Under whose influence? Had he simply pondered the issue before reconsidering his views? His motive remains unclear. In any case, he now approved Manstein's intentions concerning First Panzer Army's breakout towards the west and decided, not without regret, to reinforce

Fourth Panzer Army with an SS panzer corps (the newly formed 9th and 10th SS Panzer Divisions), as well as the 100th Chasseurs Division and the 367th Infantry Division taken from Hungary. The field marshal returned to his headquarters momentarily satisfied.[543] These fresh units would allow him to foil the trap set by Soviet commander in chief Marshal Zhukov, which would have led to the destruction of 22 German divisions, among which were a few of Germany's best armored divisions, a total of 200,000 men. The First Panzer Army escaped the noose that was tightening more and more around it by reversing its march and rearranging its units in such a way that it was able to meet up with the reinforcements that were coming to its aid through the rear of the Soviet forces that had been surprised by the brilliant maneuver. Without knowing it, however, Manstein had just achieved his last victory. Hitler had had more than enough of working with this gifted but obstinate soldier. Six days later, he would relieve him of his command.

Hitler was annoyed at having made concessions, particularly after his initial refusal before a large audience, to a commander who, from his perspective, had been a troublemaker during the preceding weeks and, moreover, ineffective in the management of operations. It was not that Manstein had ever been defeated on the battlefield, but the continuous loss of territory in the East—albeit in the face of enorous odds—was viewed by Hitler as a failure. Apart from the disasters of the air war which did not affect the position of Reich Field Marshal Göring, his old political friend and commander of the Luftwaffe, Hitler invariably reacted to every great military setback by laying responsibility on the relevant commander. His practice was to replace the "failed" commander with another who was likely to boost the morale of the troops and to reinvigorate their will and fighting spirit. The time had thus come for him to part with Manstein, just as with another field marshal, Kleist, who, two days after his colleague, came to the Berghof to finally obtain authorization to withdraw Army Group A from the Bug, onto the coast of the Black Sea, towards the lower Dniester.

On March 30, the Führer's personal plane, a four-engine Condor, picked up Field Marshals Manstein and Kleist to take them to the Berghof. Upon their arrival, they met with Colonel General Zeitzler, who informed them that the Führer wanted to relieve them of their command. He also confided to Manstein that, during recent conversations at the Berghof, Göring, Himmler, and most likely Keitel, had set Hitler up against him, which had certainly contributed towards inciting him to drop not only him but Kleist. He added that, after learning of the decision, he had also immediately requested to be relieved of his duties as chief of the OKH general staff, because he had always agreed with Manstein and could not honorably remain if he were to leave. But his request had been summarily rejected, just as his subsequent attempt in writing was denied.

General Schmundt saw to it that the two field marshals were dismissed with dignity in order to prevent them from having any resentment toward Hitler. Manstein and Kleist were replaced, respectively, by Colonel General Walter Model and General Ferdinand Schorner, both tough and energetic commanders, and favorites of the Führer. He deemed them both perfect to arouse the fervor of the troops and fill them with the strict fighting spirit of National Socialism. Model, who had halted the collapse of Army Group North after the liberation of Leningrad, and Schorner, who was close to the party and had been recommended by Himmler, were both staunch Nazis who were to dedicate their abilities to bringing their troops back to servile submission under the Führer's orders. At the same time, Army Groups South and A were renamed "Army Group Northern Ukraine" and "Southern Ukraine."[544]

During their meeting, Hitler paid homage to Manstein by adding the swords to his Knight's Cross. But he declared of him that, in the East, the period of large-scale operations, in which he particularly excelled, was now over. What was henceforth needed was no longer a master of mobile warfare and armored breakthroughs, but a new commander who was an expert in static defensive strategy, who would know how to fire up the enthusiasm of his troops in combat so that they would fight tenaciously for each foot of ground. He considered Colonel General Model perfectly qualified for this new stage of the war, claiming that he would "dash around the divisions" to inspire them. Manstein responded to this with the only icy note during the conversation, saying, "The Army Group's divisions had long been giving of their best under my command and that no one else could get them to give anything more." Nevertheless, he agreed that Model was a proper choice for his replacement, given his skill at obstinate defense, and especially now that the crisis involving First Panzer Army had been solved.

Hitler let it be understood that he would call upon Manstein's services in the near future, or in other words as soon as the Germans could once again launch large-scale offensives, and that he should remain from this point on available to him. He even held out the possibility of appointing him commander in chief of the Western Front, a position still held by Field Marshal Rundstedt. He then wished him the best for an upcoming operation on his right eye and a speedy recovery. Throughout their conversation Hitler appeared courteous, even cordial, and assured Manstein that there was no dissension between them. He clearly did not want to count him among his enemies.[545]

On the evening of March 30, the OKH sent a telex to Army Group South to inform it that its commander in chief, Field Marshal Manstein, was on leave of absence for health reasons. It is true that he suffered from cataracts and that he had been postponing for an operation for quite some time, but the suffering had not yet become so unbearable that he could no longer fulfill his duties. In fact, his dismissal was due to other reasons, notably for a series of altercations with Hitler concerning the management of the war.

Manstein certainly knew that Göring and Himmler had been working towards his downfall for some time. He nevertheless attributed the main reason for his discharge to the fact that Hitler had been forced, on March 25, to concede to his reviews, shortly after having refuted them in front of a large audience. To this he could have added the January 27, 1944 episode, during which he had interrupted the Führer during his speech. All things considered, his dismissal was the logical conclusion of an extended series of disputes. "No one else has clashed so much with Hitler than Manstein," declared Kielmansegg after the war. Blumentritt also asserted that, convinced of the accuracy of his operational theories, the field marshal did not hesitate on occasion to characterize those of the Führer as nonsense, even in the presence of other officers during military conferences.[546] His discharge was also due to the fact that Hitler was insisting more than ever that the Wehrmacht must in no way retreat, which meant commanders not specializing in maneuver, but at holding the front at all costs. To the Führer, generals were only inclined to maneuver in order to stage more successful retreats.

That Hitler waited so long to abandon Manstein's services is clear testimony to his high opinion of the field marshal's operational abilities. Indeed, on several earlier occasions he had juggled with the idea of dismissing him. However, each time he decided otherwise, not believing himself to be in a position to manage without his military knowledge, by which he was always profoundly impressed.

When Goebbels, Göring, and Himmler exerted pressure on him in February 1943, in order to obtain Manstein's dismissal, Hitler restrained himself from agreement, fearing that the departure of his most gifted commander would further inflame the military situation. On March 2, 1943, Goebbels noted in his diary: "The Führer was in fact intending, during his trip to the southern front, to replace Manstein. But, for the moment, he had not achieved this desire." In the autumn of 1943, Hitler shared the almost pathological distrust that Goebbels and Himmler felt towards Manstein after his failure to restore a solid defensive line on the Dnieper. And for Hitler, such a failure was primarily attributable to the field marshal's lack of political direction or worldview (*Weltanschauung*)—and not to the fatigue of the troops, to Hitler's contradictory orders, or to the inadequacy of supplies, particularly fuel. However, Manstein was not relieved of the command of Army Group South.

On October 19, 1943, Goebbels wrote that Manstein "is anything but a partisan of the National Socialist regime. But, for the moment, we are unable to carry out anything against him, this is at least what the Führer claims." The following week, Goebbels noted: "The Führer is expecting to find an immediate solution to a personal crisis in Army Group South [...]. He wants to grant Colonel General Model Field Marshal Manstein's position and to entrust to him the command of the army group." But, two months later, he remarked in his diary about his growing impatience, because the Führer had still not relieved Manstein of his command. "He is called," Goebbels wrote concerning Manstein, "[...] the in and out field marshal."[547]

Himmler, Göring, and Goebbels, who for quite some time had all been suspecting Manstein of wanting to take command of the German Army, undoubtedly succeeded in March 1944 at convincing Hitler to remove him once and for all. His dismissal was to their great relief, moreover, for they had feared that the Führer would eventually acquiesce to Manstein's demands by granting him complete responsibility of military operations. This would have given rise to a new center of military power, and equally so political power, which could have competed with their own positions.[548]

That the American weekly news magazine *Time* devoted its January 10, 1944 cover story to Manstein could have only further aroused their jealousy and mistrust. Indeed, in this issue, the title of which, to say the least, was evocative—"Field Marshal Fritz Erich von Manstein: Retreat may be Masterly, but Victory is in the Opposite Direction"—the analysis concerned Manstein's exceptional military knowledge and his numerous achievements on the Eastern Front, particularly during the winter of 1943–44. The field marshal's relationship with his Führer was also discussed under the subtitle: "A German Pétain?" Faced with the prospect of imminent defeat, as was mentioned in the article, the highly conservative Prussian military caste might be tempted to get rid of Hitler and demand a Junker like Field Marshal Manstein to play the same role in Germany as Marshal Pétain in Vichy France. "Despite defeat and desperation, the German citizen of today has no greater military idol than Manstein."[549]

Even if he had discharged his field marshal, Hitler continued to have a great amount of esteem for his remarkable military talent, as Goebbels' remark in his diary on April 18, 1944, proves: "The Führer has absolutely nothing against Manstein, as I had initially assumed. Of course, he does not consider him as an enthusiastic army chief who is able to greatly inspire the troops, but rather as a shrewdly intelligent tactician. He even envisions relying upon him whenever we will once again be in a position of launching offensives. But there still remains a good amount of time before arriving at this point and when this does occur, we will then dissuade the Führer of this."[550]

In the spring of 1944, shortly after he relieved Manstein of his command, Hitler expressed to Jodl his own opinion of the field marshal: "In my eyes Manstein has a tremendous talent for operations. There's no doubt about that. And if I had an army of, say, twenty divisions at full strength and in peacetime conditions, I couldn't think of a better commander for them than Manstein. He knows how to handle them, and will do it. He would move like lightening—but always under the condition that he has first-class material, petrol, plenty of ammunition. If something breaks down [...] he doesn't get things done. If I got hold of another army today I'm not at all sure that I wouldn't employ Manstein because he is certainly one of our most competent officers [...]. [He] can operate with divisions as long as they are in good shape. If the divisions are roughly handled I have to take them away from him in a hurry; he can't handle such a situation."[551]

If the compliments expressed by Hitler with respect to Manstein were justified, it was not the same, however, for his criticisms. In fact, beginning in November 1942, the field marshal was almost always required to fight on the Eastern Front with units that were incomplete, numerically inferior to the enemy, and often in a sorry state. By making such unfounded remarks about Manstein, Hitler appears to have been looking to justify his decision to bring an end to his services.

Kleist was received by Hitler immediately after Manstein and was released in a similar manner. When the two dismissed field marshals left the Berghof, their successors, Colonel General Model and General Schorner, were already waiting at the door. On April 2, Manstein officially handed his command over to Model. The escape of the First Panzer Army and its regrouping with the Fourth Panzer Army between the Carpathians and the Pripyat swamps had become certain, even though they still needed to fight tough battles. On April 5, Raus' panzers were able to move to the attack and, on April 9, Hube's armored units were liberated.

Soon enough, it was to appear clear that the change in command and name would not be enough to avoid a German collapse. The new commanders proved to be no more capable of stopping the inexorable advance of the Red Army than Manstein and Kleist. Despite the Führer's repeated directives to hold the front at all costs, Model's forces were driven out of Galicia and the Carpathians, whereas Schorner had to abandon Odessa and then the entire Crimea. When the battles ended with the spring 1944 *rasputitsa*, the Germans had retreated, in certain sectors, more than 900 kilometers since the beginning of the year. Between March and mid-April, the German southern wing retreated a distance of 220 kilometers.[552]

When he left his Lemberg (Lvov) headquarters on April 3, Manstein was not thinking that his military career had just come to an end. At this particular moment, he was still hoping, of course with a surprising naivety, that the Führer would decide sooner or later to call upon his services by entrusting him with the leadership of military operations over all the theaters of operations, or at least over that of the East, in order to spare Germany a total military collapse. After the operation on his right eye, he would furthermore do everything possible to recover as quickly as possible so that he would be ready for when his Führer would call upon him. But his dream of one day becoming chief of general staff or commander in chief was not to be realized.

During the sixteen months he had commanded Army Group Don and Army Group South, Manstein had led an orderly and methodical retreat of nearly 1,300 kilometers on a front that was at times some 800 kilometers wide. Indeed, from the steppes of the Don all the way to Galicia, he had known how to preserve cohesion within his command.[553] This was a veritable achievement in itself. And even more so if one considers that he had been able to spare his troops from the fate of Stalingrad, by simultaneously fighting against an enemy greatly superior in number and against Hitler's stubbornness with the idea of fighting for every inch of ground. Contrary to Hitler's belief in the omnipotence of pure willpower, the field marshal believed—like the majority of the other German military chiefs—that success could only be achieved through mobile operations, the only area where the superiority of German officers and soldiers could be applied with full effect. If he had not succeeded, for the most part, at imposing his perspective, and if, consequently, his hopes of finally defeating the enemy were not accomplished, Manstein nevertheless achieved positive results. The Red Army was indeed unable to complete the encirclement of the entire southern wing of the German front, even though the operational situation and the enemy's enormous numerical superiority had given it the upper hand.

In short, Manstein's series of defensive successes achieved at six-to-one odds, occasionally greater, after the encirclement of Paulus' Sixth Army in Stalingrad, represented a remarkable achievement. It demonstrated the extent to which it would have been possible for the *Ostheer* to prolong the war and wear the Soviets out, if its defensive strategy had been at the level of its tactical skill. But its chances were compromised by Hitler's insistence upon not undertaking any sort of retreat without his authorization, an authorization that he would only issue under the most extreme reluctance and often only when an initial problem had become a severe crisis. The army chiefs who took such initiative without the Führer's prerequisite authorization were threatened with court martial, even if it were a matter of withdrawing a small battalion from a dangerously isolated position. Hitler's slogan was always the same: it was necessary to hold one's ground while fighting in place. Such a rigid principle had certainly allowed the Wehrmacht to overcome the crisis of the first Russian winter, but it became fatal once the German troops began to lack sufficient resources to remain in control of vast Soviet territories, along with the fact that the enemy continually improved its own skill, command, and mobility. He denied the German commanders the essential flexibility in order to evade, regroup, and implement the doctrine of maneuver so that they could inflict blows, not simply absorb them. Manstein's counteroffensives in February–March 1943, between the Dnieper and the Donetz, which permitted him to recapture Kharkov and Bielgorod, and those of November in the Kiev sector, which made possible the re-conquest of Jitomir and Korosten, had demonstrated the extent to which such a doctrine could prove to be extremely effective if it were well implemented.

The conduct of operations involving "backhand" attacks or counteroffensives, after allowing the Soviets to commit forces first, such as Manstein had proposed on several occasions during the winter and spring of 1943, would have forced Hitler to accept enormous risks in other theaters and on other sectors of the Eastern Front, as well as significant political and economic disadvantages. It was, however, the only way to succeed at exhausting the offensive power of the Russians in 1943, and thus to open the path to a political compromise, an option which Hitler was clearly in no way willing to embrace.

The July 20, 1944 putsch: Manstein's search for an alibi

The bomb attack of July 20, 1944, perpetrated against Hitler by Colonel Stauffenberg, is too well known for us to dwell on here. However, after he came out almost unscathed, the Führer, overcome in a fit of rage and with an unquenchable thirst for vengeance, assigned *Reichsführer-SS* Himmler to tirelessly hunt down all those who had dared, in any manner, to conspire against him. He demanded swift and implacable action. For traitors, there was no question of granting a soldier's honorable death before a firing squad. They would be dismissed from the Wehrmacht, then tried as civilians and executed within two hours of their sentencing. He thus issued the order to create an Army Court of Honor to weed from the army all those who had been involved in the conspiracy. As for those that the People's Court would later condemn to death, they would be hanged in prison as common criminals.

The investigations and the executions by the Gestapo continued non-stop until the final days of the war, and the trials of the People's Court, presided over by the fanatical Nazi judge Roland Freisler, lasted for months. With a few exceptions, primarily due to luck—particularly for Lieutenant Colonel Gersdorff or Captain Schlabrendorff—anyone who had remotely participated in the plot, from either the civilian or the military side, thus some 200 people overall, were arrested, tortured, and executed. Field Marshal Witzleben, Colonel General Hoepner (unemployed ever since the Führer had relieved him of the command of the 4th Panzer Group in January 1942), General Erich Fellgiebel (chief of communications for the OKW), General Paul von Hase (commander of Berlin), and Colonel Schulze-Büttger were sentenced to death and hanged. On the eve of capitulation, Admiral Wilhelm Canaris, victim of his own ambiguous behavior, and Major General Oster were each executed in their internment camp. For having blown as much hot as cold, Colonel General Fromm was also executed under orders from Himmler, who immediately succeeded him at the head of the reserves.

Other officers chose to commit suicide, such as Colonel General Beck, Major General Tresckow, and Field Marshal Kluge. The latter, if he had not committed suicide, would apparently have been arrested by the Gestapo for having lent a willing ear to the conspirators, even more so since he had been denounced in the testimony of certain conspirators who had been broken down by torture. For his part, General Stülpnagel, military governor of France, was hanged after his failed suicide attempt. Finally, Field Marshal Rommel, like Kluge implicated by the confessions of various conspirators, was arrested and accused of high treason. Hitler, however, let one of his favorite field marshals, one of the most popular in all Germany, to commit suicide. He even granted him a national funeral with complete military honors. In order to avoid scandal, Rommel's supposed participation in the conspiracy was concealed from the public, and his death was attributed to wounds inflicted by enemy aircraft on July 17, 1944.

Despite the small number of generals who participated in the conspiracy, the officers' corps of the German Army emerged humiliated from the purge. It found itself obliged to remain passive while some of its members were thrown into Gestapo prisons or executed after a semblance of a trial before the People's Court. In such an unprecedented situation and in spite of its secular traditions, the officers' corps did not close ranks. To the contrary, it sought to regain the Führer's confidence by being party to the purge. Field Marshal Rundstedt even agreed to preside over the Army Court of Honor created by Hitler on August 2,

1944, in order to expel from the Wehrmacht all officers suspected of complicity in the putsch, which would allow him to refuse them a court martial and to defer them to the People's Court. Not having the authorization to hear an accused officer present his own defense, the Army Court of Honor gave its verdict exclusively on the supposed evidence provided by the Gestapo. However, Rundstedt did not protest against such a restriction, no more than the other judges, who were all high-ranking officers, including Field Marshal Keitel and Colonel General Guderian.[554]

Guderian, who had replaced Colonel General Zeitzler in the position of chief of general staff of the OKH the day after the assassination attempt, confessed in his *Memoirs* that he had received orders to sit on the court, which he reluctantly did and as seldom as possible. He even brought up the troubles of conscience caused by such an unpleasant job, which consisted in sending dozens of colleagues to certain execution, after having them demoted by removal from the army.[555] And yet he did even more. As chief of general staff, he drafted two sensational items of agenda in order to express to the supreme chief of the German armed forces the unshakeable loyalty of the officers' corps.

The first, put forth on July 23, 1944, accused the conspirators of being "a small number of officers among whom some were reserves, who had lost all bravery and, out of cowardice and weakness, had preferred to commit themselves to the path of shame rather than on the only path open to a soldier worthy of the name—that of duty and honor." Upon which he solemnly assured his Führer of "the unity of the generals, the officers' corps, and the soldiers."

In the second, which he presented on July 29, 1944, he warned all of the general staff officers that henceforth they were required to set an example and become good National Socialists, who were loyal and faithful to their leader. "Each general staff officer must be a National Socialist officer, not only [...] through his attitude regarding political matters, but by actively cooperating in the political indoctrination of the youngest officers, in conformity with the Führer's principles [...]."[556] Quite obviously, Guderian made no mention of such memorandums in his *Memoirs*.

On July 20, 1944, Field Marshal Manstein had been in Usedom, a peninsula on the Baltic coast, located approximately fifty kilometers northwest of Stettin, for a week with his wife and adjutant. This trip, taken in order to relax, proved to be a fortunate coincidence, for it spared him, at least for the moment, of being suspected of any sort of participation in the putsch. If, on this particular day, he had remained at home in Liegnitz, where he had stayed since his dismissal, or even worse, if he had gone to Berlin to learn about the newly deteriorating situation on all the fronts, as he was occasionally in the habit of doing, he would have most likely become subject to interrogation by the Gestapo, all the more so since his name was possibly mentioned in certain compromising documents.

Before these few days of vacation in Usedom, on the highway between Liegnitz and Breslau, Stahlberg had announced to Manstein that an assassination attempt against Hitler was being prepared. In Stahlberg's *Memoirs*, he dedicates a rather interesting passage to the episode: "*Herr* Field Marshal, I think that it is my duty to report to you that the Führer will be killed today or during the following days." A pause. A long pause. No response. After an amount of time that seemed an eternity to me, a response came forth: 'Tell me that again!' I repeated word for word. Another long pause. [...] After another 'eternity,' came the question that I was expecting and the answer to which I had thought about for many hours the night before. 'Who gave you this news?' I immediately responded: 'General Fellgiebel.' After another pause, he had me repeat once again my reply: 'General Fellgiebel.' After a silence that lasted for several kilometers, I thought that the time had come to ask the field marshal a question: '*Herr* Field Marshal, I would like to ask you if it would not have been better not to report this information to you?' His response came quickly: 'Of course not! It was your duty to tell me!' I took another breath. After another long silence [...] the field marshal suddenly broke the silence and declared: 'Stahlberg, what we both know is really something.' [...] On the way back to Liegnitz, Manstein said nothing else to me. When we arrived at his house, he immediately went upstairs to his room. [...] During lunch, he suddenly asked me if I knew of a pretty house on the shores of the Baltic where we could all take two or three weeks of vacation. I gave him the name of the hotel and inn 'Seeschloss' in Bansin on the island of Usedom."[557] It clearly appeared to be an opportune time for Manstein to leave on a vacation some distance away in order to take cover from any suspicion, should a coup d'état actually occur, and especially if it were to fail.

The field marshal remained no less upset by the creation of an Army Court of Honor for which the task was to remove from the Wehrmacht all officers suspected of having participated in the coup d'état Hitler or to have had knowledge of its preparation. The suspects were then refused a court martial. Handed over to the Gestapo, they were immediately deferred to the People's Court. The demoted officers were then taken to the Plötzensee prison in Berlin, where they were executed by hanging. Having been solicited on several occasions by the conspirators, Manstein had reason to be worried, all the more so since he was a good friend of General Fellgiebel. Knowing that something had been brewing against Hitler since the winter of 1942–43, he could be accused of being an accomplice. But, out of a spirit of camaraderie, he had preferred not to abandon his fellow officers who had tried to convince him to join the conspiracy. He then endeavored to create for himself a solid alibi that would shelter him from any suspicion. The effort was not in vain for, in its investigation of Manstein, the Gestapo was unable to find any sort of connection with the conspirators' activities of July 20. As a result, it left him alone until the end of the war.[558]

Even after the war, he sought to diminish the importance of what he knew at the time concerning the plot against Hitler. At Nuremberg, during the trial against the high command of the Wehrmacht, he even claimed to have never been aware that the circle of men from July 20 had made contact with him. This was quite obviously a flagrant lie. He declared to the court: "I never had knowledge of this. I once received a letter from [Colonel] General Beck in the winter of 1942, in which he expressed his opinion on the strategic situation in relation to Stalingrad, and was of the opinion that the war could, with some difficulty, be brought to an end. I responded to him that I could not refuse his presentation, but that defeat was not a reason to consider the war as lost, that a war was only truly lost if one recognized it as such; that the front furthermore made me so anxious that I could not take much time to discuss such matters for long. It is now, after the fact, that it has become clear that different attempts had been made in view of probing, or understanding the depths of my thoughts. It was thus that one day General von Gersdorff came to find me, carrying—as he later revealed to me—Goerderler's letters, I believe, and Popitz's, which he would have shown me if I had been ripe for a coup d'état. As I had always been of the opinion that the removal or suppression of Hitler could only, in the middle of a war, lead to chaos, he did not show me the letters. That all of this represented an attempt to probe for information, later appeared clear to me. I thus never gave my consent to anyone to participate in such an undertaking."⁵⁵⁹

After the war, Stahlberg recounted Manstein's violent reaction when he learned from him, after he had listened to the Führer's speech, shortly after midnight, that it was Stauffenberg who had committed the assassination attempt: "He had not yet gone to bed, and sat down at the table with his wife. I informed him that Hitler had spoken and announced that it was Stauffenberg. He looked at me for a short time, as if he were stunned, then he began to shout like I had never before heard. He fumed: 'Has he gone mad? How could he do such a thing!' He repeated these words over and over. When he calmed down, I asked if he had other orders for me. I then wished him a good night."⁵⁶⁰ For Manstein, the assassination attempt against Hitler was a betrayal, an illegal act against the official leadership of the state.⁵⁶¹

The appointment of Colonel General Guderian to the position of army chief of general staff, in place of Colonel General Zeitzler after the July 20, 1944, coup d'état had profoundly affected Field Marshal Manstein. Not only had he aspired to that position for quite some time, he had been intending to take advantage of such a role to persuade Hitler to grant him full and complete authority in the conduct of military operations and, if possible, to entrust to him the responsibility of the three branches of the Wehrmacht. Yet with the appointment of Guderian, who was recognized for his unfailing devotion to the Führer, there was no longer a possibility of creating a position of chief of general staff of the Wehrmacht which would include the three branches. Manstein was yet even more disappointed when Field Marshal Kluge was granted command of the Western Front on July 11, 1944, after the replacement of Field Marshal Rundstedt. However, at the time Manstein had been dismissed from his duties on March 30, 1944, Hitler had given him the impression that he would probably call upon his services as commander in chief of the Western Front.

Clearly, Hitler never had any intention of entrusting him with anything further, at least not as long as the Reich was unable to launch large-scale offensives. In March 1945, two months before Germany's surrender, he would make the following remarks concerning Manstein: "If I had forty offensive divisions to decisively fight the enemy, I would only consider Manstein to command these troops. But I am unable to utilize him in the current situation. He lacks faith in National Socialism. He is unable to withstand the pressure with which a general in command is confronted by the current military situation."[562]

At the end of August 1944, Manstein began to realize that the war was perhaps definitively over for him. He informed Guderian of his great disappointment at not having been appointed commander of the Western Front: "When Hitler spoke to me at the end of March, he said that he would again call upon my services in the foreseeable future. Yet, since then, the position of commander in chief of the Western Front has already been occupied on two occasions, and almost all of the army groups have new commanders, and this, without calling upon me. I must thus come to the conclusion that, for the moment, the Führer has not the slightest intention of using my services. You must know, in light of your own experience, how painful this period of inactivity is for me."[563]

In his *Memoirs*, Guderian stated that he asked the Führer on several occasions to appoint Manstein as chief of the OKW, in place, of Keitel and each time endured a point-blank refusal for the simple reason that "Hitler could not tolerate the presence of so capable and soldierly a person as Manstein in his environment."

According to the new chief of staff of the OKH, the reason was a result of the incompatible personalities of Hitler and Manstein: "Their characters were too opposed: on the one hand Hitler, with his great willpower and fertile imagination; on the other, Manstein, a man of most distinguished military talents, a product of the German general staff corps, [...] who was our finest operational brain. [...] when I was entrusted with the duties of Chief of the Army General Staff, I frequently proposed to Hitler that Manstein be appointed chief of the OKW in place of Keitel, but always in vain. It is true that Keitel made life easy for Hitler; he sought to anticipate and fulfill Hitler's every wish before it had even been uttered. Manstein was not so comfortable a man to deal with; he formed his own opinions and spoke them aloud. Hitler finally answered my repeated proposal with the words: 'Manstein is perhaps the best brain that the general staff has produced. But he can only operate with fresh, good divisions and not with the remnants of divisions, which are all that are now available to us. Since I can't find him any fresh, operationally capable formations, there's no point in giving him the job.' But the truth is that he did not wish to do so and was trying to justify his refusal by such circuitous excuses."[564]

That Manstein thought that he would be able to avoid the worst for Germany, due to the superiority of his operational talent in relation to that of his fellow generals, is without a doubt. After his dismissal in the spring of 1944, he proved this once again when he broached the question of the Mediterranean theater of operations with Lieutenant Stahlberg, who was now the field marshal's adjutant. If he did not have very much esteem for his colleague Kesselring, commander of the German forces in Italy, Manstein had even less admiration for the commanders of the Allied forces. Concerning this, he declared to Stahlberg: "These men in Italy lead their command like little runts. They are squandering their troops. One should not at all go to war in Italy with modern weapons, for one would destroy the artistic treasures and waste the blood of the soldiers. If they believe that they must absolutely fight in Italy, they should rather conduct a decisive battle in the Po Valley. If I were commander in chief of the Allies, I would hold the Germans back in southern Italy with a minimum number of forces and land the bulk of my forces in Genoa in order to cut off Kesselring's entire army group at its root. Italy would thus fall from the sky like a ripe fruit."

When Stahlberg asked him how he would lead the war in Italy if he were in charge of this theater, Manstein replied that he would bring back into Germany the bulk of the forces stationed on Italian soil, and this as quickly as possible so that the Americans and the English would not be able to catch them. He would then defend the Alpine crossings with only a few troops. As for the mobile units of Kesselring's army group, they could be reformed in Germany, then prepared for offensive action as strategic reserves. But Manstein's strict adherence to his military code was revealed once again when Stahlberg asked him whether, should the highly expected Allied invasion of France occur, he would give priority to the Eastern or Western Front in a strategic defense of the Reich: "This is a political decision and the soldier is at the service of politics," stated the field marshal. He then added, "We must restrict ourselves to discussions regarding military issues and not to rack our brains over political problems."[565] This was a response quite clearly characteristic of Manstein's personality.

An estate for Manstein as a gift from the Führer to ensure his loyalty?

Even though he was constantly worried about being arrested by the
Gestapo, and then transferred before the Army Court of Honor,
Manstein assigned a particular job to Stahlberg. In the autumn of 1944,
he informed him of his intention to acquire some land and an estate, if
possible in East Pomerania, where he had friends, which would ensure
him a pleasant lifestyle. The beauty of Pomerania had pleased him since
he had been commander of a battalion in Kolberg. When his adjutant
asked if it would not be better to look for an estate somewhere in
Schleswig-Holstein or in Westphalia, due to a likely transfer to the west
of the Polish border, Manstein argued that if Pomerania were lost, they
would all be lost. Such a response clearly demonstrated the extent to
which the field marshal was a man who held delusions about the outcome of the war. At that very moment, hundreds of thousands of
Germans were being driven out of East Prussia, and soon, a large part
of Pomerania would no longer belong to the Reich.[566]

Stahlberg thus contacted Dr. Albert Hagemann, a highly respected
agronomist from Pomerania, in order to find an estate corresponding to
the field marshal's tastes. Accompanied by Hagemann, with whom they
had many appointments, Manstein and Stahlberg covered the
Pomerania countryside by car. However, the only estates available were
in a poor financial state; the owners of the prosperous farms were in no
way inclined to sell.

On October 7, 1944, after having participated in a state ceremony
at the Monument of Tannenberg in East Prussia, Field Marshal
Manstein went to dinner with his good friend Colonel General
Guderian, chief of the OKH general staff. Stahlberg had reserved for
that evening a table for four. The two high-ranking officers and their
respective adjutants discussed the worrying military situation: The Red
Army had driven Army Group Center back to the border of East
Prussia. After dinner, the conversation became more relaxed with the
help of one or two bottles of wine. Then, unexpectedly, Manstein asked:
"Tell me, Guderian, I heard someone say that you got an estate in
Poznan. How did you do that?" Guderian said quite simply that he had
been provided a list of beautiful Polish estates that he visited for a few
days before choosing the property most suitable for him. Manstein was
taken aback and wanted to know if the Polish owners were still alive at

this very moment. When Guderian responded yes, Manstein immediately asked what happened to them. The colonel general stated that he did not know. When he took possession of the estate, he added, the Polish had already left. He thus did not have the slightest idea what happened to them. The field marshal was speechless, stupefied by what he had just heard. "He raised an eyebrow once or twice. I recognized this too well to not know what it meant: such a way of getting an estate was not at all in his style," recounted Stahlberg in his *Memoirs*.[567]

Manstein's approach to finding an estate nevertheless demonstrated the extent to which he was an opportunist. Like several army colleagues, he wanted to take advantage of the Führer's endowment system and get his slice of the pie. Above the tax-free monthly stipends that he granted to his colonel generals and field marshals, as well as to commanders of divisions, corps, army, and army groups, Hitler awarded other gifts to his military elite, particularly on their birthdays, when the senior officers turned 50, 55, 60, 65, or 70 years old, to reward their service to National Socialist Germany. Such endowments appeared most often as sums of tax-free money, and also at times as properties or estates, or even objects of art. Discretion in the delivery of gifts was deemed necessary in order not to incite jealousy or resentment. Granting such presents to the high-ranking generals of the Wehrmacht was standard practice, and paid witness to a corrupt political regime.[568]

Field Marshal Manstein, who ranked among the greatest critics of Hitler concerning issues relative to the management of military operations and to the structure of the Wehrmacht high command, did not receive any sort of gift for his 55th birthday on November 24, 1942. At the very least there is nothing regarding this in the archives. In Nuremberg, when he was asked if he had received an endowment, he responded in the negative.[569] However, some of his contemporaries claimed that he had indeed received from Hitler an enormous estate in the autumn of 1944.[570] But such an assertion has still not been proven. In fact, the question remains to this day a veritable enigma. It is completely possible that Manstein did not begin his search for an estate without having previously received an endowment from the Führer. Moreover, it is highly likely that the estate gifts which benefited Kleist in October 1942, Guderian in October 1943, Leeb in July 1944, and Keitel in October 1944, encouraged Manstein to apply to Hitler with the aim of acquiring one for himself.

There exists a document in which it is mentioned that the Führer would have entrusted to Herbert Backe, minister of the Reich, the job of granting an estate to Manstein. In fact, Backe, who was the head of the Ministry of Food and Agriculture, wrote to Field Marshal Manstein on October 17, 1944 to inform him of the "Führer's wish to help him in the search for a suitable property." The choice of words employed by Backe implies that Manstein had perhaps previously received a gift, for Hitler often appeared ready, in light of the style of wording, to assist those who, after obtaining a cash gift, wanted to use it to acquire a piece of land or an estate. Whatever the case may be, Backe recommended to Manstein, "after serious consideration and his particular interests," to take a look at purchasing a wooded estate. However, nothing permits us to know if the field marshal's efforts were successful. It is possible that the Ministry of Food and Agriculture was forced to dismiss all requests relative to the acquisition of estates in the eastern regions of the Reich due to the deterioration of the military situation on the Eastern Front. In the summer of 1944, Backe's secretary, Werner Willikens, furthermore proposed to him to postpone until the end of the war all estate endowments in the East or, at the very least, to wait until the Wehrmacht had driven the Red Army back from the eastern region of the Reich.[571]

"Manstein, save Germany!"

At the end of January 1945, with Silesia becoming the scene of fighting, Manstein decided to leave Liegnitz for Achterberg, a manor located to the west of the army training region of Bergen, not far from Celle in Lüneburg Heath. It was with his family and Stahlberg that he settled into this residence which had not been inhabited for several years. In fact, the last person to have lived there was the former commander in chief of the army, Colonel General Fritsch, who had died during the Polish campaign in September 1939. On January 25 the field marshal, his family, and Stahlberg thus left Liegnitz for Achterberg. Due to Allied aerial bombing, they had to make a detour via Berlin and Hanover.

On January 29 Manstein, who had been in Berlin for two days, took advantage of this to go to the Reich Chancellery in order to meet with the Führer. Was he hoping to convince him to hand over the management of military operations to save Germany from disaster? Was he aspiring to become the savior of the German homeland and nation, even though he had already declared the contrary to Stahlberg? With defeat looming on the horizon, Manstein actually seemed to want to go down in history as the savior of Germany in its confrontation with the Red Army and Bolshevism. "When he is up to his neck, he will call upon me," he confided to Stahlberg on several occasions when speaking of Hitler. Despite the late hour, Manstein was still convinced that the Führer could not indefinitely do without him, by far the best commander in the German Army.[572]

That Hitler had entrusted, a few months earlier, the Ardennes offensive to Field Marshal Rundstedt had more than likely incited resentment on his part. Unleashed on December 16, 1944, this last German offensive of the war failed in less than ten days, for a lack of reserves. Even though the operational concept of the offensive curiously resembled the Sickle Cut Plan, Hitler did not judge it necessary to call upon Manstein's services to conduct it, despite the fact that he informed him on March 30, 1944 of his intention to confer upon him new assignments as soon as the Wehrmacht was again in a position to undertake offensives. At the end of 1944, he had even refused Rundstedt the services of Manstein, Leeb, or Kleist to assist him in supervising the operations on the Western Front.[573]

Nevertheless, when Manstein entered the Reich Chancellery, accompanied by his adjutant, two SS men seated at a table rose and saluted him. Manstein responded by raising his field marshal's baton: "I am Field Marshal Manstein. Would you please be so kind as to announce [my arrival] to the Führer." One of the two SS men asked: "Do you have an appointment, *Herr* Field Marshal?" Manstein stated that he did not have one, but that he had come on important business. He was asked, as well as his adjutant, to take a seat and wait patiently while one of the two SS men left the room After half an hour, the latter returned and declared: "I have orders to inform you that the Führer is not seeing anyone." Having difficulty containing his anger, Manstein then asked: "Did you tell the Führer or one of his adjutants who I am? –I did, *Herr* Field Marshal! –Then I want to speak with one of the adjutants. –I am sorry, *Herr* Field Marshal, I am ordered not to allow anyone to enter." Manstein rose abruptly and left the room without saluting. He took it as an insult that not a single one of the Führer's adjutants would see him. The fact must have been clear: the supreme commander had no use for "the most dangerous enemy of the Allies."[574] Likewise, he must have become aware that he had no chance of saving Germany.

On May 1, 1945, when Stahlberg learned from the radio of the death of the Führer, who had committed suicide on the preceding day, he rushed immediately to Manstein to tell him the news. The field marshal was sitting at a table with his wife, reading a book. "*Herr* Field Marshal, exclaimed Stahlberg, the Führer is dead!" The field marshal stared at him for several seconds without saying anything, stunned speechless. Then came a cry from his wife, a great admirer of the Führer and a highly involved member of the Nazi party: "No! This cannot be true!" While Manstein was trying to console his wife, Stahlberg mentioned the appointment of Grand Admiral Dönitz to succeed the Führer as head of state.[575]

In mid-April, Field Marshal Manstein moved to Weißenhaus, a property close to Bad Oldesloe, a small town in Schleswig-Holstein, so as to avoid being taken prisoner before the capitulation of the Reich. Another of his inactive army colleagues, Field Marshal Bock, also moved into this region of northern Germany, to Lensahn. At the end of April, both men attempted to contact the commander in chief of Germany's Army Group North, Field Marshal Busch, to advise him to join his forces with those of the Western Front, with the goal of saving the troops of the Eastern Front and the civilian population of the east German regions. Next, they visited Grand Admiral Dönitz, commander in chief of the Kriegsmarine, now head of the Third Reich, who had transferred his headquarters from Berlin to Plon, in Schleswig-Holstein. They recommended that he gradually withdraw the armies of the Eastern Front closer to the American and British fronts. However, they did not utter a word about the necessity of bringing the war to an end. Manstein and Bock were apparently speculating on an eventual breakup of the alliance among the enemies, which would perhaps provide Germany with new opportunities to negotiate.

On his way back, at the crossroads of Lübeck and Weißenhaus, a military patrol stopped Manstein's car and urged him to return immediately to Dönitz's headquarters. The latter was asking Manstein to meet him again, for he wanted to appoint him as commander in chief of the OKW, in place of Field Marshal Keitel, and to place him in charge of negotiating the conditions relative to the military surrender of Germany. Quite clearly, Dönitz was hoping that Manstein, as the new commander in chief of the OKW, and thanks to his great prestige, could mitigate the conditions of capitulation from the Allied powers, and, perhaps even spare a large part of the *Ostheer* soldiers from being taken captive by the Soviets.

But shortly before his arrival in Plon, Manstein passed the car of *ReichsFührer-SS* Himmler. The chief of the SS, the Gestapo, and the reserves had just come from meeting with Dönitz and had dissuaded him from granting Manstein command of the Wehrmacht. And so, when Manstein arrived in Plon, a few officers informed him immediately that he was too late to be able to take on the duties of chief of the OKW. As a result, he was unable to meet with Dönitz. He was indeed too late to have the possibility of changing in any way the outcome of the war. Furthermore, Manstein did not find very enticing the idea of now being included among those who were participating in the decline of the Reich. That he had been solicited to take the supreme command of the German Army not only by the July 20 conspirators, but also by the new chief of the Third Reich reveals the admiration for his enormous operational talent that his colleagues from the Wehrmacht held for him. Moreover, in the final days of the war, a good number of German officers were still placing their last hopes in him.[576]

After the war, Dönitz claimed that difficulties in communication had prevented Manstein from taking command of the German armed forces during the final days of the war: "In the last days of April, Field Marshals von Bock and von Manstein came to me. We discussed the military situation. On this occasion, Manstein had insisted upon the necessity of gradually withdrawing armies from the Eastern Front closer to the American and English fronts. This fully coincided with my intentions. On May 1, I requested to be in touch with Manstein. I wanted to offer him the leadership of the Wehrmacht high command in place of Keitel. But I was not successful at reaching Manstein. The leadership of the OKW thus remained in Keitel's and Jodl's hands."[577] It nevertheless seems more likely that the true reason was due more to Himmler's pressures than to a supposed communication problem.[578]

On May 3, 1945, Field Marshal Bock went to Weißenhaus to meet with Field Marshal Manstein. He wanted to discuss with him Germany's imminent surrender. During his trip from Lensahn to Weißenhaus, Bock's car was attacked by a British fighter. The field marshal was gravely wounded and transported to a hospital in Oldenburg.

His wife and daughter were killed. Immediately informed of the tragedy, Manstein and Stahlberg went to the hospital. Bock was lying in bed, wrapped in bandages. When the doctor announced the identity of those who were at the foot of his bed, the latter could only say a few words, the last that he was to utter before dying: "Manstein, save Germany!" Bock was the third field marshal, after Kluge and Rommel, to consider Manstein, though less senior in rank, as the *primus inter pares*.[579] It was nevertheless too late for him to save Germany, which surrendered on May 8, 1945.

For Manstein, the capitulation, which he believed he could have prevented had Hitler decided to hand over to him full and complete leadership of military operations, was a veritable catastrophe. On May 8, the day of the surrender, he assigned Stahlberg the duty of informing the British Field Marshal Bernard Montgomery of the place where he was staying. Not only did he not want to hide like a criminal, but he was persuaded that perhaps he would be needed, in case of a breakup of the alliance of convenience between the Western Allies and the U.S.S.R.[580] Of course, he was once again deluding himself. On August 26, 1945, he was instead imprisoned by the British Army, a captivity that would last until May 7, 1953.

THE LEGEND OF AN "HONORABLE AND UPRIGHT" WEHRMACHT

Recognized for his apolitical attitude, Field Marshal Manstein remained loyal to Hitler until the very end of the war, even if he had felt compelled to stand up to him on occasion regarding the management of operations. It was only after the complete and utter collapse of the Third Reich that he distanced himself from Hitler, vigorously protesting his innocence and insisting that he only be regarded as a soldier who was only doing his duty. More than any of his colleagues from the officers' corps, Manstein substantiated after the war, through his testimony and his *Memoirs*, the following myths: the German Army had only been the victim of expansionist Nazi policy; the generals had only done their duty by obeying their orders; Hitler was the only one responsible for the military defeat of the Reich; and the Wehrmacht would have never participated in the criminal actions of the regime.

During the trial of major war criminals before the International Military Tribunal at Nuremberg, many observers claimed that Manstein had become known "as the most brilliant" witness to fight for the cause of the Wehrmacht.[581] His testimony, combined with that of several other former combatants, greatly influenced researchers who were inspired by him and the others. Manstein thus became after 1945 one of the principal moral supporters of Wehrmacht integrity, which explains the fact that he was among those who, at the request of Chancellor Konrad Adenauer, participated in supervising the reconstruction of the German Army within the framework of NATO in 1956.

He had, however, been sentenced in Hamburg, on December 19, 1949, by a British military tribunal, to eighteen years in prison for his responsibility as commander of the Eleventh Army in the Crimea, where violations of the rules of war had been committed by his soldiers. He was released on May 7, 1953, after having received leave for medical reasons. Some in West Germany thus thought that he had been nothing more than a victim of "victors' justice," purging a collective offense and not that of a simple war criminal. Yet, the field marshal was answerable for the Wehrmacht and its actions, thus placing himself in the shadow of the image by which he preferred to be remembered.[582]

Manstein and the duty to defend the honor and integrity of the Wehrmacht in Nuremberg

With the intention of punishing those responsible for launching the war, and the crimes of unparalleled violence that it spawned, a special inter-allied tribunal was formed in Nuremberg from November 20, 1945 to September 30, 1946. Of course, its primary concern was to prove National Socialist Germany's responsibility for unleashing of the conflict, but above all it was necessary to judge the acts of barbarism practiced on a massive scale against civilian populations and the organized genocide of entire groups of people. Composed of judges from the four victorious powers, the court held four charges against twenty-two high Nazi dignitaries: the concerted plan or plot aimed at the domination of the European continent by way of a war of aggression; crimes against peace as defined by the violation of international treaties; war crimes that entailed pillaging, enslavement, and assassinations; and crimes against humanity as characterized by the systematic persecution and extermination of political adversaries and racial and religious minorities. If the last charge was itself a new legal idea, the trying of the six major Third Reich entities (the National Socialist Party, the Reich cabinet, the SS, SA, the Gestapo and the SD, the general staff, and the military high command) also represented an innovation.

Among the primary leaders of the National Socialist regime called to appear in court, five were from the military: Göring, Reichsmarshal and commander in chief of the Luftwaffe; Keitel, field marshal and chief of the OKW general staff; Jodl, colonel general and chief of the OKW operations department; Raeder, grand admiral and commander in chief of the Kriegsmarine until 1943; and Dönitz, grand admiral, commander in chief of the Kriegsmarine from 1943 until the end of the war, and last chief of the Reich following Hitler's death.

On October 1, 1946, Göring, Keitel, and Jodl were sentenced to death, while Raeder and Dönitz were sentenced, respectively, to life in prison and ten years in custody. As for the general staff and the high command, accused of having abetted a criminal organization, Sir Geoffrey Lawrence, president of the International Military Tribunal, immediately declared after having read the decisions: "The Tribunal believes that no declaration of criminality should be made with respect to the General Staff and High Command." He then stated the same grounds for the Reich cabinet, that nothing permitted them to declare it as a criminal organization: "The number of persons charged, while larger than that of the Reich Cabinet, is still so small that individual trials of these officers would accomplish the purpose here sought better than a declaration such as requested." He added, however: "But a more compelling reason is that in the opinion of the Tribunal the General Staff and High Command is neither an organization nor a group within the meaning of these terms as used in Article 9 of the Charter."[583]

For several observers, such an acquittal was due in large measure to a field marshal named Erich von Manstein, commander in chief of Army Group South until March 30, 1944. Called to the stand as a witness for the defense, he strove to defend the honor and integrity of the German Army. Because of his prestige as the most talented campaign commander of the Wehrmacht, he greatly contributed towards the exoneration of the general staff and the high command of accusations of having formed a criminal organization in the same way as the National Socialist party, the SS, the SD, and the Gestapo. One thus characterized him as the "strategic brain" (*strategische Kopf*) of the defense. According to General Westphal, "The soul of our defense was Field Marshal Manstein, the most gifted of our military leaders. Inventive, always courageous in combat, the acquittal of the general staff in October 1946 was largely due to his tireless and intelligent actions." And for others, Manstein was quite simply the "savior of the general staff and the honor of the German soldier."[584]

In fact, he became the spokesman for an entire group of senior officers, which included Field Marshal Brauchitsch, commander in chief of the OKH until December 19, 1941, Colonel General Halder, chief of the OKH general staff until September 24, 1942, General Warlimont, Jodl's adjutant to the operations department of the OKW until September 6, 1944, and General Westphal, chief of staff of the supreme command in the West until May 7, 1945. In his deposition given at Nuremberg, Manstein summarized, more or less, the arguments of the memorandum that he had drafted in the autumn of 1945, in collaboration with Brauchitsch, Halder, Warlimont, and Westphal, and which their lawyers utilized for their defense.

Known better under the name of the "generals' memorandum," the deposition, entitled *The German Army from 1920 to 1945 (Das Deutsche Heer von 1920–1945)*, dated November 19, 1945, and intended for the International Military Tribunal, relieved the officers and soldiers of the Wehrmacht of all responsibilities for the facts relating to the four charges. It came out from the memorandum that the generals had only done their soldierly duties by obeying orders and restricting themselves exclusively to military issues, and that they had been prohibited to rebel due to the apolitical military tradition of a subservient devotion in service to the state, the Reich, and the nation. According to the memorandum, the Wehrmacht had been an institution distinct from the Nazi apparatus and was impervious to the National Socialist ideology by remaining loyal to the chivalrous values of a long Prussian military tradition. Not only had it been hostile to the National Socialist Party and the SS, but it was equally opposed to almost all of Hitler's important decisions, whether it was the commencement of the war or the implementation of criminal orders on the Eastern Front. According to the authors of the document in question, the German Army had distanced itself with regard to the criminal actions committed by units of the SS and the SD, even standing in opposition to them when it had been possible, even though it ignored, in general, what was occurring behind the front, and as a result, the true nature and magnitude of the massacres perpetrated in the East.[585]

Clearly, none of the authors were taking responsibility for their actions. The "Generals' memorandum" remains no less one of the most significant documents aimed at minimizing as much as possible the responsibility of the OKW and the OKH in the unleashing of the Second World War, in the preparation and conduct of the wars of aggression, and in the planning and execution of criminal orders. In actuality, this "Generals' memorandum" contributed largely to the birth of the legend of an "honorable and upright Wehrmacht." Due precisely to the fact that it was written by key generals most certainly ensured the transmission of this defensive version of the Wehrmacht's role under the Third

Reich to Western public opinion during the following decades. It goes without saying that the judgment of the inter-allied military tribunal according to which the general staff and the high command had not formed a criminal organization tremendously reinforces this legend of an "irreproachable Wehrmacht."[586]

However, even before the Nuremberg trials, the victorious powers had no doubt as to the complicity of German military leaders with the National Socialist government. Without them, Hitler would not have had the means to fulfill his aggressive, expansionist ambitions, and his criminal measures could not have been implemented on such a large scale. After all, had Hitler not already termed the Wehrmacht as the second pillar of the regime after only the Nazi Party? Despite the abundant material proof incriminating them that was presented at Nuremberg, the general staff and the high command were nevertheless acquitted of all charges brought against them.

If one takes into consideration that twenty million Germans fought or served in the German Army at one time or another during the Second World War and that, of this number, thirteen million served on the Eastern Front, the condemnation of the general staff and the high command would have, to a certain extent, been viewed as a curse over a significant portion of German society. A general amnesty would have thus become necessary to legitimize the reconstruction of the German nation on the ashes of the Third Reich.[587] It would have been extremely difficult to subsequently legitimize the rearmament of the German Federal Republic undertaken within the scope of NATO during the second half of the 1950s. Concerning this, General Walther Wenck, who gained fame on the Eastern Front during the war, mentioned that if the defense had not succeeded at exonerating the general staff and the high command of the accusation of having formed a criminal organization, "there most likely would not have been a Bundeswehr or any German contribution to Euro-Atlantic security ten years later."[588]

After having presented his arguments against the general staff and the high command, Brigadier General Telford Taylor, an American prosecuting attorney at Nuremberg, endeavored to bring to the court's attention the manner in which witnesses such as Manstein and Rundstedt saw the present and the future: "The first steps toward the revival of German militarism have been taken right here in this courtroom. The German General Staff has had plenty of time to think since the spring of 1945, and it well knows what is at stake here. The German militarists know that their future depends on re-establishing the faith of the German people in their military powers and in disassociating themselves from the atrocities which they committed in the service of the Third Reich. [...] The documents and testimony show that theirs are transparent fabrications. But here, in embryo, are the myths and legends which the German militarists will seek to propagate in the German mind. These lies must be stamped and labeled for what they are now while the proof is fresh."

He continued his speech, asserting that the war had been anchored by certain German generals. To substantiate his remarks, he declared, and rightly so, that Manstein "considered the glory of the war as something great." According to Taylor, Manstein was not thinking any differently than Jodl who, in a memorandum formulating the "considered opinion" of the OKW, wrote in 1939: "Despite all attempts to outlaw it, war is still a law of nature which may be challenged but not eliminated. It serves the survival of the race and state and the assurance of its historical future. This high moral purpose gives war its total character and its ethical justification."

Taylor concluded with a condemnation of militarism, insisting upon its destructive consequences: "The truth is spread on the record before us, and all we have to do is state the truth plainly. The German militarists joined forces with Hitler and with him created the Third Reich; with him they deliberately made a world in which might was all that mattered; with him they plunged the world into war, and spread terror and devastation over the continent of Europe. They dealt a blow to all mankind; a blow so savage and foul that the conscience of the world will reel for years to come. This was not war; it was crime. This was not soldiering; it was savagery. We cannot here make history over again, but we can see that it is written true."

It was feared that the public would take the International Military Court's recommendation for an acquittal of the German military hierarchy badly. As president of the court, Lawrence took care to emphasize the responsibility of the German military leadership. He wanted, by making such a declaration, to ensure that the court's conclusion would not prohibit the individual prosecutions of generals or junior ranking officers, whose criminal actions had been proven: "Although the Tribunal is of the opinion that the term 'group' in Article 9 must mean something more than this collection of military officers, it has heard much evidence as to the participation of these officers in planning and waging aggressive war, and in committing war crimes and crimes against humanity. This evidence is, as to many of them, clear and convincing.

"They have been responsible in large measure for the miseries and suffering that have fallen on millions of men, women, and children. They have been a disgrace to the honorable profession of arms [...]. Although they were not a group falling within the words of the Charter, they were certainly a ruthless military caste [...].

"Many of these men have made a mockery of the soldier's oath of obedience to military orders. When it suits their defense they say they had to obey; when confronted with Hitler's brutal crimes [...] they say they disobeyed. The truth is that they actively participated in all these crimes, or sat silent or acquiescent, witnessing the commission of crimes on a scale larger and more shocking than the world has ever had the misfortune to know. This must be said.

"Where the facts warrant it, these men should be brought to trial so that those among them who are guilty of these crimes should not escape punishment."[589]

After the International Military Court's decision not to incriminate the general staff and the high command as a criminal organization, the American authorities in Germany decided to proceed with the individual cases in their zone of occupation. In other words, instead of holding the German Army responsible in its entirety, they preferred to bring to justice the senior military leadership accused of crimes against peace, war crimes, or crimes against humanity, and who had not been judged by the International Military Tribunal of Nuremberg. Of the twelve subsequent trials, three involved officers: the trial of Milch (case 2), the trial against the generals of the Southeast (case 7), and the trial against the OKW (case 12).

If the trial against the generals of the Southeast dealt with a specific theater of operations, that of the Balkans, the trial against the OKW, for its part, was directed at both the representatives of the Wehrmacht supreme command and the primary commanders of the Army, the Luftwaffe, and the Kriegsmarine. In fact, only three out of the fourteen accused high-ranking generals had served in the OKW: Colonel General Rudolf Lehmann, General Hermann Reinecke, and General Warlimont.

The others were: Field Marshal Leeb, Field Marshal Sperrle, Field Marshal Küchler, Colonel General Blaskowitz, Colonel General Hoth, Colonel General Reinhardt, Colonel General Salmuth, Colonel General Hollidt, Admiral Otto Schniewind, General Karl von Rocques, and General Wöhler.

The trial against the OKW took place from December 30, 1947 to October 29, 1948. With Blaskowitz having committed suicide on the first day of the hearing, February 5, 1948, the remaining thirteen defendants were tried for crimes against peace, war crimes, and crimes against humanity. The last two charges were the most significant, considering the brutal and disgraceful treatment that the Wehrmacht reserved for Soviet prisoners of war, the political commissars of the Red Army, as well as the civilian population and the Jews of Eastern Europe. As was to be expected, the defendants refused to take the slightest personal responsibility, taking refuge behind the traditional argument that they had been forced to obey orders or feigning to be unaware of the true character and magnitude of the crimes committed by the Nazi regime.

For the charge concerning the preparations for a war of aggression, more commonly referred to as crimes against peace, they were declared not guilty. Even though certain ones among them had participated in the preparations for Hitler's wars of aggression, the court judged that they did not hold any duties at the level of political leadership. However, Keitel and Raeder were both sentenced for crimes against peace by the International Military Tribunal. As for the charges of war crimes and crimes against humanity, eleven of the defendants were found guilty: life in prison for Generals Warlimont and Reinecke; twenty years in prison for Field Marshal Küchler, Colonel General Salmuth, and General Rocques; fifteen years in prison for Colonel Generals Reinhardt and Hoth; between five and eight years custody for Colonel Generals Lehmann and Hollidt, as well as for General Wöhler. Field Marshal Leeb was sentenced to three years in prison, a sentence that was dismissed as soon as it was pronounced. As for Field Marshal Sperrle and Admiral Schniewind, they were both declared not guilty.[590]

The penultimate case to bring the Nuremberg trials to a close was that of the former Reich secretary of state, Ernst von Weizsacker, which lasted until April 1949. But the trial against the Wehrmacht generals was not completely over. The case that was to receive the most media coverage, and would take place throughout 1949 in the British zone of occupation, was that of Field Marshal Erich von Manstein.

Manstein brought before the tribunal for war crimes?

More than two years after the Wehrmacht's capitulation and more than a year after the International Military Tribunal rendered its verdict at Nuremberg, the British government was still confronted with the question of whether or not to try the German senior officers whom it had been holding in captivity since the end of the war, for war crimes and crimes against humanity. Such an issue was not unusual in itself, for it concerned four high-ranking officers of the Wehrmacht: Field Marshal Manstein, Field Marshal Brauchitsch, Field Marshal Rundstedt, and Colonel General Strauß, who had all been detained by the British authorities since the summer of 1945.

During the summer of 1947, Brigadier General Taylor, who had succeeded Robert H. Jackson to the position of public prosecutor of the United States for war crimes, was preparing the trial against the OKW in order to judge the primary leaders of the Wehrmacht imprisoned by the American authorities and who had not been brought before the International Military Tribunal. During the process of researching the fourteen defendants, Taylor's team had amassed a significant amount of proof incriminating Manstein, Brauchitsch, Rundstedt, and Strauß.

On August 6, 1947, Taylor communicated the evidence to Sir Hartley Shawcross, Great Britain's public prosecutor, in the form of a long memorandum. The principal charges gathered against the four senior officers cited in the document were the following: 1. elimination of Soviet political commissars, in view of the "Commissar Order"; 2. execution of prisoners of war and poor treatment inflicted upon them; 3. execution of hostages, excessive retaliatory measures, deportation of civilians in order to create a slave labor force, the extermination of Slavs, Jews, and Communists. In the memorandum, Taylor suggested to Shawcross that the British follow the example of the Americans. To this end, he submitted judicial procedures to follow in order to carry out such an action.[591]

Taylor's memorandum left the British authorities rather perplexed, particularly when he urged them to judge their Wehrmacht prisoners of war, like the Americans, who, at this particular moment, were preparing to engage in judicial procedures against the generals held in captivity in their zone of occupation. Shawcross, who had been the chief English prosecutor during the Nuremberg trials, submitted Taylor's memorandum to the War Ministry, for the matter fell primarily under its jurisdiction, and suggested that the Ministry of Foreign Affairs be consulted on this case.

After having read the memorandum, War Minister Frederick Bellenger wrote on October 3, 1947 to Ernest Bevin, minister of Foreign Affairs, that the evidence gathered by Taylor against Manstein, Brauchitsch, Rundstedt, and Strauß represented an admissible case that unfortunately could not be ignored. "We were all hoping that there would be no more of these trials of German generals," he added bitterly. However, Bellenger mentioned to Bevin that the army could not begin such proceedings, for he did not have available to him officers having the required legal expertise and experience, as well as the linguistic qualifications necessary in order to interrogate the defendants, nor a qualified research team to examine the German documents to prepare the case. "For these reasons," concluded Bellenger, "I do not recommend that we should take on the trials." According to him, the best solution was to hand the four generals over to the Polish or the Russians, those who were principally concerned with their crimes, or even to request the Americans to include them in the trial against the OKW, which they were preparing in Nuremberg against the high leadership of the Wehrmacht detained in captivity in their zone of occupation.

The Taylor memorandum raised issues that exceeded to a large extent the scope of administrative difficulties of the War Ministry. Because of the stature of the officers concerned and of their crimes during the war, the memorandum also had implications on the level of international policy. Due to this, Bellenger transferred the case to his colleague at the Ministry of Foreign Affairs. Bevin did not hesitate to take over the situation. On October 15, 1947, his Ministry sent a telegraph to Field Marshal Sir Sholdo Douglas, the military governor of the British zone of occupation. He requested him to ask his American counterpart, General Lucius Clay, if the Americans would be willing to include Field Marshals Manstein, Brauchitsch, Rundstedt, and Colonel General Strauß in the trial against the OKW for which proceedings were soon to commence in order to judge the fourteen high-ranking military leaders accused of having committed similar offenses.

Douglas did not respond to the telegraph for eight days. The indignation of the British Army regarding the judgment rendered against Field Marshal Albert Kesselring was certainly not unrelated to his apathy. Judged by a British military tribunal in Venice in the spring of 1947, Kesselring had been sentenced to death. But the protests in the British military circles were such that the sentence was commuted to life in prison. Field Marshal Harold George Alexander had been one of the many British officers to write to the prime minister, Labour Party member Clement Attlee, apropos of Kesselring's irreproachable performance, explaining that the retaliatory measures to which he had resorted in Italy in his role as commander in chief of the theater, were unfortunate, but understandable in wartime.

Douglas was apparently convinced that the appearance in court of other German generals before a British military tribunal would provoke protests in the British Army that were just as intense. Before consulting General Clay on the matter, he first wanted to ascertain that the proposal had been carefully considered. Evidently, he had serious reservations, and expressed them in a telegraph addressed to the minister of Foreign Affairs on October 23, 1947.[592]

Field Marshal Douglas next assigned his adjutant in Berlin, Lieutenant General Sir Brian Robertson, to speak about this sensitive case to General Clay. The latter stated to him that he was hardly inclined to accept the British proposal, for the indictments had already been carried out and the OKW trial was about to commence. He had even led him to believe that not only did he not want to take the four generals and bring them before the tribunal, but he was hoping that the British would come to the conclusion that it was preferable not to try them. Such a commentary led Robertson to ensure the Ministry of Foreign Affairs that there would be no criticism on the part of the Americans if the decision was made to abandon the idea of going to trial against Manstein, Brauchitsch, Rundstedt, and Strauß. In private, he declared: "I am certain that we would be well advised to act in such a way."[593]

However, for Bevin, this was not a conceivable solution, all the more so since Taylor was putting more and more pressure on the British to persuade them to accept his request. The minister of Foreign Affairs actually found himself in a highly delicate situation. If the British government were to choose to do nothing, and if the evidence gathered against the four German generals were to end up being exposed to international opinion, it goes without saying that it would automatically provoke an angry response from the latter for sheltering and protecting war criminals. On the other hand, there was no question of handing them over to the U.S.S.R. or Poland, while an iron curtain was crashing down on central Europe in the context of an international cold war between the Western and the Soviet blocs.

On December 3, 1947, Bevin came to the conclusion that there was no other solution for the British authorities than to try the officers. But as soon as he learned this, the Lord Chancellor of England, William Jowitt, was immediately opposed to this decision. He wrote to Bevin to inform him that he had recently spoken to Robertson, who was in London for a conference of ministers of Foreign Affairs of the four victorious powers, for which the objective was to achieve a definitive ruling on the German issue, and that he had assured him that the evidence against the four German military chiefs was hardly convincing. Accompanied by Shawcross, Bevin then met with Jowitt and presented the memorandum to him. After having been briefed, the Lord Chancellor recognized that there was indeed enough material for a trial against Field Marshals Manstein, Brauchitsch, and Rundstedt, as well as against Colonel General Strauß.

Robertson was nevertheless hoping to convince Emanuel Shinwell, who had succeeded Bellenger to the position of Minister of War, that trials of the generals or any other dignitary from the Third Reich must be brought to an end. To the Minister of War, on December 13, 1947, Robertson asserted to Shinwell that it was ridiculous to engage in legal proceedings to punish the men of crimes that they had committed more than two years ago. Reconciliation with Germany seemed to him much more important that the legal pursuit of her former military leaders. In his view, the support of the West German leaders in the fight against Communism, within the context of the cold war, depended precisely on the termination of such trials. But, like Bevin, Shinwell remained convinced that the accusations against the four generals were admissible and that it was necessary to proceed with this case.[594]

Meanwhile, medical examinations of the four generals would encourage him to have a change of heart. At the beginning of 1948, the Ministry of War conducted a medical exam on the four prisoners in order to determine if, due to their age, their health would allow them to endure a trial. The three doctors of the British Army who had given the medical exam to the four Wehrmacht commanders unanimously declared that they were incapable of suffering through a trial. Shinwell then stated to Bevin that it would be preferable to send these four men back to Germany.

The public prosecutor Shawcross was nevertheless opposed to letting them leave on the strength of a medical report that he considered to be more than dubious, particularly since it was the work of an army medical commission. Consequently, he demanded a new medical exam of the defendants, this time by prison doctors from the Ministry of the Interior according to the criteria of the English criminal court. On March 22, 1948, Bevin, Shinwell, Shawcross, and Jowitt agreed to the new medical exam and to leave in the cabinet's hands the decision whether the four officers were to be tried or not. According to the new medical report, only Manstein, Rundstedt, and Strauß were considered to be in sufficiently good health to bear a long trial, whereas Brauchitsch was deemed too ill.

During this time, while the pressure to reach a decision was being increasingly felt, the problem confronting the British ministers was further complicated due to Russian and American interventions in this highly embarrassing matter. On March 11, 1948, the Soviet military administration in Germany requested that Field Marshals Manstein and Rundstedt be handed over for the purpose of trying them for war crimes committed against Soviet citizens. Barely a month later, the United States' public prosecutor for war crimes also called for the men, along with Brauchitsch, as defense witnesses in the OKW trial in Nuremberg.

At the request of Marshal Vassili Sokolovsky, military governor of the Soviet zone of occupation, to extradite Manstein and Rundstedt, Lieutenant General Robertson responded negatively, bringing up the necessity of detaining them in England for reasons similar to those formulated by his counterpart. If, however, the four generals were to be repatriated to Germany as suggested by Shinwell, they would certainly be subject to any new extradition request. Robertson was thus opposed to their return to Germany. A solution to the dilemma was found with the decision made by London on April 12, 1948 to conclude all legal procedures against the German war criminals beginning on September 1, 1948, and to no longer consider extradition requests presented after this date other than exceptional cases.

As for Brigadier General Taylor's request, it too posed a serious problem. If they were to be called to the stand as defense witnesses, Manstein and Rundstedt would necessarily have to face a cross-examination from the prosecution, which would most likely implicate them as much as the defendants. Even if they were permitted not to respond to questions that could incriminate them, their presence alone at Nuremberg would suffice to cause trouble for the British government or lead it to precipitate its decision regarding its intention to try them or not. Due to this, the medical reasons could no longer be invoked to justify the decision not to bring them before the tribunal. As a result, the response to the American request was to be deferred until the cabinet had reached its decision concerning this sensitive issue.

When the cabinet finally turned its attention to the question on July 5, 1948, it was decided, in order to spare Great Britain the possibility of being open to international criticism, to hold another trial that would be held in Hamburg as soon as preparations were completed. Shinwell was invited to participate in the legal proceedings against the four generals. The Brauchitsch case was to be reassessed in light of his health, in case the evidence gathered against him were to justify a trial. During this time, Manstein and Rundstedt would be placed at the disposal of the American authorities so that they could bring them before the tribunal in Nuremberg as defense witnesses within the framework of the OKW trial.[595]

On July 14, 1948, Field Marshal Brauchitsch and Colonel General Strauß were transferred to the Münsterlager Hospital in Hamburg, where Field Marshals Manstein and Rundstedt joined them a few days later after their refusal, on the advice of their defense attorneys, to testify at Leeb's trial. While the prosecution was preparing their respective trials, the four men were placed in hospital rooms under permanent surveillance to prevent any attempt at suicide. As to the fate that was awaiting them, they were held in complete ignorance until the arrival of the new year. Three among them, specifically Manstein, Rundstedt, and Strauß, were then informed that they would be charged with war crimes and crimes against humanity. Regarding Brauchitsch, he had died in the interim of thrombosis on October 18, 1948.

The cabinet's decision to transfer the four senior officers of the Wehrmacht to the Münsterlager Hospital in Hamburg was completed with the greatest discretion so as to prevent an outcry of protests in Great Britain. But it would not be long before the entire case would be known to the public. Manstein had been deliberately authorized to write to his new friend, the British military historian Basil Henry Liddell Hart, to whom, during his captivity in England, he had related his many feats of arms. He wrote a letter to him, published later in *The Manchester Guardian*, which recounted his suffering. Indeed, he described in it what he called his "torment" and his "torture." His wife could only visit him one hour per day, while his children were absolutely not allowed. Kept in ignorance concerning the fate that was reserved for him, he relentlessly complained of his humiliations: "We are being confined like criminals," he wrote.

The publication of the letter had the desired effect. It raised a wave of protests and indignation in British public opinion against the supposed shameful treatment being doled to the four prisoners, just as it created a flood of sympathy towards them. However, when Winston Churchill, now the head of the opposition, threatened to protest publicly in the Commons should it arise that the government would announce its decision to try the four German generals, Bevin remained cold and unshakeable. To his political advisors who, in light of the outcry provoked by the case, asked if it were not preferable to backtrack, the minister of Foreign Affairs promptly responded: "We have tried the corporals, now the generals must be tried too." After having tried those who had executed the criminal orders, declared Bevin, one can now only do the same thing with those who had issued them.[596]

But the magnitude of the protests had clearly caught him by surprise. Furthermore, following Shinwell's refusal to announce publicly in the Commons that a trial would be held against the four senior officers of the Wehrmacht, Bevin insisted upon the necessity of convening once again the cabinet in order to reassert the decision that it had previously made and to approve the declaration that it was prepared to express in the Commons on September 22, 1948.

The reaction from the Commons to Bevin's declaration was resolutely hostile. Not a single opinion was voiced in support of the government's decision. Among the party leaders who were criticizing this decision, besides Churchill, were Parliament members Reginald Paget and Richard Stokes. The latter was nicknamed the "deputy of the Hamburg parliament," due to his persistent criticism against the Allies' German policy, which he considered negative. During the war, he led a campaign, along with Paget, against the bombing of Reich towns and of the German civilian population, asserting that this represented a war crime, for they comprised no military objective. At the announcement of the government's decision to bring before the tribunal Field Marshals Manstein, Brauchitsch, and Rundstedt, as well as Colonel General Strauß, deputies Paget and Stokes were among those who sprung up in the Commons to express their indignation. Among the members of Parliament denouncing the decision to try the "old and sick" generals, there were even some among them who had suffered during the war, a fact that was revealing of the magnitude of the opposition.

The discontent also reached the ranks of the House of Lords, particularly the person of Bell, the Bishop of Chichester who, throughout the war, had been one of the principal spokesmen against the bombings of the civilian population and towns in Germany. In the crusade that he led against the government's decision to try the four Wehrmacht generals, he was supported by the Viscount de L'Isle, Viscount Maugham, who, until 1945, had been the primary critic of the government for its laxity in preparations for the war crimes trials, and Lord Hankey, former secretary to the cabinet, as well as a large number of conservative colleagues, among whom were several former supporters in favor of a policy of appeasement.

Outside of Parliament, the most visible militant was the Jewish editor Victor Gollancz, a philanthropist who asserted that reconciliation was of capital importance. The radical and resolutely socialist pacifist denounced the trials for crimes of war as an "appalling mix of hypocrisy, time-limits, and thirst for vengeance." Gollancz also protested against the conditions in which the four generals were living and which he described as degrading, even citing, to reinforce his stance, the letter that Manstein had addressed to Liddell Hart.[597]

If the large majority of the protest movement stemmed from the political right and the conservative-leaning public, it was, however, not without liberal circles and the left in which ruled a virulent sentiment of anti-Communism, fueled by the advent of the cold war. Some, born of the political center and the left, preferred that these former dignitaries of the Wehrmacht not be tried in order to carefully manage the West Germans, whom they were hoping would participate in a trans-Atlantic military alliance to provide defense for Western Europe against the Soviet bloc, at a moment when the cold war was at its climax. To reach such a political objective, several British were actually ready to brush the war crimes committed by the former German generals under the carpet and present a completely honorable image of the Wehrmacht. In their eyes, the latter did not behave any differently than other armies. It had led a "proper war" and its soldiers had earned respect and dignity by fighting under a chivalrous code of honor.[598]

Far from fading with time, the criticisms gained strength, notably in the debates in the House of Commons that took place during the following weeks. Among other things, they focused on the opportunity of holding such a trial, on the cabinet's reasons for undertaking it, and on the prison conditions of the defendants, particularly since their return to Germany. On October 10, 1948, on behalf of the opposition, Churchill condemned the government's decision as being an "unfavorable and malicious enterprise" for "military, humane, and legal" reasons. He even characterized it as "stupid," "demented" and "mad." In his view, it was only more or less the result of a thirst for vengeance on the part of the victors. Two weeks later, he returned to the attack: "Retributive persecution is of all policies the most pernicious [...] British policy should henceforth be to wipe a sponge over the past—hard as that may be—and look for the sake of our salvation to our future."[599]

Despite the vehement criticisms, the government decided to proceed, just as its members had decided, with preparations for the trial. Completion of the charges demanded a colossal amount of work involving the interrogation of witnesses in Germany and the examination of German documents retained in Nuremberg, Berlin, London, and Washington. In the spring of 1949, while preparations were underway, worrying news came about the health of Rundstedt and Strauß. The Minister of War ordered another medical exam of the three surviving officers by a commission from the army and the Ministry of Interior. The four military and civilian doctors who composed the commission unanimously came to the decision that only Manstein remained capable of enduring a trial. On May 5, 1949, the cabinet thus decided to free Rundstedt and Stauß for health reasons. As for the accusations set forth against Manstein, it was expecting to announce them shortly. In fact, it was on May 24, 1949, that it would inform Manstein of the charges held against him.[600] The decision to bring him before a tribunal would arouse an outcry of protests in both West Germany and Great Britain.

A wave of sympathy for Manstein due to political considerations?

The Manchester Guardian described the government's announcement to try Manstein for war crimes as an "inglorious decision." Its editorial continued in the following terms: "Heaven is weary of the hollow words, which States and Kingdoms utter, when they talk of truth and justice." For the news weekly *The Economist*, the trying "of one of the most gifted German commanders of the war in Russia and in Poland would be rather incompatible with winning Germany over to the cause of the West in the cold war [...]. The result of the delay [...] was most likely due to the reluctance for a trial of such importance for which all of the evidence originated from the other side of the iron curtain."

Notably among those proposing to draw a definitive line on any undertaking aimed at trying German generals for war crimes, there was the philosopher Bertrand Russell who, in the *Hamburger Abendblatt*, asserted that Manstein had already fully served his time since he had been detained all of these years by the British Army. In his opinion, to advance with the trial against Manstein would risk stirring up National Socialist sympathy in Germany, all the more so since the war crimes of the victorious powers, for their part, had not in any way been punished. Not only was it necessary to avoid arousing German nationalism, but it was above all important to gain West Germany as a trustworthy partner to fight against communism in the context of the cold war which was raging at the time.

The bishop of Chichester, who had been advocating for some time the adoption of a moderate policy with respect to the "good Germans," who had opposed the Nazis, denounced the government's decision for "questions of justice, humanity, and political wisdom." Highly critical towards the Charter of the International Military Tribunal, particularly for the exclusion of any defense resting on the argument of obedience to orders from above, Bishop Bell pleaded for a general amnesty, in addition to the unconditional liberation of the commanders of the Wehrmacht. "After all this time, after such an interval since the Moscow Declaration, after four years of imprisonment, let them leave," he declared.

Such a point of view was shared by those who, while supporting the motion, emphasized other aspects of the debate. Viscount Simon, for example, challenged the political grounds of the government's decision, indicating that the British concept of trials against war crimes, the elaboration of which he himself had contributed, had the objective of establishing justice through a small number of examples. He thus asked himself what further advantage could the government gain by making another example, this time with Manstein. Others even spoke of a dangerous precedent, about confusing the concept of justice with that of vengeance, and about blind adherence to international agreements that had already been violated by the Soviets. The decision to bring Manstein before a tribunal for war crimes appeared all the more political since the war crimes of the victorious powers had not been pursued.[601]

The sympathy towards Manstein quickly gained momentum in British public opinion, even more so since the majority of British still did not grasp at the time the entire scope and true significance of the policy of extermination of the Jews carried out by the National Socialist regime. For their part, the senior officers of the British armed forces were refusing to see in Manstein anything other than the incarnation of traditional, chivalrous Prussian military virtues. Indeed, as much in public opinion as in the view of British officers, Manstein was quite simply an officer born into the old Prussian military caste, and a representative of the most traditional military tradition there ever was.

It goes without saying that British senior officers must have inevitably felt a spirit of camaraderie for their former enemy. Remembering the "proper" military campaign led in North Africa by Rommel, a field marshal for whom they had tremendous respect, the British military elite could only believe that the other German field marshals or generals, whose military achievements had primarily been accomplished in Soviet territory, had performed similarly. In addition, the impending creation of NATO, the trans-Atlantic military alliance destined to contain the Soviet threat from the other side of the iron curtain, and the negotiations that ensued in the Western camp on the necessity of having a remilitarized West Germany participate, was certainly not unrelated to this sympathy towards Manstein. In fact, the British military leaders considered that it was in the interest of their country to demonstrate clemency towards the German field marshal so as not to compromise the rearmament of the Federal Republic of Germany and its membership in NATO. Called upon to become the bastion of the West against the Soviet threat, due to its geostrategic location in Europe, the Republic was considered a crucial partner to effectively counter, with credibility, the propagation of communism.[602]

It was a situation that would be brilliantly exploited by Dr. Paul Leverkuehn and Hans Laternser, the two German attorneys assigned to defend Manstein at his trial. For several months, they attempted to convince the British Ministry of Foreign Affairs that Manstein should be able to count on a British attorney to provide his defense and that the latter should be paid straight from government funds in London, for the field marshal did not have any financial resources in Great Britain. Like his fellow officers, his pension had been suspended and his fortune confiscated. But the Ministry of Foreign Affairs rejected such a proposal.

On July 11, 1949, with the assistance of the Viscount de l'Isle, Leverkuehn addressed a letter to *The Times* newspaper in order to obtain a British attorney for the defense of his client, stating that the German attorneys were at a disadvantage with regard to the English language and English law, specifically Common Law, and the procedural techniques of Anglo-Saxon tribunals. However, the two German attorneys had spent the last years arguing quite remarkably their cases before the Nuremberg International Military Tribunal, and during the trials had interrogated Field Marshal Manstein in his role as witness for the defense. They had also defended Field Marshal Leeb's case before an American military tribunal in Nuremberg within the framework of the OKW trial, as well as that of Field Marshal Kesselring before a British military tribunal in Venice. If Laternser understood the English language, he could, however, not speak it. This was in contrast to Leverkuehn, who was very familiar with England and the United States since he had already lived there and had perfect mastery of English, even speaking without the slightest German accent.

The letter nevertheless achieved an immense success. Two days later, Lord Bridgeman and the viscounts de L'Isle and Dudley organized a public fund-raising event to defray the costs of the defense. Churchill, who denounced the "belated trial of an aged German general," was one of the first to contribute to it by making a donation of 25£ (300DM). In all, the event raised a sum of 2,000£ (24,000DM) to adequately provide for Manstein's defense.

Even though they were delighted by the support from a personality as eminent as Churchill, the Germans remained perplexed by the sympathy felt by many British for Manstein. Among his supporters was even an exceptional poet, critic, and playwright, T.S. Eliot. Several Germans interpreted such a wave of sympathy for Manstein not as a gesture of amends, nor the result of a thought process according to which it was absurd to commence legal proceedings for war crimes, but rather as overwhelming proof of the British desire to take advantage of the knowledge of a German officer of Manstein's unparalleled caliber, whose principal military achievements had taken place in the East, and to make the most of it against the Russians within the context of the cold war. The Soviet leadership interpreted similarly the benevolence that the British were showing to Manstein, even accusing Churchill of being "Warmonger No. 1." The British embassy's proposal to Moscow to win the cooperation of the Russians in the case was thus formally rejected.[603]

Manstein's trial with the cold war in the background

Manstein's trial took place before a British military tribunal in Hamburg, in the Curio House, on August 24, 1949. The walls of the courtroom were covered with maps illustrating where Manstein's armies were located at each point in the war in the East. In the hallways it was recounted that, if Manstein had surrendered to the Polish, he would have been hanged, whereas if he had handed himself over to the Russians, he would have been placed at the head of an army group, while the British were having difficulties at choosing which of the two options they liked the least.

To provide for his defense, Manstein had at his disposal, besides the German attorneys Leverkuehn and Laternser, the British attorneys Reginald Paget and Samuel C. Silkin, both members of the Labour Party which formed the government in London. Attorney to the Crown and former officer of the Royal Navy, Paget had accepted Leverkuehn's invitation to take charge of Manstein's defense, but had refused to receive any honorariums for his services. To assist him in his job, he called upon Silkin, who had reached the rank of lieutenant colonel in the British Army. German propagandists would not hesitate to reveal that Silkin, who had also refused to receive any honorarium for his work, was Jewish. It goes without saying that the fact that a Jew was involved in the defense of a field marshal of the Wehrmacht caused great commotion in Germany. Public opinion was deeply moved by this, just as the newspapers which saw in Silkin's participation the proof of Manstein's innocence.

During the trial, a third British attorney named Bill Croome, a defense specialist, would join the team gathered around Manstein. General Busse, Manstein's former chief of staff and close friend, and three secretaries also devoted their body and soul to the field marshal's defense.[604]

The principal attorney of the Crown was Sir Arthur Comyns-Carr, who had been Great Britain's public prosecutor during the war crimes trials in Tokyo. He was assisted by Elwyn Jones, the private parliamentary secretary of Great Britain's public prosecutor and one of the prosecutors at the International Military Tribunal in Nuremberg, as well as by Colonel Gerald Draper. Lieutenant General Sir Frank Simpson acted as the president of the tribunal. Judge Justice Collingwood sat next to them as legal counsel and assessor to the president.

Until the end of May 1949, the accused Manstein was refused the right to know the charges brought against him, as well as the evidence that had been gathered. He had equally been denied the right to contest the court's jurisdiction or to oppose any of its members, or to even appeal the judgment. Paget and his team of attorneys were unable to prepare the defense properly before the opening of the trial, for they did not learn of the charges against their client until the last hour. This, representing a major breach in the English practice of law, revolted Paget. Furthermore, it was for all of these reasons, if one believed his remarks, that he had agreed to take charge of the field marshal's defense. During their first meeting at the Münsterlager Hospital, Paget explained to Manstein that, if he had come to Hamburg, it was for the one and only reason that he considered it contrary to the honor of his country that a defendant should be prevented from obtaining a suitable defense.

Manstein responded that he had followed Paget's activities in the House of Commons and that he was very impressed by what he considered to be an honorable attitude towards the defeated. He expressed to him all of his gratitude. He then stated that all that counted in his eyes, within the framework of his trial, was to preserve the honor of the German Army: "I am not particularly concerned as to what happens to me; in any event my life is over. I am concerned for my honour and the honour of the German army I led. Your soldiers know that when they met us we fought like honourable soldiers. You have been convinced by

Bolshevik propaganda that in Russia we fought like savages. That is untrue. In a terribly hard winter we maintained firm discipline and fought honourably. I am determined to defend the honour of the German army."[605] Just as at Nuremberg, three years earlier, Manstein was devoted to the mission of preserving the honor of the Wehrmacht, an honor that it had, however, tarnished by being party to the National Socialist regime and its criminal policies.

On August 24, 1949, Comyns-Carr, prosecuting attorney, opened the trial by stating the charges against Field Marshal Manstein. These were based on the allegation that he committed acts that infringed upon the laws and customs of war as defined by the Hague Convention of 1907. The charges reached a total of seventeen.

The first three charges concerned the Polish campaign, during which Manstein had been Rundstedt's chief of staff, at the headquarters of Army Group South. They underlined several incidents in which civilians and Polish soldiers had been executed. The murders had been committed, in certain cases, by soldiers of the army and, in others, by members of the *Einsatzgruppen*, the SS, the SD, and the police force, while these Nazi paramilitary organizations were under direct military control. Manstein's responsibility was based on his duties as chief of staff of an army group which entrusted him with the opportunity, if he desired it, to plan or, at least, oppose such crimes, and on the fact that he was very well aware of the criminal policy that the Nazi war machine was intending to implement in Poland, having been informed of this by Hitler himself during the military conference that the latter had held at the Berghof on August 22, 1939, before the Wehrmacht generals.

The fourth charge was in relation to the treatment of prisoners of war in the Crimea, at the time when Manstein was commander in chief of the Eleventh Army. It was alleged that the field marshal, in his role as commander of this army, had neglected, in a deliberate and heedless manner, his duty to ensure the humane treatment of Soviet prisoners of war detained by the forces under his command. Consequently, several thousand of them had died of exposure, hunger, or abuse. Others had been handed over by his troops to *Einsatzgruppe D*, SS units, SD units, or the police, which were operating in the military region under his direct command, to be killed on the spot. Manstein was thus blamed for having consented to the elimination of certain groups of prisoners of war, primarily Communists and Jews, for ideological and racial reasons expressed by the National Socialist regime. Within nine months in the Crimea, his troops had handed over to Nazi paramilitary organizations some 3,300 prisoners of war who were considered undesirable elements.

The three following charges also dealt with the question of Soviet prisoners of war. It was claimed that they had been illegally treated as partisans and that, as a result, several thousand among them had been killed without a trial by soldiers of the Eleventh Army, in conformity with criminal orders issued by the high command of the army and by Manstein himself. It was also mentioned that the Germans had forcefully enlisted Soviet prisoners into the German Army and that Manstein did not oppose this procedure. It was also alleged that Soviet prisoners had been used by the Germans for prohibited and dangerous jobs. The prosecution therefore referred to the clauses of the Hague Convention of 1907, which stipulated that prisoners of war could be utilized for labor, but only insofar as it was not excessive nor related to military operations. According to the prosecution, Manstein made use of prisoners of war in Russia under circumstances that contravened the following four clauses: 1. supporting German combat troops; 2. the construction and maintenance of bridges, roads, and railroads; 3. minesweeping; 4. construction of fortifications. Moreover, the prisoners were regularly utilized in the advanced zones of the front where they were under fire from their own troops.

The eighth charge referred to the Commissar Order, which enjoined Wehrmacht troops to summarily execute all Communist Party members found in the Red Army, for the purpose of eradicating Bolshevik terror. The prosecution put forth that Manstein had received this order shortly before the invasion of the U.S.S.R., and that it had been implemented during the three principal commands that the defendant had overseen in Soviet Russia. In addition, it was alleged that Manstein's directive of November 20, 1941, issued as commander in chief of the Eleventh Army in the Crimea, corresponded entirely to the spirit of the Commissar Order. According to the prosecution, Manstein's directive had the objective of further inciting his troops to execute on the spot the political commissars who fell into their hands, or to hand them over as soon as possible to *Einsatzgruppe D*, the SS, SD, or the police for the same end. The November 20 directive was thus invoked as evidence that Manstein indeed had his troops execute the Commissar Order, of which he fully approved.

Characterized as "anti-Jewish charges," the following four charges dealt with the issue of the extermination of the Jews, in reference to the activities of *Einsatzgruppe D* in the rear of Eleventh Army in southern Ukraine and on the Crimean peninsula. They attributed Manstein with the responsibility of 33,000 out of some 100,000 Jews assassinated in this southern region of Bolshevik Russia. More precisely, he was accused of having authorized a large-scale execution of Jews, and even having encouraged it by issuing his orders of November 20, 1941 to his troops. Not only was he accused of having incited his troops to act brutally against the Jews, but also of having ordered them to hand over the Jews who were captured in occupied territories to the units of *Einsatzgruppe D*, knowing full well that this would lead to their deaths. For these reasons, he was blamed, as commander in chief of an army, for having neglected, in a deliberate and heedless manner, his duty to ensure order and public safety, as well as respecting the rights and honor of individual life. In addition, he was incriminated for having done nothing to prevent *Einsatzgruppe D* from carrying out its job, even though he was responsible for the maneuvering and resupplying of this organization that was attached directly to his army. Although the orders relative to its activities came under the chief of the SD or the police force, the commander in chief of the army also had the right to issue his own orders if the course of operations demanded it. According to the prosecution, Manstein was thus well informed of the activities of *Einsatzgruppe D*, all the more so since his own troops had assisted in its mission of eliminating all the Jews of the region.

The thirteenth and fourteenth charges concerned the "Barbarossa decree," according to which crimes committed against civilians or prisoners of war would only be court martialed if a breach in the discipline of combat troops demanded it. Because of this, Manstein was accused of having issued orders enjoining his troops to execute hostages under the guise of retaliatory measures for guerilla warfare against German soldiers or for sabotage against German military infrastructure. Hostages were chosen at random among the civilian population of the area where resistance had been perceived. He was thus blamed for having executed without trial innocent civilians for offenses committed by others. It was also alleged that the retaliatory measures were excessive in relation to the offenses committed, most of the time fifty civilians being executed for every German soldier killed. As if this were not enough, on

November 16, 1941, the staff of Eleventh Army ordered that for every attempt or act of sabotage perpetrated against the German occupier, 100 inhabitants would be executed as a retaliatory measure, which paid witness to the undeniable arbitrary nature of the retaliation. Moreover, Manstein was accused of having ordered his troops to execute without trial civilians who were simply suspected of belonging to partisan groups. Thousands of innocent people had thus been killed under the pretext that they were partisans, guerillas, or bandits.

The last three charges concerned the period of war during which the German Army was retreating from the vast territories of the Soviet Union it had previously occupied. The prosecution referred to them as "charges of forced labor." They accused Manstein of having issued his troops a certain number of directives relative to the forced labor of Soviet civilians, following which several thousand of them had been used in the construction of fortifications and other military works. The charges alleged that such work had been conducted, in several cases, very close to the front line, and that they involved on occasion pregnant women, children, and elderly. The prosecution invoked an OKH order, dated from February 1943, which decreed that all inhabitants of the operations zone from 14 to 64 years old and capable of working were subject to forced labor by the German forces. Manstein was also accused of having given various orders for the forced deportation of Soviet civilians from the occupied territories to Germany, where they would be forced to work in weapons and ammunition factories, under the framework of an obligatory Nazi work program led by Fritz Sauckel. He was thus blamed for having cooperated in the removal of men, women, and children who were sent to Germany to work as slaves. In any case, only the close cooperation of the Wehrmacht had made possible the forced deportation into Germany of some three million Russian civilians forced to work as slave laborers. Finally, Manstein was accused of having issued orders to size livestock and foodstuffs, destroy houses and factories, and deport civilians who were able to work. He was incriminated him for having participated in a "scorched earth" policy adopted by the Wehrmacht during its retreat.[606]

With the assistance of Laternser and Leverkuehn, Paget and Silkin prepared their arguments according to the major points of the "generals' memorandum" drafted in November 1945 by Manstein, Brauchitsch, Halder, Warlimont, and Westphal. The defense launched a "crusade" aimed at denouncing the humiliation inflicted by the Allies on the German generals and, as a result, on the honor of the Wehrmacht. Quite clearly, it minimized the war of annihilation led by the Wehrmacht in the East, particularly its political and ideological objectives, as well as its participation in the extermination of Jews, political commissars, and Soviet prisoners, which it attributed to the context of anti-partisan warfare. Likewise, it evaded the military elite's contribution to the planning and conducting of this war of aggression, simultaneously criminal and barbaric. Moreover, it labeled as Soviet propaganda allegations claiming that the Wehrmacht had committed atrocities in Eastern Europe.

In short, according to the defense, far from infringing upon the principles of the Hague Convention of 1907, Manstein maintained order and discipline within his command. He had quite simply participated in an honorable and chivalrous battle, treating appropriately the prisoners of war and the civilian populations of the occupied territories. In addition, Manstein had refused to execute the criminal orders put forth by his superiors, such as the Commissar Order, and was unaware of the extermination of Jews by the units of the SD or the SS, all his time having been monopolized by military matters due to his responsibilities as commander of the front.[607]

It is nonetheless surprising that a man like Manstein, recognized for his exceptional intellectual capacities, and for his remarkable memory of the slightest detail, was clumsy in his testimony, contradicting himself on several occasions. He defended himself by arguing that he had been forced, through his duty as a soldier, to obey the orders of his superiors. Yet, this was an argument that the judgment rendered by the Nuremberg International Military Tribunal had categorically rejected. Coming from a field marshal who boasted about having confronted Hitler on several occasions about the conduct of military operations, such an argument hardly conformed to the heroic image of the Prussian officer as with which many had characterized him. If this argument had been accepted, it would have meant that, excluding Hitler and the primary figures of the Nazi regime, very few Germans, out of a population of nearly seventy million, would have been able to be held responsible for anything.

By insisting upon the criticisms that he had addressed to Hitler about his conduct of military operations, Manstein was implying, with-

out realizing it, that he had accepted everything else that he did not criticize, such as the regime's policy of annihilation in the East, which is to
say the extermination of the Jews, the elimination of the political commissars, the physical abuse inflicted upon prisoners and the civilian population, as well as the brutal exploitation of the occupied territories.[608]

At the conclusion of the trial, Paget's closing statements summarized
his main arguments aimed at exonerating Manstein from the seventeen
charges against him. They were essentially based on three primary
points: 1. the duty of a general was to obey the orders that his government had issued to him; 2. the Hague Convention could not be applied
to the war in Bolshevik Russia, for the latter was not an adherent; 3.
Manstein was not implicated in any of the war crimes of the National
Socialist regime, including those relative to the extermination of the
Jews.

Paget concluded by denouncing the political objective of the trial:
"An attempt has been made to tarnish the reputation of the German
Army and its greatest commander. [...] When we engaged in battle
against the Wehrmacht in Africa, Italy, and in France, it always fought
honorably. Because of the Russian propaganda about which we heard
so much, we think that the Germans fought like savages in the East. [...]
This has not been proven by the documents that we presented here. In
my opinion, they have demonstrated that the Wehrmacht demonstrated,
in large measure, restraint and discipline, and this, under circumstances
of unimaginable cruelty."

Implicitly making reference to the context of the cold war, which
was prevailing at the time of the trial and, in particular, to imperatives
linked to the defense of Western Europe, notably to West Germany's
envisioned rearmament, Paget asked for Manstein's discharge: "I hope
that we will all become friends in the future. If Western Europe must
genuinely be defended, then we must be friends. I do not believe [...]
that it is the conquerors' right, that it is our right, to tarnish the reputation of the vanquished. For Germany, Manstein will never be a war
criminal. He is a hero to his people and will remain so. He was the
architect of German victory and the Hector in Germany's defeat, the
man who commanded the great retreat while in his heart and in his soul
he knew that Troy would fall. And, here, before the tribunal, he has
now delivered his last battle for the honor of the men that he led and
who fell in combat under his command."

Paget continued his speech, declaring that if the tribunal made the decision to condemn Manstein, one could not hesitate to consider him as a victim of the "victors' justice," born out of a spirit of revenge: "If we condemn him, then we will be damaging not his reputation, but ours. The conquerors do not have the right to damage the reputation of the defeated. Caesar condemned Vercingetorix. History has forgotten the Roman colonists who were massacred by the insurgent Gauls. It only remembers the noble Gaul who died from the conquerors' triumph. Only Caesar's reputation and Rome's honor were tainted. It has always been easy to condemn the vanquished as war criminals. After the South African war, we were able to condemn the Boer generals who had shot the kaffir prisoners. We have instead taken a more noble and intelligent path. Five hundred years ago, we condemned a female enemy military leader. At that time we acted in such a way for political reasons. We wanted to denounce her for being a witch, but we made of her a saint. I hope [...] that the decision of this tribunal will mark a return in Europe to a more generous and civilized lifestyle."

Paget ended his remarks by asking for Manstein's acquittal. In his eyes, the German was an honorable field marshal who had only done his soldierly duty by obeying the orders his superiors had issued to him: "I do not believe that there is one among you who, for a single second, dares to imagine that Manstein is an evil man. He was appreciated by his staff and his soldiers. This is at least what has been clearly demonstrated. No one casts doubt on the fact that he possessed all the traditional moral qualities. [...] The accusation that is brought against him is that he executed the desires of his commander in chief, but this is Germany's crime. [...] In my opinion [...] it is utterly and completely unjust to condemn a person who did nothing more than execute the desires of his government. Consequently, such a symbolic expiation negates the individual. [...] I am asking for Manstein's acquittal, because I believe that his acquittal will be honorable for my country."[609]

Such an argument served to vindicate a war criminal. The passage where Paget states that Manstein had been "the architect of German victory" and not of "German victories" is quite striking, for it represents an interpretation of the history of the Second World War which was not without ulterior motive. This was very clear: it was a matter of implicitly emphasizing Manstein's contribution to the fight against Bolshevism, and implied that, without his military accomplishments in

Soviet Russia, Western Europe would probably have been consumed by Bolshevism, just like Eastern Europe. In the context of the cold war at the time—Germany's division, that of the European continent into two antagonistic blocks, and the creation of a Western military alliance to fend off the threat of Bolshevism—such an allusion could not leave the members of the tribunal indifferent. Moreover, the comparison with Troy revived the myth of a Germany that had been conquered on the battlefield only through trickery. It even suggested that Germany had conducted a defensive war, whereas in reality she had unleashed the war and invaded most of the countries of the European continent. Finally, the comparison with Hector made of Manstein the greatest defender of Germany, which had resisted an enemy largely superior in number. In short, the roles of assailant and defender had been inverted: Germany and Manstein were the victims, whereas Bolshevik Russia was the aggressor.

In his closing remarks, Comyns-Carr summarized the evidence that he had gathered regarding each of the charges against Manstein. According to the prosecuting attorney, the field marshal was guilty of having supported out of conviction the criminal war led by Hitler in both Poland and the U.S.S.R., as his attitude in relation to the extermination of the Jews and the elimination of political commissars demonstrated. If he had desired, added Comyns-Carr, he could have prevented or, at the very least, opposed the criminal actions that occurred in the military region under his command without running any personal risks. He ended his speech with the following words: "I am asking you to ignore the political considerations [of the defense] and to declare that this defendant is guilty of the charges for which he has been charged."[610]

After the closing arguments, the tribunal adjourned for three weeks in order to allow Collingwood, the legal counsel and Simpson's assessor, to prepare a recapitulation of the trial. The latter first recommended that the tribunal adopt the Nuremberg decisions in order render its own judgment. As a result, neither the orders given by superiors nor the laws adopted by the state could be claimed by the defense as motives likely to exonerate their client for criminal actions. In addition, the execution of prisoners of war as retaliation was declared an illegal act under all circumstances. It was also clarified that the principles of the Hague Convention applied to the war against the U.S.S.R., whether the latter was an adherent to it or not, and that the concept relative to the necessity of war was valid only in the cases specifically put forth by the Convention. Finally, it was mentioned that Manstein was responsible for exercising executive power in the region under his military command, and that any ignorance or violation of his military prerogatives was not an excuse. Collingwood then presented a recapitulation of both the prosecution and the defense.

On December 19, 1949, the tribunal finally rendered its verdict. Field Marshal Manstein was acquitted of eight charges and found guilty of nine others. After having pronounced the judgment before the defendant, the president of the tribunal, Lieutenant General Simpson, added the following personal remark: "I was forced to act, for the first time in my life, in a manner contrary to my convictions. If I had been in the field marshal's situation, I would not have acted any differently than him. But I must sentence him in accordance with the laws in place."[611]

Although there was no doubt as to his culpability, Manstein was declared not guilty of the three charges concerning Poland, with the tribunal arguing that his duties as chief of staff of an army group made him in no way responsible for the crimes that had been committed during this campaign. Despite the facts presented before the tribunal, he was also judged not guilty of the accusation of having proceeded with the forced recruitment of Soviet prisoners of war for the Wehrmacht. The tribunal, however, declared him guilty of having used Soviet prisoners of war for minesweeping and the construction of military fortifications, and of having forcefully deported civilians from the zone of his army command towards the Reich in order for them to be used as slave labor.

Contrary to all expectations, he was acquitted of the three charges related to the extermination of the Jews, despite the overwhelming evidence presented to the tribunal that incriminated him beyond doubt, particularly in relation to his order of November 20, 1941. The tribunal decided that the prosecution had not proven with any certainty that Manstein had approved the extermination of the Jews or that he had actively participated by either inciting or authorizing his troops to execute Jews or hand them over to SD or SS units to accomplish the job. However, for these three charges, he was indicted for having neglected his duty to ensure, as commander of the campaign, order and public safety, as well as respect for the rights and honor of the family and individual life in the military region placed under his command, a result of which a considerable number of Jews had been exterminated. But the tribunal declared that it was not a matter of deliberate and heedless negligence, as the prosecution stated. Such a sentence revealed, however, Manstein's actual responsibility in the war crimes that occurred in the region of operations falling under his command.

It was a rather surprising fact that Manstein was exonerated by the tribunal for the massive execution of civilians who were labeled as partisans, whereas his comrades-in-arms had been previously sentenced for this same charge during the OKW trial. Indeed, the tribunal declared that Manstein had absolutely no responsibility for the application of the "Barbarossa decree." As for the charges concerning the ravages caused by the German Army during its retreat, Manstein was acquitted. Yet he was held responsible for the poor treatment inflicted upon Soviet prisoners of war, for the execution of several among them, for surrendering them over to SD or SS units, and for the execution of Red Army political commissars. The tribunal undoubtedly considered that the execution of commissars was a crime greater than the execution of civilians deemed as partisans and that it deserved being sanctioned. Finally, Manstein was found guilty of the execution of civilians as a retaliatory measure, as well as for the actions of his subordinate officers who were acting in accordance to orders issued by the OKH, but not of those that he had himself set forth.[612]

The tribunal sentenced Field Marshal Manstein to eighteen years in prison. In light of current historical research on the Wehrmacht's responsibility in the extermination of the Jews in Eastern Europe, and concerning the massive execution of Soviet political commissars and prisoners, as well as in relation to the poor treatment inflicted upon the civilian population of this region, such a sentence appears quite insignificant. The order of November 20, 1941, issued by Manstein to his troops, was nevertheless fully sufficient to prove his consent and participation in the Jewish Holocaust.

The sentence provoked an outcry as much in Germany as in Great Britain. In fact, it would make of Manstein nothing less than a genuine martyr. Some in West Germany thought he had been nothing more than a victim of "victors' justice," having to endure a collective punishment rather being personally guilty as a war criminal. The simple fact that he had been tried was perceived as an insult to the honor of the German soldier, for he was considered as being above suspicion. German political leadership feared that the sentence would call into question the foothold that the Republic held in the West. On the British side, public opinion expressed *grosso modo* the same sentiments, dreading the emergence of a new nationalism in the Federal Republic of Germany, which would weaken her integration into the community of Western democracies.[613]

In the *Hamburger Allgemeine Zeitung*, a highly liberal newspaper of anti-militarist tradition, Manstein's sentencing was denounced as a political decision: "In the same way as the Nuremberg trials, this trial against Field-Marshal von Manstein was foremost a political trial. A trial not directed against some high-ranking German officer, but against a man who in the opinion of British military critics was called the most outstanding German army leader of the Second World War. As such he was a member of that Wehrmacht whose honour is identical with the honour of all those Germans who in the meaning of that word regarded themselves as soldiers. Millions of them died for that honour, but millions of survivors forever remain tied to the idea of German soldierly honour, although they laid down their arms. After the Nuremberg precedents an honourable acquittal for Manstein could hardly be expected, but all Germans watching the Manstein trial in all its phases were hoping for a mild judgment. The political gesture of such a judgment was sure to have had a warm welcome. That this gesture was not made is something we shall have to put up with, but is also a factor no politically aware German man or woman will be able to overlook."

In *The Times*, the celebrated military author Liddell Hart spoke of his profound indignation concerning the sentence pronounced against Manstein:

> It is now clear that Manstein never initiated any policy of brutality [...]. Although the Russia war became a barbarous fight, Manstein's corps abstained from complying with the drastic orders of the High Command. No fault has been found until he was transferred to command an army in a region where those orders were *already* in operation. It is absurd to assume that a mere army commander, newly arrived [...], could publicly annul orders already made known to his new subordinates *and* to the S.S. there. Even so, there is much evidence that he curbed their

severity. Most significant is a note in the diary of Goebbels, who
frequently warned Hitler of Manstein's opposition to his orders:
'Manstein and Kleist have introduced more humane treatment
of the inhabitants in regions that have again come under military administration as a result of our retreat.' (4/28/1943)

It is evident that Manstein took the initiative in mitigating
inhumane measures. One may hope, not least for our own reputation, that we shall be led to show a similar sense of humanity in mitigating the savage sentence inflicted upon him.

I have studied the records of warfare long enough to realize
that few men who have commanded armies in a hard struggle
could have come through such a searching examination, of their
deeds and words, as well as Manstein did. His condemnation
appears a glaring example either of gross ignorance or gross
hypocrisy."[614]

Manstein was incarcerated in the Werl prison for war criminals,
close to Dortmund in Westphalia, where ten other German generals
were confined, in particular Field Marshal Kesselring and Colonel
General von Mackensen. Manstein had placed at his disposal a secretary to assist in compiling his *Memoirs*. It should be noted that not a
single one of the 632 war criminals executed after their sentencing by
the British and American tribunals was a general. Those who were executed were all subordinates who, in their trial, had invoked an obligation to obey orders given by their superiors.[615]

After a long internal debate, as a result of the outcry unleashed by
the field marshal's sentencing, his prison term was reduced to twelve
years in February 1950. This however, did not bring the protests to an
end. Indeed, numerous interest groups led a campaign to have Manstein
freed, simultaneously provoking a much more widespread debate on
German war criminals incarcerated in the prisons of the Western Allies
in the Republic. Public interest in Manstein's fate would thus accelerate
the search for a solution to the issue of releasing the former German military elite imprisoned for war crimes.

Field Marshal Manstein's liberation, as well as Field Marshal
Kesselring's, was negotiated at the highest level by Churchill, who was
once again prime minister (1951–55), and by Adenauer, the West
German chancellor (1949–63). The issue was of course the object of

countless conversations throughout the British administration. As a result of the cold war, Great Britain and the Federal Republic had become allies of convenience. It was thus in the former's interest not to offend the latter so as not to weaken its position in Europe. As was stated by Lieutenant General Robertson, one of the most visible militants in England fighting to free Manstein, it was not only necessary to prevent him from becoming a martyr to the Germans, but equally so to prevent the emergence of a new nationalism in the Republic. Although the liberation of German war criminals incarcerated in British prisons was not beyond dispute, the two men would nevertheless be released before the end of their prison terms. In Manstein's case, this occurred on May 7, 1953, after receiving a leave the previous year for medical reasons. For his part, Field Marshal Kesselring had been released shortly earlier, in 1952, also for medical reasons. Besides a serious eye operation, protests from leading personalities such as the statesman Churchill, Field Marshal Montgomery, and the famous military author Liddell Hart, were largely responsible for Manstein's early release.[616]

Already at the time of Manstein's trial, Bevin had undertaken steps to prevent his government from once again being confronted with such an embarrassing and explosive situation. Discussion occurred between London, Paris, and Washington in order to define a general policy concerning the sensitive case of German war criminals. At their conclusion, it was agreed that Great Britain would cease, after Manstein's trial, to try anyone who was accused of war crimes. War crimes or crimes against humanity would only be tried before German tribunals and according to legal procedures under German criminal law. If the British policy of prosecuting all those charged of crimes against peace remained in force, the extradition of those charged with murders in the countries that were requesting them remained possible, as long as the extradition requests included sufficiently admissible proof in order to permit exceptions to the deadline of September 1, 1948. Manstein's trial was thus the last British trial held against a German war criminal in Germany.[617]

The Memoirs, the Cold War and the legend of an "irreproachable" Wehrmacht

In 1951, Paget published a work in which he presented his views that were, to say the least, in defense of Manstein's conduct of the war, as well as his trial, a work that would appear in German the following year. Describing the verdict rendered against Manstein by the British tribunal in Hamburg as "victors' justice," he thus contributed towards, as much in Great Britain as in Germany, the emergence of the legend of an "irreproachable" Wehrmacht. Consequently, one must keep in mind that this legend of the supposed "untarnished shield" of the Wehrmacht was not only propagated by the German generals, but also by eminent personalities from countries that were once enemies, such as Churchill, Liddell Hart, and Paget.[618]

The generals of the Wehrmacht reinforced this myth of a "proper" Wehrmacht by publishing their memoirs during the 1950s. Written during a period of reconstruction, economic prosperity, and political stability, they were written with the cold war and anti-communism in the background. In this context, the consolidation of the image of a Wehrmacht that claimed to be a victim of Nazi policy was thus facilitated. It certainly had an influence on those conducting the research. Among the most significant memoirs were those of Halder (*Hitler als Feldherr*, or *Hitler as Miltary Leader*, 1949), Guderian (*Erinnerungen eines Soldaten*, or *Reminiscences of a Soldier*, 1951), Kesselring (*Soldat bis zum letzten Tag*, or *Soldier to the Last Day*, 1953) and Dönitz (*Zehn Jahre und zwanzig Tage*, or *Ten Years and Twenty Days*, 1958), as well as Manstein's, published in two volumes, the first under the title of *Verlorene Siege* (*Lost Victories*, 1955), the second under the title *Aus einem Soldatenleben 1887–1939* (*A Soldier's Life, 1887–1939*, published in 1958).

It is true that the cold war and, more specifically, the tensions between the Soviet Union and the United States, contributed towards overshadowing the role and responsibility of the members of the high command of the German Army in the planning and conduct of wars of aggression, as well as in the criminal actions committed in the East. The need to legitimize the rearmament of the Republic and the necessity to call upon former officers, non-commissioned officers, and soldiers from the Wehrmacht in order to create the ranks of the Bundeswehr, which was accepted into NATO in 1955, demanded the support of a positive image of the German Army.

A declaration of the American President (and former Supreme Allied Commander) Dwight D. Eisenhower on January 23, 1951, and one by West German Chancellor Konrad Adenauer on April 5, 1951, on the honor of the German soldiers of the Second World War would support this direction. Furthermore, former officers were dependent upon such declarations for their use in the enlistment of new armed forces for West Germany. It was Adenauer himself who intervened in favor of Manstein to Eisenhower so that the latter would make a statement about the honor of the German soldiers who had fought during the war from 1939 to 1945.

The liberation of prisoners of war also became one of the conditions for membership into NATO drawn up by the West German government. The closing of the last military prison, that of Landsberg, in 1958, lifted the moral burden that was weighing over the German population, and even more over the former members of the Wehrmacht. It strengthened the myth that the officers of the Wehrmacht had been unjustly incarcerated and that the war in the East had taken place within the norms of the most pure military tradition. Indeed, according to German and Anglo-Saxon opinion, it was unimaginable that German soldiers could have dared to overstep the code of honor and ethics of the Prussian military caste. The German Army, it was believed, could not have behaved in a way that was worse than the others.[619]

It was in this context that Manstein was invited by the Adenauer government to participate as an advisor in the creation of the Bundeswehr. Furthermore, he was the only one of Hitler's field marshals to be consulted by Bonn concerning the creation of a West German Army. But his influence over the studies and theories in relation to the construction of the Bundeswehr has at times been overestimated in the literature. His insufficient comprehension of the political situation at the time led to repeated discussions with General Heusinger, who served in the office of Theodor Blank and was the former chief of operations for the OKH. He was nevertheless the object of several tributes made by the Bundeswehr for having offered his expertise, notably on his 80th and 85th birthdays.[620]

On June 10, 1973, Manstein died from a stroke at the age of 85 in the town of Irschenhausen, near Munich, where he had been living since 1958, after having successively lived in Allmendingen, near Ulm in Essen, and Münster. He was interred on June 15, 1973, with full military honors, in Dorfmark, near Soltau in the Lüneburg Heath. His body was placed next to his wife's, who had died seven years earlier. Until his death, Manstein demonstrated a keen interest in the discussion and studies about him, even participating in a few of them. More than a quarter of century after the end of the war, he was still making it his duty to defend the honor of the German soldiers who had fought under the Third Reich.

CONCLUSION:
THE MAN AND THE SOLDIER

In the first volume of his *Memoirs*, Manstein presents and explains the war from a strictly strategic point of view. Despite the high positions that he held in the Wehrmacht, he fails to pose the question of moral and political responsibility. In the preface, he clarifies the reasons for this silence: "The present book recalls the memories of a soldier. I thus deliberately abstained from speaking about any political problems that did not have a direct and immediate rapport with military events. As one recalls the words of the British military author Liddell Hart: "The German generals of this war were the best-finished product of their profession—anywhere. They could have been better if their outlook had been wider and their understanding deeper. *But if they had become philosophers they would have ceased to be soldiers.*"[621]

Liddell Hart's reflection on the generals of the Wehrmacht is remarkably pertinent in arriving at an understanding of Manstein, as much the man as the soldier. Indeed, it describes perfectly the character and the worldview of an officer who was the most accomplished product of the Prussian military caste of his time, and who was thus extremely representative of his milieu. Through him emerges quite simply the destiny of the large majority of his colleagues in the German officers' corps.

By confining himself only to the military aspects of the global conflict, Manstein avoided, undoubtedly with full knowledge of the facts, addressing the question of the moral and political responsibility of the disastrous consequences of the war, of millions of deaths, and the war's criminal character. Likewise, by citing Liddell Hart's thoughts on the generals of Hitler's army, he justified his assertion that he was only a simple soldier at the service of politics. In this respect, the British military author was not incorrect to claim that the majority of German generals were essentially technicians who were absorbed in their professional work and hardly interested in anything that did not directly concern their jobs or their duties.[622]

Field Marshal Manstein recounts the unfolding of the Second World War, particularly the Russian campaign and the crucial role that he played there, with a surprising absence of any sort of relationship to politics, even more so since he does not question the meaning of the events and his share of the responsibility in them. On this account, Joachim Wieder, who witnessed the tragedy of Stalingrad as a soldier in the Sixth Army, recalled, after the war, his ambivalent thoughts on the man and the soldier that was Manstein: "He held the military success of the great operations over which he had control closer to his heart than worrying about the ethics of politics. Even if he were honestly convinced out of loyalty to his soldiers to serve only the German people, he was, and will remain—and this is precisely his tragedy—a man who can rightly called 'the most uncomfortable general of the devil.' The master abilities of Manstein the strategist have perhaps contributed towards prolonging the fate that was looming over Germany. This was one of the great disappointments of the former chief of general staff, Ludwig Beck, to notice that even the disastrous events tied to the Stalingrad tragedy were not enough to open the eyes of the great military chiefs to the fateful signs of the threatening German collapse."

Wieder continues his analysis of Manstein's behavior and attitude during the war by citing Beck, who, in his military testament written in 1938 in anticipation of the misfortune that was going to crash down upon Germany, set forth the criteria according to which the war chiefs should be judged: "It is a lack of the scale and knowledge of his mission for a high-ranking soldier in a similar time to see his duties and his job within the limited framework of his military missions, without being aware of his significant responsibilities before all of the people. Exceptional times demand exceptional actions!"[623]

Of course, Manstein expresses, in his memories of the war, his conviction that restoring the military situation, on the condition of a political change of heart, would have been possible after Stalingrad, even after Kursk. His own operational ideas would have offered an opportunity for this. But, after Hitler brushed them away with the back of his hand, military defeat had become unavoidable. Manstein's theories lead one to suppose that he overestimated his strategic ability on the battlefield, and moreover, had a complete lack of comprehension of the psychological, political, and ideological aspects linked to the person of Hitler.

The field marshal appears to have considered the battlefield as a sort of autonomous territory upon which his mastery and conduct of military operations would be of decisive importance for the outcome of the war. Faced with such an exaggerated emphasis of only the military dimension and from a strictly strategic point of view, it is enough to recall Colonel General Beck's statements, written in 1938: "The actual concept, which many have remarked, that a great war can only be won through an armed victory is erroneous, harmful and, at a time when, before the entire world, one only speaks of the supposed 'all-encompassing war,' absolutely incomprehensible."

Even after the overpowering advance of the Red Army towards the eastern regions of the Reich, the Anglo-American landing on the Normandy coast, and the failed assassination attempt against Hitler, Field Marshal Manstein still did not consider the war as lost and believed that a retrieval of the military situation was possible, and with this, a political recovery as well. However, he never presented in a convincing and detailed manner how such an evolution was able to occur under Hitler's control, particularly after all of the crimes committed by Germany.

It is indeed difficult to understand how a personality such as Manstein, holding such high positions and with such intelligence, never recognized the precise gravity of Germany's entwined political and military fate. However, after the Stalingrad disaster, certain senior officers were aware, like a weight on their conscience, of the impossibility of a favorable outcome of the war. For well founded reasons, a good number of them even claimed the war was lost. In the conservative-leaning German resistance movement, there were men who endeavored to bring an end to a hopeless war and to spare the German people the appalling sacrifices that were threatening them. Among such men were Colonel General Beck, whom the historian Friedrich Meinecke described as "one of these too few numerous high ranking officers who can be considered the authentic inheritors of Scharnhorst, not only as unyielding and vigorous soldiers, but also as highly cultivated patriots who knew how to see into the distance."[624] Clearly, Manstein was not one of these high-ranking officers who knew how to see into the distance.

In his analysis of Manstein, Wieder also raises the issue of the moral and political responsibility for the war: "Manstein's memoirs can be considered representative of the great majority of texts and memoirs written by the primary German generals of Hitler's time in order to justify themselves. An overall view of this literature, which honestly remains an eloquent source of contemporary history, shows us an alarming amount of unshakeable self-confidence, impenitence, and lack of judgment. The British military writer Liddell Hart gives a striking description of the German officer of the Hitler era, exclusively attached to his professional, technical, and military world, obeying without discussing, and that the difficult problems of political responsibility were of absolutely no concern to him. "He appears to be," he states, "like a modern Pontius Pilate who washes his hands of all responsibility concerning the orders that he must execute. There is almost never any question, in this genre of memoir, of personal failing or of a higher level of awareness. One almost never sees in them how the war was conducted overall and one never asks [in such memoirs] the question of underlying political plans of the event." By placing the responsibility for all the misfortunes on Hitler, he adds, one "does not mention the entire hierarchy of responsibilities that go from the supreme leader to the least senior ranks while moving through the commanders of the front."[625]

After the war, some would blame Manstein for having wanted to create a "myth of the German field marshals" through the publication of his *Memoirs*, and for having wanted to become, by this very fact, a "second Hindenburg." The title of the first volume of his *Memoirs*, *Verlorene Siege* (*Lost Victories*), indeed implies that the generals only lost the war because of Hitler. Beyond the title, Manstein presents in his book the image of an exceptional military high command, as much from a strategic as a tractical viewpoint, but which had been the victim of the Führer's incompetency and his incessant interference in the conduct of operations. Thus, if Hitler had given his generals complete freedom, they would not have lost the war. Through such arguments, Manstein contributed, to a certain extent, to the emergence of a new legend of being "stabbed in the back." The enormous success in sales of his autobiography, and the fact that he had even been approached about being the successor of the first president of the Federal Republic of Germany,

Theodor Heuss, demonstrates the extent to which he was venerated by the public. In truth, during the two decades that followed the end of the war, Manstein had quite simply become a figurehead who was the subject of a veritable military cult.[626]

In 1956, in an article titled "Manstein" published in the *Frankfurter Hefte*, Konrad von Hammerstein, the son of the former army commander in chief Colonel General Kurt Freiherr von Hammerstein-Equord, challenged this cult concerning certain Wehrmacht field marshals, beginning with Manstein: "The army chiefs of the Second World War, who were not National Socialists for the most part, carry a very heavy responsibility in the fate of their people which they cannot pass off on Hitler, because of their extensive knowledge of the situation, their education, and their position. This is why one cannot invent a myth of the army chiefs by promoting the creation of a new Wehrmacht."[627]

Such remarks raised an interesting question: is one able to absolve the generals of the Wehrmacht from all responsibility for the political situation borne from the war that they waged in Europe? On Manstein's death in June 1973, in a commemorative article published in the *Frankfurter Allgemeine Zeitung*, Jürgen Busche responded precisely to this question: "Perfection in the art of war [...] becomes ridiculous when a criminal mentality dominates so greatly the political leadership, especially when the officer, through his extreme competency, thus prolongs the butchery of the war. It is in Germany, during this century, that such a dilemma clearly occurred in the person and fate of Field Marshal Erich von Lewinski, named von Manstein. [...] The victories that Manstein described as "lost" in his autobiography have increased the misery instead of alleviating it. Military expertise has thus degenerated into [nothing more] than a contribution towards the pursuit of inhumanity."[628]

On November 24, 1967, on Manstein's eightieth birthday, the military inspector of the Bundeswehr at the time, Lieutenant General Ernst Ferber, invited the young German soldiers not to mythologize the most brilliant field marshal of the Wehrmacht. In his view, the young generation of Bundeswehr soldiers should rather see in Field Marshal Manstein a tragedy of his time.[629] It goes without saying that, for the leadership of the Bundeswehr, it was important to instill in the young German soldiers a completely new idea of one's military service. At the time of the Wehrmacht, the soldier's ultimate duty was his unconditional obedience to the supreme command of the armed forces and to the head of state, specifically Hitler. At the time of the Bundeswehr, to the contrary, the soldier's priority was to serve Germany and the German people.

The traditional Prussian military virtues, embodied in the sense of duty, obedience, and loyalty prevented Manstein the soldier from understanding the repercussions that were emerging in order to spare his country a total military defeat that was nevertheless inevitable: to leave his position as commander in chief of Army Group South as a form of protest against the Führer's conduct of the war or to actively support the conspiracy with the idea of ensuring the success of a coup d'état against the Nazi regime. It was as an apolitical soldier filled with the spirit of Moltke that he considered his duty of obedience and loyalty to Hitler, who embodied legal authority. He thus respected one of the major principles that he had been taught in the cadets' corps during the time of Imperial Germany. As a soldier, he would have thus fulfilled his duty. But nothing else. One can apply the phrase of Berthold Brecht to Manstein: "First comes obedience, then ethics."[630]

Instead of rebellion, Manstein, the most talented of the Wehrmacht field marshals, chose subordination. Until the very end of the war, he thus remained loyal to the Führer and the Nazi regime. But by refusing to join the ranks of the military resistance, Manstein acted no differently than the other generals, for his position with respect to the opposition movement was the rule and not the exception. Indeed, any sort of resistance that the apolitical soldier that was Manstein made towards Hitler, if there was any, was limited to the domain of military operations. "[…] Manstein's opposition to Hitler," Wieder justly recalls in his post-war reflections, "was that of the military technician in his sovereign superiority against the dilettante. It primarily occurred from the point of view of his military duties and not for reasons of a higher ethical nature."[631]

Concerning Manstein's attitude with respect to the resistance, Guido Knopp makes these highly revealing remarks: "He was a soldier—no less, no more."[632] In addition, Manstein's two autobiographical works are both highly suggestive on this subject, for they only address his life as a soldier. The first, *Verlorene Siege* (*Lost Victories*), appeared in 1955, and covers the period from the Polish campaign to his discharge from the command of Army Group South on March 30,

1944. As for the second, *Aus einem Soldatenleben 1887–1939* (*A Soldier's Life*), published three years later, he describes his military career until the summer of 1939. Clearly, for Manstein, to be a soldier was not a simple job, but rather a *raison d'être*, a way of living that was intimately linked to his worldview.

In his *Memoirs*, Gersdorff presents an enlightening analysis of the character of the highest ranking generals of the Wehrmacht: "I have the personal conviction that the commanders in chief of the army groups and the army of the First World War were in no way able to measure up to such genius strategists, for example, as Field Marshals von Bock, von Manstein, and von Rundstedt. But they were superior in terms of the character of the commanders of the Second World War. I do not, however, underrate that it was easier for the generals who were working within the high spheres of the monarchic system to safeguard their character, for they could count on the fact that there would be no orders issued by the political and military leadership that would place in question the soldier's honor.

"From the memory that I have of my father and of several of my former officers of the old army, I am convinced that the officers' corps of Imperial Germany would have reacted, in such a case, much more forcefully, resolutely, and assuredly than the officers' corps of the Wehrmacht. Contrary to many other opinions, I believe that the idea of resistance, thus of the obligation to overstep on occasion the duty of obedience, was much more deeply anchored in the past and even more so at the time of Imperial Germany than during the Third Reich. Prussian history alone includes several examples where officers in fact resorted to such resistance. The various oaths repeatedly offered—to the emperor and the king, to [Friedrich] Ebert, to Hindenburg, and finally to Hitler—have perhaps negatively influenced the sense of values and character of the highest generals of the Wehrmacht."[633]

By quite simply transposing the fundamental values of the Prussian military tradition in relation to the sense of duty from the time of the Imperial Reich to that of Hitler's state, the field marshal found himself in a situation where he was required to obey orders. For this reason, he was unable to admit that he could serve under orders from a criminal or, at the very least, for an unjust cause. This explains in part his passive attitude with respect to the policies and criminal actions of the Wehrmacht in Eastern Europe, as well as towards the Holocaust.

Manstein's sense of responsibility has always been tarnished by his political indifference and his personal ambitions, which led him to stand in support of Hitler's wars of aggression, particularly the wars of destruction and extermination led in Eastern Europe that were racial and ideological in nature, and which were in absolute contradiction to chivalrous military traditions. Like the large majority of high-ranking officers, Manstein accepted, or at least did nothing to prevent, the Wehrmacht's participation in the crimes of the *Einsatzgruppen*, the SS, and the SD. The German Army was greatly assimilated into Hitler's demented program of exploitation and extermination aimed at creating *Lebensraum*, harnessing economic resources from the Soviet Union, the use of slave labor, and the elimination of the Jews and members of the Communist Party.

When one analyzes Manstein, as much the man as the soldier, one can only recall Jehuda L. Wallach's brief description of the field marshal: "[...] von Manstein was in all likelihood a good technician and a good expert, but he was undeniably a little man." As Raymond Aron has asserted, if Manstein was a "great soldier," he was nevertheless a "lame politician." In addition, Aron has added that he was "one of the most indulgent of the German generals with respect to Hitler," and never succeeded at "realizing the contradiction between the intended goal and the methods applied by Hitler," as well as fully comprehending "the substitution of a 'racial' state for a traditional state."[634] In this sense, Field Marshal Manstein most likely erred out of naiveté by not entirely grasping the implications of his actions, which is to say the consequences of his key military role in favor of the National Socialist regime, and by becoming, without truly wanting to admit it, an obedient instrument in a criminal enterprise.

NOTES

INTRODUCTION

[1] Philippe Masson, *Histoire de l'armée allemande 1939–1945* (Paris: Perrin, 1944), 474.

[2] Basil Henry Liddell Hart, *The Other Side of the Hill. Germany's Generals. Their Rise and Fall. With Their Own Account of Military Events 1939–1945* (London: Cassel, 1951), 94; Liddell Hart, *Histoire de la Second Guerre mondiale* (Paris: Fayard, 1973), 42.

[3] John Keegan, *La Deuxième Guerre mondiale* (Paris: Perrin, 1990), 62; Christian Schneider, "Denkmal Manstein. Psychogramm eines Befehlshabers," in Hannes Heer and Klaus Naumann, eds., *Vernichtungskrieg. Verbrechen der Wehrmacht 1941–1944*, (Hamburg: Hamburger Edition, 1995), 402; Guido Knopp, *Hitlers Krieger* (Munich: Goldmann, 2000), 235; David Irving, *Hitler's War* (New York: Viking, 1977), 81; Albert Seaton, *The German Army 1933 – 1945* (London: Weidenfeld and Nicolson, 1982), 215.

[4] Liddell Hart, "Forward,"in Erich von Manstein, *Lost Victories* (London: Methuen, 1958),13; Richard Brett-Smith, *Hitler's Generals* (London: Osprey, 1976), 221.

[5] Brett-Smith, *Hitler's Generals*, 234; Heinz Guderian, *Panzer Leader* (Washington D.C.: Zenger, 1979), 302; Liddell Hart, *The Other Side of the Hill*, p 98; Walther Görlitz, ed., *The Memoirs of Field Marshal Keitel* (London: Kimber, 1965), 53.

[6] Samuel W. Mitcham, *Hitler's Field Marshals and their Battles* (London: Grafton, 1988), 241; Lord Carver, "Manstein,"in Correlli Barnett, ed., *Hitler's Generals* (London: Weidenfeld and Nicolson, 1989), 221.

[7] Marcel Stein, *Generalfeldmarschall Erich von Manstein. Kritische Betrachtung des Soldaten und Menschen* (Mayence: Hase & Koehler, 2002), 10-11.

[8] Manfred Messerschmidt, "Das Bild der Wehrmacht in Deutschland seit 1945," *Revue de l'Allemagne et des pays de langue allemande*, 30, no. 2 (April-

483

May 1998): 117-119.

[9] The first volume of the *Memoirs* of Field Marshal Erich von Manstein appeared in 1955, *Verlorene Siege,* 16th ed. (Bonn: Bernard & Graefe, 2000), the second volume in 1958, *Aus einem Soldatenleben 1887 – 1939* (Bonn: Athenäum, 1958).

CHAPTER 1

[10] Manstein, *Aus einem Soldatenleben,* 13-14.

[11] ibid., 22-23.

[12] Knopp, *Hitlers Krieger,* 178.

[13] Manfred Messerschmidt, "German Staff Officers' Education since the Beginning of the 19th Century. Innovations and Traditions," *Militärhistorik Tidskrift,* 187 (1983): 9-13.

[14] Manstein, *Aus einem Soldatenleben,* 51-57.

[15] Andreas Hillgruber, "In der Sicht des Kritischen Historikers," in *Nie ausser Dienst. Zum achtzigsten Geburtstag von Generalfeldmarschall Erich von Manstein* (Cologne: Greven & Bechtold, 1967), 68.

[16] Manstein, *Aus einem Soldatenleben,* 54; Knopp, *Hitlers Krieger,* 182.

[17] Manstein, *Aus einem Soldatenleben,* 77-84 (81 for the citation).

[18] ibid., 46.

[19] ibid., 115.

[20] Wolfram Wette, *Die Wehrmacht, Feinbilder. Vernichtungskrieg. Legenden* (Frankfurt-am-Main: Fischer, 2002), 141-150 (144-145 and 150 for the citations).

[21] Edward W. Bennett, *German Rearmament and the West, 1932–1933* (Princeton: Princeton University, 1979), 506-507; Michael Geyer, *Aufrüstung oder Sicherheit. Die Reichswehr in die Krise der Machtpolitik 1924–1936* (Wiesbaden: Steiner, 1980), 41; Geoffrey P. Megargee, *Inside Hitler's High Command* (Kansas City: University Press of Kansas, 2000), 12; Klaus-Jürgen Müller, "Deutsche Militär-Elite in der Vorgeschichte des Zweiten Weltkrieges," in Martin Broszat and Klaus Schwabe, eds., *Deutsche Eliten und der Weg in den Zweiten Weltkrieg* (Munich: Beck, 1989), 246-247.

[22] Carl Dirks and Karl-Heinz Janßen, *Der Krieg der Generäle. Hitler als Werkzeug der Wehrmacht* (Berlin: Propyläen, 1999), 11-33 (25 for the citation). See also Karle-Heinz Janßen, "Politische und militärische Zielvorstellungen der Wehrmachtführung," in Rolf-Dieter Müller and Hans-Erich Volkmann, eds., *Die Wehrmacht. Mythos und Realität* (Munich: Oldenburg, 1999), 75-84.

[23] Manstein, *Aus einem Soldatenleben,* 159.

CHAPTER 2

[24] Knopp, *Hitlers Krieger,* 182.

^{25} Jean Solchany, "La lente dissipation d'une légende: La 'Wehrmacht' sous le regard de l'histoire," *Revue d'histoire moderne et contemporaine*, 47, no. 2 (April-June 2000): 347.

^{26} Klaus-Jürgen Müller, "Deutsche Militär-Elite," 257-260; Wilhelm Deist, *The Wehrmacht and German Rearmament* (Toronto: University of Toronto, 1981), 26.

^{27} Manstein, *Aus einem Soldatenleben*, 167-168.

^{28} Manfred Messerschmidt, "The Wehrmacht and the Volksgemeinschaft," *Journal of Contemporary History*, 18, no. 4 (October 1983): 721, 730-731.

^{29} Manfred Messerschmidt, *Die Wehrmacht im NS-Staat: Zeit der Indoktrination* (Hamburg: Decker, 1969), 15; Wilhelm Deist, "The Rearmament of the Wehrmacht," in Wilhelm Deist et al., *Germany and the Second World War*, vol. 1, *The Build-up of German Aggression* (Oxford: Clarendon, 1990), 521; Klaus-Jürgen Müller, *Das Heer und Hitler: Armee und nationalsozialistisches Regime 1933–1940* (Stuttgart: Deutsche Verlags-Anstalt, 1969), 67.

^{30} Messerschmidt, "The Wehrmacht," 730; Messerschmidt, "Forward Defense: The 'Memorandum of the Generals' for the Nuremberg Court," in Hannes Heer and Klaus Naumann, eds., *War of Extermination. The German Military in World War II, 1941 - 1944* (New York: Berghahn, 2000), 383-384; Deist, "The Rearmament," 523.

^{31} Manstein, *Verlorene Siege*, 73-74.

^{32} Bryan Mark Rigg, *Hitler's Jewish Soldiers. The Untold Story of Nazi Racial Laws and Men of Jewish Descent in the German Military* (Kansas City: University Press of Kansas, 2002), 77-81; Klaus-Jürgen Müller, *Armee und Dtrittes Reich 1933–1939. Darstellung und Dokumentation* (Paderborn: Schoningh, 1989), 57-58.

^{33} Rigg, *Hitler's Jewish Soldiers*, 83; Hans Breithaupt, *Zwischen Front und Widerstand. Ein Beitrag zur Diskussion um den Feldmarschall von Manstein* (Bonn: Bernard & Graefe Verlag, 1994), 123.

^{34} MGFA/DZ: II H 1008/1.

^{35} Rigg, *Hitler's Jewish Soldiers*, 98; Enrico Syring, "Erich von Manstein—Das operative Genie," in Ronald Smelser and Enrico Syring, eds., *Die Militärelite des Dritten Reiches* (Berlin: Ullstein, 1997), 330.

^{36} BA-MA, BMRS, Rüdiger von Manstein file, Manstein to Rigg, July 21, 2001; BA-MA, BMRS, interview with Rüdiger von Manstein, November 17, 1994, T-54; BA-MA, BMRS, interview with Alexander Stahlberg, December 3-4, 1994, T-68; BA-B, NS 19/2177. See also Rigg, *Hitler's Jewish Soldiers*, 85, 314 (note 62) and 316 (note 91); Alexander Stahlberg, *Die verdammte Pflicht. Erinnerungen 1932 bis 1945* (Berlin: Ullstein, 1994), 344-345; Wette, *Die Wehrmacht*, 79-80. According to Gerald Reitlinger, *The SS Alibi of a Nation 1922–1945* (London: Heinemann, 1956), 377, Reichsführer-SS Heinrich Himmler would have discovered that Field Marshal Manstein and SS-Obergruppenführer Erich von dem Bach-Zelewski both had in the sixteenth century a common ancestor of Slavic origin.

[37] Bernd Boll, "Generalfeldmarschall Erich von Lewinski, gen. von Manstein," in Gerd Rolf Ueberschär, ed., *Hitlers militärische Elite*, vol. 2, *Vom Kriegsbeginn bis zum Weltkriegsende* (Darmstadt: Wissenschaftliche Buchgesellschaft, 1988), 145; Knopp, *Hitlers Krieger*, 182-183; Syring, "Erich von Manstein," 329-330; Erich Kosthorst, *Die Geburt der Tragödie aus dem Geist des Gehorsams. Deutschlands Generäle und Hitler—Erfahrungen und Reflexionen eines Frontoffiziers* (Bonn: Bouvier, 1998), 184-185; Müller, *Das Heer und Hitler*, 84; Stein, *Gernalfeldmarschall Erich von Manstein*, 27.

[38] Müller, *Armee und Drittes Reich*, 57-60.

[39] Manstein, *Aus einem Soldatenleben*, 185.

[40] ibid., 187.

[41] Boll, "Generalfeldmarschall Erich von Lewinski," 144; Müller, *Armee und Drittes Reich*, 69.

[42] Wette, *Die Wehrmacht*, 153; Kosthorst, *Die Geburt der Tragödie*, 202-203.

[43] Ian Kershaw, *Hitler 1889–1936: Hubris* (Paris: Flammarion, 1999), 743-744; William L. Shirer, *Le IIIe Reich* (Paris: Stock, 1990), 249.

CHAPTER 3

[44] Stein, *Generalfeldmarschall Erich von Manstein*, 27-28. The officers' corps saw an increase in its numbers from 3,724 in May 1932, to 21,793 in October 1938. Bernhard R. Kroener, "Auf dem Weg zu einer 'nationalsozialistischen Volksarmee.' Die soziale Öffnung des Heeresoffizierkorps im Zweiten Weltkrieg," in Martin Broszat et al. ed., *Von Stalingrad zur Währungsreform. Zur Sozialgeschichte des Umbruchs in Deutschland* (Munich: Oldenburg, 1988), 652.

[45] Manstein, *Aus einem Soldatenleben*, 350. See also Messerschmidt, "Forward Defense," 384.

[46] Michael Geyer, "The Dynamics of Military Revisionism in the Interwar Years. Military Politics between Rearmament and Diplomacy," in Wilhelm Deist, ed., *The German Military in the Age of Total War* (Leamington Spa: Berg, 1985), 109-110, 121; Klaus-Jürgen Müller, "Le réarmament allemand et le problème de la sécurité nationale face à la politique du révisionnisme (1933–1937)," *Guerres mondiales*, 154 (April 1989): 63-67; Deist, "The Rearmament," 402-404, 416-423.

[47] Müller, "Le réarmement allemand," 76. See also Müller, "Deutsche Militär-Elite," 267-270; Deist, *The Wehrmacht*, 46-49; Deist, "The Rearmament," 434-435, 438-439, 454; Messerschmidt, "Forward Defense," 384; Geoffrey P. Megargee, *Inside Hitler's High Command* (Kansas City: University Press of Kansas, 2000), 30-32.

⁴⁸ Guderian, *Panzer Leader*, 21-22; Manstein, *Aus einem Soldatenleben*, 240-243.

⁴⁹ Manstein, *Aus einem Soldatenleben*, 243-250; Albert Seaton, "Field-Marshal Erich von Manstein,"in Michael Carver, ed., *Military Commanders of the Twentieth Century. The War Lords* (London: Weidenfeld and Nicholson, 1976), 233-234; Seaton, *The German Army*, 167-168; Carver, "Manstein," 225-226; Matthew Cooper, *The German Army, 1933–1945: Its Political and Military Failure* (New York: Stein and Day, 1978), 277-278.

⁵⁰ Ian Kershaw, *Hitler 1936–1945: Nemesis* (Paris: Flammarion, 2000), 21.

⁵¹ Ibid., 25, 49-50.

⁵² F.W. Mellenthin, *German Generals of World War Two as I Saw Them* (Norman: University of Oklahoma), 23; Cooper, *The German Army*, 51-52.

⁵³ Klaus-Jürgen Müller, *General Ludwig Beck. Studien und Dokumente zur politischmilitärischen Vorstellungswelt und Tätigkeit des Generalstabschefs des deutschen Heeres 1933–1938* (Boppard: Boldt, 1980), 249-253; Karl-Heinz Janßen and Fritz Tobians, *Der Sturz der Generäle: Hitler und die Blomberg-Fritsch-Krise 1938* (Munich: Beck, 1994), 9-12. Called to testify at the Nuremberg trial, Manstein declared, without successfully convincing the panel, that he knew nothing of the November 5, 1937, conference. TMIN, vol. XX, p. 645. See also similar remarks made by Manstein in *Aus einem Soldatenleben*, 320-321.

⁵⁴ ibid, 281.

⁵⁵ Janßen and Tobias, *Der Sturz der Generäle*, 9-21, 90; Kershaw, *Hitler 1936–1945*, 108-124.

⁵⁶ Knopp, *Hitlers Krieger*, 184-185.

⁵⁷ Manstein, *Aus einem Soldatenleben*, 317-318.

⁵⁸ ibid., 280-295 (291 for the citation).

⁵⁹ Syring, "Erich von Manstein," 331-333.

⁶⁰ Nicolaus von Below, *Als Hitlers Adjutant 1937–1945* (Mayence: Hase & Koehler, 1980), 114. See also Stein, *Generalfeldmarschall Erich von Manstein*, 31.

⁶¹ Manstein, *Aus einem Soldatenleben*, 318-319.

⁶² Christian Hartmann, *Halder: Generalstabschef Hitlers 1938–1942* (Paderborn: Schoningh, 1991), 55.

⁶³ Manstein, *Aus einem Soldatenleben*, 323-332 (323 for the citation).

⁶⁴ Kershaw, *Hitler 1936–1945*, 109-110, 162-163; Müller, "Le réarmement allemand," 75.

⁶⁵ Müller, *General Ludwig Beck*, 289-311, 521-535.

⁶⁶ BA-MA, H 08-28/4 (Nachlaß Beck). See also Müller, *Das Heer und Hitler*, 335-337, 656-665.

⁶⁷ Müller, *General Ludwig Beck*, 310-311, 580.

⁶⁸ TMIN, vol. XX, 647.

CHAPTER 4

[69] Manstein, *Verlorene Siege*, 12-17, 20-21, 68 (12, 16, 20, and 68 for the citations). Called to testify after the war at the Nuremberg trial, Manstein suggested before the International Military Tribunal similar arguments in order to justify his impression that no war of aggression had been envisioned by the Reich. TMIN, vol. XX, 647-648.

[70] Horst Rohde, "Hitler's First *Blitzkrieg* and its Consequences for North-Eastern Europe," in Klaus A. Maier, et al., *Germany and the Second World War*, vol. 2, *Germany's Initial Conquests in Europe* (Oxford: Clarendon, 1991), 69, 71-72,81-82.

[71] Mellenthin, *German Generals*, 25; Mitcham, *Hitler's Field Marshals*, 243.

[72] Manstein, *Verlorene Siege*, 37-38.

[73] Manstein, *Verlorene* Siege, 24-28; Hans Umbreit, "The Battle for Hegemony in Western Europe," in Klaus A. Maier et al., *Germany and the Second World War*, p. 266; Rohde, "Hitler's First *Blitzkrieg*," 101.

[74] Donald Cameron Watt, *How War Came. The Immediate Origins of the Second World War, 1938–1939* (London: Mandarin, 1991), 69.

[75] Christian Hartmann and Sergej Slutsch, "Franz Halder und die Kriegsvorbereitungen im Frühjahr 1939. Eine Ansprache des Generalstabschefs des Heeres," *Vierteljahrshefte für Zeitgeschichte*, 45 (July 1997): 467-495 (for the citation, 495). See also Dirks and Janßen, *Der Krieg der Generäle*, 136; Carl Dirks and Karl-Heinz Janßen, "Plan Otto," *Die Zeit*, 38 (September 19, 1997): 16. After the war, Halder declared to have been opposed to Hitler's intention to attack Poland. He acknowledged that he and the other generals were powerless with regards to stopping Hitler. Hartmann and Slutsch, "Franz Halder," 471.

[76] Manstein, *Verlorene Siege*, 14-15.

[77] Diks and Janßen, *Der Krieg der Generäle*, 71-72; Rohde, "Hitler's First Blitzkrieg," 76-77.

[78] Rohde, "Hitler's First Blitzkrieg," 124; Kershaw, *Hitler 1936–1945*, 367.

[79] ibid., 366.

[80] ibid., 371.

[81] Manstein, *Verlorene Siege*, 56-57.

[82] Rohde, "Hitler's First *Blitzkrieg*," 99-100.

[83] Manstein, *Verlorene Siege*, 30.

[84] Manstein, *Verlorene Siege*, 31-33. See also Philippe Masson, *Une guerre totale 1939–1945. Stratégies, moyens, controverses* (Paris: Tallandier, 1990), 104; Rohde, "Hitler's First Blitzkrieg," 124-125; Liddell Hart, *Histoire de la Seconde Guerre mondiale*, 29-30.

[85] Manstein, *Verlorene Siege*, 56.

[86] Umbreit, "The Battle for Hegemony," 265-266; Philippe Masson, *Histoire de l'armée française de 1914 à nos jours* (Paris: Perrin), 184, 188.

[87] Manstein, *Verlorene siege*, 20.

[88] Czeslaw Madajczyk, "Die Verantwortung der Wehrmacht für die Verbrechen während des Krieges mit Polen," in Wolfram Wette and Gerd Rolf Ueberschär, ed., *Kriegsverbrechen im 20. Jahrhundert* (Darmstadt: Wissenschaftliche Buchgesellschaft, 2001), 113-115, 117; Bernd Boll, Hannes Heer, and Walter Manoschek, "Prelude to a Crime: The German Army in the National Socialist State, 1933–1939," in The Hamburg Institute for Social Research, ed., *The German Army and Genocide. Crimes Against War Prisoners, Jews, and Other Civilians, 1939–1944* (New York: The New Press, 1999), 23; Omer Bartov, *L'Armée d'Hitler. La Wehrmacht, les nazis et la guerre* (Paris: Hachette Littérature, 1999), 95-105; Helmut Krausnick and Hans-Heinrich Wilhelm, *Die Truppe des Weltanschauungskrieges: Die Einsatzgruppen der Sicherheitspolizei und des SD 1938–1942* (Stuttgart: Deutsche Verlags-Anstalt, 1981), 76-77.

[89] Manstein, *Verlorene Siege*, 57.

[90] Boll, Heer, and Manoschek, "Prelude to a Crime," 25-26.

[91] Boll, Heer, and Manoschek, "Prelude to a Crime," 24; Krausnick and Wilhelm, *Die Truppe des Weltanschauungskrieges*, 103-104. See also Bartov, *L'Armée d'Hitler*, 100-103.

[92] Dirks and Janßen, *Der Krieg der Generäle*, 135.

[93] Müller, *Das Heer und Hitler*, 437-450; Wette, *Die Wehrmacht*, 106.

[94] Stein, *Generalfeldmarschall Erich von Manstein*, 35, 216, 218-219; Krausnick and Wilhelm, *Die Truppe des Weltanschauungskrieges*, 77, 103; Madajczyk, "Die Verantwortung der Wehrmacht," 122 (note 21); Oliver von Wrochem, "Die Auseinandersetzung mit Wehrmachtsverbrechen in Prozeß gegen den Generalfeldmarschall Erich von Manstein 1949," *Zeitschrift für Geschichtswissenschaft*, 46, no. 4 (1998): 337. During Manstein's trial in Hamburg in 1949, his attorneys proposed an unconvincing argument in order to explain his refusal to endorse Langhaeuser's draft. They claimed that, when the draft was presented to their client, the latter asked its author if he had any proof that the soldiers of the Wehrmacht had indeed committed such criminal atrocities. With Langhaeuser replying to him that he had only heard rumors, Manstein thus asserted that he could not approve such a draft so long as one had not presented to him concrete proof. Reginald Thomas Paget, *Manstein: His Campaigns and His Trial* (London: Collins, 1951), 129-130. However, he had already received several memorandums mentioning the numerous abuses perpetrated by soldiers of the German Army with respect to Polish civilians, Jews, and prisoners of war.

[95] Stein, *Generalfeldmarschall Erich von Manstein*, 219, 318-320; Krausnick and Wilhelm, *Die Truppe des Weltanschauungskrieges*, 46-47, 77, 81.

[96] Manstein, *Verlorene Siege*, 43-44.

[97] Stein, *Generalfeldmarschall Erich von Manstein*, 219-220.

[98] Stein, *Generalfeldmarschall Erich von Manstein*, 218-219; Krausnick and

Wilhelm, *Die Truppe des Weltanschauungskrieges*, 98.
[99] Kershaw, *Hitler 1936–1945*, 385.

CHAPTER 5
[100] Below, *Als Hitlers Adjutant*, 210; Umbreit, "The Battle for Hegemony," 232.
[101] Karl-Heinz Frieser, *Le Mythe de la guerre éclair. La campagne de l'Ouest de 1940* (Paris: Belen, 2003), 34,72-73; Karl-Heinz Frieser, "Der Westfeldzug und die 'Blitzkrieg'—Legende," in Militärgeschichtliches Forschungsamt, Frieburg im Breisgau, ed., *Ideen und Strategien 1940. Ausgewählte Operationen und deren militärgeschichtliche Aufarbeitung* (Bonn: Mittler & Sohn, 1990), 169; Masson, *Histoire de l'armée allemande*, 82-83; Umbreit, "The Battle for Hegemony," 236.
[102] Müller, *Das Heer und Hitler*, 481, 502, 507-508; Hans-Adolf Jacobsen, *Fall Gelb: Der Kampf um den deutschen Operationsplan zur Westoffensive 1940* (Wiesbaden: Steiner, 1957), 25-26, 44-49.
[103] Jacobsen, *Fall Gelb*, 46-47; Müller, *Das Heer und Hitler*, 520-521; Kershaw, *Hitler 1936–1945*, 415-416; Frieser, *Le Mythe de la guerre éclair*, 74-75.
[104] Manstein, *Verlorene Siege*, 84.
[105] ibid., 79, 89.
[106] Only Leeb implored Brauchitsch to intercede with the Führer in order to find a political solution to the war. Umbreit, "The Battle for Hegemony," 237.
[107] Manstein, *Verlorene Siege*, 86-89.
[108] TMIN, vol. XX, 649.
[109] Frieser, *Le Mythe de la guerre éclair*, 78.
[110] BA-MA, RH 6/1. See also Manstein, *Verlorene Siege*, 93-96, 620-623.
[111] BA-MA, RH 6/2. See also Manstein, *Verlorene Siege*, 93-96, 623-625. The capture of the Netherlands was restored in mid-November, upon the insistance of the Luftwaffe. The latter feared that the British, in case of a German invasion of Belgium, would transfer its aerial forces into Holland, which would represent a direct threat to the Ruhr. As a result, the Luftwaffe deemed it more appropriate that the Netherlands be occupied by Germany, all the more so since it could serve as a springboard for operations against England. Ernest R. May, *Strange Victory. Hitler's Conquest of France* (New York: Hill and Wang, 2000), 230; Umbreit, "The Battle for Hegemony," 242; Cooper, *The German Army*, 198.
[112] Manstein, *Verlorene Siege*, 96-100. See also Günther Roth, "Operational Thinking in Schlieffen and Manstein," in Militärgeschichtliches Forschungsamt, Freiburg im Breisgau, ed., *Development, Planning and Realization of Operational Conceptions in World Wars I and II* (Herford: Mittler & Sohn, 1989), 9, 12, 18-23.
[113] BA-MA, RH 19 I/26. See also Manstein, *Verlorene Siege*, 100-105, 625-626.

[114] Günther Roth, "The Campaign Plan 'Case Yellow' for the German Offensive in the West in 1940," in Militärgeschichtliches Forschungsamt, Freiburg im Breisgau, ed., *Operational Thinking in Clausewitz, Moltke, Schlieffen and Manstein* (Herford: Mittler & Sohn, 1988), 48-50; Roth, "Operational Thinking," 9-12, 25; Frieser, *Le Mythe de la guerre éclair*, 91-92, 96, 362-364; Raymnd Aron, *Penser la guerre, Clausewitz*, vol. 2, *L'Âge planétaire* (Paris: Gallimard, 1976), 88.

[115] Roland G. Foerster, "Operational Thinking of the Elder Moltke and its Consequences," in Militärgeschichtliches Forschungsamt, Freiburg im Breisgau, ed., *Operational Thinking in Clausewitz*, 27.

[116] Manstein, *Verlorene Siege*, 97.

[117] Roth, "Operational Thinking," 17-18, 21; Frieser, *Le Mythe de la guerre éclair*, 97-98, 406 (note 70); Aron, *Penser la guerre*, 43-44.

[118] Stein, *Generalfeldmarschall Erich von Manstein*, 36-37, 87.

[119] BA-MA, RH 19 I/26. See also Manstein, *Verlorene Siege*, 105.

[120] BA-MA, RH 6/3. See also Frieser, *Le Mythe de la guerre éclair*, 79, 93.

[121] Jacobsen, *Fall Gelb*, 32, 40, 273-274; Cooper, *The German Army*, 196, 200; Frieser, *Le Mythe de la guerre éclair*, 88, 92; May, *Strange Victory*, 238.

[122] Umbreit, "The Battle for Hegemony," 240-241.

[123] Frieser, *Le Mythe de la guerre éclair*, 93; Jacobsen, *Fall Gelb*, 118.

[124] Manstein, *Verlorene Siege*, 107; Liddell Hart, *The Other Side of the Hill*, 153; Guderian, *Panzer Leader*, 89.

[125] BA-MA, RH 19 I/26. See also Manstein, *Verlorene Siege*, 107, 627-631.

[126] BA-MA, RH 19 I/26. See also Manstein, *Verlorene Siege*, 109-110, 631-633.

[127] BA-MA, RH 19 I/26. See also Manstein, *Verlorene Siege*, 110, 633-637.

[128] David Downing, *The Devil's Virtuosos: German Gernals at War, 1940–1945* (New York: St. Martin's Press, 1977), 26.

[129] Manstein, *Verlorene Siege*, 110; Stein, *Generalfeldmarschall Erich von Manstein*, 36-37, 87; Knopp, *Hitlers Krieger*, 190-191; Frieser, *Le Mythe de la guerre éclair*, 82. According to Umbreit, "The Battle for Hegemony," 245, Manstein's operational concept had been known by Hitler since December 1939, but he does not state how he was informed. For his part, Kershaw, *Hitler 1936–1945*, 440, claims that the Führer had a few reverberations in the major points of the plan drafted by Manstein in the second half of December. Like Umbreit, he does not clarify, however, how he would have caught wind of the ideas of Army Group A's chief of staff. According to Liddell Hart, *Histoire de la Deuxième Guerre mondiale*, 43, after the conversation that he had with Manstein in mid-December, Warlimont would have presented the latter's ideas to Lieutenant General Jodl, chief of the OKW's operations bureau, who would have then spoken to Hitler about them. However, it is unlikely that the Führer would have caught wind of these ideas, if not for the reason of the professional jealousy felt by Jodl towards Manstein. Furthermore, he had not demonstrated

much interest for the operations plan of Army Group A's chief of staff when he was informed about it by Warlimont. Regarding this matter, see Liddell Hart, *The Other Side of the Hill*, 154.

[130] Manstein, *Verlorene Siege*, 110-112 (112 for the citation).

[131] BA-MA, RH 19 I/26. See also Manstein, *Verlorene Siege*, 112-113, 637-641.

[132] BA-MA, RH 19 I/26. See also Manstein, *Verlorene Siege*, 113-114, 641-648.

[133] Liddell Hart, *The Other Side of the Hill*, 155; Liddell Hart, *Histoire de la Seconde Guerre Mondiale*, 41.

[134] BA-MA, RH 19 II/21. See also Jacobsen, *Fall Gelb*, 99-100.

[135] Manstein, *Verlorene Siege*, 117.

[136] Frieser, *Le Mythe de la guerre éclair*, 80-81.

CHAPTER 6

[137] Frieser, *Le Mythe de la guerre éclair*, 82-83.

[138] Manstein, *Verlorene Siege*, 118. Such an opinion is accepted by practically every author who discusses this episode. On the other hand, Masson, *Histoire de l'armée allemande*, 96, suggests that it was in no way a question of dismissing him on the part of the OKH, but an appointment that had been planned since the autumn of 1939. However, the pressure exerted by Manstein on the OKH so that it would accept his operations plan had indeed commenced in the summer of 1939. Stein, *Generalfeldmarschall Erich von Manstein*, 37-38, moves in the same direction as Masson.

[139] Syring, "Erich von Manstein," 335; Hillgruber, "In der Sicht," 74.

[140] Frieser, *Le Mythe de la guerre éclair*, 86-87.

[141] May, *Strange Victory*, 230-231.

[142] Manstein, *Verlorene Siege*, 71-73, 76.

[143] BA-MA RH 19 I/25. See also Guderian, *Panzer Leader*, 90.

[144] Manstein, *Verlorene Siege*, 86-89.

[145] Frieser, "Der Westfeldzug," 174; Frieser, *Le Mythe de la guerre éclair*, 112.

[146] Frieser, *Le Mythe de la guerre éclair*, 83-84 (for the citation), 94; Knopp, *Hitlers Krieger*, 191; Umbreit, "The Battle for Hegemony," 247; Irving, *Hitler's War*, 81; Cooper, *The German Army*, 201; Keegan, *La Deuxième Guerre mondiale*, 64; Masson, *Histoire de l'armée allemande*, 95; Liddell Hart, *Histoire de la Seconde Guerre Mondiale*, 43.

[147] BA-MA, RH 19 I/41; BA-MA, RH 19 I/26. See also Manstein, *Verlorene Siege*, 118-120.

[148] Knopp, *Hitlers Krieger*, 192. See also Frieser, "The Execution of 'Case Yellow'," 59.

[149] BA-MA, RH 19 I/38.

[150] Frieser, "Der Westfeldzug," 174; Frieser, "The Execution of 'Case Yellow'," 59.

[151] Frieser, *Le Mythe de la Guerre éclair*, 111, 115.

[152] Umbreit, "The Battle for Hegemony," 270-271.

[153] Liddell Hart, *Histoire de la Seconde Guerre Mondiale*, 42.

[154] Frieser, *Le Mythe de la Guerre éclair*, 153-154, 410 (note 73).

[155] ibid., 108-109.

[156] Liddell Hart, *Histoire de la Seconde Guerre mondiale*, 44.

[157] Frieser, *Le Mythe de la Guerre éclair*, 92.

[158] Roth, "The Campaign Plan," 54-55; Frieser, *Le Mythe de la Guerre éclair*, 88.

[159] Manstein, *Verlorene Siege*, 106-107.

[160] Frieser, *Le Mythe de la Guerre éclair*, 92-95.

[161] Roth, "The Campaign Plan," 54-55; Frieser, *Le Mythe de la Guerre éclair*, 88.

[162] Syring, "Erich von Manstein," 335; Otto E. Moll, *Die deutschen Generalfeldmarschälle 1939–1945* (Rastatt: Pabel, 1961), 119.

[163] Mellenthin, *German Generals*, 25.

CHAPTER 7

[164] Frieser, *Le Mythe de la Guerre éclair*, 51-53, 59-64. See also Jacobsen, *Fall Gelb*, 258-259; Umbreit, "The Battle for Hegemony," 279.

[165] Masson, *Histoire de l'armée allemande*, 112-114; Umbreit, "The Battle for Hegemony," 284-285; Frieser, "The Execution," 67.

[166] Frieser, "Der Westfeldzug," 176-177, 182, 185; Frieser, *Le Mythe de la Guerre éclair*, 119, 132, 157, 174, 194-196, 211-213.

[167] ibid., 77, 209.

[168] Frieser, *Le Mythe de la Guerre éclair*, 89-90, 209-210, 225-226, 287-295; Umbreit, "The Battle for Hegemony," 247, 286.

[169] Frieser, *Le Mythe de la Guerre éclair*, 77, 212.

[170] Masson, *Histoire de l'armée française*, 223-226. See also Umbreit, "The Battle for Hegemony," 287.

[171] Manstein, *Verlorene Siege*, 122, 127.

[172] Frieser, *Le Mythe de la guerre éclair*, 275, 421 (note 19).

[173] Umbreit, "The Battle for Hegemony," 289-291, 293-294; Kershaw, *Hitler 1936–1945*, 447-449; Masson, *Histoire de l'armée allemande*, 116-118; Liddell Hart, *Histoire de la Seconde Guerre mondiale*, 86-89; Shirer, *Le IIIᵉ Reich*, 772-774; Cooper, *The German Army*, 230-232; Frieser, *Le Mythe de la guerre éclair*, 336.

[174] Frieser, *Le Mythe de la guerre éclair*, 323-326; Umbreit, "The Battle for Hegemony," 293-295.

[175] Shirer, *Le IIIᵉ Reich*, 772, 776; Liddell Hart, *Histoire de la Seconde Guerre mondiale*, 85; Bevin Alexander, *How Hitler Could Have Won World War II: The Fatal Errors that Led to Nazi Defeat* (New York: Three Rivers, 2000), 31-32.

[176] Karl-Heinz Frieser, "Die deutschen Blitzkriege: Operativer Triumph—strategische Tragödie," in Rolf-Dieter Müller and Hans-Erich Volkmann, eds., *Die Wehrmacht*, 191; Frieser, "The Execution of 'Case Yellow'," 80; Roth, "Operational Thinking," 40; Frieser, "*Le Mythe de la guerre éclair*, 339; Knopp, *Hitlers Krieger*, 193-194.

[177] Manstein, *Verlorene Siege*, 122-124, 126-128 (122 for the citation).

[178] Frieser, *Le Mythe de la guerre éclair*, 328-329; J. Lukacs, *Le Duel Churchill-Hitler, 10 mai–31 juillet 1940* (Paris: Laffont, 1992), 125-126.

[179] Roth, "Operational Thinking," 38; Frieser, "The Execution of 'Case Yellow'," 80.

[180] Manstein, *Verlorene Siege*, 125-126.

[181] ibid., 122-123, 126-129 (122-123 for the citations).

[182] ibid., 127-133.

[183] Manstein, *Verlorene Siege*, 140; Liddell Hart, *The Other Side of the Hill*, 95.

[184] Jeremy Noakes and Geoffrey Pridham, *Nazism 1919–1945: A Documentary Reader*, vol. 3, *Foreign Policy, War, and Racial Extermination* (Exeter: University of Exeter, 1997), 778.

[185] Knopp, *Hitlers Krieger*, 195.

[186] Frieser, *Le Mythe de la guerre éclair*, 210.

[187] Stefan Martens, "La défaite française: une heureuse surprise allemande?" in Christine Levisse-Touzé, ed., *La Campagne de 1940. Actes du colloque: 16 to 18 novembre 2000* (Paris: Tallandier, 2001), 410; Jürgen Förster, "Hitler's Decision in Favour of War Against the Soviet Union," in Horst Boog et al., *Germany and the Second World War*, vol. 4, *The Attack on the Soviet Union* (Oxford: Clarendon, 1998), 13.

[188] Manstein, *Verlorene Siege*, 149-150. See also Stein, *Generalfeldmarschall Erich von Manstein*, 314-315.

[189] Joachim Wieder, *Stalingrad ou la responsabilité du soldat* (Paris: Albin Michel, 1983), 243.

[190] Gerd Rolf Ueberschär and Winfried Vogel, *Dienen und Verdienen. Hitlers Geschenke an seine Eliten* (Frankfurt-am-Main, Fischer, 1999), 13-34, 71-75 (75 for the citation). See also Norman J. W. Goda, "Black Marks: Hitler's Bribery of His Senior Officers during World War II," *The Journal of Modern History*, 72 (June 2000): 423-424; Winfried Vogel, "...schlechthin unwürdig," *Die Zeit*, 14 (March 28, 1997): 44; Wette, *Die Wehrmacht*, 154-155.

[191] Ueberschär and Vogel, *Dienen und Vergienen*, 72-73, 98-99, 101-110, 193-195, 243-247; Goda, "Black Marks," 418-423; Megargee, *Inside Hitler's High Command*, 126.

[192] Goda, "Black Marks," 424-426, 429.

CHAPTER 8
[193] Lukacs, *Le Duel Churchill-Hitler*, 201.

[194] Dirks and Janßen, *Der Krieg der Generäle*, 128-129.

[195] Shirer, *Le IIIe Reich*, 799-802; Liddell Hart, *Histoire de la Seconde Guerre mondiale*, 94-95.

[196] In his *Memoirs*, Manstein mentioned that his army corps was to regroup three infantry divisions for the landing operation in England. Manstein, *Verlorene Siege*, 150. However, in his distribution of forces for the first invasion wave, Umbreit, "Plans and Preparations for a Landing in England," in Klaus A. Maier et al., *Germany and the Second World War*, vol. 2, *Germany's Initial Conquests*, 370, only assigns two infantry divisions to the 38th army corps.

[197] Shirer, *Le IIIe Reich*, 799-803 (803 for the citation). See also Masson, *Histoire de l'armée allemande*, 141-142; Liddell Hart, *Histoire de la Seconde Guerre mondiale*, 95.

[198] Manstein, *Verlorene Siege*, 157.

[199] ibid., 159.

[200] Heinz Magenheimer, *Hitler's War. Germany's Key Strategic Decisions 1940–1945. Could Germany Have Won World War Two?* (London: Arms & Armour, 1998), 29-30.

[201] Manstein, *Verlorene Siege*, 161-162.

[202] Andreas Hillgruber, *Hitlers Strategie. Politik und Kriegsführung, 1940–1941* (Frankfurt-am-Main: Bernard & Graefe, 1965), 188-192. See also Magenheimer, *Hitler's War*, 30-31, 70; Alexander, *How Hitler Could Have Won World War II*, xi, 48-50; Kershaw, *Hitler 1936–1945*, 492-493.

[203] Frieser, *Le Mythe de la Guerre éclair*, 323-326; Umbreit, "The Battle for Hegemony," 293-295.

[204] Manstein, *Verlorene Siege*, 163-171 (163-165, 168-169, 171 for the citations). Called to testify at Nuremberg, Manstein once again claimed to have considered the war against Russia as a preventative war on Germany's part. TMIN, vol. XX, 649.

[205] Manstein, *Verlorene Siege*, 171.

[206] Magenheimer, *Hitler's War*, 23, 28-29, 32; Shirer, *Le IIIe Reich*, 805.

[207] Manstein, *Verlorene Siege*, 147, 154-156, 170, 179-180, 304.

[208] Ernst Klink, "The Military Concept of the War Against the Soviet Union," in Horst Boog et al., *Germany and the Second World War*, vol. 4, *The Attack on the Soviet Union*, 225-325.

[209] Dirks and Janßen, *Der Krieg der Generäle*, 127-138; Dirks and Janßen, "Plan Otto," 16.

[210] Dirks and Janßen, *Der Krieg der Generäle*, 136-142; Dirks and Janßen, "Plan Otto," 16.

[211] Dirks and Janßen, *Der Krieg der Generäle*, 142-143.

[212] Förster, "Hitler's Decision," 26-27; Klink, "the Military Concept," 232-233; Kershaw, *Hitler 1936–1945*, 461, 466-467; Hillgruber, *Hitlers Strategie*, 213-214; Megargee, *Inside Hitler's High Command*, 103.

213 Manstein, *Verlorene Siege*, 174.
214 Klink, "The Military Concept," 257-265, 270-285; Megargee, *Inside Hitler's High Command*, 104-105, 111-112, 124, 131-132.
215 Manstein, *Verlorene Siege*, 171.
216 Keegan, *La Deuxième Guerre mondiale*, 134.
217 Manstein, *Verlorene Siege*, 173-174.
218 Noakes and Pridham, *Nazism 1919–1945*, 817-818; David M. Glantz and Jonathan House, *When Titans Clashed. How the Red Army Stopped Hitler* (Kansas: University Press of Kansas, 1995), 31; Barry A. Leach, *German Strategy against Russia 1939–1941* (Oxford, Clarendon, 1973), 192.
219 Joachim Hoffmann, "The Soviet Union up to the Eve of the German Attack," in Horst Boog et al., *Germany and the Second World War*, vol. 4, *The Attack on the Soviet Union*, 92-93; Klink, "The Military Concept," 323-325; Magenheimer, *Hitler's War*, 76-80; Leach, *German Strategy*, 192.
220 Megargee, *Inside Hitler's High Command*, 110-111, 114.
221 Manstein, *Verlorene Seige*, 173.
222 Förster, "Hitler's Decision," 13-38; Kershaw, *Hitler 1936–1945*, 509-514, 576-578.
223 Krausnick and Wilhelm, *Die Truppe des Weltanschauungskrieges*, 115; Jürgen Förster, "Operation Barbarossa as a War of Conquest and Annihilation," in Horst Boog et al., *Germany and the Second World War*, vol. 4, *The Attack on the Soviet Union*, 482-485; Kershaw, *Hitler 1936–1945*, 527-528.
224 Förster, "Operation Barbarossa," 485, 491-492 (485 for the citation). See also Kershaw, *Hitler 1936–1945*, 530.
225 Förster, "Operation Barbarossa," 492, 497 (497 for the citation); Gerd Rolf Ueberschär and Wolfram Wette, eds., *"Unternehmen Barbarossa." Der deutsche Überfall auf die Sowjetunion 1941. Berichte, Analysen, Dokumente* (Paderborn: Schoningh, 1984), 248. See also Christian Streit, *Keine Kameraden: Die Wehrmacht und die sowjetischen Kriegsgefangenen 1941–1945* (Stuttgart: Deutsche Verlags-Anstalt, 1978), 36; Wette, *Die Wehrmacht*, 95.
226 Förster, "Operation Barbarossa," 498.
227 Ueberschär and Wette, eds., "Unternehmen Barbarossa," 249; Förster, "Operation Barbarossa," 491-496.
228 Ueberschär and Wette, eds., "Unternehmen Barbarossa," 252-254, 259-260; Förster, "Operation Barbarossa," 501-510.
229 Förster, "Hitler's Decision," 37; Förster, "Operation Barbarossa," 519-520; Ueberschär et Wette, eds., "Unternehmen Barbarossa," 251.
230 Stein, *Generalfeldmarschall Erich von Manstein*, 238.
231 Manstein, *Verlorene Siege*, 176.
232 Kershaw, *Hitler 1936–1945*, 535; Förster, "Operation Barbarossa," 520.

233 Förster, "Operation Barbarossa," 518-519; Jürgen Förster, "New Wine in Old Skins? The Wehrmacht and the War of 'Weltanschauungen,' 1941," in Wilhelm Deist, ed., *The German Military in the Age of Total War* (Leamington Spa: Berg, 1985), 312; Solchany, "La lente dissipation d'une légende," 340-341.

234 Kershaw, *Hitler 1936–1945*, 578.

CHAPTER 9

235 Manstein, *Verlorene Siege*, 182-186 (184 for the citation). See also Paget, *Manstein*, 32; Cooper, *The German Army*, 290, 300-302.

236 Syring, "Erich von Manstein," 335-336.

237 Manstein, *Verlorene Siege*, 208.

238 ibid., 214-218.

239 Mitcham, *Hitler's Field Marshals*, 244.

240 Porter Randall Blakemore, *Manstein in the Crimea: The Eleventh Army Campaign, 1941–1942*, Ph.D. dissertation, University of Georgia, 1978, 56-58. See also Manstein, *Verlorene Siege*, 218-223.

241 ibid., 223-225.

242 Ernst Klink, "The Conduct of Operations," in Horst Boog et al., *Germany and the Second World War*, vol. 4, *The Attack on the Soviet Union*, 612-613; Blakemore, *Manstein in the Crimea*, 78-79.

243 Manstein, *Verlorene Siege*, 227-331 (229 for the citation).

244 Manstein, *Verlorene Siege*, 235-240; Klink, "The Conduct of Operations," 628-629.

245 Masson, *Une guerre totale*, 126; Liddell Hart, *Histoire de la Seconde Guerre mondiale*, 172; Alan Clark, *Barbarossa. The Russian-German Conflict, 1941–1945* (New York: Morrow, 1965), 182-183.

246 Kershaw, *Hitler 1936–1945*, 662-664, 1380 (note 370) (663 for the ciation); Megargee, *Inside Hitler's High Command*, 138-139, 147; Irving, *Hitler's War*, 351, 359-360.

247 Knopp, *Hitlers Krieger*, 213. See also Liddell Hart, *The Other Side of the Hill*, 96.

248 Manstein, *Verlorene Siege*, 240-243; Blakemore, *Manstein in the Crimea*, 140, 236.

249 Blakemore, *Manstein in the Crimea*, 129-131; Manstein, *Verlorene Siege*, 244-245; Knopp, *Hitlers Krieger*, 198.

250 Klink, "The Conduct of Operations," 759; Blakemore, *Manstein in the Crimea*, 131-132.

251 Manstein, *Verlorene Siege*, 245; Blakemore, *Manstein in the Crimea*, 132; Stein, *Generalfeldmarschall Erich von Manstein*, 39-40; Eberhard Einbeck, *Das Exempel Graf Sponeck. Ein Beitrag zum Thema Hitler und die Generäle* (Bremen: Schünemann, 1970), 8-10.

252 Blakemore, *Manstein in the Crimea*, 133-134; Klink, "The Conduct of

Operations," 630-631; Knopp, *Hitlers Krieger*, 198; Stein, *Generalfeldmarschall Erich von Manstein*, 41-42.

[253] Manstein, *Verlorene Siege*, 248-250. See also Blakemore, *Manstein in the Crimea*, 149-150.

[254] Manstein, *Verlorene Siege*, 254, 261 (261 for the citation).

[255] Manstein, *Verlorene Siege*, 254-255; Bernd Wegner, "The War Against the Soviet Union 1942–1943," in Horst Boog et al., *Germany and the Second World War*, vol. 6, *The Global War, Widening of the Conflict into a World War and the Shift of the Initiative 1941–1943* (Oxford: Clarendon, 2001), 930-932; Blakemore, *Manstein in the Crimea*, 175.

[256] Joel Hayward, "A Case Study in Early Joint Warfare: An Analysis of the Wehrmacht's Crimean Campaign of 1942," *The Journal of Strategic Studies*, 22, no. 4 (December 1999): 115.

[257] Blakemore, *Manstein in the Crimea*, 197.

[258] Wallace P. Franz, "Operational Concepts," *Military Review*, 64, no. 7 (1984): 2-15.

[259] Wegner, "The War Against the Soviet Union," 933.

[260] Manstein, *Verlorene Siege*, 262.

[261] Manstein, *Verlorene Siege*, 262, 265-269; Wegner, "The War Against the Soviet Union," 935, 940; Blakemore, *Manstein in the Crimea*, 201-202; Mellenthin, *German Generals*, 33-34; Brett-Smith, *Hitler's Generals*, 224-225.

[262] Manstein, *Verlorene Siege*, 277-278; Wegner, "The War Against the Soviet Union," 938.

[263] Mitcham, *Hitler's Field Marshals*, 246; Brett-Smith, *Hitler's Generals*, 225; Seaton, "Field-Marshal Erich von Manstein," 238; Blakemore, *Manstein in the Crimea*, 220.

[264] Manstein, *Verlorene Siege*, 283.

[265] Heuer, *Die deutschen Generalfeldmarschälle*, 92; Stein, *Generalfeldmarschall Erich von Manstein*, 315.

[266] Manstein, *Verlorene Siege*, 290-291; Blakemore, *Manstein in the Crimea*, 236-237.

[267] Seaton, "Field-Marshal Erich von Manstein," 238; Blakemore, *Manstein in the Crimea*, 236; Knopp, *Hitlers Krieger*, 203-204; Irving, *Hitler's War*, 417; Wegner, "The War Against the Soviet Union," 993.

[268] Manstein, *Verlorene Siege*, 291-292.

[269] BA-MA, RH 19 III/185; Wegner, "The War Against the Soviet Union," 993; Boll, "Generalfeldmarschall Erich von Lewinski," 147; Knopp, *Hitlers Krieger*, 204.

[270] Only Grand Admiral Raeder opposed the complete destruction of Leningrad. His reservations were, however, of a purely military nature, for all that he wished was to preserve the infrastructure of the harbors vital to the Kriegsmarine. Wegner, "The War Against the Soviet Union," 993, 995.

271 Idem. Manstein does not allude to these conversations in his *Memoirs*.

272 Manstein, *Verlorene Siege*, 294-295; Wegner, "The War Against the Soviet Union," 998-1,000; Mitcham, *Hitler's Field Marshals*, 246.

273 Manstein, *Verlorene Siege*, 297.

274 Mellenthin, *German Generals*, 30; Knopp, *Hitlers Krieger*, 196.

CHAPTER 10

275 TMIN, vol. XX, 668.

276 Jürgen Förster, "The German Army and the Ideological War against the Soviet Union," in Gerhard Hirschfeld, ed., *The Politics of Genocide: Jews and Soviet Prisoners of War in Nazi Germany* (Boston: Allen & Unwin, 1986), 15; Förster, "New Wine in Old Skins?" 304, 319; Kershaw, *Hitler 1936–1945*, 671-672.

277 Kershaw, *Hitler 1936–1945*, 677 (for the citation); Krausnick and Wilhelm, *Die Truppe des Weltanschauungskrieges*, 223-243; Streit, *Keine Kameraden*, 109-127; Jürgen Förster, "Securing 'Living-Space'," in Horst Boog et al., *Germany and the Second World War*, vol. 4, *The Attack on the Soviet Union*, 1,205.

278 Krausnick and Wilhelm, *Die Truppe des Weltanschauungskrieges*, 621; Förster, "The German Army," 22; Kershaw, *Hitler 1936–1945*, 680-681. In April 1942, reports from the four *Einsatzgruppen* took into account the execution of at least 461,500 Soviet Jews: 229,052 for *Einsatzgruppe A* (in February 1942), 45,467 for *Einsatzgruppe B* (from November 14, 1941), 95,000 for *Einsatzgruppe C* (from April 4, 1942). Christian Streit, "The German Army and the Policies of Genocide," in Gerhard Hirschfeld, ed., *The Policies of Genocide*, 7, 13-14 (note 31).

279 In order to ensure a greater "pacification" from the occupied territories, additional police battalions were put into place beginning at the end of July 1941. At the end of 1941, members of the execution platoons were eleven times greater than at the beginning of Operation Barbarossa. In June 1942, these platoons included within their ranks 165,000 members; in January 1943, the numbers had reached 300,000. Christopher Browning, *The Path to Genocide. Essays on Launching the Final Solution* (Cambridge: Cambridge University, 1992), 106.

280 Timm C. Richter, "Die Wehrmacht und der Partisanenkrieg," in Rolf-Dieter Müller and Hans-Erich Volkmann, eds., *Die Wehrmacht*, 846 (for the citation); Hannes Heer, "Killing Fields: The Wehrmacht and the Holocaust in Belorussia, 1941–42," in Hannes Heer and Klaus Naumann, eds., *War of Extermination*, 72-73; Jürgen Förster, "Wehrmacht, Krieg und Holocaust," in Rolf-Dieter Müller and Hans-Erich Volkmann, eds., *Die Wehrmacht*, 963; Streit, "The German Army," 10; Solchany, "La Lente dissipation d'une légende," 343.

281 TMIN, vol. XX, 652.

[282] Christian Streit, "Soviet Prisoners of War in the Hands of the Wehrmacht," in Hannes Heer and Klaus Naumann, eds., *War of Extermination*, 80-81; Streit, *Keine Kameraden*, 10, 131, 293; Rolf-Dieter Müller, "The Failure of the Economic '*Blitzkrieg*' Strategy," in Horst Boog et al., *Germany and the Second World War*, vol. 4, *The Attack on the Soviet Union*, 1,173 and 1,176-1,177.

[283] Streit, "Soviet Prisoners of War," 81; Solchany, "La lente dissipation d'une légende," 344.

[284] TMIN, vol. XX, 652-653.

[285] Solchany, "La lente dissipation d'une légende," 344-345; Streit, "Soviet Prisoners of War," 81-83, 86-88.

[286] Referring to Halder's diary from August 1 to September 21, 1941, Streit asserts that only one unit on the Eastern Front would not have carried out the Commissar Order, that of Lieutenant General Hans-Jürgen von Arnim's 17th armored division. Streit, *Keine Kameraden*, 83-87. However, Förster and Krausnick claim that reports from the 17th armored division concerning the execution of political commissars in August and September 1941 would completely prove the culpability of Arnim's troops in the application of the Commissar Order. Förster, "Securing 'Living-Space'," 1,226; Förster, "The German Army," 23; Helmut Krausnick, "Kommissarbefehl und 'Gerichtsbarkeitserlaß Barbarossa' in neuer Sicht," *Vierteljahrschefte für Zeitgeschichte*, 25 (1977): 734-735, in particular note 261 on the reports from the 17th armored division attesting to the execution of some 26 political commissars furing the period from August 17 to September 26, 1941.

[287] Streit, *Keine Kameraden*, 105; Streit, "The German Army," 4-7; Streit, "Soviet Prisoners of War," 85-86; Bartov, *L'Armée d'Hitler*, 126-127; Förster, "Securing 'Living-Space'," 1228-1231; Förster, "The German Army," 20-21; Solchany, "La lente dissipation d'une légende," 345.

[288] Manstein, *Verlorene Siege*, 176-177. At Nuremberg and during his trial at Hamburg, he reiterated that he refused to implement the Commissar Order by roughly invoking the same arguments. TMIN, vol. XX, 650; Wrochem, "Die Auseinandersetzung mit Wehrmachtsverbrechen," 341; Paul Leverkuehn, *Verteidigung Manstein* (Hamburg: Nölke, 1950), 11-12, 25, 31.

[289] NOKW 1674; Krausnick, "Kommissarbefehl," 733 (note 257); Stein *Generalfeldmarschall Erich von Manstein*, 200-201; Jörg Friedrich, *Das Gesetz des Krieges. Das deutsche Heer in Rußland 1941 bis 1945. Der Prozeß gegen das Oberkommando der Wehrmacht* (Munich: Piper, 1993), 596, 600.

[290] Jörg Friedrich, *Das Gesetz des Krieges*, 596-601; Wrochem, "Die Auseinandersetzung mit Wehrmachtsverbrechen," 340-341; Stein, *Generalfeldmarschall Erich von Manstein*, 205; Boll, "Generalfeldmarschall Erich von Lewinski," 146.

[291] Manstein, *Verlorene Siege*, 177.

[292] Stein, *Generalfeldmarschall Erich von Manstein*, 202, 207, 210, 211;

Knopp, *Hitlers Krieger*, 195.

293 Friedrich, *Das Gesetz des Krieges*, 597.

294 Streit, "The German Army," 8-9; Heer, "Killing Fields," 64-68; Wette, *Die Wehrmacht*, 100.

295 Kershaw, *Hitler 1936–1945*, 677.

296 Streit, *Keine Kameraden*, 115; Förster, "Securing 'Living-Space'," 1,211-1,212; Bartov, *L'Armée d'Hitler*, 188; Ueberschär and Wette, eds., "Unternehmen Barbarossa," 285.

297 Förster, "Securing 'Living-Space'," 1,211-1,213; Streit, *Keine Kameraden*, 115; Streit, "The German Army," 7; Krausnick and Wilhelm, *Die Truppe des Weltanschauungskrieges*, 260.

298 Streit, *Keine Kameraden*, 116-117; Förster, "Securing 'Living-Space'," 1,214-1,215; Bartov, *L'Armée d'Hitler*, 189-190.

299 BA-MA, RH 20-11/519. See also TMIN, vol. XX, 684-685; Förster, "Securing 'Living-Space'," 1,215-1,216; Jehuda L. Wallach, "Feldmarschall Erich von Manstein und die deutsche Judenaustrottung in Rußland," *Jahrbuch des Instituts für Deutsche Geschichte*, 4 (1975): 462-464; Ueberschär and Wette, eds., "*Unternehmen Barbarossa*," 289.

300 Streit, *Keine Kameraden*, 125; Streit, "The German Army," 9; Krausnick and Wilhelm, *Die Truppe des Weltanschauungskrieges*, 248; Bartov, *L'Armée d'Hitler*, 134-135, 139.

301 Wette, *Die Wehrmacht*, 205; Messerschmidt, "Forward Defense," 382; Messerschmidt, "The Wehrmacht," 736; Förster, "The German Army," 23-24. At Nuremberg, when one asked him if he had known that the goal of the war against the partisans was to exterminate the Jews and the Slavs, Manstein responded with a categorical no. TMIN, vol. XX, 656.

302 Bartov, *L'Armée d'Hitler*, 190.

303 Wette, *Die Wehrmacht*, 40-46, 49-50; Solchany, "La lente dissipation d'une légende," 348, 351; Martin Kitchen, *The Silent Dictatorship. The Politics of the German High Command under Hindenburg and Ludendorff, 1916–1918* (London: Croom Helm, 1976), 142, 194, 211; Heer, "Killing Fields," 67.

304 Nicolas Reynold, "Der Fritsch-Brief vom 11. Dezember 1938," *Vierteljahreshefte für Zeitgeschichte*, 28 (1980): 362-363, 370.

305 Stein, *Generalfeldmarschall Erich von Manstein*, 243.

306 Wette, *Die Wehrmacht*, 51-52, 101; Solchany, "La lente dissipation d'une légende," 348-351.

307 Rigg, *Hitler's Jewish Soldiers*, 268-269; Bryan Mark Rigg, "Riggs Liste. Warum gehorchten Soldaten jüdischer Herkunft einem Regime, das ihre Familien umbrachte?" *Die Zeit*, 15 (April 4, 1997): 11. See also Wette, *Die Wehrmacht*, 86.

308 Förster, "Securing 'Living-Space'," 1,216.

309 TMIN, vol. XX, 683, 686, 688.

CHAPTER 11

[310] Wallach, "Feldmarschall Erich von Manstein," 464-465.

[311] Stein, *Generalfeldmarschall Erich von Manstein*, 212-213; TMIN, vol. XX, 659, 661, 676.

[312] Werner Maser, *Der Nürnberger Prozeß* (Cologne: Markus Verlagsgesellschaft, 1958), 419.

[313] TMIN, vol. IV, 321, 323-325, 356-357 (324, 325, 357 for the citations).

[314] Wallach, "Feldmarschall Erich von Manstein," 469-470; Stein, *Generalfeldmarschall Eric von Manstein*, 214-215; Boll, "Generalfeldmarschall Erich von Lewinski," 147; Knopp, *Hitlers Krieger*, 200; Wrochem, "Die Auseinandersetzung mit Wehrmachtsverbrechen," 342; Friedrich, *Das Gesetz des Krieges*, 596, 959. Invited during the Nuremberg trial to clarify if he had had any dealings with Ohlendorf during the Crimean campaign, Manstein appeared very evasive, asserting to have perhaps seen him, but not to have remembered. TMIN, vol. XX, 659-660.

[315] NOKW 3234; NOKW 12.

[316] Friedrich, *Das Gesetz des Krieges*, 634, 665. See also Stein, *Generalfeldmarschall Erich von Manstein*, 241.

[317] Manstein, *Verlorene Siege*, 283.

[318] NOKW 1284; NOKW 1286; BA-MA, RH 23/69; BA-MA, RH 20-11/337.

[319] BA-MA, RH 20-11/488.

[320] BA-MA, RH 20-11/488.

[321] BA-MA, RH 20-11/488.

[322] BA-MA, RH 20-11/488.

[323] BA-MA, RH 20-11/488.

[324] BA-MA, RH 20-11/488.

[325] BA-MA, RH 20-11/488.

[326] BA-MA, RH 20-11/488.

[327] Wrochem, "Die Auseinandersetzung mit Wehrmachtsverbrechen," 344-345.

[328] NOKW 641.

[329] BA-MA, RH 20-11/341.

[330] BA-MA, RH 23-72; NOKW 1632.

[331] BA-MA, RH 23/69.

[332] BA-MA, RH 23/72.

[333] NOKW 1529.

[334] NOKW 1532.

[335] Stein, *Generalfeldmarschall Erich von Manstein*, 272.

[336] BA-MA, RH 23/72; NOKW 1628.

[337] Stein, *Generalfeldmarschall Erich von Manstein*, 273; Wrochem, "Die Auseinandersetzung mit Wehrmachtsverbrechen," 342; Friedrich, *Das Gesetz des Krieges*, 661-662.

[338] NOKW 1573.

339 BA-MA, RH 23/72; NOKW 1573.

340 BA-MA, RH 23/72; BA-MA, RH 23/80; BA-MA, RH 23/86.

341 TMIN, vol. XX, 661.

342 Friedrich, *Das Gesetz des Krieges*, 628-629, 631; Stein, *Generalfeldmarschall Erich von Manstein*, 293-294 (note 672).

343 NOKW 3422; NOKW 3439.

344 Friedrich, *Das Gesetz des Krieges*, 632.

345 NOKW 2834.

346 Stein, *Generalfeldmarschall Erich von Manstein*, 276-277.

347 BA-MA, RH 23/86.

348 Wrochem, "Die Auseinandersetzung mit Wehrmachtsverbrechen," 347; Friedrich, *Das Gesetz des Krieges*, 652-653; Stein, *Generalfeldmarschall Erich von Manstein*, 275.

349 BA-MA, RH 23/86; NOKW 3453.

350 BA-MA, RH 20-11/488.

351 BA-MA, RH 20-11/488.

352 Stein, *Generalfeldmarschall Erich von Manstein*, 277-280. See also Friedrich, *Das Gesetz des Krieges*, 669-670; Wallach, "Feldmarschall Erich von Manstein," 467-468.

353 Leverkuehn, *Verteidigung Manstein*, 37; Stein, *Generalfeldmarschall Erich von Manstein*, 280 (note 629); Wrochem, "Die Auseinandersetzung mit Wehrmachtsverbrechen," 345 (note 114); TMIN, vol. XX, 662; TMIN, vol. XXI, 9.

354 NOKW 5905. See also Friedrich, *Das Gesetz des Krieges*, 670-671; Stein, *Generalfeldmarschall Erich von Manstein*, 281-282.

355 NOKW 1259; NOKW 1590.

356 BA-MA, RH 20-11/341.

357 BA-MA, RH 20-11/341.

358 BA-MA, RH 20-11/341.

359 BA-MA, RH 20-11/342.

360 BA-MA, RH 20-11/342.

361 BA-MA, RH 20-11/341.

362 BA-MA, RH 20-11/342.

363 BA-MA, RH 20-11/341.

364 BA-MA, RH 23/80; NOKW 1872.

365 BA-MA, RH 20-11/341.

366 BA-MA, RH 20-11/342.

367 Manstein, *Verlorene Siege*, 249; Leverkuehn, *Verteidigung Manstein*, 51; Paget, *Manstein*, 148-150 (149-150 for the citation).

368 NOKW 584

369 Friedrich, *Das Gesetz des Krieges*, 648, 654; Wrochem, "Die Auseinandersetzung mit Wehrmachtsverbrechen," 347.

370 BA-MA, RH 23/80.
371 NOKW 1283.
372 BA-MA, RH 23/75; BA-MA, RH 23/79.
373 BA-MA, RH 23/75.
374 BA-MA, RH 23/72.
375 BA-MA, RH 23/79.
376 Stein, *Generalfeldmarschall Erich von Manstein*, 289.
377 BA-MA, RH 20-11/342.
378 Krausnick and Wilhelm, *Die Truppe des Weltanschauungskrieges*, 204.
379 BA-MA, RH 23/79.
380 BA-MA, RH 20-21/488.
381 NOKW 1717.
382 BA-MA, RH 20-11/342; BA-MA, RH 23/91.
383 BA-MA, RH 20-11/342.
384 Krausnick and Wilhelm, *Die Truppe des Weltanschauungskrieges*, 276.
385 BA-MA, RH 20-11/488; NOKW 6281.
386 Raul Hilberg, *Die Vernichtung der europäischen Juden* (Frankfurt-am-Main: Fischer, 1990), 1,294; Friedrich, *Das Gesetz des Krieges*, 665; Stein, *Generalfeldmarschall Erich von Manstein*, 240-241, 296.
387 BA-MA, RH 20-11/342.
388 BA-MA, RH 20-11/342.
389 BA-MA, RH 20-11/342.
390 BA-MA, RH 20-11/337.
391 BA-MA, RH 20-11/337.
392 BA-MA, RH 20-11/337.
393 BA-MA, RH 20-11/342.
394 BA-MA, RH 20-11/337.
395 Regarding this, see NOKW 1878; Friedrich, *Das Gesetz des Krieges*, 420-421, 638-639.
396 TMIN, vol. XX, 660-661, 665.
397 Stahlberg, *Die verdammte Pflicht*, 234-235; Stein, *Generalfeldmarschall Erich von Manstein*, 262.
398 Knopp, *Hitlers Krieger*, 199.
399 Wrochem, "Die Auseinandersetzung mit Wehrmachtsverbrechen," 344.
400 Stein, *Generalfeldmarschall Erich von Manstein*, 292-294, 305-306 (note 698), 320 (note 733).
401 Stahlberg, *Die verdammte Pflicht*, 314-315.
402 Knopp, *Hitlers Krieger*, 202. In a documentary on Hitler's soldiers, Stahlberg confirmed the version of this episode related in his *Memoirs*, then added regarding the extermination of the Jews: "He [Manstein] knew everything." Stein, *Generalfeldmarschall Erich von Manstein*, 259.
403 Stahlberg, *Die verdammte Pflicht*, 354-356.

[404] Knopp, *Hitlers Krieger*, 203. See also Stein, *Generalfeldmarschall Erich von Manstein*, 261.

[405] Stahlberg, *Die verdammte Pflicht*, 351-353, 376-378.

[406] TMIN, vol. XX, 656.

[407] Stein, *Generalfeldmarschall Erich von Manstein*, 294-295.

[408] Boll, "Generalfeldmarschall Erich von Lewinski," 143.

CHAPTER 12

[409] Manstein, *Verlorene Siege*, 262, 322-323 (262, 322 for the citations).

[410] Magenheimer, *Hitler's War*, 153.

[411] Manstein, *Verlorene Siege*, 323-325 (323, 325 for the citations).

[412] Magenheimer, *Hitler's War*, 156-157, 159-161, 281-282.

[413] Megargee, *Inside Hitler's High Command*, 181-183; Walter Warlimont, *Inside Hitler's Headquarters 1939–1945* (New York: Praeger, 1964), 259-260; Below, *Als Hitlers Adjutant*, 315; Irving, *Hitler's War*, 424; Cooper, *The German Army*, 445.

[414] Dana V. Sadarananda, *Beyond Stalingrad. Manstein and the Operations of Army Group Don* (New York: Praeger, 1990), 12.

[415] Manfred Kehring, *Stalingrad. Analyse und Dokumentation einer Schlacht* (Stuttgart: Deutsche Verlags-Anstalt, 1974), 163, 183, 219-220; Kershaw, *Hitler 1936–1945*, 786-787; Below, *Als Hitlers Adjutant*, 323-324.

[416] Manstein, *Verlorene Siege*, 328-330.

[417] Sadarananda, *Beyond Stalingrad*, 17-18; Wegner, "The War Against the Soviet Union," 1,136; Downing, *The Devil's Virtuosos*, 121; Kershaw, *Hitler 1936–1945*, 787-788; Irving, *Hitler's War*, 458.

[418] Manstein, *Verlorene Siege*, 333-336 (333-334 for the citation).

[419] Manstein, *Verlorene Siege*, 334, 344; Knopp, *Hitlers Krieger*, 208-209; Downing, *The Devil's Virtuosos*, 120; Alexander, *How Hitler*, 156; Brett-Smith, *Hitler's Generals*, 227; Magenheimer, *Hitler's War*, 166.

[420] Manstein, *Verlorene Siege*, 341-342.

[421] Stahlberg, *Die verdammte Pflicht*, 242-249. See also Sadarananda, *Beyond Stalingrad*, 19; Manstein, *Verlorene Siege*, 346, 351.

[422] Manstein, *Verlorene Siege*, 351-354; Sadarananda, *Beyond Stalingrad*, 21-24.

[423] ibid., 30-31.

[424] Noakes and Pridham, *Nazism 1919–1945*, 843; John Erickson, *The Road to Berlin. Stalin's War with Germany* (London: Weidenfeld and Nicolson, 1983), 7-8; Manstein, *Verlorene Siege*, 357-361.

[425] Wieder, *Stalingrad*, 154; Wegner, "The War Against the Soviet Union," 1,143-1,145.

[426] Antony Beevor, *Stalingrad. The Fateful Siege: 1942–1943* (New York: Viking, 1998), 297-298.

[427] Wieder, *Stalingrad*, 64.

[428] Sadarananda, *Beyond Stalingrad*, 36-42; Manstein, *Verlorene Siege*, 360-363, 376-379; Cooper, *The German Army*, 429-430.

[429] Sadarananda, *Beyond Stalingrad*, 42-43.

[430] Beevor, *Stalingrad*, 299.

[431] Stahlberg, *Die verdammte Pflicht*, 250.

[432] Manstein, *Verlorene Siege*, 369-371 (371 for the citation); Kershaw, *Hitler 1936–1939*, 788-789; Kehring, *Stalingrad*, 406-410; Sadarananda, *Beyond Stalingrad*, 43; Wieder, *Stalingrad*, 69, 142.

[433] Beevor, *Stalingrad*, 309-310.

[434] Manstein, *Verlorene Siege*, 371-372.

[435] Stein, *Generalfeldmarschall Erich von Manstein*, 45, 135-136.

[436] Knopp, *Hitlers Krieger*, 209.

[437] Wieder, *Stalingrad*, 34; Sadarananda, *Beyond Stalingrad*, 46; Downing, *The Devil's Virtuosos*, 129; Irving, *Hitler's War*, 488; Knopp, *Hitlers Krieger*, 208-209.

[438] Manstein, *Verlorene Siege*, 373-377.

[439] Magenheimer, *Hitler's War*, 167-168. The extent of German losses in the Stalingrad sector constituted a surprise to the Red Army high command who, at the end of November, had estimated the number of soldiers trapped in the pocket to only be 80,000–90,000 men. Magenheimer, *Hitler's War*, 165.

[440] Magenheimer, *Hitler's War*, 166-167; Masson, *Histoire de l'armée allemande*, 236; Liddell Hart, *Histoire de la Seconde Guerre mondiale*, 482; Hillgruber, "In der Sicht," 78.

[441] Manstein, *Verlorene Siege*, 383-385.

[442] Manstein, *Verlorene Siege*, 384; Cooper, *The German Army*, 439-440. According to the OKH intelligence office, the Sixth Army could have held back around Stalingrad up to 107 large Red Army units including 13 armored units. Irving, *Hitler's War*, 482.

[443] Wegner, "The War Against the Soviet Union," 1,163, ,171; Kershaw, *Hitler 1936–1945*, 795.

[444] Manstein, *Verlorene Siege*, 395.

CHAPTER 13

[445] Manstein, *Verlorene Siege*, 400.

[446] Stahlberg, *Die verdammte Pflicht*, 245-249.

[447] Magenheimer, *Hitler's War*, 304 (note 89); Sadarananda, *Beyond Stalingrad*, 53-54; Manstein, *Verlorene Siege*, 409-413; Wegner, "The War Against the Soviet Union," 1,173-1,174.

[448] Manstein, *Verlorene Siege*, 402-408.

[449] Manstein, *Verlorene Siege*, 415-421; Sadarananda, *Beyond Stalingrad*, 62-72.

[450] Manstein, *Verlorene Siege*, 394, 424-426.

[451] Wegner, "The War Against the Soviet Union," 1,176-1,177.

[452] Manstein, *Verlorene Siege*, 437-483; Hayward, "A Case Study," 105-106.

[453] Sadarananda, *Beyond Stalingrad*, 98; Hayward, "A Case Study," 105-106; Irving, *Hitler's War*, 483-484; Knopp, *Hitlers Krieger*, 222-223.

[454] Below, *Als Hitlers Adjutant*, 329; Irving, *Hitler's War*, 477, 483; Guderian, *Panzer Leader*, 302; Kershaw, *Hitler 1936–1945*, 831-832; Wegner, "The War Against the Soviet Union," 1,185; Cooper, *The German Army*, 444; Knopp, *Hitlers Krieger*, 235.

[455] Manstein, *Verlorene Siege*, 437-444; Sadarananda, *Beyond Stalingrad*, 98-101; Eberhard Schwarz, *Die Stabilisierung der Ostfront nach Stalingrad. Mansteins Gegenschlag zwischen Donez und Dnjepr im Frühjahr 1943* (Göttingen, Münster-Schmidt, 1985), 69-73.

[456] Manstein, *Verlorene Siege*, 445-451; Sadarananda, *Beyond Stalingrad*, 102-103, 108; Wegner, "The War Against the Soviet Union," 1,184; Moll, *Die deutschen generalfeldmarschälle*, 126.

[457] Wegner, "The War Against the Soviet Union," 1,183-1,184; Schwarz, *Die Stabilisierung*, 110-120; Manstein, *Verlorene Siege*, 451-454; Sadarananda, *Beyond Stalingrad*, 108-109; Downing, *The Devil's Virtuosos*, 143; Brett-Smith, *Hitler's Generals*, 228; Seaton, "Field-Marshall Erich von Manstein," 240; Carver, "Manstein," 237.

[458] Manstein, *Verlorene Siege*, 454-459; Sadarananda, *Beyond Stalingrad*, 109-111; Schwarz, *Die Stabilisierung*, 254-258; Wegner, "The War Against the Soviet Union," 1,185, 1,188-1,189.

[459] Sadarananda, *Beyond Stalingrad*, 116-126, 140-146; Wegner, "The War Against the Soviet Union," 1,189-1,192; Manstein, *Verlorene Siege*, 459-464; Glantz and House, *When Titans Clashed*, 144; Liddell Hart, *Histoire de la Seconde Guerre mondiale*, 485-486; Erickson, *The Road to Berlin*, 64.

[460] Sadarananda, *Beyond Stalingrad*, 146.

[461] Erickson, *The Road to Berlin*, 52-55. In his *Memoirs*, Marshal Vassilevski, chief of general staff of the Red Army, asserted that Field Marshal Manstein's counter-attack had represented a true surprise for the Soviet high command, thus explaining in part the reason for his clear success. Seaton, "Field-Marshal Erich von Manstein," 241.

[462] The expression is from Masson, *Une guerre totale*, 135. For his part, Humble, *Hitler's Generals*, 109, uses the expression, "miracle of the Marne."

[463] Glantz and House, *When Titans Clashed*, 151.

[464] Warlimont, *Inside Hitler's Headquarters*, 312; Knopp, *Hitlers Krieger*, 216.

[465] Roth, "Operational Thinking," 31-33; Humble, *Hitler's Generals*, 109-110; Seaton, "Field-Marshal Erich von Manstein," 240.

[466] Manstein, *Verlorene Siege*, 468-469.

[467] Kershaw, *Hitler 1936–1945*, 831; Below, *Als Hitlers Adjutant*, 330; Gerhard

L. Weinberg, *A World at Arms. A Global History of World War II* (Cambridge: Cambridge University, 1994), 482; Irving, *Hitler's War*, 478 (note 4).
[468] Manstein, *Verlorene Siege*, 474-475.
[469] Syring, "Erich von Manstein," 339.

CHAPTER 14
[470] Manstein, *Verlorene Siege*, 305-306.
[471] Clark, *Barbarossa*, 251. See also Stahlberg, *Die verdammte Pflicht*, 233.
[472] Aron, *Penser la guerre*, 77.
[473] Manstein, *Verlorene Siege*, 306-307, 313.
[474] Aron, *Penser la guerre*, 91-92.
[475] Manstein, *Verlorene Siege*, 476.
[476] Knopp, *Hitlers Krieger*, 217.
[477] Manstein, *Verlorene Siege*, 477, 479-480.
[478] Manstein, *Verlorene Siege*, 480-484; Rüdiger von Manstein and Teodor Fuchs, *Manstein. Soldat im 20. Jahrhundert. Militärisch-politische Nachlese* (Munich: Bernard & Graefe, 1981), 170-172; Liddell Hart, *The Other Side of the Hill*, 318-319; Downing, *The Devil's Virtuosos*, 156-158; Paget, *Manstein*, 57-58; Cooper, *The German Army*, 456; Erickson, *The Road to Berlin*, 63-64. See also Magenheimer, *Hitler's War*, 207, 284, 307 (note 71), who considers this idea of Manstein's as being "the most brilliant solution," and Alexander, *How Hitler*, 204-205, who speaks of him as being the "best strategic plan."
[479] Kershaw, *Hitler 1936–1945*, 833; Guderian, *Panzer Leader*, 306; Magenheimer, *Hitler's War*, 207.
[480] Manstein, *Verlorene Siege*, 484-488; Noakes and Pridham, *Nazism 1919–1945*, 863.
[481] Kershaw, *Hitler 1936–1945*, 834-835; Manstein, *Verlorene Siege*, 488-491; Guderian, *Panzer Leader*, 306-309.
[482] Roth, "Operational Thinking," 37; Downing, *The Devil's Virtuosos*, 168.
[483] Manstein, *Verlorene Siege*, 488, 494-495.
[484] Magenheimer, *Hitler's War*, 207-209, 211-212, 308 (note 80); Masson, *Histoire de l'armée allemande*, 246; Noakes and Pridham, *Nazism 1919–1945*, 862-863; Kershaw, *Hitler 1936–1945*, 851-852.
[485] Masson, *Histoire de l'armée allemande*, 251-255; Noakes and Pridham, *Nazism 1919–1945*, 863-864; Keegan, *La Deuxième Guerre mondiale*, 458-460; Downing, *The Devil's Virtuosos*, 169-177; Manstein, *Verlorene Siege*, 499-501.
[486] Manstein, *Verlorene Siege*, 501-503; Brett-Smith, *Hitler's Generals*, 228-229; Below, *Als Hitlers Adjutant*, 341; Weinberg, *A World at Arms*, 603; Irving, *Hitler's War*, 535, 538.
[487] Manstein, *Verlorene Siege*, 504.
[488] ibid., 506.

489 Roth, "Operational Thinking," 37-38; Magenheimer, *Hitler's War*, 212-213, 284-285; Seaton, *The German Army*, 206.

490 Keegan, *La Deuxième Guerre mondiale*, 460; Irving, *Hitler's War*, 538.

491 Manstein, *Verlorene Siege*, 505-506.

492 Masson, *Histoire de l'armée allemande*, 256.

493 Manstein, *Verlorene Siege*, 504.

CHAPTER 15

494 Dirks and Janßen, *Der Kriege der Generäle*, 190. See also Knopp, *Hitlers Krieger*, 228-229.

495 Rüdiger von Manstein, "Mansteins Argumentation zum Staatsstreich," *Frankfurter Allgemeine Zeitung*, January 10, 1988.

496 Stahlberg, *Die verdammte Pflicht*, 322-323.

497 Stein, *Gereralfeldmarschall Erich von Manstein*, 61 (note 106); Kosthorst, *Die Geburt der Tragödie*, 197; Bodo Scheurig, *Spiegelbilder der Zeitgeschichte* (Oldenburg: Stalling, 1978), 140.

498 Stahlberg, *Die verdammte Pflicht*, 457; Stein, *Generalfeldmarschall Erich von Manstein*, 172 (note 366), 300, 315.

499 Manstein, *Verlorene Siege*, 8.

500 Stein, *Generalfeldmarschall Erich von Manstein*, 172 (notes 365 and 367).

501 Manstein, *Verlorene Siege*, 381, 392, 574.

502 Engert Jürgen, *Soldaten für Hitler* (Reinbeck: Rowohlt, 1999), 162. See also Hillgruber, "In der Sicht," 78-79, 81.

503 Manstein, *Aus einem Soldatenleben*, 353; Guderian, *Panzer Leader*, 276; Shirer, *Le IIIe Reich*, 1,112.

504 Manstein, *Aus einem Soldatenleben*, 354. One finds the same arguments in Guderian, *Panzer Leader*, 458-464; Albert Kesselring, *The Memoirs of Field-Marshal Kesselring* (London: Leventhal, 1988), 314-315; Karl Dönitz, *Memoirs: Ten Years and Twenty Days* (London: Greenhill, 1990), 299-314.

505 Joachim Fest, *Plotting Hitler's Death. The Story of the German Resistance* (New york: Henry Holt, 1997), 331.

506 Manstein, *Verlorene Siege*, 603.

507 ibid., 603-604.

508 Stein, *Generalfeldmarschall Erich von Manstein*, 174.

509 Stahlberg, *Die verdammte Pflicht*, 224-227,234 (234 for the citation). See also Beevor, *Stalingrad*, 273-274; Seaton, *The German Army*, 232.

510 Beevor, *Stalingrad*, 275-276 (276 for the citation).

511 Stahlberg, *Die verdammte Pflicht*, 262-270.

512 Stein, *Generalfeldmarschall Erich von Manstein*, 186; Knopp, *Hitlers Krieger*, 212.

513 Stahlberg, *Die verdammte Pflicht*, 262-263, 270-272 (271 for the citation). See also Scheurig, *Spiegelbilder der Zeitgeschichte*, 137.

514 Peter Hoffmann, *Claus Schenk Graf von Stauffenberg und seine Brüder* (Stuttgart: Deutsche Verlags-Anstalt, 1992), 267.

515 Kosthorst, *Die Geburt der Tragödie*, 191.

516 Stahlberg, *Die verdammte Pflicht*, 281; Manstein, *Verlorene Siege*, 62.

517 Manstein, *Verlorene Siege*, 282. See also Scheurig, *Spiegelbilder der Zeitgeschichte*, 137-138; Fabian von Schlabrendorff, *Offiziere gegen Hitler* (Berlin: Siedler, 1984), 159-160.

518 Manstein and Fuchs, *Manstein*, 205-207.

519 Stahlberg, *Die verdammte Pflicht*, 281-282.

520 Manstein, *Verlorene Siege*, 62.

521 Breithaupt, *Zwischen Front und Widerstand*, 86.

522 Schlabrendorff, *Offiziere gegen Hitler*, 114.

523 Breithaupt, *Zwischen Front und Widerstand*, 84.

524 Stahlberg, *Die verdammte Pflicht*, 282-283, 310 (310 for the citation).

525 Scheurig, *Spiegelbilder der Zeitgeschichte*, 137.

526 Scheurig, *Spiegelbilder der Zeitgeschichte*, 136; Schlabrendorff, *Offiziere gegen Hitler*, 160.

527 Manstein and Fuchs, *Manstein*, 207-210. See also Stahlberg, *Die verdammte Pflicht*, 315

528 Beevor, *Stalingrad*, 347.

529 Gersdorff, *Soldat im Untergang*, 133-136.

530 Peter Hoffmann, *Widertand-Staatsstreich-Attentat. Der Kampf der Opposition gegen Hitler* (Munich: Piper, 1985),340-341; Scheurig, *Spiegelbilder der Zeitgeschichte*, 138; Schlabrendorff, *Offiziere gegen Hitler*, 160; Kosthorst, *Die Geburt der Tragödie*, 192-195, 199; Schneider, "Denkmal Manstein," 406-407.

531 Manstein and Fuchs, *Manstein*, 185-186.

532 Knopp, *Hitlers Krieger*, 226-227.

533 Stahlberg, *Die verdammte Pflicht*, 338-339.

534 Knopp, *Hitlers Krieger*, 229. See also Manstein, *Verlorene Siege*, 524-525.

535 Kershaw, *Hitler 1936–1945*, 887-888; Irving, *Hitler's War*, 595; Manstein, *Verlorene Siege*, 569-570, 572-574.

536 Knopp, *Hitlers Krieger*, 228. See also Kosthorst, *Die Geburt der Tragödie*, 197; Scheurig, *Spiegelbilder der Zeitgeschichte*, 138.

537 Stahlberg, *Die verdammte Pflicht*, 376-381.

538 Kershaw, *Hitler 1936–1945*, 889-890. See also Manstein, *Verlorene Siege*, 579-580.

539 Manstein, *Verlorene Siege*, 580. See also Kershaw, *Hitler 1936–1945*, 890; Irving, *Hitler's War*, 597-598; Mitcham, *Hitler's Field Marshals*, 252; Stahlberg, *Die verdammte Pflicht*, 357.

540 Manstein, *Verlorene Siege*, 580-581. See also Kershaw, *Hitler 1936 –1945*, 890-891.

[541] Stahlberg, *Die verdammte Pflicht*, 358.

[542] Stahlberg, *Die verdammte Pflicht*, 360-363; Kosthorst, *Die Geburt der Tragödie*, 195-196; Knopp, *Hitlers Krieger*, 232; Kershaw, *Hitler 1936–1945*, 903-904, 1,441 (note 90).

[543] Manstein, *Verlorene Siege*, 608-614; Knopp, *Hitlers Krieger*, 234; Kershaw, *Hitler 1936–1945*, 904-905.

[544] Kershaw, *Hitler 1936–1945*, 905-906; Keegan, *La Deuxième Guerre mondiale*, 467-468; Irving, *Hitler's War*, 616.

[545] Manstein, *Verlorene Siege*, 614-616. See also Carver, "Manstein," 242; Seaton, "Field-Marshal Erich von Manstein," 242; Seaton, *The German Army*, 216; Mellenthin, *German Generals*, 38; Mitcham, *Hitler's Field Marshals*, 253; Stahlberg, *Die verdammte Pflicht*, 369-372; Knopp, *Hitlers Krieger*, 174.

[546] Manstein, *Verlorene Siege*, 616; Knopp, *Hitlers Krieger*, 172-173, 218 (218 for the citation); Liddell Hart, *The Other Side of the Hill*, 98.

[547] Goda, "Black Marks," 441-443; Knopp, *Hitlers Krieger*, 172, 220, 224, 230

[548] Syring, "Erich von Manstein," 340.

[549] Manstein and Fuchs, *Manstein*, 193-194. See also Knopp, *Hitlers Krieger*, 224.

[550] Syring, "Erich von Manstein," 340.

[551] Brett-Smith, *Hitler's Generals*, 234-235.

[552] Kershaw, *Hitler 1936–1945*, 906; Keegan, *La Deuxième Guerre mondiale*, 467.

[553] R.D. Palsokar, *Manstein: The Master General* (Poona: The Beg, 1970), 154; Paget, *Manstein*, 65; Seaton, "Field-Marshal Eric von Manstein," 242-243.

[554] Shirer, *Le IIIe Reich*, 1,110.

[555] Guderian, *Panzer Leader*, 345-347.

[556] Shirer, *Le IIIe Reich*, 1,110.

[557] Stahlberg, *Die verdammte Pflicht*, 391-392.

[558] Syring, "Erich von Manstein," 342. See also Boll, "Generalfeldmarschall Erich von Lewinski," 149.

[559] TMIN, vol. XX, 667.

[560] Stahlberg, *Die verdammte Pflicht*, 395.

[561] Knopp, *Hitlers Krieger*, 234.

[562] ibid., 235.

[563] Manstein and Fuchs, *Manstein*, 200.

[564] Guderian, *Panzer Leader*, 302.

[565] Stahlberg, *Die verdammte Pflicht*, 375-376.

[566] Stahlberg, *Die verdammte Pflicht*, 401; Kosthorst, *Die Geburt der Tragödie*, 200; Knopp, *Hitlers Krieger*, 235.

[567] Stahlberg, *Die verdammte Pflicht*, 401-405 (405 for the citation).

[568] Ueberschär and Vogel, *Dienen und Verdienen*, 74-83.

[569] TMIN, vol. XX, 667.

570 Kunrat Freiherr von Hammerstein, *Spähtrupp* (Stuttgart: Deutsche Verlags-Anstalt, 1963), 140; Rolf-Dieter Müller, *Hitlers Ostkrieg und die deutsche Siedlungspolitik. Die Zusammenarbeit von Wehrmacht, Wirtschaft und SS* (Frankfurt-am-Main: Fischer, 1991), 35; Alan Bullock, *Hitler et Staline. Vie Parallèles*, vol. 2 (Paris: Albin Michel/Robert Laffont, 1994), 295; Irving, *Hitler's War*, 616, 729; Mitcham, *Hitler's Field Marshals*, 253.

571 BA-B, NS 19/909: Letter from Backe to Manstein, October 17, 1944. See also Ueberschär and Vogel, *Dienen und Verdienen*, 180-181, 238 (for a copy of Backe's letter addressed to Manstein on October 17, 1944); Boll, "Generalfeldmarschall Erich von Lewinski," 149. After the war, Otto John, who was the plaintiff's adviser in German law, confirmed the steps carried out by Manstein with the Führer which were intended at finding an estate. He reported a conversation that he had a few weeks earlier with the real estate agent Schlange-Schöningen. The latter told him that Manstein had clearly received an endowment and that he had the intention of utilizing it in January 1945 in order to acquire an estate. To Manstein, Schlange-Schöningen responded: "But *Herr* Field Marshall, the Russians will probably be here in the following week." Manstein's repsonse, if one is to believe the testimony, would demonstrate the extent to which he was deluded regarding the outcome of the war: "They will soon be once again driven back by the Führer." Stein, *Generalfeldmarschall Erich von Manstein*, 48.

572 Stahlberg, *Die verdammte Pflicht*, 423. See also Boll, "Generalfeldmarschall Erich von Lewinski," 149; Knopp, *Hitlers Krieger*, 234.

573 Irving, *Hitler's War*, 729.

574 Stahlberg, *Die verdammte Pflicht*, 423-425; Knopp, *Hitlers Krieger*, 236.

575 Stahlberg, *Die verdammte Pflicht*, 434-435.

576 Manstein and Fuchs, *Manstein*, 213-214; Knopp, *Hitlers Krieger*, 236; Hillgruber, "In der Sicht," 81; Boll, "Generalfeldmarschall Erich von Lewinski," 149; Stahlberg, *Die verdammte Pflicht*, 435.

577 Dönitz, *Memoirs*, 447.

578 Manstein and Fuchs, *Manstein*, 213-214.

579 Stahlberg, *Die verdammte Pflicht*, 435-436; Manstein and Fuchs, *Manstein*, 215.

580 Knopp, *Hitlers Krieger*, 236-237.

CHAPTER 16
581 Kosthorst, *Die Geburt der Tragödie*, 178.

582 Paul Létourneau, "Le maréchal Erich von Manstein: à l'ombre de l'image de la Wehrmacht," *Revue d'Allemagne et des pays de langue allemande*, 30, no. 2 (April-June 1998): 128.

583 Telford Taylor, *Procureur à Nuremberg* (Paris: Seuil, 1995), 536 (note 13), 599-601 (601 for the citations).

[584] Syring, "Erich von Manstein," 342-343; Siegfried Westphal, *Der deutsche Generalstab auf der Anklagebank Nürnberg 1945–1948* (Mayence: Hase & Koehler, 1978), 92; Schneider, "Denkmal Manstein," 415.

[585] Westphal, *Der deutsche Generalstab*, 28-87.

[586] Messerschmidt, "Forward Defense," 381-399; Wette, *Die Wehrmacht*, 205-207; Georg Meyer, "Zur Situation der deutschen militärischen Führungsschicht im Vorfeld des westdeutschen Verteidigungsbeitrages 1945–1950/51," in Roland G. Foerster et al., *Anfänge westdeutscher Sicherheitspolitik 1945–1956*, vol. 1, *Von der Kapitulation bis zum Pleven-Plan* (Munich: Oldenburg, 1982), 672.

[587] Omer Bartov, "German Soldiers and the Holocaust. Historiography, Research and Implications," *History & Memory*, 9, nos. 1-2 (1997): 163.

[588] Walther Wenck, "Nie Ausser Dienst," in *Nie Ausser Dienst*, 86.

[589] Taylor, *Procureur à Nuremberg*, 545-546, 601-602.

[590] Wette, *Die Wehrmacht*, 208, 212-216. See also Georg Meyer, "Soldaten ohne Armee. Berufssoldaten im Kampf um Standesehre und Versorgung," in Martin Broszat et al., ed., *Von Stalingrad zur Währungsreform*, 709-710; Meyer, "Zur Situation der deutschen militärischen Führungsschicht," 621-624.

[591] Telford Taylor, *Final Report to the Secretary of the Army on the Nuremberg War Crimes Trials under Control Council Law No. 10* (Washington D.C.: US Government Print Office, 1949), 80-83. See also J.H. Hoffman, "German Field Marshals as War Criminals? A British Embarrassment," *Journal of Contemporary History*, 23, no. 1 (January 1988): 17-18, 32 (note 3); Oliver von Wrochem, "Rehabilitation oder Strafverfolgung. Kriegsverbrecherprozeß gegen Generalfeldmarschall Erich von Manstein im Widerstreit britischer Interessen," *Mittelweg 36*, 6, no. 3 (1997): 26.

[592] Tom Bower, *The Pledge Betrayed. America and Britain and the Denazification of Postwar Germany* (Garden City: Doubleday, 1982), 227-228.

[593] Hoffman, "German Field Marshals," 20; Bower, *The Pledge Betrayed*, 228-229; Taylor, *Final Report*, 82; Wrochem, "Rehabilitation oder Strafverfolgung," 27.

[594] Bower, *The Pledge Betrayed*, 222, 230-231.

[595] Hoffman, "German Field Marshals," 22-24; Bower, *The Pledge Betrayed*, 235-236; Wrochem, "Rehabilitation oder Strafverfolgung," 27-28.

[596] Bower, *The Pledge Betrayed*, 237-238.

[597] Bower, *The Pledge Betrayed*, 233, 238; Meyer, "Zur Situation der deutschen militärischen Führungsschicht," 625; Jörg Friedrich, *Die kalte Amnestie. NS-Täter in der Bundesrepublik* (Frankfurt-am-Main: Fischer, 1984), 132.

[598] Wette, *Die Wehrmacht*, 221.

[599] Meyer, "Zur Situation der deutscher militärischen Führungsschicht," 624; Bower, *The Pledge Betrayed*, 239.

[600] Hoffman, "German Field Marshals," 26-28, 35 (note 52); Leverkuehn,

Verteidigung Manstein, 9; Wrochem, "Rehabilitation oder Strafverfolgung," 28.

601 Bower, *The Pledge Betrayed*, 240; Wrochem, "Rehabilitation oder Strafverfolgung," 29; Hoffman, "German Field Marshals," 28-29; Wette, *Die Wehrmacht*, 223.

602 Friedrich, *Die kalte Amnestie*, 131; Wallach, "Feldmarshall Erich von Manstein," 471; Stein, *Generalfeldmarschall Erich von Manstein*, 51; Wrochem, "Rehabilitation oder Strafverfolgung," 26-28.

603 Bower, *The Pledge Betrayed*, 241.

604 Paget, *Manstein*, 74, 107, 132-133; Bower, *The Pledge Betrayed*, 241; Wrochem, "Die Auseinandersetzung mit Wehrmachtsverbrechen," 32; Wrochem, "Rehabilitation oder Strafverfolgung," 30.

605 Paget, *Manstein*, 69-70, 75-76 (75-76 for the citation).

606 Leverkuehn, *Verteidigung Manstein*, 10-16; Paget, *Manstein*, 88-104; Wrochem, "Die Auseinandersetzung mit Wehrmachtsverbrechen," 335-349; Wrochem, "Rehabilitation oder Strafverfolgung," 28-29.

607 Leverkuehn, *Verteidigung Manstein*, 33-35.

608 Bower, *The Pledge Betrayed*, 224, 244.

609 Leverkuehn, *Verteidigung Manstein*, 45-46.

610 Wrochem, "Die Auseinandersetzung mit Wehrmachtsverbrechen," 350.

611 Meyer, "Zur Situation der deutschen militärischen Führungsschicht," 628; Manstein and Fuchs, *Manstein*, 302.

612 Wrochem, "Die Auseinandersetzung mit Wehrmachtsverbrechen," 351-352.

613 Friedrich, *Die kalte Amnestie*, 131; Wrochem, "Die Auseinandersetzung mit Wehrmachtsverbrechen," 352.

614 Paget, *Manstein*, 195-199.

615 Bower, *The Pledge Betrayed*, 247.

616 Wrochem, "Die Auseinandersetzung mit Wehrmachtsverbrechen," 352; Wrochem, "Rehabilitation oder Strafverfolgung," 33-36; Kosthorst, *Die Geburt der Tragödie*, 179.

617 Hoffman, "German Field Marshals," 30; Wrochem, "Die Auseinandersetzung mit Wehrmachtsverbrechen," 329; Boll, "Generalfeldmarschall Erich von Lewinski," 150.

618 Wette, *Die Wehrmacht*, 222-223.

619 See Norbert Frei, "Das ganz normale Grauen," *Der Spiegel*, 16 (April 14, 1997): 64-67; Wette, *Die Wehrmacht*, 232-234.

620 Heuer, *Die deutschen Generalfeldmarschälle*, 92; Stein, *Generalfeldmarschall Erich von Manstein*, 52; Boll, "Generalfeldmarschall Erich von Lewinski," 150; Syring, "Erich von Manstein," 343-344.

CONCLUSION

621 Manstein, *Verlorene Siege*, 7. For Liddell Hart's citation, see his work *The

Other Side of the Hill, 471. Emphasis is mine.

622 ibid., 7-8.

623 Wieder, *Stalingrad*, 175.

624 ibid., 169, 171.

625 ibid., 249.

626 Syring, "Erich von Manstein," 343-344; Knopp, *Hitlers Krieger*, 240.

627 Konrad von Hammerstein, "Manstein," *Frankfurter Hefte*, 11 (1956): 449-454 (454 for the citation).

628 Kosthorst, *Die Geburt des Tragödie*, 180.

629 Joachim Engelmann, *Manstein. Stratege und Truppenführer. Ein Lebensricht in Bildern*, (Friedberg: Podzun-Pallas, 1981), 175.

630 Knopp, *Hitlers Krieger*, 176. See also Kosthorst, *Die Geburt der Tragödie*, 201.

631 Wieder, *Stalingrad*, 175. See also Scheurig, *Spiegelbilder der Zeitgeschichte*, 142; Knopp, *Hitlers Krieger*, 228-229.

632 ibid., 226, 241.

633 Gersdorff, *Soldat im Untergang*, 137.

634 Wallach, "Feldmarschall Erich von Manstein", 472.

BIBLIOGRAPHY

PRIMARY SOURCES

Bundesarchiv-Militärarchiv-Freiburg (BA-MA)
AOK 11:
RH 20-11/337 (Gruppe Geheime Feldpolizei)
RH 20-11/341 (Partisanenbekämpfung)
RH 20-11/342 (Meldung des Stabes für Partisanenbekämpfung)
RH 20-11/488 (Einsatzgruppe D)
RH 20-11/519 (Manstein-Befehl 20.11.1941)

Korück 553
RH 23/69	RH 23/70	RH 23/71	RH 23/72
RH 23/77	RH 23/78	RH 23/79	RH 23/80
RH 23/83	RH 23/84	RH 23/86	RH 23/88
RH 23/91			

AOK HGr A:
RH 19 I/25	RH 19 I/26	RH 19 I/38	RH 19 I/41

OKH:
RH 6/1	RH 6/2	RH 6/3	RH 6/3
RH 19 II/21			

MGFA/DZ: II H 1008/1
H 08-28/4 (Nachlaß Beck)

Bryan Mark Rigg-Sammlung:
BMRS, Interview Rüdiger von Manstein, 17.11.1994, T-54
BMRS, Akte Rüdiger von Manstein, Manstein an Rigg, 21.7.2001

BMRS, Interview Alexander Stahlberg, 3-4.12.1994, T-68

Bundesarchiv-Berlin (BA-B)
Persönlicher Stab Reichsführer-SS:
NS 19/909 (Backe an Manstein, 17.10.1944)
NS 19/2177

Nürnberger Oberkommando der Wehrmacht – Dokumente (NOKW). Der Prozeß der Vereinigten Staaten von Amerika gegen Wilhelm von Leeb und andere (OKW-Prozeß, High Command-Case: Fall12)

19-156 (Opening Statement der Anklage)
156-1743 (Beweisverfahren der Anklage)
1743-2642 (Fall Leeb mit allen Zeugenverhören inclusive Halder)
2642-2992 (Fall Küchler mit allen Zeugenverhören)
2992-3277 (Fall Hoth mit allen Zeugenverhören)
3277-3832 (Fall Reinhardt mit allen Zeugenverhören)
5469-5962 (Fall Wöhler mit allen Zeugenverhören)
6126-6979 (Fall Warlimont mit allen Zeugenverhören)

Trial of the major war criminals before the International Military Tribunal of Nuremberg (TMIN), November 14, 1945–October 1, 1946, Nuremberg, 1949, 42 volumes:
Volume IV
Volume XX
Volume XXI

SECONDARY SOURCES

BOOKS

Alexander, Bevin. *How Hitler Could Have Won World War II: The Fatal Errors that Led to Nazi Defeat.* New York: Three Rivers, 2000.
Bartov, Orner. *L'Armée d'Hitler. La Wehrmacht, les nazis et la guerre.* Paris: Hachette Littérature, 1999.
Beevor, Antony. *Stalingrad: The Fateful Siege, 1942–1943.* New York: Viking, 1998.
Below, Nicolaus von. *Als Hitlers Adjutant 1937–1945.* Mayence: Hase & Koehler, 1980.
Blakemore, Porter Randall. 1978. *Manstein in the Crimea: The Eleventh Army Campaign, 1941–1942.* Ph.D. diss., University of Georgia.

Bower, Tom. *The Pledge Betrayed: America and Britain and the Denazification of Postwar Germany*. Garden City, Doubleday, 1982.

Breithaupt, Hans. *Zwischen Front und Widerstand. Ein Beitrag zur Diskussion um den Feldmarschall von Manstein*. Bonn: Bernard & Graefe, 1994.

Brett-Smith, Richard. *Hitler's Generals*. London: Osprey, 1976.

Cooper, Matthew. *The German Army, 1933–1945: Its Political and Military Failure*. New York: Stein and Day, 1978.

Deist, Wilhelm, ed. *The German Military in the Age of Total War*. Leamington Spa: Berg, 1985.

Dirks, Carl et Janßen, Karl-Heinz. *Der Krieg der Generäle. Hitler als Werkzeug der Wehrmacht*. Berlin: Propyläen, 1999.

Downing, David. *The Devil's Virtuosos: German Generals at War, 1940–1945*. New York: St. Martin's Press, 1977.

Freiser, Karl-Heinz. *Le Mythe de la guerre éclair. La campagne de l'Ouest de 1940*. Paris: Belin, 2003.

Friedrich, Jörg. *Die kalte Amnestie. NS-Täter in der Bundesrepublik*. Francfurt-am-Main: Fischer, 1984.

____. *Das Gesetz des Krieges. Das deutsche Heer in Rußland 1941–1945. Der Prozeß gegen das Oberkommando der Wehrmacht*. Munich: Piper, 1995.

Gersdorff, Rudolf-Christoph Freiheer von. *Soldat im Untergang. Lebensbilder*. Berlin: Ullstein, 1977.

Geyer, Michael. *Aufrüstung oder Sicherheit. Die Reichswehr in der Krise der Machtpolitik 1924–1936*. Wiesbaden: Steiner, 1980.

Guderian, Heinz. *Panzer Leader*. Washington, DC: Zenger, 1979.

Heer, Hannes and Naumann, Klaus, eds. *War of Extermination: The German Military in World War II, 1941–1994*. New York: Berghahn, 2000.

Heuer, Gerd F. *Die deutschen Generalfeldmarschälle und Grossadmirale*. Rastatt: Pabel, 1978.

Hirschfeld, Gerhard, ed. *The Policies of Genocide: Jews and Soviet Prisoners of War in Nazi Germany*. Boston: Allen & Unwin, 1986.

Humble, Richard. *Hitler's Generals*. London: Arthur Barker, 1974.

Irving, David. *Hitler's War*. New York: Viking, 1977.

Keegan, John. *La Deuxième Guerre mondiale*. Paris: Perrin, 1990.

Kershaw, Ian. *Hitler, 1889–1936: Hubris*. Paris: Flammarion, 1999.

____. *Hitler, 1936 – 1945: Nemesis*. Paris: Flammarion, 2000.

Knopp, Guido. *Hitlers Krieger*. Munich: Goldmann, 2000.

Kosthors, Erich. *Die Geburt der Tragödie aus dem Geist des Gehorsams. Deutschlands Generäle und Hitler—Erfahrungen und Reflexionen eines Frontoffiziers*. Bonn: Bouvier, 1998.

Krausnick, Helmut and Wilhelm, Hans-Heinrich. *Die Truppe des Welt-anschauungskrieges: Die Einsatzgruppen der Sicherheitspolizei und des SD 1938–1942*. Stuttgart: Deutsche Verlags-Anstalt, 1981.

Liddell Hart, Basil Henry. The Other Side of the Hill: *Germany's Generals, Their Rise and Fall. With their own Account of Military Events, 1939–1945*. London: Cassel, 1951.

____. *Histoire de la Seconde Guerre mondiale*. Paris: Fayard, 1973.

Leverkuehn, Paul. *Verteidigung Manstein*. Hamburg: Nolke, 1950.

Magenheimer, Heinz. *Hitler's War: Germany's Key Strategic Decisions 1940–1945: Could Germany have won World War Two?* London: Arms & Armour, 1998.

Manstein, Erich von. *Aus Einem Soldatenleben, 1887–1939*. Bonn: Athenäum, 1958.

____. *Verlorene Siege*. Bonn: Bernard & Graefe, 2000.

Manstein, Rüdiger von and Fuchs, Theodor. *Manstein: Soldat im 20. Jahrhundert. Militärisch-politische Nachlese*. Munich: Bernard & Graefe, 1981.

Masson, Philippe. *Histoire de l'armée allemande, 1939–1945*. Paris: Perrin, 1994.

Mellenthin, F.W. von. *German Generals of World War Two as I Saw Them*. Norman: University of Oklahoma, 1977.

Messerschmidt, Manfred. *Die Wehrmacht im NS-Staat: Zeit der Indoktrination*. Hamburg: Decker, 1969.

Militärgeschichtliches Forschungsamt (MGFA). *Germany and the Second World War. Vol. 1, The Build-up of German Aggression. Vol. 2, Germany's Initial Conquests in Europe. Vol. 4, The Attack on the Soviet Union. Vol. 6, The Global War. Widening of the Conflict into a World War and the Shift of the Initiative 1941–1943*. Oxford: Clarendon, 1990, 1991, 1998, and 2001.

Mitcham, Samuel W. *Hitler's Field Marshals and their Battles*. London: Grafton, 1988.

Moll, Otto E. *Die deutschen Generalfeldmarschälle 1935–1945*. Rastatt: Pabel, 1961.

Müller, Klaus-Jürgen. *Das Heer und Hitler: Armee und nationalsozialistisches Regime 1933–1940*. Stuttgart: Deutsche Verlags-Anstalt, 1969.

____. *Armee, Politik und Gesellschaft in Deutschland 1933–1945: Studien zum Verhältnis von Armee und NS-System*. Paderborn: Schöningh, 1979.

Müller, Rolf-Dieter and Volkmann, Hans-Erich, eds. *Die Wehrmacht. Mythos und Realität*. Munich: Oldenbourg, 1999.

Paget, Reginald. *Manstein: His Campaigns and His Trial*. London: Collins, 1951.

Palsokar, R. D. *Manstein: The Master General*. Poona: The Beg, 1970.

Rigg, Bryan Mark. *Hitler's Jewish Soldiers. The Untold Story of Nazi Racial Laws and Men of Jewish Descent in the German Military*. Kansas City: Unversity Press of Kansas, 2002.

Sadarananda, Dana V. *Beyond Stalingrad: Manstein and the Operations of Army Group Don*. New York: Praeger, 1990.

Sscheurig, Bodo. *Spiegelbilder der Zeitgeschichte*. Oldenburg: Stalling, 1978.

Schwarz, Eberhard. *Die Stabilisierung der Ostfront nach Stalingrad. Mansteins Gegenschlag zwischen Donez und Dnjepr im Frühjahr 1943*. Gottingen: Münster-Schmidt, 1985.

Seaton, Albert. *The German Army 1933–1945*. London: Weidenfeld and Nicolson, 1982.

Shirer, William L. *Le IIIe Reich*. Paris: Stock, 1990.

Stahlberg, Alexander. *Die verdammte Pflicht. Erinnerungen 1932 bis 1945*. Berlin: Ullstein, 1994.

Stein, Marcel. *Generalfeldmarschall Erich von Manstein. Kritische Betrachtung des Soldaten und Menschen*. Mayence: Hase & Koehler, 2002.

Streit, Christian. *Keine Kameraden: Die Wehrmacht und die sowjetischen Kriegsgefangenen 1941–1945*. Stuttgart: Deutsche Verlags-Anstalt, 1978.

Taylor, Telford. *Procureur à Nuremberg*. Paris: Seuil, 1995.

Ueberschär, Gerd Rolf and Wette, Wolfram, eds. *"Unternehmen Barbarossa." Der deutsche Überfall auf die Sowjetunion 1941. Berichte, Analysen, Dokumente*. Paderborn: Schoningh, 1984.

Ueberschär, Gerd Rolf and Vogel, Winfried. *Dienen und Verdienen*. Frankfurt-am-Main: Fischer, 1999.

Warlimont, Walter. *Inside Hitler's Headquarters 1939–1945*. New York: Praeger, 1964.

Wette, Wolfram. *Die Wehrmacht. Feinbilder. Vernichtungskrieg. Legenden*. Frankfurt-am-Main: Fischer, 2002.

Wette, Wolfram and Ueberschär, Gerd Rolf, eds. *Kriegsverbrechen im 20. Jahrhundert*. Darmstadt: Wissenschaftliche Buchgesellschaft, 2001.

Wieder, Joachim. *Stalingrad ou la responsabilité du soldat*. Paris: Albin Michel, 1983.

ARTICLES

Boll, Bernd. "Generalfeldmarschall Erich von Lewinski, gen. von Manstein." In *Hitlers militärische Elite*.

Edited by Gerd Rolf Ueberschär. Vol 2, "Yom Kriegsbeginn bis zum Weltkriegsende." Darmstadt: Wissenschaftliche Buchgesellschaft, 1998.

Carver, Lord. Manstein. "Hitler's Generals." Edited by Correlli Barnett. London: Weidenfeld and Nicholson,1989.

Dirks, Carl and Janßen, Karl-Heinz. 1997. "Plan Otto. Die Zeit, 19 September, 16."

Frieser, Karl-Heinz. "Der Westfeldzug und die 'Blitzkrieg'—Legende." *Ideen und Strategien 1940*.

"Ausgewählte Operationen und deren militärgeschichtliche Aufarbeitung." In *Militärgeschichtliches Forschungsamt*. Edited by Freiburg im Breisgau. Bonn: Mittler & Sohn, 1990.

Goda, Norman J.W. 2000. "Black Marks: Hitler's Bribery of His Senior Officers during World War II." *The Journal of Modern History*, 72: 413-452.

Hayward, Joel. 1999. "A Case Study in Early Joint Warfare: An Analysis of the Wehrmacht's Crimean Campaign of 1942." *The Journal of Strategic Studies*, 22, no. 4: 103-130.

Hartmann, Christian and Slutch, Sergej. 1997. "Franz Halder und die Kriegsvorbereitungen im Frühjahr 1939. Dokumentation." *Vierteijahrshefte für Zeitgeschichte*, 45, no. 3: 467-495.

Hillgruber, Andreas. "In der Sicht des Kritischen Historikers. In Nie ausser Dienst. Zum achtzigsten Geburtstag von Generalfeldmarschall Erich von Manstein." Cologne: Greven & Bechtold, 1967.

Hoffman, J. H. 1988. "German Field Marshals as War Criminals? A British Embarrassment." *Journal of Contemporary History*, 23, no. 1: 17-35.

Létourneau, Paul. 1998. "Le maréchal Erich von Manstein: à l'ombre de l'image de la Wehrmacht." *Revue d'Allemagne et des pays de langue allemande*, 30, no. 2:127-135.

Manstein, Rüdiger von. "Mansteins Argumentation zum Staatsstreich." *Frankfurter Allgemeine Zeitung*, 10 January 1988.

Martens, Stefan. "La défaite française: une heureuse surprise allemande?" In *La Campagne de 1940*.

"Actes du colloque: 16 au 18 novembre 2000." Edited by Christine Levisse-Touzé. Paris: Tallandier, 2001.

Messerschmidt, Manfred. 1983. "The Wehrmacht and the Volksgemeinschaft." *Journal of Contemporary History*, 18, no. 4: 719-740.

———. 1983. "German Staff Officers' Education since the Beginning of the 19th Century: Innovations and Traditions." *Militärhistorisk Tidskrift*, 187: 9-19.

Müller, Klaus-Jürgen. "Deutsche Militär-Elite in der Vorgeschichte des Zweiten Weltkrieges." In *Die deutschen Eliten und der Weg in den Zweiten Weltkrieg*. Edited by Martin Broszat et Klaus Schwabe. Munich: Beck, 1989.

———. 1989. "Le réarmement allemand et le problème de la sécurité nationale face à la politique du révisionnisme (1933–1937)." *Guerres mondiales*, 154: 63-77.

Rigg, Bryan Mark. 1997. "Warum gehorchten Soldaten jüdischer Herkunft einem Regime, das ihre Familien umbrachte?" *Die Zeit*, no. 15: 7.

Roth, Günther. "The Campaign Plan 'Case Yellow' for the German Offensive in the West in 1940. The Operational Thinking of Clausewitz, Moltke, Schlieffen, and Manstein. In *Militargeschichtliches Forschungsamt*. Edited by Freiburg im Breisgau. Herford: Mittler & Sohn, 1988.

____. "Operational Thinking of Schlieffen and Manstein. The Development, Planning and Realization of Operational Conceptions in World Wars I and II." In *Militargeschichtliches Forschungsamt*. Edited by Freiburg im Breisgau. Herford: Mittler & Sohn, 1989.

Schnieder, Christian. "Denkmal Manstein. Psychogramm cines Befehlshabers. In Vernichtungskrieg Verbrechen der Wehrmacht, 1941 bis 1944." Edited by Hannes Heer and Klaus Naumann. Hamburg: Hamburger Edition, 1995.

Seaton, Albert. "Field-Marshal Erich von Manstein." In *Military Commanders of the Twentieth Century*. Edited by Michael Carver. London: Weidenfeld and Nicholson, 1976.

Solchany, Jean. 2000. "La lente dissipation d'une légende: la 'Wehrmacht' sous le regard de l'Histoire." *Revue d'histoire moderne et contemporaine*, 47, no. 2: 323-353.

Syring, Enrico. "Erich von Manstein—Das operative Genie." In *Die Militärelite des Dritten Reiches*. Edited by Ronald Smelser and Enrico Syring. Berlin: Ullstein, 1997.

Wallach, Jehuda L. 1975. "Feldmarschall Erich von Manstein und die deutsche Judenausrottung in Rußland." *Jahrbuch des Instituts für Deutsche Geschichte*, 4: 457-472.

Wrochem, Oliver von. 1997. "Rehabilitation oder Strafverfolgung. Kriegsverbrecherprozeß gegen Generalfeldmarschall Erich von Manstein im Widerstreit britischer Interessen." *Mittelweg*, 36 6, no. 3: 26-36.

____. 1998. "Die Auseinandersetzung mit Wehrmachtsverbrechen in Prozeß gegen den Generalfeldmarschsall Erich von Manstein, 1949." *Zeitschrift für Geschichtswissenschaft*, 46, no. 4: 329-353

INDEX

Greece, 177, 180, 194
Green Plan, 52, 60, 63
Greiffenberg, Colonel Hans von, 68, 96
Groddek Brigade, 231
Guderian, Major General Heinz, 3, 48,
    77-78, 91, 110-114, 123-124, 129,
    133-134, 141-147, 150-154, 160,
    165, 189, 197, 209, 219, 226, 337,
    369, 384, 424, 427-428, 430-431,
    472; hesitation to commence
    western campaign, 92; opinion of
    Manstein, 3; role in France cam-
    paign, 160; strategic use of Panzer
    divisions, 48; support of Ardennes
    traversal, 112; *Reminiscences of a
    Soldier*, 472
Gulf of Finland, 240, 360
Gunzert, Captain Ulrich, 292

Hagemann, Dr. Albert, 430
Hague Convention, 204, 207, 249,
    459-460, 463-464, 466
Halbjude, 33
Halder, Colonel General Franz, 4, 56-
    57, 63, 68, 72, 75, 76, 90-94, 96,
    98-99, 102, 110-112, 114-116, 119-
    123, 126, 129-130, 134, 137, 143,
    146-147, 149, 151-152, 161, 173,
    188-192, 194, 201, 219-220, 226,
    239, 241, 248-249, 262, 266, 299,
    439-440, 462, 472; hesitation to
    commence Western campaign, 92;
    Hitler as Military Leader, 472;
    involvement in Yellow Plan, 79;
    opposition to Hitler's Dunkirk halt-
    order, 112; rejection of Manstein
    Plan, 99; role in Otto Plan, 188-189
Hamburg, 6, 262, 267, 280, 289, 437,
    450-451, 454, 457-458, 469, 472
Hamburger Abendblatt, 454
Hamburger Allgemeine Zeitung, 469
Hammerstein, Konrad von, 479
Hammerstein-Equord, Colonel General
    Kurt Freiherr von, 14, 44, 57, 479
Hannibal, 106, 133, 153
Hansen, General Christian, 211, 213
Hart, Basil Henry Liddell, 2-3, 132,
    451-452, 469, 471-472, 475, 478

Hase, General Paul von, 423
Hausser, Lieutenant General Paul, 342,
    346
Heydrich, *SS-Gruppenführer*
    Reinhardt, 200, 202, 268
Hillgrüber, Andreas, 4
Himmler, *Reichsführer-SS* Heinrich, 4,
    7, 39, 200, 221, 227, 247, 267,
    291, 293, 415-418, 422-423, 435
Hindenburg, President Paul Von, 3,
    12, 14-15, 17, 30, 33, 38-39, 41,
    191, 260, 389, 413, 478, 481
Hitler, Adolf, 2-6, 8-9, 11, 14, 18-19,
    23-26, 28-33, 36, 38-47, 49-56, 58-
    67, 71, 73, 74-75, 80-81, 83-84, 86,
    90, 92-97, 110-119, 121, 123, 125-
    127, 134-136, 143, 145-146, 148-
    156, 159-167, 169-170, 172-174,
    177-178, 180-182, 184-192, 194-
    196, 198, 200-202, 205-208, 210,
    217-221, 225-227, 229-230, 233,
    237-243, 245, 252-253, 255, 258,
    260-261, 264-265, 289, 291, 293,
    296-299, 301, 303-304, 307, 310-
    311, 313-317, 319-322, 326-330,
    334-339, 341-343, 347-348, 351-
    353, 355-358, 361-363, 365-371,
    373-374, 377, 379-382, 384-387,
    390, 394-423, 425-428, 431-433,
    436-438, 440-444, 459, 463, 466,
    470, 472-473, 475-482; approval of
    Manstein Plan, 127-128, 134-135;
    as author of Sickle Cut Plan, 134;
    characterized as "Bohemian corpo-
    ral," 165; conquest of living space,
    52; dismissal of Kleist, 415-416; dis-
    missal of Manstein, 5, 418; fear of
    Manstein, 4-5; halt-order of
    Dunkirk, 120 146, 148-149; halt-
    order of Montcornet, 146-147;
    granting of expense accounts to high
    leaders, 164-165; granting of pro-
    motions after France campaign,
    163-164; naming himself as Führer
    and Reich Chancellor, 41; opinion
    of Manstein, 2-3, 14, 126, 419;
    postponement of Operation Sea
    Lion, 174; preference to attack

losses, 76; Manstein's denial of atrocities in, 85-86; Manstein's participation in plans for invasion of, 73, 76-81; policy of extermination in, 81; response to Wehrmacht massacres in, 86-87; Soviet invasion of, 77-78; Tenth Army in, 56, 62; Third Army in, 69, 76; Waffen SS in, 71; Wehrmacht massacres in, 85; policy of extermination, 163-166, 168-169, 202; Army Group North's role in, 203, 207; Barbarossa decree and, 203-204; complicity of German generals in, 204-205; Eleventh Army's complicity in, 203, 270-273; Himmler's complicity in, 198; Manstein's denial of, 273-274; Manstein's role in, 201, 206-207; OKH and, 247, 251, 253, 255, 262-263; OKW and the, 247, 254, 262-263; role of Einsatzgruppen in, 203, 208; Wehrmacht's complicity in, 250-254, 256

Policy of racial purification, 82, 84

Polish Army, 23, 68-72, 76-77, 79, 87, 91

political commissars, 7, 26, 198, 202, 204-206, 208, 246, 249-253, 267, 271, 278, 286-287, 444-445, 460, 463-464, 468

Poltava, Ukraine, 342, 344-345

Poltava-Dniepropetrovsk line, 340-341

Pomerania, 22, 28, 57, 67-69, 79, 91, 119, 153, 430

Popitz, Johannes, 400-402, 426

Port of Sevastopol, 212

Potemkinskaya, Ukraine, 333

Praskoveya, Russia, 328

Prételat, General André Gaston, 133

Pripyat swamps, 196, 420

Proletarsk, Russia, 332

Prussia, King of, 13, 16, 42, 163, 389, 395

Prussian military tradition, 394-395, 403, 440, 481

Psel River, Ukraine, 374

Raeder, Admiral Erich, 32, 52, 161,

172-173, 176, 178-179, 186, 438-439, 444; commentary on relationship between army and National Socialist Party, 32; skepticism of England invasion, 172-173; strategy for Mediterranean, 178-179

Rapallo Treaty, 23

rasputitsa, 360, 362, 364, 420

Rastenburg, Hitler's headquarters, 229, 291, 336, 348, 370, 405, 407, 412

Raus, General Erhard, 413, 420

Red Army, 2, 6-7, 23, 26-27, 49, 87, 187-190, 192-198, 202, 204-206, 208, 212-213, 226, 232-233, 248-252, 256-257, 262, 271, 274, 282, 285-286, 298, 300, 302, 304-305, 309-310, 312, 316-317, 321, 325, 328, 334, 339-341, 434-344, 346-350, 352, 355, 357-358, 360, 362-364, 371-372, 375, 377-378, 380, 382, 420-421, 430, 432-433

Red Plan, 51, 105, 148, 156; Manstein's development of, 51-52, 156

Reich Chancellery, 28, 50, 52, 58-59, 93-94, 126, 161, 164, 166, 170, 200, 411, 432-433

Reichenau, Field Marshal Walter von, 8, 33, 36, 39-42, 54-55, 69, 76-77, 86-87, 91, 140, 161, 171, 197, 219, 221, 225, 227, 253-260, 262-265; commentary on relationship between army and National Socialist Party, 33; complicity in war of extermination, 254-255, 257-258, 261

Reichswehr, 14, 15, 18, 20-27, 29-32, 34-42, 44-46, 78, 385

Reinecke, General Hermann, 443-444

Reinhardt, Colonel General Georg-Hans, 119, 129, 141, 144, 200, 252, 444

Reminiscences of a Soldier, 472

Rethondes Armistice, 260

Rhineland, remilitarization of, 44, 46, 49-51

Richthofen, Colonel General Wolfram Freiherr von, 231-232, 234, 240, 301, 306, 337, 344